13th Edition

UNDERSTANDING COMPUTERS:
TODAY AND TOMORROW

INTRODUCTORY

DEBORAH MORLEY

CHARLES S. PARKER

COURSE TECHNOLOGY
CENGAGE Learning™

Australia • Brazil • Japan • Korea • Mexico • Singapore • Spain • United Kingdom • United States

COURSE TECHNOLOGY
CENGAGE Learning™

Understanding Computers: Today and Tomorrow, 13th Edition
Deborah Morley and Charles S. Parker

Vice President of Publishing: Nicole Jones Pinard

Executive Editor: Marie Lee

Associate Acquisitions Editor: Brandi Shailer

Product Manager: Katherine C. Russillo

Product Manager: Leigh Heffron

Associate Product Manager: Julia Leroux-Lindsey

Editorial Assistant: Zina Kresin

Senior Marketing Manager: Ryan DeGrote

Marketing Coordinator: Kristen Panciocco

Development Editor: Pam Conrad

Content Project Manager: Heather Hopkins

Print Buyer: Fola Orekoya

Proofreader: Brandy Lilly

Indexer: Elizabeth Cunningham

Composition: Integra Software Services

Text and Cover Designer: Marissa Falco

For product information and technology assistance, contact us at
Cengage Learning Customer & Sales Support, 1-800-354-9706

For permission to use material from this text or product, submit all requests online at **cengage.com/permissions**
Further permissions questions can be emailed to
permissionrequest@cengage.com

Library of Congress Control Number: 2010920338

Student Edition ISBN 13: 978-0-538-74811-7

Student Edition ISBN 10: 0-538-74811-7

Course Technology
20 Channel Center Street
Boston, MA 02210
USA

Cengage Learning is a leading provider of customized learning solutions with office locations around the globe, including Singapore, the United Kingdom, Australia, Mexico, Brazil, and Japan. Locate your local office at:
international.cengage.com/region

Cengage Learning products are represented in Canada by Nelson Education, Ltd.

For your course and learning solutions, visit **www.cengage.com**

Purchase any of our products at your local college store or at our preferred online store **www.CengageBrain.com**

Printed in the United States of America
1 2 3 4 5 6 7 16 15 14 13 12 11 10

PREFACE

In today's computer-oriented society, computers and technology impact virtually everyone's life. *Understanding Computers: Today and Tomorrow, 13ᵗʰ Edition* is designed to ensure that students are current and informed in order to thrive in our technologically oriented, global society. With this new edition, students not only learn about relevant cutting-edge technology trends, but they also gain a better understanding of technology in general and the important issues surrounding technology today. This information gives students the knowledge they need to succeed in today's world.

This nontechnical, introductory text explains in straightforward terms the importance of learning about computers, the various types of computer systems and their components, the principles by which computer systems work, the practical applications of computers and related technologies, the ways in which the world is being changed by these technologies, and the associated risks and other potential implications of computers and related technologies. The goal of this text is to provide readers with a solid knowledge of computer fundamentals, an understanding of the impact of our computer-oriented society, and a framework for using this knowledge effectively in their lives.

KEY FEATURES

The Introductory version of *Understanding Computers: Today and Tomorrow, 13ᵗʰ Edition* contains the first nine chapters of the sixteen-chapter Comprehensive version. This textbook provides current and comprehensive coverage of important topics, flexible organization and an engaging presentation, as well as a variety of learning tools associated with each chapter to help each student master important concepts. Numerous marginal notations direct students to the Understanding Computers Web site where they can access **Online Videos**, **Podcasts**, **Video Podcasts**, and **Further Exploration** links, as well as other **Interactive Activities**, **Testing Activities**, **Study Tools**, and **Additional Resources**.

Currency and Accuracy

The state-of-the-art content of this book and its Web site reflect the latest technologies, trends, and classroom needs. To ensure the content is as accurate and up to date as possible, numerous **Industry Expert Reviewers** provided feedback and suggestions for improvements to the content in their areas of expertise. Throughout the writing and production stages, enhancements were continually made to ensure that the final product is as current and accurate as possible.

Comprehensiveness and Depth

Accommodating a wide range of teaching styles, *Understanding Computers: Today and Tomorrow, 13ᵗʰ Edition* provides comprehensive coverage of traditional topics while also covering relevant, up-to-the-minute new technologies and important societal issues, such as netbooks, graphene chips, UMPCs, 3D mice, USB monitors, Wi-Fi SD cards, and other new and emerging types of hardware; wireless power, one-time password (OTP) cards, TransferJet, gesture input, and other hardware technologies; cloud computing, thumb drive PCs, and other computing concepts; new software products and technologies, such as Windows 7, Google Chrome, cloudware, Microsoft Office 2010, and browser-based operating systems; new communications technologies, such as 4G cellular standards, emerging Wi-Fi standards, G.hn, personal mobile hotspots, and unified communications (UC); new and growing Internet applications, such as mobile voice search, Web notebooks, Twittering, social network management services, online financial alerts, mobile phone check deposits, and geobrowsing; and new security threats (such as real-time credit card data theft, rogue antivirus programs, and drive-by pharming) and new security trends (such as social engineering tests, people-driven security, and two-factor authentication).

Readability

We remember more about a subject if it is presented in a straightforward way and made interesting and exciting. This book is written in a conversational, down-to-earth style—one designed to be accurate without being intimidating. Concepts are explained clearly and simply, without the use of overly technical terminology. More complex concepts are explained in an understandable manner and with realistic examples from everyday life.

Chapter Learning Tools

1. **Outline**, **Learning Objectives**, and **Overview**: For each chapter, an **Outline** of the major topics covered, a list of student **Learning Objectives**, and a **Chapter Overview** help instructors put the subject matter of the chapter in perspective and let students know what they will be reading about.

2. **Boldfaced Key Terms and Running Glossary**: Important terms appear in boldface type as they are introduced in the chapter. These terms are defined at the bottom of the page on which they appear and in the end-of-text glossary.

3. **Chapter Boxes**: In each chapter, a **Trend** box provides students with a look at current and upcoming developments in the world of computers; an **Inside the Industry** box provides insight into some of the practices that have made the computer industry unique and fascinating; a **How It Works** box explains in detail how a technology or product works; and a **Technology and You** box takes a look at how computers and technology are used in everyday life.

4. **Ask the Expert Boxes**: In each chapter, three **Ask the Expert** boxes feature a question about a computing concept, a trend, or how computers are used on the job or otherwise in the real world along with the response from an expert. Experts for this edition include a former Navy pilot, a guitarist from a rock band, a software engineer from Walt Disney Imagineering, and executives from notable companies like McDonald's, Jack in the Box, Google, SanDisk, Kingston, Seagate, The Linux Foundation, ACM, and Symantec.

NEW 5. **Marginal Tips and Caution Elements**: **Tip** marginal elements feature time-saving tips or ways to avoid a common problem or terminology mistake, or present students with interesting additional information related to the chapter content. New **Caution** elements warn of a possible problem students should avoid.

6. **Illustrations and Photographs**: Instructive, current, full-color illustrations and photographs are used to illustrate important concepts. Figures and screenshots show the latest hardware and software and are annotated to convey important information.

✓ **TIP**

If your Internet connection slows down, try *power cycling* your modem and router: Unplug the modem and router for 30 seconds, then plug in the modem and wait for 30 seconds, then plug in the router.

CAUTION CAUTION CAUTIC

When upgrading your mobile phone, be c phone to others. Before disposing of or re settings to clear all personal data from the

7. **Online Video Marginal Element**: **Online Video** marginal elements direct students to the Understanding Computers Web site to watch a short video (provided by Google, IBM, Symantec, and other companies) related to the topic in that section of the text.

NEW 8. **Video Podcast Marginal Elements**: **Video Podcast** marginal elements direct students to the Understanding Computers Web site to download and watch a practical "How To" video podcast related to the chapter content. Audio podcasts of the Expert Insight features are also available via this book's Web site.

9. **Summary and Key Terms**: The end-of-chapter material includes a concise, section-by-section **Summary** of the main points in the chapter. The chapter's Learning Objectives appear in the margin next to the relevant section of the summary so that students are better able to relate the Learning Objectives to the chapter material. Every boldfaced key term in the chapter also appears in boldface type in the summary.

10. **Review Activities**: End-of-chapter **Review Activities** allow students to test themselves on what they have just read. A matching exercise of selected **Key Terms** helps students test their retention of the chapter material. A **Self-Quiz** (with the answers listed at the end of the book) consists of ten true-false and completion questions. Five additional easily graded matching and short-answer **Exercises** are included for instructors who would like to assign graded homework. Two short **Discussion Questions** for each chapter provide a springboard to jump-start classroom discussions.

NEW 11. **Projects**: End-of-chapter **Projects** require students to extend their knowledge by doing research and activities beyond merely reading the book. Organized into six types of projects (**Hot Topics**, **Short Answer/Research**, **Hands On**, **Presentation/Demonstration**, **Web Activities**, and a new **Ethics in Action** project), the projects feature explicit instructions so that students can work through them without additional directions from instructors. A special marginal icon denotes projects that require Internet access.

12. **Understanding Computers Web Site**: Throughout each chapter, **Further Exploration** marginal elements direct students to the Understanding Computers Web site where they can access collections of links to Web sites containing more in-depth information on a given topic from the text, as well as streaming videos and downloadable podcasts. At the end of every chapter, students are directed to the Understanding Computers Web site to access a variety of other **Interactive Activities**, as well as **Testing Activities**, **Study Tools**, and **Additional Resources**.

References and Resources Guide

A **References and Resources Guide** at the end of the book brings together in one convenient location a collection of computer-related references and resources, including a **Computer History Timeline**, a **Guide to Buying a PC**, **A Closer Look at Numbering Systems** feature, and a **Coding Charts** feature.

NEW and Updated Expert Insight Features

In this exciting feature located at the end of each module, industry experts provide students with personal insights on topics presented in the book, including their personal experiences with technology, key points to remember, and advice for the future. The experts, professionals from **D-Link**, **Acer**, **Microsoft**, and **Symantec** for the Introductory version of this text, provide a unique perspective on the module content and how the topics discussed in the module impact their lives and their industry, what it means for the future, and more!

ONLINE VIDEO

Go to the Chapter 1 page at **www.cengage.com/computerconcepts/np/uc13** to watch the "Searching the Web on Your iPhone" video clip.

VIDEO PODCAST

Go to the Chapter 1 page at **www.cengage.com/computerconcepts/np/uc13** to download or listen to the "How To: Control Your Computer with Twitter" video podcast.

FURTHER EXPLORATION   Go

Go to the Chapter 1 page at **www.cengage.com/computerconcepts/np/uc13** for links to information about computer certification programs.

Expanded Web Site Content

The **Understanding Computers Web site** includes a wealth of information at your fingertips to help enhance the classroom experience and to help students master the material covered in the book. Some of the content featured on the site includes new and updated **Key Term Matching, Self-Quizzes, Exercises,** and **Practice Tests**; interactive activities, such as **Student Edition Labs, Crossword Puzzles, Video Podcasts, Podcasts, Online Videos,** and **Further Exploration** links; and many other resources, including **Online Study Guides, Online Summaries, Online Glossaries, Expert Insights,** and **Online References and Resources Guide** content.

Student and Instructor Support Materials

Understanding Computers: Today and Tomorrow, 13th Edition is available with a complete package of support materials for instructors and students. Included in the package are the Understanding Computers Web site, Instructor Resources (available on CD and online), and SAM Computer Concepts.

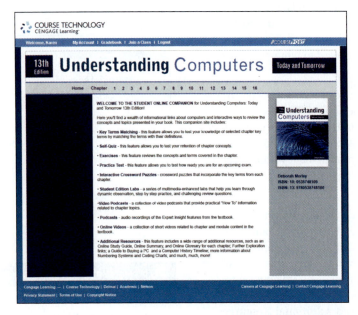

The Understanding Computers Web Site

The Understanding Computers Web site, which is located at **www.cengage.com/computerconcepts/np/uc13**, provides media-rich support for each chapter of the book. The Web site includes the following:

➤ **Key Term Matching**—this feature allows students to test their knowledge of selected chapter key terms.

➤ **Self-Quiz**—this feature allows students to test their retention of chapter concepts.

➤ **Exercises**—this feature reviews the concepts and terms covered in the chapter.

➤ **Practice Test**—this feature allows students to test how ready they are for upcoming exams.

➤ **Crossword Puzzles**—this feature incorporates the key terms from each chapter into an online interactive crossword puzzle.

➤ **Student Edition Labs**—this interactive feature reinforces and expands the concepts covered in the chapters.

➤ **Video Podcasts**—this feature includes several downloadable video podcasts per chapter that provide practical "How To" information related to chapter topics.

➤ **Podcasts**—this feature includes downloadable audio podcasts of the Expert Insight features.

➤ **Online Videos**—this feature includes several streaming videos per chapter related to the topics in that chapter.

➤ **Further Exploration**—this feature includes links to additional information about content covered in each chapter.

➤ **Additional Resources**—this feature includes a wide range of additional resources, such as **Expert Insights**; an **Online Study Guide, Online Summary,** and **Online Glossary** for each chapter; a **Guide to Buying a PC** and a **Computer History Timeline**; and more information about **Numbering Systems** and **Coding Charts**.

Instructor Resources

Course Technology instructional resources and technology tools provide instructors with a wide range of tools that enhance teaching and learning. These tools can be accessed from the Instructor Resources CD or at **www.cengage.com/coursetechnology**.

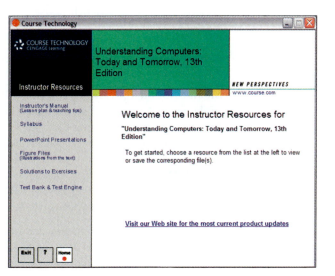

Electronic Instructor's Manual

The Instructor's Manual is written to provide instructors with practical suggestions for enhancing classroom presentations. For each of the 9 chapters in the Introductory book and 16 chapters in the Comprehensive book, the Instructor's Manual provides: **Lecture Notes**, **Teacher Tips**, **Quick Quizzes**, **Classroom Activities**, **Discussion Questions**, **Key Terms**, a **Chapter Quiz**, and more!

ExamView Test Bank

This textbook is accompanied by ExamView, a powerful testing software package that allows instructors to create and administer printed, computer (LAN-based), and Internet exams. ExamView includes 1,600 questions that correspond to the topics covered in this text, enabling instructors to create exams mapping exactly to the content they cover. The computer-based and Internet testing components allow instructors to administer exams over the computer and also save time by grading each exam automatically.

PowerPoint Presentations

This book comes with **Microsoft PowerPoint presentations** for each chapter. These are included as a teaching aid for classroom presentation, to make available to students on a network for chapter review, or to be printed for classroom distribution. Instructors can customize these presentations to cover any additional topics they introduce to the class. **Figure Files** for all figures in the textbook are also on the Instructor Resource CD.

Online Learning:

Course Technology has partnered with the leading distance learning solution providers and class-management platforms today. To access this material, Instructors can go to **www.cengage.com/coursetechnology** to visit our password-protected instructor resources. Instructor resources include the following: additional case projects, sample syllabi, PowerPoint presentations per chapter, and more. For additional information or for an instructor username and password, please contact your sales representative. For students to access this material, they must have purchased a WebTutor PIN-code specific to this title and your campus platform. The resources for students may include (based on instructor preferences) but are not limited to topic review, review questions, and practice tests.

SAM: Skills Assessment Manager

SAM 2007 is designed to help bring students from the classroom to the real world. It allows students to train and test on important computer skills in an active, hands-on environment. SAM's easy-to-use system includes powerful interactive exams, training and projects on the most commonly used Microsoft Office applications. SAM simulates the Office 2007 application environment, allowing students to demonstrate their knowledge and think through the skills by performing real-world tasks such as bolding text in Word or setting up slide transitions in PowerPoint. Add in live-in-the-application projects and students are on their way to truly learning and applying skills to business-centric documents.

Designed to be used with the New Perspectives Series, SAM includes handy page references, so students can print helpful study guides that match the New Perspectives Series textbooks used in class. For instructors, SAM also includes robust scheduling and reporting features.

ACKNOWLEDGEMENTS

We would like to extend a special thank you to all of the industry professionals who reviewed module content and provided their expertise for the **Expert Insight** features:

Introduction Module: Joe Melfi, Associate Director of Business Solutions, D-Link Systems
Hardware Module: Sumit Agnihotry, Vice President, Product Marketing, Acer Pan America
Software Module: Graham Watson, Senior Community Lead, Technical Audience Global Marketing, Microsoft
Networks and the Internet Module: Collin Davis, Senior Development Manager, Consumer Product Solutions, Symantec Corporation
Business on the Web Module: Jim Griffith, Dean of eBay Education, eBay
Systems Module: Stuart Feldman, Past President of ACM and Vice President, Engineering, Google
Computers and Society Module: Frank Molsberry, Technologist, Dell Inc.

In addition, we are very grateful to the numerous Industry Expert Reviewers that performed technical reviews and provided helpful suggestions to ensure this book is as accurate and current as possible. We would also like to thank the Educational Reviewers, who have helped to define and improve the quality of this text over the years. In particular, we would like to thank the following individuals:

Industry Expert Reviewers—13th Edition

Mike Hall, Corporate Communications, Seagate Technology
Kevin Curtis, CTO, InPhase Technologies
Sriram K. Peruvemba, Vice President, Marketing, E Ink Corporation
Jim Sherhart, Senior Director of Marketing, Data Robotics
Jack Dollard, Marketing, Mitek Systems
Joe Melfi, Associate Director of Business Solutions, D-Link Systems
Dave Gelvin, President, Tranzeo Wireless USA
Kevin Raineri, Director, Sales and Marketing, Innovative Card Technologies
Bill Shribman, Executive Producer, WGBH Interactive
Mike Markham, Vice President of Sales, Cadre Technologies
Renee Cassata, Marketing Manager, iDashboards
Russell T. Cross, Vice President of AAC Products, Prentke Romich Company
Dr. Kimberly Young, Director, The Center for Internet Addiction Recovery

Industry Expert Reviewers–Previous Editions

Jason Taylor, Worldwide Director of Corporate Communications, MobiTV; Nicole Rodrigues, Public Relations Manager, MobiTV; Stephen Yeo, Worldwide Strategic Marketing Director, IGEL Technology; Bob Hirschfeld, Public Information Officer, Lawrence Livermore National Lab; Bryan Crum, Vice President of Communication, Omnilert, LLC; David Bondurant, MRAM Product Manager, Freescale Semiconductor, Inc.; Rick McGowan, Vice President & Senior Software Engineer, Unicode, Inc.; Margaret Lewis, Director of Commercial Solutions, AMD; Mark Tekunoff, Senior Technology Manager, Kingston Technology; Billy Rudock, Customer Service Staff Engineer, Seagate Technology; James M. DePuydt, Ph.D., Technology Director, Imation Corporation; Dan Bloom, Sr. PR Manager, SanDisk; Kevin Curtis, CTO, InPhase Technologies; Gail Levy, Director of Marketing, TabletKiosk; Novell Marketing; John McCreesh, Marketing Project Lead, OpenOffice.org; Jackson Dunlap, ESP Systems; Laura Abram, Director of Corporate Marketing, Dust Networks; Kevin Schader, Communications Director, ZigBee Alliance; Mauro Dresti, Linksys Product Marketing Manager; Lianne Caetano, Executive Director, WirelessHD, LLC; Brad Booth; Howard Frazier; Bob Grow; Michael McCormack; George Cravens, Technical Marketing, D-Link; Christiaan Stoudt, Founder, HomeNetworkHelp.Info; Douglas M. Winneg, President, Software Secure, Inc.; Frank Archambeault, Director of Network Services, Dartmouth College; Adam Goldstein, IT Security Engineer, Dartmouth College; Ellen Young, Manager of Consulting Services, Dartmouth College; Becky Waring, Executive Editor, JiWire.com; Ellen Craw, General Manager, Ilium Software; Michael Behr, Senior Architect, TIBCO; Joe McGlynn, Director of Product Management, CodeGear; John Nash, Vice President of Marketing, Visible Systems; Josh Shaul, Director of Technology Strategy, Application Security, Inc.; Jodi Florence, Marketing Director, IDology, Inc.; Dr. Maressa Hecht Orzack, Director, Computer Addiction Services; Janice K. Mahon, Vice President of Technology Commercialization, Universal Display Corporation; Dr. Nhon Quach, Next Generation Processor Architect, AMD; Jos van Haaren, Department Head Storage Physics, Philips Research Laboratories; Terry O'Kelly, Technical Communications Manager, Memorex;

Randy Culpepper, Texas Instruments RFID Systems; Aaron Newman, CTO and Co-Founder, Application Security Inc.; Alan Charlesworth, Staff Engineer, Sun Microsystems; Khaled A. Elamrawi, Senior Marketing Engineer, Intel Corporation; Timothy D. O'Brien, Senior Systems Engineer, Fujitsu Software; John Paulson, Manager, Product Communications, Seagate Technology; Omid Rahmat, Editor in Chief, Tom's Hardware Guide; Jeremy Bates, Multimedia Developer, R & L Multimedia Developers; Charles Hayes, Product Marketing Manager, SimpleTech, Inc.; Rick McGowan, Vice President & Senior Software Engineer, Unicode, Inc.; Russell Reynolds, Chief Operating Officer & Web Designer, R & L Multimedia Developers; Rob Stephens, Director, Technology Strategies, SAS; Dave Stow, Database Specialist, OSE Systems, Inc.

Educational Reviewers

Marc Forestiere, Fresno City College; Beverly Amer, Northern Arizona University; James Ambroise Jr., Southern University, Louisiana; Virginia Anderson, University of North Dakota; Robert Andree, Indiana University Northwest; Linda Armbruster, Rancho Santiago College; Michael Atherton, Mankato State University; Gary E. Baker, Marshalltown Community College; Richard Batt, Saint Louis Community College at Meremec; Luverne Bierle, Iowa Central Community College; Fariba Bolandhemat, Santa Monica College; Jerry Booher, Scottsdale Community College; Frederick W. Bounds, Georgia Perimeter College; James Bradley, University of Calgary; Curtis Bring, Moorhead State University; Brenda K. Britt, Fayetteville Technical Community College; Cathy Brotherton, Riverside Community College; Chris Brown, Bemidji State University; Janice Burke, South Suburban College; James Buxton, Tidewater Community College, Virginia; Gena Casas, Florida Community College, Jacksonville; Thomas Case, Georgia Southern University; John E. Castek, University of Wisconsin-La Crosse; Mario E. Cecchetti, Westmoreland County Community College; Jack W. Chandler, San Joaquin Delta College; Alan Charlesworth, Staff Engineer, Sun Microsystems; Jerry M. Chin, Southwest Missouri State University; Edward W. Christensen, Monmouth University; Carl Clavadetscher, California State Polytechnic University; Vernon Clodfelter, Rowan Technical College, North Carolina; Joann C. Cook, College of DuPage; Laura Cooper, College of the Mainland, Texas; Cynthia Corritore, University of Nebraska at Omaha; Sandra Cunningham, Ranger College; Marvin Daugherty, Indiana Vocational Technical College; Donald L. Davis, University of Mississippi; Garrace De Groot, University of Wyoming; Jackie Dennis, Prairie State College; Donald Dershem, Mountain View College; John DiElsi, Marcy College, New York; Mark Dishaw, Boston University; Eugene T. Dolan, University of the District of Columbia; Bennie Allen Dooley, Pasadena City College; Robert H. Dependahl Jr.; Santa Barbara City College; William Dorin, Indiana University Northwest; Mike Doroshow, Eastfield College; Jackie O. Duncan, Hopkinsville Community College; John Dunn, Palo Alto College; John W. Durham, Fort Hays State University; Hyun B. Eom, Middle Tennessee State University; Michael Feiler, Merritt College; Terry Felke, WR Harper College; J. Patrick Fenton, West Valley Community College; James H. Finger, University of South Carolina at Columbia; William C. Fink, Lewis and Clark Community College, Illinois; Ronald W. Fordonski, College of Du Page; Connie Morris Fox, West Virginia Institute of Technology; Paula S. Funkhouser, Truckee Meadows Community College; Janos T. Fustos, Metropolitan State; Gene Garza, University of Montevallo; Timothy Gottleber, North Lake College; Dwight Graham, Prairie State College; Wade Graves, Grayson County College; Kay H. Gray, Jacksonville State University; David W. Green, Nashville State Technical Institute, Tennessee; George P. Grill, University of North Carolina, Greensboro; John Groh, San Joaquin Delta College; Rosemary C. Gross, Creighton University; Dennis Guster, Saint Louis Community College at Meremec; Joe Hagarty, Raritan Valley Community College; Donald Hall, Manatee Community College; Jim Hanson, Austin Community College; Sallyann Z. Hanson, Mercer County Community College; L. D. Harber, Volunteer State Community College, Tennessee; Hank Hartman, Iowa State University; Richard Hatch, San Diego State University; Mary Lou Hawkins, Del Mar College; Ricci L. Heishman, Northern Virginia Community College; William Hightower, Elon College, North Carolina; Sharon A. Hill, Prince George's Community College, Maryland; Alyse Hollingsworth, Brevard College; Fred C. Homeyer, Angelo State University; Stanley P. Honacki, Moraine Valley Community College; L. Wayne Horn, Pensacola Junior College; J. William Howorth, Seneca College, Ontario, Canada; Mark W. Huber, East Carolina University; Peter L. Irwin, Richland College, Texas; John Jasma, Palo Alto College; Elizabeth Swoope Johnson, Louisiana State University; Jim Johnson, Valencia Community College; Mary T. Johnson, Mt. San Antonio College; Susan M. Jones, Southwest State University; Amardeep K. Kahlon, Austin Community College; Robert T. Keim, Arizona State University; Mary Louise Kelly, Palm Beach Community College; William R. Kenney, San Diego Mesa College; Richard Kerns, East Carolina University, North Carolina; Glenn Kersnick, Sinclair Community College, Ohio; Richard Kiger, Dallas Baptist University; Gordon C. Kimbell, Everett Community College, Washington; Robert Kirklin, Los Angeles Harbor Community College; Judith A. Knapp, Indiana University Northwest; Mary Veronica Kolesar, Utah State University; James G. Kriz, Cuyahoga Community College, Ohio; Joan Krone, Denison University; Fran Kubicek, Kalamazoo Valley Community College; Rose M. Laird, Northern Virginia Community College; Robert Landrum, Jones Junior College; Shelly Langman, Bellevue Community College; James F. LaSalle, The University of Arizona; Chang-Yang Lin, Eastern Kentucky University; Linda J. Lindaman, Black Hawk College; Alden Lorents,

Northern Arizona University; Paul M. Lou, Diablo Valley College; Deborah R. Ludford, Glendale Community College; Kent Lundin, Brigham Young University-Idaho; Barbara J. Maccarone, North Shore Community College; Wayne Madison, Clemson University, South Carolina; Donna L. Madsen, Kirkwood Community College; Randy Marak, Hill College; Gary Marks, Austin Community College, Texas; Kathryn A. Marold, Ph.D., Metropolitan State College of Denver; Cesar Marron, University of Wyoming; Ed Martin, Kingsborough Community College; Vickie McCullough, Palomar College; James W. McGuffee, Austin Community College; James McMahon, Community College of Rhode Island; William A. McMillan, Madonna University; Don B. Medley, California State Polytechnic University; John Melrose, University of Wisconsin—Eau Claire; Dixie Mercer, Kirkwood Community College; Mary Meredith, University of Southwestern Louisiana; Marilyn Meyer, Fresno City College; Carolyn H. Monroe, Baylor University; William J. Moon, Palm Beach Community College; Marilyn Moore, Purdue University; Marty Murray, Portland Community College; Don Nielsen, Golden West College; George Novotny, Ferris State University; Richard Okezie, Mesa Community College; Joseph D. Oldham, University of Kentucky; Dennis J. Olsen, Pikes Peak Community College; Bob Palank, Florissant Community College; James Payne, Kellogg Community College; Lisa B. Perez, San Joaquin Delta College; Savitha Pinnepalli, Louisiana State University; Delores Pusins, Hillsborough CC; Mike Rabaut, Hillsborough CC; Robert Ralph, Fayetteville Technical Institute, North Carolina; Herbert F. Rebhun, University of Houston-Downtown; Nicholas John Robak, Saint Joseph's University; Arthur E. Rowland, Shasta College; Kenneth R. Ruhrup, St. Petersburg Junior College; John F. Sanford, Philadelphia College of Textiles and Science; Kammy Sanghera, George Mason University; Carol A. Schwab, Webster University; Larry Schwartzman, Trident Technical College; Benito R. Serenil, South Seattle Community College; Allanagh Sewell, Southeastern Louisiana University; Tom Seymour, Minot State University; John J. Shuler, San Antonio College, Texas; Gayla Jo Slauson, Mesa State College; Harold Smith, Brigham Young University; Willard A. Smith, Tennessee State University; David Spaisman, Katherine Gibbs; Elizabeth Spooner, Holmes Community College; Timothy M. Stanford, City University; Alfred C. St. Onge, Springfield Technical Community College, Massachusetts; Michael L. Stratford, Charles County Community College, Maryland; Karen Studniarz, Kishwaukee College; Sandra Swanson, Lewis & Clark Community College; Tim Sylvester, Glendale Community College; Semih Tahaoglu, Southeastern Louisiana University; Jane J. Thompson, Solano Community College; Sue Traynor, Clarion University of Pennsylvania; William H. Trueheart, New Hampshire College; James D. Van Tassel, Mission College; James R. Walters, Pikes Peak Community College; Joyce V. Walton, Seneca College, Ontario, Canada; Diane B. Walz, University of Texas at San Antonio; Joseph Waters, Santa Rosa Junior College, California; Liang Chee Wee, University of Arizona; Merrill Wells, Red Rocks Community College; Fred J. Wilke, Saint Louis Community College; Charles M. Williams, Georgia State University; Roseanne Witkowski, Orange County Community College; David Womack, University of Texas, San Antonio; George Woodbury, College of the Sequoias; Nan Woodsome, Araphoe Community College; James D. Woolever, Cerritos College; Patricia Joann Wykoff, Western Michigan University; A. James Wynne, Virginia Commonwealth University; Robert D. Yearout, University of North Carolina at Asheville; Israel Yost, University of New Hampshire; and Vic Zamora, Mt. San Antonio College.

We would also like to thank the people on the Course team—their professionalism, attention to detail, and enormous enthusiasm make working with them a pleasure. In particular, we'd like to thank Marie Lee, Kate Russillo, Heather Hopkins, Brandi Shailer, Leigh Hefferon, and Pam Conrad for all their ideas, support, and tireless efforts during the design, writing, rewriting, and production of this book. Thanks to Julia Leroux-Lindsey for managing the instructor resources and Ryan DeGrote and Kristen Panciocco for their efforts on marketing this text. We would also like to thank Marissa Falco for the new interior and cover design, and Tintu Thomas for all her help managing the production of the book. Thanks also to Nicole Jones Pinard.

We are also very appreciative of the numerous individuals and organizations that were kind enough to supply information and photographs for this text, the many organizations that generously allowed us to use their videos in conjunction with this text to continue to include the Online Video feature, and Daniel Davis of Tinkernut.com who kindly permitted us to incorporate his video podcasts into this edition of the text to create the new Video Podcast feature.

We sincerely hope you find this book interesting, informative, and enjoyable to read. If you have any suggestions for improvement, or corrections that you'd like to be considered for future editions, please send them to deborah.morley@cengage.com.

Deborah Morley
Charles S. Parker

BRIEF CONTENTS

CONTENTS

13th Edition

UNDERSTANDING COMPUTERS:

TODAY AND TOMORROW

⏻ module

Introduction

Today, computers are virtually everywhere in our society. People encounter and use computers and computing technology many times during the average day. Individuals use personal computers and mobile devices both at home and while on the go to perform a variety of important daily tasks, such as to pay bills, shop, manage investments, communicate with others, research products, make travel arrangements, check current news and weather, look up phone numbers, and view maps of locations. Individuals also increasingly use these devices for a growing number of entertainment purposes, such as playing games, downloading and listening to music, and watching TV shows. Businesses, schools, government agencies, and other organizations use computers and related technologies to facilitate day-to-day transactions, provide better services to customers, communicate with others, retrieve and disseminate information, and assist managers in making good decisions. Because they are so embedded in our society today, it is essential for everyone to know something about computers and what they can do.

This module introduces you to computers and some of their uses. Chapter 1 helps you to understand what computers are, how they work, and how people use them today. Chapter 1 also provides an overview of common computer terms and concepts that you will encounter throughout this text, as well as gives you a brief look at how to use a computer to perform basic tasks and to access resources on the Internet and the World Wide Web.

"Embrace computers as productivity tools and entertainment appliances, in whatever form they take."

For more comments from Guest Expert **Joe Melfi** of D-Link Systems, see the **Expert Insight on . . . Personal Computers** feature at the end of the module.

chapter 1

Introduction to the World of Computers

After completing this chapter, you will be able to do the following:

1. Explain why it is essential to learn about computers today and discuss several ways computers are integrated into our business and personal lives.

2. Define a computer and describe its primary operations.

3. List some important milestones in computer evolution.

4. Identify the major parts of a personal computer, including input, processing, output, storage, and communications hardware.

5. Define software and understand how it is used to instruct the computer what to do.

6. List the six basic types of computers, giving at least one example of each type of computer and stating what that computer might be used for.

7. Explain what a network, the Internet, and the World Wide Web are, as well as how computers, people, and Web pages are identified on the Internet.

8. Describe how to access a Web page and navigate through a Web site.

9. Discuss the societal impact of computers, including some benefits and risks related to their prominence in our society.

OVERVIEW

Computers and other forms of technology impact our daily lives in a multitude of ways. We encounter computers in stores, restaurants, and other retail establishments. We use computers and the Internet regularly to obtain information, experience online entertainment, buy products and services, and communicate with others. Many of us carry a mobile phone or other mobile device with us at all times so we can remain in touch with others on a continual basis and can access Internet information as we need it. It is even possible to use these portable devices to pay for purchases, play online games with others, watch TV and movies, and much, much more.

Businesses also use computers extensively, such as to maintain employee and customer records, manage inventories, maintain online stores and other Web sites, process sales, control robots and other machines in factories, and provide business executives with the up-to-date information they need to make decisions. The government uses computers to support our nation's defense systems, for space exploration, for storing and organizing vital information about citizens, for law enforcement and military purposes, and other important tasks. In short, computers and computing technology are used in an endless number of ways.

Understanding Computers: Today and Tomorrow is a guide to computers and related technology and how they are being used in the world today. It will provide you with a comprehensive introduction to computer concepts and terminology and give you a solid foundation for any future courses you may take that are related to computers or their use in the world today. It will also provide you with the basic knowledge you need to understand and use computers in school, on the job, and in your personal life, as well as give you an overview of the various societal issues related to technology, such as security and privacy issues, ethical considerations, and environmental concerns.

Chapter 1 is designed to help you understand what computers are, how they work, and how people use them. It introduces the important terms and concepts that you will encounter throughout this text and in discussions about computers with others, as well as includes an overview of the history of computers. It also takes a brief look at how to use a computer to perform basic tasks and to access resources on the Internet and the World Wide Web, in order to provide you with the knowledge, skills, and tools you need to complete the projects and online activities that accompany this textbook. The chapter closes with an overview of the societal impact of computers. ■

TIP ✓

Most of the computer concepts introduced in this chapter are discussed in more detail in subsequent chapters of this text.

PODCAST

Go to **www.cengage.com/ computerconcepts/np/uc13** to download or listen to the "Expert Insight on Personal Computers" podcast.

COMPUTERS IN YOUR LIFE

Computers today are used in virtually every aspect of most individuals' lives—at home, at school, at work, and while on the go. The next few sections provide an overview of the importance of computers and some of the most common computer-related activities that individuals may encounter every day.

Why Learn About Computers?

Fifty years ago, computers were used primarily by researchers and scientists. Today, computers are an integral part of our lives. Experts call this trend *pervasive computing*, in which few aspects of daily life remain untouched by computers and computing technology. With pervasive computing—also referred to as *ubiquitous computing*—computers are found virtually everywhere and computing technology is integrated into an ever-increasing number of devices to give those devices additional functionality, such as enabling them to communicate with other devices on an on-going basis. Because of the prominence of computers in our society, it is important to understand what a computer is, a little about how a computer works, and the implications of living in a computer-oriented society.

Prior to about 1980, computers were large and expensive, and few people had access to them. Most computers used in organizations were equipped to do little more than carry out high-volume processing tasks, such as issuing bills and keeping track of product inventories. The average person did not need to know how to use a computer for his or her job, and it was uncommon to have a computer at home. Furthermore, the use of computers generally required a lot of technical knowledge and the use of the *Internet* was reserved primarily for researchers and educational institutions. Because there were few good reasons or opportunities for learning how to use computers, the average person was unfamiliar with them.

Beginning in the early 1980s, things began to change. *Microcomputers*—inexpensive *personal computers* that you will read about later in this chapter—were invented and computer use increased dramatically. The creation of the *World Wide Web* (*WWW*) in the late 1980s and the graphical *Web browser* in the 1990s brought personal computing to a whole new level and began the trend of individuals buying and using computers for personal use. Today, more than 80% of all U.S. households include a personal computer, and most individuals use some type of computer on the job. Whether you become a teacher, attorney, doctor, engineer, restaurant manager, salesperson, professional athlete, musician, executive, or skilled tradesperson, you will likely use a computer to obtain and evaluate information, to facilitate necessary on-the-job tasks, and to communicate with others. Today's computers are very useful tools for these purposes; they are also taking on new roles in our society, such as delivering entertainment on demand. In fact, computers and the traditional communication and entertainment devices that we use every day—such as telephones, televisions, and home entertainment systems—are *converging* into single units with multiple capabilities. For instance, you can check your *e-mail* (electronic messages), watch videos, and view other Internet content on your living room TV; you can make telephone calls via your personal computer; and you can view Internet content and watch TV on your *mobile phone*. As a result of this *convergence* trend (see Figure 1-1), the personal computer has moved beyond an isolated productivity tool to become an integral part of our daily lives.

Just as you can learn to drive a car without knowing much about car engines, you can learn to use a computer without understanding the technical details of how a computer works. However, a little knowledge gives you a big advantage. Knowing something about cars can help you make wise purchasing decisions and save money on repairs. Likewise, knowing something about computers can help you buy the right one for your needs, get the most efficient use out of it, be able to properly *upgrade* it as your needs change, and have a much higher level of comfort and confidence along the way. Therefore, basic **computer literacy**—knowing about and understanding computers and their uses—is an essential skill today for everyone.

Ⓥ **FIGURE 1-1**

Convergence.

Today's computers typically take on the role of multiple devices.

MOBILE DEVICES
Typically include the functions of a telephone, organizer, digital media player, gaming device, Web browser, and digital camera.

HOME COMPUTERS
Can often be used as a telephone, television, and stereo system, in addition to their regular computing functions.

>**Computer literacy.** The knowledge and understanding of basic computer fundamentals.

Computers in the Home

Home computing has increased dramatically over the last few years as computers and Internet access have become less expensive and as an increasing number of computer-related consumer activities have become available. Use of the Internet at home to look up information, exchange e-mail, shop, watch TV and videos, download music and movies, research products, pay bills and manage bank accounts, check news and weather, store and organize *digital photos*, play games, make vacation plans, and so forth is now the norm for many individuals (see Figure 1-2). Many individuals also use a computer at home for work-related tasks, such as to review work-related documents or check work e-mail from home.

As computers, the Internet, television, *digital video recorders* (*DVRs*), and *gaming consoles* continue to converge, the computer is also becoming a central part of home entertainment. *Wireless networking* has added to the convenience of home computing, allowing the use of computers in virtually any location and the ability to stream content wirelessly from one device to another. You can also use a computer to make telephone calls (referred to as *Voice over IP* or *VoIP*) via a personal computer, a special telephone adapter connected to your *landline phone*, or a *dual-mode mobile phone* (a mobile phone that can make phone calls over the Internet via a *Wi-Fi network*, in addition to making phone calls via a *cellular network*, as described in more detail in Chapter 7).

Computing technologies also make it possible to have *smart appliances*—traditional appliances (such as refrigerators or ovens) with some type of built-in computer or communications technology that allows them to be controlled by the user via a telephone or the Internet, to access and display Internet information, or to perform other computer-related functions. *Smart homes*—homes in which household tasks (such as watering the lawn, turning the air conditioning on or off, making coffee, monitoring the security of the home and grounds, and managing home entertainment content) are controlled by a main computer in the home or by the homeowner remotely via a mobile phone—have arrived, and they are expected to be the norm in less than a decade. Some believe that one primary focus of smart appliances and smart homes will be energy conservation—for instance, the ability to perform tasks (such as running the dishwasher and watering the lawn) during non-peak energy periods and to potentially transfer waste heat from one appliance (such as an oven) to another appliance (such as a dishwasher) as needed.

Computers in Education

Today's youth can definitely be called the *computing generation*. From *handheld gaming devices* to mobile phones to computers at school and home, most children and teens today have been exposed to computers and related technology all their lives. Although the amount of computer use varies from school to school and from grade level to grade level, most students today have access to computers either in a classroom or in a computer lab. Many schools (particularly college campuses) today also have *wireless hotspots* that allow students to use their personal computers to connect wirelessly to the college network and the Internet from anywhere on campus (see Figure 1-3). Today, students at all levels are typically required to use a computer to some extent as part of their normal coursework—such as for preparing papers, practicing skills, doing Internet research, accessing Internet content (for instance, class *Web pages* or their campus *YouTube* channel), or delivering presentations—and some colleges require a computer for enrollment. For a look at how mobile phones are beginning to be used as a teaching tool at some colleges, see the Technology and You box.

Computers are also used to facilitate *distance learning*—an alternative to traditional classroom learning in which students participate, typically at their own pace, from their

REFERENCE AND COMMUNICATIONS
Many individuals today have access to the Internet at home; retrieving information, obtaining news, viewing recipes, shopping online, and exchanging e-mail are popular home computer activities.

PRODUCTIVITY
Home computers are frequently used for editing and managing digital photos and home videos, creating and editing work-related documents, and other productivity tasks.

ENTERTAINMENT
Home computers and gaming consoles are becoming a central hub for entertainment, such as the delivery of photos, videos, music, games, and recorded TV.

FIGURE 1-2
Computer use at home.

COMPUTER LABS AND CLASSROOMS
Many schools today have computers available in a lab or the library, as well as computers or Internet connections in classrooms, for student use.

CAMPUS WIRELESS HOTSPOTS
Many college students can access the Internet from anywhere on campus to do research, check e-mail, and more, via a campus hotspot.

DISTANCE LEARNING
With distance learning, students—such as these U.S. Army soldiers—can take classes from home or wherever they happen to be at the moment.

⚠ **FIGURE 1-3**
Computer use in education.

▽ **FIGURE 1-4**
Computer use on the job.

current location (via their computers and Internet connections) instead of physically going to class. Consequently, distance learning gives students greater flexibility to schedule class time around their personal, family, and work commitments, as well as allows individuals located in very rural areas or stationed at military posts overseas to take courses when they are not able to attend classes physically.

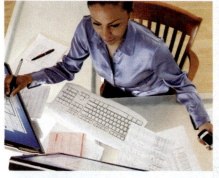

DECISION MAKING
Many individuals today use a computer to help them make on-the-job decisions.

PRODUCTIVITY
Many individuals today use a computer to perform on-the-job tasks efficiently and accurately.

Computers on the Job

Although computers have been used on the job for years, their role is continually evolving. Computers were originally used as research tools for computer experts and scientists and then as productivity tools for office workers. Today, computers are used by all types of employees in all types of businesses—including corporate executives, retail store clerks, traveling sales professionals, artists and musicians, engineers, police officers, insurance adjusters, delivery workers, doctors and nurses, auto mechanics and repair personnel, and professional athletes. In essence, the computer has become a universal tool for on-the-job decision making, productivity, and communications (see Figure 1-4). Computers are also used extensively for access control at many businesses and organizations, such as *authentication systems* that allow only authorized individuals to enter an office building, punch in or out of work, or access the company network via an access card or a fingerprint or hand scan, as shown in Figure 1-4 and discussed in detail in Chapter 9. In addition to jobs that require the use of computers by employees, many new jobs have been created simply because computers

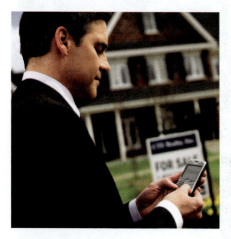

OFFSITE COMMUNICATIONS
Many individuals use portable computers or mobile devices to record data, access data, or communicate with others when they are out of the office.

AUTHENTICATION
Many individuals use authentication systems to punch in and out of work, access facilities, log on to company computers, or perform other security-related tasks.

TECHNOLOGY AND YOU

M-Learning on Campus

While mobile phones have been banned from many classrooms in past years, the tide may be turning. Despite concerns about cheating and distractions, some educators are now viewing mobile phones as a tool to enhance learning. One such school is Abilene Christian University (ACU) in Texas where entering freshman receive either an *iPhone 3G* or an *iPod Touch.* The devices are being used to facilitate *m-learning* (*mobile learning*) by providing the means for students to access class schedules, podcasts, flashcards, Google Apps, campus directories, news, and other student tools, as well as to facilitate real-time class polls, live assessments, and other in-class activities. These in-class activities can provide both instructors and students with immediate feedback, as well as keep students engaged and interested in the content being presented and discussed in class. ACU has a special mobile learning Web site (see the accompanying figure) to help students access available resources, which are expected to grow as the program evolves.

While notebook and tablet computers are used more often than mobile phones for m-learning activities on college campuses today, the time for mobile phone-based learning may have arrived. ACU considered notebook computers as their m-learning platform, but determined that the screens created a barrier between the teacher and the students and so selected the mobile phone as their m-learning platform instead. With the vast majority of college students already owning a mobile phone, and with Web-enabled mobile phones becoming the norm, m-learning could be the next logical step for education.

exist, such as jobs in electronics manufacturing, online retailing, and technology-related computer support.

Computers are also used extensively by military personnel for communications and navigational purposes, as well as to control missiles and other weapons, identify terrorists and other potential enemies, and perform other necessary national security tasks. To update their computer skills, many employees in all lines of work periodically take computer training classes or enroll in computer certification programs.

FURTHER EXPLORATION Go

Go to the Chapter 1 page at
**www.cengage.com/
computerconcepts/np/uc13**
for links to information about
computer certification programs.

Computers on the Go

In addition to using computers in the home, at school, and on the job, most people encounter and use all types of computers in other aspects of day-to-day life. For example, it is common for consumers to use *consumer kiosks* (small self-service computer-based stations that provide information or other services to the public, including those used for ATM transactions, bridal registries, ticketing systems, and more), *point-of-sale (POS) systems* (such as

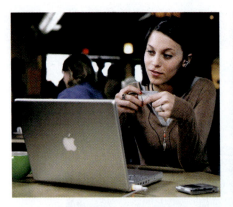

PORTABLE COMPUTERS
Many people today carry a portable computer or mobile device with them at all times or when they travel in order to remain in touch with others and Internet resources.

CONSUMER KIOSKS
Electronic kiosks are widely available to view conference or gift registry information, print photographs, order products or services, and more.

M-COMMERCE SYSTEMS
Allow individuals to pay for purchases using a mobile phone or other device.

CONSUMER AUTHENTICATION SYSTEMS
Allow access to facilities for authorized members only, such as for theme park annual pass holders, as shown here.

FIGURE 1-5
Computer use while on the go.

those found at most retail stores to check customers out), and *self-checkout systems* (which allow retail store customers to scan their purchases and pay for them without a salesclerk) while in retail stores and other public locations. Individuals may also need to use a computer-based consumer authentication system to gain access to a local health club, theme park, or other membership-based facility (see Figure 1-5).

In addition, many individuals carry a *portable computer* or Web-enabled *mobile device* with them on a regular basis to remain electronically in touch with others and to access information (such as stock quotes, driving directions, airline flight updates, movie times, news headlines, and more) as needed while on the go. These portable devices are also increasingly being used to watch TV, download and listen to music, access *Facebook* and other *social networking sites*, and perform other mobile entertainment options, as well as to pay for products and services via *m-commerce systems* (refer again to Figure 1-5). GPS (*global positioning system*) capabilities are also frequently built into mobile phones, cars, and other devices to provide individuals with driving directions and other navigational aids while traveling or hiking.

WHAT IS A COMPUTER AND WHAT DOES IT DO?

A **computer** can be defined as a programmable, electronic device that accepts data, performs operations on that data, presents the results, and stores the data or results as needed. The fact that a computer is *programmable* means that a computer will do whatever the instructions—called the *program*—tell it to do. The programs used with a computer determine the tasks the computer is able to perform.

The four operations described in this definition are more technically referred to as *input*, *processing*, *output*, and *storage*. These four primary operations of a computer can be defined as follows:

➤ **Input**—entering data into the computer.

➤ **Processing**—performing operations on the data.

> **Computer.** A programmable, electronic device that accepts data input, performs processing operations on that data, and outputs and stores the results. > **Input.** The process of entering data into a computer; can also refer to the data itself. > **Processing.** Performing operations on data that has been input into a computer to convert that input to output.

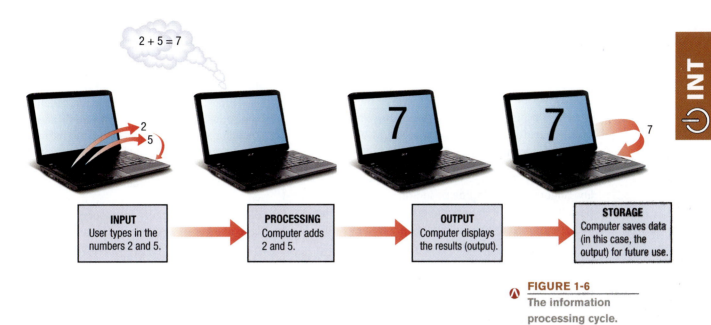

2 + 5 = 7

INPUT	PROCESSING	OUTPUT	STORAGE
User types in the numbers 2 and 5.	Computer adds 2 and 5.	Computer displays the results (output).	Computer saves data (in this case, the output) for future use.

FIGURE 1-6
The information processing cycle.

➤ **Output**—presenting the results.

➤ **Storage**—saving data, programs, or output for future use.

For example, assume that you have a computer that has been programmed to add two numbers. As shown in Figure 1-6, input occurs when data (in this example, the numbers 2 and 5) is entered into the computer, processing takes place when the computer program adds those two numbers, and output happens when the sum of 7 is displayed on the computer screen. The storage operation occurs any time the data, a change to a program, or some output is saved for future use.

For an additional example, look at a supermarket *barcode reader* to see how it fits this definition of a computer. First, the grocery item being purchased is passed over the barcode reader—input. Next, the description and price of the item are looked up—processing. Finally, the item description and price are displayed on the cash register and printed on the receipt—output—and the inventory, ordering, and sales records are updated—storage.

This progression of input, processing, output, and storage is sometimes referred to as the *IPOS cycle* or the *information processing cycle.* In addition to these four primary computer operations, today's computers also typically perform **communications** functions, such as sending or retrieving data via the Internet, accessing information located in a shared company database, or exchanging e-mail messages. Therefore, communications—technically an input or output operation, depending on which direction the information is going—is increasingly considered the fifth primary computer operation.

Data vs. Information

As just discussed, a user inputs **data** into a computer, and then the computer processes it. Almost any kind of fact or set of facts can become computer data, such as the words in a letter to a friend, the numbers in a monthly budget, the images in a photograph, the notes in a song, or the facts stored in an employee record. When data is processed into a meaningful form, it becomes **information**.

>**Output.** The process of presenting the results of processing; can also refer to the results themselves. >**Storage.** The operation of saving data, programs, or output for future use. >**Communications.** The transmission of data from one device to another. >**Data.** Raw, unorganized facts. >**Information.** Data that has been processed into a meaningful form.

ASK THE EXPERT

Paul Baker, Senior Principal Software Engineer, Walt Disney Imagineering.

Would a college student graduating with a computer degree qualify for a job at Walt Disney Imagineering?

Computers play a large role at Walt Disney Imagineering, so a degree based on computers could be a great match if the course load includes science, math, and engineering courses. Every Disney ride is run by a computer and in many cases by several computers. In fact, some of the rides have computers on each and every vehicle. Unlike typical desktop computers, these "ride computers" are specialized for performing specific, distinct tasks and interfacing to the electronic devices that control and monitor mechanical equipment. Consequently, the algorithms used to run these rides—and ensure they operate in a dependable, predictable manner—are heavily based on engineering and physics. Two types of computer-related jobs that exist at Imagineering are Ride Engineering and Pre-Visualization—both require computer skills, as well as strong math, science, and engineering skills.

Information is frequently generated to answer some type of question, such as how many of a restaurant's employees work less than 20 hours per week, how many seats are available on a particular flight from Los Angeles to San Francisco, or what is Hank Aaron's lifetime home run total. Of course, you don't need a computer system to process data into information; for example, anyone can go through time cards or employee files and make a list of people who work a certain number of hours. If this work is done by hand, however, it could take a lot of time, especially for a company with a large number of employees. Computers, however, can perform such tasks almost instantly, with accurate results. *Information processing* (the conversion of data into information) is a vital activity today for all computer users, as well as for businesses and other organizations.

Computers Then and Now

The basic ideas of computing and calculating are very old, going back thousands of years. However, the computer in the form in which it is recognized today is a fairly recent invention. In fact, personal computers have only been around since the late 1970s. The history of computers is often referred to in terms of *generations*, with each new generation characterized by a major technological development. The next sections summarize some early calculating devices and the different computer generations.

Precomputers and Early Computers (before approximately 1946)

Based on archeological finds, such as notched bones, knotted twine, and hieroglyphics, experts have concluded that ancient civilizations had the ability to count and compute. The *abacus* is considered by many to be the earliest recorded calculating device; it was used primarily as an aid for basic arithmetic calculations. Other early computing devices include the *slide rule*, the *mechanical calculator*, and Dr. Herman Hollerith's *Punch Card Tabulating Machine and Sorter*. This latter device (see Figure 1-7) was the first electromechanical machine that could read *punch cards*—special cards with holes punched in them to represent data. Hollerith's machine was used to process the 1890 U.S. Census data and it was able to complete the task in two and one half years, instead of the decade it usually took to process the data manually. Consequently, this is considered to be the first successful case of an information processing system replacing a paper-and-pen-based system. Hollerith's company eventually became *International Business Machines* (*IBM*).

First-Generation Computers (approximately 1946—1957)

The first computers were enormous, often taking up entire rooms. They were powered by thousands of *vacuum tubes*—glass tubes that look similar to large, cylindrical light bulbs—which needed replacing constantly, required a great deal of electricity, and generated a lot of heat. *First-generation computers* could solve only one problem at a time since they needed to be physically rewired with cables to be reprogrammed (see Figure 1-7), which typically took several days (sometimes even weeks) to complete and several more days to check before the computer could be used. Usually paper punch cards and paper tape were used for input, and output was printed on paper.

Two of the most significant examples of first-generation computers were *ENIAC* and *UNIVAC*. ENIAC, shown in Figure 1-7, was the world's first large-scale, general-purpose computer. Although it was not completed until 1946, ENIAC was developed during World War II to compute artillery-firing tables for the U.S. Army. Instead of the 40 hours required for a person to compute the optimal settings for a single weapon under a single set of conditions using manual calculations, ENIAC could complete the same calculations in less than two minutes. UNIVAC, released in 1951, was initially built for the U.S. Census Bureau and was used to analyze votes in the 1952 U.S. presidential election. Interestingly, its correct prediction of an Eisenhower victory only 45 minutes after the polls closed was not publicly aired because the results were not trusted. Despite this initial mistrust of its capabilities, UNIVAC did go on to become the first computer to be mass produced for general commercial use.

PRECOMPUTERS AND EARLY COMPUTERS
Dr. Herman Hollerith's Punch Card Tabulating Machine and Sorter is an example of an early computing device. It was used to process the 1890 U.S. Census data.

FIRST-GENERATION COMPUTERS
First-generation computers, such as ENIAC shown here, were large and bulky, used vacuum tubes, and had to be physically wired and reset to run programs.

SECOND-GENERATION COMPUTERS
Second-generation computers, such as the IBM 1401 mainframe shown here, used transistors instead of vacuum tubes so they were smaller, faster, and more reliable than first-generation computers.

THIRD-GENERATION COMPUTERS
Third-generation computers used integrated circuits which allowed the introduction of smaller computers, such as the IBM System/360 mainframe shown here.

FOURTH-GENERATION COMPUTERS
Fourth-generation computers, such as the original IBM PC shown here, are based on microprocessors. Most of today's computers fall into this category.

Second-Generation Computers (approximately 1958–1963)

The second generation of computers began when the *transistor*—a small device made of *semiconductor* material that acts like a switch to open or close *electronic circuits*—started to replace the vacuum tube. Transistors allowed *second-generation computers* to be physically smaller, less expensive, more powerful, more energy-efficient, and more reliable than first-generation computers. Typically, programs and data were input on punch cards and *magnetic tape*, output was on punch cards and paper printouts, and magnetic tape was used for storage (see Figure 1-7). *Magnetic hard drives* and *programming languages* (such as *FORTRAN* and *COBOL*) were developed and implemented during this generation.

FIGURE 1-7
A brief look at computer generations.

Third-Generation Computers (approximately 1964–1970)

The replacement of the transistor with *integrated circuits* (*ICs*) marked the beginning of the third generation of computers. Integrated circuits incorporate many transistors and electronic circuits on a single tiny silicon *chip*, allowing *third-generation computers* to be even smaller and more reliable than computers in the earlier computer generations. Instead of punch cards and paper printouts, *keyboards* and *monitors* were introduced for input and output; magnetic hard drives were typically used for storage. An example of a widely used third-generation computer is shown in Figure 1-7.

TIP

For a more detailed timeline regarding the development of computers, see the "Computer History Timeline" located in the References and Resources Guide at the end of this book.

FURTHER EXPLORATION

Go to the Chapter 1 page at www.cengage.com/computerconcepts/np/uc13 for links to information about the history of computers.

Fourth-Generation Computers (approximately 1971–present)

A technological breakthrough in the early 1970s made it possible to place an increasing number of transistors on a single chip. This led to the invention of the *microprocessor* in 1971, which ushered in the fourth generation of computers. In essence, a microprocessor contains the core processing capabilities of an entire computer on one single chip. The original *IBM PC* (see Figure 1-7) and *Apple Macintosh* computers, and most of today's modern computers, fall into this category. *Fourth-generation computers* typically use a keyboard and *mouse* for input, a monitor and *printer* for output, and magnetic *hard drives*, *flash memory media*, and *optical discs* for storage. This generation also witnessed the development of *computer networks*, *wireless technologies*, and the Internet.

Fifth-Generation Computers (now and the future)

Although some people believe that the fifth generation of computers has not yet begun, most think it is in its infancy stage. *Fifth-generation computers* have no precise classification, since experts tend to disagree about the definition for this generation of computers. However, one common opinion is that fifth-generation computers will be based on *artificial intelligence*, allowing them to think, reason, and learn. Voice and touch are expected to be a primary means of input, and computers may be constructed differently than they are today, such as in the form of *optical computers* that process data using light instead of electrons, tiny computers that utilize *nanotechnology*, or as entire general-purpose computers built into desks, home appliances, and other everyday devices.

Hardware

The physical parts of a computer (the parts you can touch and discussed next) are called **hardware**. The instructions or programs used with a computer—called *software*—are discussed shortly. Hardware components can be *internal* (located inside the main box or *system unit* of the computer) or *external* (located outside the system unit and connected to the system unit via a wired or wireless connection). There are hardware devices associated with each of the five computer operations previously discussed (input, processing, output, storage, and communications), as summarized in Figure 1-8 and illustrated in Figure 1-9.

FIGURE 1-8
Common hardware listed by operation.

INPUT	PROCESSING
Keyboard	CPU
Mouse	**OUTPUT**
Microphone	Monitor
Scanner	Printer
Digital camera	Speakers
Digital pen/stylus	Headphones/headsets
Touch pad/touch screen	Data projector
Joystick	**STORAGE**
Fingerprint reader	Hard drive
COMMUNICATIONS	CD/DVD disc
Modem	CD/DVD drive
Network adapter	Flash memory card
	Flash memory card reader
	USB flash drive

Input Devices

An *input device* is any piece of equipment that is used to input data into the computer. The input devices shown in Figure 1-9 are the *keyboard*, *mouse*, and *microphone*. Other common input devices include *scanners*, *digital cameras*, *digital pens* and *styluses*, *touch pads* and *touch screens*, *fingerprint readers*, and *joysticks*. Input devices are discussed in more detail in Chapter 4.

Processing Devices

The main *processing device* for a computer is the *central processing unit* (*CPU*). The CPU is a *computer chip* located inside the system unit that performs the calculations and comparisons

> **Hardware.** The physical parts of a computer system, such as the keyboard, monitor, printer, and so forth.

FLASH MEMORY CARD READER
Reads and writes flash memory cards.

DVD DRIVE
Reads and writes CD and DVD discs.

HARD DRIVE
Located inside the system unit; stores programs and most data.

SYSTEM UNIT
Case that contains the CPU, memory, power supply, disk drives, and all other internal hardware.

MONITOR
Lets you see your work as you go; a primary output device.

PRINTER
Produces printed copies of computer output.

MICROPHONE
Captures spoken input.

SPEAKERS
Produce audio output.

MODEM
Connects the computer to the Internet.

USB FLASH DRIVE
Used to store documents, digital photos, music files, and other content to be moved from one PC to another.

KEYBOARD
Used to type instructions into the computer; a primary input device.

USB PORTS
Connect external devices that use the USB interface.

CD AND DVD DISCS
Deliver programs and store large multimedia files.

MOUSE
Used to make on-screen selections; a primary pointing device.

FLASH MEMORY CARDS
Used to store digital photos, music files, and other content.

FIGURE 1-9
Typical computer hardware.

needed for processing; it also controls the computer's operations. For these reasons, the CPU is often considered the "brain" of the computer. Also involved in processing are various types of *memory*—additional chips located inside the system unit that the computer uses to store data and instructions while it is working with them. The CPU, memory, and processing are discussed in detail in Chapter 2.

Output Devices

An *output device* accepts processed data from the computer and presents the results to the user, most of the time on the computer screen (*monitor*), on paper (via a *printer*), or through a *speaker*. Other common output devices include *headphones* and *headsets* (used to deliver audio output to a single user) and *data projectors* (used to project computer images onto a projection screen). Output devices are covered in more detail in Chapter 4.

Storage Devices

Storage devices (such as *CD/DVD drives* and *flash memory card readers*) are used to store data on or access data from *storage media* (such as *CD discs*, *DVD discs*, or *flash memory cards*). Some storage hardware (such as a *hard drive* or a *USB flash drive*) includes both a storage device and storage medium in a single piece of hardware. Storage devices are used to save data, program settings, or output for future use; they can be installed inside the computer, attached to the computer as an external device, or accessed remotely through a network or wireless connection. Storage is discussed in more detail in Chapter 3.

Communications Devices

Communications devices allow users to communicate electronically with others and to access remote information via the Internet or a home, school, or company computer network. Communications hardware includes *modems* (used to connect a computer to the Internet) and *network adapters* (used to connect a computer to a computer network). A variety of modems and network adapters are available because there are different types of Internet and network connections—a modem used to connect to the Internet via a cable connection is shown in Figure 1-9. Communications hardware and computer networks are discussed in more detail in Chapter 7; connecting to the Internet is covered in Chapter 8.

Software

The term **software** refers to the programs or instructions used to tell the computer hardware what to do. Software is traditionally purchased on a CD or DVD or is downloaded from the Internet; in either case, the software needs to be *installed* on a computer before it can be used. A rapidly growing alternative is running programs directly from the Internet (via Web pages) without installing them on your computer—referred to as *Web-based software*, *Software as a Service* (*SaaS*), and *cloud computing* (see the Trend box) and discussed in more detail in Chapter 6.

Computers use two basic types of software: *system software* and *application software.* The differences between these types of software are discussed next.

VIDEO PODCAST

Go to the Chapter 1 page at **www.cengage.com/ computerconcepts/np/uc13** to download or listen to the "How To: Control Your Computer with Twitter" video podcast.

System Software

The programs that allow a computer to operate are collectively referred to as *system software.* The main system software is the **operating system**, which starts up the computer and controls its operation. Common operating system tasks include setting up new hardware, allowing users to run other software, and allowing users to manage the documents stored on their computers. Without an operating system, a computer cannot function. Common operating systems for personal computers are *Windows*, *Mac OS*, and *Linux*; these and other operating systems are discussed in detail in Chapter 5.

To use a computer, first turn on the power to the computer by pressing the power button, and then the computer begins to **boot**. During the *boot process*, part of the computer's operating system is loaded into memory, the computer does a quick diagnostic of itself, and then it launches any programs—such as an *antivirus* or *instant messaging* (*IM*) program—designated to run each time the computer starts up. You may need to *log on* to your computer or the appropriate computer network to finish the boot process.

Once a computer has booted, it is ready to be used and waits for input from the user. Most software today uses a variety of graphical objects (such as *icons* and *buttons*) that are selected with the mouse (or with a finger or stylus for a computer that supports touch or pen input) to tell the computer what to do. For instance, the **Windows desktop** (the basic workspace for computers running the Windows operating system; that is, the place where documents, folders, programs, and other objects are displayed when they are being used), along with some common graphical objects used in Windows and many other software programs, are shown in Figure 1-10.

>Software. The instructions, also called computer programs, that are used to tell a computer what it should do. **>Operating system.** A type of system software that enables a computer to operate and manage its resources and activities. **>Boot.** To start up a computer. **>Windows desktop.** The background work area displayed on the screen in Microsoft Windows.

WINDOWS DESKTOP
Provides the backdrop for icons, windows, and other objects.

ICONS
Represent folders, documents, or other items that can be opened.

WINDOWS
Rectangular areas containing programs, documents, or other data.

DIALOG BOX
Displayed when needed to request information from the user.

MENU BAR
Opens menus that can be used to issue commands.

RIBBON
Replaces menus and toolbars in some programs.

TOOLBAR
Contains buttons or icons that can be used to issue commands.

SIZING BUTTONS
Minimize, maximize, or close a window.

HYPERLINK
Issues a command to the computer when clicked.

TASKBAR
Usually located at the bottom of the desktop.

START BUTTON
Opens the Start menu that is used to launch programs.

TASKBAR TOOLBAR
Contains icons that can start programs.

TASKBAR BUTTONS
Correspond to open windows; can be used to change the active window.

SYSTEM TRAY
Shows the clock and other indicators.

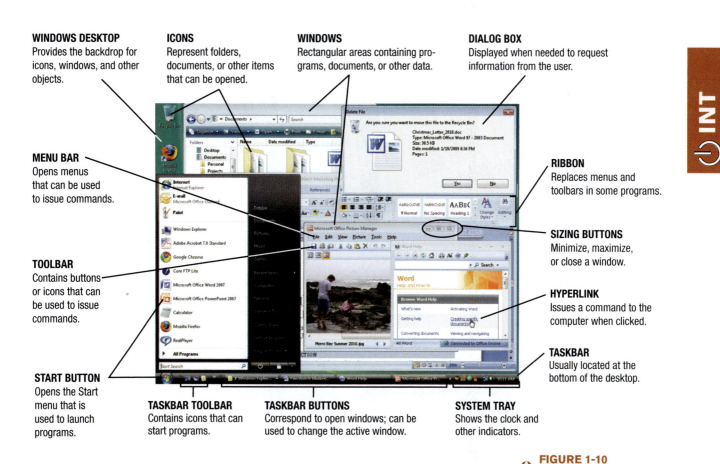

FIGURE 1-10
The Windows desktop.

Application Software

Application software (see Figure 1-11) consists of programs designed to allow people to perform specific tasks using a computer, such as creating letters, preparing budgets, managing inventory and customer databases, playing games, watching videos, listening to music, scheduling appointments, editing digital photographs, designing homes, viewing Web pages, burning DVDs, and exchanging e-mail. Application software is launched via the operating system (such as by using the *Windows Start* menu shown in Figure 1-10 for Windows computers) and is discussed in greater detail in Chapter 6.

There are also application programs that help users write their own programs in a form the computer can understand using a *programming language* like *BASIC*, *Visual Basic*, *COBOL*, *C++*, *Java*, or *Python*. Some languages are traditional programming languages for developing applications; others are designed for use with Web pages or multimedia programming. *Markup* and *scripting* languages (such as *HTML*, *XHTML*, and *JavaScript*) used to create Web pages are covered in Chapter 10; traditional programming languages are discussed in detail in Chapter 13.

Computer Users and Professionals

In addition to hardware, software, data, and *procedures* (the predetermined steps to be carried out in particular situations), a computer system includes people. *Computer users*, or *end users*, are the people who use computers to perform tasks or obtain information.

TIP

To launch a program on a Windows computer quickly, begin to type the name of the desired program in the Search box at the bottom of the Start menu and then click the link to the desired program when it is displayed (or press Enter when the proper program name is highlighted).

> **Application software.** Programs that enable users to perform specific tasks on a computer, such as writing letters or playing games.

WORD PROCESSING PROGRAMS
Allow users to create written documents, such as reports, letters, and memos.

MULTIMEDIA PROGRAMS
Allow users to perform tasks, such as playing music or videos and transferring content to CDs and DVDs.

WEB BROWSERS
Allow users to view Web pages and other information located on the Internet.

E-MAIL PROGRAMS
Allow users to compose, send, receive, and manage electronic messages sent over the Internet or a private network.

FIGURE 1-11
Examples of application software.

Anyone who uses a computer is a computer user, including an accountant electronically preparing a client's taxes, an office worker using a word processing program to create a letter, a supervisor using a computer to check and see whether or not manufacturing workers have met the day's quotas, a parent e-mailing his or her child's teacher, a college student analyzing science lab data, a child playing a computer game, and a person bidding at an *online auction* over the Internet.

Programmers, on the other hand, are computer professionals who write the programs that computers use. Other *computer professionals* include *systems analysts* (who design computer systems to be used within their companies as discussed in Chapter 12), *computer operations personnel* (who are responsible for the day-to-day computer operations at a company, such as maintaining systems or troubleshooting user-related problems), and *security specialists* (who are responsible for securing the company computers and networks against *hackers* and other intruders who are discussed in more detail in Chapter 9). Computer professionals are discussed in more detail in Chapter 12.

TREND

Cloud Computing

In general, the term *cloud computing* refers to computing in which tasks are performed by a "cloud" of servers, typically via the Internet. This type of network has been used for several years to create the supercomputer-level power needed for research and other power-hungry applications, but it was more typically referred to as *grid computing* in this context. Today, *cloud computing* typically refers to accessing Web-based applications and data using a personal computer, mobile phone, or any other Internet-enabled device (see the accompanying illustration). While many of today's cloud applications (such as Google Apps, Windows Live, Facebook, and YouTube) are consumer-oriented, business applications are also available and are expected to grow in the near future. Consequently, the term is also used to refer to businesses purchasing computing capabilities as they need them, such as through the *Amazon Elastic Compute Cloud* (*Amazon EC2*) service or other *cloud providers* that provide Web-based applications, computing power, *cloud storage,* and other cloud services.

Advantages of cloud computing include easy scalability, lower capital expenditure, and access to data from anywhere. It is also beneficial to business travelers and other individuals whose computers, mobile phones, or other devices may be lost or otherwise compromised while the individual is on the go—if no personal or business data is stored on the device, none can be compromised. Disadvantages include a possible reduction in performance of applications if they run more slowly via the cloud than they would run if installed locally, and the potentially high expense related to data transfer for companies with high bandwidth applications. In addition, numerous security concerns exist, such as how the data is protected against unauthorized access and data loss.

Despite the potential risks, many believe that cloud computing is the wave of the future and will consist of millions of computers located in data centers around the world that are connected together via the Internet. They also view cloud computing as a way to enable all of an individual's devices to stay synchronized and, and as a result, allow an individual to work with his or her data and applications on a continual basis.

THE INTERNET

END USERS   CLOUD PROVIDERS

Cloud providers provide services via the Internet.

COMPUTERS TO FIT EVERY NEED

The types of computers available today vary widely—from the tiny computers embedded in consumer devices and appliances, to the pocket-sized computers and mobile phones that do a limited number of computing tasks, to the powerful and versatile *desktop computers* and *portable computers* found in homes and businesses, to the superpowerful computers used to control the country's defense systems. Computers are generally classified in one of six categories, based on size, capability, and price.

➤ *Embedded computers*—tiny computers embedded into products to perform specific functions or tasks for that product.

➤ *Mobile devices*—mobile phones and other small personal devices that contain built-in computing or Internet capabilities.

➤ *Personal computers*—fully-functioning portable or desktop computers that are designed to be used by a single individual at a time.

> ➤ *Midrange servers*—computers that host data and programs available to a small group of users.

> ➤ *Mainframe computers*—powerful computers used to host a large amount of data and programs available to a wide group of users.

> ➤ *Supercomputers*—extremely powerful computers used for complex computations and processing.

In practice, classifying a computer into one of these six categories is not always easy or straightforward. For example, some high-end personal computers today are as powerful as midrange servers, and some personal computers today are nearly as small as a mobile phone. In addition, technology changes too fast to have precisely defined categories and the computer of the future may not look anything like today's computers. In fact, future predictions envision personal computers built into a variety of useful objects to best fit a person's lifestyle—such as a ring or watch for an older person, eyeglasses for a technical worker, and a flexible mobile device that can physically change its shape as needed (as discussed in the Chapter 2 Technology and You box) for general consumer use. Future devices are also expected to use voice, touch, or gesture input instead of a keyboard and mouse, and to project output on any appropriate surface instead of using a monitor. Nevertheless, these six categories are commonly used today to refer to groups of computers designed for similar purposes.

FIGURE 1-12

Embedded computers. This car's embedded computers control numerous features, such as notifying the driver when a car enters his or her blind spot.

A light indicates that a moving vehicle is in the driver's blind spot.

A camera located under the mirror detects moving vehicles in the driver's blind spot.

Embedded Computers

An **embedded computer** is a tiny computer embedded into a product designed to perform specific tasks or functions for that product. For example, computers are often embedded into household appliances (such as dishwashers, microwaves, ovens, coffee makers, and so forth), as well as into other everyday objects (such as thermostats, answering machines, treadmills, sewing machines, DVD players, and televisions), to help those appliances and objects perform their designated tasks. Typically, cars also use many embedded computers to assist with diagnostics, to notify the user of important conditions (such as an underinflated tire or an oil filter that needs changing), to control the use of the airbag and other safety devices (such as cameras that alert a driver that a vehicle is in his or her blind spot—see Figure 1-12—or auto braking systems that engage when a front collision is imminent, as discussed in the Chapter 5 Inside the Industry box), to facilitate the car's navigational or entertainment systems, and to help the driver perform tasks. Embedded computers are designed for specific tasks and specific products and so cannot be used as general-purpose computers.

ONLINE VIDEO

Go to the Chapter 1 page at **www.cengage.com/ computerconcepts/np/uc13** to watch the "Wireless O ROKR Sunglasses" video clip.

Mobile Devices

A **mobile device** is loosely defined as a very small communications device (such as a mobile phone) that has built-in computing or Internet capability. Mobile devices can typically be used to make telephone calls, send *text messages* (short text-based messages), view Web pages, take digital photos, play games, download and play music, watch TV shows, and access calendars and other personal productivity features. Most (but not all) mobile phones today include computing and Internet capabilities; these phones (such as the one in Figure 1-13) are sometimes referred to as **smartphones**; an older term is *PDA*

> **Embedded computer.** A tiny computer embedded in a product and designed to perform specific tasks or functions for that product. > **Mobile device.** A very small communications device that has built-in computing or Internet capability. > **Smartphone.** A mobile device based on a mobile phone.

(*personal digital assistant*), though some devices referred to as PDAs do not include telephone capabilities. Handheld gaming devices (such as the *Sony PSP* and the *Nintendo DSi*) and *portable digital media players* (such as the *iPod Touch* and *Zune*) that include Internet capabilities can also be referred to as mobile devices, though they have less overall capabilities than conventional mobile devices.

Today's mobile devices typically have small screens and keyboards. Because of this, mobile devices are most appropriate for individuals wanting continual access to e-mail, timely Web content (such as breaking news, weather forecasts, driving directions, and updates from Web sites like Facebook), and music collections rather than for those individuals wanting general Web browsing and computing capabilities. This is beginning to change, however, as mobile devices continue to grow in capabilities, as wireless communications continue to become faster, and as mobile input options (such as voice input) continue to improve. For instance, some mobile devices can perform Internet searches and other tasks via voice commands (as discussed in Chapter 6), some can be used to pay for purchases while you are on the go (as discussed in Chapter 11), and many can view and edit documents stored in a common format, such as *Microsoft Office* documents. For a look at some recent issues surrounding the use of mobile devices on the job, see the Inside the Industry box.

FIGURE 1-13

Smartphones. Most mobile devices today are based on the mobile phone.

Personal Computers (PCs)

A **personal computer** (**PC**) or **microcomputer** is a small computer designed to be used by one person at a time. Personal computers are widely used by individuals and businesses today and range in size from *desktop computers* to *ultra-mobile PCs* (*UMPCs*), as discussed next. Because many personal computers today are continually connected to the Internet, securing those computers—such as protecting them against *computer viruses* and *hackers* as discussed more later in this chapter and in Chapter 9—is an essential concern for both individuals and businesses.

Desktop Computers

Conventional personal computers that are designed to fit on or next to a desk (see Figure 1-14) are often referred to as **desktop computers**. The most common style of desktop computer today uses a *tower case*; that is, a system unit that is designed to sit vertically, typically on the floor. Desktop computers can also have a *desktop case* that is designed to be placed horizontally on a desk's surface, or an *all-in-one case* that incorporates the monitor and system unit into a single piece of hardware (a tower case and all-in-one case are shown in Figure 1-14).

FIGURE 1-14

Desktop computers.

Desktop computers typically cost between $350 and $1,000 and usually conform to one of two standards or *platforms*: *PC-compatible* or *Macintosh*. PC-compatible computers (sometimes referred to as *Windows PCs* or *IBM-compatible PCs*) evolved from the original IBM PC—the first personal computer widely accepted for business

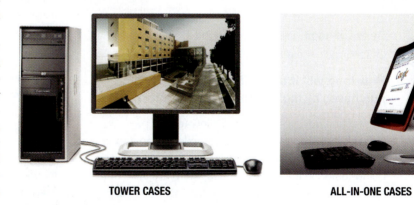

TOWER CASES   **ALL-IN-ONE CASES**

INSIDE THE INDUSTRY

Mobile Phone Use on the Job?

While there are numerous jobs for which having access to a mobile phone and the Internet are needed and extremely useful, there are times when this isn't necessarily the case. One of the most well-known recent issues surrounding mobile phone use on the job was the decision involving President Obama's desire to continue to use his Blackberry after taking office. While the President was eventually allowed to keep his device to stay in touch with senior staff and a small group of personal friends—a first for any U.S. president—the decision brought the issue of mobile phone use on the job to the forefront, especially as it relates to security issues. Security experts stress the importance of protecting the content on mobile phones by using tools such as logon passwords, encryption, remote wiping features, and other security tools discussed in detail in Chapter 9.

In addition to security concerns, the issue of the appropriateness of mobile phone use on the job is also under scrutiny. While the ability to stay in touch with others and post information on a regular basis is often a useful business and personal tool, it can also violate company policy, laws, and even social norms. For instance, one professional basketball player was recently reprimanded for posting a Twitter update during halftime from the locker room and judges across the country are having to deal with the issue of mobile phone use by jurors to obtain and disseminate information about cases during trials.

From researching defendants online, to using Google Maps to determine walking or driving time between locations discussed in the trial, to Twittering about upcoming verdicts, juror mobile phone use is resulting in numerous mistrials and is raising many questions about jury instructions and juror access to technology during trials. Another issue is discretion and taste, as in the case of a newspaper reporter who recently posted Twitter updates during the funeral of a three-year-old boy. Mobile phone use is already prohibited in some public locations (see the accompanying illustration), such as theaters (for courtesy reasons) and airplanes and hospitals (for safety reasons). With mobile phones becoming ubiquitous, it is increasingly important for individuals to ensure that they use their mobile phones only in an appropriate and secure manner, both on the job and off.

ASK THE EXPERT

Debra Jensen, Vice President and Chief Information Officer, Jack in the Box Inc.

How long will it be until paying for fast-food purchases by mobile phone is the norm?

The technology exists today to allow for the payment of fast-food purchases by mobile phone and it's being used in Europe and Japan. Though it's also being tested in the United States, there are still some hurdles, primarily the adoption of the technology by cell phone providers and retailers, and consumers' willingness to use it. Another hurdle is consumer concerns about the technology being secure. It will likely be 2011 before there is widespread use.

use—and are the most common type of personal computer used today. In general, PC-compatible hardware and software are compatible with all brands of PC-compatible computers—such as those made by Dell, Hewlett-Packard, NEC, Acer, Lenovo, Fujitsu, and Gateway—and these computers typically run the Microsoft Windows operating system. Macintosh (*Mac*) computers are made by Apple, use the Mac OS operating system, and often use different hardware and software than PC-compatible computers. Although PC-compatible computers are by far the most widely used in the United States, the Mac is traditionally the computer of choice for artists, designers, and others who require advanced graphics capabilities. Extra powerful desktop computers designed for computer users running graphics, music, film, architecture, science, and other powerful applications are sometimes referred to as *workstations*.

Portable Computers

Portable computers are computers that are designed to be carried around easily, such as in a briefcase or pocket, depending on their size. Like mobile devices, portable computers are designed to be powered by rechargeable batteries so they can be used while on the go, though many can also be powered by electricity. Portable computers now outsell desktop computers and are often the computer of choice for students and for individuals buying a new home computer, as well as for many businesses. In fact, portable computers are essential for many workers, such as salespeople who need to make presentations or take orders from clients off-site, agents who need to collect data at remote locations, and managers who need computing and communications resources as they travel. Portable computers are available in a variety of configurations, as discussed next and shown in Figure 1-15.

NOTEBOOKS

SLATE TABLETS

NETBOOKS

ULTRA-MOBILE PCS (UMPCs)

FIGURE 1-15
Portable computers.

> ➤ **Notebook computers** (also called **laptop computers**)—computers that are about the size of a paper notebook and open to reveal a screen on the top half of the computer and a keyboard on the bottom. They are typically comparable to desktop computers in features and capabilities.

> ➤ **Tablet computers**—notebook-sized computers that are designed to be used with a digital pen or stylus. They can be either *slate tablets* (which are one-piece computers with just a screen on top and no keyboard, such as the one shown in Figure 1-15) or *convertible tablets* (which use the same *clamshell* design as notebook computers but the top half of the computer can be rotated and folded shut so it can also be used as a slate tablet.

> ➤ **Netbooks** (also called *mini-notebooks*, *mini-laptops*, and *ultraportable computers*)—notebook computers that are smaller (a 10-inch-wide screen is common), lighter (typically less than three pounds), and less expensive than conventional notebooks, so they are especially appropriate for students and business travelers. They typically don't include a CD or DVD drive and they have a smaller keyboard than a notebook computer. The market for this new category of portable computer is growing rapidly and it is expected to reach 50 million by 2012, according to the research firm Gartner.

> ➤ **Ultra-mobile PCs (UMPCs)** (also sometimes called **handheld computers**)—computers that are small enough to fit in one hand. UMPCs are smaller (with a typical screen size of seven inches or smaller) and lighter (usually less than two pounds) than netbooks. They can support keyboard, touch, and/or pen input, depending on the particular design being used.

It is important to realize that while a portable computer offers the convenience of mobility, it typically isn't as comfortable to use for a primary home or work computer as a desktop computer is, without additional hardware. For instance, many individuals find it more convenient to connect and use a conventional monitor, keyboard, and mouse when using a notebook

TIP

For tips on buying a personal computer, see the "Guide to Buying a PC" in the References and Resources Guide located at the end of this book.

TIP

Computers that allow pen input—such as tablet computers and some ultra-mobile PCs—are convenient in crowded situations, as well as in places where the clicking of a keyboard would be annoying to others.

>**Portable computer.** A small personal computer, such as a notebook, tablet, netbook, or ultra-mobile PC (UMPC), designed to be carried around easily. >**Notebook computer.** A fully functioning portable computer that opens to reveal a screen and keyboard; also called a **laptop computer**. >**Tablet computer.** A portable computer about the size of a notebook that is designed to be used with an electronic pen. >**Netbook.** A very small notebook computer. >**Ultra-mobile PC (UMPC).** A portable personal computer that is small enough to fit in one hand; also called a **handheld computer.**

ASK THE EXPERT

Martin Smekal, President and Founder, TabletKiosk

How will personal computers five years from now be different than today?

I believe that five years from now people will rely even more on their computers than they do today. They will likely create a personal computing ecosystem that combines the stability of a desktop system with the portability of a mobile computer and that has full wireless access to key files and applications. Hopefully, this will evolve to one single adaptable computing device that is capable of meeting all of these needs by incorporating "always-on" wireless connectivity and a touch screen interface.

In general, the computers of the future will be smaller, lighter, and have a much longer battery life than today's models. Traditional modes of input like the keyboard and mouse could become obsolete as we begin to rely more on touch input, speech recognition, and improved handwriting recognition.

computer at a desk for a long computer session. This hardware can be connected individually to many portable computers via a wired or wireless connection; there are also special *docking stations* that can be used to connect a portable computer easily to the hardware devices that are attached to the docking station. Docking stations and other *ergonomic*-related topics are discussed in more detail in Chapter 16.

Thin Clients and Internet Appliances

Most personal computers today are sold as stand-alone, self-sufficient units that are equipped with all the necessary hardware and software needed to operate independently. In other words, they can perform input, processing, output, and storage without being connected to a network, although they can be networked if desired. In contrast, a device that must be connected to a network to perform processing or storage tasks is referred to as a *dumb terminal*. Two types of personal computers that may be able to perform a limited amount of independent processing (like a desktop or notebook computer) but are designed to be used with a network (like a dumb terminal) are *thin clients* and *Internet appliances*.

A **thin client**—also called a *network computer* (*NC*)—is a device that is designed to be used in conjunction with a company network. Instead of using local hard drives for storage, programs are typically accessed from and data is stored on a *network server*. The main advantage of thin clients over desktop computers is lower cost (such as for overall hardware and software, computer maintenance, and power and cooling costs), increased security (since data is not stored locally), and easier maintenance (since all software is located on a central server). Disadvantages include having limited or no local storage (although this is an advantage for companies with highly secure data that need to prevent data from leaving the facility) and not being able to function as a stand-alone computer when the network is not working. Thin clients are used by businesses to provide employees with access to network applications; they are also sometimes used to provide Internet access to the public. For instance, the thin client shown in Figure 1-16 is installed in a hotel in Boston, Massachusetts, and is used to provide guests with Internet access, hotel and conference information, room-to-room calling, and free phone calls via the Internet.

Network computers or other devices designed primarily for accessing Web pages and/or exchanging e-mail are called **Internet appliances** (sometimes referred to as *Internet devices*). Typically, Internet appliances are designed to be located in the home and can be built into another product (such as a refrigerator or telephone console) or can be stand-alone Internet devices (such as the *Chumby* device shown in Figure 1-16 that is designed to deliver news, sports scores, weather, and other personalized Web-based information). Gaming consoles (such as the *Nintendo Wii* shown in Figure 1-16 and the *Sony*

>**Thin client.** A personal computer designed to access a network for processing and data storage, instead of performing those tasks locally; also called a network computer (NC). >**Internet appliance.** A specialized network computer designed primarily for Internet access and/or e-mail exchange.

THIN CLIENTS   **STAND-ALONE INTERNET DEVICES**   **INTERNET-ENABLED GAMING CONSOLES**

PlayStation 3) that can be used to view Internet content, in addition to their gaming abilities, can also be classified as Internet appliances when they are used to access the Internet. There are also Internet capabilities beginning to be built into television sets, which make these TVs Internet appliances, as well.

FIGURE 1-16
Thin clients and
Internet appliances.

Midrange Servers

A **midrange server**—also sometimes called a *minicomputer* or *midrange computer*—is a medium-sized computer used to host programs and data for a small network. Typically larger, more powerful, and more expensive than a desktop computer, a midrange server is usually located in a closet or other out-of-the-way place and can serve many users at one time. Users connect to the server through a network, using their desktop computer, portable computer, thin client, or a dumb terminal consisting of just a monitor and keyboard (see Figure 1-17). Midrange servers are often used in small- to medium-sized businesses (such as medical or dental offices), as well as in school computer labs. There are also special *home servers* designed for home use, which are often used to *back up* (make duplicate copies of) the content located on all the computers in the home automatically and to host music, photos, movies, and other media to be shared via a *home network*.

FIGURE 1-17
Midrange servers.
Midrange servers are
used to host data and
programs on a small
network, such as a
school computer lab or
medical office network.

Some midrange servers consist of a collection of individual *circuit boards* called *blades*; each blade contains the hardware necessary to provide the complete processing power of one personal computer. These servers—called *blade servers*—are much easier to expand and upgrade than traditional servers, have lower overall power and cooling costs, and are more secure. With some blade servers, the processing power of the blades is shared among users. With others, each user has an individual blade, which functions as that individual's personal computer, but the blades are locked in a secure location instead of having that hardware located on each employee's desk. In either case, the thin client designed specifically to access a blade server is sometimes called a *blade workstation*.

One trend involving midrange servers (as well as the *mainframe computers* discussed next) today is **virtualization**—creating *virtual* (rather than actual) versions of a computing resource; in this case, separate server environments that, although physically located on the same computer, function

Users connect to the
server using computers, thin
clients, or dumb terminals.

The server is typically
stored in a nearby closet or
other out-of-the way place.

>**Midrange server.** A medium-sized computer used to host programs and data for a small network. >**Virtualization.** Creating virtual (rather than actual) versions of a computing resource, such as several separate environments that are located on a single server but act like different servers.

as separate servers and do not interact with each other. For instance, all applications for an organization can be installed in virtual environments on one or more physical servers instead of using a separate server for each application. Using a separate server for each application often wastes resources since the servers are typically not used to full capacity—one estimate is that about only 10% of server capability is frequently utilized. With virtualization, companies can fulfill their computing needs with fewer servers, which translates into reduced costs for hardware and server management, as well as lower power and cooling costs. Consequently, one of the most significant appeals of *server virtualization* today is increased efficiency. The concepts of virtualization are also beginning to be applied to other computing areas, such as networking and storage.

Mainframe Computers

A **mainframe computer** is a powerful computer used by many large organizations—such as hospitals, universities, large businesses, banks, and government offices—that need to manage large amounts of centralized data. Larger, more expensive, and more powerful than midrange servers, mainframes can serve thousands of users connected to the mainframe via personal computers, thin clients, or dumb terminals, in a manner similar to the way users connect to midrange servers. Mainframe computers are typically located in climate-controlled *data centers* and connect to the rest of the company computers via a computer network. During regular business hours, a mainframe typically runs the programs needed to meet the different needs of its wide variety of users. At night, it commonly performs large processing tasks, such as payroll and billing. Today's mainframes are sometimes referred to as *high-end servers* or *enterprise-class servers* and they usually cost at least several hundred thousand dollars each.

One issue facing businesses today is the high cost of electricity to power and cool the mainframes, servers, and personal computers used in an organization. Consequently, making the computers located in a business—particularly mainframes and servers—more energy efficient is a high priority today. For example, IBM recently consolidated approximately 4,000 servers located in its data centers into just 30 mainframes (one of the new mainframes is shown in Figure 1-18). This new environment is expected to consume approximately 80 percent less energy and result in significant savings in energy, software, and system support costs. Energy efficiency and other *green computing* topics are discussed in more detail in Chapter 16.

FIGURE 1-18
Mainframe computers.

Supercomputers

Some applications require extraordinary speed, accuracy, and processing capabilities—for example, sending astronauts into space, controlling missile guidance systems and satellites, forecasting the weather, exploring for oil, and assisting with some kinds of scientific research. **Supercomputers**—the most powerful and most expensive type of computer available—were developed to fill this need. Some relatively new supercomputing applications include hosting extremely complex Web sites and *decision support systems* for corporate executives, as well as *three-dimensional applications* (such as 3D medical imaging, 3D image projections, and 3D architectural modeling). Unlike mainframe computers, which typically run multiple applications simultaneously to serve a wide variety of users, supercomputers generally run one program at a time, as fast as possible.

Conventional supercomputers can cost several million dollars each. To reduce the cost, supercomputers today are often built by connecting hundreds of smaller and less

---

>**Mainframe computer.** A computer used in large organizations (such as hospitals, large businesses, and colleges) that need to manage large amounts of centralized data and run multiple programs simultaneously. >**Supercomputer.** The fastest, most expensive, and most powerful type of computer.

expensive computers (increasingly midrange servers) into a **supercomputing cluster** that acts as a single supercomputer. The computers in the cluster usually contain multiple CPUs each and are dedicated to processing cluster applications. For example, IBM's *Roadrunner* supercomputer (shown in Figure 1-19)— currently the fastest computer in the world—contains approximately 19,000 CPUs. This supercomputing cluster, built for the U.S. Department of Energy, is installed at Los Alamos National Lab in California and is used primarily to ensure the safety and reliability of the nation's nuclear weapons stockpile. Roadrunner, which cost about $100 million and occupies about 5,200 square feet, is the first supercomputer to reach *petaflop* (quadrillions of *floating point operations per second*) speeds. This supercomputer is also one of the most energy efficient computers in the *TOP500* list of the 500 fastest computers in the world. A new IBM supercomputer named *Sequoia* that is currently under development for the Lawrence Livermore National Laboratory is expected to use approximately 1.6 million CPUs and perform at 20 petaflops.

FIGURE 1-19
The Roadrunner supercomputer. Supercomputers are used for specialized situations in which immense processing speed is required.

COMPUTER NETWORKS AND THE INTERNET

A **computer network** is a collection of computers and other devices that are connected together to enable users to share hardware, software, and data, as well as to communicate electronically with each other. Computer networks exist in many sizes and types. For instance, home networks are commonly used to allow home computers to share a single printer and Internet connection, as well as to exchange files. Small office networks enable workers to access company records stored on a *network server*, communicate with other employees, share a high-speed printer, and access the Internet (see Figure 1-20). School networks allow students and teachers to access the Internet and school resources, and large corporate networks often connect all of the offices or retail stores in the corporation, creating a network that spans several cities or states. Public wireless networks—such as those available at some coffeehouses, restaurants, public libraries, and parks—provide Internet access to individuals via their portable computers and mobile devices. Most computers today connect to a computer network. Chapter 7 discusses networks in greater detail.

What Are the Internet and the World Wide Web?

The **Internet** is the largest and most well-known computer network in the world. It is technically a network of networks, since it consists of thousands of networks that can all access each other via the main *backbone* infrastructure of the Internet. Individual users connect to the Internet by connecting their computers to servers belonging to an **Internet service provider (ISP)**—a company that provides Internet access, usually for a fee. ISPs (which include conventional and mobile telephone companies like AT&T, Verizon, and Sprint; cable providers like Comcast and Time Warner; and stand-alone ISPs like NetZero and EarthLink) function as gateways or onramps to the Internet, providing Internet access to their subscribers. ISP servers are continually connected to a larger network, called a *regional network*, which, in turn, is connected to one of the major high-speed networks within a country, called a *backbone network*. Backbone networks within a country are connected to each other and to backbone networks in other countries. Together they form one enormous network of networks—the Internet. Tips for selecting an ISP are included in Chapter 8.

> **Supercomputing cluster.** A supercomputer comprised of numerous smaller computers connected together to act as a single computer.
> **Computer network.** A collection of computers and other hardware devices that are connected together to share hardware, software, and data, as well as to communicate electronically with one another. > **Internet.** The largest and most well-known computer network, linking millions of computers all over the world. > **Internet service provider (ISP).** A business or other organization that provides Internet access to others, typically for a fee.

BETTY'S PC

WEB PAGE
(for Mary)

THE
INTERNET

FILES
(for Tom)

INTERNET
CONNECTION

WEB PAGE
(for Mary)

E-MAIL
(to a customer)

MARY'S PC

NETWORK
SERVER

SHARED PRINTER

TOM'S PC

FILES
(for Tom)

E-MAIL
(to a customer)

FIGURE 1-20

Example of a
computer network.

Millions of people and organizations all over the world are connected to the Internet. Some of the most common Internet activities today are exchanging e-mail and instant messages (IMs), and accessing content located on *Web pages*. While the term *Internet* refers to the physical structure of that network, the **World Wide Web** (**WWW**) refers to one resource—a collection of documents called **Web pages**—available through the Internet. A group of Web pages belonging to one individual or company is called a **Web site**. Web pages are stored on computers (called **Web servers**) that are continually connected to the Internet; they can be accessed at any time by anyone with a computer (or other Web-enabled device) and an Internet connection. A wide variety of information is available via Web pages, such as company and product information, government forms and publications, maps, telephone directories, news, weather, sports results, airline schedules, and much, much more. You can also use Web pages to shop, bank, trade stock, and perform other types of online financial transactions; access *social networks* like *Facebook* and *MySpace*; and listen to music, play games, watch television shows, and perform other entertainment-oriented activities (see Figure 1-21). Web pages are viewed using a **Web browser**, such as *Internet Explorer* (*IE*), *Chrome*, *Safari*, *Opera*, or *Firefox*.

>**World Wide Web (WWW).** The collection of Web pages available through the Internet. >**Web page.** A document, typically containing hyperlinks to other documents, located on a Web server and available through the World Wide Web. >**Web site.** A collection of related Web pages usually belonging to an organization or individual. >**Web server.** A computer that is continually connected to the Internet and hosts Web pages that are accessible through the Internet. >**Web browser.** A program used to view Web pages.

ACCESSING PRODUCT INFORMATION

LOOKING UP REFERENCE INFORMATION

READING NEWS

SHOPPING

ACCESSING SOCIAL NETWORKS

WATCHING TV SHOWS AND MOVIES

Accessing a Network or the Internet

To access a local computer network (such as a home network, a school or company network, or a public wireless hotspot), you need to use a network adapter (either built into your computer or attached to it) to connect your computer to the network. With some computer networks you need to supply logon information (such as a *username* and a password) to *log on* to a network. Once you are connected to the network, you can access network resources, including the network's Internet connection. If you are connecting to the Internet without going through a computer network, your computer needs to use a modem to connect to the communications media (such as a telephone line or cable connection) used by your ISP. Network adapters and modems are discussed in more detail in Chapter 7.

Most Internet connections today are *direct* (or *always-on*) *connections*, which means the computer or other device being used to access the Internet is continually connected to the ISP's computer. With a direct connection, you only need to open your Web browser to begin using the Internet. With a dial-up connection, you must start the program that instructs your computer to dial and connect to the ISP's server via a telephone line, and then open a Web browser, each time you want to access the Internet.

To request a Web page or other resource located on the Internet, its **Internet address**—a unique numeric or text-based address—is used. The most common types of Internet addresses are *IP addresses* and *domain names* (to identify computers), *URLs* (to identify Web pages), and *e-mail addresses* (to identify people).

> **FIGURE 1-21**
> Some common Web activities.

> **Internet address.** An address that identifies a computer, person, or Web page on the Internet, such as an IP address, domain name, or e-mail address.

IP Addresses and Domain Names

IP addresses and their corresponding **domain names** are used to identify computers available through the Internet. IP (short for *Internet Protocol*) addresses are numeric, such as *207.46.197.32*, and are commonly used by computers to refer to other computers. A computer that hosts information available through the Internet (such as a Web server hosting Web pages) usually has a unique text-based domain name (such as *microsoft.com*) that corresponds to that computer's IP address in order to make it easier for people to request Web pages located on that computer. IP addresses and domain names are unique; that is, there cannot be two computers on the Internet using the exact same IP address or exact same domain name. To ensure this, specific IP addresses are allocated to each network (such as a company network or an ISP) to be used with the computers on that network, and there is a worldwide registration system for domain name registration. When a domain name is registered, the IP address of the computer that will be hosting the Web site associated with that domain name is also registered; the Web site can be accessed using either its domain name or corresponding IP address. When a Web site is requested using its domain name, the corresponding IP address is looked up using one of the Internet's *domain name system* (*DNS*) *servers* and then the appropriate Web page is displayed.

ORIGINAL TLDS	INTENDED USE
.com	Commercial businesses
.edu	Educational institutions
.gov	Government organizations
.int	International treaty organizations
.mil	Military organizations
.net	Network providers and ISPs
.org	Noncommercial organizations

NEWER TLDS	INTENDED USE
.aero	Aviation industry
.biz	Businesses
.fr	French businesses
.info	Resource sites
.jobs	Employment sites
.mobi	Sites optimized for mobile devices
.name	Individuals
.pro	Licensed professionals
.uk	United Kingdom businesses

FIGURE 1-22
Sample top-level domains (TLDs).

Domain names typically reflect the name of the individual or organization associated with that Web site and the different parts of a domain name are separated by a period. The far right part of the domain name (beginning with the rightmost period) is called the *top-level domain* (*TLD*) and traditionally identifies the type of organization or its location (such as *.com* for businesses, *.edu* for educational institutions, *.jp* for Web sites located in Japan, or *.fr* for Web sites located in France). There were seven original TLDs used in the United States; additional TLDs and numerous two-letter *country code TLDs* have since been created (see some examples in Figure 1-22). A new proposal allows for the creation of new TLDs that can be virtually any combination of up to 64 characters and that can use non-Latin characters. While custom TLDs are possible (such as to better represent a company name or personal name), they are also expected to be expensive to register (one estimate is about $100,000 each). Consequently, the initial interest in custom TLDs is by countries (such as Russia) whose native languages use non-Latin characters, groups of businesses and organizations that are interested in new activity-oriented TLDs like *.sports* and *.shop*, and community organizations interested in city-based TLDs like *.nyc* and *.paris* (for New York City and Paris businesses, respectively). Assuming the new plan is implemented, the new TLDs are expected to become available in 2010.

Uniform Resource Locators (URLs)

Similar to the way an IP address or domain name uniquely identifies a computer on the Internet, a **uniform resource locator** (**URL**) uniquely identifies a specific Web page

TIP

Only the legitimate holder of a trademarked name (such as Microsoft) can use that trademarked name as a domain name (such as microsoft.com); trademarks are discussed in detail in Chapter 16.

>**IP address.** A numeric Internet address used to uniquely identify a computer on the Internet. >**Domain name.** A text-based Internet address used to uniquely identify a computer on the Internet. >**Uniform resource locator (URL).** An Internet address (usually beginning with http://) that uniquely identifies a Web page.

(including the *protocol* or standard being used to display the Web page, the Web server hosting the Web page, the name of any folders on the Web server in which the Web page file is stored, and the Web page's filename, if needed).

The most common Web page protocols are *Hypertext Transfer Protocol* (*http://*) for regular Web pages or *Secure Hypertext Transfer Protocol* (*https://*) for *secure Web pages* that can safely be used to transmit sensitive information, such as credit card numbers. *File Transfer Protocol* (*ftp://*) is sometimes used to upload and download files. The *file extension* used for the Web page file indicates the type of Web page that will be displayed (such as *.html* and *.htm* for standard Web pages created using *Hypertext Markup Language*, as discussed in Chapter 10). For example, looking at the URL for the Web page shown in Figure 1-23 from right to left, we can see that the Web page is called *index.html*, is stored in a folder called *jobs* on the Web server associated with the *twitter.com* domain, and is a regular (nonsecure) Web page since the standard *http://* protocol is being used.

Web page URLs usually begin with the standard protocol identifier http://.

This part of the URL identifies the Web server hosting the Web page.

Next comes the folder(s) in which the Web page is stored, if necessary.

This is the Web page document that is to be retrieved and displayed.

FIGURE 1-23
A Web page URL.

TIP

Be sure that any Web page used to send sensitive data (such as your social security number or credit card information) is secure. Look for a URL that starts with *https* instead of *http* and a locked padlock icon on the Address bar.

E-Mail Addresses

To contact people using the Internet, you most often use their **e-mail addresses**. An e-mail address consists of a **username** (an identifying name), followed by the @ symbol, followed by the domain name for the computer that will be handling that person's e-mail (called a *mail server*). For example,

jsmith@cengage.com
maria_s@cengage.com
sam.peterson@cengage.com

are the e-mail addresses assigned respectively to jsmith (John Smith), maria_s (Maria Sanchez), and sam.peterson (Sam Peterson), three hypothetical employees at Cengage Learning, the publisher of this textbook. Usernames are typically a combination of the person's first and last names and sometimes include periods, underscores, and numbers, but cannot include blank spaces. To ensure a unique e-mail address for everyone in the world, usernames must be unique within each domain name. So, even though there could be a *jsmith* at Cengage Learning using the e-mail address *jsmith@cengage.com* and a *jsmith* at Stanford University using the e-mail address *jsmith@stanford.edu*, the two e-mail addresses are unique. It is up to each organization with a registered domain name to ensure that one—and only one—exact same username is assigned to its domain. Using e-mail addresses to send e-mail messages is discussed later in this chapter; other forms of online communications—such as instant messaging (IM)—are covered in Chapter 8. For a look at how online communications are being used to help keep college students safe, see the How It Works box.

> **E-mail address.** An Internet address consisting of a username and computer domain name that uniquely identifies a person on the Internet.
> **Username.** A name that uniquely identifies a user on a specific computer network.

HOW IT WORKS

Campus Emergency Notification Systems

Recent on-campus tragedies, such as the Virginia Tech shootings in 2007, have increased attention on ways organizations can quickly and effectively notify a large number of individuals. Following the Virginia Tech tragedy, which involved a shooting rampage lasting about two hours and killing more than 30 individuals, the *Higher Education Opportunity Act* was signed into law. The law provides grants and other assistance to colleges and universities to create an emergency communications system that can be used to contact students when a significant emergency or dangerous situation emerges. In response, colleges across the U.S. are implementing emergency notification systems to notify students, faculty, staff, and campus visitors of an emergency, severe weather condition, campus closure, or other critical event.

Since nearly all college students in the U.S. today have mobile phones, sending emergency alerts via text message is a natural option for many colleges. To be able to send a text message to an entire campus typically requires the use of a company who specializes in this type of mass communications. One such company is *Omnilert*, which has systems installed in more than 600 colleges and universities around the country. With the Omnilert campus notification system—called *e2Campus*—the contact information of the students, faculty, and staff to be notified is entered into the system and then the individuals can be divided into groups, depending on the types of messages each individual should receive. When an alert needs to be sent, an administrator sends the message (via a mobile phone or computer) and it is distributed to the appropriate individuals (see the accompanying illustration). In addition to text messages, alerts can also be sent simultaneously and automatically via virtually any voice or text communications medium, such as voice

messages, e-mail messages, RSS feeds, instant messages, Twitter feeds, Facebook pages, school Web pages, personal portal pages, desktop pop-up alerts, digital signage systems (such as signs located inside dorms and the student union), indoor and outdoor campus public address (PA) systems, and more.

To facilitate campus emergency notification systems, some colleges now require all undergraduate students to have a mobile phone. Some campuses also implement other useful mobile services, such as tracking campus shuttle buses, participating in class polls, and accessing class assignments and grades. An additional safety feature available at some schools is the ability to use the phones to activate an alert whenever a student feels unsafe on campus; these alerts automatically send the student's physical location (determined via the phone's GPS coordinates) to the campus police so the student can be quickly located.

Pronouncing Internet Addresses

Because Internet addresses are frequently given verbally, it is important to know how to pronounce them. A few guidelines are listed next, and Figure 1-24 shows some examples of Internet addresses and their proper pronunciations.

> ➤ If a portion of the address forms a recognizable word or name, it is spoken; otherwise, it is spelled out.

> ➤ The @ sign is pronounced *at*.

> ➤ The period (.) is pronounced *dot*.

> ➤ The forward slash (/) is pronounced *slash*.

TYPE OF ADDRESS	SAMPLE ADDRESS	PRONUNCIATION
Domain name	berkeley.edu	berkeley dot e d u
URL	microsoft.com/windows/ie/default.asp	microsoft dot com slash windows slash i e slash default dot a s p
E-mail address	president@whitehouse.gov	president at whitehouse dot gov

FIGURE 1-24
Pronouncing
Internet addresses.

Surfing the Web

Once you have an Internet connection, you are ready to begin *surfing the Web*—that is, using a Web browser to view Web pages. The first page that your Web browser displays when it is opened is your browser's starting page or *home page.* Often this is the home page for the Web site belonging to your browser, school, or ISP. However, you can use your browser's customization options to change the current home page to any page that you plan to visit regularly. From your browser's home page, you can move to any Web page you desire, as discussed next.

Using URLs and Hyperlinks

To navigate to a new Web page for which you know the URL, type that URL in the appropriate location for your Web browser (such as Internet Explorer's *Address bar*, as shown in Figure 1-25) and press Enter. Once that page is displayed, you can use the *hyperlinks*— graphics or text linked to other Web pages—located on that page to display other Web pages. In addition to Web pages, hyperlinks can also be linked to other types of files, such as to enable Web visitors to view or download images, listen to or download music files, view video clips, or download software programs.

The most commonly used Web browsers include Internet Explorer (shown in Figure 1-25), Chrome (shown in Figure 1-26), and Firefox. The newest versions of these browsers include *tabbed browsing* (which allows you to have multiple Web pages open at the same time), improved *crash recovery* and security, and improved ability to search for and *bookmark* Web pages, as discussed shortly. *Internet Explorer 8 (IE 8)* also includes the ability to subscribe to *Web Slices*—small pieces of a Web site, such as a particular online

TIP

If you get an error message when typing a URL, first check to make sure you typed it correctly. If it is correct, edit the URL to remove any folder or filenames and press Enter to try to load the home page of that site.

FIGURE 1-25
Surfing the Web with IE 8. URLs, hyperlinks, and favorites can be used to display Web pages.

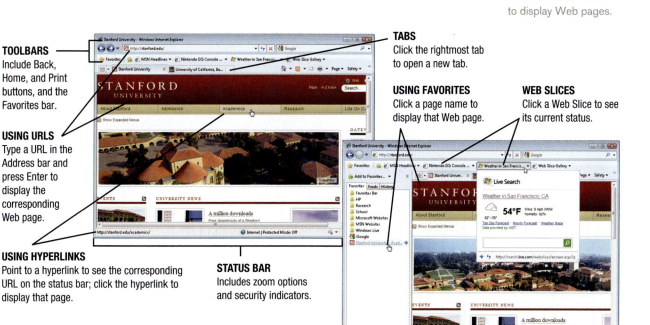

TOOLBARS
Include Back, Home, and Print buttons, and the Favorites bar.

USING URLS
Type a URL in the Address bar and press Enter to display the corresponding Web page.

USING HYPERLINKS
Point to a hyperlink to see the corresponding URL on the status bar; click the hyperlink to display that page.

STATUS BAR
Includes zoom options and security indicators.

TABS
Click the rightmost tab to open a new tab.

USING FAVORITES
Click a page name to display that Web page.

WEB SLICES
Click a Web Slice to see its current status.

auction or a particular Facebook page—and see the current status of that Web Slice without leaving your current page (refer again to Figure 1-25). In any browser, you can use the Back button on the browser's toolbar to return to a previous page. To print the current Web page, click the browser's Print button or select *Print* from the browser's menu or toolbar.

Using Favorites and the History List

All Web browsers have a feature (usually called *Favorites* or *Bookmarks* and accessed via a Favorites or Bookmarks menu or button) that you can use to save Web page URLs. Once a Web page is saved as a favorite or a bookmark, you can redisplay that page without typing its URL—you simply select its link from the Favorites or Bookmarks list. You can also use this feature to save a group of tabbed Web pages to open the entire group again at a later time. Web browsers also maintain a *History list*, which is a record of all Web pages visited during a period of time specified in the browser settings; you can revisit a Web page located on the History list by displaying the History list and selecting that page.

Most Web browsers today allow you to delete, move into folders, and otherwise organize your favorites/bookmarks, as well as to search your favorites/bookmarks or History list to help you find pages more easily. Chrome goes one step further by displaying thumbnails of your most visited sites, a list of your most recent bookmarks, and a history search box each time you open a new browser tab.

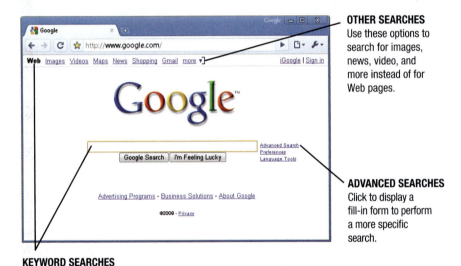

OTHER SEARCHES
Use these options to search for images, news, video, and more instead of for Web pages.

ADVANCED SEARCHES
Click to display a fill-in form to perform a more specific search.

KEYWORD SEARCHES
Since the Web option is selected, type keywords here and press Enter to see a list of Web pages matching your search criteria.

FIGURE 1-26
The Google search site displayed in the Chrome browser.

Searching the Web

People typically turn to the Web to find specific types of information. There are a number of special Web pages, called *search sites*, available to help you locate what you are looking for on the Internet. One of the most popular search sites—*Google*—is shown in Figure 1-26. To conduct a search, you typically type one or more *keywords* into the search box on a search site, and a list of links to Web pages matching your search criteria is displayed (many browsers also allow you to type search terms in the Address bar instead of a URL and an Internet search will be performed). There are also numerous *reference sites* available on the Web to look up addresses, phone numbers, ZIP codes, maps, and other information. To find a reference site, type the information you are looking for (such as "ZIP code lookup" or "topographical maps") in a search site's search box to see links to sites with that information. Searching the Web is discussed in more detail in Chapter 8.

E-Mail

Electronic mail (more commonly called **e-mail**) is the process of exchanging electronic messages between computers over a network—usually the Internet. E-mail is one of the

> **Electronic mail (e-mail).** Electronic messages sent from one user to another over the Internet or other network.

most widely used Internet applications—Americans alone send billions of e-mail messages daily and worldwide e-mail traffic is expected to exceed one-half trillion messages per day by 2013, according to the Radicati Group. You can send an e-mail message from any Internet-enabled device (such as a desktop computer, portable computer, or mobile device) to anyone who has an Internet e-mail address. As illustrated in Figure 1-27, e-mail messages travel from the sender's computer to his or her ISP's *mail server*, and then through the Internet to the mail server being used by the recipient's ISP. When the recipient logs on to the Internet and requests his or her e-mail, it is displayed on the computer he or she is using. In addition to text, e-mail messages can include attached files, such as photos and other documents.

E-mail can be sent and received via an *e-mail program*, such as *Microsoft Outlook*, installed on the computer being used (sometimes referred to as *conventional e-mail*) or via a Web page belonging to a Web mail provider such as *Gmail* or *Windows Live Mail* (referred to as *Web-based e-mail* or just *Web mail*). Using an installed e-mail program is convenient for individuals who use e-mail often and want to have copies of sent and received e-mail messages stored on their computer. To use an installed e-mail program, however, it must first be set up with the user's name, e-mail address, incoming mail server, and outgoing mail server information. Web-based e-mail does not require this set up and a user's e-mail can be accessed from any computer with an Internet connection by just displaying the appropriate Web mail page and logging on. Consequently, Web-based e-mail is more flexible than conventional e-mail since it can be accessed easily from any computer with an Internet connection. However, Web-based e-mail is typically slower than conventional e-mail and messages can only be viewed when the user is online and logged on to his or her Web mail account, unless the Web-based e-mail provider offers *offline e-mail* service. Despite these limitations, use of Web-based e-mail for both personal and business use is growing and, according to a Gartner estimate, as much as 20% of business e-mail accounts are expected to be Web-based by 2012—up from only 2% in 2007.

Web-based e-mail is typically free and virtually all ISPs used with personal computers include e-mail service in their monthly fee. Some plans from mobile phone providers that provide Internet service for mobile phones include a limit on the number and/or size of e-mail messages that can be sent or received during a billing period; messages after that point result in additional fees. Other types of mobile communications, such as text messages that typically use the *Short Message Service* (*SMS*) protocol when sent between mobile phones, may also incur a fee. Messaging and other types of online communications that can be used in addition to e-mail are discussed in Chapter 8.

FIGURE 1-27
How e-mail works.

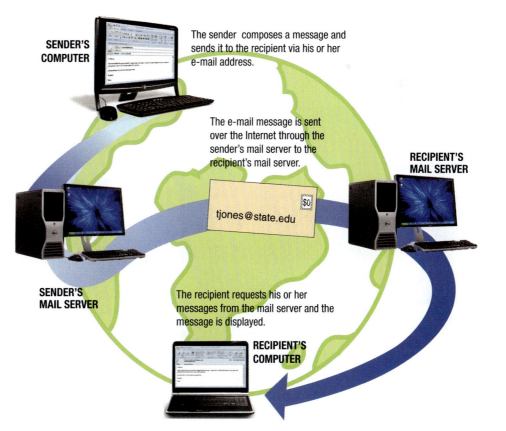

SENDER'S COMPUTER

The sender composes a message and sends it to the recipient via his or her e-mail address.

The e-mail message is sent over the Internet through the sender's mail server to the recipient's mail server.

RECIPIENT'S MAIL SERVER

tjones@state.edu

$0

SENDER'S MAIL SERVER

The recipient requests his or her messages from the mail server and the message is displayed.

RECIPIENT'S COMPUTER

COMPUTERS AND SOCIETY

The vast improvements in technology over the past decade have had a distinct impact on daily life, both at home and at work. Computers have become indispensable tools in our personal and professional lives, and related technological advancements have changed the way our everyday items—cars, microwaves, coffee pots, toys, exercise bikes, telephones, televisions, and more—look and function. As computers and everyday devices become smarter, they tend to do their intended jobs faster, better, and more reliably than before, as well as take on additional capabilities. In addition to affecting individuals, computerization and technological advances have changed society as a whole. Without computers, banks would be overwhelmed by the job of tracking all the transactions they process, moon exploration and the space shuttle would still belong to science fiction, and some scientific advances—such as DNA analysis and gene mapping—would be nonexistent. In addition, we as individuals are getting accustomed to the increased automation of everyday activities, such as shopping and banking, and we depend on having fast and easy access to information via the Internet and rapid communications via e-mail and instant messaging. In addition, many of us would not think about making a major purchase without first researching it online. In fact, it is surprising how fast the Internet and its resources have become an integral part of our society. But despite all its benefits, *cyberspace* has some risks. Some of the most important societal implications related to computers and the Internet are introduced next; many of these issues are covered in more detail in later chapters of this text.

Benefits of a Computer-Oriented Society

The benefits of having such a computer-oriented society are numerous, as touched on throughout this chapter. The capability to virtually design, build, and test new buildings, cars, and airplanes before the actual construction begins helps professionals create safer end products. Technological advances in medicine allow for earlier diagnosis and more effective treatment of diseases than ever before. The benefit of beginning medical students performing virtual surgery using a computer instead of performing actual surgery on a patient is obvious. The ability to shop, pay bills, research products, participate in online courses, and look up vast amounts of information 24 hours a day, 7 days a week, 365 days a year via the Internet is a huge convenience. In addition, a computer-oriented society generates new opportunities. For example, technologies—such as *speech recognition software* and Braille input and output devices—enable physically- or visually-challenged individuals to perform necessary job tasks and to communicate with others more easily.

In general, technology has also made a huge number of tasks in our lives go much faster. Instead of experiencing a long delay for a credit check, an applicant can get approved for a purchase, loan, or credit card almost immediately. Documents and photographs can be e-mailed or faxed in mere moments, instead of taking at least a day to be mailed physically. We can watch many of our favorite TVs shows online (see Figure 1-28) and access up-to-minute news at our convenience. And we can download information, programs, music files, movies, and more on demand when we want or need them, instead of having to order them and then wait for delivery or physically go to a store to purchase the desired items.

▼ FIGURE 1-28

Episodes of many televisions shows are available online to be viewed at the user's convenience.

Risks of a Computer-Oriented Society

Although there are a great number of benefits from having a computer-oriented society and a *networked economy*, there are risks as well. A variety of problems have emerged from our extensive computer use, ranging from stress and health concerns, to the proliferation of *spam* (unsolicited e-mails) and *malware* (harmful programs that can be installed on our computers without our knowledge), to security and privacy issues, to legal and ethical dilemmas. Many of the security and privacy concerns stem from the fact that so much of our personal business takes place online—or at least ends up as data in a computer database somewhere—and the potential for misuse of this data is enormous. Another concern is the repercussions of collecting such vast amounts of information electronically. Some people worry about creating a "Big Brother" situation, in which the government or another organization is watching everything that we do. Although the accumulation and distribution of information is a necessary factor of our networked economy, it is one area of great concern to many individuals. And some Internet behavior, such as downloading music or movies from an unauthorized source or viewing pornography on an office computer, can get you arrested or fired.

Security Issues

One of the most common online security risks today is your computer becoming infected with a malware program, such as a *computer virus*—a malicious software program designed to change the way a computer operates. Malware often causes damage to the infected computer, such as erasing data or bogging down the computer so it does not function well; it can also be used to try to locate sensitive data on your computer (such as Web site passwords or credit card numbers) and send that data to the malware creator. Malware can be attached to a program (such as one downloaded from a Web page), as well as attached to, or contained within, an e-mail message. To help protect your computer, never open an e-mail attachment from someone you do not know or that has an executable *file extension* (the last three letters in the filename preceded by a period), such as *.exe*, *.com*, or *.vbs*, without checking with the sender first to make sure the attachment is legitimate. You should also be careful about what files you download from the Internet. In addition, it is crucial to install *security software* on your computer and to set up the program to monitor your computer on a continual basis (see Figure 1-29). If a virus or other type of malware attempts to install itself on your computer (such as through an e-mail message attachment or a downloaded file), the antivirus program will block it. If malware does find its way onto your computer, the antivirus program will detect it during a regular scan, notify you, and attempt to remove it.

Another ongoing security problem is *identity theft*—in which someone else uses your identity, typically to purchase goods or services. Identity theft can stem from personal information discovered from offline means—like discarded papers or stolen mail—or from information found online, stolen from an online database, or obtained via a malware program. *Phishing*—in which identity thieves send fraudulent e-mails to people masquerading as legitimate businesses to obtain social security numbers or other information needed for identity theft—is also a major security issue today. Common security concerns and precautions, such as protecting your computer from malware and protecting yourself against identity theft and phishing schemes, are discussed in detail in Chapter 9.

FIGURE 1-29

Antivirus software.

Antivirus software is crucial for protecting your computer from viruses and other types of malware.

Privacy Issues

Some individuals view the potential risk to personal privacy as one of the most important issues regarding our networked society. As more and more data about our everyday activities is collected and stored on computers accessible via the Internet, our privacy is at risk because the potential for privacy violations increases. Today, data is collected about practically anything we buy online or offline, although offline purchases may not be associated with our identity unless we use a credit card or a membership or loyalty card. At issue is not that data is collected—with virtually all organizations using computers for recordkeeping, that is unavoidable—but rather how the collected data is used and how secure it is. Data collected by businesses may be used only by that company or, depending on the businesses' *privacy policy*, may be shared with others. Data shared with others often results in *spam*—unsolicited e-mails. Spam is an enormous problem for individuals and businesses today, and it is considered by many to be a violation of personal privacy. Privacy concerns and precautions are discussed in detail in Chapter 15.

> **CAUTION CAUTION CAUTION CAUTION CAUTION CAUTION CAUT**
>
> Using your primary e-mail address when shopping online or signing up for a sweepstake or other online activity will undoubtedly result in spam being sent to that e-mail address. Use a *throw-away e-mail address* (a free e-mail address from Gmail or another free e-mail provider that you can change easily) for these activities instead to help protect your privacy and cut back on the amount of spam delivered to your regular e-mail account.

Differences in Online Communications

There is no doubt that e-mail, instant messaging, and other online communications methods have helped speed up both personal and business communications and have made them more efficient (such as avoiding the telephone tag problem). As you spend more and more time communicating online, you will probably notice some differences between online communications methods (such as e-mail and instant messaging) and traditional communications methods (such as telephone calls and written letters). In general, online communications tend to be much less formal. This may be because people usually compose e-mail messages quickly and just send them off, without taking the time to reread the message content or check the spelling or grammar. However, you need to be careful not to be so casual—particularly in business—that your communications appear unprofessional or become too personal with people you do not know.

To help in that regard, a special etiquette—referred to as *netiquette*—has evolved to guide online behavior. A good rule of thumb is always to be polite and considerate of others and to refrain from offensive remarks. This holds true whether you are asking a question via a company's e-mail address, posting a message on someone's *Facebook Wall*, or IMing a friend. When the communication involves business, you should also be very careful with your grammar and spelling, to avoid embarrassing yourself. Some specific guidelines for what is considered to be proper online behavior are listed in Figure 1-30.

Another trend in online communications is the use of abbreviations and *emoticons*. Abbreviations or *acronyms*, such as BTW for "by the way," are commonly used to save time in all types of communications today. They are being used with increased frequency in text messaging and e-mail exchanged via mobile phones to speed up the text entry process. Emoticons are illustrations of faces showing smiles, frowns, and other expressions that are created with keyboard symbols—such as the popular :-) smile emoticon—and allow people to add an emotional tone to written online communications. Without these symbols, it is sometimes difficult to tell if the person who sent the online communication is serious or joking, since you

▼ FIGURE 1-30

Netiquette. Use these netiquette guidelines and common sense when communicating online.

RULE	EXPLANATION
Use descriptive subject lines	Use short, descriptive subject lines for e-mail messages and discussion group posts. For example, "Question regarding MP3 downloads" is much better than a vague title, such as "Question".
Don't shout	SHOUTING REFERS TO TYPING YOUR ENTIRE E-MAIL MESSAGE OR DISCUSSION GROUP POST USING CAPITAL LETTERS. Use capital letters only when it is grammatically correct to do so or for emphasizing a few words.
Watch what you say	Things that you say or write online can be interpreted as being sexist, racist, ethnocentric, xenophobic, or in just general bad taste. Also check spelling and grammar—typos look unprofessional and nobody likes wading through poorly written materials.
Avoid e-mail overload	Don't send spam mail, which is unsolicated bulk e-mail and the Internet equivalent of junk mail. The same goes for forwarding e-mail chain letters or every joke you run across to everyone in your address book.
Be cautious	Don't give out personal information—such as your real name, telephone number, or credit card information—to people you meet in a chat room or other online meeting place.
Think before you send	Once you send an e-mail or text message or post something online, you lose control of it. Don't send messages that include content (such as compromising photos) that you would not want shared with others.

cannot see the individual's face or hear his or her tone of voice. While most people would agree that using abbreviations and emoticons with personal communications is fine, they are not usually viewed as appropriate for formal business communications.

The Anonymity Factor

By their very nature, online communications lend themselves to *anonymity*. Since recipients usually do not hear senders' voices or see their handwriting, it is difficult to know for sure who the sender is. Particularly on *message boards* (online discussions in which users post messages and respond to other posts), in *virtual worlds* (online worlds that users can explore), and other online activities where individuals use made-up names instead of real names, there is an anonymous feel to being online.

Being anonymous gives many individuals a sense of freedom, which makes them feel able to say or do anything online. This sense of true freedom of speech can be beneficial. For example, a reserved individual who might never complain about a poor product or service in person may feel comfortable lodging a complaint by e-mail. In political discussion groups, many people feel they can be completely honest about what they think and can introduce new ideas and points of view without inhibition. Anonymous e-mail is also a safe way for an employee to blow the whistle on a questionable business practice, or for an individual to tip off police to a crime or potential terrorist attack.

But, like all good things, online anonymity can be abused. Using the Internet as their shield, some people use rude comments, ridicule, profanity, and even slander to attack people, places, and things they do not like or agree with. Others may use multiple online identities (such as multiple usernames on a message board) to give the appearance of increased support for their points of view. Still others may use multiple identities to try to manipulate stock prices (by posting false information about a company to drive the price down, for instance), to get buyers to trust an online auction seller (by posting fictitious positive feedback about themselves), or to commit other illegal or unethical acts.

It is possible to hide your true identity while browsing or sending e-mail by removing personal information from your browser and e-mail program or by using privacy software that acts as a middleman between you and Web sites and hides your identity, as discussed in more detail in Chapter 15. But, in fact, even when personal information is removed, ISPs and the government may still be able to trace communications back to a particular computer when a crime has occurred, so it is difficult—perhaps impossible—to be completely anonymous online.

Information Integrity

The Web contains a vast amount of information on a wide variety of topics. While much of the information is factual, other information may be misleading, biased, or just plain wrong. As more and more people turn to the Web for information, it is crucial that they take the time to determine if the information they obtain and pass on to others is accurate. There have been numerous cases of information intended as a joke being restated on a Web site as fact, statements being quoted out of context (which changed the meaning from the original intent), and hoaxes circulated via e-mail. Consequently, use common sense when evaluating what you read online, and double-check information before passing it on to others.

One way to evaluate online content is by its source. If you obtain information from a news source that you trust, you should feel confident that the accuracy of its online information is close to that of its offline counterpart. For information about a particular product, go to the originating company. For government information, government Web sites are your best source for fact checking. There are also independent Web sites (such as the *Snopes* Web site shown in Figure 1-31) that report on the validity of current online rumors and stories.

FIGURE 1-31

Snopes.com. This Web site can be used to check out online rumors.

SUMMARY

COMPUTERS IN YOUR LIFE

Computers appear almost everywhere in today's world, and most people need to use a computer or a computerized device frequently on the job, at home, at school, or while on the go. **Computer literacy**, which is being familiar with basic computer concepts, helps individuals feel comfortable using computers and is a necessary skill for everyone today.

Computers abound in today's homes, schools, workplaces, and other locations. Most students and employees need to use a computer for productivity, research, or other important tasks. Individuals often use computers at home and/or carry portable computers or devices with them to remain in touch with others or to use Internet resources on a continual basis. Individuals also frequently encounter computers while on the go, such as *consumer kiosks* and *point-of-sale* (*POS*) *systems.*

WHAT IS A COMPUTER AND WHAT DOES IT DO?

A **computer** is a *programmable* electronic device that accepts **input**; performs **processing** operations; **outputs** the results; and provides **storage** for data, programs, or output when needed. Most computers today also have **communications** capabilities. This progression of input, processing, output, and storage is sometimes called the *information processing cycle.*

Data is the raw, unorganized facts that are input into the computer to be processed. Data that the computer has processed into a useful form is called **information**. Data can exist in many forms, representing *text*, *graphics*, *audio*, and *video.*

One of the first calculating devices was the *abacus.* Early computing devices that predate today's computers include the *slide rule*, the *mechanical calculator*, and Dr. Herman Hollerith's *Punch Card Tabulating Machine and Sorter. First-generation computers*, such as *ENIAC* and *UNIVAC*, were powered by *vacuum tubes*; *second-generation computers* used *transistors*; and *third-generation computers* were possible because of the invention of the *integrated circuit* (*IC*). Today's *fourth-generation computers* use *microprocessors* and are frequently connected to the *Internet* and other *networks*. Some people believe that *fifth-generation computers* will likely be based on *artificial intelligence.*

A computer is made up of **hardware** (the actual physical equipment that makes up the computer system) and **software** (the computer's programs). Common hardware components include the *keyboard* and *mouse* (*input devices*), the *CPU* (a *processing device*), *monitors* and *printers* (*output devices*), and *storage devices* and *storage media* (such as *CDs*, *DVD drives, hard drives, USB flash drives*, and *flash memory cards*). Most computers today also include a *modem, network adapter*, or other type of *communications device* to allow users to connect to the Internet or other network.

All computers need *system software*, namely an **operating system** (usually *Windows*, *Mac OS*, or *Linux*), to function. The operating system assists with the **boot** process, and then controls the operation of the computer, such as to allow users to run other types of software and to manage their files. Most software programs today use a variety of graphical objects that are selected to tell the computer what to do. The basic workspace for a Windows' users is the **Windows desktop**.

Application software consists of programs designed to allow people to perform specific tasks or applications, such as word processing, Web browsing, photo touch-up, and so on. Software programs are written using a *programming language*. Programs are written by *programmers*; *computer users* are the people who use computers to perform tasks or obtain information.

INT

COMPUTERS TO FIT EVERY NEED

Embedded computers are built into products (such as cars and household appliances) to give them added functionality. **Mobile devices** are small devices with computing or Internet capabilities; a mobile device based on a mobile phone is called a **smartphone**.

Small computers used by individuals at home or work are called **personal computers** (**PCs**) or **microcomputers**. Most personal computers today are either **desktop computers** or **portable computers** (**notebook computers**, **laptop computers**, **tablet computers**, **netbooks**, or **ultra-mobile PCs** (**UMPC**)—also called **handheld computers**) and typically conform to either the *PC-compatible* or *Macintosh* standard. Tablet computers come in both *slate tablet* and *convertible tablet* formats. **Thin clients** are designed solely to access a network; **Internet appliances** are designed specifically for accessing the Internet and e-mail.

Medium-sized computers, or **midrange servers**, are used in many businesses to host data and programs to be accessed via the company network. A growing trend is **virtualization**—creating separate virtual environments on a single server that act as separate servers. The powerful computers used by most large businesses and organizations to perform the information processing necessary for day-to-day operations are called **mainframe computers**. The very largest, most powerful computers, which typically run one application at a time, are **supercomputers**. A supercomputer comprised of numerous smaller computers connected together to act as a single computer is a **supercomputing cluster**.

COMPUTER NETWORKS AND THE INTERNET

Computer networks are used to connect individual computers and related devices so that users can share hardware, software, and data as well as communicate with one another. The **Internet** is a worldwide collection of networks. Typically, individual users connect to the Internet by connecting to computers belonging to an **Internet service provider** (**ISP**)—a company that provides Internet access, usually for a fee. One resource available through the Internet is the **World Wide Web** (**WWW**)—an enormous collection of **Web pages** located on **Web servers**. The starting page for a **Web site** (a related group of Web pages) is called the *home page* for that site. Web pages are viewed with a **Web browser**, are connected with *hyperlinks*, and can be used for many helpful activities.

To access a computer network, you need some type of *modem* or *network adapter*. To access the Internet, an Internet service provider (ISP) is also used. **Internet addresses** are used to identify resources on the Internet and include numerical **IP addresses** and text-based **domain names** (used to identify computers), **uniform resource locators** or **URLs** (used to identify Web pages), and **e-mail addresses** (a combination of a **username** and domain name that is used to send an individual e-mail messages).

Web pages are displayed by clicking hyperlinks or by typing appropriate URLs in the browser's *Address bar. Favorites/Bookmarks* and the *History list* can be used to redisplay a previously-visited Web page and *search sites* can be used to locate Web pages matching specified criteria. **Electronic mail** (**e-mail**) is used to send electronic messages over the Internet.

COMPUTERS AND SOCIETY

Computers and devices based on related technology have become indispensable tools for modern life, making ordinary tasks easier and quicker than ever before and helping make today's worker more productive than ever before. In addition to the benefits, however, there are many risks and societal implications related to our heavy use of the Internet and the vast amount of information available through the Internet. Issues include privacy and security risks and concerns (such as *malware*, *identity theft*, *phishing*, and *spam*), the differences in online and offline communications, the anonymity factor, and the amount of unreliable information that can be found on the Internet.

Chapter Objective 6:
List the six basic types of computers, giving at least one example of each type of computer and stating what that computer might be used for.

Chapter Objective 7:
Explain what a network, the Internet, and the World Wide Web are, as well as how computers, people, and Web pages are identified on the Internet.

Chapter Objective 8:
Describe how to access a Web page and navigate through a Web site.

Chapter Objective 9:
Discuss the societal impact of computers, including some benefits and risks related to their prominence in our society.

REVIEW ACTIVITIES

KEY TERM MATCHING

a. computer

b. hardware

c. Internet

d. netbook

e. processing

f. software

g. storage

h. supercomputer

i. uniform resource locator (URL)

j. Web site

Instructions: Match each key term on the left with the definition on the right that best describes it.

1. _____ A collection of related Web pages usually belonging to an organization or individual.

2. _____ An Internet address, usually beginning with http://, that uniquely identifies a Web page.

3. _____ A programmable, electronic device that accepts data input, performs processing operations on that data, and outputs and stores the results.

4. _____ A very small notebook computer.

5. _____ Performing operations on data that have been input into a computer to convert that input to output.

6. _____ The operation of saving data, programs, or output for future use.

7. _____ The fastest, most expensive, and most powerful type of computer.

8. _____ The instructions, also called computer programs, that are used to tell a computer what it should do.

9. _____ The largest and most well-known computer network, linking millions of computers all over the world.

10. _____ The physical parts of a computer system, such as the keyboard, monitor, printer, and so forth.

SELF-QUIZ

Instructions: Circle **T** if the statement is true, **F** if the statement is false, or write the best answer in the space provided. **Answers for the self-quiz are located in the References and Resources Guide at the end of the book.**

1. **T   F**   A mouse is one common input device.

2. **T   F**   Software includes all the physical equipment in a computer system.

3. **T   F**   A computer can run without an operating system if it has good application software.

4. **T   F**   One of the most common types of home computers is the midrange server.

5. **T   F**   An example of a domain name is *microsoft.com.*

6. _____ is the operation in which data is entered into the computer.

7. A(n) _____ computer can come in convertible or slate form.

8. _____ is frequently used with servers today to create several separate environments on a single server that act as separate servers.

9. Electronic messages sent over the Internet that can be retrieved by the recipient at his or her convenience are called _____.

10. Write the number of the term that best matches each of the following descriptions in the blank to the left of its description.

    a. _____ Allows access to resources located on the Internet.

    b. _____ Supervises the running of all other programs on the computer.

    c. _____ Enables users to perform specific tasks on a computer.

    d. _____ Allows the creation of application programs.

1. Application software
2. Operating system
3. Programming language
4. Web browser

INT

EXERCISES

1. For the following list of computer hardware devices, indicate the principal function of each device by writing the appropriate letter—I (input device), O (output device), S (storage device), P (processing device), or C (communications device)—in the space provided.

    a. CPU _____   d. Keyboard _____   g. Speakers _____

    b. Monitor _____   e. Hard drive _____   h. DVD drive _____

    c. Mouse _____   f. Modem _____   i. Microphone _____

2. Supply the missing words to complete the following statements.

    a. The Internet is an example of a(n) _____, a collection of computers and other devices connected together to share resources and communicate with each other.

    b. The starting page for a Web site is called the site's _____.

    c. For the e-mail address *jsmith@cengage.com*, *jsmith* is the _____ and *cengage.com* is the _____ name.

    d. The e-mail address pronounced *bill gee at microsoft dot com* is written _____.

3. What are three differences between a desktop computer and an ultra-mobile PC (UMPC)?

4. List two reasons why a business may choose to network its employees' computers.

5. If a computer manufacturer called Apex created a home page for the Web, what would its URL likely be? Also, supply an appropriate e-mail address for yourself, assuming that you are employed by that company.

DISCUSSION QUESTIONS

1. There is usually a positive side and a negative side to each new technological improvement. Select a technology you use every day and consider its benefits and risks. What benefits does the technology provide? Are there any risks involved and, if so, how can they be minimized? If you chose not to use this technology because of the possible risks associated with it, how would your life be affected? Who should determine if the benefits of a new technology outweigh the potential risks? Consumers? The government?

2. The ubiquitous nature of mobile phones today brings tremendous convenience to our lives, but will misuse of new improvements to this technology result in the loss of that convenience? For instance, camera phones are now banned in many fitness centers, park restrooms, and other similar facilities because some people have used them inappropriately to take compromising photos, and mobile phones are banned in many classrooms because of the disruption of constant text messaging and the use of the phone by dishonest students to cheat on exams. Do you think these reactions to mobile phone misuse are justified? Is there another way to ensure the appropriate use of mobile phones without banning their use for all individuals? Should there be more stringent consequences for those who use technology for illegal or unethical purposes?

PROJECTS

1. **Mobile TV** As discussed in this chapter, TV is one of the newest entertainment options available for mobile phones. From live TV to video clips and movies, mobile TV is taking off.

   For this project, investigate the mobile TV options available today. Find at least two services and compare features, such as cost, compatibility, channels, and programming. Do your selected services offer live TV, video-on-demand, or both? If you have a mobile phone, are any of the services available through your mobile provider? Are there currently Web sites where mobile users can view episodes of TV shows for free, like personal computer users can? What is the current status of the push by the *Open Mobile Video Coalition* to have a free mobile TV standard across the United States? Have you ever watched TV on a mobile phone? If so, how do you rate your experience and would you do it again? If not, would you want to watch TV on a mobile phone? Do you think mobile TV is the wave of the future? Why or why not? At the conclusion of your research, prepare a one-page summary of your findings and opinions and submit it to your instructor.

2. **Buying a New PC** New personal computers are widely available directly from manufacturers, as well as in retail, computer, electronic, and warehouse stores. Some stores carry only standard configurations as set up by the manufacturers; others allow you to customize a system.

   For this project, assume that you are in the market for a new personal computer. Give some thought to the type of computer (such as desktop, notebook, or netbook computer) that best fits your lifestyle and the tasks you wish to perform (such as the application programs you wish to use, how many programs you wish to use at one time, and how fast you desire the response time to be). Make a list of your hardware and software requirements (refer to the "Guide for Buying a PC" in the References and Resources Guide at the end of this book, if needed), being as specific as possible. By researching newspaper ads, manufacturer Web sites, and/or systems for sale at local stores, find three systems that meet your minimum requirements. Prepare a one-page comparison chart, listing each requirement and how each system meets or exceeds it. Also include any additional features each system has, and information regarding the brand, price, delivery time, shipping, sales tax, and warranty for each system. On your comparison sheet, mark the system that you would prefer to buy and write one paragraph explaining why. Turn in your comparison sheet and summary to your instructor, stapled to copies of the printed ads, specifications printed from Web sites, or other written documentation that you collected during this project.

3. **The Internet** The Internet and World Wide Web are handy tools that can help you research topics covered in this textbook, complete many of the projects, and perform the online activities available via the textbook's Web site that are designed to enhance your learning and help you prepare for exams on the content covered in this textbook.

   For this project, find an Internet-enabled computer on your campus, at home, or at your public library and access the Understanding Computers Web site located at **www.cengage.com/ computerconcepts/np/uc13**. Once you are at the site, note the types of information and activities that are available to you as a student and select a few of them by using your mouse to click the hyperlinks corresponding to the options you want to explore. At the conclusion of this task, prepare a one-page summary describing the resources available through this textbook's Web site, and your opinion about their usefulness in enhancing your learning experience and/or preparing for exams related to this text, and submit it to your instructor.

4. **Gossip Sites** A recent trend on college campuses today is the use of campus gossip sites, where students can post campus related news, rumors, and basic gossip. These sites were originally set up to promote free speech and to allow participants to publish comments anonymously without repercussions from school administrators, professors, and other officials. However, they are now being used to post vicious comments about others. What do you think of campus gossip sites? Is it ethical to post a rumor about another individual on these sites? How would you feel if you read a posting about yourself on a gossip site? School administrators cannot regulate the content since the sites are not sponsored or run by the college, and federal law prohibits Web hosts from being liable for the content posted by its users. Is this ethical? What if a posting leads to a criminal act, such as a rape, murder, or suicide? Who, if anyone, should be held responsible?

   For this project, form an opinion about the ethical ramifications of gossip Web sites and be prepared to discuss your position (in class, via an online class discussion group, in a class chat room, or via a class blog, depending on your instructor's directions). You may also be asked to write a short paper expressing your opinion.

ETHICS IN ACTION

5. **Online Education** The amount of distance learning available through the Internet and World Wide Web has exploded in the last couple of years. A few years ago, it was possible to take an occasional course online—now, an entire college degree can be earned online.

   For this project, look into the online education options available at your school and two other colleges or universities. Compare and contrast the programs in general, including whether or not the institution is accredited, the types of courses available online, whether or not an entire certificate or degree can be earned online, and the required fees. Next, select one online course and research it more closely. Find out how the course works in an online format—including whether or not any face-to-face class time is required, whether assignments and exams are submitted online, which software programs are required, and other course requirements—and determine if you would be interested in taking that course. Share your findings with the class in the form of a short presentation. The presentation should not exceed 10 minutes and should make use of one or more presentation aids, such as the chalkboard, handouts, overhead transparencies, or a computer-based slide presentation (your instructor may provide additional requirements). You may also be asked to submit a summary of the presentation to your instructor.

PRESENTATION/ DEMONSTRATION

Instructions: Go to the Chapter 1 page at **www.cengage.com/computerconcepts/np/uc13** to work the following Web Activities.

WEB ACTIVITIES

6. **Interactive Activities** Work the interactive **Crossword Puzzle**, watch the **Video Podcasts** and **Online Videos**, and explore the **Further Exploration** links associated with this chapter.

   If you have a SAM user profile, you may have access to hands-on instruction, practice, and assessment of the skills covered in this chapter. Check with your instructor for instructions and the correct URL/Web site to access those assignments.

7. **Student Edition Labs** Work the following interactive **Student Edition Labs.**
   - ➤ **Using Windows**   ➤ **E-Mail**

8. **Test Yourself** Review the **Online Study Guide** for this chapter, then test your knowledge of the terms and concepts covered in this chapter by completing the **Key Term Matching** exercise, the **Self-Quiz**, the **Exercises**, and the **Practice Test**.

SAM

Student Edition Labs

Personal Computers

A conversation with JOE MELFI
Associate Director of Business Solutions, D-Link Systems

> *". . . it is important to be cautious about what information is shared online because, once it is out there, it can't be taken back."*

D-Link®
Building Networks for People

Joe Melfi is the Associate Director of Business Solutions for D-Link Systems. He has worked in the area of communications and electronics technologies for more than 25 years, including as a Systems Engineer, Software Engineer, Application Engineer, and Technical Marketing Engineer, before accepting his current position at D-Link. Joe holds a Bachelor of Science degree in Electrical Engineering, as well as several technical certificates. He has also been a college instructor, teaching courses in microprocessor systems, data communications, and digital electronics.

My Background . . .

In my youth, I had an endless curiosity about how things worked. I took everything apart to see what was inside, which led me down the path to become an electrical engineer. Eventually, I found my calling in computer communications. All in all, I have more than 25 years of applied experience in a wide range of communications and electronics technologies. Currently, I serve as Associate Director of Business Solutions for D-Link, a leading company in the area of business and consumer networking hardware. My primary responsibilities include driving marketing programs, creating sales materials, and overseeing technical aspects of the marketing department.

Throughout my career, I've found I favor roles that merge technology with marketing. I credit my engineering education and experience; my hands-on experience as a technician and hobbyist; my teaching experience; and my experience as a techie working with sales teams and making presentations with giving me the experience and skills needed to succeed in my chosen career.

It's Important to Know . . .

Computers are everywhere, and take many forms. Computers are more than the PC on your desk. They are in your cars, your televisions, your phones, and so many other places. The smartphone is one current technology that may end up having the biggest impact on our lives. Today's mobile phones typically can be used for much more than placing phone calls. They often include a camera, GPS capabilities, a voice recorder, Internet connectivity, multimedia functions, and access to e-mail, calendars, contact information, and more. It will be interesting to see how far this technology goes.

Computers are ubiquitous on the job. They are an integral part of almost any job today. Therefore, you can never know enough about computers and how to utilize them effectively.

Computers have also affected social behavior. While computers increase productivity and enhance functionality, we should not forget that sometimes human interaction is needed. And, when dealing with people, we should remember that people are not computers and shouldn't be treated as such—they require patience and emotional consideration.

How I Use this Technology . . .

I use computers in almost every aspect of my life, both professional and personal. My home is completely networked with computers on every floor, cameras for surveillance, servers and storage devices for managing all my data, and centralized printers and scanners accessible throughout the network. I also have networked media players that deliver video and audio from my home computers, storage devices, or the Internet to my big screen TV and entertainment systems. In addition, I have wireless home control, which is something that I expect to become more popular in the near future. My mobile phone also syncs data from my network so I can take essential information with me wherever I go.

What the Future Holds . . .

There was a time when individuals and businesses hesitated to embrace the Internet, but that has clearly changed in recent years. We are surely becoming a connected society and computers, computer communications, and the Internet have changed the way businesses operate in so many ways. Mobile phones are quickly replacing landline phones, and they are becoming handheld computers that bring us amazing capabilities, including allowing us to be more mobile than ever before. And, with Internet usage becoming such an integral part of our business and personal lives, high-speed networking is changing from optional to commonplace.

But there is more change to come. The new wireless standards that are on the horizon will continue to improve communication performance and functionality in the near future. We will have Internet access everywhere, anytime, via handheld devices, and entertainment will use the Internet as a significant method of delivery. This continued evolution of computers and communications will provide us with easier access to goods and services, instant accomplishment of tasks, and an endless assortment of entertainment and productivity options at our disposal.

It is important to remember, however, that while our increasingly connected society has many benefits, it also brings additional security and privacy risks. Computers and the Internet allow more ways for the curious and the deviant to peek into our lives and access data that has traditionally been private. In addition, many individuals today voluntarily provide personal data without hesitation, and social networking has made it so easy for a person's voice to be heard that many people spend a great deal of time posting their opinions online. But it is important to be cautious about what information is shared online because, once it is out there, it can't be taken back.

> *Computers are an integral part of almost any job today. Therefore, you can never know enough about computers and how to utilize them effectively.*

My Advice to Students . . .

Embrace computers as productivity tools and entertainment appliances, in whatever form they take. Overcome the fear that keeps many people from taking full advantage of computers. I highly recommend learning how computers function by learning what hardware is located inside. In fact, I build computers for fun and learning; there is no better way to learn than with a hands-on experience.

Discussion Question

Joe Melfi views the mobile phone as one current technology that may end up having the biggest impact on our lives in the future. Think about which tasks you use your mobile phone for and which ones you cannot. What changes need to be made in the future in order to perform all of these tasks on a mobile phone? Will they be primarily hardware or software changes? Is the mobile phone the computer of the future? Be prepared to discuss your position (in class, via an online class discussion group, in a class chat room, or via a class blog, depending on your instructor's directions). You may also be asked to write a short paper expressing your opinion.

> **For more information on D-Link Systems, visit www.dlink.com.**

module

Hardware

When most people think of computers, images of hardware usually fill their minds. Hardware includes the system unit, keyboard, mouse, monitor, and all the other interesting pieces of equipment that make up a computer system. This module explores the rich variety of computer hardware available today. But, as you already know, hardware needs instructions from software in order to function. Hardware without software is like a car without a driver or a canvas and paintbrush without an artist. Software is discussed in detail in the next module.

This module divides coverage of hardware into three parts. Chapter 2 describes the hardware located inside the system unit, which is the main box of the computer and where most of the work of a computer is performed. Chapter 3 discusses the different types of devices that can be used for data storage. Chapter 4 covers the wide variety of hardware that can be used for input and output.

"Technology has to adapt to market needs, not the other way around."

For more comments from Guest Expert **Sumit Agnihotry** of Acer Pan America, see the **Expert Insight on . . . Hardware** feature at the end of the module.

chapter 2

The System Unit: Processing and Memory

After completing this chapter, you will be able to do the following:

1. Understand how data and programs are represented to a computer and be able to identify a few of the coding systems used to accomplish this.

2. Explain the functions of the hardware components commonly found inside the system unit, such as the CPU, memory, buses, and expansion cards.

3. Describe how peripheral devices or other hardware can be added to a computer.

4. Understand how a computer's CPU and memory components process program instructions and data.

5. Name and evaluate several strategies that can be used today for speeding up the operations of a computer.

6. List some processing technologies that may be used in future computers.

OVERVIEW

The system unit of a computer is sometimes thought of as a mysterious "black box" and often the user does not have much understanding of what happens inside it. In this chapter, we demystify the system unit by looking inside the box and closely examining the functions of the parts. Consequently, the chapter gives you a feel for what the CPU, memory, and other devices commonly found inside the system unit do and how they work together to perform the tasks that the user requests.

To start, we discuss how a computer system represents data and program instructions. Here we talk about the codes that computers use to translate data back and forth from the symbols that computers can manipulate, to the symbols that people are accustomed to using. These topics lead to a discussion of how the CPU and memory are arranged with other components inside the system unit, the characteristics of those components, and how a CPU performs processing tasks. Finally, we look at strategies that can be used today to speed up a computer, plus some strategies that may be used to create faster and better computers in the future.

Many of you will apply this chapter's content to conventional personal computers—such as desktop and notebook computers. However, it is important to realize that the principles and procedures discussed in this chapter apply to other types of computers as well, such as those embedded in toys, consumer devices, household appliances, cars, and other devices, and those used with mobile devices, powerful servers, mainframes, and supercomputers. ∎

DATA AND PROGRAM REPRESENTATION

In order to be understood by a computer, data and software programs need to be represented appropriately. Consequently, *coding systems* are used to represent data and programs in a manner that can be understood by the computer. These concepts are discussed in the next few sections.

Digital Data Representation

Virtually all computers today—such as the embedded computers, mobile devices, personal computers, midrange servers, mainframes, and supercomputers discussed in Chapter 1—are *digital computers*. Most digital computers are *binary computers*, which can understand only two states, usually thought of as *off* and *on* and represented by the digits 0 and 1. Consequently, all data processed by a binary computer must be in binary form (0s and 1s). The 0s and 1s used to represent data can be represented in a variety of ways, such as with an open or closed circuit, the absence or presence of electronic current, two different types of magnetic alignment on a storage medium, and so on (see Figure 2-1).

Regardless of their physical representations, these 0s and 1s are commonly referred to as *bits*, a computing term derived

FIGURE 2-1

Ways of representing 0 and 1. Binary computers recognize only two states—off and on—usually represented by 0 and 1.

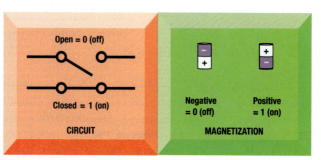

Open = 0 (off)
Closed = 1 (on)
CIRCUIT

Negative = 0 (off)
Positive = 1 (on)
MAGNETIZATION

from the phrase *binary digits*. A **bit** is the smallest unit of data that a binary computer can recognize. Therefore, the input you enter via a keyboard, the software program you use to play your music collection, the term paper stored on your computer, and the digital photos located on your mobile phone are all just groups of bits. Representing data in a form that can be understood by a digital computer is called *digital data representation.*

Because most computers can only understand data and instructions in binary form, binary can be thought of as the computer's *natural language*. People, of course, do not speak in binary. For example, you are not likely to go up to a friend and say,

0100100001001001

which translates into the word "HI" using one binary coding system. People communicate with one another in their natural languages, such as English, Chinese, Spanish, and French. For example, this book is written in English, which uses a 26-character alphabet. In addition, most countries use a numbering system with 10 possible symbols—0 through 9. As already mentioned, however, binary computers understand only 0s and 1s. For us to interact with a computer, a translation process from our natural language to 0s and 1s and then back again to our natural language is required. When we enter data into a computer system, the computer translates the natural-language symbols we input into binary 0s and 1s. After processing the data, the computer translates and outputs the resulting information in a form that we can understand.

A bit by itself typically represents only a fraction of a piece of data. Consequently, large numbers of bits are needed to represent a written document, computer program, digital photo, music file, or virtually any other type of data. Eight bits grouped together are collectively referred to as a **byte**. It is important to be familiar with this concept because *byte* terminology is frequently used in a variety of computer contexts, such as to indicate the size of a document or digital photo, the amount of memory a computer has, or the amount of room left on a storage medium. Since these quantities often involve thousands or millions of bytes, prefixes are commonly used in conjunction with the term *byte* to represent larger amounts of data (see Figure 2-2). For instance, a **kilobyte** (**KB**) is equal to 1,024 bytes, but is usually thought of as approximately 1,000 bytes; a **megabyte** (**MB**) is about 1 million bytes; a **gigabyte** (**GB**) is about 1 billion bytes; a **terabyte** (**TB**) is about 1 trillion bytes; a **petabyte** (**PB**) is about 1,000 terabytes (2^{50} bytes); an **exabyte** (**EB**) is about 1,000 petabytes (2^{60} bytes); a **zettabyte** (**ZB**) is about 1,000 exabytes (2^{70} bytes); and a **yottabyte** (**YB**) is about 1,000 zettabytes (2^{80} bytes). Using these definitions, 5 KB is about 5,000 bytes, 10 MB is about 10 million bytes, and 2 TB is about 2 trillion bytes.

Computers represent programs and data through a variety of binary-based coding systems. The coding system used depends primarily on the type of data that needs to be represented; the most common coding systems are discussed in the next few sections.

Representing Numerical Data: The Binary Numbering System

A *numbering system* is a way of representing numbers. The numbering system we commonly use is called the **decimal numbering system** because it uses 10 symbols—the digits 0, 1, 2, 3, 4, 5, 6, 7, 8, and 9—to represent all possible numbers. Numbers greater than nine, such as 21 and 683, are represented using combinations of these 10 symbols. The **binary numbering system** uses only two symbols—the digits 0 and 1—to represent all

FIGURE 2-2

Bits and bytes. Document size, storage capacity, and memory capacity are all measured in bytes.

| Bit |
| 0 0 1 1 0 0 0 0 |
| Byte |

Abbreviation	Approximate Size
KB	1 thousand bytes
MB	1 million bytes
GB	1 billion bytes
TB	1 trillion bytes
PB	1,000 terabytes

>**Bit.** The smallest unit of data a digital computer can recognize; represented by a 0 or a 1. >**Byte.** A group of 8 bits. >**Kilobyte (KB).** Approximately 1 thousand bytes (1,024 bytes to be precise). >**Megabyte (MB).** Approximately 1 million bytes. >**Gigabyte (GB).** Approximately 1 billion bytes. >**Terabyte (TB).** Approximately 1 trillion bytes. >**Petabyte (PB).** Approximately 1,000 terabytes. >**Exabyte (EB).** Approximately 1,000 petabytes. >**Zettabyte (ZB).** Approximately 1,000 exabytes. >**Yottabyte (YB).** Approximately 1,000 zettabytes. >**Decimal numbering system.** The numbering system that represents all numbers using 10 symbols (0–9). >**Binary numbering system.** The numbering system that represents all numbers using just two symbols (0 and 1).

HW

DECIMAL NUMBERING SYSTEM
Each place value in a decimal number represents 10 raised to the appropriate power.

The decimal number **7216**

10 raised to different powers

means 6 x 1   =   6
means 1 x 10   =   10
means 2 x 100   =   200
means 7 x 1,000   = 7,000
    7,216

BINARY NUMBERING SYSTEM
Each place value in a binary number represents 2 raised to the appropriate power.

The binary number **1001**

2 raised to different powers

means 1 x 1 = 1
means 0 x 2 = 0
means 0 x 4 = 0
means 1 x 8 = 8
    9

Decimal equivalent

FIGURE 2-3
Examples of using the decimal and binary numbering systems.

possible numbers. Consequently, binary computers use the binary numbering system to represent numbers and to perform math computations.

In both numbering systems, the position of each digit determines the power, or exponent, to which the *base number* (10 for decimal or 2 for binary) is raised. In the decimal numbering system, going from right to left, the first position or column (the ones column) represents 10^0 or 1; the second column (the tens column) represents 10^1 or 10; the third column (the hundreds column) represents 10^2 or 100; and so forth. Therefore, as Figure 2-3 shows, the decimal number 7,216 is understood as $7 \times 10^3 + 2 \times 10^2 + 1 \times 10^1 + 6 \times 10^0$ or 7,000 + 200 + 10 + 6 or 7,216. In binary, the concept is the same but the columns have different place values. For example, the far-right column is the ones column (for 2^0), the second column is the twos column (2^1), the third column is the fours column (2^2), and so on. Therefore, although 1001 represents "one thousand one" in decimal notation, 1001 represents "nine" ($1 \times 2^3 + 0 \times 2^2 + 0 \times 2^1 + 1 \times 2^0$ or 8 + 0 + 0 + 1 or 9) in the binary numbering system, as illustrated in the bottom half of Figure 2-3.

Coding Systems for Text-Based Data

While numeric data is represented by the binary numbering system, text-based data is represented by binary coding systems specifically developed for text-based data—namely, *ASCII*, *EBCDIC*, and *Unicode*. These codes are used to represent all characters that can appear in text data—such as numbers, letters, and special characters and symbols like the dollar sign, comma, percent symbol and many mathematical characters.

TIP

For more information about and examples of converting between numbering systems, see the "A Guide to Numbering Systems" section in the References and Resources Guide at the end of this book.

CHARACTER	ACSII
0	00110000
1	00110001
2	00110010
3	00110011
4	00110100
5	00110101
A	01000001
B	01000010
C	01000011
D	01000100
E	01000101
F	01000110
+	00101011
!	00100001
#	00100011

FIGURE 2-4

Some extended ASCII code examples.

CHINESE GREEK HEBREW

AMHARIC TIBETAN RUSSIAN

FIGURE 2-5

Unicode. Many characters, such as these, can be represented by Unicode but not by ASCII or EBCDIC.

ASCII and EBCDIC

ASCII (**American Standard Code for Information Interchange**) is the coding system traditionally used with personal computers. *EBCDIC* (*Extended Binary-Coded Decimal Interchange Code*) was developed by IBM, primarily for use with mainframes. ASCII is a 7-digit (7-bit) code, although there are several different 8-bit *extended versions* of ASCII that contain additional symbols not included in the 7-bit ASCII code. The extended ASCII character sets (see some examples of 8-bit ASCII codes in Figure 2-4) and EBCDIC represent each character as a unique combination of 8 bits. One group of 8 bits (1 byte) allows 256 (2^8) unique combinations. Therefore, an 8-bit code can represent up to 256 characters (twice as many as a 7-bit code)—enough to include the characters used in the English alphabet, as well as some non-English characters, the 10 decimal digits, the other characters usually found on a keyboard, and many special characters not included on a keyboard such as mathematical symbols, graphic symbols, additional punctuation marks, and other symbols.

Unicode

Unlike ASCII and EBCDIC, which are limited to only the Latin alphabet used with the English language, **Unicode** is a universal international coding standard designed to represent text-based data written in any ancient or modern language, including those with different alphabets, such as Chinese, Greek, Hebrew, Amharic, Tibetan, and Russian (see Figure 2-5). Unicode uniquely identifies each character using 0s and 1s, no matter which language, program, or computer platform is being used. It is a longer code, consisting of 1 to 4 bytes (8 to 32 bits) per character, and can represent over one million characters, which is more than enough unique combinations to represent the standard characters in all the world's written languages, as well as thousands of mathematical and technical symbols, punctuation marks, and other symbols and signs. The biggest advantage of Unicode is that it can be used worldwide with consistent and unambiguous results.

Unicode is quickly replacing ASCII as the primary text-coding system. In fact, Unicode includes the ASCII character set so ASCII data can be converted easily to Unicode when needed. Unicode is used by most Web browsers and is widely used for Web pages and Web applications (Google data, for instance, is stored exclusively in Unicode). Most recent software programs, including the latest versions of Microsoft Windows, Mac OS, and Microsoft Office, also use Unicode, as do modern programming languages, such as Java and Python. Unicode is updated regularly to add new characters and new languages not originally encoded—the most recent version is *Unicode 5.2*.

Coding Systems for Other Types of Data

So far, our discussion of data coding schemes has focused on numeric and text-based data, which consists of alphanumeric characters and special symbols, such as the comma and dollar sign. Multimedia data, such as graphics, audio, and video data, must also be represented in binary form in order to be used with a computer, as discussed next.

Graphics Data

Graphics data consists of still images, such as photographs or drawings. One of the most common methods for storing graphics data is in the form of a *bitmap image*—an image comprised of a grid of small dots, called *pixels* (short for *picture elements*), that are colored appropriately to represent an image. The color to be displayed at each pixel is represented by some combination of 0s and 1s, and the number of bits required to store the color for each pixel ranges from 1 to 24 bits. For example, each pixel in a *monochrome graphic* can be only one of two possible colors (such as black or white). These monochrome images require only one bit of storage space per pixel (for instance, the bit would contain a 1 when representing a pixel that should display as white, and the bit would contain a 0 for a pixel that should display as black). Images with more than two colors can use 4, 8, or 24 bits to store the color data for each pixel—this allows for 16 (2^4), 256 (2^8), or 16,777,216 (2^{24}) colors respectively, as shown in Figure 2-6.

The number of bits used per pixel depends on the type of image being stored; for instance, the *JPEG* images taken by most digital cameras today use 24-bit *true color images*. While this can result in large file sizes, some images (like JPEGs) can be *compressed* when needed, such as to reduce the amount of storage space required to store that image or to allow faster transmission over the Internet.

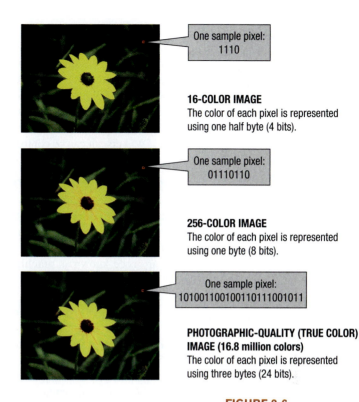

One sample pixel:
1110

16-COLOR IMAGE
The color of each pixel is represented using one half byte (4 bits).

One sample pixel:
01110110

256-COLOR IMAGE
The color of each pixel is represented using one byte (8 bits).

One sample pixel:
101001100100110111001011

PHOTOGRAPHIC-QUALITY (TRUE COLOR) IMAGE (16.8 million colors)
The color of each pixel is represented using three bytes (24 bits).

FIGURE 2-6

Representing graphics data.
With bitmapped images, the color of each pixel is represented by bits; the more bits used, the better the image quality.

Audio Data

Like graphics data, *audio data*—such as a song or the sound of someone speaking—must be in digital form in order to be stored on a storage medium or processed by a computer. To convert analog sound to digital sound, several thousand *samples*—digital representations of the sound at particular moments—are taken every second. When the samples are played back in the proper order, they recreate the sound of the voice or music. For example, audio CDs record sound using 2-byte samples, which are sampled at a rate of 44,100 times per second. When these samples are played back at a rate of 44,100 samples per second, they sound like continuous voice or music. With so many samples, however, sound files take up a great deal of storage space—about 32 MB for a 3-minute stereo song (44,100 times × 2 bytes × 180 seconds × 2 channels).

Because of its large size, audio data is usually compressed to reduce its file size when it is transmitted over the Internet or stored on an iPod or other portable digital media player. For example, files that are *MP3-encoded*—that is, compressed with the *MP3 compression algorithm* developed by the *Motion Pictures Expert Group* (*MPEG*)—are about 10 times smaller than their uncompressed digital versions, so they download 10 times faster and take up one-tenth of the storage space. The actual storage size required depends on the *bit rate*—the number of bits to be transferred per second when the file is played—used when the file is initially created; audio files using the common bit rate of 128 *Kbps* (thousands of bits per second) are about one-tenth the size of the original CD-quality recording.

TIP

For more examples of ASCII, EBCDIC, and Unicode, see the "Coding Charts" section in the References and Resources Guide at the end of this book.

ASK THE EXPERT

Mark Davis, President, The Unicode Consortium

What should the average computer user know about Unicode?

Whenever you read or write anything on a computer, you're using Unicode. Whenever you search on Google, Yahoo!, MSN, Wikipedia, or other Web sites, you're using Unicode. It's the way that text in all the world's languages can be stored and processed on computers.

Video Data

Video data—such as home movies, feature films, video clips, and television shows—is displayed using a collection of frames; each frame contains a still image. When the frames are projected one after the other (typically at a rate of 24 frames per second), the illusion of movement is created. With so many frames, the amount of data involved in showing a two-hour feature film can be substantial. Fortunately, like audio data, video data can be compressed to reduce it to a manageable size. For example, a two-hour movie can be compressed to fit on a single DVD disc; it can be compressed even further to be delivered over the Web.

Representing Software Programs: Machine Language

Just as numbers, text, and multimedia data must be represented by 0s and 1s, software programs must also be represented by 0s and 1s. Before a computer can execute any program instruction, such as requesting input from the user, moving a file from one storage device to another, or opening a new window on the screen, it must convert the instruction into a binary code known as **machine language**. An example of a typical machine language instruction is as follows:

$$01011000011100000000000100000010$$

A machine language instruction might look like a meaningless string of 0s and 1s, but it actually represents specific operations and storage locations. The 32-bit instruction shown here, for instance, moves data between two specific memory locations on one type of computer system. Early computers required programs to be written in machine language, but today's computers allow programs to be written in a programming language, which is then translated by the computer into machine language in order to be understood by the computer. Programming languages and *language translators* are discussed in detail in Chapter 13.

INSIDE THE SYSTEM UNIT

The **system unit** is the main case of a computer. It houses the processing hardware for that computer, as well as a few other devices, such as storage devices, the power supply, and cooling fans. The system unit for a desktop computer often looks like a rectangular box, although other shapes and sizes are available, such as the all-in-one computer illustrated in Figure 1-14. The inside of a system unit for a typical desktop computer system is shown in Figure 2-7. In general, the system unit contains a *CPU*, several types of *memory*, interfaces to connect external *peripheral devices* (such as printers), and other components all interconnected through sets of wires called *buses* on the *motherboard*. These components are discussed in detail in the next few sections. Portable computers (like notebook computers and ultra-mobile PCs (UMPCs)) and mobile devices have similar components, but the system unit and components are usually smaller and the system unit is usually combined with the computer screen to form a single piece of hardware. The components typically found inside a system unit are discussed next.

The Motherboard

A *circuit board* is a thin board containing *computer chips* and other electronic components. Computer chips are very small pieces of silicon or other semiconducting material that contain *integrated circuits* (*ICs*)—collections of electronic circuits containing microscopic

CPU
Performs the calculations and does the comparisons needed for processing, as well as controls the other parts of the computer system.

POWER SUPPLY
Converts standard electrical power into a form the computer can use.

FAN
Cools the CPU.

HARD DRIVE
Stores data and programs; the principal storage device for most computers.

EXPANSION CARD
Connects peripheral devices or adds new capabilities to a computer.

DRIVE BAYS
Hold storage devices, such as the DVD and hard drives shown here.

EXPANSION SLOTS
Connect expansion cards to the motherboard to add additional capabilities.

DVD DRIVE
Accesses data stored on CDs or DVDs.

MOTHERBOARD
Connects all components of the computer system; the computer's main circuit board.

FLASH MEMORY CARD READER
Accesses data stored on flash memory cards.

MEMORY (RAM) MODULES
Store data temporarily while you are working with it.

MEMORY SLOTS
Connect memory modules to the motherboard.

USB PORTS
Connect USB devices to the computer.

FIGURE 2-7

Inside a typical system unit. The system unit houses the CPU, memory, and other important pieces of hardware.

pathways along which electrical current can travel—and *transistors*—switches controlling the flow of electrons along the pathways. The main circuit board inside the system unit is called the **motherboard**.

As shown in Figure 2-7, the motherboard has a variety of chips, boards, and connectors attached to it. All devices used with a computer need to be connected via a wired or wireless connection to the motherboard. Typically, *external devices* (such as monitors, keyboards, mice, and printers) connect to the motherboard by plugging into a *port*—a special connector exposed through the exterior of the system unit case. The port is either built directly into the motherboard or created via an *expansion card* inserted into an *expansion slot* on the motherboard. Wireless external devices typically use a *transceiver* that plugs into a port on the computer to transmit data between the wireless device and the motherboard or they use wireless networking technology (such as *Bluetooth*) built into the motherboard. Ports and system expansion are discussed in more detail later in this chapter; wireless networking is covered in Chapter 7.

The Power Supply and Drive Bays
Most personal computers plug into a standard electrical outlet. The *power supply* inside a desktop computer connects to the motherboard to deliver electricity to the computer. Portable computers almost always contain a *rechargeable battery pack* to power the computer when it is not connected to a power outlet, as well as an external power supply adapter that connects the computer to a power outlet to recharge the battery when needed. One issue with newer portable computers and mobile devices is the growing use

> **Motherboard.** The main circuit board of a computer, located inside the system unit, to which all computer system components connect.

of nonremovable batteries. Although these batteries allow the devices to be lighter and are supposed to last for the typical life of the device, they are more difficult and expensive to replace if they fail—and often it is not worth the trouble and expense to replace them in some mobile devices like mobile phones and portable digital media players. The ramifications of the growing amount of *electronic trash* (*e-trash*), such as discarded mobile phones and other electronics, that is being generated worldwide is discussed in Chapter 16.

Most conventional computers (such as desktop computers) also contain *drive bays* (rectangular metal racks) inside the system unit into which storage devices (a *hard drive*, *DVD drive*, and *flash memory card reader*, for instance) can be inserted and secured. Storage devices inside the system unit are connected via a cable to the motherboard, as well as to the internal power supply, if necessary. Storage devices with removable media that need to be inserted into and removed from the drive (such as a DVD drive), are accessible through the front of the system unit (refer again to Figure 2-7). Storage devices that are not used in conjunction with removable storage media (such as an internal hard drive) are not visible outside the system unit. Many desktop computers come with empty drive bays so users can add additional storage devices as needed.

The CPU

The **central processing unit** (**CPU**) consists of a variety of circuitry and components that are packaged together and connected directly to the motherboard. The CPU—also called the **microprocessor** (when talking about personal computers) or just the **processor** (when speaking in general terms for any computer)—does the vast majority of the processing for a computer. Most personal computers today use CPUs manufactured by Intel or Advanced Micro Devices (AMD); some examples of their processors are shown in Figure 2-8. For a look inside a computer that may one day be able to compete with human contestants on the *Jeopardy!* TV show, see the How It Works box.

As shown in Figure 2-8, there are processors designed for desktop computers, servers and workstations, conventional portable computers (like notebook and tablet computers), and very small portable computers (like netbooks and UMPCs). In addition, there are also processors designed for mobile phones and embedded computers. Many CPUs today are **multi-core CPUs**; that is, CPUs that contain the processing components or *cores* of multiple independent processors on a single CPU. For example, **dual-core CPUs** contain two cores and **quad-core CPUs** contain four cores. Up until just a few years ago, most CPUs designed for desktop computers had only a

FIGURE 2-8

CPUs. CPUs today typically have multiple cores.

Four cores

Shared Level 3 cache memory

DESKTOP PROCESSORS
Typically have 2 to 4 cores and are designed for performance.

SERVER AND WORKSTATION PROCESSORS
Typically have at least 4 cores and are designed for very high performance.

NOTEBOOK PROCESSORS
Typically have 2 to 4 cores and are designed for performance and increased battery life.

NETBOOK PROCESSORS
Typically have 1 to 2 cores, are small in size, and are designed for extended battery life.

> **Central processing unit (CPU).** The chip located on the motherboard of a computer that performs the processing for a computer. Also called the **processor**. > **Microprocessor.** A central processing unit (CPU) for a personal computer. > **Multi-core CPU.** A CPU that contains the processing components or core of more than one processor in a single CPU. > **Dual-core CPU.** A CPU that contains two separate processing cores. > **Quad-core CPU.** A CPU that contains four separate processing cores.

HOW IT WORKS

Watson, the Ultimate Future *Jeopardy!* Contestant

While game shows traditionally have human contestants, IBM is working on an advanced computing system that will be capable of competing with humans on the popular quiz show, *Jeopardy!* (see the accompanying illustration). This system, codenamed *Watson*, uses software called *Question Answering* (*QA*) and is designed to understand complex questions and answer them with enough precision and speed to make it a viable *Jeopardy!* contestant. Like human contestants, Watson will not have access to the Internet or any other outside assistance. However, it will have access to its self-contained data, and researchers are teaching it how to go beyond basic data retrieval and analyze its data deeply. For example, they are teaching Watson to use context to "understand" how words relate to each other, to consider factors such as keywords and statistical paraphrasing, and to deal with puns and wordplay in order to come up with a proper response to a question (or to come up with a question to match an answer, as is the case with *Jeopardy!*). To achieve this with the speed and accuracy required for *Jeopardy!*, Watson will need to be based on a supercomputer platform, such as the IBM Blue Gene/P platform, which can contain over one million CPU cores to obtain close to petaflop performance.

While creating a computer that can play *Jeopardy!* is entertaining and newsworthy, IBM plans to make the same technology available for other, perhaps more practical, applications, such as in medical systems used to diagnose patients and in business intelligence systems used for making business decisions. IBM also envisions the technology being used with consumer applications—most likely via cloud computing on a fee per question or fee per minute basis. But, before that happens, we can enjoy Watson's *Jeopardy!* debut—currently targeted for late 2010.

single core; as a result, a common way to increase the amount of processing performed by the CPU was to increase the speed of the CPU. However, heat constraints are making it progressively more difficult to continue to increase CPU speed, so CPU manufacturers today are focusing on multi-core CPUs to increase the amount of processing that a CPU can do in a given time period.

Multi-core CPUs allow computers to work simultaneously on more than one task at a time, such as burning a DVD while surfing the Web, as well as to work faster within a single application if the software is designed to take advantage of multiple cores. Another benefit of multi-core CPUs is that they typically experience fewer heat problems than *single-core CPUs* because each core typically runs slower than a single-core CPU, although the total processing power of the multi-core CPU is greater. In addition to heat reduction, goals of CPU manufacturers today include creating CPUs that are as energy-efficient as possible (in order to reduce power consumption and increase battery life) and that use materials that are not toxic when disposed of (in order to lessen the e-trash impact of computers, as discussed in detail in Chapter 16).

CPUs commonly used with desktop computers include the Intel *Core i7* (quad-core) and AMD *Phenom II* (available in dual-core, *triple-core*, and quad-core versions). Lower-end home computers may use a dual-core CPU, such as the Intel *Core 2 Duo* or the AMD *Athlon X2*. Workstations and servers use more powerful processors, such as the Intel *Xeon* or the AMD *Opteron* processors. Notebook computers can use the same CPUs as desktop computers (more common with notebooks designed as *desktop replacements* than those

ONLINE VIDEO

Go to the Chapter 2 page at **www.cengage.com/ computerconcepts/np/uc13** to watch the "A Look at Watson, the Ultimate Future *Jeopardy!* Contestant" video clip.

TYPE OF PROCESSOR	NAME	NUMBER OF CORES	CLOCK SPEED	TOTAL CACHE MEMORY		
				LEVEL 1	LEVEL 2	LEVEL 3
DESKTOP	Intel Core i7	4	2.66–3.33 GHz	64 KB*	256 KB*	8 MB
	AMD Phenom II	2–4	2.4–3.2 GHz	128 KB*	512 KB*	4–6 MB
SERVER/ WORKSTATION	Intel Xeon (5500 series) AMD Opteron (3rd generation)	2 or 4 4 or 6	1.86–3.2 GHz 2.0–3.1 GHz	64 KB* 128 KB*	256 KB* 512 KB*	4–8 MB 6 MB
NOTEBOOK	Intel Core 2 Mobile	1, 2, or 4	1.06–3.06 GHz	64 KB*	1–12 MB	none
	AMD Turion X2 Mobile	2	2.0–2.5 GHz	128 KB*	1–2 MB*	none
NETBOOK	Intel Atom	1–2	800 MHz–2 GHz	56 KB*	512 KB*	none
	AMD Athlon Neo	1	1.6 MHz	128 KB*	512 KB*	none

*Per core

FIGURE 2-9

Some examples of current Intel and AMD CPUs.

ONLINE VIDEO

Go to the Chapter 2 page at **www.cengage.com/ computerconcepts/np/uc13** to watch the "The Computing Power of the IBM Roadrunner Supercomputer" video clip.

designed for lightweight traveling notebooks), or a CPU designed specifically for portable computers. CPUs designed specifically for notebook and tablet computers (such as the Intel *Core 2* mobile processors and the AMD *Turion X2* mobile processors) typically run a little slower than comparable desktop CPUs, but run cooler and consume less power to allow the portable computers to run longer on battery power without a recharge. CPUs designed specifically for netbooks (such as the Intel *Atom* processor shown in Figure 2-8 and the AMD *Athlon Neo*) are typically much lower in power, performance, and price than other CPUs. Some examples of current CPUs and their characteristics (which are defined and discussed shortly) are shown in Figure 2-9.

In addition to computers, CPUs are incorporated into a number of other devices, such as mobile phones, portable digital media players, consumer appliances, cars, gaming consoles, exercise machines, and more. The CPUs for these devices (such as the *Cell* processor used in the Sony PlayStation 3 gaming console) are typically different from the ones used in personal computers.

Processing Speed

One measurement of the *processing speed* of a CPU is the *CPU clock speed*, which is typically rated in *megahertz* (*MHz*) or *gigahertz* (*GHz*). A higher CPU clock speed means that more instructions can be processed per second than the same CPU with a lower CPU clock speed. For instance, a Core i7 processor running at 3.2 GHz would be faster than a Core i7 processor running at 2.66 GHz if all other components remain the same. CPUs for the earliest personal computers ran at less than 5 MHz; today's fastest CPUs have a clock speed of more than 3 GHz. Although CPU clock speed is an important factor in computer performance, other factors (such as the number of cores, the amount of *RAM* and *cache memory*, the speed of external storage devices, and the *bus width* and *bus speed*) greatly affect the overall processing speed of the computer. As a result, computers today are beginning to be classified less by CPU clock speed and more by the computer's overall processing speed or performance.

One measurement of overall processing speed is the maximum number of instructions the CPU can process per second—such as *megaflops*, *gigaflops*, and *teraflops* (millions, billions, and trillions of floating-point operations per second, respectively). It is also common for experts associated with computer journals, technical Web sites, and other organizations to test the performance of CPUs. These tests—called *benchmark tests*—typically run the same series of programs on several computer systems that are identical except for one component (such as the CPU) and measure how long each task takes in order to determine the overall relative performance of the component being tested. Because the large number of factors affecting computer performance today makes it increasingly difficult for consumers to evaluate the performance of CPUs and computers, benchmark tests are becoming an extremely important resource for computer shoppers.

Word Size

A computer word is the amount of data (measured in bits or bytes) that a CPU can manipulate at one time. While CPUs just a few years ago used 32-bit words (referred to as *32-bit processors*), most CPUs today are *64-bit processors* (that is, they are capable of using 64-bit words, in addition to 32-bit words). Usually, a larger word size allows for faster processing and the use of more RAM, provided the software being used is written to take advantage of 64-bit processing. For instance, a computer with a 64-bit processor running the 64-bit version of the Windows operating system can use more RAM and has a higher performance than the same computer running the regular 32-bit version of Windows. However, much of today's software is still 32-bit software.

ASK THE EXPERT

Chris Angelini, Managing Editor, Tom's Hardware

How can benchmark tests help when shopping for a new PC?

Like any major purchase, research is very important when buying a new PC and benchmark tests should play a big role in an informed computer purchase. You see, software behaves differently depending on the hardware behind it. By testing the most popular programs across a wide range of components, benchmark tests help consumers quantify the benefit of spending more money on a higher-end computer versus the additional cost. You can take testing one step further by zeroing in on specific components and applications. Games, for example, are most sensitive to powerful graphics cards. Video editing software runs best on a computer with plenty of RAM and a fast processor. We know these things because benchmarking clearly illustrates the gains enabled by a given upgrade, and this information can help individuals select the right system for their needs.

Cache Memory

Cache memory is a special group of very fast memory circuitry located on or close to the CPU. Cache memory is used to speed up processing by storing the data and instructions that may be needed next by the CPU in handy locations. In theory, it works the same way you might work at your desk; that is, with the file folders or documents you need most often placed within an arm's length and with other useful materials placed farther away but still within easy reach. The computer works in a similar manner. Although it can access materials (data, instructions, and programs, for instance) in RAM relatively quickly, it can work much faster if it places the most urgently needed materials into areas—cache memory—that allow even faster access. When cache memory is full and the CPU calls for additional data or a new instruction, the system overwrites as much data in cache memory as needed to make room for the new data or instruction. This allows the data and instructions that are most likely still needed to remain in cache memory.

Cache memory today is usually *internal cache* (built right into the CPU chip). In the past, some cache memory was *external cache* (located close to, but not inside, the CPU), but that is less common today because the continued miniaturization of CPU components

FURTHER EXPLORATION

Go to the Chapter 2 page at **www.cengage.com/ computerconcepts/np/uc13** for links to information about CPUs.

> **Cache memory.** A group of fast memory circuitry located on or near the CPU to help speed up processing.

allows for more room inside the CPU. Cache memory level numbers indicate the order in which the various caches are accessed by the CPU when it requires new data or instructions. *Level 1 (L1) cache* (which is the fastest type of cache but typically holds less data than other levels of cache) is checked first, followed by *Level 2 (L2) cache*, followed by *Level 3 (L3) cache* if it exists. If the data or instructions are not found in cache memory, the computer looks for them in RAM, which is slower than cache memory. If the data or instructions cannot be found in RAM, then they are retrieved from the hard drive—an even slower operation. Typically, more cache memory results in faster processing. Most multi-core CPUs today have some cache memory (such as a L1 and L2 cache) dedicated to each core; they may also use a larger shared cache memory (such as L3 cache) that can be accessed by any core as needed.

8-BIT BUS

16-BIT BUS

FIGURE 2-10
Bus width. A wider bus can transfer more data at one time than a narrower bus.

Bus Width, Bus Speed, and Bandwidth

A *bus* is an electronic path over which data can travel. There are buses inside the CPU, as well as on the motherboard. You can picture a bus as a highway with several lanes; each wire in the bus acts as a separate lane, transmitting one bit at a time. The number of bits being transmitted at one time is dependent on the *bus width*—the number of wires in the bus over which data can travel. Just as a wider highway allows more cars to travel at one time, a wider bus allows more data to be transferred at one time (see Figure 2-10). The *bus speed* is also a very important factor, since the bus width and bus speed together determine the bus's **throughput** or **bandwidth**; that is, the amount of data that can be transferred via the bus in a given time period.

Memory

Memory refers to chip-based storage. When the term *memory* is used alone, it refers to chip-based storage used by the computer—usually the amount of the computer's main memory (called *random access memory* or *RAM*, as discussed next), which is located inside the system unit. In contrast, the term *storage* refers to the amount of long-term storage available to a computer—usually in the form of the computer's hard drive or removable storage media, such as CDs, DVDs, flash memory cards, and USB flash drives, all discussed in the next chapter.

In addition to RAM, computer users should be familiar with four other types of computer memory. Two of these—*cache memory* and *registers*—are **volatile** like RAM, which means that their content is erased when power to the memory ceases; the other two—*read-only memory (ROM)* and *flash memory*—are **nonvolatile**. Cache memory has already been discussed; the other four types of memory are explained next.

Random Access Memory (RAM)

RAM (random access memory), also called *main memory*, is used to store the essential parts of the operating system while the computer is running, as well as the programs and data that the computer is currently using. When someone uses the term *memory* in reference to computers, that person is usually referring to RAM. Since RAM is volatile, its content is lost when the computer is shut off. Data in RAM is also deleted when it is no

---

>**Bandwidth.** The amount of data that can be transferred in a given period of time; also referred to as **throughput**. >**Memory.** Chip-based storage. >**Volatile.** A characteristic of memory or storage in which data is not retained when the power to the computer is turned off.
>**Nonvolatile.** A characteristic of memory or storage in which data is retained even when the power to the computer is turned off.
>**RAM (random access memory).** Chips connected to the motherboard that provide a temporary location for the computer to hold data and program instructions while they are needed.

longer needed, such as when the program using that data is closed. If you want to retrieve a document later, you need to save the document on a storage medium before closing it, as discussed in more detail in Chapter 3. After the document is saved to a storage medium, it can be retrieved from the storage medium when it is needed, even though the document is erased from RAM when the document or the program being used to create that document is closed.

Like the CPU, RAM consists of electronic circuits etched onto chips. These chips are arranged onto circuit boards called *memory modules* (see Figure 2-11), which, in turn, are plugged into the motherboard. Most desktop and server memory modules today are *dual in-line memory modules* or *DIMMs*; notebook computers typically use a smaller type of memory module referred to as a *small outline DIMM* or *SO-DIMM* (an example of each is shown in Figure 2-11). Most personal computers sold today have slots for two to four memory modules and at least one slot will be filled. For example, in the motherboard shown in Figure 2-7, there are two memory modules already installed and room to add an additional two modules, if needed. If you want to add more RAM to a computer and no empty slots are available, you must replace at least one of the existing memory modules with higher capacity modules in order to increase the amount of RAM in that computer.

RAM capacity is measured in bytes. The amount of RAM that can be installed in a computer system depends on both the CPU in that computer and the operating system being used. For instance, while computers using 64-bit CPUs today can utilize a virtually unlimited amount of RAM (older 32-bit CPUs can use up to only 4 GB of RAM), a 64-bit operating system is needed in order to use more than 4 GB of RAM. In addition, different versions of a 64-bit operating system may support different amounts of RAM; for instance, the 64-bit versions of Windows Vista can use up to 8 GB, up to 16 GB, or more than 128 GB of RAM, depending on the edition of Windows Vista being used. Consequently, when you are considering adding more RAM to a computer, it is important to determine that your computer can support it. More RAM allows more applications to run at one time and the computer to respond more quickly when a user switches from task to task. Most notebook and desktop computers sold today have at least 1 GB of RAM and 2 to 8 GB of RAM is generally considered a normal amount for home computers.

In addition to knowing the type of memory module and the amount of memory your computer can support, it is also important to select the proper type and speed of RAM when adding new memory. Most personal computers today use *SDRAM* (*synchronous dynamic RAM*). SDRAM is commonly available in *DDR* (*double-data rate*), *DDR2*, and *DDR3* versions. DDR memory sends data twice as often as ordinary SDRAM to increase throughput, DDR2 transmits twice as much data in the same time period as DDR, and DDR3 is about twice as fast as the highest-speed DDR2 memory available today. Each type of SDRAM is typically available in a variety of speeds (measured in MHz)—for optimal performance, you should use the type and speed of RAM your computer was designed to use.

To further improve memory performance, memory today typically uses a *dual-channel memory architecture*, which has two paths that go to and from memory and so it can transfer twice as much data at one time as *single-channel memory architecture* of the same speed. *Tri-channel* (three paths) and *quad-channel* (four paths) *memory architecture* are also beginning to be used for higher performance. In order to take advantage of the improved performance of using multiple paths, multi-channel RAM typically needs to be installed in matched sets, such as two 1 GB dual-channel memory modules instead of a single 2 GB dual-channel memory module. As the number of cores used with CPUs grows,

The memory module contains memory chips.

DESKTOP RAM (DIMM)

NOTEBOOK RAM (SO-DIMM)

This part of the memory module is plugged into a memory slot on the motherboard.

FIGURE 2-11
RAM memory modules.

ASK THE EXPERT

Kingston

Mark Tekunoff, Senior Technology Manager, Kingston Technology

What's the best way to find out if more memory can be added to a particular computer and the type of memory that is needed?

The best way to upgrade is to go to a Web site that has a list of PCs and other products along with a list of the memory options available to support those PCs and products. A good example is Kingston's Web site at www.kingston.com, where Kingston supports over 20,000 products with a variety of memory solutions.

In general, Windows Vista and basic Windows 7 users typically will want at least 2 GB of memory for good functionality. For advanced 32-bit Windows 7 users, we recommend 3 to 4 GB of RAM; power users with 64-bit Windows 7 are better off with 4 to 8 GB of RAM.

RAM performance is becoming increasingly important to ensure that data can be delivered to the CPU fast enough to match its processing capabilities.

While RAM as we know it today is volatile, there are several forms of *nonvolatile RAM* (*NVRAM*)—that is, memory that retains its data when the power to the device is off—becoming available or under development. Two of the most promising types of nonvolatile RAM are *magnetic RAM* (or more precisely, *magnetoresistive RAM*), and *memristor-based RAM*. Magnetoresistive RAM (commonly referred to as *MRAM*) uses *magnetic polarization* rather than an electrical charge to store data; memristor-based RAM uses *memristors* (short for *memory resistors*) that change their resistance in response to current flowing through them. Two other emerging types of nonvolatile memory are *PRAM* (*phase change random access memory*), which has a special coating that changes its physical state when heat is applied (similar to the recordable CDs and DVDs discussed in Chapter 4), and *NRAM*, which uses *carbon nanotubes* (which are discussed later in this chapter).

The most common applications for nonvolatile RAM today include storing critical data for enterprise systems as they operate to guard against data loss and saving the data necessary to help industrial automation and robotics systems recover quickly from a power loss. Future applications include "instant-on" computers and mobile devices that can be turned on and off like an electric light, without any loss of data. It is possible that a form of nonvolatile RAM (such as one of the types discussed in this section or *flash memory*, discussed shortly) will eventually replace SDRAM as the main memory for a computer.

Regardless of the type of RAM used, the CPU must be able to find data and programs located in memory when they are needed. To accomplish this, each location in memory has an address. Whenever a block of data, instruction, program, or result of a calculation is stored in memory, it is usually stored in one or more consecutive addresses, depending on its size (each address typically holds only one byte). The computer system sets up and maintains directory tables that keep track of where data is stored in memory, in order to facilitate the retrieval of that data. When the computer has finished using a program or set of data, it frees up that memory space to hold other programs and data. Therefore, the content of each memory location constantly changes. This process can be roughly compared with the handling of the mailboxes in your local post office: the number on each P.O. box (memory location) remains the same, but the mail (data) stored inside changes as patrons remove their mail and as new mail arrives (see Figure 2-12).

▼ FIGURE 2-12

Memory addressing.

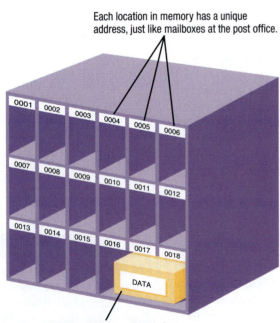

Each location in memory has a unique address, just like mailboxes at the post office.

0001 0002 0003 0004 0005 0006
0007 0008 0009 0010 0011 0012
0013 0014 0015 0016 0017 0018

DATA

Programs and blocks of data are almost always too big to fit in a single address. A directory keeps track of the first address used to store each program and data block and the number of addresses each block spans.

Registers

A **register** is high-speed memory built into the CPU. Registers are used by the CPU to store data and intermediary results temporarily during processing. Registers are the fastest type of memory used by the CPU, even faster than Level 1 cache. Generally, more registers and larger registers result in increased CPU performance. Most CPUs contain multiple registers; registers are discussed in more detail later in this chapter.

Read-Only Memory (ROM)

ROM (**read-only memory**) consists of nonvolatile chips that permanently store data or programs. Like RAM, these chips are attached to the motherboard inside the system unit, and the data or programs are retrieved by the computer when they are needed. An important difference, however, is that you can neither write over the data or programs in ROM chips (which is the reason ROM chips are called *read-only*), nor erase their content when you shut off the computer's power. ROM is used for storing permanent instructions used by a computer (referred to as *firmware*). However, ROM is increasingly being replaced with *flash memory*, as discussed next, for any data that may need to be updated during the life of the computer.

Flash Memory

Flash memory consists of nonvolatile memory chips that can be used for storage by the computer or the user. Flash memory chips have begun to replace ROM for storing system information, such as a computer's *BIOS* or *basic input/output system*—the sequence of instructions the computer follows during the boot process. For instance, one of the computer's first activities when you turn on the power is to perform a *power-on self-test* or *POST*. The POST takes an inventory of system components, checks each component for proper functioning, and initializes system settings, which produces the beeps you may hear as your computer boots. Traditionally, the instructions for the POST have been stored in ROM. By storing this information in flash memory instead of ROM, however, the BIOS information can be updated as needed. Similarly, firmware for personal computers and other devices (such as mobile phones and networking hardware) are now typically stored in flash memory that is embedded in the device so the firmware can be updated over the life of the product.

Flash memory chips are also built into many types of devices (such as portable computers, mobile phones, digital cameras, and portable digital media players) for user storage, as well as built into storage media and devices (such as flash memory cards and USB flash drives). Flash memory media and devices used for storage purposes are discussed in more detail in Chapter 3.

Fans, Heat Sinks, and Other Cooling Components

One byproduct of packing an increasing amount of technology in a smaller system unit is heat, an ongoing problem for CPU and computer manufacturers. Since heat can damage components and cooler chips can run faster, virtually all computers today employ *fans*, *heat sinks* (small components typically made out of aluminum with fins that help to dissipate heat), or other methods to cool the CPU and system unit. For instance, desktop computers today typically include several fans, such as one fan on the power supply that can be seen on the back of the computer and one fan and a heat sink on top of the CPU, and notebook computers typically include at least one fan. One of the newest cooling methods

FURTHER EXPLORATION Go

Go to the Chapter 2 page at
**www.cengage.com/
computerconcepts/np/uc13**
for links to information about memory.

> **Register.** High-speed memory built into the CPU that temporarily stores data during processing. > **ROM (read-only memory).** Nonvolatile chips located on the motherboard into which data or programs have been permanently stored. > **Flash memory.** Nonvolatile memory chips that can be used for storage by the computer or user; can be built into a computer or a storage medium.

Built-in fan is powered by a USB cable on the bottom of the stand.

Fans on the back of the system unit

Fan on top of the CPU

Water cooling tubes

FANS AND WATER COOLING SYSTEMS
These cooling methods and heat sinks are used with computers today to cool the inside of the computer.

NOTEBOOK COOLING STANDS
These stands cool the underside of a notebook computer by allowing for better air circulation; some stands also include a fan.

FIGURE 2-13

Computer cooling methods.

being used with desktop computers consists of liquid-filled tubes that draw heat away from processors. Although initially expensive, difficult to install, and complicated to use, these *water cooling systems* are now available in simpler and less expensive formats. An added bonus of water-cooled computers is that they are quieter than conventional systems. As shown in Figure 2-13, some desktop computers use a combination of fans and water cooling systems. When a notebook's built-in fan isn't sufficient to cool the underside of the computer—one of the problem areas with many notebook computers—a *notebook cooling stand* (such as the one shown in Figure 2-13) can be used to help cool this part of the computer.

Because heat is an ongoing problem with computers, new cooling technologies are continually being developed. One possibility for the future is the *ion pump cooling system* that strips electrons from molecules of oxygen and nitrogen in the air, resulting in positively charged ions; the positively charged ions then flow to a negatively charged collector electrode, resulting in a flow of air that cools nearby components. Ion pump cooling systems have no moving parts, use minimal energy consumption, and could potentially be integrated into CPUs and other computer components during manufacturing because they can be made of silicon.

Expansion Slots, Expansion Cards, and ExpressCard Modules

Expansion slots are locations on the motherboard into which **expansion cards** (also called *interface cards*) can be inserted to connect those cards to the motherboard. Expansion cards are used to give desktop computers additional capabilities, such as to connect the computer to a network, to add a TV tuner to allow television shows to be watched and recorded on the computer, or to connect a monitor to the computer. Today, some basic capabilities (such as the necessary connectors for speakers and monitors) are being integrated directly into the motherboard instead of requiring the use of an expansion card. However, an expansion card can be added and used instead, if needed. For instance, a *video graphics card* can be added to a computer to add additional capabilities not allowed by the computer's *integrated graphics* feature. Most new desktop computers come with a few empty expansion slots on the motherboard so that new expansion cards can be added when new capabilities are needed. There are several different types of expansion cards, such as *PCI* and *PCIe*—each corresponds to a specific type of expansion slot, as discussed in the next section, and they are not interchangeable.

Traditionally, *PC Cards* were used for notebook expansion. Today, however, most notebook and netbook computers use the newer **ExpressCard modules** instead. ExpressCard modules are inserted into the computer's *ExpressCard slot* in order to be used; they can also be used with any desktop computer that has an ExpressCard slot. ExpressCard modules and ExpressCard slots are available in two widths: 34 mm and 54 mm, referred to as *ExpressCard/34* and *ExpressCard/54*, respectively. While ExpressCard/34 modules can be used in both sized slots, ExpressCard/54 modules can only be used with ExpressCard/54 slots.

Figure 2-14 shows a typical expansion card and ExpressCard module, and lists some examples of common uses for expansion cards and ExpressCard modules. Expansion cards or ExpressCard modules designed to connect external devices (such as a monitor or piece of networking hardware) have a port accessible to connect that device; cards that do not need to connect to additional hardware (such as wireless networking cards) do not have an exposed port. Expansion for UMPCs and mobile devices is usually much more limited and is often restricted to devices that can plug into a *USB port* or *flash memory card slot*; desktop and portable computers can connect some peripherals using these ports as well. Ports are discussed in more detail shortly.

FIGURE 2-14

Expansion cards and ExpressCard modules. These are most often used with desktop and notebook computers, respectively.

EXPANSION CARD
This part of the card plugs into an empty PCI Express slot on the motherboard.

The port on this network interface card is accessible through the exterior of the system unit's case.

EXPRESSCARD MODULE
This end of the card is inserted into an ExpressCard/34 slot. There is no external port because this is a wireless networking card.

COMMON EXPANSION CARDS/MODULES	
CARD TYPE	**PURPOSE**
Disk controller card	Enables a particular type of disk drive to interface with the computer.
Modem	Provides communications capabilities to connect to a network or the Internet.
Network adapter	Enables a computer to connect to a network.
Sound card	Enables users to attach speakers to a computer and provides sound capabilities.
TV tuner card	Allows a computer to pick up television signals.
USB/FireWire card	Adds one or both of these ports to a computer.
Video graphics card	Enables the connection of a monitor; can provide additional graphics capabilities not available with graphics integrated into the motherboard.

>**ExpressCard module.** A module that can be inserted into a computer's ExpressCard slot to add additional functionality or to connect a peripheral device to that computer; commonly used with notebook computers.

Buses

As already discussed, a **bus** in a computer is an electronic path over which data travels. There are buses located within the CPU to move data between CPU components; there are also a variety of buses etched onto the motherboard to tie the CPU to memory and to peripheral devices (one possible design is shown in Figure 2-15). The buses that connect peripheral (typically input and output) devices to the motherboard are often called **expansion buses**. Expansion buses connect directly to ports on the system unit case or

◢ FIGURE 2-15

Buses and expansion slots. Buses transport bits and bytes from one component to another, including the CPU, RAM, and peripheral devices.

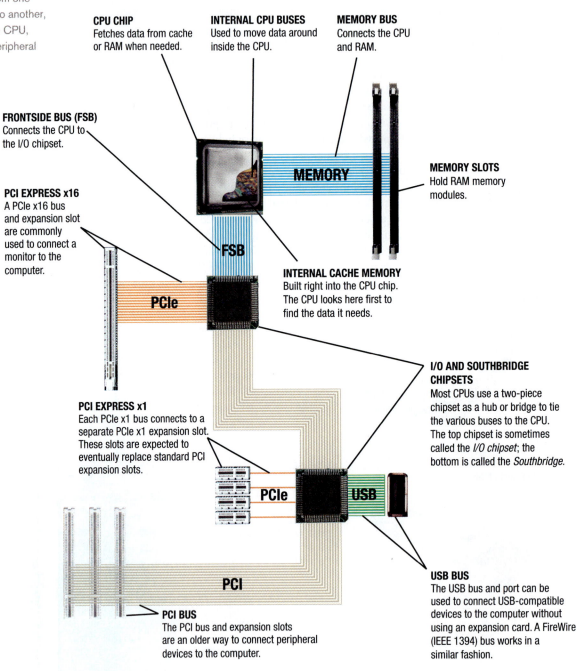

CPU CHIP
Fetches data from cache or RAM when needed.

INTERNAL CPU BUSES
Used to move data around inside the CPU.

MEMORY BUS
Connects the CPU and RAM.

FRONTSIDE BUS (FSB)
Connects the CPU to the I/O chipset.

MEMORY SLOTS
Hold RAM memory modules.

PCI EXPRESS x16
A PCIe x16 bus and expansion slot are commonly used to connect a monitor to the computer.

INTERNAL CACHE MEMORY
Built right into the CPU chip. The CPU looks here first to find the data it needs.

I/O AND SOUTHBRIDGE CHIPSETS
Most CPUs use a two-piece chipset as a hub or bridge to tie the various buses to the CPU. The top chipset is sometimes called the *I/O chipset*; the bottom is called the *Southbridge*.

PCI EXPRESS x1
Each PCIe x1 bus connects to a separate PCIe x1 expansion slot. These slots are expected to eventually replace standard PCI expansion slots.

USB BUS
The USB bus and port can be used to connect USB-compatible devices to the computer without using an expansion card. A FireWire (IEEE 1394) bus works in a similar fashion.

PCI BUS
The PCI bus and expansion slots are an older way to connect peripheral devices to the computer.

>**Bus.** An electronic path on the motherboard or within the CPU or other computer component along which data is transferred. >**Expansion bus.** A bus on the motherboard used to connects peripheral devices.

to expansion slots on the motherboard (some of the most common expansion buses and expansion slots are illustrated in Figure 2-15). It is important to realize that expansion slots are not interchangeable—that is, each type of expansion slot is designed for a specific type of expansion card, such as *PCI* or *PCI Express* (*PCIe*). The specific buses shown in Figure 2-15 are discussed next.

Memory Bus

One recent change in the bus architecture used with most new personal computers today is connecting the CPU directly to RAM, as shown in Figure 2-15. This change allows for increased performance; the bus used to connect the CPU to RAM is typically called the **memory bus**.

Frontside Bus (FSB)

The **frontside bus** (**FSB**) connects the CPU to the chipset (most often called the *I/O bridge* today, though sometimes the older term *Northbridge* is still used) that connects the CPU to the rest of the *bus architecture*. Because of the importance of this connection, CPU manufacturers typically use special high-speed technologies: Intel uses its *QuickPath Interconnect* (*QPI*) technology; AMD uses its *HyperTransport Technology*.

PCI and PCI Express Bus

The *PCI* (*Peripheral Component Interconnect*) *bus* has been one of the most common types of expansion buses in past years. In new computers, the PCI bus has essentially been replaced with the **PCI Express** (**PCIe**) **bus**. The PCIe bus is available in several different widths. The 16-bit version of PCIe (referred to as *PCIe x16*) is commonly used with video graphics cards to connect a monitor to a computer; expansion cards for other peripherals often connect via the 1-bit PCIe bus (referred to as *PCIe x1*). PCIe is extremely fast—the 1-bit PCIe bus, at 5 *Gbps* (billions of bits per second), is approximately four times faster than the standard PCI bus; PCIe x16 is significantly faster at 80 Gbps. The emerging *PCI 2.0* standard essentially doubles the speed of each PCIe bus. PCIe buses are also increasingly being used with *mini cards* (such as *PCIe Mini*) that are smaller than conventional expansion cards and that are used in UMPCs and other small portable computers.

USB Bus

One of the more versatile bus architectures is the **Universal Serial Bus** (**USB**). The USB standard allows 127 different devices to connect to a computer via a single USB port on the computer's system unit. At 12 *Mbps* (millions of bits per second), the original *USB 1.0* standard is slow. However, the newer *USB 2.0* standard supports data transfer rates of 480 Mbps and the emerging 4.8 Gbps *USB 3.0* standard (also called *SuperSpeed USB*) is about 10 times as fast as USB 2.0. The convenience and universal support of USB have made it one of the most widely used standards for connecting peripherals today.

FireWire/IEEE 1394 Bus

FireWire (also known as *IEEE 1394*) is a high-speed bus standard developed by Apple for connecting devices—particularly multimedia devices like digital video cameras—to a computer. Like USB, FireWire can connect multiple external devices via a single port. FireWire is relatively fast—the original FireWire standard supports data transfer rates of up to 320 Mbps, the newer FireWire standard (called *FireWire 800*) standard supports data

---

>**Memory bus.** The connection between the CPU and RAM. >**Frontside bus (FSB).** The bus that connects the CPU (via the I/O bridge) to the rest of the bus architecture. >**PCI Express (PCIe) bus.** One of the buses most commonly used to connect peripheral devices. >**Universal Serial Bus (USB).** A universal bus used to connect up to 127 peripheral devices to a computer without requiring the use of additional expansion cards. >**FireWire.** A high-speed bus standard often used to connect digital video cameras and other multimedia hardware to a computer.

transfer rates up to 800 Mbps, and the emerging *FireWire 3200* standard offers 3.2 Gbps transfer rates.

Ports and Connectors

As already mentioned, **ports** are the connectors located on the exterior of the system unit that are used to connect external hardware devices. Each port is attached to the appropriate bus on the motherboard so that when a device is plugged into a port, the device can communicate with the CPU and other computer components. Several of the original ports used with desktop computers—such as the *parallel ports* traditionally used to connect printers—are now considered *legacy ports* and so are not typically included on newer computers. Typical ports for a desktop computer and the connectors used with those ports are shown in Figure 2-16; these and additional ports you might find on your computer are discussed next.

➤ *Monitor ports* are used to connect a monitor to a computer. Traditionally, monitors connect via a *VGA connector*; today's *flat-panel monitors* typically connect via a *Digital Video Interface* (*DVI*) connector and *high-definition monitors* connect via an *HDMI* (*High-Definition Multimedia Interface*). Monitors and emerging options for connecting them to a computer are discussed in Chapter 4.

➤ *Network ports* are used to connect a computer to a computer network via a networking cable—typically a cable using an *RJ-45 connector*, which looks similar to a telephone connector but is larger. Networks and networking hardware are discussed in detail in Chapter 7.

FIGURE 2-16

Typical ports for desktop computers and examples of connectors.

POWER CONNECTOR
Connects the computer to a power outlet.

VGA MONITOR PORT
Connects a VGA monitor.

USB PORTS
Connect a keyboard, mouse, scanner, flash memory drive, printer, digital camera, or other USB devices.

HDMI PORT
Connects a high-definition monitor.

FIREWIRE PORT
Connects FireWire devices.

NETWORK PORT
Connects the computer to a network.

AUDIO PORTS
Connect speakers, headphones, and a microphone.

EMPTY SLOTS
Ports located on new expansion cards added to the computer will be accessible here.

CONNECTORS

Monitor (VGA)

USB

Monitor (HDMI)

FireWire

Network (RJ-45)

Audio (3.5mm)

> **Port.** A connector on the exterior of a computer to which a device may be attached.

➤ *Modem ports* are used to connect a computer to a phone outlet via telephone connectors, as discussed in Chapter 7.

➤ *USB ports* are used to connect USB devices (such as keyboards, mice, printers, hard drives, and digital cameras) to a computer via a USB connector. Multiple USB devices can connect to a single USB port via a *USB hub.* USB hubs can either be wired or wireless; a wireless USB hub is shown in Figure 2-17.

➤ *FireWire (IEEE 1394) ports* are used to connect FireWire devices to the computer via a FireWire connector. Similar to USB, a *FireWire hub* can be used to connect multiple devices to a single port. FireWire connections are most often used with digital video cameras and other multimedia peripherals.

➤ *Keyboard ports* and *mouse ports* (also called *PS/2 ports*) are used to connect a keyboard and mouse with a *PS/2 connector* to the system unit. Many computers today do not include PS/2 ports; instead, they are designed to be used with USB keyboards and mice.

➤ *SCSI (Small Computer System Interface) ports* are high-speed parallel ports sometimes used to attach printers, scanners, and hard drives.

➤ *MIDI ports* are used to connect *MIDI (musical instrument digital interface)* devices (such as a musical keyboard) to the computer.

➤ *IrDA (Infrared Data Association) ports* and *Bluetooth ports* are used to receive wireless transmissions from devices; since the transmissions are wireless, these ports do not use a plug. IrDA ports are commonly used to "beam" data from a portable computer or mobile device to a computer; Bluetooth ports are most often used with wireless keyboards, mice, and headsets. Wireless data transmission is discussed in more detail in Chapter 7.

➤ *Flash memory card slots* are used to connect flash media cards or other hardware using a flash media interface. As discussed shortly, some hardware for portable computers is designed to connect using these slots.

➤ *Game ports* are used to connect a joystick, game pad, steering wheel, or other device commonly used with computer gaming programs.

➤ *Audio ports* are used to connect speakers or a microphone to the computer.

➤ *eSATA (external SATA) ports* are used to connect external SATA devices (most commonly, an external hard drive). External hard drives that connect via eSATA are much faster than external hard drives that connect via a USB or FireWire connection. Hard drives are discussed in detail in Chapter 3.

Most computers today support the *Plug and Play* standard, which means the computer automatically configures new devices as soon as they are installed and the computer is powered up. If you want to add a new device to your desktop computer and there is an available port for the device you want to add, then you just need to plug it in (shut down the computer first, unless the device uses a USB or FireWire port). If the appropriate port is not available, you need to either install the appropriate expansion card to create the necessary port or use a USB or FireWire version of the device, if you have one of those two ports available on your computer. USB and FireWire devices are *hot-swappable*, meaning they can be plugged into their respective ports while the computer is powered up. Hot-swappable devices—along with some removable storage media, such as flash memory

Plug this adapter into the computer's USB port to connect the wireless USB hub to the computer.

Plug up to four USB devices to this hub to connect them wirelessly to the computer.

FIGURE 2-17

USB hubs. A USB hub can be used to connect multiple USB devices to a single USB port.

HW

Right panel ports
(not shown):
SD card slot
eSATA port

HDMI
monitor port

VGA
monitor port

USB
ports

FireWire
port

Network
port

ExpressCard
slot

PC Card
slot

SDIO
barcode
reader

SD slot

SD flash
memory
card

NOTEBOOK COMPUTERS

MOBILE DEVICES

FIGURE 2-18
Typical ports for
portable computers.

cards—are recognized by the computer as soon as they are connected to it and can be used right away. Other devices are recognized by the computer when the computer is first powered up after the device has been added.

Notebook and netbook computers have ports similar to desktop computers (see Figure 2-18), but sometimes have less of them. UMPCs and mobile devices have a more limited amount of expandability. However, they usually come with at least one built-in expansion slot—typically a USB port or an *SD slot*, which can be used with both the postage-stamp-sized *Secure Digital* (*SD*) flash memory cards, as well as with peripheral devices adhering to the *Secure Digital Input/Output* (*SDIO*) *standard* (see Figure 2-18).

HOW THE CPU WORKS

As already discussed, a CPU consists of a variety of circuitry and components packaged together into a single component. The key element of the processor is the *transistor*—a device made of semiconductor material that controls the flow of electrons inside a chip. Today's CPUs contain hundreds of millions of transistors, and the number doubles approximately every 18 months. This phenomenon is known as *Moore's Law* and is explained in the Inside the Industry box. The primary components of a typical CPU are discussed next.

Typical CPU Components

To begin to understand how a CPU works, you need to know how the CPU is organized and what components it includes. This information will help you understand how electronic impulses move from one part of the CPU to another to process data. The architecture and components included in a CPU (referred to as *microarchitecture*) vary from processor to processor. A simplified example of the principal components that might be included in a single core of a typical CPU is shown in Figure 2-19 and discussed next. There are also additional components that are typically located inside the CPU, but not within each core. For instance, there are buses to connect the CPU cores to each other (typically via QuickPath Interconnect (QPI) or HyperTransport Technology connections), buses to connect each core to the CPU's *memory controller* (which controls the communication between the CPU cores and RAM), and buses to connect each core to any cache memory that is shared between the cores. For a look at the companies that are used to examine the parts of the CPU or other computer components to gather evidence for patent lawsuits and other official actions, see the Trend box.

CONTROL UNIT
Is in charge of the entire process, making sure everything happens at the right time. It instructs the ALU, FPU, and registers what to do, based on instructions from the decode unit.

PREFETCH UNIT
Requests instructions and data from cache or RAM and makes sure they are in the proper order for processing; it attempts to fetch instructions and data ahead of time so that the other components don't have to wait.

ARITHMETIC/LOGIC UNIT AND FLOATING POINT UNIT
Performs the arithmetic and logical operations, as directed by the control unit.

REGISTERS
Hold the results of processing.

DECODE UNIT
Takes instructions from the prefetch unit and translates them into a form that the control unit can understand.

BUS INTERFACE UNIT
The place where data and instructions enter or leave the core.

INTERNAL CACHE MEMORY
Stores data and instructions before and during processing.

FIGURE 2-19
Inside a CPU core.

Arithmetic/Logic Unit (ALU) and Floating Point Unit (FPU)

The **arithmetic/logic unit** (**ALU**) is the section of a CPU core that performs arithmetic (addition, subtraction, multiplication, and division) involving integers and logical operations (such as comparing two pieces of data to see if they are equal or determining if a specific condition is true or false). Arithmetic requiring decimals is usually performed by the **floating point unit** (**FPU**). Arithmetic operations are performed when mathematical calculations are requested by the user, as well as when many other common computing tasks are performed. For example, editing a digital photograph in an image editing program, running the spell checker in a word processing program, and burning a music CD are all performed by the ALU, with help from the FPU when needed, using only arithmetic and logical operations. Most CPUs today have multiple ALUs and FPUs that work together to perform the necessary operations.

Control Unit

The **control unit** coordinates and controls the operations and activities taking place within a CPU core, such as retrieving data and instructions and passing them on to the ALU or FPU for execution. In other words, it directs the flow of electronic traffic within the core, much like a traffic cop controls the flow of vehicles on a roadway. Essentially, the control unit tells the ALU and FPU what to do and makes sure that everything happens at the right time in order for the appropriate processing to take place.

Prefetch Unit

The **prefetch unit** orders data and instructions from cache or RAM based on the current task. The prefetch unit tries to predict what data and instructions will be needed and retrieves them ahead of time, in order to help avoid delays in processing.

> **Arithmetic/logic unit (ALU).** The part of a CPU core that performs logical operations and integer arithmetic. > **Floating point unit (FPU).** The part of a CPU core that performs decimal arithmetic. > **Control unit.** The part of a CPU core that coordinates its operations. > **Prefetch unit.** The part of a CPU core that attempts to retrieve data and instructions before they are needed for processing in order to avoid delays.

INSIDE THE INDUSTRY

Moore's Law

In 1965, Gordon Moore, the cofounder of Intel and shown in the accompanying photograph, observed that the number of transistors per square inch on chips had doubled every two years since the integrated circuit was invented. He then made a now-famous prediction—that this doubling trend would continue for at least 10 more years. Here we are, about 45 years later, and transistor density still doubles about every 18 months. Due to technological breakthroughs, *Moore's Law* has been maintained for far longer than the original prediction and most experts, including Moore himself, expect the doubling trend to continue for at least another decade. In fact, Intel states that the mission of its technology development team is to continue to break barriers to Moore's Law.

Interestingly, other computer components also follow Moore's Law. For example, storage capacity doubles approximately every 20 months, and chip speed doubles about every 24 months. Consequently, the term *Moore's Law* has been expanded and is now used to describe the amount of time it takes components to double in capacity or speed. Many experts predict that, eventually, a physical limit to the number of transistors that can be crammed onto a chip will end Moore's Law. But the end is not yet in sight.

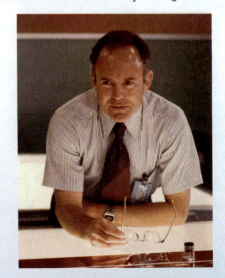

Gordon Moore (1970).

ONLINE VIDEO

Go to the Chapter 2 page at **www.cengage.com/ computerconcepts/np/uc13** to watch the "The Impact of Moore's Law" video clip.

Decode Unit

The **decode unit** takes the instructions fetched by the prefetch unit and translates them into a form that can be understood by the control unit, ALU, and FPU. The decoded instructions go to the control unit for processing.

Registers and Internal Cache Memory

As mentioned earlier, registers and cache memory are both types of memory used by the CPU. Registers are groups of high-speed memory located within the CPU that are used during processing. The ALU and FPU use registers to store data, intermediary calculations, and the results of processing temporarily. CPUs today typically have a variety of other registers used for specific purposes. Internal cache memory (such as the Level 1 and Level 2 cache typically built into each core of a CPU and the Level 3 cache that is often shared by all cores of the CPU) is used to store instructions and data for the CPU, to avoid retrieving them from RAM or the hard drive.

Bus Interface Unit

The **bus interface unit** allows the core to communicate with other CPU components, such as the memory controller and other cores. As previously mentioned, the memory controller controls the flow of instructions and data going between the CPU cores and RAM.

>**Decode unit.** The part of a CPU core that translates instructions into a form that can be processed by the ALU and FPU. >**Bus interface unit.** The part of a CPU core that allows it to communicate with other CPU components.

TREND

High-Tech Investigators

With the high value of technology today and claims of stolen technology and patent infringements happening all the time, what can companies in the computer industry do to find out the truth? Increasingly, they turn to reverse engineering companies, such as TAEUS International. Short for "Tear Apart Everything Under the Stars," TAEUS is a leader in the area of applying engineering skills and industry knowledge in order to analyze products and evaluate patent claims. In a nutshell, companies like TAEUS tear products apart to hunt for patented technologies that should not be there. Just as with criminal investigations, patent infringement claims require physical proof, and TAEUS engineers inspect and photograph critical elements of a product (see the accompanying photo) to compare that product to existing patents.

In just the past few years, TAEUS has helped to settle numerous patent infringement claims. For instance, it helped Intel avoid litigation when it was sued by Digital Equipment Corporation (DEC) for a share of Intel's Pentium CPU profits. After TAEUS found patented Intel technology inside DEC's servers, the case was settled with no money changing hands. TAEUS also does preemptive work helping tech companies avoid patent liabilities by searching through existing patents to determine which technology patents are enforceable before a problem arises. At a rate of $100,000 to reverse engineer one computer chip, services such as the ones TAEUS provide are not cheap, but with patent lawsuits often exceeding $100 million, for tech companies that avoid litigation by using TAEUS services, it is money well spent.

Other companies in the area of *computer forensics* specialize in finding other types of digital evidence needed for legal proceedings, such as recovering files deleted from a computer or storage medium, determining activities previously performed on a computer, unlocking encrypted files, and so forth. Computer forensics experts are often hired by individual companies, as well as by law enforcement agencies.

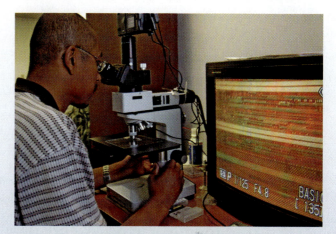

A TAEUS engineer at work.

The System Clock and the Machine Cycle

As mentioned at the beginning of this chapter, every instruction that you issue to a computer—by either typing a command or clicking something with the mouse—is converted into machine language. In turn, each machine language instruction in a CPU's *instruction set* (the collection of basic machine language commands that the CPU can understand) is broken down into several smaller, machine-level instructions called *microcode*. Microcode instructions, such as moving a single piece of data from one part of the computer system to another or adding the numbers located in two specific registers, are built into the CPU and are the basic instructions used by the CPU.

In order to synchronize all of a computer's operations, a **system clock**—a small quartz crystal located on the motherboard—is used. The system clock sends out a signal on a regular basis to all other computer components, similar to a musician's metronome or a person's heartbeat. Each signal is referred to as a *cycle*. The number of cycles per second is measured in *hertz* (*Hz*). One megahertz (MHz) is equal to one million ticks of the system clock.

> **System clock.** The timing mechanism within the computer system that synchronizes the computer's operations.

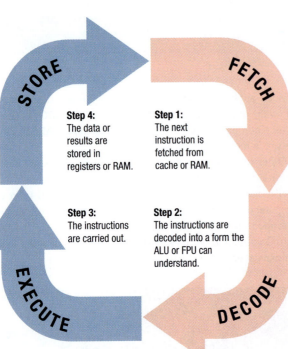

STORE

Step 4:
The data or
results are
stored in
registers or RAM.

FETCH

Step 1:
The next
instruction is
fetched from
cache or RAM.

Step 3:
The instructions
are carried out.

Step 2:
The instructions are
decoded into a form the
ALU or FPU can
understand.

EXECUTE

DECODE

FIGURE 2-20

A machine cycle.
A machine cycle is
typically accomplished
in four steps.

Many personal computers today have system clocks that run at 200 MHz, and all devices (such as CPUs) that are synchronized with these system clocks run at either the system clock speed or at a multiple of or a fraction of the system clock speed. For example, a CPU with a *CPU clock speed* of 2 GHz uses a multiplier of 10, meaning that the CPU clock essentially "ticks" 10 times during each system clock tick. During each CPU clock tick, the CPU can execute one or more pieces of microcode. Most computers today can process more than one piece of microcode at one time—a characteristic known as *superscalar*, which is the ability to process multiple *instructions per cycle* (*IPC*). A CPU with a higher CPU clock speed processes more instructions per second than the same CPU with a lower CPU clock speed.

Whenever the CPU processes a single piece of microcode, it is referred to as a **machine cycle**. Each machine cycle consists of the four general operations illustrated in Figure 2-20 and discussed next.

1. *Fetch*—the program instruction is fetched.

2. *Decode*—the instructions are decoded so the control unit, ALU, and FPU can understand them.

3. *Execute*—the instructions are carried out.

4. *Store*—the original data or the result from the ALU or FPU execution is stored in the CPU's registers.

Because each machine cycle processes only a single microcode instruction, many seemingly simple commands (such as multiplying two numbers) might require more than one machine cycle, and a computer might need to go through thousands, millions, or even billions of machine cycles to complete a user command or program instruction. For instance, a CPU processing the command 2 + 3 would typically require at least four machine cycles, such as to:

1. Fetch the number 2 from RAM, decode it, and store it in register X.

2. Fetch the number 3 from RAM, decode it, and store it in a register Y.

3. Fetch and decode the addition instruction, then add the two numbers (currently stored in registers X and Y) and store the sum in register Z.

4. Fetch and decode the instruction to display the sum, and then output the sum (currently stored in register Z) to RAM.

MAKING COMPUTERS FASTER AND BETTER NOW AND IN THE FUTURE

Over the years, computer designers have developed a number of strategies to achieve faster, more powerful, and more reliable computing performance. Researchers are also constantly working on ways to improve the performance of computers of the future. There are several ways computer users can speed up their existing computers today, and a number of technologies are being developed by manufacturers to improve computers both today and in the future.

Improving the Performance of Your System Today

Several strategies you can use to try to improve the performance of your current computer are discussed next.

Add More Memory

With today's graphic-intensive interfaces and applications, much more memory is required than was necessary even a couple of years ago. If your computer is just a few years old, slows down significantly when you have multiple programs open, and has less than 2 GB of RAM installed, you should consider adding more memory to your system. To accomplish this, first check to see if there is room inside your computer for additional memory modules (either by looking inside the computer or by using a scanning utility like the one shown in Figure 2-21 that is available on some memory manufacturers' Web sites). You can then determine (either by the scan information or by checking with your computer's manufacturer) how much memory can be added to your computer and what type and speed of RAM your computer requires. If you do not have enough empty memory slots in your computer, you will need to remove some of the old memory modules and replace them with newer, higher capacity ones in order to add more memory to your system. Remember that some memory modules must be added in sets (such as pairs or triplets) for optimal performance.

Details the quantity and type of RAM that is currently installed.

Lists the options for memory expansion.

FIGURE 2-21
Online memory scanners can help you determine what memory can be added to your computer.

CAUTION   CAUTION   CAUTION   CAUTION   CAUTION   CAUTION   CAU

Never open the case of your computer when it is powered up or plugged into an electrical outlet. To avoid damaging your computer with the static electricity stored in your body, consider wearing an *antistatic wristband*.

Perform System Maintenance

As you work and use your hard drive to store and retrieve data, and as you install and uninstall programs, most computers tend to become less efficient. One reason for this is because as large documents are stored, retrieved, and then stored again, they often become *fragmented*—that is, not stored in contiguous (adjacent) storage areas. Because the different pieces of the document are physically located in different places, it takes longer for the computer to retrieve or store them. Another reason a computer might become inefficient is that when programs are uninstalled, pieces of the program are sometimes left behind or references to these programs are left in operating system files, such as the *Windows registry*. Yet another reason is that as a hard drive begins to get full, it takes longer to locate and manipulate the data stored on the hard drive. All of these factors can result in a system performing more slowly than it should.

To avoid some of these problems, regular system maintenance should be performed. Some system maintenance tips every computer user should be aware of are:

> ► Uninstall any programs that you no longer want on your computer in order to free up space on your hard drive. Be sure to use the proper removal process, such as the *Uninstall a program* option in the Windows Control Panel or an Uninstall option for that program located on the Start menu. Windows users can also periodically use a

VIDEO PODCAST

Go to the Chapter 2 page at **www.cengage.com/ computerconcepts/np/uc13** to download or listen to the "How To: Deal with a Blue Screen of Death" video podcast.

FIGURE 2-22

Windows Disk Cleanup. Running the Disk Cleanup program can help free up room on your hard drive.

registry cleaner (a number of free registry cleaners are available online) to clean the Windows registry to remove references to nonexistent programs.

➤ If you have large files (such as digital photos or videos) stored on your computer that you do not need on a regular basis but want to keep, consider moving them to a removable storage medium, such as a DVD disc or an external hard drive. Once copied onto the new medium, the files can be deleted from your hard drive to free up space. Be sure to open the files from the storage medium to confirm that the transfer was successful before deleting the files from your hard drive, and consider copying important files to two different storage mediums. Backing up files, deleting files, and types of storage media are discussed in more detail in later chapters.

➤ Delete the temporary files (such as installation files, Web browsing history, and files in the Recycle Bin) stored by your computer and Web browser to free up room on your hard drive. You can delete these files manually, if desired, but the *Windows Disk Cleanup* program shown in Figure 2-22 can locate and delete these temporary files for you.

➤ *Error-check* and *defragment* your hard drive periodically to make it work more efficiently. Windows users can right-click a hard drive icon in Windows Explorer, select *Properties*, and then select the *Check Now* option on the Tools tab to check that hard drive for errors, or select *Defragment Now* to defragment that hard drive.

➤ Scan for *computer viruses* and *spyware* continually. A computer that suddenly slows down might be the result of a computer virus, spyware program, or other threat. *Antivirus* and *antispyware programs* can help detect and correct these problems and are discussed in more detail in Chapter 9.

➤ Clean out the dust from inside the system unit of desktop computers once or twice a year using a can of compressed air or a small vacuum cleaner. Although the dust may not slow down your system by itself, it can slow down the fans that cool your computer as well cause the components inside your computer to run hotter than they should, which can cause problems with your computer such as overheating, burned out components, and periodic shutting down without warning. Notebook users should check the bottom of their computers to see if there is a removable dust filter—if there is one, it should be cleaned periodically.

Buy a Larger or Second Hard Drive

As already mentioned, hard drives become less efficient as they fill up. If your hard drive is almost full and you do not have any data or programs that you can remove, consider buying and installing a second hard drive. The new hard drive can be an internal hard drive if you have an empty drive bay inside your computer. It can also be an external hard drive that connects via an available (typically USB) port. Alternatively, you can replace your existing hard drive with a larger one, although the data transfer process will be a little more complicated. Hard drives are discussed in detail in Chapter 3.

Upgrade Your Internet Connection

If your system seems slow primarily when you are using the Internet, the culprit might be your Internet connection. If you are using a *conventional dial-up connection* (the relatively slow Internet access available via your telephone line), you may wish to upgrade to a faster type of connection. Switching to *cable, satellite, DSL, fixed wireless,* or another type of *broadband Internet service* is more expensive than dial-up, but is significantly faster. The differences between these and other types of Internet connections are described in Chapters 7 and 8.

Upgrade Your Video Graphics Card

If programs, documents, and other items seem sluggish as they are displayed on your monitor, you can check to see if a video upgrade might help. First, determine if your computer uses *shared video memory* (in which some of your computer's RAM is used for video memory instead of separate dedicated memory located on a video graphics card). If so, then installing a separate video card containing adequate video memory may speed up your system since it will free up the RAM currently being used for video memory. You may also want to buy and install a new video card (assuming your computer has an available appropriate expansion slot) if it is necessary to connect a second monitor to your computer, or if you are a gamer, computer artist, graphical engineer, or otherwise use 3D-graphic-intensive applications.

Strategies for Making Faster and Better Computers

Researchers and manufacturers are using several strategies today to continue to build faster and better personal computers. Some relate to technology in general (such as the *virtualization* trend discussed in Chapter 1); others are techniques used specifically to speed up the CPU. Some of these strategies are described in the next few sections.

Improved Architecture

Computer manufacturers are continually working to improve the basic architecture of computers, such as to make them faster, cooler, quieter, more energy efficient, and more reliable. For example, new designs for motherboards and CPUs are always under development, and computer components are continually being built smaller, so more power and capabilities can be contained in the same size package. In fact, today's CPUs—which are formed using a process called *lithography* that imprints patterns on semiconductor materials—typically contain transistors that are 45 *nanometers* (*nm*) in size (one nanometer is a billionth of a meter); 32 nm chips are becoming available, and transistors as small as 10 nm have been created in lab settings. As lithography techniques continue to improve, transistors will likely continue to shrink, allowing more transistors to fit on the same-sized CPU. Creating components smaller than 100 nm fits the definition of *nanotechnology*, which is discussed in more detail shortly.

Other improvements include faster memory and faster bus speeds to help speed up processing and to help reduce or eliminate bottlenecks, and creating CPUs with multiple cores. CPUs are also increasingly including additional technology to meet new needs, such as support for virtualization and increased 3D graphics processing. Improvements to CPU instruction set designs are made as needed to expand the instruction set design for new applications—particularly the growing use of multimedia applications, such as editing digital movies and photos, and burning music CDs. For example, *MMX* (*Multimedia Extensions*) is a set of 57 multimedia instructions for handling many common multimedia operations. In addition, new *streaming SIMD extensions* (*SSEs*) are implemented on a regular basis to help CPUs perform floating-point-intensive applications (such as video and audio handling, 3D modeling, and physical simulations) much more quickly than before, provided the software being used supports the SSEs being used.

Improved Materials

Traditionally, CPU chips used aluminum circuitry etched onto a silicon chip. As the number of aluminum circuits that can be packed onto a silicon chip without heat damage or interference approached its limit, chipmakers began to look for alternate materials. Copper was one of the next choices since it is a far better electrical conductor, and it can produce chips containing more circuitry at a lower price. As transistors have continued to shrink (which results in an increased leakage of current), CPU manufacturers have looked to new materials that reduce current leakage to allow more reliable high-speed operation. For instance, Intel switched to a new material called *high-k* for some of the silicon components in its 45 nm and 32 nm CPUs.

A possibility for an entirely new material is the *graphene chip*, which uses *graphene*—flat sheets of carbon, such as those used to create *carbon nanotubes* (which are discussed shortly)—instead of silicon. However, instead of rolling up graphene, which is the process used when making carbon nanotubes, the graphene for chips is cut into strips. According to Georgia Tech physics professor Walter de Heer, one of the leading researchers in this area, silicon can't keep up with the current growth in chip technology and graphene may be the answer. Since electrons move through graphene with almost no resistance, they generate little heat; graphene also allows any heat that is generated to dissipate quickly. As a result, graphene-based chips can operate at much higher speeds than silicon. While de Heer estimates that graphene chips are likely at least 10 years away, he estimates that graphene can be 100 times faster than silicon—in the *terahertz* (*THz*) range.

For integrating computer components into clothing and other flexible materials (such as to create clothing, backpacks, and other objects that can control your electronic devices or display content on demand), a number of companies are developing flexible electronic components, such as the flexible processor shown in Figure 2-23. In addition to the ability to be bent without damaging the circuitry, flexible processors are thinner, lighter, generate little heat, and consume significantly less energy than conventional processors. In addition, if the processors are made from plastic (which some researchers believe is a viable alternative to silicon), it means that future CPUs could be printed on plastic sheets and be much faster than, but cost about the same as, today's silicon chips.

FIGURE 2-23
Flexible processors.

Pipelining

In older computer systems, the CPU had to finish processing one instruction completely before starting another. Today's computers, however, can process multiple instructions at one time. One way to accomplish this is through **pipelining**. With pipelining, a new instruction begins executing as soon as the previous one reaches the next stage of the pipeline. Figure 2-24 illustrates this process with a 4-stage pipeline. Notice that while the pipelined CPU is executing one instruction, it is simultaneously fetching and getting the next instruction ready for execution. Without a pipeline, the ALU and FPU would be idle while an instruction is being fetched and decoded.

Pipelines for CPUs today usually have between 10 and 20 stages, and the machine cycle is broken down in as many parts as needed to match the number of stages used. For example, with a 10-stage pipeline, the 4 steps of the machine cycle would be broken down into a total of 10 steps so that all stages of the pipeline can be used at one time. Pipelining increases the number of machine cycles completed per second, which increases the number of instructions performed per second, which improves performance.

Multiprocessing and Parallel Processing

The use of more than one processor or processing core in a computer (such as using multiple CPUs in a server, mainframe, or supercomputer, or using a multi-core CPU in a personal computer) is common today. When two or more processors or processing cores are located within a single computer, techniques that perform operations simultaneously—such

> **Pipelining.** The capability of a CPU to begin processing a new instruction as soon as the previous instruction completes the first stage of the machine cycle.

Stages

Fetch Instruction 1	Decode Instruction 1	Execute Instruction 1	Store Result Instruction 1	Fetch Instruction 2	Decode Instruction 2	Execute Instruction 2

WITHOUT PIPELINING
Without pipelining, an instruction finishes an entire machine cycle before another instruction is started.

Stages

Fetch Instruction 1	Fetch Instruction 2	Fetch Instruction 3	Fetch Instruction 4	Fetch Instruction 5	Fetch Instruction 6	Fetch Instruction 7
	Decode Instruction 1	Decode Instruction 2	Decode Instruction 3	Decode Instruction 4	Decode Instruction 5	Decode Instruction 6
		Execute Instruction 1	Execute Instruction 2	Execute Instruction 3	Execute Instruction 4	Execute Instruction 5
			Store Result Instruction 1	Store Result Instruction 2	Store Result Instruction 3	Store Result Instruction 4

WITH PIPELINING
With pipelining, a new instruction is started when the preceding instruction moves to the next stage of the pipeline.

FIGURE 2-24
Pipelining. Pipelining streamlines the machine cycle by executing different stages of multiple instructions at the same time so that the different parts of the CPU are idle less often.

HW

as **multiprocessing** (where each processor or core typically works on a different job) and **parallel processing** (where multiple processors or cores work together to make one single job finish sooner) are possible.

The use of multiprocessing and parallel processing can increase astronomically the number of calculations performed in any given time period. For example, IBM's Roadrunner supercomputer (shown in Figure 1-19 in Chapter 1) uses approximately 19,000 processors and operates at more than 1 petaflop; that is, it is able to process more than one quadrillion operations per second. To increase efficiency in multiprocessing systems, CPUs specifically designed to work with a particular number of processors (such as two or eight) can be used. These CPUs include technology (such as direct links between the processors) to improve communications and increase efficiency.

A concept related to multiprocessing is *Hyper-Threading Technology*—a technology developed by Intel to enable software to treat a single processing core as two cores. Since it utilizes processing power in the chip that would otherwise go unused, this technology lets the chip operate more efficiently, resulting in faster processing, provided the software being used supports Hyper-Threading Technology.

Future Trends

Some of the strategies discussed in the prior sections are currently being used, but some ideas are further from being implemented on a wide-scale basis. Selected trends we will likely see more of in the near future are discussed next.

Nanotechnology

Although there are varying definitions, most agree that **nanotechnology** involves creating computer components, machines, and other structures that are less than 100 nanometers in size. As already discussed, today's CPUs contain components that fit the definition of nanotechnology. However, some experts believe that, eventually, current technology

---

> **Multiprocessing.** The capability to use multiple processors or multiple processing cores in a single computer, usually to process multiple jobs at one time faster than could be performed with a single processor. > **Parallel processing.** A processing technique that uses multiple processors or multiple processing cores simultaneously, usually to process a single job as fast as possible. > **Nanotechnology.** The science of creating tiny computers and components by working at the individual atomic and molecular levels.

TECHNOLOGY AND YOU

The "Morph" Concept

While still a concept device, the *Morph* concept (developed by researchers at Nokia and the University of Cambridge Nanoscience Centre) demonstrates how nanotechnology may allow future mobile devices to be stretchable and flexible, allowing users to transform their mobile devices into radically different shapes. For instance, the Morph concept can be worn on the wrist, folded into a phone, or opened into a larger handheld device that features a touch pad or keyboard (see the accompanying illustration). Nanotechnology enables the material to repel water, dirt, and fingerprints and to be self-cleaning. Integrated sensors can monitor pollution and chemicals and notify the user as needed of any possible risks. The device is solar-powered via a covering of *Nanograss* that harvests solar power. According to Dr. Bob Iannucci, Chief Technology Officer, Nokia, "Nokia Research Center is looking at ways to reinvent the form and function of mobile devices; the Morph concept shows what might be possible."

Possible configurations for the Morph concept device.

ONLINE VIDEO

Go to the Chapter 2 page at **www.cengage.com/ computerconcepts/np/uc13** to watch the "Introducing the Morph Concept" video clip.

will reach its limits. At that point, transistors and other computer components may need to be built at the atomic and molecular level—starting with single atoms or molecules to construct the components. Prototypes of computer products built in this fashion include a single switch that can be turned on and off like a transistor but is made from a single organic molecule, as well as tiny nickel-based *nanodots* that would, theoretically, allow about 5 TB of data to be stored on a hard drive roughly the size of a postage stamp. In other nanotechnology developments, researchers at the University of Arizona recently discovered how to turn single molecules into working transistors and they created transistors as small as a single nanometer. In addition, prototypes of tiny *nanogenerators* have been developed that may someday power mobile devices with low-frequency vibrations, such as a heartbeat or simple body movements like walking. For a look at a concept mobile device that nanotechnology may make possible in the future, see the Technology and You box.

One nanotechnology development that is already being used in a variety of products available today is **carbon nanotubes**—tiny, hollow tubes made up of carbon atoms. The wall of a single-walled carbon nanotube is only one carbon atom thick and the tube diameter is approximately 10,000 times smaller than a human hair. Carbon nanotubes have great potential for future computing products since they can conduct electricity better than copper, are stronger than steel, conduct heat better than diamonds, and can transmit electronic impulses faster than silicon. Lithium ion batteries that use nanotubes are currently on the

> **Carbon nanotubes.** Tiny, hollow tubes made of carbon atoms.

market and several nanotube-based computing products—like nanotube-based display screens and memory—are currently under development. Since carbon nanotubes can transmit electricity and are transparent, they are also being used for product development in the areas of TVs, solar cells, light bulbs, and other similar non-computing applications. In addition, because of their strength and lightness for their size, carbon nanotubes are being integrated into products that benefit from those characteristics, such as automobile panels, airplanes, tennis rackets, and racing bikes. In fact, the frame of a bike model that several professional cyclists ride is built with carbon nanotubes (see Figure 2-25)—the entire bike frame weighs less than one kilogram (2.2 pounds). Carbon nanotubes are also beginning to be combined with other materials, such as plastic, to increase the durability of materials used to produce other consumer items, such as surfboards.

Two other recent developments are *nanoparticles* that can remove contaminants from water sources and *nanosensors* that can detect small amounts of cancer-causing toxins or cancer drugs inside single living cells. Possible future applications of nanotechnology include disposing of e-trash by rearranging dangerous components at the atomic level into inert substances, microscopic devices that can enter the bloodstream and perform tests or irradiate cancerous tumors, improved military uniforms that protect against bullets and germ warfare, and computers and sensors that are small enough to be woven into the fibers of clothing or embedded into paint and other materials. Some of the devices generated by nanotechnology research may contain or be constructed out of organic material. Complete *organic computers* (discussed shortly) are a long way off, but researchers have already created biological computing devices—such as the *MAYA-II* computer that uses strands of DNA to perform computations. Although very slow and only programmed to play tic-tac-toe, the computer has never lost at that game.

Quantum Computing

The idea of **quantum computing** emerged in the 1970s, but it has received renewed interest lately. Quantum computing applies the principles of quantum physics and quantum mechanics to computers, going beyond traditional physics to work at the subatomic level. Quantum computers differ from conventional computers in that they utilize atoms or nuclei working together as *quantum bits* or *qubits*. Qubits function simultaneously as both the computer's processor and memory, and each qubit can represent more than just the two states (one and zero) available to today's electronic bits; a qubit can even represent many states at one time. Quantum computers can perform computations on many numbers at one time, making them, theoretically, exponentially faster than conventional computers. Physically, quantum computers in the future might consist of a thimbleful of liquid whose atoms are used to perform calculations as instructed by an external device.

While quantum computers are still in the pioneering stage, working quantum computers do exist. For instance, in 2001 the researchers at IBM's Almaden Research Center created a 7-qubit quantum computer (see Figure 2-26) composed of the nuclei of seven atoms that can interact with each other and be programmed by radio frequency pulses. This quantum computer successfully factored the number 15—not a complicated computation for a conventional computer, but the fact that a quantum computer was able to understand the problem and compute the correct answer is viewed as a highly significant event in the area of quantum computer research.

FIGURE 2-25
Carbon nanotubes make this bike frame very strong, but light.

FIGURE 2-26
Quantum computers. The vial of liquid shown here contains the 7-qubit computer used by IBM researchers in 2001 to perform the most complicated computation by a quantum computer to date—factoring the number 15.

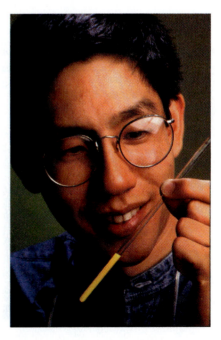

>**Quantum computing.** A technology that applies the principles of quantum physics and quantum mechanics to computers to direct atoms or nuclei to work together as quantum bits (qubits), which function simultaneously as the computer's processor and memory.

More recently, Canadian scientists developed a 16-qubit quantum computer that can solve Sudoku puzzles, and Yale University researchers developed the first rudimentary electronic quantum processor (based on a 2-qubit chip) that can successfully perform a few simple tasks. In addition, Hewlett-Packard scientists have developed a *crossbar latch*—a switch just a single molecule thick that can store binary data and might one day function as a transistor in a quantum computer. One of the obstacles to creating a fully functional quantum computer has been the inability of researchers to control the actions of a single qubit inside a matrix of other qubits. In 2009, researchers successfully accomplished this in an experiment; this breakthrough is viewed as a significant step toward the ability to create more sophisticated working quantum computers in the future.

Quantum computing is not well suited for general computing tasks but is ideal for, and expected to be widely used in, the areas of *encryption* (discussed in Chapter 9) and code breaking.

Optical Computing

Optical chips, which use light waves to transmit data, are also currently in development. A possibility for the future is the **optical computer**—a computer that uses light, such as from laser beams or infrared beams—to perform digital computations. Because light beams do not interfere with each other, optical computers can be much smaller and faster than electronic computers. For instance, according to one NASA senior research scientist, an optical computer could solve a problem in one hour that would take an electronic computer 11 years to solve. While some researchers are working on developing an all-optical computer, others believe that a mix of optical and electronic components—or an *opto-electronic computer*—may be the best bet for the future. Opto-electronic technology is already being used to improve long-distance fiber-optic communications. Initial opto-electronic computer applications are expected to be applied to the area of speeding up communications between computers and other devices, as well as between computer components. In fact, prototypes of chips that have both optical and electrical functions combined on a single silicon chip—a feat that was thought to be impossible until recently—already exist. One recent breakthrough in optical computing is the development by researchers of ways to make lasers smaller than was originally thought possible. These *nanolasers* could conceivably be incorporated into small electronic components in order to speed up communications inside a computer, such as within a CPU or between a CPU and other computer components.

⌄ FIGURE 2-27

Avalanche
Photodetector
(APD) silicon
light sensor.

Silicon Photonics

Silicon photonics refers to the process of sending optical information among computers and other electronic devices using standard silicon manufacturing techniques—essentially converging *photonics* (the control and manipulation of light) and electronics. This technology is viewed as one possible low-cost solution to future data-intensive computing applications, such as *telemedicine* and lifelike *3D virtual worlds* (which are both discussed in later chapters). According to Patrick Gelsinger, a senior vice president at Intel, "Today, optics is a niche technology. Tomorrow, it's the mainstream of every chip that we build."

One recent development in this area from Intel Labs researchers is the creation of a silicon-based light sensor (called an *Avalanche Photodetector* or *APD* and shown in Figure 2-27) that achieved world-record performance in a recent test. This test showed that a silicon photonics device could exceed the performance of a device made with more expensive optical materials, such as indium phosphide. Silicon photonics technology has great potential in the area of transferring large amounts of data very quickly between chips inside computers, in addition to between computers; it is expected to begin being incorporated in some personal computer components by 2011.

Terascale Computing

As demand by consumers and businesses for online software, services, and media-rich experiences continues to increase, some experts predict that *terascale computing*—the ability of a CPU to process one trillion floating-point operations per second (teraflops) will eventually be needed. While supercomputers currently reach teraflop and petaflop speeds, much of today's terascale research is focusing on creating multi-core processors with tens to hundreds of cores used in conjunction with multithreaded hardware and software to achieve teraflop performance. The research also includes working on developing higher-speed communications between computers, such as between Web servers and high-performance mobile devices or computers, to help facilitate high-performance cloud computing.

Intel, one of the leaders in terascale research, has created a *teraflop processor* that contains 80 cores to test strategies for moving terabytes of data rapidly from core to core and between cores and memory. It has also developed a 20-megabyte SRAM memory chip that is attached directly to the processor in order to speed up communication between processors and memory. This design allows thousands of interconnections, which enable data to travel at more than one *terabyte per second* (*TBps*) between memory and the processor cores. It is expected that this speed will be needed to handle the terabytes of data used by applications in the near future.

3D Chips

Three-dimensional (3D) chips are another technique for packing an increasing number of components onto small chips. With 3D chips, the transistors are layered, which cuts down on the surface area required. Typically, 3D chips are created by layering individual silicon wafers on top of one another. The layering is typically accomplished via a special machine that uses cameras to align the wafers properly. However, researchers at the University of Southampton, UK, have recently developed wafers that contain matching sets of pegs and holes, similar to the way Lego bricks fit together. In preliminary tests, the researchers lined up the edges of two chips by hand and pressed them together—images taken with an electron microscope show that the two chips aligned roughly five times better than with the camera-based technique. While still in the research stage, the researchers believe that this new design could aid the development of 3D chips and other 3D electronic components.

3D chips are now available for some applications (such as video) and are expected to be used for other applications (such as stacking up chips and memory controllers in some CPU architectures) in the near future. One hurdle in 3D chips is the amount of heat generated. Some new cooling methods (such as the ion pump method discussed earlier in this chapter) can't be used with 3D chips so other alternatives—such as IBM's prototype water cooling systems that can cool between the layers of a chip (see Figure 2-28)—are in development.

FIGURE 2-28

3D chips. IBM's interlayer water cooling system cools between the layers in the chip.

SUMMARY

DATA AND PROGRAM REPRESENTATION

Chapter Objective 1:
Understand how data and
programs are represented
to a computer and be able
to identify a few of the
coding systems used to
accomplish this.

Most *digital computers* work in a two-state, or *binary*, fashion. It is convenient to think of these binary states in terms of 0s and 1s. Computer people refer to these 0s and 1s as bits. Converting data to these 0s and 1s is called *digital data representation*.

While most individuals use the **decimal number system** to represent numbers and perform numeric computations, computers use the **binary numbering system**. Text-based data can be represented with one of several fixed-length binary codes (such as **ASCII** (**American Standard Code for Information Interchange**) or **Unicode**) that represent single characters of data—a numeric digit, alphabetic character, or special symbol—as strings of **bits**. Each string of eight bits is called a **byte**. Use of Unicode is growing since it can represent text in all written languages, including those that use alphabets different from English, such as Chinese, Greek, and Russian.

The storage capacity of computers is often expressed using prefixes in conjunction with the term *byte* to convey the approximate quantity being represented, such as using **kilobyte (KB)**, about one thousand bytes; **megabyte (MB)**, about one million bytes; **gigabyte (GB)**, about one billion bytes; or **terabyte (TB)**, about one trillion bytes. Other possibilities are **petabyte (PB)**, about 1,000 terabytes; **exabyte (EB)**, about 1,000 petabytes; **zettabyte (ZB)**, about 1,000 exabytes; and **yottabyte (YB)**, about 1,000 zettabytes.

The binary system can represent not only text but also graphics, audio, and video data. **Machine language** is the binary-based code through which computers represent program instructions. A program must be translated into machine language before the computer can execute it.

INSIDE THE SYSTEM UNIT

Chapter Objective 2:
Explain the functions of the
hardware components com-
monly found inside the system unit, such as the CPU,
memory, buses, and expan-
sion cards.

Personal computers typically contain a variety of hardware components located inside the **system unit**. For instance, *chips* are mounted onto *circuit boards*, and those boards are positioned in slots on the **motherboard**—the main circuit board for a computer. Every computer has a **central processing unit** (**CPU**) or **processor**—also called a **microprocessor** when referring to personal computers—attached to its motherboard that performs the processing for the computer. CPU chips differ in many respects, such as what types of computer the CPU is designed for, its *clock speed*, and *word size*. They can also be **multi-core CPUs**, such as the **dual-core** (two cores) and **quad-core** (four cores) **CPUs** now available. Another difference is the amount of **cache memory**—memory located on or very close to the CPU chip to help speed up processing. Other important differences are the general architecture of the CPU and the bus speed and width being used. The overall *processing speed* of the computer determines its performance. One of the most consistent measurements of overall performance is a *benchmark test*.

Memory refers to chip-based storage. The main memory for a personal computer is **RAM** (**random access memory**). Traditional RAM is **volatile** and used to hold programs and data temporarily while they are needed; **nonvolatile** RAM is under development. RAM is available in different types and speeds, and is measured in bytes. **ROM** (**read-only memory**) is a type of nonvolatile memory that stores nonerasable programs. **Flash memory** is a type of nonvolatile memory that can be used for storage by the computer or the user. Flash memory chips can be found in many personal computers and mobile devices; flash memory chips are also integrated into storage media and devices. **Registers** are memory built into the CPU chip to hold data before or during processing. *Fans*, *heat sinks*, and other techniques are used to compensate for the heat that CPUs and other components generate.

Most desktop computers contain internal **expansion slots**, into which users can insert **expansion cards** to give the computer added functionality. **ExpressCard modules** can be used to add additional capabilities to computers containing an *ExpressCard slot*.

A computer **bus** is an electronic path along which bits are transmitted. The **memory bus** moves data between the CPU and RAM. The **frontside bus** (**FSB**) connects the CPU to the *I/O bridge*, which connects the CPU and memory to the rest of the *bus architecture*. Common **expansion buses** include *PCI*, **PCI Express** (**PCIe**) **bus**, **Universal Serial Bus** (**USB**), and **FireWire**. The performance of a bus can be measured by the the bus's **throughput** or **bandwidth**; that is, the amount of data that can be transferred via the bus in a given time period.

System units typically have external **ports** that are used to connect peripheral devices to the computer. Notebook, tablet, and netbook computers may have fewer ports than desktop computers. Ultra-mobile PCs and mobile device users often add new capabilities via USB ports or *Secure Digital* (*SD*) *cards* or other types of flash memory cards.

Chapter Objective 3:
Describe how peripheral devices or other hardware can be added to a computer.

HOW THE CPU WORKS

CPUs today include at least one **arithmetic/logic unit** (**ALU**), which performs integer arithmetic and logical operations on data, and most include at least one **floating point unit** (**FPU**), which performs decimal arithmetic. The **control unit** directs the flow of electronic traffic between memory and the ALU/FPU and also between the CPU and input and output devices. Registers—high-speed temporary holding places within the CPU that hold program instructions and data immediately before and during processing—are used to enhance the computer's performance. The **prefetch unit** requests data and instructions before or as they are needed, the **decode unit** decodes the instructions input into the CPU, internal cache stores frequently used instructions and data, and the **bus interface unit** allows the various parts of the CPU to communicate with each other.

The CPU processes instructions in a sequence called a **machine cycle**, consisting of four basic steps. Each machine language instruction is broken down into several smaller instructions called *microcode*, and each piece of microcode corresponds to an operation (such as adding two numbers located in the CPU's registers) that can be performed inside the CPU. The computer system has a built-in **system clock** that synchronizes all of the computer's activities.

Chapter Objective 4:
Understand how the computer's CPU and memory components process program instructions and data.

MAKING COMPUTERS FASTER AND BETTER NOW AND IN THE FUTURE

There are several possible remedies for a computer that is performing too slowly, including adding more memory, performing system maintenance to clean up the computer's hard drive, buying a larger or additional hard drive, and upgrading the computer's Internet connection or video card, depending on the primary role of the computer and where the processing bottleneck appears to be. To make computers work faster overall, computer designers have developed a number of strategies over the years, and researchers are continually working on new strategies. Some of the strategies already being implemented include improved architecture, **pipelining**, **multiprocessing**, **parallel processing**, and the use of new or improved materials.

One possibility for future computers is **nanotechnology** research, which focuses on building computer components at the individual atomic and molecular levels. Some computer and consumer products (such as NRAM, solar cells, tennis rackets, and bikes) using **carbon nanotubes** (tiny hollow tubes made of carbon atoms) are currently on the market. **Quantum computing** and **optical computers** are other possibilities being researched, along with *silicon photonics*, *terascale computing*, and *three-dimensional* (*3D*) *chips*.

Chapter Objective 5:
Name and evaluate several strategies that can be used today for speeding up the operations of a computer.

Chapter Objective 6:
List some processing technologies that may be used in future computers.

REVIEW ACTIVITIES

a. ASCII

b. binary numbering system

c. byte

d. central processing unit (CPU)

e. control unit

f. motherboard

g. nanotechnology

h. parallel processing

i. RAM (random access memory)

j. Universal Serial Bus (USB)

Instructions: Match each key term on the left with the definition on the right that best describes it.

1. _____ A processing technique that uses multiple processors or processing cores simultaneously, usually to process a single job as fast as possible.

2. _____ A fixed-length, binary coding system used to represent text-based data for computer processing on many types of computers.

3. _____ A group of 8 bits.

4. _____ A universal bus used to connect up to 127 peripheral devices to a computer without requiring the use of additional expansion cards.

5. _____ Chips connected to the motherboard that provide a temporary location for the computer to hold data and program instructions while they are needed.

6. _____ The chip located on the motherboard of a computer that performs the processing for a computer.

7. _____ The main circuit board of a computer, located inside the system unit, to which all computer system components connect.

8. _____ The numbering system that represents all numbers using just two symbols (0 and 1).

9. _____ The part of the CPU that coordinates its operations.

10. _____ The science of creating tiny computers and components by working at the individual atomic and molecular levels.

SELF-QUIZ

Instructions: Circle **T** if the statement is true, **F** if the statement is false, or write the best answer in the space provided. **Answers for the self-quiz are located in the References and Resources Guide at the end of the book.**

1. **T F**   A storage medium that can hold 256 GB can hold about 256 billion characters.

2. **T F**   The amount of data that can be transferred over a bus in a given time period determines the bus's volatility.

3. **T F**   Cache memory is typically built into a CPU.

4. **T F**   A bus is a pathway, such as on the motherboard or inside the CPU, along which bits can be transferred.

5. **T F**   Computers that process data with light are referred to as quantum computers.

6. The binary number 1101 is equivalent to the decimal number _____.

7. A CPU with four separate processing cores is referred to as a(n) _____ CPU.

8. A(n) _____ is a connector on the exterior of a computer into which a peripheral device may be plugged.

9. Multi-core CPUs allow _____, in which the CPU is able to work on multiple jobs at one time.

10. Number the following terms from 1 to 9 to indicate their size from smallest to largest.

a. _____ Petabyte   d. _____ Yottabyte   g. _____ Zettabyte

b. _____ Kilobyte   e. _____ Exabyte   h. _____ Terabyte

c. _____ Gigabyte   f. _____ Byte   i. _____ Megabyte

EXERCISES

HW

1. What do each of the following acronyms stand for?

a. KB _____   c. ROM _____   e. PCIe _____

b. RAM _____   d. USB _____   f. CPU _____

2. Using the ASCII code chart in this chapter or in the References and Resources Guide at the end of the book, decode the following word. What does it say?

01000011   01000001   01000110   01000101

_____   _____   _____   _____

3. Supply the missing words to complete the following statements.

a. The smallest piece of data that can be represented by a computer (a 0 or 1) is called a(n) _____.

b. _____ is an international coding system for text-based data using any written language.

c. L1 is a type of _____.

d. The part of the CPU that performs logical operations and integer arithmetic is the _____.

4. Assume you have a USB mouse, USB keyboard, and USB printer to connect to a computer, but you have only two USB ports. Explain one solution to this problem that does not involve buying a new mouse, keyboard, or printer.

5. If your computer seems sluggish, list two things you could do to try to speed it up without resorting to purchasing an entirely new system.

DISCUSSION QUESTIONS

1. As discussed in the chapter, one push by computer manufacturers is making computers run as efficiently as possible to save battery power and electricity. What do you think is the motivation behind this trend? Is it social responsibility or a response to consumer demands? Should the energy consumption of electronic devices be regulated and controlled by the government or another organization? Why or why not? How responsible should consumers be for energy conservation in relation to electronic use? In your opinion, what, if anything, should all computer users do to practice *green computing*?

2. In addition to being used with computers and consumer products, there are also processors and other components designed to be implanted inside the human body, such as the *VeriChip* (discussed in Project 4), implantable wafers containing medication and a processor that delivers the medication at the appropriate time and dosage, *camera pills* that are swallowed to transmit images of an individual's digestive system to a receiving unit, and pacemakers designed to regulate an individual's heart rate. One step further is *brain-to-computer interfacing (BCI)*, which involves implanting electrodes directly into the human brain to restore lost functionality or to facilitate the communication ability of severely disabled individuals, such as by enabling them to control a mouse using only their thoughts. What do you think about these implantable chip applications? Are the benefits worth the risk of something going wrong with the chips implanted inside your body? Are there any privacy risks? Would you consider using an implanted device? Why or why not?

PROJECTS

1. **Wearable PCs** There are some computers available today that are designed to be worn on a belt or wrist. As mentioned in the Technology and You box, computers in the future may be able to morph into different configurations, such as a wristband, upon demand. Today's wearable computers are primarily designed for mobile workers, surgeons, military personnel, and other individuals who need hands-free access to a computer.

   For this project, locate one wearable computer on the market and determine its purpose, cost, and capabilities. What tasks can it perform? Who would use this computer? Is it geared for consumer use? If so, would you wear this computer in public? Why or why not? If not, what would need to change in order for you to be willing to wear it? Think about your chosen profession—would a wearable computer be needed or be useful? At the conclusion of your research, prepare a one-page summary of your findings and opinions and submit it to your instructor.

2. **Adding Memory** Adding additional RAM to a computer is one of the most common computer upgrades. Before purchasing additional memory, however, it is important to make sure that the memory about to be purchased is compatible with the computer.

   For this project, select a computer (such as your own computer, a school computer, or a computer at a local store) and then determine (by looking at the computer or asking an appropriate individual—such as a lab aide in the school computer lab or a salesperson at the local store) the following: manufacturer and model number, CPU, current amount of memory, total memory slots, and the number of available memory slots. (If you look inside the computer, be sure to unplug the power cord first and do not touch any components inside the system unit.) Once you have the necessary information, call a local store or use your information and a memory supplier's Web site to determine the appropriate type of memory needed for your selected computer. What choices do you have in terms of capacity and configuration? Can you add just one memory module, or do you have to add memory in pairs? Can you keep the old memory modules, or do they have to be removed? At the conclusion of your research, prepare a one-page summary of your findings and recommendations and submit it to your instructor.

3. **Intel Museum Tour** Intel Corporation has a great deal of interesting information about processors on its Web site, including information available through its online museum.

   For this project, go to the Intel Museum at **www.intel.com/museum/index.htm** (if this URL no longer works, go to the Intel home page at www.intel.com and search for "Intel Museum"). Once you are at the Intel Museum home page, select either the *Online Exhibits* option or the *Intel Corporate Archives* option to locate an exhibit or documents related to processors or memory, such as *From Sand to Circuits*, *Memory Technology*, or *Moore's Law*, and then tour the exhibit or read through the available information, making a note of at least three interesting facts you didn't know before. At the conclusion of this task, prepare a short summary listing the tour you took and the interesting facts you recorded and submit it to your instructor.

4. People Chips The *VeriChip* is a tiny chip that is designed to be implanted under a person's skin, such as on the forearm. Currently, VeriChips are used primarily for identification purposes—the unique number contained in a VeriChip can be read by a proprietary scanner and can be used in conjunction with a database, such as to provide hospital emergency room personnel with health information about an unconscious patient. However, implanted chips can also be used to control access to secure areas and for electronic payment purposes. What do you think of implanted devices, such as the VeriChip, being used for access control (such as for government buildings or highly-secure facilities), for expediting passage through security check points (such as at airports), or for making electronic payments (such as at a grocery store)? Would you be willing to be "chipped" if it made some tasks (such as unlocking your home or car) easier or some types of transactions (such as ATM withdrawals) more secure? Is it ethical for a government to require its citizens to be chipped, similar to a national ID card? Is it ethical for a business to request that its employees be chipped for security purposes? Should businesses be allowed to require chipping as a condition of employment?

For this project, form an opinion about the ethical use and ramifications of human-implantable chips and be prepared to discuss your position (in class, via an online class discussion group, in a class chat room, or via a class blog, depending on your instructor's directions). You may also be asked to write a short paper expressing your opinion.

ETHICS IN ACTION

5. Binary Conversions As discussed in the chapter, all numbers processed by the CPU must be represented in a binary format. Binary (base 2) represents all numbers using 2 digits, decimal uses 10 digits, and hexadecimal uses 16 digits.

For this project, research how to convert a three-digit decimal number to both binary and hexadecimal and back again, without the use of a calculator (refer to the "A Look at Numbering Systems" feature located in the References and Resources Guide at the end of this book if needed). Next, determine how to represent the decimal number 10 in base 3 (the numbering system that uses only the digits 0, 1, and 2). Share your findings with the class in the form of a short presentation, including a demonstration of the conversions between binary and hexadecimal and the representation of the decimal number 10 in base 3. The presentation should not exceed 10 minutes and should make use of one or more presentation aids such as the chalkboard, handouts, overhead transparencies, or a computer-based slide presentation (your instructor may provide additional requirements). You may also be asked to submit a summary of the presentation to your instructor.

PRESENTATION/ DEMONSTRATION

Instructions: Go to the Chapter 2 page at **www.cengage.com/computerconcepts/np/uc13** to work the following Web Activities.

WEB ACTIVITIES

6. Interactive Activities Work the interactive **Crossword Puzzle**, watch the **Video Podcasts** and **Online Videos**, and explore the **Further Exploration** links associated with this chapter.

If you have a SAM user profile, you may have access to hands-on instruction, practice, and assessment of the skills covered in this chapter. Check with your instructor for instructions and the correct URL/Web site to access those assignments.

7. Student Edition Labs Work the following interactive **Student Edition Labs**.
   ➤ **Binary Numbers**   ➤ **Understanding the Motherboard**

8. Test Yourself Review the **Online Study Guide** for this chapter, then test your knowledge of the terms and concepts covered in this chapter by completing the **Key Term Matching** exercise, the **Self-Quiz**, the **Exercises**, and the **Practice Test**.

chapter 3

Storage

After completing this chapter, you will be able to do the following:

1. Name several general characteristics of storage systems.

2. Describe the two most common types of hard drives and what they are used for today.

3. Discuss the various types of optical discs available today and how they differ from each other.

4. Identify some flash memory storage devices and media and explain how they are used today.

5. List at least three other types of storage systems.

6. Summarize the storage alternatives for a typical personal computer.

OVERVIEW

In Chapter 2, we discussed the role of RAM, the computer's main memory. RAM temporarily holds program instructions, data, and output while they are needed by the computer. For instance, when you first create a letter or other word processing document on your computer, both the word processing program and the document are temporarily stored in RAM. But when the word processing program is closed, the computer no longer needs to work with the program or the document, and so they are both erased from RAM. Consequently, anything (such as your word processing document) that needs to be preserved for future use needs to be stored on a more permanent medium. Storage systems fill this role.

We begin this chapter with a look at the characteristics common among all storage systems. Then, we discuss the primary storage for most personal computers—the hard drive. From there, we turn our attention to optical discs, including how they work and the various types of CDs and DVDs available today. Next, we discuss flash memory storage systems, followed by a look at a few other types of storage systems, including network and online/cloud storage, smart cards, holographic storage, and the storage systems used with large computer systems. The chapter concludes with a summary of the storage alternatives for a typical personal computer. ■

STORAGE SYSTEMS CHARACTERISTICS

All *storage systems* have specific characteristics, including having a *storage medium* and a *storage device*, *portability*, *volatility*, how data is accessed and represented, the type of storage technology used, and so on. These characteristics are discussed in the next few sections.

Storage Media and Storage Devices

There are two parts to any storage system: the **storage medium** and the **storage device**. A storage medium is the hardware where data is actually stored (for example, a *CD* or a *flash memory card*); a storage medium is inserted into its corresponding storage device (such as a *CD drive* or a *flash memory card reader*) in order to be read from or written to. Often the storage device and storage medium are two separate pieces of hardware (that is, the storage medium is *removable*), although with some systems—such as a *hard drive* or most *USB flash drives*—the two parts are permanently sealed together to form one piece of hardware.

Storage devices can be *internal* (located inside the system unit), *external* (plugged into an external port on the system unit), or *remote* (located on another computer, such as a network server). Internal devices have the advantage of requiring no additional desk space and

---

> **Storage medium.** The part of a storage system where data is stored, such as a DVD disc. > **Storage device.** A piece of hardware, such as a DVD drive, into which a storage medium is inserted to be read from or written to.

CD/DVD drives are usually assigned letters after the hard drives, such as D and E in this example.

The letter C is usually assigned to the first hard drive.

The various slots in a built-in flash memory card reader are typically assigned next, such as the letters F, G, H and I, in this example.

Other letters, beginning with J in this example, are used for any other storage devices attached to the computer, such as via these USB ports.

⚠ **FIGURE 3-1**

Storage device identifiers. To keep track of storage devices in an unambiguous way, the computer system assigns letters of the alphabet or names to each of them.

✓ **TIP**

Although most computers today typically do not include a floppy drive, the drive letters A and B are still often reserved for floppy drives so you may not have a drive A or B on your computer.

are usually faster than their external counterparts. External devices, however, can be easily transported from one location to another (such as to share data with others, to transfer data between a work computer and a home computer, or to take digital photos to a photo store). They can also be removed from the computer and stored in a secure area, when needed (such as for backup purposes or to protect sensitive data). Remote devices are accessed over a network. Some remote storage devices, such as those accessed via the Internet, have the additional advantage of being able to be accessible from any computer with an Internet connection.

Regardless of how storage devices are connected to a computer, letters of the alphabet and/or names are typically assigned to each storage device so that the user can identify each device easily when it needs to be used (see Figure 3-1). Some drive letters, such as the letter *C* typically used with the primary hard drive, are usually consistent from computer to computer and do not change even if more storage devices are added to a computer. The rest of the drive letters on a computer may change as new devices are added either permanently (such as when an additional hard drive is installed inside the computer) or temporarily (such as when a USB flash drive, digital camera, or portable digital media player is connected to the computer). When a new storage device is detected, the computer just assigns and reassigns drive letters, as needed.

Volatility

As discussed in Chapter 2, conventional RAM is volatile so programs and documents held in RAM are erased when they are no longer needed by the computer or when the power to the computer is turned off. Storage media, however, are nonvolatile, so the data remains on the media even when the power to the computer or storage device is off. Consequently, storage media are used for anything that needs to be saved for future use.

Random vs. Sequential Access

When the computer receives an instruction that requires data located on a storage medium, it must go to the designated location on the appropriate storage medium and retrieve the requested data. This procedure is referred to as access. Two basic access methods are available: *random* and *sequential*.

Random access, also called *direct access*, means that data can be retrieved directly from any location on the storage medium, in any order. A random access device works in a manner similar to a CD or DVD player used to play music or movies; that is, it can jump directly to a particular location on the medium when data located at that location is needed. Most storage devices used with computers today—including hard drives, CD/DVD drives, and USB flash drives—are random access devices.

Media that allow random access are sometimes referred to as *addressable* media. This means that the storage system can locate each piece of stored data at a unique *address*, which is determined by the computer system. With *sequential access*, however, the data can only be retrieved in the order in which it is physically stored on the medium. One type of storage device that is sometimes used with computers and that uses sequential access is a *magnetic tape drive*. Computer tapes work like audiocassette tapes or videotapes—to get to a specific location on the tape, you must play or fast forward through all of the tape before it.

Logical vs. Physical Representation

Anything (such as a program, letter, digital photograph, or song) stored on a storage medium is referred to as a **file**. Data files are also often called *documents*. When a document that was just created (such as a memo or letter in a word processing program) is saved, it is stored as a new file on the storage medium that the user designates. During the storage process, the user is required to give the file a name, called a **filename**; that filename is used to retrieve the file when it is needed at a later time.

To keep files organized, related documents are often stored in **folders** (also called *directories*) located on the storage medium. For example, one folder might contain memos to business associates while another might hold a set of budgets (see Figure 3-2). To organize files further, you can create *subfolders* (*subdirectories*) within a folder. For instance, you might create a subfolder within the *Budgets* subfolder for each fiscal year. In Figure 3-2, both *Budgets* and *Memos* are subfolders inside the *Documents* folder; the *Budgets* subfolder contains two additional subfolders (*2010* and *2011*).

Although both the user and the computer use drive letters, folder names, and filenames to save and retrieve documents, they perceive them differently. The user typically views how data is stored (what has been discussed so far in this section and what appears in the *Windows Explorer file management program* screen shown in Figure 3-2) using *logical file representation*. That is, individuals view a document stored as one complete unit in a particular folder on a particular drive. Computers, however, use *physical file representation*; that is, they access a particular document stored on a storage medium using its physical location or locations. For example, the *ABC Industries Proposal Memo* file shown in Figure 3-2 is *logically* located in the *Memos* folders in the *Documents* and *Debbie* folders on the hard drive C, but the content of this file could be *physically* stored in many different pieces scattered across that hard drive. When this occurs, the computer keeps track of the various physical locations used to store that file, as well as the logical representations (filename, folder names, and drive letter) used to identify that file, in order to retrieve the entire file when needed. Fortunately, users do not have to be concerned with how files are physically stored on a storage medium because the computer keeps track of that information and uses it to retrieve files whenever they are requested.

FIGURE 3-2

Organizing data.

Folders are used to organize related items on a storage medium.

Folders

Files

2010

2011

BUDGETS

MEMOS

DOCUMENTS

Folders; the Memos folder is selected.

Files in the Memos folder.

> **File.** Something stored on a storage medium, such as a program, a document, or an image. > **Filename.** A name given to a file by the user; it is used to retrieve the file at a later time. > **Folder.** A named place on a storage medium into which files can be stored to keep the files stored on that medium organized.

Type of Storage Technology Used

Data is stored *magnetically* or *optically* on many types of storage media. With magnetic storage systems, such as conventional hard drives, data is stored magnetically on the storage medium, which means the data (0s and 1s) is represented using different magnetic alignments. The storage device can change the magnetic alignment when needed, so data can be written to the medium, deleted from the medium, or rewritten to the medium. Optical storage media (such as CDs and DVDs) store data optically using laser beams. On some optical media, the laser burns permanent marks to represent 0s and 1s into the surface of the medium so the data cannot be erased or rewritten. With *rewritable* optical media, the laser changes the reflectivity of the medium to represent 0s and 1s but it does not permanently alter the disc surface so the reflectivity of the medium can be changed back again as needed. Consequently, the data stored on a rewritable optical disc can be changed.

Some storage systems use a combination of magnetic and optical technology. Others use a different technology altogether, such as *flash memory storage systems* that represent data using *electrons* (electrons are either trapped or not trapped inside *flash memory cells* to represent 0s and 1s). Some of the most widely used storage systems are discussed next.

HARD DRIVES

With the exception of computers designed to use only network storage devices (such as network computers and some Internet appliances), virtually all personal computers come with a **hard drive** that is used to store most programs and data. *Internal hard drives* (those located inside the system unit) are not designed to be removed, unless they need to be repaired or replaced. *External hard drives* typically connect to a computer via a USB or FireWire port and are frequently used for additional storage (such as for digital photos, videos, and other large multimedia files), to move files between computers, and for backup purposes. In addition to being used with computers, hard drives are also increasingly being incorporated into other consumer products, such as mobile phones, portable digital media players, digital video recorders (DVRs), gaming consoles, digital camcorders, and more.

For security purposes, both internal and external hard drives today are increasingly coming with built-in *encryption* that automatically encrypts all data stored on the hard drive and protects access to the hard drive with a *secure password*; external hard drives may use a built-in *fingerprint reader* to grant only authorized users access to the hard drive. Encryption, secure passwords, and fingerprint readers are discussed in detail in Chapter 9.

Magnetic Hard Drives and Solid-State Drives (SSDs)

Traditional hard drives are *magnetic hard drives* that contain *magnetic hard disks*, *read/write heads*, and an *access mechanism*. Data is written to the magnetic hard disks by read/write heads, which magnetize particles a certain way on the surface of the disks to represent the data's 0s and 1s. The particles retain their magnetic orientation until the orientation is changed again, so files can be stored, retrieved, rewritten, and deleted as needed. Storing data on a magnetic disk is illustrated in Figure 3-3.

A newer type of hard drive is the *solid-state drive* (*SSD*) that uses flash memory technology instead of magnetic technology to store data (for a look at how flash memory technology works, see the How It Works box). While magnetic hard drives are currently less expensive and are currently available in larger capacities than SSDs, the use of SSDs is growing rapidly—especially with portable computers like notebook and netbook computers. This is because the flash memory technology that SSDs are based on allows for faster operation

---

> **Hard drive.** The primary storage system for most computers; used to store most programs and data used with a computer.

(one study showed a nine-fold increase in performance over conventional magnetic hard drives), reduced power consumption (SSDs use at least 50% less power than magnetic hard drives use), and increased shock-resistance.

Magnetic Hard Drives

A **magnetic hard drive** (usually what individuals are referring to when they use the term *hard drive*) contains one or more round pieces of metal (called *hard disks* or *platters*) that are coated with a magnetizable substance. These hard disks are permanently sealed inside the hard drive case, along with the *read/write heads* used to store (*write*) and retrieve (*read*) data and an *access mechanism* used to move the read/write heads in and out over the surface of the hard disks (see Figure 3-4). Hard drives designed for desktop computers (sometimes referred to as *desktop hard drives*) typically use 2.5-inch or 3.5-inch hard disks and notebook hard drives typically use 2.5-inch hard disks. Portable digital media players, mobile phones, and other mobile devices that include a magnetic hard drive typically use tiny 1.5-inch or smaller hard drives instead. Regardless of the size, one hard drive usually contains a stack of several hard disks; if so, there is a read/write head for each hard disk surface (top and bottom), as illustrated in Figure 3-4, and these heads move in and out over the disk surfaces simultaneously.

Disk surface

The read/write head inscribes data by aligning each of the magnetic particles in one of two ways.

Particles aligned one way represent 0s; the other way represent 1s.

FIGURE 3-3
Storing data on magnetic disks.

MOUNTING SHAFT
The mounting shaft spins the hard disks at a speed of several thousand revolutions per minute while the computer is turned on.

SEALED DRIVE
The hard disks and the drive mechanism are hermetically sealed inside a case to keep them free from contamination.

2.5-INCH HARD DRIVE LOCATED INSIDE A NOTEBOOK COMPUTER

READ/WRITE HEADS
There is a read/write head for each hard disk surface, and they move in and out over the disks together.

HARD DISKS
There are usually several hard disk surfaces on which to store data. Most hard drives store data on both sides of each disk.

ACCESS MECHANISM
The access mechanism moves the read/write heads in and out together between the hard disk surfaces to access required data.

INSIDE A 3.5-INCH HARD DRIVE

FIGURE 3-4
Magnetic hard drives.

> **Magnetic hard drive.** A hard drive consisting of one or more metal magnetic disks permanently sealed, with an access mechanism and read/write heads, inside its drive.

HOW IT WORKS

Flash Memory

Instead of representing data magnetically or optically, flash memory devices represent data with electrical charges stored within *flash memory cells*. Flash memory cells are arranged in grids of rows and columns with two *gates* (the parts of a transistor that can allow electrical current to flow through the transistor's circuits) within each cell and two *lines* or wires connecting the flash memory cell to the circuitry surrounding the flash memory cell. One of the gates (the *control gate*) is connected to one of the wires (typically called the *control line* or *word line*). The other gate (the *floating gate*) is completely surrounded by an *oxide* layer and is not connected electrically to the other flash memory cell components. Since the floating gate is isolated electrically from the rest of the cell components, any electrical charge placed on the floating gate remains there until it is removed, even when the power to the flash memory device is off. The cell also has a *source* and *drain* that are connected via a wire (usually called the *bit line*) to the circuitry surrounding the flash memory cell. Under certain conditions, as described shortly, electrical current can flow from the source to the drain; this current is controlled by the voltage applied to the control gate.

To store data in a flash memory cell, a large amount of voltage is applied to the control gate. When the appropriate amount

of voltage is applied, electrons are able to tunnel through the oxide layer surrounding the floating gate and become trapped on the floating gate. To remove those electrons, voltage of the opposite polarity is applied to the control gate and the electrons tunnel off the floating gate back through the oxide.

To read data stored in a flash memory cell, a smaller amount of voltage is applied to the control gate. When this occurs, it causes current to flow from the source to the drain if there are no electrons trapped on the floating gate. If electrons are trapped on the floating gate, they will prevent the current from flowing. Whether or not the current flows from the source to the drain (and therefore, whether or not there are electrons on the floating gate) determines the value of the data (0 or 1) stored in that cell, as shown in the accompanying illustration.

Flash memory originally held a single bit per memory cell, called *single-level cell* (*SLC*) *flash*. To increase storage capacity and reduce its cost, manufacturers are increasingly using multiple bits per cell, called *multilevel cell* (*MLC*) *flash*. To increase speed, *NAND flash memory* (the type of memory used in flash memory cards, USB flash drives, and most other types of flash memory-based storage media and devices) reads and writes data in small blocks called pages, instead of in single bytes.

1 STATE

No electrons are trapped on the floating gate.

V_T

Control line

1. The appropriate voltage is applied to the control gate via the control line to read the contents of the cell.

Control gate

Bit line

Floating gate

Source — Current → Drain

Flash memory cell

2. The current flows from the source to the drain, so the value of the cell is 1.

0 STATE

Electrons are trapped on the floating gate.

V_T

Control line

1. The appropriate voltage is applied to the control gate via the control line to read the contents of the cell.

Control gate

Bit line

⊖ ⊖ ⊖ ⊖ Floating gate

Source No current Drain

Flash memory cell

2. The current does not flow from the source to the drain, so the value of the cell is 0.

How flash memory reads data.

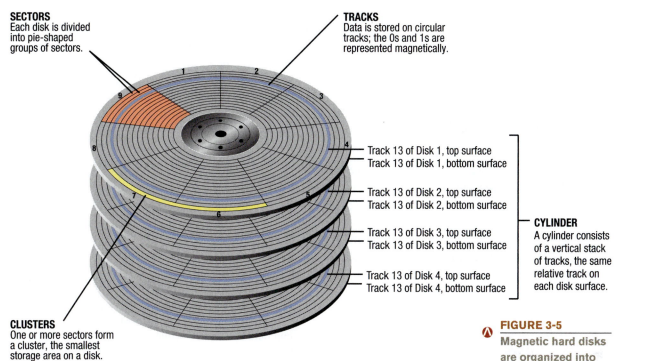

SECTORS
Each disk is divided into pie-shaped groups of sectors.

TRACKS
Data is stored on circular tracks; the 0s and 1s are represented magnetically.

Track 13 of Disk 1, top surface
Track 13 of Disk 1, bottom surface

Track 13 of Disk 2, top surface
Track 13 of Disk 2, bottom surface

Track 13 of Disk 3, top surface
Track 13 of Disk 3, bottom surface

Track 13 of Disk 4, top surface
Track 13 of Disk 4, bottom surface

CYLINDER
A cylinder consists of a vertical stack of tracks, the same relative track on each disk surface.

CLUSTERS
One or more sectors form a cluster, the smallest storage area on a disk.

FIGURE 3-5
Magnetic hard disks are organized into sectors, tracks, clusters, and cylinders.

The surface of a hard disk is organized into **tracks** (concentric rings) and pie-shaped groups of **sectors** (small pieces of tracks), as shown in Figure 3-5. On most computer systems, the smallest storage area on a hard drive is a **cluster**—one or more sectors. The computer numbers the tracks, sectors, and clusters so it can keep track of where data is stored. The computer uses a *file system* to record where each file is physically stored on the hard drive and what filename the user has assigned to it. When the user requests a document (always by filename), the computer uses its file system to retrieve it. Since a cluster is the smallest area on a hard drive that a computer can access, everything stored on a hard drive always takes up at least one cluster of storage space.

In addition to tracks, sectors, and clusters, hard drives are also organized into **cylinders** (refer again to Figure 3-5). A cylinder is the collection of one particular track, such as the first track or the tenth track, on each hard disk surface. In other words, it is the area on all of the hard disks inside a hard drive that can be accessed without moving the read/write access mechanism, once it has been moved to the proper position. For example, the hard drive shown in Figure 3-5 contains four hard disks, which means there are eight possible recording surfaces (using both sides of each hard disk). A cylinder for that hard drive would consist of eight tracks, such as track 13 on all eight surfaces. Because all of the read/write heads move together, all of the tracks in a cylinder are accessible at the same time.

Traditionally, the magnetic particles on a hard disk have been aligned horizontally, parallel to the hard disk's surface (referred to as *longitudinal magnetic recording*). To increase capacity and reliability, most new hard drives today use *perpendicular magnetic recording* (*PMR*), in which the bits are placed upright (as in Figure 3-3) to allow them to be closer together than is possible with a horizontal layout. For instance, PMR currently allows a recording density up to 400 *gigabits per square inch* (*Gb/inch²*), which results in internal hard drives with capacities up to 2 TB. Researchers believe that the theoretical limit for

>**Track.** A concentric path on a disk where data is recorded. >**Sector.** A small piece of a track. >**Cluster.** One or more sectors; the smallest addressable area of a disk. >**Cylinder.** The collection of tracks located in the same location on a set of hard disk surfaces.

ASK THE EXPERT

 Josh Tinker, Market Development Manager, Seagate Technology

What do you expect will be the capacity of a typical internal desktop hard drive in five years?

The top capacity of an internal desktop hard drive today is 2 TB, but by 2015 we expect the top capacity of internal desktop hard drives to exceed 10 TB and possibly approach 15 TB. Today, a common consumer internal desktop hard drive capacity is 500 GB. By 2015, the hard drive industry could provide a similarly priced internal hard drive that holds 2 TB or even 3 TB.

ONLINE VIDEO

Go to the Chapter 3 page at **www.cengage.com/ computerconcepts/np/uc13** to watch the "The DriveSavers Data Recovery Service" video clip.

recording density with today's hard drive technology will be 1 *terabit per square inch* (*Tb/ inch²*), which translates into about 4 TB of storage for a 3.5-inch hard drive, 1 TB for a 2.5-inch hard drive, and 100 GB for a 1-inch hard drive.

To allow for higher capacities in the future, new hard drive technologies are under development. For instance, *Heat-Assisted Magnetic Recording* (*HAMR*), which uses lasers to temporarily heat the surface of the hard disks when storing data in order to pack more data onto the surface than is normally possible, may eventually boost the storage capacity of a hard drive to 50 Tb/inch². Another emerging possibility for high-capacity storage—*holographic storage*— is discussed later in this chapter.

It is important to realize that a magnetic hard drive's read/write heads never touch the surface of the hard disks at any time, even during reading and writing. If the read/write heads do touch the surface—for example, if a desktop computer is bumped while the hard drive is spinning or if a foreign object gets onto the surface of a hard disk, a *head crash* occurs, which may do permanent damage to the hard drive. Because the read/write heads are located extremely close to the surface of the hard disks (less than one-half millionth of an inch above the surface), the presence of a foreign object the width of a human hair or even a smoke particle on the surface of a hard disk is like placing a huge boulder on a road and then trying to drive over it with your car. When hard drives containing critical data become damaged, *data recovery firms* may be able to help out, as discussed in the Inside the Industry box.

CAUTION   CAUTION   CAUTION   CAUTION   CAUTION   CAUTION   CAUT

Because you never know when a head crash or other hard drive failure will occur—there may be no warning whatsoever—be sure to *back up* the data on your hard drive on a regular basis. Backing up data—that is, creating a second copy of important files—is critical not only for businesses but also for individuals and is discussed in detail in Chapter 5 and Chapter 15.

Solid-State Drives (SSDs)

Solid-state drives (SSDs) are hard drives that use flash memory technology instead of spinning hard disk platters and magnetic technology; consequently, data is stored as electrical charges on flash memory media and SSDs have no moving parts. These characteristics mean that SSDs (along with the other types of flash memory storage systems discussed later in this chapter) are not subject to mechanical failures like magnetic hard drives, and are, therefore, more resistant to shock and vibration. They also consume less power, make no noise, and boot faster. Consequently, SSDs are an especially attractive option for portable computers and mobile devices. Although previously too expensive for all but specialty applications, prices of SSDs (also sometimes called *flash memory hard drives*) have fallen significantly over the past few years and they are becoming the norm for netbooks and other very portable computers.

> **Solid-state drive (SSD).** A hard drive that uses flash memory media instead of metal magnetic hard disks.

INSIDE THE INDUSTRY

Data Recovery Experts

It happens far more often than most people imagine. A computer's hard drive quits working the day before a big report is due, a notebook computer is dropped in the parking lot and then run over by a car, a mobile phone falls into a lake or fountain, or a business burns down taking the computer containing the only copy of the company records with it. If the data on a device was recently backed up, the data can be installed on a new hard drive or device with just a little expense and a short delay. When critical data located on a potentially destroyed hard drive or device is not backed up, it is time to seek help from a professional data recovery expert.

Data recovery firms, such as DriveSavers in California, specialize in recovering data from severely damaged storage media (see the accompanying photos). The damaged storage media (such as a computer's hard drive or the storage media integrated into a mobile phone) are taken apart in a *clean room* (a sealed room similar to the ones in which computer chips are manufactured) and temporarily repaired in order to copy all of the data (bit by bit) from the media onto a server. The copied data is then used to reconstruct the information located on the damaged drive or device. If the file directory is not recovered, engineers try to match the jumbled data to file types in order to reconstruct the original files. DriveSavers' celebrity clients have included Bruce Willis, Harrison Ford, and Sean Connery; the executive producer of *The Simpsons*, whose computer crashed taking scripts for 12 episodes of the show with it; an individual whose notebook computer was trapped for two days beneath a sunken cruise ship in the Amazon River; a MacWorld attendee whose notebook computer containing a sales presentation due in two days was run over and crushed by a shuttle bus; and a Fortune 500 company, which lost all its financial data and stockholder information when its server went down. In all of these cases, DriveSavers was able to recover all of the lost data.

In addition to these dramatic examples, data recovery firms are also frequently used when hard drives and other storage media just stop functioning. In fact, DriveSavers estimates that 75% of its business is due to malfunctioning devices. And with the vast amounts of digital data (such as digital photos, music, home videos, personal documents, and school papers) that the average person stores today, data recovery firms are increasingly being used by individuals to recover personal data, in addition to being used by businesses to recover important business data.

Data recovery firms stress the importance of backing up data to avoid data loss when a malfunction occurs. According to Scott Gaidano, president of DriveSavers, "The first thing we tell people is back up, back up, back up. It's amazing how many people don't back up." It is also important to make sure the backup procedure is working. For instance, the Fortune 500 company mentioned previously performed regular backups and kept the backup media in a fire-resistant safe, but when they went to use the backup after their server crashed, they discovered that the backup media were all blank.

Because potentially losing all the data on a storage medium can be so stressful and traumatic, DriveSavers has its own data-crisis counselor, a former suicide hotline worker. Fortunately for its clients, DriveSavers has a 90% recovery rate. The services of data recovery experts are not cheap, but when the lost data is irreplaceable, they are a bargain.

Data recovery. All the data located on the hard drive of this computer (left) that was virtually destroyed in a fire was recovered by data recovery experts in less than 24 hours. Recovery takes place in a clean room (right).

SSDs are available in the same dimensions as a conventional magnetic 2.5-inch hard drive (see Figure 3-6) so they can easily be used instead of conventional magnetic hard drives in notebooks, netbooks, and other personal computers. There are also smaller 1.8-inch SSDs available that can be used when a smaller physical size is needed, such as for a portable digital media player or mobile phone. SSDs are currently available in capacities up to 512 GB.

Data is stored in flash memory chips located inside the drive; there are no moving parts like in magnetic hard drives.

A   FIGURE 3-6
Solid-state drives (SSDs).

Internal and External Hard Drives

Internal hard drives are permanently located inside a computer's system unit and typically are not removed unless there is a problem with them. Virtually all computers have at least one internal hard drive (either a magnetic hard drive or an SSD) that is used to store programs and data. In addition, a variety of *external hard drives* are available (see Figure 3-7). External hard drives are commonly used to transport a large amount of data from one computer to another (by moving the entire hard drive to another computer), for backup purposes, and for additional storage.

Today, because of their large capacity, full-sized external hard drives (which typically are magnetic hard drives and hold between 500 GB and 4 TB) are often used by individuals to store their digital photos, digital music, home movies, recorded TV shows, and other multimedia content to be distributed to the computers and entertainment devices located in the home. In fact, special hard drive products (typically called *home servers* or *media servers*) are available that are designed to be connected to a home network to serve as a centralized storage device for all the computers in the home, as well as to back up the data on those computers automatically. There are also *DVR extender* hard drives designed to add additional storage to an individual's digital video recorder (DVR).

V   FIGURE 3-7
External hard drives.

FULL-SIZED EXTERNAL HARD DRIVES
Are about the size of a 5 by 7-inch picture frame, but thicker; this drive holds 1.5 TB.

PORTABLE HARD DRIVES (MAGNETIC)
Are about the size of a 3 by 5-inch index card, but thicker; this drive holds 500 GB.

PORTABLE HARD DRIVES (SSD)
Are about the size of a credit card, but thicker; this drive holds 18 MB.

EXPRESSCARD HARD DRIVES
Fit into an ExpressCard slot; this drive holds 32 GB.

While full-sized external hard drives can be moved from computer to computer when needed, *portable hard drives* are smaller external hard drives specifically designed for that purpose. Unlike full-sized hard drives (which typically need to be plugged into a power outlet to be used), portable hard drives are often powered via the computer they are being used with instead. Portable magnetic hard drives typically hold up to 500 GB; the capacity of portable SSD hard drives at the present time is smaller—up to 128 GB. Most external desktop and portable hard drives connect to the computer via a USB connection. However, some can connect via a wired or wireless networking connection instead, and *ExpressCard hard drives* connect via an ExpressCard slot (refer again to Figure 3-7).

Hard Drive Speed, Disk Caching, and Hybrid Hard Drives

The hard disks inside a magnetic hard drive typically spin continually at a rate of between 7,200 and 15,000 revolutions per minute. The total time that it takes for a hard drive to read or write data is called the **disk access time** and requires the following three steps:

1. Move the read/write heads to the cylinder that contains (or will contain) the desired data—called *seek time*.

2. Rotate the hard disks into the proper position so that the read/write heads are located over the part of the cylinder to be used—called *rotational delay*.

3. Move the data, such as reading the data from the hard disk and transferring it to memory, or transferring the data from memory and storing it on the hard disk—called *data movement time*.

A typical disk access time is around 8.5 milliseconds (ms). To minimize disk access time, magnetic hard drives usually store related data on the same cylinder. This strategy reduces seek time and, therefore, improves the overall access time. Because SSDs do not have to move any parts to store or retrieve data, they don't require seek time or rotational delay and their access time is much faster than magnetic hard drives—essentially instantaneous at about 0.1 ms on some benchmark tests. To speed up magnetic hard drive performance, *disk caching* is often used.

A *cache* (pronounced "cash") is a place to store something temporarily. For instance, in Chapter 2 we learned that cache memory is very fast memory used by the CPU to store data and instructions that might be needed in order to speed up processing. A **disk cache** is similar in concept—it stores copies of data or programs that are located on the hard drive and that might be needed soon in memory chips in order to avoid having to retrieve the data or programs from the hard drive when they are requested. Since the hard disks do not have to be accessed if the requested data is located in the disk cache and since retrieving data from memory is much faster than from a magnetic hard disk, disk caching can speed up performance. Disk caching also saves wear and tear on the hard drive and, in portable computers, can also extend battery life.

While the memory used for disk caching can be a designated portion of RAM, today's hard drives typically use a disk cache consisting of memory chips located on a circuit board inside the hard drive case. When a magnetic hard drive uses disk caching (as most do today), any time the hard drive is accessed the computer copies the requested data, as well as extra data located in neighboring areas of the hard drive (such as all of the data located on the cylinder being accessed), to the disk cache. When the next data is requested, the computer checks the disk cache first to see if the data it needs is already there. If it is, the data is retrieved for processing; if not, the computer retrieves the requested data from the hard disks.

Most conventional magnetic hard drives today include a flash memory-based disk cache ranging in size from 2 MB to 16 MB built into the hard drive case. However, **hybrid hard drives**—essentially a combination flash memory/magnetic hard drive (see Figure 3-8)—use a much larger amount of flash memory (up to 1 GB today). In addition to using the flash

FIGURE 3-8

Hybrid hard drives. Hybrid hard drives contain both magnetic hard disks and a large quantity of flash memory for increased performance.

MAGNETIC HARD DRIVE
This drive contains 2 hard disks and 4 read/write heads that operate in a manner similar to a conventional hard drive.

FLASH MEMORY DISK CACHE
This drive uses 256 MB of flash memory disk cache to duplicate data as it is stored on the hard disks so the data can be accessed when hard disks are not spinning.

> **Disk access time.** The time it takes to locate and read data from (or position and write data to) a storage medium. > **Disk cache.** Memory used in conjunction with a magnetic hard drive to improve system performance. > **Hybrid hard drive.** A hard drive that contains both a large amount of flash memory and magnetic hard disks.

memory to reduce the number of times the hard disks in a hybrid hard drive need to be read, hybrid hard drives can also use the flash memory to temporarily store (cache) data to be written to the hard disks, which can further extend the battery life of portable computers and mobile devices. The additional flash memory in a hybrid hard drive can also allow encryption or other security measures to be built into the drive (encryption is discussed in Chapter 9).

Hard Drive Partitioning and File Systems

Partitioning a hard drive enables you to divide the physical capacity of a single hard drive logically into separate areas, called *partitions* or *volumes*. Partitions function as independent hard drives and are sometimes referred to as *logical drives* because each partition is labeled and treated separately (such as C drive and D drive) when viewed in a file management program such as Windows Explorer, but they are still physically one hard drive. One or more partitions are created when a hard drive is first *formatted* (prepared for data storage). For instance, many new personal computers come with a C drive partition ready to use for programs and data and another logical drive (such as a D drive) set up as a *recovery partition*. A recovery partition (see Figure 3-9) contains the data necessary to restore a hard drive back to its state at the time the computer was purchased and is designed to be used only if the computer malfunctions.

FIGURE 3-9

Hard drive partitions. New personal computers today often come with the primary hard drive divided into two partitions.

In the past, operating systems could only use hard drives up to 512 MB, so hard drives larger than that limit had to use multiple partitions. While today's operating systems can use much larger hard drives and, therefore, do not require the use of multiple partitions, partitioning a large hard drive can make it function more efficiently. This is because operating systems typically use a larger cluster size with a larger hard drive. Since even tiny files have to use up one entire cluster of storage space, disk space is often wasted when a large cluster size is used. When a hard drive is partitioned, each logical drive can use a smaller cluster size, since each logical drive is smaller than the original hard drive.

Users can create additional partitions on a hard drive, if desired, but should be careful when partitioning a computer's primary hard drive, since deleting a partition erases all data contained on that partition. One reason advanced users may partition a primary hard drive is to be able to use two different operating systems on the same hard drive—such as Windows and Linux (these and other operating systems are discussed in detail in Chapter 5). With a *dual-boot system* such as this, the user specifies the operating system to be run each time the computer boots. Another reason for partitioning a hard drive is to create the appearance of having separate hard drives for file management, multiple users, or other purposes. For instance, some users choose to partition a new second or external hard drive into multiple logical drives to organize their data before storing data on that hard drive. Storing data files on a separate physical hard drive or logical partition makes it easier for the user to locate data files. It also enables users to back up all data files simply by backing up the entire hard drive or partition containing the data.

The partition size, cluster size (on magnetic hard drives), maximum drive size, and maximum file size that can be used with a hard drive are determined by the *file system* being used. For instance, Windows users have three file system options to choose from: the original *FAT* file system (not commonly used with hard drives today, though it is used with some removable storage devices like USB flash drives), the newer *FAT32* file system, and the newest *NTFS* file system. The recommended file system for computers running current versions of Windows is NTFS because it supports much larger hard drives and files than either FAT or FAT32 and it includes better security and error-recovery capabilities. Computers with older versions of Windows have to use FAT32, which has a maximum partition size of 32 GB and a maximum file size of 4 GB.

Hard Drive Interface Standards

Hard drives connect, or interface, with a computer using one of several different standards. The most common internal *hard drive interface standard* for desktop computers today is *serial ATA* (*SATA*). The SATA standard was designed to replace the older, slower *parallel ATA* (*PATA*) standard, which is also referred to as *Fast ATA* and *EIDE* (*Enhanced Integrated Drive Electronics*). SATA is faster (up to 6 Gbps) than PATA and uses thinner cables, which means SATA hard drives take up less room inside the system unit. External hard drives most often connect to the computer via a USB or FireWire port, though an *eSATA* (*External SATA*) interface can be used to connect to the computer via an eSATA expansion card if faster speeds are desired.

The most common hard drive interfaces used with servers are *serial attached SCSI* (*SAS*), which is a newer version of the SCSI interface, and *Fibre Channel*, which is a reliable, flexible, and very fast standard geared for long-distance, high-bandwidth applications. For network storage, new standards, such as *Internet SCSI* (*iSCSI*) and *Fibre Channel over Ethernet* (*FCoE*), have evolved that communicate over the Internet or another network using the *TCP/IP* networking standard.

FURTHER EXPLORATION Go

Go to the Chapter 3 page at **www.cengage.com/ computerconcepts/np/uc13** for links to information about hard drives.

OPTICAL DISCS

Data on **optical discs** (such as *CDs* and *DVDs*) is stored and read *optically*; that is, using laser beams. General characteristics of optical discs are discussed next, followed by a look at the various types of optical discs available today.

Optical Disc Characteristics

Optical discs are thin circular discs made out of *polycarbonate substrate*—essentially a type of very strong plastic—that are topped with layers of other materials and coatings used to store data and protect the disc. Data can be stored on one or both sides of an optical disc, depending on the disc design, and some types of discs use multiple recording layers on each side of the disc to increase capacity. An optical disc contains a single spiral track (instead of multiple tracks like magnetic disks), and the track is divided into sectors to keep data organized. As shown in Figure 3-10, this track (sometimes referred to as a *groove* in order to avoid confusion with the

FIGURE 3-10
How recorded optical discs work.

TRACK
A single track spirals from the center of the disc outward; recorded data is stored on the track.

SECTORS
The track is divided into sectors for data organization.

LAND

PIT

WRITING DATA
When data is written to the disc, a laser beam creates pits, represented by dark, nonreflective areas on the disc.

READING DATA
A low intensity laser beam reads the disc. A transition between a pit and a land is interpreted as a 1; a set period of time between transitions is interpreted as a 0.

>**Optical disc.** A type of storage medium read from and written to using a laser beam.

term *tracks* used to refer to songs on an audio CD) begins at the center of the disc and spirals out to the edge of the disc.

Advantages of optical discs include relatively large capacity for their size (as discussed shortly) and durability (they are more durable than magnetic media and don't degrade with use, like some magnetic media does). However, the discs should be handled carefully and stored in their cases when they are not in use, in order to protect the recorded surfaces of the discs from scratches, fingerprints, and other marks that can interfere with the usability of the discs. Optical discs are the standard today for software delivery; they are also commonly used for backup purposes, and for storing and/or transporting music, photo, video, and other large files.

Representing Data on an Optical Disc

Data is written to an optical disc in one of two ways. With *read-only optical discs* like movie, music, and software CDs and DVDs, the surface of the disc is molded or stamped appropriately to represent the data. With *recordable* or *rewritable optical discs* that can be written to using an *optical drive* such as a *CD drive* or *DVD drive*, as discussed shortly, the reflectivity of the disc is changed using a laser to represent the data. In either case, the disc is read with a laser and the computer interprets the reflection of the laser off the disc surface as 1s and 0s.

To accomplish this with molded or stamped optical discs, tiny depressions (when viewed from the top side of the disc) or bumps (when viewed from the bottom) are created on the disc's surface. These bumps are called *pits*; the areas on the disc that are not changed are called *lands*. Although many people think that each individual pit and land represents a 1 or 0 that is not completely accurate—it is the transition between a pit and land that represents a 1. When the disc is read, the amount of laser light reflected back from the disc changes when the laser reaches a transition between a pit and a land. When the optical drive detects a transition, it is interpreted as a 1; no transition for a specific period of time indicates a 0.

With a CD or DVD that is recorded using a CD or DVD drive, the recording laser beam changes the reflectivity of the appropriate areas on the disc to represent the data stored there—dark, nonreflective areas are pits; reflective areas are lands, as illustrated in Figure 3-10. The transition between a pit and a land still represents a 1 and no transition for a specific distance along the track represents a 0. Different types of optical discs use different types of laser beams. Conventional **CD discs** use *infrared* lasers; conventional **DVD discs** use *red* lasers, which allow data to be stored more compactly on the same size disc; and high-definition **Blu-ray Discs (BD)** use *blue-violet lasers*, which can store data even more compactly on a disc.

Optical Drives

Optical discs in each of the three categories (CD, DVD, and BD) can be read-only, recordable, or rewritable; they can use the + or – standard; and they can be either *single-layer* or *dual-layer* (*DL*) *discs*. Optical discs are designed to be read by **optical drives**, such as *CD*, *DVD*, and *BD drives*, and the type of optical drive being used must support the type of optical disc being used. Most optical drives today support multiple types of optical discs— some support all possible types. Optical drives are almost always *downward-compatible*, meaning they can be used with lower (older) types of discs but not higher (newer) ones. So, while a DVD drive would likely support all types of CD and DVD discs, it cannot be used with BD discs, but most BD drives today support all types of CD, DVD, and Blu-ray Discs.

> **CD disc.** A low capacity (typically 650 MB) optical disc that is often used to deliver music and software, as well as to store user data.
> **DVD disc.** A medium capacity (typically 4.7 MB or 8.5 MB) optical disc that is often used to deliver software and movies, as well as to store user data. > **Blu-ray Disc (BD).** A high-capacity (typically 25 MB or 50 MB) that is often used to deliver high-definition movies, as well as to store user data. > **Optical drive.** A drive used with optical discs, such as CD or DVD discs.

To use an optical disc, it is inserted into an appropriate optical drive. Purchased optical discs often have a title and other text printed on one side; if so, they are inserted into the optical drive with the printed side facing up. Two-sided commercial discs typically identify each side of a disc by printing that information on the disc close to the inner circle.

The process of recording data onto an optical disc is called *burning*. To burn an optical disc (such as a *CD-R* or a *DVD-R disc*), the optical drive being used must support burning and the type of disc being used. In addition, *CD-burning* or *DVD-burning* software is required. Many burning programs are available commercially, and recent versions of operating systems (including Windows and Mac OS) include CD and DVD burning capabilities. In addition, most CD and DVD drives come bundled with burning software. Some optical drives—such as *LightScribe-enabled drives*—are even capable of burning label information on the surface of a disc after the content has been recorded. (To do this, you first burn the data to the disc, and then you flip the disc over and burn the desired label information on the other side of the disc.) Most personal computers today come with an internal optical drive; one exception is netbooks, which typically do not include an optical drive. An *external optical drive* that connects via a USB port (see Figure 3-11) can be used with these computers whenever an optical drive is temporarily needed.

FIGURE 3-11
External optical drives. Can be connected as needed, typically via a USB port, such as to the netbook shown here.

Optical Disc Shapes, Sizes, and Capacities

Standard-sized optical discs are 120-mm (approximately 4 1/2-inch) discs. There are also smaller 80-mm (approximately 3-inch) *mini discs*, most often used in conjunction with *digital video cameras*. In addition, optical discs can be made into a variety of sizes and shapes—such as a heart, triangle, irregular shape, or the hockey-rink shape commonly used with *business card CDs*—because the track starts at the center of the disc and the track just stops when it reaches an outer edge of the disc. Standard shapes are molded and less expensive; custom shapes—such as those that match a service or product being sold (a soda can, musical instrument, saw blade, candy bar, or house, as in Figure 3-12)—are custom cut and are more costly. The practice of using optical discs to replace ordinary objects, such as business cards and mailed advertisements, is becoming more common. For marketing purposes, *flexible DVDs* and *scented discs* are also available. Flexible DVDs can be bent or rolled so they can be attached to the cover of a magazine or wrapped around a product, for example. Scented discs have a specific scent (such as a particular perfume, popcorn, pine trees, or a specific fruit) added to the label side of the disc; the scent is released when the surface of the disc is rubbed.

FIGURE 3-12
Optical discs are available in a variety of sizes, appearances, and capacities.

STANDARD 120 MM (4.7 INCH) SIZED DISC

MINI 80 MM (3.1 INCH) SIZED DISC

CUSTOM-SHAPED BUSINESS CARD DISC

FURTHER EXPLORATION

Go to the Chapter 3 page at **www.cengage.com/ computerconcepts/np/uc13** for links to information about DVD technology.

One of the biggest advantages of optical discs is their large capacity. To further increase capacity, many discs are available as *dual-layer discs* (also called *double-layer discs*) that store data in two layers on a single side of the disc, so the capacity is approximately doubled. For an even larger capacity, discs with more than two layers are in development. Standard-sized CD discs are normally single-layer and hold either 650 MB or 700 MB, standard-sized DVD discs hold 4.7 GB (single-layer discs) or 8.5 GB (dual-layer discs), and standard-sized BD discs hold either 25 GB (single-layer discs) or 50 GB (dual-layer discs). Discs can also be *double sided*, which doubles the capacity; however, the disc must be turned over to access the second side. Double-sided discs are most often used with movies and other prerecorded content, such as to store a *widescreen version* of a movie on one side of a DVD disc and a *standard version* on the other side. Small optical discs have a smaller storage capacity than their larger counterparts: typically, single-layer, single-sided 3-inch mini CD, DVD, and BD discs hold about 200 MB, 1.4 GB, and 7.5 GB, respectively, and business card-sized CD and DVD discs hold about 50 MB and 325 MB, respectively.

As with magnetic disks, researchers are continually working to increase the capacity of optical discs without increasing their physical size. One promising recent development is a discovery by a Harvard research team that narrows the width of the laser beam used to record data on an optical disc. This is significant because a narrower beam means that more data can be stored on a disc. Instead of using a lens to focus the laser light (which results in a laser beam width of 405 billionths of a meter when recording DVDs), the researchers used two tiny gold rods as antennas at the end of the laser and they were able to narrow the laser beam width to just 40 billionths of a meter. Although products based on this technology may be 10 years away, researchers predict that this new technique could eventually result in regular-sized optical discs that hold 3 TB—roughly 600 times more than a standard DVD today.

FIGURE 3-13

High-definition movies are available on Blu-ray Discs (BDs).

Read-Only Optical Discs: CD-ROM, DVD-ROM, and BD-ROM Discs

CD-ROM (*compact disc read-only memory*) **discs** and **DVD-ROM** (*digital versatile disc read-only memory*) **discs** are *read-only optical discs* that come prerecorded with commercial products, such as software programs, clip art and other types of graphics collections, music, and movies. For high-definition content (such as feature films—see Figure 3-13), **BD-ROM** (*Blu-ray Disc read-only memory*) **discs** are available. There are also additional read-only disc formats for specific gaming devices, such as the *UMD* (*Universal Media Disc*) format used with the Sony PSP handheld gaming device and the proprietary discs used with the Wii, Xbox, and Playstation gaming consoles. The data on a read-only disc cannot be erased, changed, or added to because the pits that are molded into the surface of the disc when the disc is produced are permanent.

Recordable Optical Discs: CD-R, DVD-R, DVD+R, and BD-R Discs

Recordable optical discs (also sometimes called *write-once discs*) can be written to, but the discs cannot be erased and reused. Recordable CDs are referred to as **CD-R discs**. Single-layer recordable DVDs are called either

---

> **CD-ROM disc.** A CD that can be read from, but not written to, by the user. > **DVD-ROM disc.** A DVD that can be read from, but not written to, by the user. > **BD-ROM disc.** A Blu-ray Disc that can be read from, but not written to, by the user. > **CD-R disc.** A recordable CD.

DVD-R discs or DVD+R discs, depending on the standard being used, and dual-layer recordable DVDs are called *DVD+R DL* or *DVD-R DL discs*. Recordable BD discs are also available in both single-layer and dual-layer (**BD-R discs** and *BD-R DL discs*, respectively). The capacities of recordable optical discs are the same as the read-only formats (see Figure 3-14).

Instead of having physically molded pits, most recordable optical discs have a recording layer containing organic light-sensitive dye embedded between the disc's plastic and reflective layers. One exception to this is the BD-R disc, which has a recording layer consisting of inorganic material. When data is written to a recordable disc, the recording laser inside the recordable optical drive burns the dye (for CD and DVD discs) or melts and combines the inorganic material (for BD-R discs), creating nonreflective areas that function as pits. In either case, the marks are permanent, so data on the disc cannot be erased or rewritten.

Recordable CDs are commonly used for backing up files, sending large files to others, and creating custom music CDs (for example, from MP3 files legally down-loaded from the Internet or from songs located on a music album purchased on CD). DVD-Rs can be used for similar purposes when more storage space is needed, such as for backing up large files and for storing home movies, digital photos, and other multimedia files. BD-R discs can be used when an even greater amount of storage is needed, such as very large backups or high-definition multimedia files.

Rewritable Optical Discs: CD-RW, DVD-RW, DVD+RW, and BD-RE Discs

Rewritable optical discs can be written to, erased, and overwritten just like magnetic hard disks. The most common types of rewritable optical discs are **CD-RW**, **DVD-RW**, **DVD+RW**, and **BD-RE discs**; BD-RE discs are also available as dual-layer discs (*BD-RE DL discs*). The capacities of rewritable discs are the same as their read-only and recordable counterparts. An additional, but not widely used, rewritable DVD format is *DVD-RAM*. DVD-RAM and DVD-RAM DL discs are supported by *DVD-RAM drives*, as well as by some DVD and BD drives.

To write to, erase, or overwrite rewritable optical discs, *phase change* technology is used. With this technology, the rewritable CD or DVD disc is coated with layers of a special metal alloy compound that can have two different appearances after it has been heated and then cooled, depending on the heating and cooling process used. With one process, the material *crystallizes* and that area of the disc is reflective. With another process, the area cools to a nonreflective *amorphous* state. Before any data is written to a rewritable optical disc, the disc is completely reflective. To write data to the disc, the recording laser heats the metal alloy in the appropriate locations on the spiral track and then uses the appropriate cooling process to create either the nonreflective areas (pits) or the reflective areas (lands). To erase the disc, the appropriate heating and cooling process is used to change the areas to be erased back to their original reflective state.

Rewritable optical discs are used for many of the same purposes as recordable optical discs. However, they are particularly appropriate for situations in which data written to the optical disc can be erased at a later time so the disc to be reused (such as transferring large files from one computer to another or temporarily storing TV shows recorded on your computer that you will later watch using your living room TV and DVD player).

FIGURE 3-14
Recordable CDs and DVDs.

CD-R DISCS
Hold 650 MB.

DVD+R DL DISCS
Hold 8.5 GB.

BD-R DL DISCS
Hold 50 GB.

HW

>**DVD-R/DVD+R discs.** Recordable DVDs. >**BD-R disc.** A recordable Blu-ray Disc. >**CD-RW disc.** A rewritable CD. >**DVD-RW/DVD+RW discs.** Rewritable DVDs. >**BD-RE disc.** A rewritable Blu-ray Disc.

TREND

IronKey: The World's Most Secure USB Flash Drive

Today, the security of data being carried on portable devices, such as USB flash drives, is extremely important and the use of encrypted portable devices is a growing trend. For individuals, business employees, or government employees that need today's most secure USB flash drive, *IronKey* (see the accompanying illustration) might just be the answer.

Available in three versions (Basic, Personal, and Enterprise) in capacities ranging from 1 GB to 8 GB, IronKey uses always-on, hardware-based encryption to protect all data written to the device. The encryption is enabled by an onboard *Cryptochip* that securely stores the encryption keys generated when the device is initialized and the user password is selected. There is also an internal counter to protect against password guessing attacks by an unauthorized individual trying to access the device. After 10 incorrect password attempts, the device self-destructs and erases all data and encryption keys stored on the device. The Personal and Enterprise versions contain additional features, such as a secure version of the Firefox browser that can be used for anonymous Web browsing (so no browsing data is stored on the local computer—just on the

IronKey drive) and the ability to store and use other portable applications on the device.

IronKey has received security validation for use by the U.S. and Canadian governments and is approved to carry classified government data. Overkill for personal use? Perhaps. But for anyone carrying sensitive data from computer to computer, highly secure USB flash drives like the IronKey can't be beat for security and convenience.

FLASH MEMORY

As previously discussed, **flash memory** is a chip-based storage medium that represents data using electrons. It is used in a variety of storage systems, such as the SSDs and hybrid hard drives already discussed and the additional storage systems shown in Figure 3-15. Because flash memory media is physically very small, it is increasingly being embedded directly into a variety of consumer products—such as portable digital media players, digital cameras, handheld gaming devices, GPS devices, mobile phones, and even sunglasses and wristwatches—to provide built-in data storage. In addition, a variety of types of *flash memory cards* and *USB flash drives* are available to use with computers and other devices for data storage and data transfer, as discussed next. For a look at what is billed as the world's most secure USB flash drive—*IronKey*—see the Trend box.

Flash Memory Cards

One of the most common types of flash memory media is the **flash memory card**—a small card containing one or more flash memory chips, a controller chip, other electrical components, and metal contacts to connect the card to the device or reader with which it is being used. Flash memory cards are available in a variety of formats, such as

Flash memory card

EMBEDDED FLASH MEMORY
Flash memory is often embedded into consumer products, such as this digital media player, for storage purposes.

FLASH MEMORY CARDS AND READERS
Flash memory cards are often used to store data for digital cameras and other devices; the data can be transferred to a computer via a flash memory card reader, as needed.

USB FLASH DRIVES
USB flash drives are often used to store data and transfer files from one computer to another.

FIGURE 3-15
Flash memory systems. Flash memory is used in a variety of storage systems today.

CompactFlash (*CF*), *Secure Digital* (*SD*), *Secure Digital High Capacity* (*SDHC*), *Secure Digital Extended Capacity* (*SDXC*), *MultiMedia Card* (*MMC*), *xD Picture Card* (*xD*), and *Memory Stick* (*MS*) (see Figure 3-16). These formats are not interchangeable, so the type of flash memory card used with a device is determined by the type of flash media card that device can accept. Flash memory cards are the most common type of storage media for digital cameras, portable digital media players, mobile phones, and other portable devices. They can also be used to store data for a personal computer, as needed, as well as to transfer data from a portable device to a computer. Consequently, most desktop and notebook computers today come with a *flash memory card reader* capable of reading flash memory cards; an external flash memory card reader (that typically connects via a USB port and is shown in Figure 3-16) can be used if a built-in reader is not available. The capacity of flash memory cards is continually growing and is up to about 4 GB for standard cards and 32 GB for high-capacity cards; the even higher capacity extended capacity cards are just beginning to become available and are expected to reach capacities of 2 TB by 2014.

TIP

Flash memory cards can be inserted into a reader only one way and must go in the proper slot, so be sure to check the slot type and look for the directional tips often printed on the card before inserting a card into a flash memory reader.

FIGURE 3-16
Flash memory cards. Shown here are some of the most widely used types of flash memory cards and a multicard reader.

MEMORY STICKS

COMPACTFLASH (CF) CARDS

SECURE DIGITAL (SD) CARDS

XD PICTURE CARDS

FLASH MEMORY CARD READERS
Can be built-in or external and usually support several different types of flash memory media; external readers such as this one typically connect to a computer via a USB port.

One of the most widely used types of flash memory media—Secure Digital (SD)—is available in different physical sizes, as well as in different capacities. For instance, standard-sized SD cards are often used in digital cameras and computers; the smaller *miniSD* and *microSD* (about one-half and one-quarter the size of a standard SD card, respectively, as shown in Figure 3-16) are designed to be used with mobile phones and other mobile devices. When more storage space is needed, higher capacity *miniSDHC* and *microSDHC* cards can be used. MMC cards and memory sticks are also available in mobile sizes; adapters can be used with mobile-sized flash memory cards in order to use them in a full-sized memory card reader.

While general purpose flash memory cards can be used for most applications, there are also flash memory cards designed for specific uses. For instance, *professional flash memory cards* designed for professional photographers are faster and more durable than consumer cards; *gaming flash memory cards* are specifically designed for gaming consoles and devices, such as the Nintendo Wii or Sony PSP; and *netbook flash memory cards* are designed to be used to expand the storage capabilities of a netbook computer. There are even Wi-Fi-enabled flash memory cards that can wirelessly upload digital photos taken with a camera using that card for storage, as discussed in the Technology and You box in Chapter 7.

Typically, flash memory media is purchased blank, but some flash-memory-based software (such as games, encyclopedias, and language translators) is available. A new option for portable music is *slotMusic*—music albums that come stored on microSD cards. These cards can be used with any phone or portable digital media player that has a microSD slot and they typically contain extra storage space to add additional files as desired. Movies are also beginning to be delivered via flash memory media. In fact, Panasonic and Disney have announced plans to begin releasing movies on microSD cards by 2010 and Sonic Solutions has announced movies stored on USB flash drives should begin to become available at about the same time. These new options for portable multimedia are geared toward individuals who would like access to this content via a mobile phone, car navigation system, netbook, or other device often used while on the go that has a flash memory card slot or a USB port.

USB Flash Drives

USB flash drives (sometimes called *USB flash memory drives*, *thumb drives*, or *jump drives*) consist of flash memory media integrated into a self-contained unit that connects to a computer or other device via a standard USB port and is powered via the USB port. USB flash drives are designed to be very small and very portable. In order to appeal to a wide variety of users, USB flash drives are available in a range of sizes, colors, and appearances—including those designed to be attached to backpacks or worn on a lanyard around the neck; those built into necklaces, wristbands, or wristwatches; those thin enough to fit easily into a wallet; and those made into custom shapes for promotional or novelty purposes (see Figure 3-17). When

◥ **FIGURE 3-17**
USB flash drives.

CONVENTIONAL USB FLASH DRIVES

USB FLASH DRIVE WRISTBANDS

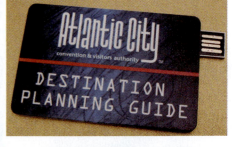

USB FLASH DRIVE WALLET CARDS

>**USB flash drive.** A small storage device that plugs into a USB port and contains flash memory media.

TECHNOLOGY AND YOU

Thumb Drive PCs

We all know that USB flash drives are a great way to transport documents from one location to another, but what about using one to take a personalized computer with you wherever you go? It's possible and easy to do with the use of *portable applications* (also called *portable apps*)—computer programs that are designed to be used with portable devices like USB flash drives. When the device is plugged into the USB port of any computer, you have access to the software and personal data (including your browser bookmarks, calendar, e-mail and instant messaging contacts, and more) stored on that device, just as you would on your own computer. And when you unplug the device, none of your personal data is left behind because all programs are run directly from the USB flash drive. Many portable applications (such as the PortableApps suite shown in the accompanying illustration) are free and include all the basics you might want in a single package. For instance, PortableApps includes a menu structure, antivirus program, Web browser, e-mail program, calendar program, the OpenOffice.org office suite, and more. To set up a USB flash drive as a portable computer, you need to perform the following steps:

1. Download your desired portable applications (such as the PortableApps suite) to your desktop or notebook computer.

2. Plug in your USB flash drive and run the portable apps installation program, using your USB flash drive as the destination folder.

3. Open a file management program such as Windows Explorer, double-click your USB flash drive, and then launch your portable apps software to test it.

4. Download and install any additional portable apps you would like to use (it is a good idea to include an antivirus program to try to prevent the USB flash drive from becoming infected with a computer virus).

To use your thumb drive computer, plug it into the USB port of any computer—many portable apps will launch automatically and display a main menu, such as the one shown in the accompanying illustration. Portable apps can also be installed on an iPod or other portable digital media player (instead of a USB flash drive) if you prefer to use that device as your portable computer.

1. USB flash drive is plugged into a computer.

2. This menu is displayed; all programs run off the USB flash drive.

the USB flash drive is built into a consumer product (such as a watch, sunglasses, or a Swiss Army knife), a retractable cord is used to connect the device to a computer when needed. Because they are becoming so widely used, additional hardware related to USB flash drives are becoming available, such as *USB duplicator systems* used by educators to copy assignments or other materials to and from a large collection of USB flash drives at one time.

To read from or write to a USB flash drive, you just plug it into a USB port. If the USB flash drive is being used with a computer, it is assigned a drive letter by the computer, just like any other type of attached drive, and files can be read from or written to the USB flash drive until it is unplugged from the USB port. The capacity of most USB flash drives today ranges from 1 GB to 64 GB. USB flash drive use has become commonplace for individuals, students, and employees to transport files from one computer to another, as well as to quickly back up important files. For a look at how you can carry your personal computer with you on a USB flash drive, see the Technology and You box.

VIDEO PODCAST

Go to the Chapter 3 page at **www.cengage.com/ computerconcepts/np/uc13** to download or listen to the "How To: Use Portable Applications with a USB Flash Drive" video podcast.

ASK THE EXPERT

Kingston

Mark Tekunoff, Senior Technology Manager, Kingston Technology

Is it better to copy a file from a USB flash drive to a hard drive for extensive editing instead of working directly with (and repeatedly saving) the document on the USB flash drive?

Flash drives use two different types of memory and can typically support 10,000 or 100,000 writes. If you take into consideration that USB flash drives have a feature called *wear leveling* to make sure that no single data location gets used over and over, the typical USB flash drive can last 7 to 10 years.

For performance, however, it's always better to process work on the hard drive. Of course, a consumer can use the USB flash drive to save or process data too, it will just be a little slower.

ONLINE VIDEO

Go to the Chapter 3 page at **www.cengage.com/computerconcepts/np/uc13** to watch the "A Look at Network Storage" video clip.

TIP

If the router used to connect devices to your home network includes a USB port, you can create an NAS by plugging a USB storage device (such as an external hard drive) directly into the router.

In addition to providing basic data storage and data portability, USB flash drives can provide additional capabilities. For instance, they can be used to lock a computer and to issue Web site passwords; they can also include *biometric features*—such as a built-in fingerprint reader—to allow only authorized individuals access to the data stored on the USB flash drive or to the computer with which the USB flash drive is being used.

OTHER TYPES OF STORAGE SYSTEMS

Other types of storage systems used with personal and business computers today include *remote storage*, *smart cards*, and *holographic storage*. There are also storage systems and technologies designed for large computer systems. These systems are discussed next.

Network Storage and Online/Cloud Storage Systems

Remote storage refers to using a storage device that is not connected directly to the user's computer; instead, the device is accessed through a local network or through the Internet. Using a remote storage device via a local network (referred to as *network storage*) works in much the same way as using *local storage* (the storage devices and media that are directly attached to the user's computer). To read data from or write data to a remote storage device (such as a hard drive in another computer being accessed via a network), the user just selects it (see Figure 3-18) and then performs the necessary tasks in the normal fashion. Network storage is common in businesses; it is also used by individuals with home networks for backup purposes or to share files with another computer in the home.

Because of the vast amount of data shared and made available over networks today, network storage has become increasingly important. Two common types of network storage used today are **network attached storage (NAS)** devices and **storage area networks (SANs)**. NAS devices are high-performance storage servers that are connected individually to a network to provide storage for the computers connected to that network. They can be large storage servers designed for a large business, or smaller NAS devices designed for a home or small business (such as the one in Figure 3-18). A growing trend, in fact, is home NAS devices designed to store multimedia data (such as downloaded music, recorded TV shows, and downloaded movies) to be distributed over a home entertainment network. NAS devices typically connect to the network via a wired networking connection, although some (like the one shown in Figure 3-18) use a wireless networking connection; networking is explained in detail in Chapter 7.

A storage area network (SAN) also provides storage for a network, but it consists of a separate network of hard drives or other storage devices, which is attached to the main network. The primary difference between network attached storage and a storage area network

>**Remote storage.** A storage device that is not directly connected to the computer being used, such as one accessed through a local network or the Internet. >**Network attached storage (NAS).** A high-performance storage device individually connected to a network to provide storage for computers on that network. >**Storage area network (SAN).** A network of hard drives or other storage devices that provide storage for another network of computers.

Computers on this network.

Items in the SharedDocs folder on the computer called NOTEBOOK.

SHARED FOLDERS
Shared folders on network computers appear and are accessed in a manner similar to local folders.

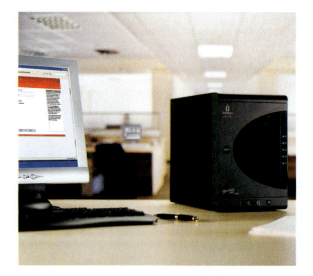

NETWORK ATTACHED STORAGE (NAS) DEVICES
This wireless NAS device holds 1 TB of data and provides storage for all computers on the network.

FIGURE 3-18
Network storage.

is how the storage devices interface with the network—that is, whether the storage devices act as individual network nodes, just like computers, printers, and other devices on the network (NAS), or whether they are located in a completely separate network of storage devices that is accessible to the main network (SAN). However, in terms of functionality, the distinction between NAS and SANs is blurring, since they both provide storage services to the network. Typically, both NAS and SAN systems are scalable, so new devices can be added as more storage is needed, and devices can be added or removed without disrupting the network.

Remote storage devices accessed via the Internet are often referred to as **online storage** or **cloud storage**. While these terms are often used interchangeably, some view cloud storage as a specific type of online storage that can be accessed on demand by various Web applications. Most online applications (such as Google Docs, the Flickr photo sharing service, and social networking sites like Facebook, for instance) provide online storage for these services. There are also sites whose primary

ASK THE EXPERT

iomega
an EMC company

Bill Hansen, Global Product Manager, Network Storage Products, Iomega Corporation

Do home networks today need network hard drives?

Definitely! Just as the Internet has changed the way we communicate, network hard drives are changing the way we share information in the home. By plugging a network hard drive into your home network, you can share files and folders easily with anyone on that network—no more walking a CD or USB flash drive around to every computer like in the past. Today's network hard drives are simple to set up and use, and they are designed to allow you to access and share your music, pictures, videos, or other files easily with the other devices on your home network. You can also use a network hard drive as a backup target for all of your computers. In a nutshell, network hard drives greatly enhance the ability to share and store your valuable digital files at home.

> **Online storage.** Remote storage devices accessed via the Internet; also called **cloud storage**.

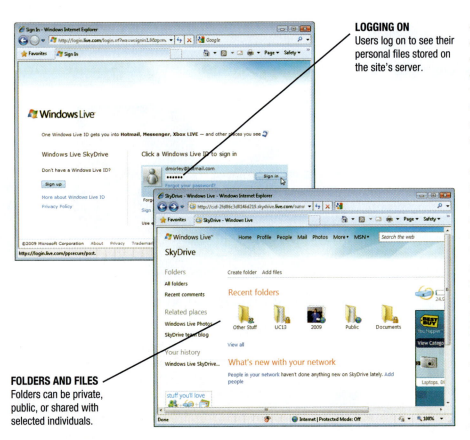

LOGGING ON
Users log on to see their personal files stored on the site's server.

FOLDERS AND FILES
Folders can be private, public, or shared with selected individuals.

FIGURE 3-19
Online storage. This site provides 25 GB of free storage.

objective is to allow users to store documents online, such as *Box.net* or Microsoft *SkyDrive*. Typically, online/cloud storage sites are password-protected (see Figure 3-19) and allow users to specify uploaded files as private files or as shared files that designated individuals can access.

The ability to store documents online (or "in the cloud") is growing in importance as more and more applications are becoming Web based and as individuals increasingly want access to their files from anywhere with any Internet-enabled device, such as a portable computer or mobile phone. Online storage is also increasingly being used for backup purposes—some online storage sites have an automatic backup option that uploads the files in designated folders on your computer to your online account at regular specified intervals, as long as your computer is connected to the Internet. Many Web sites providing online storage to individuals offer the service for free (for instance, SkyDrive gives each individual 25 GB of free storage space); others charge a small fee, such as $10 per month for 50 GB of storage space.

Business cloud storage services are also available, such as those offered in conjunction with the cloud computing services discussed in Chapter 1, which allow subscribers to access a flexible amount of both storage and computing power as needed on demand. For instance, *Amazon Simple Storage Service* (*Amazon S3*)—one of the leaders in *enterprise cloud storage*—charges a monthly fee per GB of storage used plus a fee based on the amount of data transferred that month. This service can be used alone or in conjunction with Amazon's cloud computing service, Amazon Elastic Compute Cloud (Amazon EC2). In addition to these *public cloud storage services*, businesses can also create *private clouds* designed to service just that particular business.

Smart Cards

A **smart card** is a credit card-sized piece of plastic that contains computer circuitry and components—typically a processor, memory, and storage (see Figure 3-20). Smart cards today store a relatively small amount of data (typically 64 KB or less) that can be used for payment or identification purposes. For example, a smart card can store a prepaid amount of *digital cash*, which can be used for purchases at a smart card-enabled vending machine or computer—the amount of cash available on the card is reduced each time the card is used. Smart cards are also commonly used worldwide for national and student ID cards, credit and debit cards, and cards that store identification data for accessing facilities or computer networks.

>**Smart card.** A credit card-sized piece of plastic containing a chip and other circuitry that can store data.

Although these applications have used conventional *magnetic stripe* technology in the past, the processor integrated into a smart card can perform computations—such as to authenticate the card and encrypt the data on the card to protect its integrity and secure it against unauthorized access—and data can be added to the card or modified on the card as needed. The increased capabilities of smart cards has also allowed for new applications, such as storing biometric data (such as the characteristics of a fingerprint) and other identifying data needed to accelerate airport security and to link patients to the *electronic health records* increasingly being used by hospitals.

To use a smart card, it must either be inserted into a *smart card reader* (if it is the type of card that requires contact) or placed close to a smart card reader (if it is a *contactless* card) built into or attached to a computer, keyboard, vending machine, or other device (refer again to Figure 3-20). Once a smart card has been verified by the card reader, the transaction—such as making a purchase or unlocking a door—can be completed. For an even higher level of security, some smart cards today store biometric data in the card and use that data to ensure the authenticity of the card's user before authorizing the smart card transaction (biometrics, encryption, and other security procedures are discussed in more detail in Chapter 9). An emerging trend is the use of *mobile smart cards*—smart microSD cards that are designed to add smart card capabilities to any computer or mobile device that contains a microSD slot.

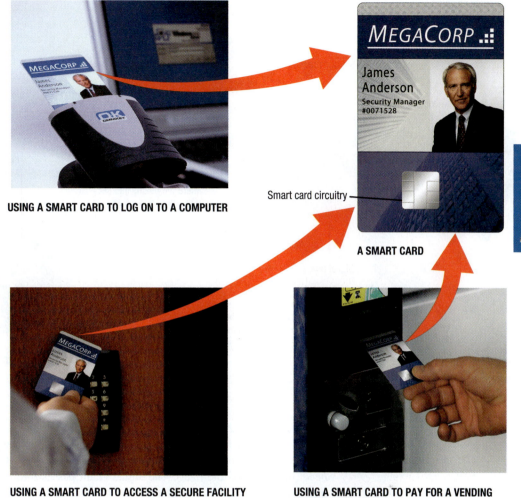

USING A SMART CARD TO LOG ON TO A COMPUTER

Smart card circuitry

A SMART CARD

USING A SMART CARD TO ACCESS A SECURE FACILITY

USING A SMART CARD TO PAY FOR A VENDING MACHINE PURCHASE

FIGURE 3-20
Smart cards. Smart cards can be used to log on to computers and networks, access facilities, pay for goods and services, and so forth.

Holographic Storage

Holographic storage is a type of three dimensional (3D) storage system that, after many years of research and development, is now a reality. *Holographic drives* typically connect to a computer via a serial attached SCSI (SAS) or Fibre Channel interface. To record data

---

>**Holographic storage.** An emerging type of storage technology that uses multiple blue laser beams to store data in three dimensions.

HOW HOLOGRAPHIC STORAGE WORKS

Detector

Storage medium

Reference beam

4. When data needs to be read, it is projected onto a detector to be reconstructed.

3. Data is converted into a hologram, which is stored where the beams intersect in the storage medium.

Holographic drive

Holographic cartridge

Spatial light modulator (SLM)

Signal beam

Laser

2. The beam is split into two beams (a reference beam and a signal beam) here, which intersect again at the storage medium.

1. A laser beam is used to write or read data.

HOLOGRAPHIC DRIVES AND CARTRIDGES

> ⚠ **FIGURE 3-21**
>
> **Holographic storage.** Holographic drives store up to one million bits of data in a single flash of light.

onto a *holographic disc* or *holographic cartridge*, the holographic drive splits the light from a blue laser beam into two beams (a *reference beam* whose angle determines the address used to store data at that particular location on the storage medium and a *signal beam* that contains the data). The signal beam passes through a device called a *spatial light modulator* (*SLM*), which translates the data's 0s and 1s into a *hologram*—a three-dimensional representation of data in the form of a checkerboard pattern of light and dark pixels. The two beams intersect within the recording medium to store the hologram at that location (see Figure 3-21) by changing the optical density of the medium.

Over one million bits of data can be stored at one time in a single flash of light, so holographic storage systems are very fast. And, because the hologram goes through the entire thickness of the medium, much more data can be stored on a holographic disc or cartridge than on a CD, DVD, or BD of the same physical size. In fact, hundreds of holograms can be stored in an overlapping manner in the same area of the medium—a different reference beam angle or position is used for each hologram so it can be uniquely stored and retrieved when needed. To read data, the reference beam projects the hologram containing the requested data onto a *detector* that reads the entire data page at one time. Today's holographic storage systems typically use removable recordable holographic cartridges that hold 300 GB per cartridge; 1.6 TB cartridges are expected by 2011.

Holographic data storage systems are particularly suited to applications in which large amounts of data need to be stored or retrieved quickly, but rarely changed, such as for business data archiving, high-speed digital video delivery, and image processing for medical, video, and military purposes. Rewritable holographic drives and media are currently in the development stage and are expected to be available by 2010.

Storage Systems for Large Computer Systems

Businesses and other organizations have tremendous storage needs. In addition to regular business data storage (such as employee files, customer and order data, business documents, and Web site content), new regulations are continually increasing the types of and

ONLINE VIDEO

Go to the Chapter 3 page at **www.cengage.com/ computerconcepts/np/uc13** to watch the "Holographic Storage: Data at the Speed of Light" video clip.

amounts of data that many businesses need to archive. For instance, the *Health Insurance Portability and Accountability Act* (*HIPAA*) requires healthcare providers to archive huge amounts of medical data, and the *Sarbanes-Oxley Act* requires certain accounting records and work papers to be archived for five years. In addition, a recent *e-discovery* federal mandate requires businesses to locate and provide to the courts in a timely manner any document stored electronically (such as e-mail messages, IM logs, and text documents) that is needed for evidence in civil litigation involving their companies. All of these requirements mean that business storage needs are growing exponentially—one forecast predicts that digital storage needs will increase by eight times in the next six years—and the documents must be stored in a manner in which they can be readily retrieved as needed.

Storage systems for large computer systems (such as those containing mainframe computers and midrange servers) utilize much of the same storage hardware, standards, and principles as those used with personal computers, but on a much larger scale. Instead of finding a single hard drive installed within the system unit, you are most likely to find a **storage server**—a separate piece of hardware containing multiple high-speed hard drives—connected to the computer system or network. Large storage servers typically contain racks (also called *chassis*) of hard drives for a large total capacity. For instance, the storage system shown in Figure 3-22 can include up to 1,280 hard drives for a total capacity of 600 TB. These types of storage systems—also referred to as *enterprise storage systems*—typically use fast Fibre Channel or iSCSI connections and are *scalable*, meaning that more racks of hard drives can be added as needed up to the maximum capacity. In addition to being used as stand-alone storage for large computer systems, storage servers may also be used in network attached storage (NAS), storage area network (SAN), and *RAID* (*redundant arrays of independent disks*) storage systems. Most storage servers are based on magnetic hard disks, although *magnetic tape storage systems* are also possible. RAID and magnetic tape systems are discussed next.

HARD DRIVES
Each drive chassis holds up to 40 individual hard drives that can store up to 1 TB each.

STORAGE SERVER
This server can manage up to 1,280 hard drives located in up to 5 cabinets like the one shown here, for a total capacity of 600 TB in a single system.

FIGURE 3-22
Storage servers.
Storage servers are usually scalable so additional hard drives can be added as needed.

RAID

RAID (redundant arrays of independent disks) is a method of storing data on two or more hard drives that work together. Although RAID can be used to increase performance, it is most often used to protect critical data on a storage server. Because RAID usually involves recording redundant (duplicate) copies of stored data, the copies can be used, when necessary, to reconstruct lost data. This helps to increase the *fault tolerance*—the ability to recover from an unexpected hardware or software failure, such as a system crash—of a storage system.

There are several different RAID designs or levels that use different combinations of RAID techniques. For example, *RAID 0* uses *disk striping*, which spreads files over two or more hard drives (see the leftmost part of Figure 3-23). Although striping improves performance since multiple hard drives can be accessed at one time to store or retrieve data, it does not provide fault tolerance. Another common RAID technique is *disk mirroring*, in which data is written to two duplicate hard drives simultaneously (see the rightmost part of Figure 3-23). The objective of disk mirroring is to increase fault tolerance—if one of the hard drives fails, the system can instantly switch to the other hard drive without any loss of

ONLINE VIDEO

Go to the Chapter 3 page at **www.cengage.com/ computerconcepts/np/uc13** to watch the "Understanding RAID" video clip.

>**Storage server.** A storage device designed for large computer systems and that typically contains multiple high-speed hard drives. >**RAID (redundant arrays of independent disks).** A storage method that uses several hard drives working together, typically to increase performance and/or fault-tolerance.

STRIPING
When a file is written to a RAID system using striping, it is split among two or more drives.

MIRRORING
When a file is written to a RAID system using mirroring, an identical copy of the file is sent to another drive in the system.

FIGURE 3-23
RAID. Two primary RAID techniques are striping and mirroring.

data or service. *RAID 1* uses disk mirroring. Levels beyond RAID 1 use some combination of disk striping and disk mirroring, with different types of error correction provisions.

One disadvantage of RAID in the past is the difficulty traditionally involved with setting up and maintaining the system. A new storage system—*Drobo*, shown in Figure 3-24—eliminates this concern. Drobo connects to an individual computer similar to an external hard drive (such as via a USB or FireWire connection) and has four empty drive bays into which hard drives with a capacity of up to 2 terabytes each can be inserted. An even newer *DroboPro* version has eight empty drive bays and can be connected directly to a network, in addition to being connected to a computer.

Like many RAID systems, Drobo and DroboPro offer continuous data redundancy, but they are much easier to use than conventional RAID systems and no special skills are needed to manage, repair, or upgrade them. For instance, hard drives just slide in and out of the Drobo devices and drives can be swapped while the devices are being used, in order to replace a bad hard drive or to increase capacity. When a drive is replaced, the system automatically copies data as needed to the new hard drive to restore the system back to its configuration before the hard drive failed or was removed. This ease of use makes the Drobo systems particularly appropriate for individuals and small businesses that need the security of data redundancy but have no IT personnel to assign to a RAID system.

FIGURE 3-24
The Drobo storage system.

Magnetic Tape Systems

Magnetic tape consists of plastic tape coated with a magnetizable substance that represents the bits and bytes of digital data, similar to magnetic hard disks. Although magnetic tape is no longer used for everyday storage applications because of its sequential-access property, it is still used today for business data archiving and backup. One advantage of magnetic tape is its low cost per megabyte.

>**Magnetic tape.** Storage media consisting of plastic tape with a magnetizable surface that stores data as a series of magnetic spots; typically comes as a cartridge.

Most computer tapes today are in the form of *cartridge tapes*, such as the one shown in Figure 3-25. Computer tapes are read by *tape drives*, which can be either an internal or an external piece of hardware. Tape drives contain one or more read/write heads over which the tape passes to allow the tape drive to read or write data. Cartridge tapes are available in a variety of sizes and formats; tape sizes and formats generally are not interchangeable. Tape cartridge capacity varies widely, from 500 MB to more than 1 TB per cartridge. When an even larger capacity is required, *tape libraries*—devices that contain multiple tape drives—can be used to boost storage capacity up to 10 PB.

FIGURE 3-25
A magnetic tape cartridge.

EVALUATING YOUR STORAGE ALTERNATIVES

Storage alternatives are often compared by weighing a number of product characteristics and cost factors. Some of these product characteristics include speed, compatibility, storage capacity, convenience, and the portability of the media. Keep in mind that each storage alternative normally involves trade-offs. For instance, most systems with removable media are slower than those with fixed media, and external drives are typically slower than internal ones. Although cost is a factor when comparing similar devices, it is often not the most compelling reason to choose a particular technology. For instance, although USB flash drives are relatively expensive per GB compared to optical discs and external hard drives, many users find them essential for transferring files between work and home or for taking presentations or other files with them as they travel. For drives that use a USB interface, the type of USB port is also significant. For example, storage devices that connect via a USB port adhering to the original USB 1.0 standard transfer data at up to 12 Mbps—USB 2.0 devices are about 40 times faster and the emerging USB 3.0 devices will be about 10 times as fast as USB 2.0 devices.

With so many different storage alternatives available, it is a good idea to research which devices and media are most appropriate for your personal situation. In general, most users today need a hard drive (for storing programs and data), some type of recordable or rewritable optical drive (for installing programs, backing up files, and sharing files with others), and a flash memory card reader (for transferring photos, music, and other content between portable devices and the computer). Users who plan to transfer music, digital photos, and other multimedia data on a regular basis between devices—such as a computer, digital camera, mobile phone, and printer—will want to select and use the flash memory media that are compatible with the devices they are using. They will also need to obtain the necessary adapter for their computer if it does not include a compatible built-in flash memory reader. Virtually all computer users today will also need at least one convenient free USB port to be used to connect external hard drives, USB flash drives, and other USB-based storage hardware, as well as USB devices that contain storage media, such as digital cameras and portable digital media players.

SUMMARY

STORAGE SYSTEM CHARACTERISTICS

Chapter Objective 1:
Name several general characteristics of storage systems.

Storage systems make it possible to save programs, data, and processing results for later use. They provide nonvolatile storage, so when the power is shut off, the data stored on the storage medium remains intact. All storage systems involve two physical parts: A **storage device** (such as a DVD drive) and a **storage medium** (such as a DVD disc). Data is often stored *magnetically* or *optically* on storage media, and storage media are read by the appropriate types of drive. Drives can be *internal*, *external*, or *remote*. Drives are typically assigned letters by the computer; these letters are used to identify the drive.

Sequential access allows a computer system to retrieve the records in a file only in the same order in which they are physically stored. *Random access* (also called *direct access*) allows the system to retrieve records in any order. In either case, **files** (sometimes called *documents*) stored on a storage medium are given a **filename** and can be organized into **folders**. This is referred to as *logical file representation*. *Physical file representation* refers to how the files are physically stored on the storage medium by the computer.

HARD DRIVES

Chapter Objective 2:
Describe the two most common types of hard drives and what they are used for today.

Hard drives are used in most computers to store programs and data. Conventional hard drives are **magnetic hard drives**; a newer type of hard drive that uses flash memory instead of magnetic disks is the **solid-state drive** (**SSD**). Hard drives can be *internal* or *external*; external hard drives can be full-sized or portable. **Hybrid hard drives** are a combination of a magnetic hard drive and an SSD, containing a large amount of flash memory that is used in conjunction with magnetic hard disks to provide increased performance while reducing power consumption.

Magnetic hard drives contain metal hard disks that are organized into concentric **tracks** encoded with magnetized spots representing 0s and 1s. **Sector** boundaries divide a magnetic disk surface into pie-shaped pieces. A **cluster**, which is the smallest amount of disk space that can be allocated to hold a file, is comprised of one or more sectors. All tracks in the same position on all surfaces of all disks in a hard drive form a **cylinder**. A separate *read/write head* that corresponds to each disk surface is used to read and write data. Hard drives can be divided into multiple *partitions* (logical drives) for efficiency or to facilitate multiple users or operating systems. Solid-state drives (SSDs) are increasingly used for portable computers because they are more shock-resistant and energy-efficient.

The total time it takes for a magnetic hard drive to read from or write to disks is called **disk access time**. A **disk cache** strategy, in which the computer transfers additional data to memory whenever disk content is retrieved, can help to speed up access time. Hard drives can connect to a computer using one of several standards, such as *serial ATA* (*SATA*), *parallel ATA* (*PATA*), *serial attached SCSI* (*SAS*), *eSATA*, *Fibre Channel*, FireWire, or USB.

OPTICAL DISCS

Chapter Objective 3:
Discuss the various types of optical discs available today and how they differ from each other.

Optical discs, such as **CD discs**, **DVD discs**, and **Blu-ray Discs** (**BDs**), store data *optically* using laser beams, and they can store data much more densely than magnetic disks. They are divided into tracks and sectors like magnetic disks, but they use a single spiral track instead of concentric tracks. Data is represented by *pits* and *lands* permanently formed on the surface of the disk. Optical discs are available in a wide variety of sizes, shapes, and capacities and are read by **optical drives**, such as *CD* or *DVD drives*. **CD-ROM discs** come with data already stored on the disc. CD-ROM discs cannot be erased or overwritten—they are *read-only.* **DVD-ROM discs** are similar to CD-ROM discs, but they hold much more data (at least 4.7 GB instead of 650 MB). High-capacity read-only optical discs designed for high-definition content are **BD-ROM discs**. *Recordable discs* (**CD-R**, **DVD-R/DVD+R**, and **BD-R discs**, for example) and *rewritable disks* (**CD-RW**, **DVD-RW/DVD+RW**, and **BD-RE discs**, for instance) can all be written to, but only rewritable discs can be erased and rewritten to, similar to a hard drive. Recordable CDs and DVDs store data by burning permanent marks onto the disc, similar to CD-ROM and DVD-ROM discs; rewritable discs typically use *phase change* technology to temporarily change the reflectivity of the disc to represent 1s and 0s.

FLASH MEMORY

Flash memory is used in a variety of storage systems. **Flash memory cards**, one of the most common types of *flash memory media*, are commonly used with digital cameras, portable computers, and other portable devices, as well as with desktop computers. Flash memory cards come in a variety of formats—the most common are *CompactFlash* (*CF*) and *Secure Digital* (*SD*) *cards*. **USB flash drives** connect to a computer or other device via a USB port and are a convenient method of transferring files between computers. They can also provide other capabilities, such as to lock a computer or control access to the data stored on the USB flash drive.

Chapter Objective 4:
Identify some flash memory storage devices and media and explain how they are used today.

OTHER TYPES OF STORAGE SYSTEMS

Remote storage involves using a storage device that is not directly connected to your computer. One example is using a *network storage* device, such as a n**etwork attached storage** (**NAS**) or **storage area network** (**SAN**). Another is **online storage** or **cloud storage**; that is, storage available via the Internet. **Smart cards** contain a chip or other circuitry usually used to store data or a monetary value. **Holographic storage**, which uses multiple blue laser beams to store data in three dimensions, is now available for high-speed data retrieval applications.

Storage systems for larger computers implement many of the same standards as the hard drives used with personal computers. Instead of finding a single set of hard disks inside a hard drive permanently installed within a system unit, however, a **storage server** is often used. **RAID** (**redundant arrays of independent disks**) technology can be used to increase *fault tolerance* and performance. **Magnetic tape** systems store data on plastic tape coated with a magnetizable substance. Magnetic tapes are usually enclosed in cartridges and are inserted into a *tape drive* in order to be accessed.

Chapter Objective 5:
List at least three other types of storage systems.

EVALUATING YOUR STORAGE ALTERNATIVES

Most personal computers today include a hard drive, some type of optical drive, a flash memory card reader, and multiple USB ports that can be used to connect USB-based storage devices, such as external hard drives and USB flash drives, as well as other USB hardware. The type of optical drive and any additional storage devices are often determined by weighing a number of factors, such as cost, speed, compatibility, storage capacity, removability, and convenience.

Chapter Objective 6:
Summarize the storage alternatives for a typical personal computer.

REVIEW ACTIVITIES

KEY TERM MATCHING

a. disk cache

b. file

c. flash memory card

d. folder

e. hard drive

f. holographic storage

g. RAID

h. remote storage

i. solid-state drive (SSD)

j. storage server

Instructions: Match each key term on the left with the definition on the right that best describes it.

1. _____ A named place on a storage medium into which files can be stored to keep the files stored on that medium organized.

2. _____ A hard drive that uses flash memory media instead of metal magnetic hard disks.

3. _____ An emerging type of storage technology that uses multiple blue laser beams to store data in three dimensions.

4. _____ A small, rectangular flash memory medium, such as a CompactFlash (CF) or Secure Digital (SD) card; often used with digital cameras and other portable devices.

5. _____ A storage device designed for large computer systems and that typically contains multiple high-speed hard drives.

6. _____ A storage device that is not directly connected to the computer being used, such as one accessed through a local network or the Internet.

7. _____ A storage method that uses several hard drives working together, typically to increase performance and/or fault-tolerance.

8. _____ Memory used in conjunction with a magnetic hard drive to improve system performance.

9. _____ Something stored on a storage medium, such as a program, a document, or an image.

10. _____ The primary storage system for most computers; used to store most programs and data used with that computer.

SELF-QUIZ

Instructions: Circle **T** if the statement is true, **F** if the statement is false, or write the best answer in the space provided. **Answers for the self-quiz are located in the References and Resources Guide at the end of the book.**

1. **T F** A computer system with a C drive and a D drive must have two physical hard drives.

2. **T F** The smallest amount of space a file on a disk can take up is one cluster.

3. **T F** External hard drives typically connect via a flash memory reader.

4. **T F** A CD-R disc can be written to by the user.

5. **T F** A hybrid hard drive contains both magnetic hard disks and optical discs.

6. The drive letter that would most likely be assigned to the primary hard drive on a typical personal computer is _____.

7. Storage media are not _____, meaning they do not lose their contents when the power is shut off.

8. A single-sided, single-layer CD disc typically holds _____.

9. A(n) _____ looks similar to a credit card but contains a chip and other circuitry that can store data.

10. Secure Digital (SD) cards are one type of _____ medium.

1. Assume, for simplicity's sake, that a kilobyte is 1,000 bytes, a megabyte is 1,000,000 bytes, and a gigabyte is 1,000,000,000 bytes. You have a 500-gigabyte hard drive with the following content:

ITEM	STORAGE SPACE USED
Operating system	65 MB
Other software	1,350 MB
Digital photos and videos	1,000 MB
Other documents	85 MB

   How much storage space is currently being used? _____ How much is left? _____

2. Supply the missing words to complete the following statements.

   a. A(n) _____ disc can hold either 25 GB or 50 GB and is designed for high-definition content, such as movies.

   b. *Thumb drive* is another name for a(n) _____.

   c. Memory used in conjunction with a magnetic hard drive to improve system performance is called a(n) disk _____.

3. Explain why CD-ROM discs are not erasable, but CD+RW discs are.

4. List two possible advantages and two possible disadvantages for using online storage.

5. Which types of storage media would be appropriate for someone who needed to exchange large (5 MB to 75 MB) files with another person? List at least three different types, stating why each might be the most appropriate under specific conditions.

1. There are a number of types of flash memory cards available, such as SD, CF, XD, and memory stick. Is there an advantage to having multiple standards or would it be beneficial to consumers if there was only one flash memory standard, such as just the various sizes of SD cards? Would having a single standard be less expensive and more convenient for consumers? If so, will a single standard naturally evolve or should it be mandated by the storage industry or the government? If you use multiple types of flash memory cards with your devices, would you prefer they all used the same type? Why or why not?

2. People send their digital photos over the Internet in different ways. For instance, digital photos are often e-mailed to others, posted on Facebook pages and other social networking sites, and uploaded to a server (such as one belonging to Snapfish, Wal-Mart, or Costco) in order to order prints, enlargements, or other photo-based items. If you have ever sent photos over the Internet, were you concerned about someone other than the intended recipient intercepting or viewing your photo files? If you have ever uploaded files to a processing service for printing, did you check to see if the Web server being used was secure? Should individuals be concerned about sending their personal photos over the Internet? There are a number of advantages, but are there privacy risks, as well?

PROJECTS

1. **Thumb Drive PCs** As discussed in the chapter Technology and You box, USB flash drives can be used to bring your personal software and settings with you to any computer with which you use that drive. In addition, USB flash drives can be used to securely store files, grant access to a computer, and more.

    For this project, research two features that USB flash drives can provide, in addition to just data storage. For your selected features, determine what the feature does, how it works, what benefits it provides, and some examples of USB flash drives that are currently being sold that include that feature. Is there an additional cost for drives that contain this feature? If so, do you think it is worth the extra cost? Do you think the feature is beneficial? Why or why not? At the conclusion of your research, prepare a one- to two-page summary of your findings and opinions and submit it to your instructor.

2. **Big Brother?** Some of the storage technology used today, such as smart cards, can help facilitate fast and secure access to locked facilities, can protect against the use of stolen credit card numbers, and, when used in conjunction with a biometric characteristic, can unequivocally identify an individual. They can also be used for employee monitoring, such as to identify the location of an employee carrying or wearing his or her smart card at any time. While some people find benefits to the applications just discussed, others worry that smart cards and other devices will be used to track our movements.

    For this project, write a short essay expressing your opinion about the use of smart cards and similar technology to identify individuals for various applications. Is the convenience of smart card technology worth the possible loss of privacy? Do you think employers or the government have the right to track individuals' movements? If so, under what conditions? What are some advantages and disadvantages for the government and your employer always knowing where you are? Have you ever used a smart card or been identified with a biometric system? If so, how do you rate the experience? Submit your opinion on this issue to your instructor in the form of a one-page paper.

3. **Online/Cloud Storage** There are a number of online or cloud storage services (such as ADrive, SkyDrive, and Box.net) designed to allow individuals to back up files online and share specific files with others; specialty online storage services designed for digital photo sharing include Flickr, Photobucket, and SnapFish.

    For this project, visit at least one online/cloud storage site designed for backup and file exchange, and at least one site designed for digital photo sharing. You can try the sites listed above or use a search site to find alternative sites. Tour your selected sites to determine the features each service offers, the cost, the amount of storage space available, and the options for sending uploaded files to others. Do the sites password protect your files, or are they available for anyone with an Internet connection to see? What are the benefits for using these types of storage services? Can you think of any drawbacks? Would you want to use any of the storage sites you visited? Why or why not? At the conclusion of this task, prepare a short summary of your findings and submit it to your instructor.

4. **Lost and Found** Portable computers, mobile phones, USB flash drives, and other portable devices are lost all the time today. They can be dropped out of a pocket or bag, inadvertently left on a table, and so forth. If the owner has identifying information (name, phone number, or e-mail address, for instance) printed on the device, the individual who finds the device can attempt to return it to the owner. But what if there is no identifying information clearly visible on the device? Should the finder look at the contents of the device to try to determine the owner? If the device is lost in a location where there is a responsible party (such as an airplane or a restaurant) the finder can turn over the device to that authority (such as a flight attendant or manager), but is it ethical for the responsible party to look at the contents in order to identify the owner? If you lost a device, would you want someone to look at the contents to try to determine your identity? Why or why not? Is looking at the contents on a found device ever ethical? Should it be illegal?

For this project, form an opinion about the ethical ramifications of lost devices and be prepared to discuss your position (in class, via an online class discussion group, in a class chat room, or via a class blog, depending on your instructor's directions). You may also be asked to write a short paper expressing your opinion.

5. **Flash Cards** There are a wide variety of flash memory card products available today and they can be used with a variety of devices.

For this project, find at least two different examples of flash memory card products in each of the following three categories: user storage; software, music, or movie delivery; and an interface for a peripheral device. Share your findings with the class in the form of a short presentation, including the products that you found, their purpose, what devices they are intended to be used with, and their cost. Be sure to also mention any additional categories or applications using flash cards (in addition to the three categories listed here) that you found doing your research. The presentation should not exceed 10 minutes and should make use of one or more presentation aids, such as the chalkboard, handouts, overhead transparencies, or a computer-based slide presentation (your instructor may provide additional requirements). You may also be asked to submit a summary of the presentation to your instructor.

Instructions: Go to the Chapter 3 page at **www.cengage.com/computerconcepts/np/uc13** to work the following Web Activities.

6. **Interactive Activities** Work the interactive **Crossword Puzzle**, watch the **Video Podcasts** and **Online Videos**, and explore the **Further Exploration** links associated with this chapter.

If you have a SAM user profile, you may have access to hands-on instruction, practice, and assessment of the skills covered in this chapter. Check with your instructor for instructions and the correct URL/Web site to access those assignments.

7. **Student Edition Labs** Work the following interactive **Student Edition Lab**.
   ➤ **Managing Files and Folders**

8. **Test Yourself** Review the **Online Study Guide** for this chapter, then test your knowledge of the terms and concepts covered in this chapter by completing the **Key Term Matching** exercise, the **Self-Quiz**, the **Exercises**, and the **Practice Test**.

chapter 4

Input and Output

After completing this chapter, you will be able to do the following:

1. Explain the purpose of a computer keyboard and the types of keyboards widely used today.

2. List several different pointing devices and describe their functions.

3. Describe the purposes of scanners and readers and list some types of scanners and readers in use today.

4. Explain what digital cameras are and how they are used today.

5. Understand the devices that can be used for audio input.

6. Describe the characteristics of a display device and explain some of the technologies used to display images.

7. List several types of printers and explain their functions.

8. Identify the hardware devices typically used for audio output.

OVERVIEW

In Chapter 2, we learned how data is processed by a computer. The focus of this chapter is on the hardware designed for inputting data into the computer, and then outputting results to the user after the data has been processed. We begin with a look at input. First we discuss the most common input devices used with personal computers—mainly, keyboards and pointing devices (such as a mouse or pen). Next, we discuss hardware designed for capturing data in electronic form (such as scanners, barcode readers, and digital cameras), followed by an overview of the devices that are used to input audio data.

The second part of this chapter explores output devices. Most output today occurs on a screen (via a display device) or on paper (via a printer). Display devices are covered first, including their basic properties and the various types of display devices that are in use today. Next, we discuss printers and then devices used for audio output. Due to the vast number of different types of input and output devices that can be used for various needs, this chapter focuses on the most common types of input and output devices in use today. ∎

KEYBOARDS

Most computers today are designed to be used with a **keyboard**—a device used to enter characters at the location on the screen marked by the *insertion point* or *cursor* (typically a blinking vertical line). Keyboards can be built into a device, attached using a wired cable (such as via a USB or keyboard port), or connected via a wireless connection (such as via a *Bluetooth* wireless networking connection, which is discussed in more detail in Chapter 7). A typical desktop computer keyboard is shown in Figure 4-1. Like most keyboards, this keyboard contains standard *alphanumeric keys* to input text and numbers, as well as additional keys used for various purposes. For instance, this keyboard contains a *numeric keypad* (for entering numbers), *function keys* (for issuing commands in some programs), *Delete* and *Backspace keys* (deleting characters), *Control* and *Alternate keys* (for issuing commands in conjunction with other keys on the keyboard, such as Ctrl+S to save the current document in some programs), and *arrow keys* (for moving around within a document). Some keyboards also contain special keys that are used for a specific purpose, such as to control the speaker volume or DVD playback, or to launch an e-mail program or favorite Web site. To allow individuals to work under a variety of lighting conditions (such as in a dark living room or in an airplane), keyboards today (such as the one in Figure 4-1) are increasingly using *illuminated keys* to light up the characters on the keyboard.

Many computer keyboards today include *touch pads*, *scroll wheels*, and other components for easier control over some functions, such as scrolling through documents. Some keyboards also include a *fingerprint reader* or other *biometric reader* that can be used for

> **Keyboard.** An input device containing numerous keys that can be used to input letters, numbers, and other symbols.

FUNCTION KEYS
Perform a different command or function in each program designed to use them.

TAB KEY
Moves to the next tab location.

CAPS LOCK KEY
Turns all caps on or off.

WINDOWS KEY
Opens the Windows Start menu.

USER PROGRAMMABLE KEYS
Perform functions as defined by the user.

CONTROL AND ALTERNATE KEYS
Used in combination with other keys to enter commands into the computer.

KEYBOARD DISPLAY
Displays images, videos, communication and gaming data, etc.

SPACE BAR
Enters a blank space.

ENTER KEY
Used to enter commands into the computer, end paragraphs, and insert blank lines in documents.

SHIFT KEY
Produces uppercase letters and symbols on the upper part of certain keys when the Caps Lock key is not on.

BACKSPACE KEY
Erases one character to the left of the insertion point.

DELETE KEY
Deletes one character to the right of the insertion point.

ALPHANUMERIC KEYS
Usually arranged in the same order as the keys on a standard typewriter.

MEDIA KEYS
Control music, videos, and images.

SCROLL WHEEL
Scrolls through documents.

INSERT KEY
Toggles between inserting text and typing over text in many programs.

NUMERIC KEYPAD
Used to efficiently enter numerical data.

ARROW KEYS
Move the cursor around a document without disturbing existing text.

PAGE UP AND PAGE DOWN KEYS
Move up or down one page or screen in most programs.

FIGURE 4-1
A typical desktop keyboard.

identification purposes, as discussed in more detail later in this chapter and in Chapter 9. In addition, some keyboards are made for languages other than English, and some keyboards are designed for special purposes, such as to allow easy input for specific systems (a library electronic card catalog or a company database, for instance), to input music into a computer (such as a *MIDI keyboard* used for piano compositions), or to be regularly and easily sterilized (such as keyboards used in hospitals).

Notebook and netbook computers usually have a keyboard that is similar to a desktop keyboard, but it is typically smaller, contains fewer keys (it often has no numeric keypad, for instance), and the keys are typically placed somewhat closer together. Notebook and netbook computer users can also connect and use a conventional keyboard to make inputting data easier if their computer contains an appropriate port (such as a USB port).

Increasingly, ultra-mobile PCs (UMPCs) and mobile devices today have a built-in keyboard; often these are *slide-out keyboards* that can be revealed when needed and hidden when not in use. Many UMPCs and mobile devices also support *pen input* and/or *touch input* (discussed shortly) and can use an *on-screen keyboard* instead of, or in addition to, a physical keyboard (see Figure 4-2). The order and layout of the keys on a mobile device may be different from the order and layout on a conventional keyboard, and the keyboard layout may vary from device to device. If a mobile device does not have a built-in keyboard, a *portable keyboard* (that folds or rolls up and connects to the device via a wired or wireless connection when needed) can often be used with the device for easier data entry. One possibility for the future is printing keyboards directly on clothing and other products that can connect wirelessly to the devices being used. For example, keyboards might be printed on jackets to allow consumers to wirelessly input data or otherwise control their mobile phones while on the go, or keyboards might be printed on soldiers' uniforms to be used with UMPCs or other small computers while in the field.

On-screen keyboard rotates as the device is rotated.

BUILT-IN KEYBOARDS   **SLIDE-OUT KEYBOARDS**   **ON-SCREEN KEYBOARDS**

FIGURE 4-2
Keyboards for mobile devices.

POINTING AND TOUCH DEVICES

In addition to a keyboard, most computers today are used in conjunction with some type of **pointing device**. Pointing devices are used to select and manipulate objects, to input certain types of data (such as handwritten data), and to issue commands to the computer. Two of the most common pointing devices are the *mouse* and the *pen/stylus*, which are used to *click* screen objects and perform *pen input*, respectively; a common pointing device that uses *touch input* is the *touch screen*. For a look at an emerging input option—*gestures*—see the Trend box.

ONLINE VIDEO

Go to the Chapter 4 page at **www.cengage.com/ computerconcepts/np/uc13** to watch the "What Is a 3D Mouse" video clip.

Mice

The **mouse** (see Figure 4-3) is the most common pointing device for a desktop computer. It typically rests on the desk or other flat surface close to the user's computer, and it is moved across the surface with the user's hand in the appropriate direction to point to and select objects on the screen. As it moves, an on-screen *mouse pointer*—usually an arrow—moves accordingly. Once the mouse pointer is pointing to the desired object on the screen, the buttons on the mouse are used to perform actions on that object (such as to open a hyperlink or to resize an image). Similar to keyboards, mice today typically connect via a USB or mouse port, or via a wireless connection.

Older *mechanical mice* have a ball exposed on the bottom surface of the mouse to control the pointer movement. Most mice today are *optical*

FIGURE 4-3
Examples of mice.

A LASER MOUSE

A 3D MOUSE

> **Pointing device.** An input device that moves an on-screen pointer, such as an arrow, to allow the user to select objects on the screen.
> **Mouse.** A common pointing device that the user slides along a flat surface to move a pointer around the screen and clicks its buttons to make selections.

mice or *laser mice* that track movements with light. For use with *virtual worlds*, *animation programs*, and other *3D* applications, *3D mice* are available that are designed to make navigation through a 3D environment easier. For example, the *3Dconnexion SpaceNavigator 3D mouse* shown in Figure 4-3 has a *controller cap*, which can be lifted up to move an object up, rotated to "fly" around objects, or tilted to "look" up. In addition to being used with desktop computers, mice can also be used with portable computers (such as notebook and netbook computers), as long as an appropriate port (such as a USB port) is available. There are also special *cordless presenter* mice that can be used by presenters to control on-screen slide shows.

Mice are used to start programs; open, move around, and edit documents; draw or edit images; and more. Some of the most common mouse commands are described in Figure 4-4.

Pens/Styluses

Many devices today, including some desktop computers and many tablet computers and mobile devices, can accept *pen input*; that is, input by writing, drawing, or tapping on the screen with a pen-like device called a **stylus**. Sometimes, the stylus (also called a *digital pen*, *electronic pen*, or *tablet pen*) is simply a plastic device with no additional functionality; more commonly, it is a pressure-sensitive device that transmits the pressure applied by the user to the device that the stylus is being used with in order to allow more precise input. These more sophisticated styluses also are typically powered by the device that it is being used with, have a smooth rounded tip so they don't scratch the screen, and contain buttons or switches to perform actions such as erasing content or right-clicking.

The idea behind pen input and *digital writing* in general is to make using a computer or other device as convenient as writing with a pen, while adding the functionality that pen input can provide (such as converting pen input to editable typed text). Pen input is being used increasingly for photography, graphic design, animation, industrial design, document processing, and healthcare applications. In addition to supporting handwritten input (referred to as *inking*), digital pens can also be used to navigate through a document and issue commands to the computer (such as to print, delete, copy, and more) via specific gestures with the pen, known as *pen flicks* in Microsoft Windows. Pen input is also a useful alternative to touch input for mobile device users who have long fingernails, who wear gloves in the winter, or who have a device with a screen that is too small to have accurate touch input via a finger. Some of the most common devices that use pen input are discussed next.

Pen-Based Computers

Although their capabilities depend on the type of computer and software being used, pen input can be used with a variety of computer types (see Figure 4-5). Most often, pens are used with mobile devices, UMPCs, and tablet computers to both input handwritten text and sketches, and to manipulate objects (such as to select an option from a menu, select text, or resize an image). They can also be used with a desktop computer if the

POINT
Move the mouse until the mouse pointer is at the desired location on the screen.

CLICK
Press and release the left mouse button.

RIGHT-CLICK
Press and release the right mouse button.

DOUBLE-CLICK
Press and release the left mouse button twice, in rapid succession.

DRAG-AND-DROP
When the mouse pointer is over the appropriate object, press and hold down the left mouse button, drag the object to the proper location on the screen by moving the mouse, and then drop the object by releasing the mouse button.

SCROLL WHEEL/BUTTON
If your mouse has a wheel or button on top, use it to scroll through the displayed document.

FIGURE 4-4
Common mouse operations.

>**Stylus.** An input device that is used to write electronically on the display screen.

TREND

Gesture Input

We already have some devices that support gestures—such as the Nintendo Wii and the Apple iPhone—but some view gesture input as the next step toward making computer input easier and more natural to use. While devices like the Wii and iPhone use special hardware (such as an *accelerometer*) to detect gestures, gesture-based input systems used with computers typically use cameras to detect input based solely on a user's movements. For instance, hand gestures can be used to select and manipulate objects on the screen, similar to the system used by Tom Cruise's character in the movie *Minority Report* to change the images on his display by gesturing with his hands. Gesture input is noncontact, which avoids the fingerprint and germ issues related to public keyboard and touch screen use; it also enables input to be performed from a slight distance (such as through a glass storefront window). In addition, gesture input allows for full body input and, because cameras are used, it can enable the user's image to be imported into the application, such as to have the user's image displayed in a game or virtual world, showing his or her current movements in real time.

Currently, gesture input devices are being used primarily with consumer gaming applications and large screen interactive displays used for advertising purposes (see the accompanying photo) or to convey information in public locations. However, they are also beginning to be used with mobile phones and personal computers and, according to the president and co-founder of Gesturetek (one of the leading companies in gesture input), 3D gesture input is expected to make its way to televisions by 2010.

Gesture input enables the user to control a computer with noncontact hand movements.

monitor supports pen input. Depending on the software being used, handwritten input can be stored as an image, stored as handwritten characters that can be recognized by the computer, or converted to editable, typed text. For the latter two options, software with **handwriting recognition** capabilities must be used.

FIGURE 4-5
Pen-based computers.

Stylus

MOBILE DEVICES

TABLET COMPUTERS

DESKTOP COMPUTERS

>**Handwriting recognition.** The ability of a device to identify handwritten characters.

With handwriting recognition, the computer interprets handwritten pen input as individual characters. For instance, handwritten notes can be converted by the computer to typed notes and data written on a *digital form* (such as the patient assessment form shown in Figure 4-6) can be handwritten and then automatically converted into typed text. The use of handwriting recognition technology in conjunction with digital forms saves time, reduces paper waste, and increases data accuracy. The use of digital forms is growing rapidly and is expected to continue to grow as companies increasingly move toward digital records and digital documents, such as *electronic health records*. In addition, the U.S. government is converting many paper forms to electronic forms. For example, the United States Department of Defense (DoD) has announced a new forms management system that allows nearly 1,000 electronic forms used by DoD entities (including the Army, Navy, Air Force, Marines, Coast Guard, Joint Chiefs of Staff, and the Office of the Secretary of Defense) to be filled out, saved, digitally signed, and submitted electronically. This new system is expected to save time and minimize the need for printed copies.

FIGURE 4-6

Digital forms. If the software supports it, the text handwritten on a digital form can be converted by the computer to typed text.

Digital Writing Systems

Digital writing systems are pen-based systems (such as the one shown in Figure 4-7, which is designed to facilitate student note taking) that capture handwritten input as it is being written. Typically, digital writing systems require the use of special paper that contains a grid of dots so the pen (which contains a camera) can determine what is being written or drawn on the paper and where that data was written on the paper. The handwritten input can be transferred to a computer, typically via a wireless connection when a Send button on the paper is selected or by docking the pen in its cradle attached to a computer. If the pen being used supports handwriting recognition capabilities and the necessary software is installed on the computer, the handwritten text can be converted to typed text.

FIGURE 4-7

Other uses for digital pens.

DIGITAL WRITING SYSTEMS
Record all input written on the paper and transfer it wirelessly to a computer upon demand.

GRAPHICS/PEN TABLETS
Transfer all input written or drawn on the tablet to the computer in real time and allow the use of pen flicks and other pen navigation tools.

SIGNATURE CAPTURE DEVICES
Record signatures for purchases, deliveries, and other applications that require recorded authorization.

Graphics Tablets

A **graphics tablet**—also called a *pen tablet* or *digitizing tablet*—is a flat, touch-sensitive tablet used in conjunction with a digital pen (see Figure 4-7). The graphics tablet is typically connected to a computer via a USB port and anything drawn or written on the graphics tablet is automatically transferred to the connected computer. The graphics tablet can also be used to issue commands to the computer. Graphic artists, photographers, and other graphics professionals often use graphics tablets in conjunction with *image editing software* to create original images or to modify digital photographs. Graphics tablets can also be used to add overall pen capabilities to a computer.

Signature Capture Devices

Another type of pen-based input device is the *signature capture device* (see Figure 4-7). These devices are found most often at checkout counters to record signatures used to authorize credit card purchases electronically. Delivery companies, restaurants, retail stores, and other service businesses may also use a signature capture device—or a portable computer with a stylus and appropriate software—to record authorizing signatures.

Touch Screens

Touch screens allow the user to touch the screen with his or her finger to select commands or otherwise provide input to the computer associated with the touch screen. Their use is becoming common with devices such as personal computers, mobile phones, mobile devices, and consumer kiosks (see Figure 4-8) in order to provide easy input. Some touch screens (such as the one used on the Apple iPhone 3G) are *multi-touch*; that is, they can recognize input from more than one finger at a time. Similar multi-touch products are used for large wall displays, such as for use in

HW

FIGURE 4-8
Touch screens.

DESKTOP COMPUTERS

MOBILE DEVICES

SURFACE COMPUTING DEVICES

CONSUMER KIOSKS

> **Graphics tablet.** A flat, rectangular input device that is used in conjunction with a stylus to transfer drawings, sketches, and anything written on the device to a computer. > **Touch screen.** A display device that is touched with the finger to issue commands or otherwise provide input to the connected device.

ASK THE EXPERT

GestureTek. Vincent John Vincent, President and Co-Founder, GestureTek, Inc.

How is surface computing being used today and how will it be used in the future?

For over 10 years, GestureTek has placed its surface computing systems in public venues, such as malls, airports, stores, and museums. The public loves interacting with multimedia displays through full body or hand gestures, either by being tracked from a distance or close to the display's surface. The intuitive, dynamic nature of these interactions is more like play than information-retrieval, so people engage with these displays much longer than ordinary touch screens. Groups of people even stop others to interact and the whole experience becomes very social. Eventually, as the technology gets cheaper, public landscapes will be filled with these types of interactive displays and the technology will move into the home where every surface of our house can potentially be this type of engaging interactive display.

ONLINE VIDEO

Go to the Chapter 4 page at **www.cengage.com/computerconcepts/np/uc13** to watch the "A Look at Gesture and Multi-Touch Displays" video clip.

museums, government command centers, and newsrooms. For instance, CNN's multi-touch *Magic Wall* was used extensively during the 2008 elections to display maps, photos, videos, charts, and other data during broadcasts, and a similar *Weather Wall* is used by Al Roker on his new *Wake Up with Al* show on The Weather Channel.

One new trend in touch screens is referred to as *surface computing*—using a combination of multi-touch input from multiple users and object recognition to interact with computers that are typically built into tabletops and other surfaces. One example is *Microsoft Surface*. This product (shown in Figure 4-8) uses touch and gestures performed via the screen, as well as objects placed on the screen, as input. It can recognize input from multiple users and multiple objects placed on the table simultaneously. According to Panos Panay, the general manager of Microsoft Surface, Microsoft Surface breaks down the barriers between people and technology—moving beyond the traditional mouse and keyboard experience to blend the physical and virtual worlds—and allows for effortless interaction with digital information in a simple, intuitive way.

Touch screens are also used in consumer kiosks and other point-of-sale (POS) systems, and they are useful for on-the-job applications (such as factory work) where it might be impractical to use a keyboard or mouse. A growing trend is to use touch screens that provide *tactile feedback*—a slight movement or other physical sensation in response to the users' touch so they know their input has been received by the computer. For a closer look at how touch screens work, see the How It Works box. While touch screens make many devices today (computers, mobile phones, televisions, and many other consumer electronics) more convenient for the majority of individuals to use, there is also concern that these devices and their applications are not accessible to blind individuals, users with limited mobility, and other individuals with a disability; accessibility is discussed in detail in Chapter 16.

Other Pointing Devices

A few other common pointing devices are described next and shown in Figure 4-9. In addition to these and the other pointing devices discussed in this chapter, pointing devices specifically designed for users with limited mobility are available. These pointing devices—along with *ergonomic keyboards*, *Braille keyboards*, and other types of input devices designed for users with special needs—are discussed in Chapter 16.

Gaming Devices

A variety of gaming devices today (such as the ones shown in Figure 4-9) can be used as controllers to supply input to a computer. For instance, the stick of a *joystick* can be moved with the hand to move an on-screen object (such as a player or vehicle in a game) and the buttons pressed to perform their assigned functions (such as jumping or firing a weapon). *Gamepads* perform similar functions but are held in the hand instead; *steering wheels* are also available for driving games. There are also input devices designed to be used with gaming consoles, such as the Wii, Xbox 360, and Playstation 3. These include gamepads and steering wheels; guitars, drums, and other musical instruments; dance pads and balance boards, and other motion sensitive controllers; and proprietary controllers such as the *Wii Remote* used with the Nintendo Wii gaming system.

Trackballs

Similar to an upside-down mechanical mouse, a *trackball* has the ball mechanism on top, instead of on the bottom. The ball is rotated with the thumb, hand, or finger to move the on-screen pointer. Because the device itself does not need to be moved, trackballs take up less space on the desktop than mice; they also are easier to use for individuals with limited hand or finger mobility.

Guitar controller

Joystick

Gamepad

Steering wheel

GAMING DEVICES
Most often used for gaming applications.

Thumb wheel

Select button

BUTTONS AND WHEELS
Commonly found on portable digital media players and other consumer devices.

TOUCH PADS
Commonly found on notebook and netbook computers.

FIGURE 4-9
Other common pointing devices.

Buttons and Wheels

Many consumer devices today, such as portable digital media players, GPS devices, and handheld gaming devices, use special buttons and wheels to select items and issue commands to the device. For instance, the portable digital media player shown in Figure 4-9 contains a *thumb wheel* that is rotated to navigate through menus and a *select button* that is used to select items in order to access music and other content stored on the device.

Touch Pads

A **touch pad** is a rectangular pad across which a fingertip or thumb slides to move the on-screen pointer; tapping the touch pad typically performs clicks and other mouse actions. Although most often found on notebook and netbook computers (see Figure 4-9), touch pads are also available as stand-alone devices to be used with desktop computers and are built into some keyboards.

>**Touch pad.** A small rectangular-shaped input device, often found on notebook computers, that is touched with the finger or thumb to control an on-screen pointer and make selections.

HOW IT WORKS

Touch Screens

A touch screen typically has three main components. First, a *touch responsive surface* is needed. Typically, touch screens today use clear (often glass) touch sensitive panels that have an electrical current or charge passing over them whenever the touch screen is on. While there are various methods that can be used to detect the touch input, usually touching the screen causes a voltage or signal change that is registered by the touch screen. Next, a *touch screen controller* uses this data to determine the physical location on the screen that the user touched and passes that information on to the computer being used with the touch screen. Finally, special software determines how to interpret the touch information sent from the controller; for example, to identify the option on the screen that the user selected (such as an item to be purchased) and what action to take as the result of the input (such as adding that item to the individual's order).

One type of touch screen (a *capacitive touch screen*) is shown in the accompanying illustration. Using this method of touch input, a small amount of voltage is present in the four corners of the touch screen at all times when the screen is on. Touching the screen draws a small amount of current from the corners of the screen to the point of contact, allowing the touch screen controller to determine the location on the screen that the user touched and then pass that information on to the computer to determine the appropriate action to be taken.

1. A small amount of voltage is applied to the four corners of the touch screen while it is on.

2. The user's finger draws a tiny amount of current from the corners to the point of contact.

3. The circuitry inside the touch screen uses the voltage change to determine the exact location on the screen that the user touched.

SCANNERS, READERS, AND DIGITAL CAMERAS

There are a variety of input devices designed to capture data in digital form so a computer can manipulate it. Some of these devices (such as *scanners* and *readers*) are designed to convert data that already exists in physical form (such as on *source documents* like order forms, photographs, invoices, checks, ID cards, or shipping labels); others (such as *digital cameras* and the digital writing systems already discussed) capture data initially in digital form. Automating the data entry process is referred to as *source data automation* and can refer to capturing data electronically from a source document or entering data directly into a computer at the time and place the data is generated (see Figure 4-10).

Source data automation can save a great deal of time and is much more accurate than recording the data on paper and then later entering it into a computer via a keyboard. It also allows the people who know the most about the events that the data represents to be the ones who input the data, which helps increase accuracy during the data-entry process. For instance, an insurance adjuster or auto mechanic entering data directly into a computer about the condition of a car involved in an accident will likely have fewer input errors than if he or she records that data on paper, and then an assistant keys the data into a computer later.

Many devices used in source data automation are *scanning* or *reading devices*, that is, devices that scan or read printed text, codes, or graphics, and then translate the results into digital form. The next few sections discuss several different types of scanning and reading devices, followed by a look at *digital cameras*, which capture images in digital form.

Scanners

A **scanner**, more officially called an *optical scanner*, captures an image of an object (usually a flat object, such as a printed document, photograph, or drawing) in digital form, and then transfers that data to a computer. Typically, the entire document (including both text and images) is input as a single graphical

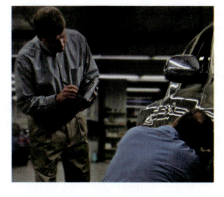

RECORDING DATA DIRECTLY INTO A COMPUTER

CAPTURING DATA FROM ITS SOURCE DOCUMENT

image that can be resized, inserted into other documents, posted on a Web page, e-mailed to someone, printed, or otherwise treated like any other graphical image. The text in the scanned image, however, cannot be edited unless *optical character recognition* (*OCR*) software is used in conjunction with the scanner to input the scanned text as individual text characters.

Individuals frequently use scanners to input printed photographs and other personal documents into a computer. Businesses are increasingly using scanners to convert paper documents into electronic format for archival or document processing purposes. Most scanners scan in color and some are *duplex scanners*—that is, they can scan both sides of a document at one time. The most common types of scanners are discussed next.

FIGURE 4-10
Source data automation. Recording data initially in digital form or capturing data directly from a source document can help reduce data input errors and save time.

Types of Scanners

Flatbed scanners are designed to scan flat objects one page at a time, and they are the most common type of scanner. Flatbed scanners work in much the same way that photocopiers do—whatever is being scanned remains stationary while the scanning mechanism moves underneath it to capture the image (see Figure 4-11). Some scanners can scan slides and

FIGURE 4-11
Optical scanners.

FLATBED SCANNERS
Used to input photos, sketches, slides, book pages, and other relatively flat documents into the computer.

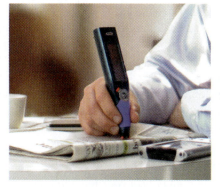

PORTABLE SCANNERS
Used to capture small amounts of text; the text is typically transferred to a computer at a later time.

INTEGRATED SCANNERS
Built into other devices, such as into the ATM machine shown here to capture images of deposited checks.

>**Scanner.** An input device that reads printed text and graphics and transfers them to a computer in digital form. >**Flatbed scanner.** An input device that scans flat objects one at a time.

▼ FIGURE 4-12

Scanning resolution.

96 dpi
(833 KB)

300 dpi
(1,818 KB)

600 dpi
(5,374 KB)

RESOLUTION

Most scanners let you specify the resolution (in dpi) to use for the scan. High-resolution images look sharper but result in larger file sizes.

film negatives, in addition to printed documents. Scanners designed for high-volume business processing come with automatic document feeders so that large quantities of paper documents can be scanned (one page after the other) with a single command.

Portable scanners are designed to capture text and other data while on the go. Some are *full-page portable scanners* that can capture images of an entire document (such as a printed document or receipt) encountered while on the go; others are *handheld scanners* designed to capture text one line at a time (such as the one shown in Figure 4-11). In either case, the scanner is typically powered by batteries, the scanned content is stored in the scanner, and the content is transferred to a computer (via a cable or a wireless connection) when needed. Some handheld scanners can also be used to translate scanned text from one language to another.

Multimedia, medical, and some business applications may require the use of a *three-dimensional (3D) scanner*, which can scan an item or person in 3D. Task-specific scanners, such as *receipt scanners* and *business card scanners*, are also available. In addition, scanning hardware is being incorporated into a growing number of products, such as ATM machines to scan the images of checks deposited into the machine (refer again to Figure 4-11); typically, the check images are printed on the deposit receipt and can be viewed online via online banking services.

Scanning Quality and Resolution

The quality of scanned images is indicated by *optical resolution*, usually measured in the number of *dots per inch* (*dpi*). When a document is scanned (typically using scanning software, though some application programs allow you to scan images directly into that program), the resolution of the scanned image can often be specified. The resolution of a scanned image can also be specified when the image is saved or if it is modified at a later time using an image editing program. Scanners today usually scan at between 2,400 × 2,400 dpi and 4,800 × 9,600 dpi. A higher resolution results in a better image but also results in a larger file size, as illustrated in Figure 4-12. A higher resolution is needed, however, if the image is to be enlarged significantly or if only one part of the image is to be extracted and enlarged. The file size of a scanned image is also determined in part by the physical size of the image. Once an image has been scanned, it can usually be resized and then saved in the appropriate file format and resolution for the application with which the image is to be used. Scanners can cost anywhere from less than one hundred dollars to several thousand dollars.

Readers

A variety of *readers* are available to read the different types of codes and marks used today, as well as to read an individual's *biometric* characteristics. Some of the most common readers are discussed next.

Barcode Readers

A **barcode** is an *optical code* that represents data with bars of varying widths or heights. Two of the most familiar barcodes are *UPC* (*Universal Product Code*), the barcode found on packaged goods in supermarkets and other retail stores, and *ISBN* (*International Standard Book Number*), the type of barcode used with printed books (see Figure 4-13). A new barcode for small consumer goods like fresh foods and jewelry is the *DataBar*,

---

> **Portable scanner.** A scanner designed to capture input while on the go. > **Barcode.** A machine-readable code that represents data as a set of bars.

also shown in Figure 4-13. Businesses and organizations can also create and use custom barcodes to fulfill their unique needs. For instance, shipping organizations (such as FedEx and UPS) use custom barcodes to mark and track packages, retailers (such as Target and Wal-Mart) use custom barcodes added to customer receipts to facilitate returns, hospitals use custom barcodes to match patients with their charts and medicines, libraries and video stores use custom barcodes for checking out and checking in books and movies, and law enforcement agencies use custom barcodes to mark evidence. In fact, any business with a *barcode printer* and appropriate software can create custom barcodes for use with its products or to classify items (such as paper files or equipment) used within its organization. The most popular barcode for these types of nonfood use is *Code 39*, which can encode both letters and numbers. Examples of the Code 39 barcode and the *Intelligent Mail barcode* (used by the U.S. Postal Service to represent destination ZIP codes, as well as shipper IDs and other identifying data specified by the shipper) are shown in Figure 4-13.

These conventional types of barcodes are referred to as *one-dimension (1D) barcodes* because they contain data only horizontally, in one direction. Newer *two-dimensional (2D) barcodes* store information both horizontally and vertically and can hold significantly more data—up to several hundred times more. One of the most common 2D barcodes—the *QR (Quick Response) code* that represents data with a matrix of small bars—is also shown in Figure 4-13. Today, 2D barcodes are beginning to be used by consumers with mobile phones for activities such as viewing a video clip or photo (stored either in the code or online) or downloading a coupon or ticket when the barcode is captured with the phone's camera. In Japan, 2D barcodes are even beginning to appear on tombstones to enable graveside visitors to access information about the deceased via their mobile phones.

Barcodes are read with **barcode readers**. Barcode readers use either light reflected from the barcode or imaging technology to interpret the bars contained in the barcode as the numbers or letters they represent. Then, data associated with that barcode—typically identifying data, such as data used to uniquely identify a product, shipped package, or other item—can be retrieved. *Fixed* barcode readers are frequently used in point-of-sale (POS) systems (see Figure 4-14); *portable* barcode readers are also available for individuals who

ISBN 1-4188-6054-9

ISBN CODES

3 456789 012340

UPC (UNIVERSAL PRODUCT CODE) CODES

DATABAR CODES

INTELLIGENT MAIL CODES

123ABC

CODE 39 CODES

QR CODES

HW

FIGURE 4-13
Common types of barcodes.

FIGURE 4-14
Barcode readers.

FIXED BARCODE READERS
Used most often in retail point-of-sale applications.

PORTABLE BARCODE READERS
Used when portability is needed.

INTEGRATED BARCODE READERS
Used most often for consumer applications.

>**Barcode reader.** An input device that reads barcodes.

need to scan barcodes while on the go, such as while walking through a warehouse, retail store, hospital, or other facility. In addition, barcode reading capabilities can be integrated into portable computers and mobile devices, such as by adding a barcode reader attachment (like the one shown in Figure 2-18 in Chapter 2) or by downloading a barcode reading software program to a camera phone (such as the one shown in Figure 4-14).

Radio Frequency Identification (RFID) Readers

Radio frequency identification (RFID) is a technology that can store, read, and transmit data located in **RFID tags**. RFID tags contain tiny chips and radio antennas (see Figure 4-15); they can be attached to objects, such as products, price tags, shipping labels, ID cards, assets (such as livestock, vehicles, computers, and other expensive equipment), and more. The data in RFID tag is read by **RFID readers**. Whenever an RFID-tagged item is within range of an RFID reader (from two inches to up to 300 feet or more, depending on the type of tag and the frequency being used), the tag's built-in antenna allows the information located within the RFID tag to be sent to the reader. Unlike barcodes, RFID tags only need to be within range (not within line of sight) of a reader. This enables RFID readers to read the data stored in many RFID tags at the same time and read them through cardboard and other materials—a definite advantage for shipping and inventory applications. Another advantage over barcodes is that the RFID tag attached to each item is unique (unlike UPC codes, for instance, that have the same code on all instances of a single product), so each tag can be identified individually and the data can be updated as needed. RFID technology is cost-prohibitive for low-cost items at the present time; however, the many advantages RFID has over barcodes make it possible that RFID may eventually replace barcodes on product labels and price tags—especially as the costs associated with RFID technology go down and its usage becomes even more commonplace. Because RFID technology can read numerous items at one time, it is also possible that, someday, RFID will allow a consumer to perform self-checkout at a retail store by just pushing a shopping cart past an RFID reader, which will ring up all items in the cart at one time.

Label for shipping carton

RFID circuitry (chip and antenna)

FIGURE 4-15
RFID tags.

RFID is used today for many different applications (see Figure 4-16 for some examples). Some of the initial RFID applications were tracking the movement of products and shipping containers during transit, managing inventory in retail stores, tagging pets and livestock, and tracking tractors and other large assets. Many of these applications use GPS technology in conjunction with the RFID tags to provide location information for the objects to which the tags are attached. For several years now, RFID has also been used for *electronic toll collection* (automatically deducting highway tolls from a payment account when an RFID-tagged car drives past the tollbooth). More recent RFID applications include tracking patients at hospitals, increasing efficiency in ticketing applications (such as train passes, concert tickets, and ski lift tickets), and speeding up the identification process of travelers at border crossings. In the United States, for instance, several states are issuing *enhanced driver's licenses* that contain RFID chips, and all *U.S. Passports* and *U.S. Passport Cards* issued today contain RFID chips. RFID is also used to facilitate *electronic payments* via RFID-enabled credit cards or mobile phones that support *Near Field Communications* (*NFC*)—a short-range wireless communication standard used in conjunction with RFID and mobile phones. For security purposes, *high-frequency RFID chips* (which requires the item containing the RFID chip to be within an inch or so of the reader) are used in electronic payment applications. Electronic payments, NFC, and *mobile commerce* are discussed in more detail in Chapter 11.

In addition, because RFID chips can be updated during the life of a product (such as to record information about a product's origin, shipping history, and the temperature range the item has been exposed to), and because that information can be read when needed (such as at a product's final destination), RFID is being used by prescription drug manufacturers to comply with government mandates, which require that the drugs be tracked throughout their life cycles. While not mandated yet (though some believe it is just a matter of time), RFID is also beginning to be used to implement life cycle tracking of food products in response to the recent food poisoning outbreaks. For instance, Hawaii recently implemented a three-year pilot RFID initiative to track all fresh produce throughout the state in order to obtain information about the grower, pesticides used, time in cold storage, and other factors when needed, as well as to facilitate recalls. RFID is also used extensively by the military, primarily for asset tracking.

INVENTORY TRACKING
This portal RFID reader reads all of the RFID tags attached to all of the items on the palette at one time.

TICKETING APPLICATIONS
This stationary RFID reader is used to automatically open ski lift entry gates for valid lift ticket holders at a ski resort in Utah.

MOBILE PAYMENTS
This stationary RFID reader is used at checkout locations to quickly process payments via RFID-enabled credit cards or mobile phones.

BORDER SECURITY
This stationary RFID reader is used at the U.S.-Mexico border crossing located in San Diego to reduce wait time.

FIGURE 4-16
RFID applications.

A variety of RFID readers—including *handheld*, *portal*, and *stationery RFID readers*—are available to fit the various RFID applications in use today. Handheld RFID readers are used by workers to read RFID tags on the go or to read RFID-enabled tickets at a venue entrance. Portal RFID readers are used to read all the RFID tags located on all the products located inside sealed shipping boxes on a palette at one time when the palette passes through the portal. Stationary RFID readers are used at checkstands, border crossings, and other locations where RFID tags need to be read on a continual basis. A portal reader and a few stationary readers are shown in Figure 4-16.

Despite all its advantages, a number of privacy and security issues need to be resolved before RFID gains widespread use at the consumer level. Precautions against fraudulent use—such as using high-frequency tags that need to be within a few inches of the reader, and requiring a *PIN code*, signature, or other type of authorization when an RFID payment system is used—are being developed. Currently, a price limit (such as $25) for completely automated purchases (without a signature or other authorization) is being debated as a compromise between convenience and security. Privacy advocates are concerned about linking RFID tag data with personally-identifiable data contained in corporate databases, such as to track consumer movements or shopping habits. As of now, no long-term solution to this issue has been reached.

▼ **FIGURE 4-17**

Optical mark readers (OMRs).

OMRs are commonly used to score tests and tally questionnaires.

CAUTION   CAUTION   CAUTION   CAUTION   CAUTION   CAUTION   CAUT

Keep your enhanced driver's license and passport in the supplied protective sleeve when not in use to protect against unauthorized reading or tracking. While currently no personal data is stored in the RFID chips used in these documents, hackers have demonstrated the ability to read these documents if they are not properly shielded. Because of this, privacy advocates recommend taking this precaution with any RFID-enabled identity document.

Optical Mark Readers (OMRs)

Optical mark readers (*OMRs*) input data from special forms to score or tally exams, questionnaires, ballots, and so forth. Typically, you use a pencil to fill in small circles or other shapes on the form to indicate your selections, and then the form is inserted into an optical mark reader (such as the one shown in Figure 4-17) to be scored or tallied. The results can be input into a computer system if the optical mark reader is connected to a computer.

Optical Character Recognition (OCR) Devices

Optical character recognition (OCR) refers to the ability of a computer to recognize text characters. The characters are read by a compatible scanning device, such as a flatbed scanner, barcode reader, or dedicated *OCR reader*, and then *OCR software* is used to identify each character and convert it to editable text. While OCR systems can recognize many typed fonts, *optical characters*—which are characters specifically designed to be identifiable by humans as well as by an OCR device—are often used on documents intended to be processed by an OCR system. For example, optical characters are widely used in processing *turnaround documents*, such as the monthly bills for credit card and

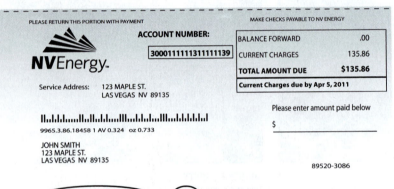

OPTICAL CHARACTERS
These OCR characters indicate the customer account number and amount due and can be read by both computers and humans.

▲ **FIGURE 4-18**

Optical characters.

The most common use of optical characters is in turnaround documents, such as on the utility bill shown here.

utility companies (see Figure 4-18). These documents contain optical characters in certain places on the bill to aid processing when consumers send it back with payment—or "turn it around."

Magnetic Ink Character Recognition (MICR) Readers

Magnetic ink character recognition (*MICR*) is a technology used primarily by the banking industry to facilitate check processing. MICR characters (such as those located on the bottom of a check that represent the bank routing number, check number, and account number) are inscribed on checks with magnetic ink when the checks are first printed.

> **Optical character recognition (OCR).** The ability of a computer to recognize scanned text characters and convert them to electronic form as text, not images.

TECHNOLOGY AND YOU

Mobile Phone Check Deposits

You use your mobile phone today for a wide number of functions—such as phone calls, texting, accessing Web information, and storing music and photos—but depositing your paychecks? Yes, now you can, thanks to a new technology developed by Mitek Systems.

While the use of remote deposit by businesses is growing, this new technology opens the door to remote deposit by individuals. In order to make a remote deposit via your mobile phone, you need to have the mobile deposit application on your mobile phone (if it is not included in your mobile banking software, you can typically download it). To make a remote deposit, you simply need to log on to your mobile banking service, and then you can enter the amount of the check and use your phone's built-in camera to take a photo of the front and back of the check (see the accompanying photo) in order to deposit that check into your bank account. After the software optimizes the image and verifies it meets the Check 21 Law image standards, the check images and deposit data are transmitted to your bank and you receive a confirmation text message. The software can be used with virtually any mobile banking system and a secure connection is used to protect the data as it is being transmitted.

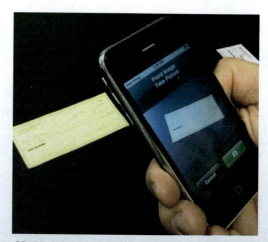

Mobile phone cameras can be used to submit check images for remote deposit.

These characters can be read and new characters (such as to reflect the check's amount) can be added by an *MICR reader* (also called a *check scanner*) when needed. High-volume MICR readers are used by banks to process checks deposited at the bank. Smaller units (such as the one shown in Figure 4-19) are used by many businesses to deposit paper checks remotely (referred to as *remote deposit* and permitted by the *Check 21 Law*, which allows financial institutions to exchange digital check images and process checks electronically). To make a remote deposit using an MICR reader, the check is scanned and then the check data is transmitted to the bank electronically for payment. There are also MICR readers incorporated in most new ATM machines today to enable the MICR information located on checks inserted into the ATM machine to be read at the time of the deposit.

Remote deposit and electronic check processing is a growing trend. It is faster and more convenient for businesses and individuals. It also helps the environment since, according to one estimate, a typical check travels 48 miles during processing, which results in an annual cost to the environment for check processing of more than 80,000 tons of paper used and more than 160 million gallons of fuel consumed. In addition to MICR readers, remote deposit can be performed by using a flat-bed scanner or, as discussed in the Technology and You box, even by using your mobile phone.

FIGURE 4-19
Magnetic ink character recognition (MICR) readers are used primarily to process checks.

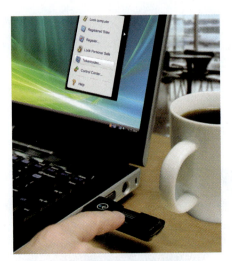

STAND-ALONE FINGERPRINT READERS
Often used to control access to facilities or computer systems, such as to the notebook computer shown here.

BUILT-IN FINGERPRINT READERS
Typically used to control access to the device into which the reader is built, such as to the external hard drive shown here.

FIGURE 4-20
Biometric readers.

Biometric Readers

Biometrics is the science of identifying individuals based on measurable biological characteristics. **Biometric readers** are used to read biometric data about a person so that the individual's identity can be verified based on a particular unique physiological characteristic (such as a fingerprint or a face) or personal trait (such as a voice or a signature). As shown in Figure 4-20, a biometric reader can be stand-alone or built into another piece of hardware, such as a keyboard, a portable computer, an external hard drive, or a USB flash drive. Biometric readers can be used to allow only authorized users access to a computer or facility or to the data stored on a storage device, as well as to authorize electronic payments, log on to secure Web sites, or punch in and out of work. Biometrics used for access control is covered in more detail in Chapter 9.

ONLINE VIDEO

Go to the Chapter 4 page at **www.cengage.com/ computerconcepts/np/uc13** to watch the "How Mobile Deposit Works" video clip.

TIP

When comparing the zoom capabilities of a digital camera, look for *optical zoom*, not *digital zoom*, specifications. Optical zoom specifications reflect how much the camera can zoom without losing image quality.

Digital Cameras

Digital cameras work much like conventional film cameras, but instead of recording images on film they record them on a digital storage medium, such as a flash memory card, digital tape cartridge, built-in hard drive, or DVD disc. Digital cameras are usually designated either as *still* cameras (which take individual still photos) or *video* cameras (which capture moving video images), although many cameras today take both still images and video. In addition to stand-alone still and video cameras, digital camera capabilities are integrated into many portable computers and mobile phones today.

Digital Still Cameras

Digital still cameras are available in a wide variety of sizes and capabilities, such as inexpensive point-and-shoot digital cameras designed for consumers, professional digital cameras, and digital cameras integrated into mobile phones and other mobile devices (see Figure 4-21). Consumer digital cameras start at about $50; professional digital cameras can cost several thousand dollars each.

The primary appeal of digital still cameras is that the images are immediately available for viewing or printing, instead of having to have the film developed first. One disadvantage of digital cameras is the slight delay between when the user presses the button and when the camera takes the photo, which is especially important when taking action shots. Although not yet as quick as conventional film cameras, the delay typically associated with digital cameras is continually being made shorter. Digital still cameras most often use flash memory cards for storage; the number of digital photos that can be stored at one

>**Biometric reader.** A device used to input biometric data, such as an individual's fingerprint or voice. >**Digital camera.** An input device that takes pictures and records them as digital images.

time depends on the capacity of the card being used, as well as the photo resolution being used.

Photos taken with a digital camera are typically transferred to a computer or printer via the flash memory card containing the images or by connecting the camera to the computer or printer using a wired or wireless connection. Some digital cameras and flash memory cards can even connect directly to photo sharing Web sites via a *Wi-Fi* connection, as discussed in the Chapter 7 Trend box, to upload your photos automatically as they are taken. Once the photos have been transferred to a computer, they can be retouched with image editing software, saved, printed, posted to a Web page, or burned onto a CD or DVD disc, just like any other digital image. The images on the storage medium can be deleted at any time to make room for more photos.

One factor affecting digital camera quality is the number of pixels (measured in *megapixels* or millions of pixels) used to store the data for each image. Today's cameras are typically between 6 and 20 megapixels. Although other factors—such as the quality of the lens and the technology used inside the camera to capture and process images— also affect the quality of digital photographs, the number of pixels does impact how large the digital photos can be printed. For instance, to print high-quality 8 by 10-inch or larger prints, at least a 5-megapixel camera is needed.

The integration of digital cameras into most mobile phones today has many advantages, such as the ability to keep your friends up to date about your current activities; to take photos of car accidents and other incidents for authorities; and to read barcodes, remotely deposit checks, and facilitate gesture input, as discussed earlier in this chapter. However, they have also created new ethical problems in our society, such as the ability to take and distribute compromising photos. For instance, there have been many cases of individuals using camera phones to take and distribute compromising photos of others, as well as cases of teenagers using camera phones to send compromising photos of themselves to others (a form of *sexting*, as discussed in more detail in Chapter 9).

PREVIEWS
Virtually all digital cameras let you display and erase images.

STORAGE MEDIA
Most cameras use removable storage media in addition to, or instead of, built-in storage.

TYPICAL CONSUMER DIGITAL CAMERAS

PROFESSIONAL DIGITAL CAMERAS

DIGITAL CAMERAS INTEGRATED INTO MOBILE PHONES

FIGURE 4-21
Digital cameras.
Digital cameras, which record images on digital media instead of on film, are available in many shapes and sizes.

ASK THE EXPERT

SanDisk® **Tanya Chuang,** Director of Worldwide Retail Product Marketing, High Performance Imaging, SanDisk

Does the speed of the flash memory card in a digital camera affect the delay factor when taking a digital photo?

The performance is important for both the camera and card. If you have a fast camera but a slow card, or vice versa, you can miss some great shots. If you've ever pressed the shutter button and have had to wait for 5 seconds to take a picture, you'll understand the frustration. At one point, up to early 2000, the cards were too slow. Now, the memory cards are much faster than the cameras so it's important to have the right card for your camera.

DIGITAL CAMCORDERS
Typically store video on a built-in hard drive (as in this camera) or on DVD discs.

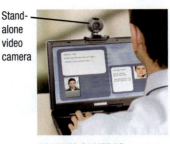

Standalone video camera

PC VIDEO CAMERAS
Commonly used to deliver video over the Internet, such as in the video chat session shown here.

FIGURE 4-22
Digital video cameras.

Digital Video Cameras

Digital video cameras (see Figure 4-22) include *digital camcorders* and small digital video cameras used in conjunction with computers and other devices. Digital video cameras are often built into portable computers and mobile devices, but they are also available as stand-alone devices that typically connect via a USB port. Digital camcorders are similar to conventional *analog* camcorders, but they store images on digital media—typically on built-in hard drives or rewritable DVDs for conventional-sized camcorders or on flash memory for pocket-sized camcorders. Many mobile phones also include digital video capabilities. Once a video is recorded, it can be transferred to a computer, edited with software as needed, and saved to a DVD or other type of storage medium. It can also be *compressed* (made smaller), if needed, and then uploaded to video-sharing sites, such as YouTube. Some digital video cameras today can take high-definition (HD) video. Video cameras used with personal computers—commonly called *PC cams* or *Web cams*—are typically used to transmit still or video images over the Internet (such as during a *Web conference* or *video phone call*) or to broadcast images continually to a Web page.

Both individuals and businesses commonly use digital video cameras today. Typical personal applications include recording home movies with a digital camcorder and making video phone calls with a PC cam. An emerging personal application is using special *home surveillance video cameras* for security purposes—such as to monitor an empty house or keep an eye on a sleeping baby. Typically, these systems either transmit the video via the Internet to a computer or mobile device, or via a wireless connection to a special display device located in the home. Their use is growing and has had some initial success. In 2009, for instance, a woman checked her home surveillance video via the Internet while at work, saw her house being robbed, and notified the police, who were able to catch the individuals in her house and charge them with burglary. Businesses also often use digital video cameras for security applications, as well as to create videos for marketing purposes and to perform *videoconferences* and *Webinars* (seminars that take place via the Web). Digital video cameras can also be used for identification purposes, such as with the *face recognition technology* used to authorize access to a secure facility or computer resource via an individual's face, as discussed in more detail in Chapter 9.

AUDIO INPUT

Audio input is the process of entering audio data into the computer. The most common types of audio input are voice and music.

Voice Input and Speech Recognition Systems

Voice input—inputting spoken words and converting them to digital form—is typically performed via a *microphone* or *headset* (a set of *headphones* with a built-in microphone). It can be used in conjunction with *sound recorder software* to store the voice in an audio file, such as to create a *podcast*—a recorded audio file that is distributed via the Internet, as discussed in Chapter 8, as well as with *Voice over IP systems* that allow individuals to place telephone calls from a computer over the Internet. It can also be used in conjunction with *speech recognition software* to provide spoken instructions to a computer.

Speech recognition systems enable the computer to recognize voice input as spoken words and require appropriate software, such as *Dragon NaturallySpeaking* or *Windows Speech Recognition*. With speech recognition, voice input can be used to control the computer, such as opening and closing programs, selecting options from a menu or list, and moving the insertion point. It can also be used to input and edit text, including dictating text to be typed, selecting text to be formatted or edited, deleting text, correcting errors, and so forth. Voice input systems are used by individuals who cannot use a keyboard, as well as by individuals who prefer not to use a keyboard or who can generate input faster via a voice input system. For instance, medical and legal transcription is the most frequently used voice input application at the present time.

To enable hands-free operation, speech recognition capabilities are increasingly incorporated into mobile phones, GPS systems, and other mobile devices. They are also commonly built into cars to enable hands-free control of navigation systems and sound systems, as well as to allow hands-free mobile phone calls to take place via the car's voice interface. Specialty speech recognition systems are frequently used to control machines, robots, and other electronic equipment, such as by surgeons during surgical procedures.

With a typical speech recognition system (see Figure 4-23), a microphone is used to input the spoken words into the computer, and then the sounds are broken into digital representations of *phonemes*—the basic elements of speech, such as *duh*, *aw*, and *guh* for the word *dog*. Next, the speech recognition software analyzes the content of the speech to convert the phonemes to words. Once words are identified, they are displayed on the screen. If a match is questionable or a homonym is encountered (such as the choice between *two*, *too*, and *to*), the program analyzes the context in which the word is used in an attempt to identify the correct word. If the program inserts an inappropriate word while converting the user's voice input to text, the user can correct it. To increase accuracy, most speech recognition software can be trained by individual users to allow the program to become accustomed to the user's speech patterns, voice, accent, and pronunciation.

The basic concept of speech recognition is also being applied to other audio input applications that enable computers and devices to recognize sounds other than voice. For instance, one type of *sound recognition* system located inside a computer could monitor the sound a hard drive is making to detect a possible malfunction before it happens, and another type could be used in conjunction with security systems to "listen" for the sound of a door opening or other suspicious sounds in order to alert security personnel.

FIGURE 4-23
Speech recognition systems.

The patient exhibits signs of...

2. An analog-to-digital converter on the sound card located inside the computer converts the spoken words to phonemes, the fundamental sounds in the language being used, and digitizes them.

The patient exhibits signs of|

1. The user speaks into a microphone that cancels out background noise and inputs the speech into the computer.

4. The spoken words appear on the screen in the application program (such as a word processor or an e-mail program) being used.

3. Voice recognition software determines the words that were spoken.

>**Speech recognition system.** A system, consisting of appropriate hardware and software, used to recognize voice input, such as dictation or audio computer commands.

Music Input Systems

Music input systems are used to input music into a computer, such as to create an original music composition or arrangement, or to create a custom music CD. Existing music can be input into a computer via a music CD or a Web download. For original compositions, microphones and *keyboard controllers*—essentially piano keyboards connected to a computer—can be used (see Figure 4-24). Original music compositions can also be created using a conventional computer keyboard with appropriate software or a special device (such as a microphone or digital pen) designed to input music and convert it to a printed musical score. Once the music is input into the computer, it can be saved, modified, played, inserted into other programs, or burned to a CD or DVD.

FIGURE 4-24

Music input systems. Musicians can input original compositions into a computer via microphones, MIDI keyboards, and other devices.

DISPLAY DEVICES

A **display device**—the most common form of output device—presents output visually on some type of screen. Because the output appears temporarily on a display device, it is sometimes referred to as *soft copy*. The display device for a desktop computer is more formally called a **monitor**; the display device for a notebook computer, netbook computer, UMPC, mobile phone, or other device for which the screen is built into the device is typically called a **display screen**. In addition to being used with computers and mobile devices, display screens are also built into handheld gaming devices, home entertainment devices (like remote controls, televisions, and portable DVD players) and kitchen appliances. They are also an important component in *digital photo frames* (stand-alone or wall mounted photo frames, which display digital photos that are typically transferred to the frame via a flash memory card or a wireless networking connection), *e-book readers* (which display electronic versions of books), portable digital media players, and other consumer products (see Figure 4-25).

Display screens also appear in public locations on *digital signage systems*—digital signs whose content can be changed throughout the day as needed. The content displayed on a digital sign can be graphics or video sent from a computer, video streamed via a camera, live Internet content, and more. For instance, the digital signage system shown in Figure 4-25 is located in Times Square in New York and displays advertising clips, live broadcasts, public service announcements, and video of special events taking place at Times Square in the main screen at the top of the display, and real-time CNN.com news feeds and weather forecasts in the bottom screen. In addition to these types of *digital billboard* applications, digital signage systems are also frequently used in office buildings and convention centers (such as for directories and other information), in retail stores and restaurants (to advertise specials and to display menus, for instance), on consumer kiosks, in lecture halls, and in sporting arenas. They are even found in displays used to target advertising to consumers when they are waiting in a checkout line, riding in an elevator or taxi, stopped at a traffic light, or some other location where they are captive for a few minutes—a trend referred to as *captive marketing*.

ONLINE VIDEO

Go to the Chapter 4 page at **www.cengage.com/ computerconcepts/np/uc13** to watch the "An Introduction to Digital Signage" video clip.

Display Device Characteristics

Several characteristics and features differentiate one type of display device from another. The following sections discuss a few of the most significant characteristics.

>**Display device.** An output device that contains a viewing screen. >**Monitor.** A display device for a desktop computer. >**Display screen.** A display device built into a notebook computer, netbook, UMPC, or other device.

PORTABLE COMPUTERS

HANDHELD GAMING DEVICES

DIGITAL PHOTO FRAMES

MOBILE DEVICES

DIGITAL SIGNAGE SYSTEMS

FIGURE 4-25

Uses for display devices.

Color vs. Monochrome Displays

Display devices form images by lighting up the proper configurations of **pixels** (the smallest colorable areas on a display device—essentially tiny dots on a display screen). A variety of technologies can be used to light up the appropriate pixels needed to display a particular image, as discussed shortly. Display devices can be *monochrome displays* (in which each pixel can only be one of two colors, such as black or white) or *color displays* (in which each pixel can display a combination of three colors—red, green, and blue—in order to display a large range of colors). Most monitors and display devices today are color displays.

CRT Monitors vs. Flat-Panel Displays

The **CRT monitor** used to be the norm for desktop computers. CRT monitors use the same *cathode-ray tube* technology used in conventional televisions in which an electron gun sealed inside a large glass tube projects an electron beam at a screen coated with red, green, and blue phosphor dots; the beam lights up the appropriate colors in each pixel to display the necessary image. As a result, CRTs are large, bulky, and heavy.

> **Pixel.** The smallest colorable area in an electronic image, such as a scanned image, a digital photograph, or an image displayed on a display screen. > **CRT monitor.** A type of display device that projects images onto a display screen using a technology similar to the one used with conventional TVs.

Four flat-panel monitors.

While CRT monitors are still in use, most computers today (as well as most television sets) use the thinner and lighter **flat-panel displays**. Flat-panel display technology is also used in the display screens integrated into mobile phones and consumer electronics. As discussed in more detail shortly, flat-panel displays form images by manipulating electronically charged chemicals or gases sandwiched between thin panes of glass or other transparent material. Flat-panel displays take up less desk space, which makes it possible to use multiple monitors working together to increase the amount of data the user can view at one time (see Figure 4-26), increasing productivity. Flat-panel displays also consume less power than CRTs and most use digital signals to display images (instead of the analog signals used with CRT monitors), which allows for sharper images. To use multiple monitors, you must have the necessary hardware to support it, such as a monitor port on a notebook computer or an appropriate video adapter, as discussed shortly. One disadvantage to a flat-panel display is that the images displayed on a flat-panel display sometimes cannot be seen clearly when viewed from certain angles.

FIGURE 4-26

Flat-panel displays. The smaller footprint of a flat-panel display makes it possible to use multiple monitors together with a single computer to increase productivity.

Size and Aspect Ratio

Display device size is measured diagonally from corner to corner, in a manner similar to the way TV screens are measured. Most desktop computer monitors today are between 17 inches and 27 inches (though larger screens—up to 60 inches and more—are becoming increasingly common); notebook and tablet displays are usually between 15 inches and 20 inches; and netbooks typically have displays that are 10 inches or smaller. To better view DVDs and other multimedia content, many monitors today are *widescreen displays*, which conform to the *16:9 aspect ratio* of widescreen televisions, instead of the conventional *4:3 aspect ratio*.

FIGURE 4-27

Screen resolution. A higher screen resolution (measured in pixels) displays more content than a lower screen resolution, but everything is displayed smaller.

Screen Resolution

Regardless of the technology used, the screen of a display device is divided into a fine grid of tiny pixels, as previously discussed. The number of pixels used on a display screen determines the *screen resolution*, which affects the amount of information that can be displayed on the screen at one time. When a higher resolution is selected, such as 1,280 pixels horizontally by 1,024 pixels vertically for a standard computer monitor (written as 1,280 × 1,024 and read as *1280 by 1024*), more information can fit on the screen, but everything will be displayed smaller than with a lower resolution, such as 1,024 × 768 (see Figure 4-27). The screen resolution on many computers today can be changed by users to match their preferences and the software being used. On Windows computers,

1,024 × 768   1,280 × 1,024

---

display options are changed using the Control Panel. When multiple monitors are used, typically the screen resolution of each display can be set independently of the others. Very high-resolution monitors are available for special applications, such as viewing digital X-rays.

Video Adapters, Interfaces, and Ports

The *video card* installed inside a computer or the integrated graphics component built directly into the motherboard of the computer houses the *graphics processing unit* (*GPU*)— the chip devoted to rendering images on a display device. The video card or the integrated graphics component determines the graphics capabilities of the computer, including the screen resolutions available, the number of bits used to store color information about each pixel (called the *bit depth*), the total number of colors that can be used to display images, the number of monitors that can be connected to the computer via that video card or component, and the types of connectors that can be used to connect a monitor to the computer. Video cards typically contain a fan and other cooling components to cool the card. Most video cards also contain memory chips (typically called *video RAM* or *VRAM*) to support graphics display, although some do not and are designed to use a portion of the com-

puter's regular RAM as video RAM instead. To support higher resolutions, higher bit depths, and a greater number of colors, a sufficient amount of video RAM is required. Most video cards today contain between 256 MB and 1 GB of video RAM. A typically video card is shown in Figure 4-28.

The three most common types of interfaces used to connect a monitor to a computer are *VGA* (*Video Graphics Array*), *DVI* (*Digital Visual Interface*), and

VGA   **DVI**   **TV-OUT**   **HDMI**

FAN
Cools the components on the video card.

GPU
Renders images on the display screen (is located beneath the fan on this card for cooling purposes).

DISPLAYPORT

PORTS
Determine how a monitor can connect.

PCI EXPRESS x16 CONNECTOR
Plugs into the PCIe x16 slot on the motherboard.

VIDEO RAM CHIPS
Provide memory for video display (are located beneath the heat sinks on this card for cooling purposes).

FIGURE 4-28
Video cards. Provide a connection to a monitor, as well as determine video capabilities.

HDMI (*High-Definition Multimedia Interface*). VGA uses a 15-pin D-shaped connector and it is commonly used with CRT monitors and many flat-panel monitors to transfer analog images to the monitor. DVI uses a more rectangular connector and it is frequently used with flat-panel displays to allow the monitor to receive clearer, more reliable digital signals than is possible with a VGA interface. HDMI uses a smaller connector and can be used with display devices that support high-definition content. A newer type of connector is *DisplayPort*, which is designed to eventually replace VGA and DVI ports on computers, video cards, and monitors. In fact, Apple already includes a smaller version—referred to as a *Mini DisplayPort*—on its newest MacBooks. The ports used with each of these possible connections are illustrated in Figure 4-28.

A video card or integrated video component in a desktop computer will have at least one port exposed through the system unit case to connect a monitor. Notebook computers and other computers with a built-in display typically contain a monitor port to connect a second monitor to the computer. An emerging option is connecting monitors to a computer via a USB port. *USB monitors* (monitors designed to connect via a USB port) can be added to a computer without requiring a video card that supports multiple monitors. Conventional monitors can also connect to a computer via a USB port if a *USB display adapter* (such

HW

A USB port on this side of the adapter connects the adapter to the computer.

A DVI cable connects the display device to the adapter.

FIGURE 4-29
A USB display adapter.

as the one shown in Figure 4-29) or a peripheral device (such as a docking station) that includes USB display capabilities is used. A USB connection allows multiple monitors to be connected easily to a device. For instance, many USB monitors are designed to be *daisy-chained* together so they all connect via a single USB port, and multiple USB display adapters (such as the one shown in Figure 4-29) can typically be used to connect multiple conventional monitors to a single computer.

Wired vs. Wireless Displays

Most computer monitors today are *wired displays*; that is, monitors that are physically connected to the system unit via a cable. Some display devices—such as digital photo frames, e-book readers, and some computer monitors and television sets, however—are designed to be wireless. *Wireless displays* connect to a computer using a wireless networking connection such as *Wi-Fi* or *Bluetooth* (discussed in more detail in Chapter 7), typically display content from a computer located within range of the monitor, and may support touch or pen input for when the display is used away from the computer.

Display is built into eyeglasses, which connect to a mobile device.

Images from the source device (an e-mail message in this example) are displayed on top of the user's normal vision.

FIGURE 4-30
3D wearable displays.

2D vs. 3D Displays

Recent improvements in flat-panel display technology and graphics processing have led to several emerging *three-dimensional (3D) output devices*, including *3D display screens* for computers. While traditional 3D displays require special 3D glasses, the newest 3D products use filters, prisms, multiple lenses, and other technologies built into the display screen to create the 3D effect and, as a result, do not require 3D glasses. Some 3D displays resemble conventional monitors; others are shaped differently, such as the dome-shaped *Perspecta* 3D display. Perspecta is used primarily for medical imaging; scientists, architects, and other professionals who routinely view detailed graphics or diagrams in the course of their work also frequently use 3D displays.

Other 3D displays are designed to be wearable. A *3D wearable display* (such as the eyeglasses-based display shown in Figure 4-30) projects the image from a mobile device (typically a mobile phone or portable digital media player) to a display screen built into the glasses. Typically, the technology allows the user to see the image as if it is on a distant large screen display, and many 3D wearable displays overlay the projected image on top of what the user is seeing in real time in order to provide situational awareness while the display is being used. While 3D wearable displays have entertainment applications, there are also wearable 3D displays designed for soldiers and other mobile workers.

Touch and Gesture Capabilities

As discussed earlier in this chapter, it is increasingly common for monitors and display screens to support touch input. Touch screen displays are commonly used with personal computers, as well as with consumer kiosks, portable gaming devices, mobile phones, portable digital media players, and other consumer devices. Gesture input is beginning to become available with these products as well. According to Francis MacDougall, Co-Founder and Chief Technology Officer of GestureTek, that company is working with major telecom companies and electronics manufacturers to enable gesture control for their set top boxes, consoles, and other consumer electronics devices.

Flat-Panel Display Technologies

The most common flat-panel technologies include *liquid crystal display* (*LCD*), various types of *light emitting diode* (*LED*), and *gas plasma*. Emerging flat-panel technologies include *interferometric modulator display* (*IMOD*) and *surface-conduction electron-emitter display* (*SED*). These display technologies are discussed next. Another technology used by some flat-panel displays (including e-book readers, some digital signage systems, and the display on some wristwatches and USB flash drives) is *e-paper* technology, discussed in the Inside the Industry box.

Liquid Crystal Displays (LCDs)

A **liquid crystal display (LCD)** uses charged liquid crystals located between two sheets of clear material (usually glass or plastic) to light up the appropriate pixels to form the image on the screen. Several layers of liquid crystals are used, and, in their normal state, the liquid crystals are aligned so that light passes through the display. When an electrical charge is applied to the liquid crystals (via an electrode grid layer contained within the LCD panel), the liquid crystals change their orientation or "twist" so that light cannot pass through the display, and the liquid crystals at the charged intersections of the electrode grid appear dark. Color LCD displays use a color filter that consists of a pattern of red, green, and blue *subpixels* for each pixel. The voltage used controls the orientation (twisting) of the liquid crystals and the amount of light that gets through, affecting the color and shade of that pixel—the three different colors blend to make the pixel the appropriate color.

LCD displays can be viewed only with reflective light, unless light is built into the display. Consequently, LCD panels used with computer monitors typically include a light inside the panel, usually at the rear of the display—a technique referred to as *backlighting*. LCDs are currently the most common type of flat-panel technology used for small- to medium-sized computer monitors (the monitors shown in Figure 4-26 are LCD monitors). However, it is expected that, someday, LCD monitors may be completely replaced by newer technologies, such as the *LED technologies* discussed next.

Light Emitting Diode (LED) and Organic Light Emitting Diode (OLED) Displays

LED (*light emitting diode*) *technology* is also commonly used with consumer products, such as alarm clocks, Christmas lights, car headlights, and more. LEDs are also beginning to be used to backlight LCD panels, although another form of LED—*OLED*—may eventually replace LCD technology entirely.

Organic light emitting diode (OLED) displays use layers of organic material, which emit a visible light when electric current is applied. Because they emit a visible light, OLED displays do not use backlighting. This characteristic makes OLEDs more energy efficient than LCDs and lengthens the battery life of portable devices using OLED displays. Other advantages of OLEDs are that OLEDs are thinner than LCDs, that they have a wider viewing angle than LCDs and so displayed content is visible from virtually all directions, and that their images are brighter and sharper than LCDs. OLED displays are incorporated into many digital cameras, mobile phones, portable digital media

---

> **Liquid crystal display (LCD).** A type of flat-panel display that uses charged liquid crystals to display images. > **Organic light emitting diode (OLED) display.** A type of flat-panel display that uses emissive organic material to display brighter and sharper images.

INSIDE THE INDUSTRY

E-Paper

Electronic paper (*e-paper*) is a type of flat panel display device that attempts to mimic the look of ordinary printed paper. The purpose of an *Electronic Paper Display* (*EPD*) is to give the user the experience of reading from paper, while providing them with the ability to update the information shown on the device electronically. EPDs display content in high-contrast, so they can be viewed in direct sunlight. They also require much less electricity than other types of displays, since they don't require a backlight and they don't require power to maintain the content shown on the display—they only require power to change the content. Because the content stored in an EPD can be erased when it is no longer needed and then replaced with new content, EPDs are more environmentally friendly than conventional paper documents. An additional benefit is portability; an *e-book reader* (such as the *Amazon Kindle* and the *Sony Reader* shown in the accompanying photograph), for instance, can hold over a thousand books stored in electronic format in a device about the size of a paperback novel. In fact, with an e-book reader, you could carry a small library in your backpack.

E-paper is also widely used for *e-signs*, which look like ordinary paper signs, but their text can be changed wirelessly. Their low power consumption means that e-signs can run off battery power for an extended period of time, even with moving data. Some e-signs don't even require a battery; instead, the wireless signal used to transmit data to the display is strong enough to update the sign content by itself. Other retail applications currently on the market include e-paper shelf price tags that can communicate electronically with the store's database so the current price is always displayed, e-paper displays on wristwatches and USB flash drives, destination displays on trains, and e-paper newspapers that can be updated periodically during the day to reflect the latest news. For instance, in late 2007, the French newspaper *Les Echos* announced an electronic paper edition. This e-newspaper is delivered automatically to subscribers via a Wi-Fi connection and it is updated every hour during the day on weekdays. The Amazon Kindle e-book reader can also receive newspaper content (in addition to e-book content)—and thanks to its proprietary high-speed wireless connection, it can download 1,000 pages in less than one minute. E-paper technology used with fabric, plastic, metal, and other materials is in development and is expected to be used to enable keyboards to be printed onto military uniform sleeves, light switches to be printed onto wallpaper, and radio circuitry and controls to be printed onto clothing and other everyday objects. It may also allow e-paper to be used on billboards, T-shirts, and even paint for easy redecorating, as well as regular-sized e-paper that can be inserted into a special computer printer to be printed electronically and then reused over and over. One improvement that has already occurred is the incorporation of touch and pen input with e-paper displays. For instance, both touch and pen input can be used in conjunction with the Sony e-book reader shown in the accompany photograph to flip the "pages" of the book and otherwise control the device.

So how does e-paper work? It is based on a display technology called *electrophoretic*, which was invented and is now manufactured and marketed by E Ink® Corporation. An electrophoretic display contains *electronic ink*—essentially charged ink that consists of millions of tiny beads or *microcapsules* about half the diameter of a human hair. These beads contain positively charged white particles and negatively charged black particles suspended in a clear fluid. When voltage is applied to the beads (through the circuitry contained within the display), either the white or the black particles rise to the top and the opposite colored particles are pulled to the bottom of the bead, depending on the polarity of the charge applied. Consequently, the beads in each pixel appears to be either white or black (see the accompanying illustration) and remain in that state until another transmission changes the pattern.

The white particles are at the top, so this pixel appears white.

AN E-BOOK   **AN E-INK MICROCAPSULE**

players, and other consumer devices (see Figure 4-31). They are also beginning to appear in television and computer displays.

There are also a few special types of OLEDs that support applications not possible with CRT or LCD technology. For instance, *flexible OLED (FOLED)* displays—a technology developed by Universal Display Corporation—are OLED displays built on flexible surfaces, such as plastic or metallic foil. Flexible displays using FOLED technology—such as displays for portable computers and mobile devices that can roll up when not in use (see Figure 4-32)—are being developed by several companies. Other possible uses for flexible screens include making lighter desktop and portable computer monitors, integrating displays on military uniform sleeves, and allowing retractable wall-mounted big screen televi-

FIGURE 4-31
How OLED displays work. Each pixel on an OLED display emits light in the necessary color.

sions and monitors. The flexibility of FOLED displays also adds to their durability, and their thinness makes FOLED technology extremely suitable for mobile devices.

Another form of OLED developed by Universal Display Corporation is *transparent OLED (TOLED)*. TOLED displays are transparent and can emit light toward the top and bottom of the display surface. The portion of the display that does not currently have an image displayed (and the entire display device when it is off) is nearly as transparent as glass, so the user can see through the screen (see Figure 4-32). TOLEDs open up the pos-

sibility of displays on home windows, car windshields, helmet face shields, and other transparent items. A third type of OLED is *Phosphorescent OLED* or *PHOLED*. The term *phosphorescence* refers to a process that results in much more conversion of electrical energy into light instead of heat; with phosphorescence, OLEDs can be up to four times more efficient than without it. Consequently, PHOLED technology is especially appropriate for use on mobile devices, consumer electronics, and other devices where power consumption is an important concern.

FOLEDS
Used to create flexible displays on plastic or another type of flexible material.

TOLEDS
Used to create transparent displays.

FIGURE 4-32
Special types of OLEDs.

Interferometric Modulator (IMOD) Displays

Another emerging flat-panel display technology is *interferometric modulator (IMOD) displays*. Designed initially for mobile phones and other portable devices, an IMOD display is essentially a complex mirror that uses external light—such as from the sun or artificial light inside a building—to display images. Because IMOD displays are utilizing light instead of fighting it the way LCD displays do, images are bright and clear even in direct sunlight (see Figure 4-33). And, because backlighting isn't used, power consumption is much less than what is needed for LCD displays. In fact, similar to e-paper, devices using IMOD displays use no power unless the image changes so they can remain on at all times without draining the device battery. Beginning to be used initially with mobile devices, IMODs could eventually be used for outdoor television screens, large digital signs, and other outdoor display devices that normally consume a great deal of power.

Plasma Displays and Surface-Conduction Electron-Emitter Displays (SEDs)

Plasma displays use a layered technology like LCD and OLEDs and look similar to LCD displays, but they use a layer of gas between two plates of glass, instead of liquid crystals or organic material. A phosphor-coated screen (with red, green, and blue phosphors for each pixel) is used, and an electron grid layer and electronic charges are used to make the gas atoms light up the appropriate phosphors to create the image on the screen. The very large displays used by businesses, as well as many large screen televisions, are typically plasma displays.

A display technology in development for high-definition displays is *surface-conduction electron-emitter display* (*SED*). SED is being developed by Toshiba and Canon. It uses millions of tiny electron guns (similar to those used in CRTs but much smaller and millions of them instead of one) to power the pixels on a flat-panel display. SED displays are thin and bright, and they have less flicker than LCD and plasma screens. Televisions based on SED technology are beginning to become available.

Data and Multimedia Projectors

A **data projector** is used to display output from a computer to a wall or projection screen. Conventional data projectors are often found in classrooms, conference rooms, and similar locations and can be freestanding units or permanently mounted onto the ceiling. While most data projectors connect via cable to a computer, *wireless projectors* that use a Wi-Fi connection are available. Some projectors (such as the one shown in Figure 4-34) also include an *iPod dock* to connect a video iPod in order to project videos stored on that device.

FIGURE 4-33
An IMOD display is bright and readable, even in direct sunlight.

FIGURE 4-34
Data projectors.

CONVENTIONAL DATA PROJECTORS
Frequently used for both business and classroom presentations.

INTEGRATED AND PORTABLE PROJECTORS
Images displayed on the device (such as the mobile phone shown here) are projected onto any surface.

HOLOGRAPHIC PROJECTORS
Project 3D images of objects or individuals.

>**Plasma display.** A type of flat-panel display that uses layers of gas to display images; most often used on large displays. >**Data projector.** A display device that projects all computer output to a wall or projection screen.

Another type of data projector is the *integrated projector*—tiny projectors that are beginning to be built into mobile phones, portable computers, portable digital media players, and other portable devices to enable the device to project an image (such as a document, presentation, or movie) onto a wall or other flat surface from up to 12 feet away (refer again to Figure 4-34). These integrated projectors typically create a display up to 10 feet wide in order to easily share information on the device with others on the go without having to crowd around a tiny screen. This same technology is also incorporated into very small stand-alone *portable projectors* that can be used for making presentations while on the go. Another type of data projector shown in Figure 4-34 is designed to project actual 3D projections or *holograms*. For instance, holograms of individuals and objects can be projected onto a stage for a presentation and hologram display devices can be used in retail stores, exhibitions, and other locations to showcase products or other items in 3D.

PRINTERS

Instead of the temporary, ever-changing soft copy output that a monitor produces, **printers** produce *hard copy*; that is, a permanent copy of the output on paper. Most desktop computers are connected to a printer; portable computers can use printers as well.

Printer Characteristics

Printers differ in a number of important respects, such as the technology used, size, speed, and print quality. Some general printer characteristics are discussed next, followed by a look at the most common types of printers.

Printing Technology

Printers produce images through either impact or nonimpact technologies. *Impact printers*, like old ribbon typewriters, have a print mechanism that actually strikes the paper to transfer ink to the paper. For example, a *dot-matrix printer* (see Figure 4-35) uses a *print head* consisting of pins that strike an inked ribbon to transfer the ink to the paper—the appropriate pins are extended (and, consequently, strike the ribbon) as the print head moves across the paper in order to form the appropriate words or images. Impact printers are used today primarily for producing multipart forms, such as invoices, packing slips, and credit card receipts.

Most printers today are *nonimpact printers*, meaning they form images without the print mechanism actually touching the paper. Nonimpact printers usually produce higher-quality images and are much quieter than impact printers are. The two most common types of printers today—*laser printers* and *ink-jet printers*—are both nonimpact printers. As discussed in more detail shortly, laser printers form images with *toner powder* (essentially ink powder) and ink-jet printers form images with liquid ink. Both impact and nonimpact printers form images with dots, in a manner similar to the way monitors display images with pixels. Because of this, printers are very versatile and can print text in virtually any size, as well as print photos and other graphical images. In addition to paper, both impact and nonimpact printers can print on transparencies, envelopes, mailing labels, and more.

FIGURE 4-35
Dot-matrix printers.
Dot-matrix printers are impact printers; today they are typically high-speed printers used in manufacturing, shipping, or similar applications.

>**Printer.** An output device that produces output on paper.

Color vs. Black and White

Both *color printers* and *black-and-white printers* are available. Color printers work similarly to black-and-white printers, except that, instead of using just black ink, they also use cyan (blue), magenta (red), and yellow ink (see Figure 4-36). Either color printers apply all of the colors in one pass, or they go through the entire printing process multiple times, applying one color during each pass. Color printers are often used in homes (to print photographs, greeting cards, flyers, and more). Businesses may use black-and-white printers for output that does not need to be in color (since it is less expensive and faster to print in black and white) and color printers for output that needs to be in color (such as product brochures and other colorful marketing materials).

> **FIGURE 4-36**
> **Color printing.**
> Color printers require multiple color cartridges or cartridges that contain multiple colors.

Personal vs. Network Printers

Printers today can be designated as *personal printers* (printers designed to be connected directly to a single computer) or *network printers* (printers designed to be connected directly to a home or an office network). Personal printers can be shared over a home network if the computer to which the printer is connected is powered up and the printer is designated as a shared device and some personal printers today include Wi-Fi capabilities to enable individuals to print from any Wi-Fi-enabled device via a home Wi-Fi network. However, network printers are designed to connect directly to a network (instead of to a single computer) so they can be used by anyone connected to the network via a wired or wireless connection. In addition, many network printers today are designed for high-volume office printing and often include other capabilities, such as to collate, staple, hole-punch, and print on both sides of the page (referred to as *duplex printing*). Networking is discussed in detail in Chapter 7.

Print Resolution

Most printing technologies today form images with dots of liquid ink or flecks of toner powder. The number of dots per inch (dpi)—called the *print resolution*—affects the quality of the printed output. Printers with a higher print resolution tend to produce sharper text and images than printers with a lower resolution tend to produce, although other factors (such as the technology and number of colors used) also affect the quality of a printout. Guidelines for acceptable print resolution are typically 300 dpi for general-purpose printouts, 600 dpi for higher-quality documents, 1,200 dpi for photographs, and 2,400 dpi for professional applications.

Print Speed

Print speed is typically measured in *pages per minute* (*ppm*). How long it takes a document to print depends on the actual printer being used, the selected print resolution, and the content being printed. For instance, pages containing photographs or other images typically take longer to print than pages containing only text, and full-color pages take longer to print than black-and-white pages. Common speeds for personal printers today range from about 15 to 35 ppm; network printers typically print from 40 to 100 ppm.

Connection Options

Most personal printers today connect to a computer via a USB connection; some have the option of connecting via a Wi-Fi wireless connection as well. In addition, many personal printers can receive data to be printed via a flash memory card, a cable connected to a digital camera (such as for printers and cameras adhering to the *PictBridge standard*), or a *camera docking station* (a device connected to a printer into which a digital camera is placed so images stored in the camera can be printed). Most network printers connect via a wired *Ethernet* networking connection or a wireless Wi-Fi connection. Networking connections are discussed in detail in Chapter 7.

Multifunction Capabilities

Some printers today offer more than just printing capabilities. These units—referred to as **multifunction devices (MFDs)** or *all-in-ones*—typically copy, scan, fax, and print documents. MFDs (see Figure 4-37) can be based on ink-jet printer or laser printer technology, and they are available as both color and black-and-white devices. Although multifunction devices have traditionally been desktop units used in small offices and home offices, larger workgroup multifunction devices are now available that are designed for multiple users, either as stand-alone stations or as networked units.

Laser Printers

Laser printers are the standard for business documents and come in both personal and network versions; they are also available as both color and black-and-white printers. To print a document, the laser printer first uses a laser beam to charge the appropriate locations on a drum to form the page's image, and then *toner powder* (powdered ink) is released from a *toner cartridge* and sticks to the drum. The toner is then transferred to a piece of paper when the paper is rolled over the drum, and a heating unit fuses the toner powder to the paper to permanently form the image (see Figure 4-38). Laser printers print one entire

FIGURE 4-37
A multifunction device (MFD).

FIGURE 4-38
How black-and-white laser printers work.

HW

1. The paper enters the printer, and then it is given an electrical charge so the toner can stick to the paper, as explained in step 5.

2. The printer's microprocessor decodes page data sent from the computer.

3. Instructions from the printer's microprocessor control a laser beam that charges the appropriate locations on the drum so the toner will stick to the drum, as explained in step 4.

4. Toner powder is applied to the drum and sticks only to the charged areas on the drum.

5. The paper rolls over the drum and the toner is transferred to the paper, forming the image for the entire page.

6. The paper goes through the fusing unit, at which point the toner is permanently affixed to the paper through heat and pressure.

7. The paper exits the printer.

> **Multifunction device (MFD).** A device that offers multiple functions (such as printing, scanning, and faxing) in a single unit. > **Laser printer.** An output device that uses toner powder and technology similar to that of a photocopier to produce images on paper.

page at a time and are typically faster and have better quality output than *ink-jet printers*, discussed next. Common print resolutions for laser printers are between 600 and 2,400 dpi; speeds for personal laser printers range from about 15 to 30 ppm. Black-and-white laser printers start at about $100; color laser printers start at about $300.

Ink-Jet Printers

Ink-jet printers form images by spraying tiny drops of liquid ink from one or more *ink cartridges* onto the page, one printed line at a time (see Figure 4-39). Some printers print with one single-sized ink droplet; others print using different-sized ink droplets and using multiple nozzles or varying electrical charges for more precise printing. The print head for an ink-jet printer typically travels back and forth across the page, which is one reason why ink-jet printers are slower than laser printers. However, an emerging type of ink-jet printer uses a printhead that is the full width of the paper, which allows the printhead to remain stationary while the paper feeds past it. These printers are very fast, printing up to 60 ppm for letter-sized paper.

Because they are relatively inexpensive, have good-quality output, and can print in color, ink-jet printers are usually the printer of choice for home use. With the use of special photo paper, *photo-quality ink-jet printers* can also print photograph-quality digital photos. Starting at less than $50 for a simple home printer, ink-jet printers are affordable, although the cost of the replaceable ink cartridges can add up, especially if you do a lot of color printing.

FIGURE 4-39

How ink-jet printers work.

Each ink cartridge is made up of multiple tiny ink-filled firing chambers; to print images, the appropriate color ink is ejected through the appropriate firing chamber.

Ink-jet printer

Heating element

Steam bubble

Firing chamber

Paper

Steam bubble

Ink droplet

Steam bubble

Ink droplet

1. A heating element makes the ink boil, which causes a steam bubble to form.

2. As the steam bubble expands, it pushes ink through the firing chamber.

3. The ink droplet is ejected onto the paper and the steam bubble collapses, pulling more ink into the firing chamber.

> **Ink-jet printer.** An output device that sprays droplets of ink to produce images on paper.

In addition to being used in computer printers, ink-jet technology is being applied to a number of other applications. For instance, ink-jet technology may eventually be used for dispensing liquid metals, aromas, computer chips and other circuitry, and even "printing" human tissue and other organic materials for medical purposes.

Special-Purpose Printers

Although both laser and ink-jet printers can typically print on a variety of media—including sheets of labels, envelopes, transparencies, photo paper, and even fabric, in addition to various sizes of paper—some printers are designed for a particular purpose. Some of the most common *special-purpose printers* are discussed next and illustrated in Figure 4-40.

Photo Printers

Photo printers are color printers designed to print photographs. Although many photo printers are connected to a computer to print photos stored on the hard drive, most photo printers also can print photos directly from a digital camera or a storage medium (such as a flash memory card) without transferring the photos to a computer first. Often, photo

FIGURE 4-40
Special-purpose printers.

Photos can be previewed and edited here.

Flash memory media can be inserted here.

PHOTO PRINTERS
Used to print digital photographs in a variety of sizes.

BARCODE PRINTERS
Used to print barcoded labels. This printer can also program RFID tags, when they are embedded inside the barcoded labels.

PORTABLE AND INTEGRATED PRINTERS
This printer uses no ink and is integrated into the digital camera to print digital photographs.

WIDE-FORMAT PRINTERS
Used for printouts that are too big for a standard-sized printer.

3D PRINTERS
Used to print items (such as plastic parts or models) in 3D.

> **Photo printer.** An output device designed for printing digital photographs.

printers have a preview screen (see Figure 4-40) to allow for minor editing and cropping before printing, but it is usually more efficient to do extensive editing on a computer. Some photo printers can print a variety of photo paper sizes; others—sometimes called *snapshot printers*—print only on standard 4 by 6-inch photo paper. Although photo printers offer the convenience of printing digital photos at home and whenever the need arises, the cost per photo is typically higher than using a photo printing service at a retail store or an Internet photo printing service.

Barcode, Label, and Postage Printers

Barcode printers enable businesses and other organizations to print custom barcodes on price tags, shipping labels, and other documents for identification or pricing purposes. Most barcode printers can print labels in a variety of barcode standards; some (such as the one shown in Figure 4-40) can also encode RFID tags embedded in labels. For other types of labels, such as for envelopes, packages, and file folders, regular *label printers* may come in handy. Some special-purpose label printers referred to as *postage printers* can print *electronic postage* (also called *e-stamps*). E-stamps are valid postage stamps that can be printed once a postage allotment has been purchased via the Internet or from an e-stamp vendor; postage values are deducted from your allotment as you print the e-stamps. Some e-stamp services also allow stamps to be printed directly onto shipping labels and envelopes using laser or ink-jet printers, as well.

Portable and Integrated Printers

Portable printers are small, lightweight printers that can be used on the go, such as with a notebook computer or mobile device, and connect via either a wired or wireless connection. Portable printers that can print on regular-sized (8.5 by 11-inch) paper are used by businesspeople while traveling; portable receipt and barcode printers are used in some service professions. Printers can also be integrated into other devices. For instance, the digital camera shown in Figure 4-40 contains an *integrated printer* that is based on a new technology developed by *ZINK* (for "zero ink") *Imaging*. This printer uses no ink; instead, it uses special paper that is coated with special color dye crystals. Before printing, the embedded dye crystals are clear, so *ZINK Paper* looks like regular white photo paper. The ZINK printer uses heat to activate and colorize these dye crystal when a photo is printed, creating a full color image. In addition to being integrated into a variety of consumer electronics devices, including digital cameras and digital picture frames, stand-alone *ZINK printers* are also available.

Wide-Format Ink-Jet Printers

To print charts, drawings, maps, blueprints, posters, signs, advertising banners, and other large documents in one piece, a larger printer (such as the one shown in Figure 4-40) is needed. Today, most large format printers (sometimes called *plotters*) are *wide-format ink-jet printers*, which are designed to print documents from around 24 inches to 60 inches in width. Although typically used to print on paper, some wide-format ink-jet printers can print directly on fabric and other types of materials.

3D Printers

When 3D output is required, such as to print a 3D model of a new building or prototype of a new product, **3D printers** (see Figure 4-40) can be used. Instead of printing on paper,

---

> **Barcode printer.** An output device that prints barcoded documents. > **Portable printer.** A small, lightweight printer designed to be used while on the go. > **3D printer.** An output device designed to print three-dimensional objects, such as product prototypes.

these printers typically form output in layers using molten plastic during a series of passes to build a 3D version of the desired output—a process called *fused deposition modeling (FDM)*. Some printers can produce multicolor output; others print in only one color and need to be painted by hand, if color output is desired.

AUDIO OUTPUT

Audio output includes voice, music, and other audible sounds. **Computer speakers**, the most common type of audio output device, connect to a computer and provide audio output for computer games, music, video clips and TV shows, Web conferencing, and other applications. Computer speaker systems resemble their stereo system counterparts and are available in a wide range of prices. Some speaker systems (such as the one shown in Figure 4-41) consist of only a pair of speakers. Others include additional speakers and a subwoofer to create better sound (such as surround sound) for multimedia content. Instead of being stand-alone units, the speakers for some desktop computers are built directly into, or permanently attached to, the monitor. Portable computers and mobile devices typically have speakers integrated into the device; mobile devices can also be connected to a stereo system or other consumer device (such as the treadmill shown in Figure 4-41) that contains an *iPod/MP3 dock* and integrated speakers designed to be used to play music stored on a portable digital media player. In addition, many cars can connect a portable digital media player to the car's stereo system; typically devices are connected via the device's headphone jack or USB port.

Headphones can be used instead of speakers so the audio output does not disturb others (such as in a school computer lab or public library). **Headsets** (see Figure 4-41) are headphones with a built-in microphone and are often used when dictating to a computer and when making telephone calls or participating in Web conferences using a computer; wireless headsets are commonly used in conjunction with mobile phones. Even smaller than headphones are the *earphones* and *earbuds* often used with portable digital media players, handheld gaming devices, and other mobile devices.

FIGURE 4-41
Audio output
devices.

COMPUTER SPEAKERS
Used to output sound from a computer.

IPOD/MP3 DOCK
Used to output sound from a portable
digital media player.

HEADSETS
Used when both voice input and audio
output are required.

> **Computer speakers.** Output devices connected to computers that provide audio output. > **Headphones.** A personal audio output device used by an individual so only he or she can hear the sound; headphones with a built-in microphone are typically referred to as **headsets**.

SUMMARY

KEYBOARDS

Most people use a **keyboard** to input data into a personal computer. Keyboards typically include the standard alphanumeric keys, plus other keys for special purposes. Many mobile phones and other mobile devices include a keyboard today—if not, a *portable keyboard* can often be used. *Wireless keyboards* are also available.

POINTING AND TOUCH DEVICES

Pointing devices are hardware devices that move an on-screen *mouse pointer* or similar indicator. The most widely used pointing device is the **mouse**. Another common pointing device is the **stylus**, which is used with pen-based computers, many mobile devices, and *digital writing systems* to input handwritten data and to select options; with **handwriting recognition** technology, the input can be converted to typed text. Use of *digital forms* in conjunction with handwriting recognition is a growing trend. **Touch screens** are monitors that are touched with the finger to select commands or provide input. Touch screens are commonly used in consumer kiosks, as well as with personal computers, mobile phones, mobile devices, and other consumer devices. Other pointing devices include **graphics tablets**, gaming devices, and **touch pads**.

SCANNERS, READERS, AND DIGITAL CAMERAS

There are many different input devices that can be used to convert data that already exists (such as *source documents*) to digital form or to initially capture data in digital form. A **scanner** allows users to input data that exists in physical form, such as photographs, drawings, and printed documents, into a computer. Most scanners are **flatbed scanners** or **portable scanners**. *Receipt*, *3D*, and *business card scanners* are also available. When used with **optical character recognition** (**OCR**) software, the computer can recognize scanned text characters as editable text; if not, the scanned page is input as a single image.

Barcode readers read **barcodes**, such as the *UPC codes* used to identify products in many retail stores. **Radio frequency identification** (**RFID**) is a technology used to store and transmit data located in **RFID tags**, which contain tiny chips and antennas and which are attached to items. RFID tags are read by **RFID readers** and are most often used in conjunction with shipping containers and other large assets. RFID technology can also be used to track individuals, assets, and other items, as well as be used for electronic payment systems.

Optical mark readers (*OMRs*) read specific types of marks on certain forms, such as on testing forms and voter ballots. *OCR readers* read characters, such as the specially printed *optical characters* used on bills and other *turnaround documents*. *Magnetic ink character recognition* (*MICR*) is used by the banking industry to rapidly sort, process, and route checks to the proper banks. **Biometric readers** read *biometric* characteristics (such as a fingerprint, hand geometry, or a face) in order to identify individuals.

Digital cameras work much like conventional film cameras, but they record digital images on a digital storage medium (such as a flash memory card, digital tape cartridge, built-in hard drive, or DVD disc), instead of on conventional film or videotape. The images are immediately available without processing and can be transferred to a computer for manipulation or printing, or sent directly to some printers for printing. *Digital still cameras* take still photos; *digital video cameras* are either *digital camcorders* or *PC cam/Web cam* digital video cameras that are used in conjunction with personal computers.

AUDIO INPUT

Speech recognition systems, which enable computer systems to recognize spoken words, are one means of *audio input*. Speech recognition can be used for data input, as well as for controlling a computer or other device (such as a mobile phone, car navigation system, or surgical robot). *Music input systems* are used to input music, such as original music compositions, into a computer. Music can also be input via a CD, DVD, or Web download.

DISPLAY DEVICES

Display devices (also called **monitors** and **display screens**) are the most common type of output device for a computer; they are also incorporated into a wide variety of other electronic devices. Display devices are available in a wide variety of sizes and are generally either **CRT monitors** or **flat-panel displays**. Flat-panel displays are most often **liquid crystal displays** (**LCDs**) or **plasma displays**, but these technologies are expected to be replaced by **organic light emitting diode** (**OLED**) **displays** and other new display technologies, such as *interferometric modulator* (*IMOD*) displays and *surface-conduction electron-emitter displays* (*SEDs*). Special types of OLEDs (such as *flexible, transparent,* and *Phosphorescent OLEDs*) are emerging for special applications. Regardless of the technology used, the screen of a display device is divided into a fine grid of small areas or dots called **pixels**. Monitors can be *color* or *monochrome*, *wired* or *wireless*, and are available in a wide variety of sizes. Some monitors support 3D images, and some include touch screen capabilities. The *video card* or integrated graphics component being used determines many of the graphics capabilities of the computer. **Data projectors** connect to a computer and project any output sent to the computer's monitor through the projector onto a wall or projection screen. Some projectors are integrated into mobile devices; others project *holograms*.

HW

PRINTERS

Printers produce *hard copy* output through either *impact* or *nonimpact* printing technology. Most printers today form images as matrices of dots, although with many technologies, the dots are too small to be visible. Printer quality is usually measured in *dots per inch* (*dpi*); speed is typically measured in *pages per minute* (*ppm*). Both *personal* and *network printers* are available and there are a number of options for connecting a printer to a network, computer, or other device. Some printers print in color and others print in just black and white. **Multifunction devices** (**MFDs**) incorporate the functions of multiple devices—typically a printer, scanner, and fax machine—into a single unit.

The most common printers are **laser printers** (which use *toner powder*) and **ink-jet printers** (which use liquid ink). Special-purpose printers include **photo printers**, **barcode printers**, **portable printers**, *wide-format ink-jet printers*, and **3D printers**. Some printers are integrated into other devices, such as digital cameras.

AUDIO OUTPUT

The most common *audio output* device is **computer speakers**, which output music or spoken voice. **Headphones** or **headsets** can be used to prevent the sound from disturbing other people; speakers are also integrated into some consumer devices (such as treadmills) to play music stored on portable digital media players.

REVIEW ACTIVITIES

a. digital camera

b. ink-jet printer

c. laser printer

d. mouse

e. OLED display

f. optical character recognition (OCR)

g. RFID tag

h. scanner

i. stylus

j. touch screen

Instructions: Match each key term on the left with the definition on the right that best describes it.

1. _____ A common pointing device that the user slides along a flat surface to move a pointer around the screen and clicks its buttons to make selections.

2. _____ A device containing a tiny chip and a radio antenna that is attached to an object so it can be identified using radio frequency identification technology.

3. _____ A display device that is touched with the finger to issue commands or otherwise provide input to the connected device.

4. _____ An input device that reads printed text and graphics and transfers them to a computer in digital form.

5. _____ An input device that is used to write electronically on the display screen.

6. _____ An input device that takes pictures and records them as digital images.

7. _____ An output device that uses toner powder and technology similar to that of a photocopier to produce images on paper.

8. _____ A type of flat-panel display that uses emissive organic material to display brighter and sharper images.

9. _____ An output device that sprays droplets of ink to produce images on paper.

10. _____ The ability of a scanning device to recognize scanned text characters and convert them to electronic form as text, not images.

Instructions: Circle **T** if the statement is true, **F** if the statement is false, or write the best answer in the space provided. **Answers for the self-quiz are located in the References and Resources Guide at the end of the book.**

1. **T F** A keyboard is an example of a pointing device.

2. **T F** Most digital still cameras store photos on flash memory media.

3. **T F** UPC is a type of barcode.

4. **T F** Consumer kiosks located in retail stores commonly use touch screens for input.

5. **T F** An ink-jet printer normally produces a better image than a laser printer.

6. With _____ software, pen-based computers can convert handwritten text into editable, typed text.

7. A(n) _____ can be used to convert flat printed documents, such as a drawing or photograph, into digital form.

8. The smallest colorable area in an electronic image (such as a scanned document, digital hotograph, or image displayed on a display screen) is called a(n) _____.

9. Portable computers and mobile devices virtually always use _____ displays, while some desktop computers may use the larger, more bulky _____ monitors.

10. Match each input device to its input application, and write the corresponding number in the blank to the left of the input application.

a. _____ Pen-based computing   1. Keyboard
b. _____ Consumer kiosk   2. Stylus
c. _____ Text-based data entry   3. RFID tag
d. _____ Secure facility access   4. Biometric reader
e. _____ Tracking goods   5. Touch screen

EXERCISES

WH

1. For the following list of computer input and output devices, write the appropriate abbreviation (I or O) in the space provided to indicate whether each device is used for input (I) or output (O).

a. _____ Biometric reader   f. _____ Digital camera
b. _____ Graphics tablet   g. _____ Data projector
c. _____ Speaker   h. _____ Microphone
d. _____ Photo printer   i. _____ OLED monitor
e. _____ Flat-panel display   j. _____ Joystick

2. Write the number of the type of printer that best matches each of the printing applications in the blank to the left of each printing application.

a. _____ To print inexpensive color printouts for a wide variety of documents.
b. _____ To print all output for an entire office.
c. _____ To print receipts for jet-ski rentals at the beach.
d. _____ To print high-quality black-and-white business letters and reports at home.

1. Personal laser printer
2. Network laser printer
3. Ink-jet printer
4. Portable printer

3. List three advantages of RFID technology over barcode technology.

4. Would an OLED display or an LCD display use more battery power? Explain why.

5. List one personal or business application that you believe is more appropriate for a dot-matrix printer, instead of another type of printer, and explain why.

DISCUSSION QUESTIONS

1. While gaming and texting are both popular pastimes, it is possible to become injured by performing these activities. For instance, some Wii users have developed tennis elbow and other ailments from some Wii Sports games and heavy texters have developed problems with their thumbs. Think of the devices you use regularly. Have you ever become sore or injured from their use? If so, was it the design of the input device being used, overuse, or both? What responsibilities do hardware manufacturers have in respect to creating safe input devices? If a user becomes injured due to overuse of a device, whose fault it is? Should input devices come with warning labels?

2. The choice of an appropriate input device for a product is often based on both the type of device being used and the target market for that device. For instance, a device targeted to college students and one targeted to older individuals may use different input methods. Suppose that you are developing a device to be used primarily for Internet access that will be marketed to senior citizens. What type of hardware would you select as the primary input device? Why? What are the advantages and disadvantages of your selected input device? How could the disadvantages be minimized?

PROJECTS

1. **Biometrics and Personal Privacy** Biometric input devices, such as fingerprint readers and iris scanners, are increasingly being used for security purposes, such as to clock in and out of work, or to obtain access to locked facilities, a computer, or a computer network. Other uses of biometric technology are more voluntary, such as expedited airport-screening programs used by some frequent travelers and the fingerprint payment systems used at some retail stores. While viewed as a time-saving tool by some, other individuals may object to their biometric characteristics being stored in a database for this purpose. Is convenience worth compromising some personal privacy? What about national security? Would you be willing to sign up for a voluntary program, such as an airport-screening system or a fingerprint payment system, that relies on biometric data? Would you work at a job that required you to use a biometric input device on a regular basis? Do you think a national ID card containing hard-to-forge biometric data could help prevent terrorist attacks, such as the September 11, 2001 attacks? If so, do you think most Americans would support its use?

   For this project, research the use of biometric input devices today and form an opinion about their use and any potential impact their use may have on personal privacy. At the conclusion of your research, prepare a one-page summary of your findings and opinions and submit it to your instructor.

2. **Printer Shopping** Printers today have many more features than a few years ago. These features may include improved quality, more memory, photo printing capabilities, digital camera connectivity, built-in flash memory card readers, wireless connectivity, and faster speed.

   For this project, suppose you are in the market for a new personal printer. Make a list of the most important features needed to meet your needs, and then research printers to identify the best printer for your needs. Be sure to consider both the price of the printer and the price of consumables (such as paper and ink/toner) in your evaluation process. At the conclusion of your research, prepare a one-page summary of your findings and best options and submit it to your instructor.

3. **Keyboarding Speed Test** Although voice and other alternative means of input are emerging, most data input today is still performed via the keyboard. Proper keyboarding technique can help increase speed and accuracy. Online keyboarding tests can help to evaluate your keyboarding ability.

   For this project, find a site (such as Typingtest.com) that offers a free online typing test and test your keyboarding speed and accuracy. At the conclusion of the test, rate your keyboarding ability and determine whether a keyboarding course or tutor program, or just keyboarding practice, will help you improve if your score is not at least 20 correct words per minute (cwpm). Take the test one more time to see if your speed improves now that you are familiar with how the test works. If your speed is fast, but accuracy is low, take the test once more, concentrating on accuracy. If you still test less than 20 cwpm, locate a free typing tutor program or Web site and evaluate it to see if it would help you to increase your speed and accuracy. At the conclusion of this task, prepare a short summary of your experience, including the typing test site used and your best score.

4. **Green Technology Mandates** The chapter Inside the Industry box discusses e-paper—an erasable, reusable alternative to traditional paper and ink. While e-paper has many societal benefits (such as reducing the use of traditional paper and ink and the resources needed to create and dispose of them), it has been slow to catch on. When a new technology, such as e-paper, that has obvious benefits to society is developed, who (if anyone) should be responsible for making sure it gets implemented in a timely fashion? Do we, as a society, have an ethical responsibility to ensure the new product succeeds? Should the government mandate the use of beneficial technology? Will businesses or individuals choose to use e-paper products if the only incentive is a cleaner environment? Would you be willing to switch to a new technology (such as e-paper) that is beneficial to society if it costs more than the existing technology? Is it ethical for an industry or the government to mandate the use of new technologies if they create an additional cost or inconvenience to individuals?

For this project, form an opinion about the ethical obligations individuals, businesses, and the government have in regards to the development and implementation of beneficial new technologies and be prepared to discuss your position (in class, via an online class discussion group, in a class chat room, or via a class blog, depending on your instructor's directions). You may also be asked to write a short paper expressing your opinion.

ETHICS IN ACTION

5. **Assistive Computing** In addition to the conventional input and output hardware mentioned in the chapter, there are a variety of assistive input and output devices that physically challenged individuals can use to make computing easier and more efficient.

For this project, select one type of disability, such as being blind, deaf, paraplegic, quadriplegic, or having the use of only one arm or hand. Research the hardware and software options that could be used with a new computer for someone with the selected disability. Make a list of potential limitations of any standard computer hardware and the assistive hardware and software that would be appropriate for this individual. Research each assistive option, comparing the ease of use, cost, and availability, and then prepare a recommendation for the best computer system for your selected hypothetical situation. Share your findings with the class in the form of a short presentation. The presentation should not exceed 10 minutes and should make use of one or more presentation aids, such as the chalkboard, handouts, overhead transparencies, or a computer-based slide presentation (your instructor may provide additional requirements). You may also be asked to submit a summary of the presentation to your instructor.

PRESENTATION/ DEMONSTRATION

Instructions: Go to the Chapter 4 page at **www.cengage.com/computerconcepts/np/uc13** to work the following Web Activities.

6. **Interactive Activities** Work the interactive **Crossword Puzzle**, watch the **Video Podcasts** and **Online Videos**, and explore the **Further Exploration** links associated with this chapter.

If you have a SAM user profile, you may have access to hands-on instruction, practice, and assessment of the skills covered in this chapter. Check with your instructor for instructions and the correct URL/Web site to access those assignments.

7. **Student Edition Labs** Work the following interactive **Student Edition Labs**.
   ➤ **Using Input Devices** ➤ **Peripheral Devices**

8. **Test Yourself** Review the **Online Study Guide** for this chapter, then test your knowledge of the terms and concepts covered in this chapter by completing the **Key Term Matching** exercise, the **Self-Quiz**, the **Exercises**, and the **Practice Test**.

WEB ACTIVITIES

SAM

Student Edition Labs

Hardware

A conversation with **SUMIT AGNIHOTRY**
Vice President, Product Marketing, Acer Pan America

> *". . . storage technology will need to continue to evolve to improve accessibility, performance, and capacity, and to support new high-definition and content-on-the-go applications."*

acer

Sumit Agnihotry is the Vice President of Product Marketing for Acer Pan America. In his 15+ years in the computer field, he has held various positions in computer product marketing. He started at the Acer Group in 1998 as a product manager, and has successfully helped launch numerous Acer products through U.S. consumer channels. Sumit holds a Bachelor of Science Degree in Marketing and has attended Executive Education programs in Leadership Development and Cross-Cultural Negotiation at the John Hopkins University.

My Background . . .

I started in the computer industry when I got my first job as a manufacturer's representative while still in school, marketing computer peripherals and accessories to retailers. I began my career at the Acer Group in 1998 as a product manager for mobile products. I'm now the Vice President of product marketing for the Americas region and my responsibilities include working with engineers to develop the latest cutting-edge products, and then launching those products through various channels in North, Central, and South America. I also oversee the marketing of Acer notebooks, netbooks, desktop computers, and monitors. I believe that my ability to understand consumer needs and pain points, coupled with my knowledge of this industry and technology, has helped me succeed in this field and in my current position.

It's Important to Know . . .

Moore's Law is still valid. The trend of improvements in the area of computing hardware is well described by Moore's Law, which basically says that the number of transistors that can be placed inexpensively on an integrated circuit has increased exponentially since the invention of the integrated circuit in 1958 and will continue to do so. But, in addition to the density of components and transistors, many other measures of digital technology are improving at exponential rates as well, including computing performance, power consumption, battery life, and network capacity. This growth trend is expected to continue for at least another decade.

The world is becoming wireless. Consumers today want access to information anytime and anywhere. The desire of consumers to access digital and voice information on the go dictates that emerging devices will need to have wireless connectivity and high performance, as well as be able to support popular applications such as social networking. In addition, devices will need to be ultra thin and light, and have an all-day battery life. They must also be designed to appeal to the mass market, but still be affordable.

Storage technology will continue to evolve. Optical storage media (such as DVDs and CDs) and flash storage media (such as flash memory cards and USB flash drives) are widely used today. However, storage technology will need to continue to evolve to improve accessibility, performance, and capacity, and to support new high-definition and content-on-the-go applications. The potential impact of current and future technologies on the environment will need to be taken into consideration as well.

How I Use this Technology . . .

I spend a lot of time on the road visiting suppliers and customers so I use my BlackBerry and laptop throughout the day—basically anytime I am not sleeping or flying. When I don't have access to my laptop or it's not convenient to use it, I am still able to respond to e-mail messages and perform other mission-critical tasks in a timely manner using my BlackBerry. These devices also allow me to connect with my family easily when I am away from home. Of course, another personal favorite use of technology is entertainment and I frequently download movies and TV shows to watch while I'm on the go; for instance, I watched an episode of "The Office" that I downloaded from iTunes on a recent flight from San Francisco to Taipei.

What the Future Holds . . .

Over the past few decades, computing has evolved from mainframes, to desktop computers, to luggable so-called "portable" computers, to today's laptops and mobile devices. I believe that as consumers continue to embrace digital information consumption on the go, the vision of a "laptop for every lap" will come true. However, the device may not look like today's laptop. As the cost of creating wireless and mobile devices continue to drop, we will see huge improvements in portable computing products in the near future that will enable us to provide consumers with portable, yet affordable, devices that can be used to access the types of information that are important to them, whenever they want to do so.

"The desire of consumers to access digital and voice information on the go dictates that emerging devices will need to have wireless connectivity and high performance . . ."

My Advice to Students . . .

Technology has to adapt to market needs, not the other way around. So when you think about innovative technology, it has to be centered on improving consumer experience and pain points.

Discussion Question

Sumit Agnihotry believes the vision of a "laptop for every lap" will become a reality in the near future. Think about the computing and communications tasks you wish to do on a daily basis, which tasks you prefer to do on the go, and the size and connectivity requirements for the optimal device to accomplish these tasks. What capabilities would the device need to have? Would your optimal device be based on today's mobile phone, notebook computer, netbook computer, or something entirely different? What other hardware characteristics would your optimal device need? Is the future of personal computing a mobile device? Be prepared to discuss your position (in class, via an online class discussion group, in a class chat room, or via a class blog, depending on your instructor's directions). You may also be asked to write a short paper expressing your opinion.

>**For more information on Acer and Acer products, visit us.acer.com. For news about hot technology products, trends, and ideas, visit www.engadet.com and www.ted.com.**

Module

Software

In Chapter 1, we looked at the basic software concepts involved with starting up and using a computer. We continue that focus in this module, discussing in more depth both system software—the software used to run a computer—and application software—the software that performs the specific tasks users want to accomplish using a computer.

Chapter 5 focuses on system software and how it enables the hardware of a computer system to operate and to run application software. Chapter 6 discusses application software, including some important basic concepts and characteristics, as well as an overview of some of the most common types of application software used today—namely, word processing, spreadsheet, database, presentation graphics, and multimedia software.

"Technology should be used as an enabler to achieve your goals, improve your life, and improve the lives of others."

For more comments from Guest Expert **Graham Watson** of Microsoft, see the **Expert Insight on . . . Software** feature at the end of the module.

chapter 5

System Software: Operating Systems and Utility Programs

After completing this chapter, you will be able to do the following:

1. Understand the difference between system software and application software.

2. Explain the different functions of an operating system and discuss some ways that operating systems enhance processing efficiency.

3. List several ways in which operating systems differ from one another.

4. Name today's most widely used operating systems for personal computers and servers.

5. State several devices other than personal computers and servers that require an operating system and list one possible operating system for each type of device.

6. Discuss the role of utility programs and outline several tasks that these programs perform.

7. Describe what the operating systems of the future might be like.

outline

OVERVIEW

As you already know, all computers require software in order to operate and perform basic tasks. For instance, software is needed to translate your commands into a form the computer can understand, to open and close other software programs, to manage your stored files, and to locate and set up new hardware as it is added to a computer. The type of software used to perform these tasks is system software—the focus of this chapter. System software runs in the background at all times, launching other software when needed and making it possible for you to use your computer.

We begin this chapter by looking at the difference between system software and application software. System software, the primary topic of this chapter, is usually divided into two categories: operating systems and utility programs. First we examine the operating system—the primary component of system software. We discuss the functions of and general differences between operating systems, and then we explore the specific operating systems most widely used today. Next, we look at utility programs. Utility programs typically perform support functions for the operating system, such as allowing you to manage your files, perform maintenance on your computer, check your computer for viruses, or uninstall a program you no longer want on your computer. Chapter 5 closes with a look at what the future of operating systems may hold. ■

SYSTEM SOFTWARE VS. APPLICATION SOFTWARE

Computers run two types of software: system software and application software.

> - **System software** consists of the operating system and utility programs that control a computer system and allow you to use your computer. These programs enable the computer to boot, to launch application programs, and to facilitate important jobs, such as transferring files from one storage medium to another, configuring your computer to work with the hardware connected to it, managing files on your hard drive, and protecting your computer system from unauthorized use.

> - **Application software** includes all the programs that allow you to perform specific tasks on your computer, such as writing a letter, preparing an invoice, viewing a Web page, listening to a music file, checking the inventory of a particular product, playing a game, preparing financial statements, designing a home, and so forth. Application software is discussed in detail in Chapter 6.

In practice, the difference between system and application software is not always straightforward. Some programs, such as those used to burn DVDs, were originally viewed as utility programs. Today, these programs typically contain a variety of additional features,

> **System software.** Programs, such as the operating system, that control the operation of a computer and its devices, as well as enable application software to run on the computer. > **Application software.** Programs that enable users to perform specific tasks on a computer, such as writing a letter or playing a game.

such as the ability to organize and play music and other media files, transfer videos and digital photos to a computer, edit videos and photos, create DVD movies, copy CDs and DVDs, and create slide shows. Consequently, these programs now fit the definition of application programs more closely. On the other hand, system software today typically contains several application software components. For example, the *Microsoft Windows* operating system includes a variety of application programs including a Web browser, a calculator, a calendar program, a painting program, a media player, a movie making program, an instant messaging program, and a text editing program. A program's classification as system or application software usually depends on the principal function of the program, and the distinction between the two categories is not always clear cut.

THE OPERATING SYSTEM

A computer's **operating system** is a collection of programs that manage and coordinate the activities taking place within the computer and it is the most critical piece of software installed on the computer. The operating system boots the computer, launches application software, and ensures that all actions requested by a user are valid and processed in an orderly fashion. For example, when you issue the command for your computer to store a document on your hard drive, the operating system must perform the following steps: 1) make sure that the specified hard drive exists, 2) verify that there is adequate space on the hard drive to store the document and then store the document in that location, and 3) update the hard drive's directory with the filename and disk location for that file so that the document can be retrieved again when needed. In addition to managing all of the resources associated with your local computer, the operating system also facilitates connections to the Internet and other networks.

In general, the operating system serves as an intermediary between the user and the computer, as well as between application programs and the computer system's hardware (see Figure 5-1). Without an operating system, no other program can run, and the computer cannot function. Many tasks performed by the operating system, however, go unnoticed by the user because the operating system works in the background much of the time.

Functions of an Operating System

Operating systems have a wide range of functions—some of the most important are discussed next.

FIGURE 5-1
The intermediary role of the operating system.

1. USER
The user instructs the operating system to start an application program.

2. OPERATING SYSTEM
The operating system starts the requested program.

3. USER
The user instructs the application program to print the current document.

4. APPLICATION PROGRAM
The application program hands the document over to the operating system for printing.

5. OPERATING SYSTEM
The operating system sends the document to the printer.

6. PRINTER
The printer prints the document.

> **Operating system.** The main component of system software that enables the computer to manage its activities and the resources under its control, run application programs, and interface with the user.

Interfacing with Users

As Figure 5-1 illustrates, one of the principal roles of every operating system is to translate user instructions into a form the computer can understand. It also translates any feedback from hardware—such as a signal that the printer has run out of paper or that a new hardware device has been connected to the computer—into a form that the user can understand. The means by which an operating system or any other program interacts with the user is called the *user interface*; user interfaces can be *text-based* or *graphics-based*, as discussed in more detail shortly. Most, but not all, operating systems today use a *graphical user interface* (*GUI*).

Booting the Computer

As discussed in Chapter 1, the first task your operating system performs when you power up your computer is to *boot* the computer. During the boot process, the essential portion, or core, of the operating system (called the **kernel**) is loaded into memory. The kernel remains in memory the entire time the computer is on so that it is always available; other parts of the operating system are retrieved from the hard drive and loaded into memory when they are needed. Before the boot process ends, the operating system determines the hardware devices that are connected to the computer and configured properly, and it reads an opening batch of instructions. These startup instructions (which the user can customize to some extent when necessary) assign tasks for the operating system to carry out each time the computer boots, such as prompting the user to sign in to an instant messaging program or launching a security program to run continually in the background to detect possible threats.

Typically, many programs are running in the background at any one time, even before the user launches any application software (Figure 5-2 lists all the programs running on one computer immediately after it boots). These programs are launched automatically by the operating system, and they all consume memory and processing power. In Windows, users can see some of the application programs that are running in the background by looking at the icons in the system tray. To close a program, right-click the icon and select the appropriate option. To view the programs that will run each time the computer boots or to remove a program from this *startup list*, Windows users can use the *Startup* tab on the *Microsoft System Configuration Utility*. To open this utility, type *msconfig* in the search box at the bottom of the Start menu and then click the *msconfig* program name when it is displayed. To avoid creating a problem with your computer, however, be sure not to disable a program from the startup list without knowing absolutely what the program does and that it can be safely disabled. Other system configuration information is stored in the *Windows registry* files, which should be modified only by the Windows program itself or by advanced Windows users.

TIP

Press Ctrl+Alt+Delete to open the Task Manager window shown in Figure 5-2.

TIP

Run the msconfig program on a new Windows computer to remove the many *bloatware* programs that are typically preinstalled on a new computer and set to run at start up.

SW

FIGURE 5-2

Running programs.
Many programs are launched by the operating system when the computer boots.

TASK MANAGER
These programs are running, even before any application programs are launched by the user.

SYSTEM TRAY ICONS
These programs were launched during the boot process and will show up in the system tray unless they are closed by the user (right-click an icon to see if you can close that program).

>**Kernel.** The essential portion, or core, of an operating system.

FIGURE 5-3

Finding new hardware. Most operating systems are designed to detect new hardware and to try to configure it automatically.

NETGEAR WG111v2 54Mbps Wireless USB 2.0 Adapter ✕
Device driver software installed successfully.

3:53 PM

VIDEO PODCAST

Go to the Chapter 5 page at **www.cengage.com/ computerconcepts/np/uc13** to download or listen to the "How To: Find Out What's Running on Your PC" video podcast.

FIGURE 5-4

Program malfunctions. Most operating systems attempt to close only the program causing the problem, rather than requiring a full reboot.

Microsoft Windows

Internet Explorer has stopped working

Windows can check online for a solution to the problem and try to restart the program.

➔ Check online for a solution and restart the program

➔ Restart the program

⌄ View problem details

Configuring Devices

The operating system also configures all devices connected to a computer. Small programs called **device drivers** (or simply **drivers**) are used to communicate with peripheral devices, such as monitors, printers, and keyboards. Most operating systems today include the drivers needed for the most common peripheral devices. In addition, drivers often come on a CD packaged with the peripheral device, or they can be downloaded from the manufacturer's Web site. Most operating systems today look for and recognize new devices each time the computer boots. If a new device is found, the operating system typically tries to install the appropriate driver automatically in order to get the new hardware ready to use (see Figure 5-3)—a feature called *Plug and Play*. Because USB and FireWire devices can be connected to a computer when the computer is running, those devices are recognized and configured, as needed, each time they are plugged in to the computer.

Once a device and its driver have been installed properly, they usually work fine. If the device driver file is deleted, becomes *corrupted*, or has a conflict with another piece of software, then the device will no longer work. Usually, the operating system detects problems like this during the boot process and notifies the user, and then tries to reinstall the driver automatically. If the operating system is unable to correct the problem, the user can reinstall the driver manually. You may also need to update or reinstall some device drivers if you *upgrade* your operating system to a newer version. To keep your system up-to-date, many operating systems have an option to check for operating system updates automatically—including updated driver files—on a regular basis. Enabling these *automatic updates* is a good idea to keep your system running smoothly and protected from new threats (like the *computer viruses* discussed in Chapter 9).

Managing and Monitoring Resources and Jobs

As you work on your computer, the operating system continuously manages your computer's resources (such as software, disk space, and memory) and makes them available to devices and programs when they are needed. If a problem occurs—such as a program stops functioning or too many programs are open for the amount of memory installed in the computer—the operating system notifies the user and tries to correct the problem, often by closing the offending program (see Figure 5-4). If the problem cannot be corrected by the operating system, then the user typically needs to reboot the computer.

As part of managing system resources, the operating system schedules jobs (such as documents to be printed or files to be retrieved from a hard drive) to be performed using those resources. *Scheduling routines* in the operating system determine the order in which jobs are carried out, as well as which commands get executed first if the user is working with more than one program at one time or if the computer (such as a server or mainframe) supports multiple users.

File Management

Another important task that the operating system performs is *file management*—keeping track of the files stored on a computer so that they can be retrieved when needed. As discussed in Chapter 3, you can organize the files on a storage medium into folders to simplify file management. Usually the operating system files are stored inside one folder (such as a

> **Device driver.** A program that enables an operating system to communicate with a specific hardware device; often referred to simply as a **driver**.

ROOT DIRECTORY C:\
FOR HARD DRIVE C

WINDOWS   DOCUMENTS   PROGRAM FILES   GAMES

LETTERS   SCHOOL PAPERS

JOHN   MARY   BILL   HISTORY   ENGLISH

PATHS
A path shows the folders you must travel through to get to a particular file. C:\Documents\Letters\Mary, for instance, is the path to Mary's letter.

FOLDERS AND FILES

FOLDERS
A folder (directory) stores related information and can contain both files and other folders. Folders are designated by a file folder icon.

FILES
A file (document) can contain such things as a letter, budget, or Web page. Application programs typically use unique icons so the user can quickly identify the program associated with each file.

Word
(word processing)

Excel
(spreadsheet)

WinZip
(compressed file)

Internet Explorer
(Web page)

FIGURE 5-5
A sample hard drive organization.

FIGURE 5-6
Common file extensions.

SW

Windows folder), and each application program is stored in its own separate folder inside a main programs folder (such as *Program Files*). Other folders designed for storing data files are typically created by the operating system (such as the *Documents* (or *My Documents*) and *Music* (or *My Music*) folders in Windows, depending on the version of Windows being used); individuals may create additional folders, as desired, to keep their files organized. Folders can contain both files and other folders (called *subfolders*).

Files and folders are usually viewed in a hierarchical format; the top of the hierarchy for any storage medium is called the *root directory* (such as C: for the root directory of the hard drive C shown in Figure 5-5). The root directory typically contains both files and folders. To access a file, you generally navigate to the folder containing that file by opening the appropriate drive, folder, and subfolders. Alternatively, you can specify the *path* to a file's exact location. For example, as Figure 5-5 shows, the path

C:\Documents\Letters\Mary

leads through the root directory of the C drive and the *Documents* and *Letters* folders to a file named *Mary*. A similar path can also be used to access the files *John* and *Bill*. As discussed in Chapter 3, you specify a filename for each file when you initially save the file on a storage medium; there can be only one file with the exact same filename in any particular folder on a storage medium.

Filename rules vary with each operating system. For instance, current versions of Windows support filenames that are from 1 to 260 characters long (the length includes the entire path to the file's location) and may include numbers, letters, spaces, and any special characters except / : * ? " < > and |. Filenames typically include a *file extension* at the end of the filename. File extensions are usually three or four characters preceded by a period and are automatically added to a filename by the program in which that file was created, although sometimes the user may have a choice of file extensions supported by a program. Some common file extensions are listed in Figure 5-6 (graphics, audio, and video file formats are explained in more detail in Chapter 10).

File extensions should not be changed by the user because the operating system uses them to identify the program that should be used to open the file. For instance, if you issue a command to open a file named *Letter to Mom.docx*, the file will open using the Microsoft Word program (assuming a recent version of that program is

DOCUMENTS

.doc .docx .txt .rtf .htm .html

.mhtml .xml .xls .xlsx .mdb. .accdb

.ppt .pptx .pdf .sxc .sxi .odf

PROGRAMS

.com .exe

GRAPHICS

.bmp .tif .tiff .jpg .jpe .jpeg .eps

.gif .png .pcx .svg .dib

AUDIO

.wav .au .mp3 .snd .aiff .midi

.aac .wma .ra .m4a

VIDEO

.mpg .mp2 .mp4 .mpe .mov .avi

.rm .wmv .wm .asf

COMPRESSED FILES

.zip .sit .sitx .tar

installed on the computer) because the *.docx* file extension is associated with the Microsoft Word program. Files can be opened, as well as moved, copied, renamed, and deleted, using a *file management program* such as *Windows Explorer*. You may not be able to see file extensions in your file management program, however, since they are typically hidden by default. The Windows Explorer file management program and other utilities typically included in an operating system are discussed near the end of this chapter.

Security

A computer's operating system can use *passwords*, *biometric characteristics* (such as finger-prints), and other security procedures to prevent outsiders from accessing system resources that they are not authorized to access. Most operating systems have other security features available, such as an integrated *firewall* to protect against unauthorized access via the Internet or an option to download and install *security patches* (small program updates that correct known security problems) automatically from the operating system's manufacturer on a regular basis. Operating system passwords can also be used to ensure that *administrative level* operating system tasks (such as installing programs or changing system settings) are performed only by authorized users. Passwords, biometrics, and other security issues related to networks and the Internet are discussed in detail in Chapter 9.

Processing Techniques for Increased Efficiency

Operating systems often utilize various processing techniques in order to operate more efficiently and increase the amount of processing the computer system can perform in any given time period. Some of the techniques most commonly used by operating systems to increase efficiency are discussed in the next few sections.

Multitasking

Multitasking refers to the ability of an operating system to have more than one program (also called a *task*) open at one time. For example, multitasking allows a user to edit a spreadsheet file in one window while loading a Web page in another window or to retrieve new e-mail messages in one window while a word processing document is open in another window. Without the ability to multitask, an operating system would require the user to close one program before opening another program. Virtually all of today's operating systems support multitasking.

Although multitasking enables a user to work with multiple programs at one time, a single CPU core cannot execute more than one task at one time (unless Intel's Hyper-Threading Technology or another technology that allows a single core to function as two cores is used, as discussed in Chapter 2). Consequently, the CPU rotates between processing tasks, but it works so quickly that to the user it appears as though all programs are executing at the same time.

Multithreading

A *thread* is a sequence of instructions within a program that is independent of other threads. Examples might include spell checking, printing, and opening documents in a word processing program. Operating systems that support *multithreading* have the ability to rotate between multiple threads (similar to the way multitasking can rotate between multiple programs) so that processing is completed faster and more efficiently, even though only one thread is executed by a single core at one time. An exception to this is computers using Intel's Hyper-Threading Technology, which allows more than one thread to be executed by a single CPU core at one time. Most current operating systems support multithreading.

> **Multitasking.** The capability of an operating system to run more than one program at one time.

SEQUENTIAL PROCESSING
Tasks are performed one right after the other.

SIMULTANEOUS PROCESSING
Multiple tasks are performed at the exact same time.

FIGURE 5-7
Sequential vs. simultaneous processing.

SW

Multiprocessing and Parallel Processing

As discussed in Chapter 2, both multiprocessing and parallel processing involve using two or more CPUs (or multiple cores in a single CPU) in one computer system to perform work more efficiently. The primary difference between these two techniques is that, with multiprocessing, each CPU typically works on a different job; with parallel processing, the processors usually work together to complete one job more quickly. In either case, the CPUs can perform tasks *simultaneously* (at the exactly the same time), in contrast with multitasking and multithreading which use a single CPU and process tasks *sequentially* (by rotating through tasks, as discussed previously). Figure 5-7 illustrates the difference between simultaneous and sequential processing, using tasks typical of a desktop computer.

Multiprocessing is supported by most operating systems and is used with personal computers that have multi-core CPUs (as discussed in Chapter 2), as well as with servers and mainframe computers that have multi-core CPUs and/or multiple CPUs. Parallel processing is used most often with supercomputers and supercomputing clusters.

Memory Management

Another key function of the operating system is *memory management*, which involves optimizing the use of main memory (RAM). The operating system allocates RAM to programs as needed and then reclaims that memory when the program is closed. With today's memory-intensive programs, good memory management can help speed up processing. Since each additional running program or open window consumes memory, users can also help with memory management by limiting the number of programs running in the background (as discussed in an earlier section) to only the ones that are absolutely necessary, as well as by closing windows when they are no longer needed.

One memory management technique frequently used by operating systems is **virtual memory**, which uses a portion of the computer's hard drive as additional RAM. All programs and data located in RAM are divided into fixed-length *pages* or variable-length *segments*, depending on the operating system being used. When the amount of RAM

> **TIP**
>
> Although memory used by a program or process is supposed to be released when it is no longer needed, this does not always happen. Referred to as *memory leaking*, this problem can cause your computer to run out of memory temporarily. When this occurs, reboot your computer to refresh its RAM.

>**Virtual memory.** A memory-management technique that uses hard drive space as additional RAM.

1. Pages of programs or data are copied from RAM to the virtual memory area of the hard drive.

2. Pages are copied back to RAM as they are needed for processing.

3. As more room in RAM is needed, pages are copied to virtual memory and then deleted from RAM.

4. The swapping process continues until the program finishes executing.

FIGURE 5-8

How virtual memory works.

required exceeds the amount of RAM available, the operating system moves pages from RAM to the virtual memory area of the hard drive (this area is called the *page file* or *swap file*). Consequently, as a program is executed, some of the program may be stored in RAM and some in virtual memory. As RAM gets full, pages are moved to virtual memory, and as pages stored in virtual memory are required, they are retrieved from virtual memory and moved to RAM (see Figure 5-8). This *paging* or *swapping* process continues until the program finishes executing. Virtual memory allows you to use more memory than is physically available on your computer, but using virtual memory is slower than just using RAM. Most operating systems today allow the user to specify the total amount of hard drive space to be used for virtual memory. For additional memory to speed up operations, users with computers running recent versions of Windows can also use flash memory media (such as a USB flash drive) in conjunction with Windows' *ReadyBoost* feature.

Buffering and Spooling

Some input and output devices are exceedingly slow, compared to today's CPUs. If the CPU had to wait for these slower devices to finish their work, the computer system would experience a horrendous bottleneck. For example, suppose a user sends a 100-page document to the printer. Assuming the printer can output 20 pages per minute, it would take 5 minutes for the document to finish printing. If the CPU had to wait for the print job to be completed before performing other tasks, the computer would be tied up for 5 minutes.

To avoid this problem, most operating systems use two techniques—*buffering* and *spooling*. A **buffer** is an area in RAM or on the hard drive designated to hold input and output on their way in or out of the system. For instance, a *keyboard buffer* stores characters as they are entered via the keyboard, and a *print buffer* stores documents that are waiting to be printed. The process of placing items in a buffer so they can be retrieved by the appropriate device when needed is called **spooling**. The most common use of buffering and spooling is *print spooling*. Print spooling allows multiple documents to be sent to the printer at one time and to print, one after the other, in the background while the computer and user are performing other tasks. The documents waiting to be printed are said to be in a *print queue*, which designates the order the documents will be printed. While in the print queue, most operating systems allow the user to cancel print jobs and pause the printer (see Figure 5-9); some also allow the user to prioritize the documents in the print queue.

FIGURE 5-9

A print queue.

All print jobs currently in the queue.

This print job is being cancelled.

This print job is currently printing.

>**Buffer.** An area in RAM or on the hard drive designated to hold input and output on their way in and out of the system. >**Spooling.** The process of placing items in a buffer so the appropriate device (such as a printer) can retrieve them when needed.

Although originally used primarily for keyboard input and print jobs, most computers and operating systems today use several other buffers to speed up operations. For instance, it is common today for computers to use buffers to assist in redisplaying images on the screen and to temporarily store data that is in the process of being burned onto a CD or DVD.

Differences Among Operating Systems

There are different types of operating systems available to meet different needs. Some of the major distinctions among operating systems include the type of user interface utilized, whether the operating system is targeted for personal or network use, and what type of processing the operating system is designed for.

Command Line vs. Graphical User Interface

As mentioned earlier in this chapter, a user interface is the manner in which an operating system interacts with its users. Most operating systems today use a **graphical user interface** (**GUI**). The older *DOS* operating system and some versions of the *UNIX* and *Linux* operating systems use a **command line interface** (see Figure 5-10), although graphical versions of UNIX and Linux are available. Command line interfaces require users to input commands using the keyboard; graphical user interfaces allow the user to issue commands by selecting icons, buttons, menu items, and other graphical objects with a mouse or other pointing device.

Types of Operating Systems

Operating systems used with personal computers are typically referred to as **personal operating systems** (also called *desktop operating systems*) and they are designed to be installed on a single computer. In contrast, **server operating systems** (also called *network operating systems*) are designed to be installed on a network server to grant multiple users access to a network and its resources. Each computer on a network has its own personal operating system installed (just as with a stand-alone computer) and that operating system controls the activity on that computer, while the server operating system controls access to network resources. Computers on a network may also need special *client* software to access the network and issue requests to the server.

For instance, when you boot a computer connected to a network, the personal operating system installed on your computer boots that computer; the server operating system then asks for your username and password or whatever other data is required to log on to the network, and then allows you to access to the network resources you are authorized to access. To the computers on a network, network resources (such as a shared network hard drive or printer) generally look like *local* (non-network) resources. For instance, you will see a network hard drive listed with its own identifying letter (such as F or G) along with the drives located on your computer, and you will see a network printer included in your list of available printers whenever you open a Print dialog box. If you do not log on to the network or if the network

FIGURE 5-10
Command line
vs. graphical user
interfaces.

COMMAND LINE INTERFACE
Commands are entered using the keyboard.

GRAPHICAL USER INTERFACE
Icons, buttons, menus, and other objects are selected with the mouse to issue commands to the computer.

>**Graphical user interface (GUI).** A graphically based interface that allows a user to communicate instructions to the computer easily.
>**Command line interface.** A user interface that requires the user to communicate instructions to the computer via typed commands.
>**Personal operating system.** A type of operating system designed to be installed on a single personal computer. >**Server operating system.** A type of operating system designed to be installed on a network server.

1. The client software provides a shell around your desktop operating system. The shell program enables your computer to communicate with the server operating system, which is located on the network server.

2. When you request a network activity, such as printing a document using a network printer, your application program passes the job to your desktop operating system, which sends it to the client shell, which sends it on to the server operating system, which is located on the network server.

3. The server operating system then lines up your job in its print queue and prints the job when its turn comes.

Client shell

Desktop operating system

Application software

Your print job

Your print job

Network server running a server operating system

Desktop computer running Windows and client software for the server operating system being used.

Your print job

Your print job

4. Your print job

3. Job C

2. Job B

1. Job A

Network printer   **PRINT QUEUE**

FIGURE 5-11

How operating systems are used in a network environment.

is down, you cannot access network resources, such as to launch a program located on the network server, save a document to a network hard drive, print using a shared printer, or access the Internet via a shared Internet connection. However, the personal operating system installed on your computer will allow you to work locally on that computer, just as you would on a stand-alone computer. An overview of how a typical personal operating system and a server operating system interact on a computer network is illustrated in Figure 5-11.

In addition to personal operating systems and server operating systems, there are **mobile operating systems** that are designed to be used with mobile phones and other mobile devices, and **embedded operating systems** that are built into consumer kiosks, cash registers, some consumer electronics, and other devices. Specific examples of personal, server, mobile, and embedded operating systems are covered later in this chapter.

The Types of Processors Supported

Most operating systems today are designed to be used with specific types of processors, such as mobile, desktop, or server processors, as well as specific numbers of processors. For instance, some personal operating systems (such as Microsoft Vista) can be used with only one or two processors. In addition, most operating systems are designed for either 32-bit or 64-bit CPUs. Because their word size is twice as large, 64-bit processors can process up to twice as much data per clock cycle as 32-bit processors (depending on the extent to which the application being used supports 64-bit processing), and they can address more than 4 GB of RAM. Both of these factors help to speed up processing in some applications if a 64-bit operating system is being used. Operating systems that support 64-bit CPUs often include other architectural improvements that together may result in a more efficient operating system and, consequently, faster operations. Windows, Mac OS, Linux,

> **Mobile operating system.** A type of operating system used with mobile phones and other mobile devices. > **Embedded operating system.** A type of operating system embedded into devices, such as cars and consumer devices.

TREND

SideShow and Smart Notebook Covers

Ever want to change the cover of your portable computer to reflect your mood or to check your e-mail when your computer is closed? Well, the solution is just about here. Because of the progress being made in the area of flexible electronics, experts predict that soon a variety of images and information will be able to be displayed on the cover of a portable computer, even if the computer is turned off. Possibilities include changing the color or displaying images on the entire computer for decorative purposes, as well as displaying useful content from the computer. While this feature has yet to materialize on the entire cover of a portable computer, recent versions of Windows include support for a secondary display device—such as a small display located on the cover of a portable computer, on a keyboard, or on other hardware. The technology, called *SideShow*, allows users to access content—such as e-mail messages, news updates, schedules, maps, flight information, stock quotes, address books, Wi-Fi connectivity information, digital music, and more—from the computer the SideShow display is being used with and display that information on the secondary display. The SideShow device can be a part of the computer itself or built into devices such as keyboards, monitors, laptop bags, remote controls, digital picture frames, or stand-alone displays (see the accompanying photos). In any case, the SideShow device displays information received from the associated computer. For example, a SideShow-enabled remote control can be used to retrieve TV listings or information about recorded TV shows from a Windows Media Center computer, and a SideShow-enabled digital picture frame can be used to display e-mail messages, flight information, and other information, in addition to displaying digital photos.

Because it uses minimal power, a SideShow device can be left on continually; in fact, it can be set up to access information on the computer it is being used with and refresh the content displayed on the SideShow device on a regular basis. SideShow devices typically connect to their respective computers via a wireless networking connection, and users can determine the information they would like displayed on the SideShow device by installing and configuring *gadgets*—small programs—on the SideShow device.

SECONDARY DISPLAY BUILT INTO A NOTEBOOK COVER

Each display has its own directional and selection controls.

Content, such as new e-mail messages, maps, stock quotes, or schedule information, is displayed here.

STAND-ALONE SECONDARY DISPLAY

and most other widely used operating systems are all available in 64-bit versions. Details about these and other operating systems are discussed shortly.

Support for Virtualization and Other Technologies

As new technologies or trends (such as new types of buses, virtualization, power consumption concerns, touch and gesture input, and the move to Web-based software, for example) emerge, operating systems must be updated in order to support those new technologies or trends. On the other hand, as technologies become obsolete, operating system manufacturers need to decide when support for those technologies will cease. Alternatively, hardware manufacturers also need to respond to new technologies introduced by operating systems. For instance, the latest versions of Windows support a new *SideShow* feature that requires the incorporation of a secondary display device built into hardware, such as into the cover of a notebook computer. When a new operating system feature (such as SideShow) is introduced, hardware manufacturers must decide if they want to adapt their hardware to support the new feature. For a look at SideShow and how it can be used to provide you with updates of the information you want to see on a regular basis, see the Trend box.

OPERATING SYSTEMS FOR PERSONAL COMPUTERS AND SERVERS

As previously discussed, many operating systems today are designed either for personal computers (such as desktop and notebook computers) or for network servers. The most widely used personal and server operating systems are discussed next. Mobile and embedded versions of these operating systems are discussed later in this chapter.

DOS

During the 1980s and early 1990s, **DOS (Disk Operating System)** was the dominant operating system for microcomputers. DOS traditionally used a command line interface, although newer versions of DOS support a menu-driven interface. There are two primary forms of DOS: *PC-DOS* and *MS-DOS*. PC-DOS was created originally for IBM PCs (and is owned by IBM), whereas MS-DOS was created for use with IBM-compatible PCs. Both versions were originally developed by Microsoft Corporation, but neither version is updated any longer. DOS is not widely used with personal computers today because it does not utilize a graphical user interface and does not support modern processors and processing techniques. Some computers (such as computers running the Windows operating system), however, can still understand DOS commands and users can issue these commands using the *Command Prompt* window, as shown in Figure 5-12.

CHANGE DIRECTORY (CD) COMMAND
Changes to a new location on the current drive.

DRIVE COMMAND
Changes to a new drive.

COPY COMMAND
Copies files from one location to another.

DIRECTORY (DIR) COMMAND
Displays the files and folders in the current location.

FIGURE 5-12
DOS. Even though DOS has become technologically obsolete, Windows users can still issue DOS commands via the Command Prompt.

Windows

Microsoft Windows has been the predominant personal operating system for many years and still holds about 90% of the market. There have been many different versions of **Windows** over the years; the next few sections chronicle the main developments of this operating system.

Windows 1.0 Through Windows XP

Microsoft created the original version of Windows—*Windows 1.0*—in 1985 in an effort to meet the needs of users frustrated by having to learn and use DOS commands. Windows 1.0 through *Windows 3.x* (*x* stands for the version number of the software, such as Windows 3.0, 3.1, or 3.11) were not, however, full-fledged operating systems. Instead, they were *operating environments* for the DOS operating system; that is, graphical shells that operated around the DOS operating system and were designed to make DOS easier to use.

In 1994, Microsoft announced that all versions of Windows after 3.11 would be full-fledged operating systems instead of just operating environments. The next several versions of Windows are as follows:

> *Windows 95* (released in 1995) and *Windows 98* (released in 1998)—both used a GUI similar to the one used with Windows 3.x but were easier to use than earlier versions of Windows. Both Windows 95 and Windows 98 supported multitasking, long filenames, a higher degree of Internet integration, more options for customizing the desktop user interface, larger hard drives, DVD drives, and USB devices.

> *Windows NT* (*New Technology*)—the first 32-bit version of Windows designed for high-end workstations and servers. Windows NT was built from the ground up using a different kernel than the other versions of Windows.

> *Windows Me* (*Millennium Edition*)—the replacement for Windows 98. Designed for home computers, Windows Me supported improved home networking and a shared Internet connection; it also featured improved multimedia capabilities, better system protection, a faster boot process, and more Internet-ready activities and games.

> *Windows 2000*—released in 2000 to replace Windows NT. Windows 2000 was geared toward high-end business workstations and servers, and it included support for wireless devices and other types of new hardware.

> *Windows XP*—replaced both Windows 2000 (for business use) and Windows Me (for home use) and included improved photo, video, and music editing and sharing; improved networking capabilities; and support for handwriting and voice input. While Microsoft is phasing out Windows XP and only netbooks can be purchased with that version of Windows today, there is still a large installed base of Windows XP users and Microsoft plans to support Windows XP until 2014.

Windows Vista

Windows Vista replaced Windows XP and was the current version of Windows until *Windows 7* was released in late 2009. However, Windows Vista is still widely used today. It comes in four basic editions (*Home Basic*, *Home Premium*, *Business*, and *Ultimate*) and in both 32-bit and 64-bit versions. One of the most obvious initial changes in Windows Vista is the *Aero* interface. Aero is a new visual graphical user interface that uses glass-like transparency, vibrant colors, and dynamic elements like *Live Thumbnails* of taskbar buttons and a *Flip 3D* feature to view all open windows in 3D to make the Vista experience more productive and enjoyable

ASK THE EXPERT

Tony Onorati, Former Naval Aviator and Former Commanding Officer, Strike Fighter Weapons School Pacific, NAS Lemoore

What computer experience is needed to be a U.S. Navy pilot?

While no computer experience is necessarily required to enter flight school, failure to have a solid knowledge of the Windows operating system will put the candidate well behind his/her contemporaries when they finally do reach the fleet as a pilot. All the tactical planning tools for preflight preparation, navigation, ordnance delivery, and mission planning, as well as all aircraft-specific publications, manuals, and training, are all computer based. For the FA-18 Hornet, all mission data is created on the computer, copied to a mission computer card, and plugged into the jet where it is downloaded into the aircraft's computer for use in flight. Becoming a naval aviator without computer skills is like entering flight school without ever having flown before—it can be done but it places you well behind the power curve.

AERO INTERFACE
Features translucent, glass-like windows and 3D effects.

ICONS
Represent programs, folders, documents, and other items that can be opened with the mouse.

SIDEBAR
Contains the user's selected gadgets.

WINDOWS
Contain programs, icons, documents, and so forth.

SEARCHES
Can be saved for later use.

QUICK LAUNCH TOOLBAR
Used to launch programs.

START MENU
Includes a search box to search for and open documents, programs, and Web sites.

FIGURE 5-13
Windows Vista.

(see Figure 5-13). Windows Vista also introduced the *Sidebar* feature that contains *gadgets*—small applications that are used to perform a variety of tasks, such as displaying weather information, a clock, a calendar, a calculator, sticky notes, news headlines, personal photos, e-mail messages, stock tickers, and more.

The Vista Start menu is more streamlined than in Windows XP. It also contains an *Instant Search* feature located at the bottom of the Start menu to allow users to easily search for and open programs and documents stored on their computers. Searches can be saved in *Search Folders* so that updated search results based on that search criteria can be viewed at any time just by opening the appropriate Search Folder, as discussed in more detail later in this chapter.

Vista also contains several built-in security features and much improved networking, collaboration, and synchronization tools. Improved multimedia capabilities include a new *Windows Photo Gallery*, *Windows DVD Maker*, and a *Windows Media Center* used to access digital entertainment, such as recorded TV shows and downloaded music. *Windows Speech Recognition* allows users to interact with their computers using their voice; with this program, users can control the operating system, dictate documents, and fill out Web-based forms verbally, as discussed in the Chapter 6 How It Works box.

One issue surrounding Vista is its higher level of hardware requirements when compared to earlier versions of Windows and other operating systems. Windows Vista requires a significant amount of memory in order to function at an acceptable speed; it also has specific graphics requirements that must be met in order to use the Aero interface. These limitations are one reason many individuals and businesses decided to stay with Windows XP instead of upgrading to Vista.

Windows 7

Windows 7, released in late 2009, is the newest version of Windows. Windows 7 is available in both 32-bit and 64-bit versions and in four main editions, including *Home Premium* (the primary version for home users) and *Professional* (the primary version for businesses). While the minimum suggested system requirements for Windows 7 are essentially the same as for Vista, Windows 7 is designed to start up and respond faster than Vista. In addition, Microsoft states that all versions of Windows 7 will run well on netbooks—something Vista could not do and a very important feature since netbooks are one of the fastest growing areas of the personal computer market today.

>**Windows 7.** The current version of Windows.

AERO INTERFACE
Windows are still transparent and 3D options (such as Live Thumbnails) are active.

DESKTOP GADGETS
Gadgets are now located on the desktop.

PROGRAM ICONS
Can be pinned to the taskbar.

TASKBAR BUTTONS
Can be rearranged by the user; pointing to a button displays a Live Thumbnail.

JUMP LISTS
Right-click an icon to display the most recent documents for that program.

SHOW DESKTOP
Point to the Show Desktop button to make all windows temporarily transparent.

FIGURE 5-14
Windows 7.

The appearance of Windows 7 is similar to Windows Vista—many of the improvements in Windows 7 focus on making it faster and easier to use. For instance, you can now drag taskbar buttons to rearrange them in the order you prefer, and you can *pin* (lock) a program to the taskbar so it can be launched with a single click (this feature replaces the *Quick Launch toolbar* in Windows Vista). In addition, you can view a larger version of a window by pointing to its taskbar thumbnail, and you can right-click a taskbar button (and some Start menu items) to bring up a *jump list* to show your most recent documents for that program (see Figure 5-14). To quickly arrange two windows side by side, you can drag a window to the left or right edge of the desktop to have it automatically resize and snap into place to fill half of the screen. Gadgets have moved from the Sidebar (as in Windows Vista) to the desktop in Windows 7 to free up the entire screen for documents and other content. Gadgets (and other items located on the desktop) can be viewed easily by pointing to the *Show Desktop* button in the bottom far right corner of the taskbar. This option temporarily makes all open windows transparent so items on the desktop are visible (as in the right image in Figure 5-14).

To make it easier to use and manage all of your connected devices (such as printers, portable digital media players, USB flash drives, and so forth), Windows 7 includes a new *Device Stage*. To easily stream media content stored on your computer to any networked device (such as another computer, a stereo, or an Xbox 360), Windows 7 includes a *Play To* option. In addition, Windows 7 includes a *HomeGroup* feature for improved home networking, one-click Wi-Fi connections, support for both touch and pen input, and improved accessory programs (such as a more versatile Calculator and a Paint program that uses the *Ribbon* interface found in recent versions of Microsoft Office).

TIP

With Windows 7, some programs (such as Messenger, Mail, Photo Gallery, and Movie Maker) are no longer included in the operating system but are available for free as *Windows Live Essentials* downloads from the Windows Live Web site.

Windows Server and Windows Home Server

Windows Server is the version of Windows designed for server use. *Windows Server 2008* includes *Internet Information Services 7.0*, which is a powerful Web platform for Web applications and Web services; built-in virtualization technologies; a variety of new security tools and enhancements; and streamlined configuration and management tools. The latest version of Windows Server 2008 is called *Windows Server 2008 R2* and includes features that are designed specifically to work with client computers running Windows 7.

A related operating system designed for home use is *Windows Home Server*, which is preinstalled on home server devices and designed to provide services for a home network. For instance, a home server can serve as a central storage location for all devices (computers, gaming consoles, portable digital media players, and so forth) in the home. Home servers also can be set up to back up all devices in the home on a regular basis, as well as to give users access to the data on the home server and to control the home network from any computer via the Internet.

Mac OS

Mac OS (see Figure 5-15) is the proprietary operating system for computers made by Apple Corporation. It is based on the UNIX operating system (discussed shortly) and originally set the standard for graphical user interfaces. Many of today's operating systems follow the trend that Mac OS started and, in fact, use GUIs that highly resemble the one used with Mac OS.

The latest versions of Mac OS (such as *Mac OS X Leopard* and *Mac OS X Snow Leopard*) are part of the **Mac OS X** family. Mac OS X allows multithreading and multitasking, supports dual 64-bit processors, and has a high level of multimedia functions and connectivity. In addition, it includes the *Safari* Web browser, a *Spaces* feature that allows you to organize groups of applications and windows into Spaces that can be displayed or hidden as desired, a *Stacks* feature that allows you to store files (documents, programs, and so on) in a Stack on the *Dock*, and a *Quick Look* feature that shows you previews of files without opening them. The main improvement provided by the most recent version of Mac OS X (Snow Leopard) over the previous version (Leopard) is responsiveness. For instance, the *Time Machine* automatic backup and restore system is 50% faster, *Mail* loads messages 85% faster and conducts

V **FIGURE 5-15**

Mac OS X Leopard.

QUICK LOOK
Shows previews of files without opening them.

WINDOWS
Contain programs, icons, documents, and so forth.

STACK
Contains a collection of documents stored on the dock by the user.

ICONS
Represent programs, folders, documents, or other items that can be opened with the mouse.

DOCK
Contains the user's Stacks and commonly used icons.

searches up to 90% faster, and the new 64-bit Safari browser is faster and more resistant to crashes. Snow Leopard is also more efficient, requiring only about one-half the hard drive space as previous versions.

Mac OS X Server is the server version of Mac OS X. The latest version, *Mac OS X Server Snow Leopard*, is a full 64-bit operating system that is up to twice as fast as earlier server versions. New capabilities built into Snow Leopard Server include *Podcast Producer 2* for creating and publishing podcasts, and *Mobile Access Server* for providing authorized users secure remote access to firewall protected servers via Macs, iPhones, and other Apple devices.

UNIX

UNIX was originally developed in the late 1960s at AT&T Bell Laboratories as an operating system for midrange servers. UNIX is a multiuser, multitasking operating system. Computer systems ranging from microcomputers to mainframes can run UNIX, and it can support a variety of devices from different manufacturers. This flexibility gives UNIX an advantage over competing operating systems in some situations. However, UNIX is more expensive, requires a higher level of technical knowledge, and tends to be harder to install, maintain, and upgrade than most other commonly used operating systems.

There are many versions of UNIX available, as well as many other operating systems that are based on UNIX. These operating systems—such as Mac OS—are sometimes referred to as *UNIX flavors*. In fact, the term *UNIX*, which initially referred to the original UNIX operating system, has evolved to refer today to a group of similar operating systems based on UNIX. Many UNIX flavors are not compatible with each other, which creates some problems when a program written for one UNIX computer system is moved to another computer system running a different flavor of UNIX. To avoid this incompatibility problem, the *Open Group* open source consortium is dedicated to the development and evolution of the *Single UNIX Specification*—a standardized programming environment for UNIX applications. Both personal and server versions of UNIX-based operating systems are available.

FIGURE 5-16

Linux. This version of Linux includes a 3D graphical interface to increase the user's workspace.

Linux

Linux is an operating system developed by *Linus Torvalds* in 1991 when he was a student at the University of Helsinki in Finland. The operating system resembles UNIX but was developed independently from it. Linux was released to the public as *open source software*; that is, a program whose *source code* is available to the public and can be modified to improve it or to customize it to a particular application, as discussed in more detail in Chapter 6. Over the years, the number of Linux users has grown, and volunteer programmers from all over the world have collaborated to improve it, sharing their modified code with others over the Internet. Although Linux originally used a command line interface, most recent versions of Linux programs use a graphical user interface (see Figure 5-16). Linux is widely available as a free download via

THE **LINUX** FOUNDATION

Jim Zemlin, Executive Director, The Linux Foundation

Is there a downside to installing Linux on a personal computer?

No, I don't think so. More consumers than ever are using Linux on their PCs. Recently, Microsoft introduced a new operating system that won't run well on PCs more than just a few years old. Many people are finding that Linux is well suited for these older computers. This is good for users who don't want to throw away a perfectly good computer, and it's good for the environment and our landfills. Desktop Linux is easy to install and use. In fact, the Russian government recently installed Linux on all computers in their schools. The upsides of running Linux on a personal computer are flexibility, customization, and choice, among others. It's also free and comes with all the software you need! A computer is your personal property and you should have the freedom to customize it as you see fit—both inside and out. Linux allows you this freedom.

the Internet; companies are also permitted to customize Linux and sell it as a retail product. Commercial Linux distributions (such as those available from Red Hat and Novell) come with maintenance and support materials (something that many of the free versions do not offer) making the commercial versions more attractive for corporate users.

Over the years, Linux has grown from an operating system used primarily by computer techies who disliked Microsoft to a widely accepted operating system with strong support from mainstream companies, such as IBM, HP, Dell, and Novell. Linux is available in both personal and server versions; it is also widely used with mobile phones, as discussed shortly. The use of Linux with inexpensive personal computers is growing. In fact, one Linux-based operating system (*Android*) developed for mobile phones may be extended to netbooks and other very portable personal computers in the near future.

One reason individuals and organizations are switching to Linux and other open source software is cost. Typically, using the Linux operating system and a free or low-cost office suite, Web browser program, and e-mail program can save several hundreds of dollars per computer.

OPERATING SYSTEMS FOR MOBILE PHONES AND OTHER DEVICES

While notebook, netbook, UMPCs, and other portable personal computers typically use the same operating systems as desktop computers, mobile phones and other mobile devices usually use mobile operating systems—either mobile versions of personal operating systems (such as Windows or Linux) or special operating systems (such as *Apple iPhone OS* or *Blackberry OS*) that are designed solely for mobile devices. There are also embedded operating systems designed to be used with everyday objects, such as home appliances, gaming consoles, digital cameras, toys, watches, GPS systems, home medical devices, voting terminals, and cars (for a look at some of the features now available in *smart cars*, see the Inside the Industry box). Most users select a mobile phone by considering the mobile provider, hardware, and features associated with the phone, instead of considering the operating system used. However, users should understand that the operating system used with a phone or other device determines some of the capabilities of the phone (such as whether it can accept touch input or whether its display can rotate automatically as the phone is moved from portrait to landscape orientation), the interface used, and the applications that can run on that device. The most widely used mobile and embedded operating systems are discussed next.

Mobile and Embedded Versions of Windows

The mobile and embedded versions of Windows are called *Windows Mobile* and *Windows Embedded*, respectively.

INSIDE THE INDUSTRY

Smart Cars

Computers have been integrated into cars for years to perform specific tasks, such as assisting with gear shifting and braking. Lately, however, the use of computers in cars has skyrocketed and they are also being used to add additional convenience and safety to the driving experience. Some features, such as GPS navigation systems and smart air bag systems that adjust the deployment of an air bag based on the weight of the occupant, are fairly standard today. Integrated *infotainment systems* that use Bluetooth and USB ports to tie mobile phones and portable digital media players to the car stereo system, as well as to steering wheel and voice control systems, are also now available. Some other new and emerging trends in smart cars are discussed next.

➤ *Self-parking systems*—use cameras and/or sensors to assist in parallel parking; the onboard computer completely controls the car's steering wheel during the parking process and instructs the driver when any action (such as changing gears) is needed in order to park the car correctly.

➤ *Lane departure systems*—use cameras to view the markings on the road and vibrate the steering wheel if the car begins to veer out of its lane.

➤ *Drowsiness detection systems*—use cameras to evaluate the driver's blinking pattern and eyelid movements and vibrate the seat or otherwise alert the driver if the driver becomes drowsy.

➤ *Blind spot detection systems*—use cameras mounted on the car's side mirrors to detect vehicles in the driver's blind spot and display a warning light near the mirror to notify the driver that something is in the blind spot (shown in Figure 1-12 in Chapter 1).

➤ *Adaptive cruise control and distance alert systems*—use a radar system installed on the front of the car to detect the speed and distance of the vehicle ahead of it, and then automatically decrease or increase the speed of the car to maintain a safe distance from the vehicle ahead of it.

➤ *Collision warning and auto brake systems*—use radar and camera systems installed on the front of the car to warn the driver when they are too close to the car in front of them; if a collision is imminent, the brakes are automatically activated at that point (see the accompanying illustration).

➤ *Electronic traffic sign recognition systems*—use cameras to read speed limit, one-way, and other important traffic signs and notify the driver of any potential problems (such as exceeding the speed limit or driving the wrong way on a one-way street). When used with adaptive cruise control systems, the car can be set to adjust the speed to the correct speed limit automatically.

➤ *Keyless entry and ignition systems*—use the owner's fingerprint to unlock and start the car; future applications will likely include mobile phone applications that perform these tasks.

One of the biggest challenges for smart car technologies is the safe use of all the smart gadgets being incorporated into cars. The concern stems from studies consistently showing that distracted drivers are the cause of a vast majority of crashes. Voice-controlled dashboard components, mobile phones, and other devices help because they are hands-free, although studies have found that your risk of an accident requiring a trip to the hospital quadruples when you are talking on a mobile phone—hands-free or not.

Volvo's collision warning and auto brake system.

WINDOWS MOBILE

ANDROID

IPHONE OS

BLACKBERRY OS

FIGURE 5-17

Examples of mobile
operating systems.

Windows Mobile

Windows Mobile is the version of Windows designed for mobile phones. It has some of the look and feel of the larger desktop versions of Windows (see the Start button shown in Figure 5-17), but it also has features useful to mobile users. For instance, Windows Mobile supports multitasking; includes an improved mobile Web browser; supports a free *My Phone* service that automatically syncs and backs up contacts, text messages, and other information to the Web; and supports a variety of software, including Facebook applications, mobile versions of Microsoft Word, Excel, and PowerPoint; and more. The current version of Microsoft Mobile is *Microsoft Mobile 6.1*. The next version—*Windows Mobile 6.5*, also called *Microsoft Phone*—features a new honeycomb Home screen interface that allows users to view the information most important to them at a glance and accurately select the desired item by touch, and a new *Windows Marketplace for Mobile* application store to help users locate and purchase additional mobile applications. Windows Mobile 6.5 is expected to be available in 2010.

Windows Embedded

Windows Embedded is a family of operating systems based on Windows that is designed primarily for consumer and industrial devices that are not personal computers, such as cash registers, digital photo frames, GPS devices, ATM machines, medical devices, and robots. There are multiple versions of Windows Embedded based on different versions of Windows (including Windows XP, Windows Vista, and Windows Mobile) to match the type of device the operating system is to be used with and the computers with which the devices may need to interact. There are also versions of Windows specifically designed to be embedded into cars, such as *Microsoft Auto*—an embedded version of Windows that is designed specifically for integrated in-vehicle communication, entertainment, and navigation systems. For instance, Microsoft Auto powers the *Ford SYNC* system, which enables calls from mobile phones and music from portable digital media players to be controlled by voice or with buttons on the steering wheel.

Android

Android (refer again to Figure 5-17) is a Linux-based operating system developed by the Open Handset Alliance, a group that includes Google and more than 30 technology and mobile companies. Android supports multitasking and, as a relatively new operating system, it was able to built from the ground up with current mobile device capabilities in mind, which enables developers to create mobile applications that take full advantage of all the features a mobile device has to offer. It is an open platform, so users can connect to any mobile network and mobile phone provider they choose and they can customize their mobile phones (including the home screen, dialer, and applications used) as much as desired. A large number of applications have already been developed for Android and more applications and more Android-based phones (and, potentially, Android-based personal computers) are expected to be released soon.

iPhone OS

The mobile operating system designed for Apple mobile phones and mobile devices, such as the *iPhone 3G* and the *iPod Touch*, is **iPhone OS** (see Figure 5-17). This operating system is based on Apple's OS X operating system, supports multi-touch input, and has thousands of applications available via the *App Store*. While earlier versions of iPhone OS do not allow multitasking of third-party software (reportedly to increase battery life and stability), the newest version—*iPhone 3.0*—supports limited multitasking. It also includes an improved version of the Safari Web browser; a new media player; the ability to copy, cut, and paste text; the ability to send photos via text messaging; and improved search capabilities.

BlackBerry OS

BlackBerry OS is the operating system designed for BlackBerry devices (see Figure 5-17). It supports multitasking and, like other mobile operating systems, it includes e-mail and Web browsing support, music management, video recording, calendar tools, and more. In addition, BlackBerry OS includes a *voice note* feature that allows you to send a voice note via e-mail or text message and has an integrated maps feature. The latest version is *Blackberry OS 5.0*.

Palm OS and Palm webOS

Palm OS is the original operating system designed for Palm devices. In 2009, Palm released **Palm webOS**—a new Linux-based mobile operating system developed for next-generation Palm mobile phones, such as the *Palm Pre*. Unlike Palm OS, Palm webOS supports full multitasking; it also includes *Palm Synergy* to synchronize contacts and calendars from multiple locations, an improved Web browser, and a Web-based application suite.

Symbian OS

Symbian OS is a mobile operating system that supports multithreading and multitasking; it also includes support for Web browsing, e-mail, handwriting recognition, synchronization, and a range of other applications designed for mobile communications and computing. It has a flexible user interface framework that enables mobile phone manufacturers to develop and customize user interfaces to meet the needs of their customers. While not as widely used in North America as in other locations, Symbian OS is the most widely used mobile operating system worldwide, running on nearly half of the world's mobile phones, and is used on most Nokia mobile phones. The current version is *Symbian OS 9.5*.

ONLINE VIDEO

Go to the Chapter 5 page at **www.cengage.com/ computerconcepts/np/uc13** to watch the "A Tour of the Ford SYNC System" video clip.

ONLINE VIDEO

Go to the Chapter 5 page at **www.cengage.com/ computerconcepts/np/uc13** to watch the "A Tour of the T-Mobile G1 Android Mobile Phone" video clip.

FURTHER EXPLORATION

Go to the Chapter 5 page at **www.cengage.com/ computerconcepts/np/uc13** for links to information about operating systems.

SW

>**iPhone OS.** The operating system designed for Apple mobile phones and mobile devices. >**BlackBerry OS.** The operating system designed for BlackBerry devices. >**Palm OS.** The original operating system designed for Palm devices. >**Palm webOS.** The newest operating system designed for Palm devices. >**Symbian OS.** An operating system widely used with mobile phones; primarily used outside North America.

Embedded Linux

Embedded Linux is another operating system alternative for mobile phones, GPS devices, portable digital media players, and other mobile devices. Just as with desktop and server versions of Linux, embedded Linux is available in a variety of flavors from different companies. Linux is also the basis for several other mobile operating systems, such as Android, iPhone OS, and Palm webOS.

OPERATING SYSTEMS FOR LARGER COMPUTERS

Larger computer systems—such as high-end servers, mainframes, and supercomputers—sometimes use operating systems designed solely for that type of system. For instance, IBM's *i5/OS* and *z/OS* are designed for IBM servers and mainframes, respectively. In addition, many servers and mainframes today run conventional operating systems, such as Windows, UNIX, and Linux. Linux in particular is increasingly being used with both mainframes and supercomputers; often a group of Linux computers are linked together to form a Linux supercomputing cluster, as discussed in Chapter 1. Larger computer systems may also use a customized operating system based on a conventional operating system; for instance, many IBM mainframes and Cray supercomputers use versions of UNIX developed specifically for those computers (*AIX* and *UNICOS*, respectively).

UTILITY PROGRAMS

A **utility program** is a software program that performs a specific task, usually related to managing or maintaining the computer system. Many utility programs—such as programs for finding files, diagnosing and repairing system problems, cleaning up a hard drive, viewing images, playing multimedia files, and backing up files—are built into operating systems. There are also many stand-alone utility programs available as an alternative to the operating system's utility programs (such as a *search* or a *backup program*) or to provide additional utility features not usually built into operating systems (such as an *antivirus* or a *file compression program*). Stand-alone utility programs are often available in a *suite* of related programs (such as a collection of *maintenance programs* or *security programs*, as shown in Figure 5-18). Some of the most commonly used integrated and stand-alone utility programs are discussed next. For a look at how to download and install a new utility program from the Internet, see the How It Works box.

FIGURE 5-18
Utility suites. Utility suites contain a number of related utility programs.

File Management Programs

File management programs allow you to perform file management tasks such as looking to see which files are stored on a storage medium, and copying, moving, deleting, and renaming folders and files. The file management program incorporated into Windows is **Windows Explorer**; some common file management tasks using this program are summarized next.

HOW IT WORKS

Downloading and Installing Programs

Many software programs—including utility programs—are available for download via the Web. To download a program, generally a hyperlink is clicked and then the file is downloaded to your computer. With some installations, you can specify the location where the downloaded program should be stored on your computer—a good location for Windows users is the desktop for the installation files that you want to store only temporarily or the Downloads folder for the installation files that you want to retain. To start the installation process once the installation file is downloaded, open the installation file (navigate to the folder in which the installation is located, if needed, and then double-click the file). Many programs require that you accept the terms of a license agreement at the beginning of the installation process in order for the program to install. If the product was purchased, you may also be required to type in a *registration code* or *product key* at some point during the installation process;

these codes are typically e-mailed to you (or otherwise provided to you) after your payment for the product is processed. You may also be asked to specify or verify the installation location or other settings during the installation process; once the installation process has been completed, the program can be launched. This procedure is illustrated in the accompanying illustrations.

DOWNLOADING THE PROGRAM

1. Click the download link, then click Save to start the download process.

2. Specify the download location, then click Save to download the installation file.

INSTALLING THE PROGRAM

1. Launch the installation program, click the Run button, and then follow the prompts to launch the installation program.

2. You will often have to agree to the terms of a license agreement before installation will take place.

3. Specify or verify the desired location, click Next, and then follow the prompts to install the program.

USING THE INSTALLED PROGRAM

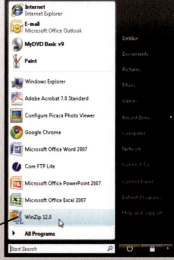

Click the program name on the Start menu to launch the installed program.

Use the Organize button to create new folders and copy files and folders.

Use the Back button to go to the previous location.

Use the Views button to specify how the items in the right pane are displayed.

The Address bar shows the current location.

Enter keywords to search for a folder or file meeting the criteria you supply.

Click a drive or folder icon in the left pane to display its contents in the right pane.

Click a dark arrow to close a folder and hide its contents.

Click a clear arrow to open a folder and display its contents.

The Navigation pane contains Favorite Links and the Folders list.

Double-click a folder to open it.

Double-click a document to open it in its associated program.

⚠ **FIGURE 5-19**
**Using Windows
Explorer to look
at the contents
of a computer.**

Looking at the Folders and Files Stored on a Computer

Once a file management program is open, you can look at the folders and files stored on your computer. For instance, you can do the following in Windows Explorer (see Figure 5-19):

➤ To see the folders and files stored on your hard drive, USB flash drive, or any other storage medium, click the appropriate letter or name for that medium in the left pane (called the *Navigation pane*).

➤ To look inside a folder, click it (in the left pane) or double-click it (in the right pane). To go back to the previous location, click the Back toolbar button.

➤ To open a file in its associated program, double-click it.

➤ To create a new folder in the current location, click the *Organize* button, select *New Folder*, and then type the name for the new folder.

Copying and Moving Files and Folders

To copy or move a file or folder using a file management program, you first need to navigate to the drive and folder where the item is located and then select the desired file or folder. Next, issue either the *Copy command* (to copy the item) or the *Cut command* (to move the item), such as by using Windows Explorer's Organize button as shown in Figure 5-20, to copy or move that item to the *Clipboard* (a temporary location used for copying items). You then need to navigate to the drive and folder where you want the file to go, and use the *Paste command* to copy or move the item to that location.

Renaming Files and Folders

You can also change the name of a file and folder using a file management program. To rename an item in Windows Explorer, select the item to be renamed, use the Organize button to issue the *Rename command* (or click a second time on the filename once the item is selected), and then retype or edit the filename.

2. Click the Organize button and select *Copy* to copy the file to the Clipboard.

3. Navigate to the drive and folder where you want the file to go.

1. Navigate to the drive and folder containing the file you want to copy or move, and then select the file.

4. Click the Organize button and select *Paste* to copy the file to the current location.

5. The file is copied.

Deleting Files and Folders

To delete a file or folder using a file management program, navigate to the drive and folder that contains the file or folder you want to delete, select the desired item, and then press the Delete key on the keyboard. You will need to select *Yes* when the Confirm File/Folder Delete dialog box opens to finish the deletion process. Deleting a folder deletes all of the contents located inside that folder.

Search Tools

As the amount of e-mail, photos, documents, and other important data individuals store on their computers continues to grow, **search tools**—utility programs that search for documents and other files on a user's hard drives—are becoming more important. Search tools are often integrated into file management programs and they are highly improved in recent versions of some operating systems, such as Mac OS and Windows. There are also a number of third-party search tools available.

Search tools typically are used to find files located somewhere on the specified storage medium that meet specific criteria, such as being in a certain folder, including certain characters in the filename, being of a particular type (a song, digital photo, or spreadsheet, for instance), and/or having a particular date associated with the file. If a document has been manually or automatically assigned *metadata tags* (information about the file, such as author, artist, or keywords), some search programs can search by those tags as well.

In Windows, for instance, users can use the *Search box* located at the top right corner of the Windows Explorer window (refer again to Figure 5-19) to search for files and folders in the current location that match the keywords entered into the Search box. Searches can be saved by clicking the Save Search button that appears on the toolbar at the top of the Windows Explorer window after a search is performed; saved searches can be run again by opening the user's *Searches folder* in the Navigation pane. For a quick search, users can also search for programs, documents, and Web pages by typing keywords in the Search box at the bottom of the Start menu.

A variety of Internet search companies—such as Google, Microsoft, and Yahoo!—have also developed *desktop search tools* that apply the technology used in their Internet search tools to an individual's computer. Typically these programs search through files,

FIGURE 5-20
Using Windows Explorer to copy files.

TIP

To *restore* a file or folder deleted from your computer's hard drive, open your computer's *Recycle Bin* and restore the file to its original location. Files and folders deleted from removable media cannot be restored in this manner, but there are special utility programs available to help you recover deleted files from flash memory cards and USB flash drives, as long as you have not written anything to the card or drive since the files were deleted.

TIP

To help you better organize and locate your files, Windows 7 uses *Libraries*—special folders designed to provide access to common types of files (such as photos, documents, music, or videos), regardless of where those items are physically stored on your computer; you just specify which folders on your computer each Library should include.

>**Search tool.** A utility program designed to search for files on the user's hard drive.

ASK THE EXPERT

John Christopher, Senior Data Recovery Engineer, DriveSavers, Inc.

How important are disk-maintenance procedures—such as defragmenting a hard drive—in preventing a hard drive failure?

It's important to run a disk maintenance program occasionally to fix minor directory corruption and repair incorrect disk or file permissions. In addition, defragmenting files—or optimizing as it is sometimes called—can help improve the performance of a hard drive.

During regular use, a computer system will always try to write data files to consecutive sectors on the hard drive. When that's not possible because the hard drive is nearing capacity or files are exceptionally large, files are fragmented—broken into logical pieces and recorded in different locations on the drive. Defragmenting reassembles the file pieces so the access time (the time needed to read all the file pieces and load them into the computer's memory) is reduced, thus improving performance.

Computer users who create large high-resolution graphics, professional audio recording, and video production files should defragment regularly; these users will see the most benefit from a regular defragmenting routine.

e-mail and chat messages, cached Web pages, and other content stored on the user's hard drive to find the items that match the user's supplied search terms. To speed up searching, most of these search tools create an index of the computer content on an ongoing basis.

Diagnostic and Disk Management Programs

Diagnostic programs evaluate your system, looking for problems and making recommendations for fixing any errors that are discovered. *Disk management programs* diagnose and repair problems related to your hard drive. Diagnostic and disk management utilities built into the Windows operating system include programs to check your hard drive for errors and programs to optimize your hard drive (by rearranging the data on the hard drive so all files are stored in contiguous locations—called *disk defragmentation*) so it works more efficiently. Third-party utility programs can perform these and other related tasks, as well.

Uninstall and Cleanup Utilities

As programs are used, temporary data is often created. When programs are *uninstalled* (removed from the hard drive), this data and other remnants of that program can be left behind on the hard drive or in system files unless an *uninstall utility* is used. If a user removes programs by deleting the program's folder (which is not the recommended method for removing programs), the extraneous data is left behind, using up valuable disk space and, sometimes, slowing down the computer. Uninstall utilities remove the programs along with related extraneous data, such as references to those programs in your system files. Some uninstall capabilities are built into most operating systems; often an uninstall option is also included in a program's folder or under that program's Start menu item when that program is originally installed.

Cleanup utilities (such as Windows *Disk Cleanup* shown in Figure 2-22 in Chapter 2) are designed to delete temporary files (such as deleted files still in the Recycle Bin, temporary Internet files, temporary installation files, and so forth) in order to free up disk space. Some specialty cleanup programs (called *registry cleaners*) are designed to locate unnecessary information in the Windows registry and other system files (such as from uninstalled programs) and delete it, making your computer run more efficiently.

CAUTION CAUTION CAUTION CAUTION CAUTION CAUTION CAUT

To avoid deleting any system files used by other programs when uninstalling a program, be sure to keep all files (such as *.dll* files) that an uninstall utility asks you about and says might be needed by another program. As an extra precaution, you can create a *System Restore point* (using the *System Restore* tools) before uninstalling a program (if you are using a Windows computer), so you can roll the computer's settings back to that point if a problem occurs after the program is uninstalled.

File Compression Programs

File compression programs reduce the size of files so they take up less storage space on a storage medium or can be transmitted faster over the Internet. The most common format for user-compressed files in the Windows environment is the *.zip* format, which is created by file compression programs such as the *WinZip* program shown in Figure 5-21. Mac users typically use *StuffIt* (which creates files in the *.sit* or *.sitx* format) or a similar program instead, although many file compression programs can open files compressed with other programs.

A file compression program is required to both compress (*zip*) and decompress (*unzip*) files, unless the zipped file is made *executable*. Executable zipped files have the extension *.exe* and decompress automatically when they are opened, even if the appropriate file compression program is not installed on the recipient's computer. File compression programs can compress either a single file or a group of files into a single compressed file. When multiple files are compressed, they are separated back into individual files when the file is decompressed. Some file compression programs can also *encrypt* your zipped files so that a password is needed to unzip them. Encryption is discussed in detail in Chapter 9.

COMPRESSION RATIOS
Certain image file formats (such as .tif) compress more than others (such as .jpg, which is already in a compressed format). Documents containing text fall somewhere in between.

FILE SIZE
The 27 files, totalling nearly 17 MB, are zipped into a single 5 MB *.zip* file.

FIGURE 5-21
File compression.
File compression can be used with both image and text files, although image files generally compress more efficiently.

Backup and Recovery Utilities

Virtually every computer veteran will warn you that, sooner or later, you will lose some critical files. This could happen due to a power outage (if the file you are working on has not yet been saved), a hardware failure (such as if your computer or hard drive stops functioning), a major disaster (such as a fire that destroys your computer), or a user error (such as accidentally deleting or overwriting a file).

Creating a **backup** means making a duplicate copy of important files so that when a problem occurs, you can restore those files using the backup copy to avoid data loss. Performing a backup can include backing up an entire computer (so it can be restored at a later date, if needed), backing up all data files (in order to restore them in case the computer is lost or damaged), or backing up only selected files (to make sure you have a clean copy of each file if the original is accidentally lost or destroyed). Depending on their size, backup data can be placed on a recordable or rewritable CD or DVD disc, an external hard drive, a USB flash drive, or virtually any other storage medium. To protect against fires and other natural disasters, backup media should be stored in a different physical location than your computer or inside a fire-resistant safe.

It is critical for a business to have backup procedures in place that back up all data on a frequent, regular basis—such as every night. A rotating collection of backup media should be used so it is possible to go back beyond the previous day's backup, if needed. While individuals tend to back up in a less formal manner, personal backups are becoming increasingly necessary as the amount of important information that users store digitally (such as home movies, music, digital photos, and tax returns) grows. Personal backups can

TIP
Be sure to save your documents frequently as you work, in case the power goes out. Creating a copy of a document with a different filename (by using the *Save As* option of the File menu, for example) before editing a document is another good idea, so you can return to the original version, if needed.

> **File compression program.** A program that reduces the size of files, typically to be stored or transmitted more efficiently. > **Backup.** A duplicate copy of data or other computer content in case the original version is destroyed.

WINDOWS BACKUP PROGRAM
Allows you to back up files to the desired backup medium manually or on a regular basis automatically.

WEB-BASED BACKUP SERVICE
Allows you to back up files to a secure Web site.

FIGURE 5-22
Backup utilities.

be as simple as copying important documents to a USB flash drive or uploading them to an online storage service Web site, or as comprehensive as backing up the entire contents of your computer.

You can perform backups by manually copying files using your file management program, but there are *backup utility* programs (both stand-alone and built-into operating systems) that make the backup process easier, such as the *Windows Backup* program shown in Figure 5-22. For convenience, many backup programs can be scheduled to back up specified files, folders, or drives on a regular basis (such as every night or every Friday night, depending on how important the contents of your computer are and how often you modify files). There are also online backup services (such as the *MozyHome* service shown in Figure 5-22) that can back up your specified files automatically to a secure Web server on a regular basis, provided you have a broadband Internet connection. Backups and *disaster recovery* are discussed in more detail in Chapter 15.

Antivirus, Antispyware, Firewalls, and Other Security Programs

As discussed in detail in Chapter 9, a *computer virus* is a software program that is designed to cause damage to the computer system or perform some other malicious act, and *spyware* is a software program installed without the user's knowledge that secretly collects information and sends it to an outside party via the user's Internet connection. Other security concerns today include *phishing* schemes that try to trick users into supplying personal information that can be used for credit card fraud, *identity theft*, and other criminal acts. Because of these threats, it is critical that all computer users today protect themselves and their computers. There are many *security programs* available, such as *antivirus programs* and *antispyware programs* (that protect against malicious software being installed on your computer) and *firewall programs* (that protect against someone accessing your computer via the Internet or a wireless connection). Increasingly, operating systems are including security software integrated into the operating system. For instance, recent versions of Windows include *Windows Firewall* and *Windows Defender* (an antispyware program). Because network and Internet security is such an important topic today, Chapter 9 is dedicated to these topics.

TECHNOLOGY AND YOU

The Browser OS

As the emphasis of personal computing moves from desktop applications to Web-based applications, it is expected that soon operating systems will be focused more on providing access to Web-based tools and applications than on running installed applications. Consequently, a Web browser could function as the operating system of the future. With the recent release of Google Chrome—Google's Web browser that was built with Web applications in mind—this prediction is becoming much closer to reality.

While Chrome is sometimes referred to as *a cloud operating system* by others, Google doesn't call Chrome an operating system, even though some features of Chrome are designed to make using Web-based applications easier. For instance, Chrome's application shortcut feature allows users to create shortcuts (such as on the desktop or Start menu, depending on their preference) to Web-based applications. Clicking an application shortcut loads the Web-based application in a streamlined Chrome window (with no browser tabs, search box, or navigation buttons, for instance) to give the user as much working room as possible while working with the application (see the accompanying illustration of how to create and use an application shortcut for the Google Docs Web-based program). This ability to launch Web-based applications as if they were installed applications is bringing us closer to the point where the browser might be an operating system that controls all your applications. And, in fact, Google has announced that they are now developing a Linux-based operating system built around Chrome. This new operating system, expected to be released in late 2010, is currently dubbed *Google Chrome OS* and is

initially targeted to the netbook market, with desktop computers a possibility for the future.

1. With Google Docs open, create the desired application shortcut using the Page menu.

2. Click the application shortcut to launch the application in a streamlined window.

3. The program can then be used in its normal fashion, such as opening and editing documents.

Creating a Google Docs application shortcut with Google Chrome.

THE FUTURE OF OPERATING SYSTEMS

The future configuration of operating systems is anyone's guess, but it is expected that they will continue to become more user-friendly and, eventually, may be driven primarily by a voice, touch, and/or gesture interface. Operating systems are also likely to continue to become more stable and self-healing, repairing or restoring system files as needed. In addition, they are expected to continue to include security and technological improvements as they become available.

Improvements will almost certainly continue to be made in the areas of synchronizing and coordinating data and activities among a person's various computing and communications devices, such as his or her personal computer and mobile phone. In addition, with the pervasiveness of the Internet, operating systems in the future may be used primarily to access software available through the Internet or other networks, instead of accessing software on the local computer. For a look at a possible operating system of the future—your Web browser—see the Technology and You box.

SUMMARY

SYSTEM SOFTWARE VS. APPLICATION SOFTWARE

Chapter Objective 1:
Understand the difference
between system software
and application software.

System software consists of the programs that coordinate the activities of a computer system. The basic role of system software is to act as a mediator between **application software** (programs that allow a user to perform specific tasks on a computer, such as word processing, playing a game, preparing taxes, browsing the Web, and so forth) and the computer system's hardware, as well as between the computer and the user.

THE OPERATING SYSTEM

Chapter Objective 2:
Explain the different functions
of an operating system and
discuss some ways that
operating systems enhance
processing efficiency.

A computer's **operating system** is the primary system software program; it manages the computer system's resources and interfaces with the user. The essential portion, or core, of an operating system is called its **kernel**. The functions of the operating system include booting the computer, configuring devices and **device drivers** (often simply called **drivers**), communicating with the user, managing and monitoring computer resources, file management, and security. *File management programs* allow the user to manage the enormous collection of files typically found on a computer's hard drive by organizing files hierarchically into folders. To access a file in any directory, the user can specify the *path* to the file; the path identifies the drive and folders the user must navigate through in order to access the file.

A variety of processing techniques can be built into operating systems to help enhance processing efficiency. **Multitasking** allows more than one program to be open at one time; *multithreading* allows for rotation between program *threads*; and multiprocessing and parallel processing involve using two or more CPUs (or CPU cores) to perform work at the same time. Operating systems typically use **virtual memory** to extend conventional memory by using a portion of the hard drive as additional memory, and **spooling** frees up the CPU from time-consuming interaction with input and output devices, such as printers, by storing input and output on the way in or out of the system in a **buffer**.

Chapter Objective 3:
List several ways in which
operating systems differ from
one another.

Some of the differences among operating systems center around whether they use a **graphical user interface** (**GUI**) or **command line interface**, whether they are a **personal operating system** designed for individual users or a **server operating system** designed for multiple users, and the types and numbers of processors supported. Operating systems that are used with mobile devices or are embedded in other devices are called **mobile operating systems** or **embedded operating systems**, respectively.

OPERATING SYSTEMS FOR PERSONAL COMPUTERS AND SERVERS

Chapter Objective 4:
Name today's most widely
used operating systems for
personal computers and
servers.

One of the original operating systems for IBM and IBM-compatible personal computers was **DOS** (**Disk Operating System**), which is still in existence but not widely used. Most desktop computers today run a version of **Windows**. *Windows 3.x*, the first widely used version of Windows, was an *operating environment* that added a GUI shell to DOS, replacing the DOS command line interface with a system of menus, icons, and screen boxes called *windows*. *Windows 95*, *Windows 98*, *Windows 98 Second Edition* (*SE*), *Windows NT*, *Windows Me*, *Windows 2000*, *Windows XP*, and *Windows Vista*—all full-fledged operating systems and successors to Windows 3.x—each included an increasing number of enhancements, such as multitasking, a better user interface, and more Internet, multimedia, and communications functions. The current personal version of Windows is **Windows 7**; the current network version of Windows (**Windows Server**) is *Windows Server 2008 R2*.

Mac OS is the operating system used on Apple computers. The current personal version is **Mac OS X** (and includes *Mac OS X Leopard* and the newer *Mac OS X Snow Leopard*); **Mac OS X Server** is designed for server use. **UNIX** is a flexible operating system that was originally developed for use with midrange servers, but is now available for a variety of devices. UNIX comes in many versions or *UNIX flavors* and is the basis of several other operating systems, including Mac OS. The open source **Linux** operating system has gathered popularity because it is distributed free over the Internet and can be used as an alternative to Windows and Mac OS. Linux has earned support as a mainstream operating system in recent years and is being used in computer systems of all sizes, from netbooks to supercomputers.

OPERATING SYSTEMS FOR MOBILE PHONES AND OTHER DEVICES

Mobile phones and mobile devices usually require a different operating system than a desktop computer or server. Widely used mobile operating systems include **Windows Mobile**, **Android**, **iPhone OS**, **BlackBerry OS**, **Palm OS** and the newer **Palm webOS**, and **Symbian OS**. Other everyday devices that contain a computer—such as cars, cash registers, and consumer electronics devices—typically use an embedded operating system, such as **Windows Embedded** and **Embedded Linux**.

OPERATING SYSTEMS FOR LARGER COMPUTERS

High-end servers, mainframes, and supercomputers may use an operating system designed specifically for that type of system, but are increasingly using customized versions of conventional operating systems, such as Windows, UNIX, and Linux.

UTILITY PROGRAMS

A **utility program** is a type of system software written to perform specific tasks usually related to maintaining or managing the computer system. **File management programs** enable users to perform file management tasks, such as copying, moving, and deleting files. The file management system built into Windows is **Windows Explorer**. **Search tools** are designed to help users find files on their hard drives; *diagnostic* and *disk management programs* are used mainly to diagnose and repair computer problems, such as hard drive errors and files deleted accidentally, as well as maintenance tasks, such as performing *disk defragmentation*. *Uninstall utilities* remove programs from a hard drive without leaving annoying remnants behind, **file compression programs** reduce the stored size of files so they can be more easily archived or sent over the Internet, and **backup** programs make it easier for users to back up the contents of their hard drive. There are also a number of security-oriented utility programs, such as *antivirus*, *antispyware*, and *firewall* programs.

THE FUTURE OF OPERATING SYSTEMS

In the future, operating systems will likely become even more user-friendly, voice-driven, and stable, repairing themselves when needed and causing errors and conflicts much less frequently. They will also likely continue to include improved security features, support for new technologies, and assistance for coordinating data and activities among a user's various computing and communications devices. They may also one day be designed primarily for accessing Web-based applications.

SW

Chapter Objective 5:
State several devices other than desktop computers and servers that require an operating system and list one possible operating system for each type of device.

Chapter Objective 6:
Discuss the role of utility programs and outline several tasks that these programs perform.

Chapter Objective 7:
Describe what the operating systems of the future might be like.

REVIEW ACTIVITIES

KEY TERM MATCHING

a. Android

b. backup

c. device driver

d. kernel

e. multitasking

f. operating system

g. spooling

h. utility program

i. virtual memory

j. Windows

Instructions: Match each key term on the left with the definition on the right that best describes it.

1. _____ A duplicate copy of data or other computer content for use in the event that the original version is destroyed.

2. _____ A Linux-based operating system designed for mobile phones and developed by a group of companies that includes Google.

3. _____ A memory-management technique that uses hard drive space as additional RAM.

4. _____ A program that enables an operating system to communicate with a specific hardware device.

5. _____ A type of software that performs a specific task, usually related to managing or maintaining the computer system.

6. _____ The capability of an operating system to run more than one program at one time.

7. _____ The essential portion, or core, of an operating system.

8. _____ The main component of system software that enables the computer to manage its activities and the resources under its control, run application programs, and interface with the user.

9. _____ The primary personal computer operating system developed by Microsoft Corporation.

10. _____ The process of placing items in a buffer so the appropriate device (such as a printer) can retrieve them when needed.

SELF-QUIZ

Instructions: Circle **T** if the statement is true, **F** if the statement is false, or write the best answer in the space provided. **Answers for the self-quiz are located in the References and Resources Guide at the end of the book.**

1. **T F** Windows 7 is an example of an operating system.

2. **T F** Most operating systems today use a command line interface.

3. **T F** Mobile devices, such as portable digital media players and mobile phones, typically require an operating system.

4. **T F** Windows Explorer is an operating system designed for mobile phones.

5. **T F** Windows Mobile is a versatile operating system designed to be used on a variety of computer types, such as mainframes, servers, personal computers, and mobile phones.

6. _____ refers to the ability of an operating system to have more than one program open at one time.

7. _____ is an operating system that is available for free over the Internet.

8. To decrease the size of a file, a(n) _____ utility program can be used.

9. To guard against losing your data if a computer problem occurs, you should _____ your data files on a regular basis.

10. Match each device to the most appropriate operating system and write the corresponding number in the blank to the left of the device.

a. _____ Home office computer   **1.** Windows Embedded

b. _____ Mainframe computer   **2.** Palm webOS

c. _____ Mobile phone   **3.** Windows 7

d. _____ Car   **4.** UNIX

EXERCISES

1. For the following path, identify the drive the document is located on, the name of the file (including its file extension), and whether or not the document is stored inside a folder. If the file is stored inside one or more folders, list the folder name(s).

C:\Documents\Resume.docx

2. Match each program or processing technique with the appropriate term and write the corresponding number in the blank to the left of each term.

a. _____ Zipped file   **1.** Spooling

b. _____ Printer   **2.** File management program

c. _____ Swap file   **3.** File compression program

d. _____ Folder   **4.** Virtual memory

3. Would a new notebook computer typically have Windows XP, Windows 7, Windows Mobile, or Windows Server 2008 R2 installed as its operating system? Explain your answer.

4. What type of utility program is designed to make duplicate copies of your hard drive content?

5. Identify the purpose of each of the following types of utility programs.

a. File management program _____

b. Uninstall utility _____

c. File compression program _____

d. Antivirus program _____

DISCUSSION QUESTIONS

1. There are a few companies, such as Microsoft and Google, that have moved into many different areas of computing, such as operating systems, application software, Web-based software, search, and more, and both of these companies have been accused of monopolistic procedures. Is there a risk for the consumer or for businesses if one company is involved with so many different aspects of computing? Should this be prohibited or should the natural order of the free market be trusted to prevent areas of computing from being monopolized by one company?

2. As discussed in the chapter, many everyday devices—including cars and other vehicles—are controlled by operating systems. There are advantages, such as avoiding possible driver errors and the ability to change the speed of or reroute trains automatically to avoid collisions. But are there potential risks, as well? For example, Thailand's Finance Minister once had to be rescued from inside his limousine after the onboard computer malfunctioned, leaving the vehicle immobilized and the door locks, power windows, and air conditioning not functioning. Do you think the benefits of increased automation of devices that could put us in danger if they malfunction outweigh the risks? What types of safeguards should be incorporated into computer-controlled cars, subway trains, and other automated vehicles? What about medication dispensers and other automated medical devices?

PROJECTS

1. **New OSs** There have been a number of new operating systems developed in the past few years, such as Android, Palm webOS, and the Google Chrome OS that was in development at the time of this writing.

   For this project, select one new or emerging operating system and research it. What is the purpose and targeted market for this operating system? What advantages does it have over any current competition for this market? If the operating system was developed to fulfill a new need, are there other operating systems that are being adapted or being developed as a result? Do you think your selected operating system will succeed? Why or why not? At the conclusion of your research, prepare a one- to two-page summary of your findings and opinions and submit it to your instructor.

2. **File Compression** As described in the chapter, compression programs can be used to reduce the size of files before they are stored or sent over the Internet. The most common compression programs create files with the file extensions *.zip*, *.sit*, *.sitx*, and *.exe*. Self-extracting compressed files decompress automatically when you download them, while compressed files must be decompressed with a version of the program that compressed them.

   For this project, identify compression programs associated with each of the file extensions listed above and determine which extensions represent a self-extracting format, as well as which extensions are associated with the Windows and Mac OS operating systems. For the type of computer you use most often, find at least two compression programs that you might use and compare their costs and capabilities. At the conclusion of your research, prepare a one-page summary of your findings and submit it to your instructor.

3. **File Practice** As discussed in the chapter, all operating systems have a file management-system, such as the Windows Explorer program illustrated in Figures 5-19 and 5-20.

   For this project, obtain a removable storage medium (such as a USB flash drive) appropriate for a computer you have access to, connect it to that computer, and perform the following tasks.

   a. Open the file management program and select the icon representing the removable storage medium being used to display its contents. Are there any files on the storage medium? How much room is available on the storage medium?

   b. Open any word processing program available on your computer (such as Word or Notepad for a Windows computer). Create a new document consisting of just your name, then save the document to your storage medium (be sure to change the save location to the appropriate drive and use an appropriate filename). In the file management program, view the content of your storage medium to see the new document. What is the file size and how much room is now left on your storage medium?

   c. Prepare a short summary of your work to submit to your instructor, listing the software programs and storage medium used, the name and size of the file, and the amount of space left on your storage medium once the file was stored on it.

   d. Return to your file management program and delete the file from your storage medium.

4. **Operating System Bugs** Most software, including operating systems, is not error-free when it is first released. Some programs, in fact, contain thousands of problems, called *bugs*. Software companies regularly release fixes (called *patches*) to correct known issues with released software. Is it ethical for software companies to release products that have known problems? Many hackers and other criminals target these bugs with computer viruses or other attacks, frequently on the day a new vulnerability is discovered—called a *zero-day attack*. Obviously, the acts by these criminals are not ethical, but what responsibility does a software company have to consumers if they are put at risk due to the company's carelessness or rush to market? What responsibility do consumers have to make sure they keep their computers patched against new vulnerabilities?

For this project, form an opinion about the ethical ramifications of software bugs and be prepared to discuss your position (in class, via an online class discussion group, in a class chat room, or via a class blog, depending on your instructor's directions). You may also be asked to write a short paper expressing your opinion.

ETHICS IN ACTION

5. **OS Support** No matter which operating system you have, it's likely you will eventually need to get some help resolving a problem. Support options typically include the following: searchable knowledge bases, technical support phone numbers and e-mail addresses, online chat, FAQs, and user discussion groups.

For this project, select one operating system and go to the manufacturer's Web site to determine which of the support options listed in the previous paragraph are available. Select one support option and find out how it is used and what type of information can be obtained. Share your findings with the class in the form of a short presentation. The presentation should not exceed 10 minutes and should make use of one or more presentation aids, such as the chalkboard, handouts, overhead transparencies, or a computer-based slide presentation (your instructor may provide additional requirements). You may also be asked to submit a summary of the presentation to your instructor.

PRESENTATION/ DEMONSTRATION

Instructions: Go to the Chapter 5 page at **www.cengage.com/computerconcepts/np/uc13** to work the following Web Activities.

WEB ACTIVITIES

6. **Interactive Activities** Work the interactive **Crossword Puzzle**, watch the **Video Podcasts** and **Online Videos**, and explore the **Further Exploration** links associated with this chapter.

If you have a SAM user profile, you may have access to hands-on instruction, practice, and assessment of the skills covered in this chapter. Check with your instructor for instructions and the correct URL/Web site to access those assignments.

7. **Student Edition Labs** Work the following interactive **Student Edition Labs**.
   ➤ **Backing up Your Computer**   ➤ **Maintaining a Hard Drive**

8. **Test Yourself** Review the **Online Study Guide** for this chapter, then test your knowledge of the terms and concepts covered in this chapter by completing the **Key Term Matching** exercise, the **Self-Quiz**, the **Exercises**, and the **Practice Test**.

chapter 6

Application Software

After completing this chapter, you will be able to do the following:

1. Describe what application software is, the different types of ownership rights, and the difference between installed and Web-based software.

2. Detail some concepts and commands that many software programs have in common.

3. Discuss word processing and explain what kinds of documents are created using this type of program.

4. Explain the purpose of spreadsheet software and the kinds of documents created using this type of program.

5. Identify some of the vocabulary used with database software and discuss the benefits of using this type of program.

6. Describe what presentation graphics and electronic slide shows are and when they might be used.

7. List some types of graphics and multimedia software that consumers use frequently.

8. Name several other types of application software programs and discuss what functions they perform.

OVERVIEW

As discussed in previous chapters, application software consists of programs designed to perform specific tasks or applications. Today, a wide variety of application software is available to meet virtually any user need. Individuals and businesses use software to perform hundreds of tasks, including to write letters, keep track of their finances, participate in videoconferences, watch videos, learn a foreign language, entertain themselves or their children, create music CDs or home movie DVDs, manage a business's inventory, create greeting cards and flyers, make business presentations, process orders, prepare payrolls and tax returns, touch up digital photos, and teach their kids the ABCs.

This chapter begins with a discussion of some general characteristics of application software. Then we look at five of the most widely used types of application software: word processing, spreadsheet, database, presentation graphics, and graphics and multimedia software. The chapter concludes with an overview of some of the other types of application software you may encounter in your personal and professional life. ■

THE BASICS OF APPLICATION SOFTWARE

All computer users should be familiar with the basic characteristics and concepts related to **application software**; for instance, the different possible ownership rights and delivery methods used with application software, how software for personal computers and mobile devices differs, and the basic commands that are common to most types of application software. Although these topics are discussed next in the context of application software, they also apply to other types of software, such as system software (discussed in Chapter 5) and programming languages (discussed in Chapter 13).

Software Ownership Rights

The *ownership rights* of a software program specify the allowable use of that program. After a software program is developed, the developer (typically an individual or an organization) holds the ownership rights for that program and decides whether or not the program can be sold, shared with others, or otherwise distributed. When a software program is purchased, the buyer is not actually buying the software. Instead, the buyer is acquiring a **software license** that permits him or her to use the software. This license specifies the conditions under which a buyer can use the software, such as the number of computers on which it may be installed (many software licenses permit the software to be installed on just one computer). In addition to being included in printed form inside the packaging of most software programs, the licensing agreement is usually displayed and must be agreed to by the end user at the beginning of the software installation process (see Figure 6-1).

PODCAST

Go to **www.cengage.com/ computerconcepts/np/uc13** to download or listen to the "Expert Insight on Software" podcast.

SW

> **Application software.** Programs that enable users to perform specific tasks on a computer, such as writing a letter or playing a game.

> **Software license.** An agreement, either included in a software package or displayed on the screen during installation, that specifies the conditions under which a buyer of the program can use it.

This statement explains that you are accepting the terms of the license agreement by installing the software.

This statement explains that the program can be tried for 14 days and then it needs to be either registered or uninstalled.

COMMERCIAL SOFTWARE PROGRAM

SHAREWARE PROGRAM

FIGURE 6-1

Software licenses. Most software programs display their licensing agreements at the beginning of the installation process.

There are four basic categories of software: *commercial software, shareware, freeware,* and *public domain software* (see Figure 6-2). Each of these types of software has different ownership rights, as discussed next. In addition, software that falls into any of these four categories can also be **open source software**—programs whose source code is available to the public. An open source program can be copyrighted, but individuals and businesses are allowed to modify the program and redistribute it—the only restrictions are that changes must be shared with the open source community and the original copyright notice must remain intact. For more information about open source software, see the Inside the Industry box.

FIGURE 6-2

Software ownership rights.

TYPE OF SOFTWARE	EXAMPLES
Commercial Software	Microsoft Office (office suite) Norton AntiVirus (antivirus program) Adobe Photoshop (image editing program) World of Warcraft (game)
Shareware	WinZip (file compression program) Ulead Video Toolbox (video editing/conversion program) Image Shrinker (image optimizer) Deluxe Ski Jump 3 (game)
Freeware	Internet Explorer (Web browser) OpenOffice.org (office suite) QuickTime Player (media player) Yahoo! Messenger (instant messaging program)
Public domain software	Lynx (text-based Web browser) Pine (e-mail program)

Commercial Software

Commercial software is software that is developed and sold for a profit. When you buy a commercial software program (such as *Microsoft Office, TurboTax,* or *GarageBand*), it typically comes with a *single-user license,* which means you cannot legally make copies of the installation CD to give to your friends and you cannot legally install the software on their computers using your CD. You cannot even install the software on a second computer that you own, unless allowed by the license. For example, some software licenses state that the program can be installed on one desktop computer and one portable computer belonging to the same individual. To determine which activities are allowable for a particular commercial software program, refer to its software license. Schools or businesses that need to install software on a large number of computers or need to have the software available to multiple users over a network can usually obtain a *site license* or *network license* for the number of users needed.

INSIDE THE INDUSTRY

Open Source Software

The use of open source software has grown over the past few years, primarily for cost reasons. One of the first widely known open source programs is the Linux operating system, which was discussed in Chapter 5. However, there are also low-cost or no-cost open source alternatives for a wide selection of application programs today. For instance, the free *OpenOffice.org* office suite (see the accompanying screen shot) can be used as an alternative to Microsoft Office, and the free *GIMP* program can be used to retouch photos instead of Adobe Photoshop or another pricey image editing program. In addition to saving you money, these alternative programs often require less disk space and memory than their commercial software counterparts require.

Other possible benefits of using open source software include increased stability and security (since they are tested and improved by a wide variety of programmers and users), and the ability to modify the application's source code. Perceived risks of using open source software include lack of support and compatibility issues. However, both Linux and open source application programs are continuing to gain acceptance and their use is growing. Some insiders feel that the open source movement is finally gathering the momentum it deserves.

An emerging trend is applying open source principles to hardware—some hardware designers are releasing designs for new hardware to the public in hopes that manufacturing companies will use the designs in new products and credit them as the original designer. Like open source software developers, open source hardware designers can possibly earn revenue from consulting work related to their designs.

The OpenOffice.org Writer word processing program.

In addition to their full versions, some commercial software is available in a *demo* or *trial version*. Typically, these versions can be used free of charge and distributed to others, but often they are missing some key features (such as the ability to save or print a document) or they will not run after the trial period expires. Since these programs are not designed as replacements for the fee-based version, it is ethical to use them only to determine if you would like to buy the full program. If the decision is made against purchasing the product, the demo or trial version should be uninstalled from your computer.

Recent trends in computing—such as multiprocessing, virtualization, and cloud computing, all discussed in earlier chapters of this book—are leading to new software licensing issues for commercial software companies. For example, software companies must decide whether the number of installations allowed by the license is counted by the number of computers on which the software is installed or by the total number of processors or CPU cores used by those computers, as well as decide how to determine the number of users in a virtualized environment. Some Microsoft software, for instance, is licensed per processor, regardless of the number of cores each processor has. And, for some server software used within a virtual environment, Microsoft computes the number of users based on a *per running instance*—that is, the number of software instances (installed or virtual) being used at any given time—instead of how many virtual environments the software is actually available to. Another software vendor (Altair Engineering) uses *license tokens* that are drawn from a central license server when the application is running and returned to the server when the application is finished. This system allows the number of tokens used by an

TIP

Ownership rights for original creative works are referred to as *copyrights* and are discussed in more detail in Chapter 16.

TIP

Businesses should periodically audit their software licenses to ensure they are not paying for too many licenses or for licenses associated with software that is not being used. They should also consider negotiating new types of licensing agreements that best fit the company, such as concurrent-user pricing instead of per-computer pricing.

individual computer to vary depending on the computing hardware (such as number of cores) being used, but still ensures that the number of users accessing the software at any one time does not exceed the limits specified in the software license. Software vendors are expected to continue to develop and implement new licensing models to address these and other trends in the future.

Shareware

Shareware programs are software programs that are distributed on the honor system. Most shareware programs are available to try free of charge, but typically require a small fee if you choose to use the program regularly (refer again to the shareware license in Figure 6-1). By paying the requested registration fee, you can use the program for as long as you want to use it and may be entitled to product support, updates, and other benefits. You can legally and ethically copy shareware programs to pass along to friends and colleagues for evaluation purposes, but those individuals are expected to pay the shareware fee if they decide to keep the product.

FIGURE 6-3

Shareware and freeware programs are typically downloaded via the Internet.

Many shareware programs have a specified trial period, such as one month. Although it is not illegal to use shareware past the specified trial period, it is unethical to do so. Ethical use of shareware dictates either paying for the program or uninstalling it from your computer at the end of the trial period. Shareware is typically much less expensive than commercial versions of similar software because it is often developed by a single programmer and because it uses the shareware marketing system to sell directly to consumers (typically via a variety of software download sites, such as the one shown in Figure 6-3) with little or no packaging or advertising expenses. Shareware authors stress that the ethical use of shareware helps to cultivate this type of software distribution. Legally, shareware and demo versions of commercial software are similar, but shareware is typically not missing key features.

Most download sites list the license type for each program.

Freeware

Freeware programs are software programs that are given away by the author for others to use free of charge. Although freeware is available without charge and can be shared with others, the author retains the ownership rights to the program, so you cannot do anything with it—such as sell it or modify it—that is not expressly allowed by the author. Freeware programs are

---

>**Shareware.** Copyrighted software that is distributed on the honor system; consumers should either pay for it or uninstall it after the trial period.
>**Freeware.** Copyrighted software that may be used free of charge.

frequently developed by individuals; commercial software companies sometimes release freeware as well, such as Microsoft's *Internet Explorer* and Real's *RealPlayer*. Like shareware programs, freeware programs are widely available over the Internet.

Public Domain Software

Public domain software is not copyrighted; instead, the ownership rights to the program have been donated to the public domain. Consequently, it is free and can be used, copied, modified, and distributed to others without restrictions.

Desktop vs. Mobile Software

Notebook computers, tablet computers, UMPCs, and other portable computers typically run the same application software as desktop computers. However, mobile phones and other mobile devices typically require *mobile software*; that is, software specifically designed for a specific type of mobile phone or other mobile device. A wide range of mobile software is available today. For instance, there are mobile versions of popular programs like Word or PowerPoint, games and media players, business tools that record inventory data or keep track of your business expenses, calendars and programs that allow you to organize notes and voice recordings, applications that allow you to broadcast your current location to friends, and Web browsers for accessing Web sites (see Figure 6-4). In fact, there are over 15,000 applications for the iPhone alone and that number is growing all the time. Many mobile applications are available free of charge.

In addition to having a more compact, efficient appearance, many mobile applications include features for easier data input, such as an on-screen keyboard, a phrase list, or handwriting recognition capabilities. Some mobile software programs are designed to be compatible with popular *desktop software*, such as Microsoft Office, to facilitate sharing documents between the two platforms. The desktop versions of the most common Microsoft Office programs are illustrated later in this chapter. For a look at a new mobile application—*mobile voice search*—see the Technology and You box.

Installed vs. Web-Based Software

Software also differs in how it is accessed by the end user. It can be installed on and run from the end user's computer (or installed on and run from a network server in a network setting), or it can be Web-based and accessed by the end user over the Internet.

FURTHER EXPLORATION Go

Go to the Chapter 6 page at **www.cengage.com/ computerconcepts/np/uc13** for links to information about free and low-cost office suites.

FIGURE 6-4

Mobile software. There is a wide variety of software available today for mobile phones and other mobile devices.

SW

>**Public domain software.** Software that is not copyrighted and may be used without restriction.

Downloaded version will be
downloaded to the buyer's computer.

Packaged version will be
shipped to the buyer.

FIGURE 6-5

Installed software.
Installed software can
be purchased in a
physical package or
downloaded via the
Internet.

Installed Software

Installed software must be installed on a computer before it is run. Desktop software can be purchased in physical form (such as on a CD or DVD) or downloaded from the Internet (see Figure 6-5); mobile software is almost always downloaded. Many mobile phone manufacturers have download sites to facilitate this, such as Apple's *App Store*, Blackberry's *App World*, and the *Android Market*. In either case, the program is installed using its *installation program* (which typically runs automatically when the software CD or DVD is inserted into the drive or when the downloaded program is opened, as explained in the Chapter 5 How It Works box). Once the software is installed, it is ready to use. Whether or not installed software requires a fee depends on whether the program is a commercial, demo/trial, shareware, freeware, or public domain program.

Web-Based Software

Instead of being available in an installed format, some software is run directly from the Internet as **Web-based software**. A Web-based software program is delivered on demand via the Web to wherever the user is at the moment, provided he or she has an Internet connection (and has paid to use the software if a payment is required). Also referred to as **Software as a Service (SaaS)** and **cloudware**, the use of Web-based software is growing rapidly. In fact, research firm Gartner predicts that 25% of new business software will be delivered via the Web by 2011, up from 5% of new software purchases in 2006. Typically, documents created using Web-based software are stored online.

There is a wide range of both free and fee-based Web-based software available (see Figure 6-6). For instance, many free interactive games are available through Web sites and there are several free online *office suites* (such as *Google Docs*, *ThinkFree Online*, and the *Zoho* suite of programs) that can be used as an alternative to the Microsoft Office office suite (discussed in more detail shortly). In addition, Microsoft has been testing an online version of Microsoft Office 2007 (code-named *Albany*) and it is planning a Web-based version of the upcoming *Microsoft Office 2010* product (as discussed in the Trend box later in this chapter). In addition, many business software services are offered as SaaS, including applications geared for collaboration, scheduling, customer service, accounting, project management, and more. Typically, business SaaS applications use a subscription (often per user, per month) pricing scheme; companies that deliver SaaS are sometimes referred to as *application service providers* (*ASPs*). As it evolves, Web-based software is beginning to move from single stand-alone applications to groups of products that can work together to fulfill a wide variety of needs. For instance, the Google Docs Home page provides access to the Google Docs applications, but it also allows easy access to other Google online services, such as Gmail, Calendar, Photos, and Web search.

One advantage of Web-based software over installed software is that the programs and your files can be accessed from any computer with an Internet connection regardless of the type of computer or operating system used; some can also be accessed via a mobile phone, portable digital media player, or other type of Internet-enabled mobile device. This makes Web-based software especially appropriate for applications like shared scheduling and collaboration applications that are time-critical because documents and other data can be shared regardless of an individual's location or device. Other advantages of Web-based

ONLINE APPLICATIONS
This program allows you to create presentations online.

WEB DATABASE APPLICATIONS
This application allows you to retrieve property information, such as home values and homes for sale.

BUSINESS SAAS APPLICATIONS
This program allows you to share documents and collaborate on projects online.

SW

> **FIGURE 6-6**
> Web-based software.

> **ONLINE VIDEO**
>
> Go to the Chapter 6 page at **www.cengage.com/ computerconcepts/np/uc13** to watch the "Zillow iPhone App" video clip.

software include the ability of individuals and businesses to try out new applications for little or no out-of-pocket costs while they decide whether or not to continue subscribing to the software, the ability of small businesses to have access to complex (and normally expensive) powerful business applications at an affordable price, and the benefit of always working with the most current version of the software without having to perform software updates on company computers. In addition, Web-based applications can easily interface with existing online databases, such as online maps and property records (for instance, the real estate applications accessible via the Zillow Web site shown in Figure 6-6 utilize maps, property record information, and real estate listing information pulled from various online databases).

Some potential disadvantages of Web-based software are that online applications tend to run more slowly than applications stored on a local hard drive, that many online applications have a limit regarding the file size of the documents you create, and that the cost may eventually exceed the cost of buying a similar installed software program. In addition, you cannot access the Web-based program and your data if the server on which they reside goes down or if you are in a location with no Internet access, such as while traveling

TECHNOLOGY AND YOU

Mobile Voice Search

You know you can do many things with your mobile phone—including accessing and searching the Web on most of today's phones. Web searching has traditionally been text based, but *mobile voice search* is now available. Mobile voice search allows you to speak, rather than type, search terms into your mobile phone, and then see the results of that search. The newest systems—such as Yahoo!'s *oneSearch* service shown in the accompanying illustration—allow the user to just press a button on the phone and speak the search terms into the phone, and then the search results are immediately displayed, just as with a text-based Web page search. Commonly requested information includes movie show times, information about and directions to local businesses, stock quotes, sports scores, weather information, airline flight updates, and more. In addition to providing the requested information, Yahoo! oneSearch also supplies other relevant information (such as displaying weather information for the departure and arrival cities when flight information is requested), as shown in the accompanying illustration. Usually, search results are filtered by proximity to the user's geographical area (which is determined by the GPS information or nearby cell tower locations relayed by the mobile phone being used)—a feature called *geobrowsing*. Geobrowsing (discussed in more detail in the Chapter 8 Trend box) is based on the assumption that mobile users are likely searching for something nearby. When used in

conjunction with geobrowsing, mobile voice search essentially turns your mobile phone into your personal concierge.

1. Hold down the appropriate button on your mobile phone and speak your search request.

2. Your spoken request is translated into typed text and the search is performed.

3. The search results are displayed.

Getting a flight update with Yahoo! oneSearch.

or in a rural area. To eliminate this last concern, a growing trend is for online applications to also function, at least in part, offline. For instance, Google Docs added offline capabilities so that users can access the Google Docs applications and their documents locally on their computers, when needed. Edits are stored locally on the computer when a user is offline and, when the user reconnects to the Internet, the changes are synchronized with the documents stored on the Google Docs servers. The technology behind some offline Web applications—*Google Gears*—is discussed in the Chapter 13 Trend box.

Software Suites

Sometimes, related software programs (such as a group of graphics programs, utility programs, or office-related software) are sold bundled together as a **software suite**. Businesses and many individuals often use *office suites*, sometimes called *productivity software suites*, to produce written documents. Typically, office suites contain the following programs;

> **Software suite.** A collection of software programs bundled together and sold as a single software package.

many also contain additional productivity tools—such as a calendar, a messaging program, or collaboration tools.

> *Word processing software*—allows users to easily create and edit complex text-based documents that can also include images and other content.

> *Spreadsheet software*—provides users with a convenient means of creating documents containing complex mathematical calculations.

> *Database software*—allows users to store and organize vast amounts of data and retrieve specific information when needed.

> *Presentation graphics software*—allows users to create visual presentations to convey information more easily to others.

One of the most widely used office software suites is **Microsoft Office**. The latest version is Microsoft Office 2007, though Office 2010 is scheduled to be released in 2010. (For a look at this new version of Office, see the Trend box.) Similar suites are available from Corel (*WordPerfect Office*) and Apple (*iWork*) (see Figure 6-7); a free alternative office suite is *OpenOffice.org*. Many office suites are available in a variety of versions, such as a home or student version that contains fewer programs than a professional version. Not all software suites are available for all operating systems, however. For example, Microsoft Office is available for both Windows and Mac OS computers; iWork is available only for Mac OS computers; and OpenOffice.org is available for Windows, Linux, and Mac OS computers. OpenOffice.org is also available in more than 30 different languages.

The primary advantages of using a software suite include a common interface among programs in the suite and a total cost that is lower than buying the programs individually. Although most programs written for the same operating system (such as Windows or Mac OS) use similar interfaces and commands, the entire command interface for a software suite is usually very similar from program to program. This similarity is not just for basic commands (such as *Save* and *Print*), but for all commands (such as adding borders and shading or inserting a row or column) that appear in more than one program in the suite. The standardization of the user interface across all programs in a suite means that once you are familiar with how to use one program in a suite, you will probably find it easy to learn another program in that suite.

Common Software Commands

One of the greatest advantages of using software instead of paper and pencil to create a document is that you do not have to recreate the entire document when you want to make changes to it. This is because the document is created in RAM and then saved on a storage medium, instead of it being created directly on paper. Consequently, the document can be retrieved, modified, saved, and printed as many times as needed. The commands used to perform these tasks are similar in most application programs; the most common ways to issue commands to application programs are discussed next.

FIGURE 6-7

Office suites. Three of the most common commercial office suites are Microsoft Office, Corel WordPerfect Office, and Apple iWork.

Toolbars, Menus, Keyboard Shortcuts, and the Ribbon

Most commands in an application program are issued through *menus*, *keyboard short-cuts*, or *command buttons* located on a *toolbar* or *Ribbon*. As shown in Figure 1-10

>**Microsoft Office.** One of the most widely used office software suites.

COMMAND	COMMAND BUTTON	KEYBOARD SHORTCUT	DESCRIPTION
Open		Ctrl+O	Opens a saved document from a storage medium, usually for editing or printing.
Save		Ctrl+S	Saves the current version of the document to a storage medium.
Print		Ctrl+P	Prints the current version of the document onto paper.
Cut		Ctrl+X	Moves the selected item to the clipboard.
Copy		Ctrl+C	Copies the selected item to the clipboard.
Paste		Ctrl+V	Pastes the contents of the clipboard to the current location.
Undo		Ctrl+Z	Undoes the last change to the document.
Close		Alt+F4	Closes the document. Any changes made to the document are lost if the document wasn't saved first.

FIGURE 6-8
Common application software commands.

FIGURE 6-9
The Microsoft Office Ribbon.

in Chapter 1, the *menu bar* appears at the top of many windows and contains text-based lists (menus), which provide access to commands that can be selected to perform actions in that program. Many programs also have toolbars—sets of *icons* or command buttons that are clicked with the mouse to issue commands. **Keyboard shortcuts** are key combinations that correspond to specific commands, such as Ctrl+S for the Save command (this keyboard shortcut is issued by holding down the Ctrl key and pressing the S key). A list of common keyboard shortcuts used in Microsoft Office and many other programs is shown in Figure 6-8, along with examples of the command buttons typically used to perform these operations.

The **Ribbon** is a new feature in versions of Microsoft Office, starting with Office 2007. The Ribbon (see Figure 6-9) consists of *tabs*, which contain *groups* of related commands for the program being used. For convenience, most programs have a *Home tab* that contains the most frequently used commands in that program. In addition to the standard Ribbon tabs that are available whenever the program is open, additional *contextual tabs* are displayed as needed, depending on the action being taken. For instance, selecting a picture or other graphic

MICROSOFT OFFICE BUTTON
Contains common document commands, such as Save and Print.

QUICK ACCESS TOOLBAR
Contains command buttons for frequently used commands; can be modified by the user.

TABS
Organize related groups of commands; the Home tab is currently selected.

GALLERY
Displays sets of options that can be selected for a particular feature; this is the Styles gallery.

COMMAND BUTTONS
Issue a command or display a list of related commands.

GROUPS
Related commands on the Ribbon are organized into groups; these are the Font and Paragraph groups.

DIALOG BOX LAUNCHER
Opens a dialog box or task pane for that group.

MORE BUTTON
Opens a gallery to display more options.

HELP BUTTON
Launches the Office Help system.

> **Keyboard shortcut.** A combination of keyboard keys that are pressed in unison to issue a specific software command. > **Ribbon.** A feature found in recent versions of Microsoft Office that uses tabs to organize groups of related commands.

TREND

Microsoft Office 2010

The upcoming version of Microsoft Office—*Office 2010*—takes advantage of the trends of cloud computing and mobile computing and has specific versions of Office available for those users, in addition to the traditional installed version. The *Web version* of Office enables users to store, access, and collaborate on documents online, such as from the Windows Live *SkyDrive* online storage service. The *Mobile version* is designed for mobile phones and other mobile devices; desktop users can also create a portable version of Office to carry with them on a USB flash drive, when needed.

The overall appearance of Office 2010 is similar to Office 2007 (see the accompanying illustration). The Ribbon is still used for most commands, though the Office button now opens a full-screen menu containing more options and information than in Office 2007. New features include improved image editing tools, improved document protection features to better manage permissions and metadata associated with documents, extended printing capabilities from within Office applications, and the *jump lists* introduced in Microsoft Windows 7 to provide quick access to commonly used tasks.

Web version of Word   Installed version of Excel

Office 2010 comes in both installed and Web versions.

in Word displays the *Picture Tools tab* that contains commands related to a picture, such as to crop, resize, rotate, or recolor the picture. Clicking a command button on the Ribbon either carries out that command or displays a *gallery* of choices from which the user can select the desired action. The *Microsoft Office Button* replaces the File menu used in older versions of Office and contains commands commonly used with documents, such as to open, save, print, send, and publish them.

Editing a Document

Editing a document refers to changing the content of the document, such as adding or deleting text. Most application programs that allow text editing have an **insertion point** that looks like a blinking vertical line on the screen and shows where the next change will be made to the document currently displayed on the screen. To insert text, just start typing and the text will appear at the insertion point location. To delete text, press the Delete key to delete one character to the right of the insertion point or press the Backspace key to delete one character to the left of the insertion point. If the insertion point is not in the proper location for the edit, it must be moved to the appropriate location in the document by using the arrow keys on the keyboard or by pointing and clicking with the mouse. To select an object or block of text, click the object or drag the mouse over the text. Usually, once an object or some text is selected, it can be manipulated, such as to be moved, deleted, copied, or *formatted*.

> **TIP**
>
> The *Quick Access Toolbar* (located to the right of the Microsoft Office Button in recent Microsoft Office programs) contains frequently used commands and can be customized by the user. Right-click a command button on the Ribbon and select *Add to Quick Access Toolbar* to add that command to your Quick Access Toolbar.

> **Editing.** Changing the content of a document, such as inserting or deleting words. > **Insertion point.** An on-screen character that looks like a blinking vertical line; indicates the current location in a document, which is where the next change will be made.

This is 10-point Arial.

This is 12-point Times New Roman.

This is 16-point Lucida Handwriting.

This is 20-point Calibri.

This 16-point Calibri text is bold and italic.

This 16-point Calibri text is red and underlined.

FIGURE 6-10
Ⓐ **Fonts.** The font face, size, style, and color used with text can be specified in many application programs.

Formatting a Document

While editing changes the actual content of a document, **formatting** changes the appearance of the document. One common type of formatting is changing the appearance of selected text in a document. You can change the *font face* or *typeface* (a named collection of text characters that share a common design, such as Calibri or Times New Roman), *font size* (which is measured in *points*), *font style* (such as bold, italic, or underline), and *font color* (see Figure 6-10). Other common types of formatting include changing the *line spacing* or *margins* of a document; adding *page numbers*; and adding *shading* or *borders* to a paragraph, image, or other item.

Getting Help

Most people have an occasional question or otherwise need some help as they work with a software program. There are various options for getting help when you need it. For instance, most application programs have a built-in help feature, typically available through a *Help button* or a *Help* option on a menu. The type and amount of built-in help available varies from program to program, but typically includes one or more of the following forms.

➤ *Table of Contents*—works much like the table of contents in a book; that is, with related help topics organized under main topics. With most help systems, selecting a main topic reveals the subtopics related to that main topic; subtopics can then be selected until the desired help topic is displayed. Selecting a help topic displays information related to that topic on the screen (see Figure 6-11).

➤ *Browsing*—allows you to click hyperlinks related to major help categories, similar to a Table of Contents but each time a topic is clicked, a new page containing links appears, similar to the way Web pages work. Clicking a link representing a help topic displays information related to that topic on the screen.

ASK THE EXPERT

OpenOffice.org

John McCreesh, Marketing Project Lead, OpenOffice.org

Can a student use the free OpenOffice.org suite at home and the Microsoft Office suite at school for the same documents? If so, would any content or formatting be lost in the translation process?

OpenOffice.org will read and write Microsoft Office file formats with a high degree of accuracy. There may be occasional slight differences in formatting—just as there are if you open old files in a newer version of Microsoft Office.

The best solution is to always store all office documents in OpenDocument Format (ODF), which is the ISO approved format for saving office files. OpenOffice.org uses this by default; Microsoft Office users can use a converter.

> **Formatting.** Changing the appearance of a document, such as changing the margins or font size.

> *Search*—allows you to search for help topics by typing a keyword or phrase, and then the help system displays a list of links to possible matching help topics; clicking a help topic link displays information related to that topic on the screen.

Some help systems automatically search for online help from the manufacturer's Web site if the program detects an Internet connection. In addition, there is a vast amount of additional information about application software programs available via the Web, such as online articles, tutorials, and *message boards* for particular software programs, and e-mail support from software companies. Of course, online and offline books are also available for many software programs.

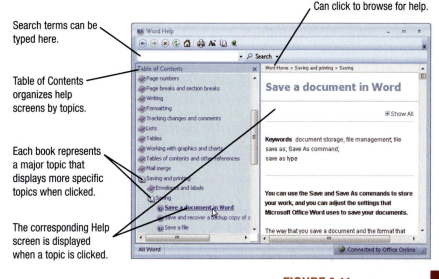

Search terms can be typed here.

Table of Contents organizes help screens by topics.

Each book represents a major topic that displays more specific topics when clicked.

The corresponding Help screen is displayed when a topic is clicked.

Can click to browse for help.

FIGURE 6-11
Getting help. Most application programs have built-in help systems.

SW

WORD PROCESSING CONCEPTS

Word processing is one of the most widely used application programs today. Although the actual commands and features vary somewhat from program to program, it is important to be familiar with the general concept of what word processing enables you to do, as well as the basic features of word processing. The following sections discuss these concepts and features.

What Is Word Processing?

Word processing refers to using a computer and **word processing software** to create, edit, save, and print written documents, such as letters, contracts, manuscripts, newsletters, invoices, marketing material, and reports. At its most basic level, word processing is used to do what was done on a typewriter before computers were commonplace. Many documents created with word processing software also include content that was not possible to create using a typewriter, such as photos, drawn objects, clip art images, hyperlinks, video clips, and text in a variety of sizes and appearances. Like any document created with software instead of paper and pencil, word processing documents can be retrieved, modified, and printed as many times as needed.

Word processing programs today typically include improved collaboration, security, and *rights-management tools* (tools used to protect original content from misuse by others). Rights management and intellectual property rights are discussed in more detail in Chapter 16; *digital signatures*, *encryption*, and other security tools that are now used to secure word processing documents are discussed in Chapter 9. Word processing programs today also typically include a variety of Web-related tools, as well as support for speech and pen input. For a look at how to use speech input with Microsoft Word on a Windows Vista computer, see the How It Works box.

FURTHER EXPLORATION Go

Go to the Chapter 6 page at **www.cengage.com/ computerconcepts/np/uc13** for links to information about application software resources.

TIP ✓

When selecting font size in a document, 72 points equals one-inch-tall text.

VIDEO PODCAST

Go to the Chapter 6 page at **www.cengage.com/ computerconcepts/np/uc13** to download or listen to the "How To: Create Your Own Customized Fonts" video podcast.

> **Word processing.** Using a computer and word processing software to create, edit, save, and print written documents, such as letters, contracts, and manuscripts. > **Word processing software.** Application software used to create, edit, save, and print written documents.

HOW IT WORKS

Windows Vista Speech Recognition with Microsoft Word

Speech recognition has arrived. Surgeons use it to control surgical robotic equipment, individuals use it to dial their mobile phones, and now you can use it to control your computer.

The Speech Recognition feature built into recent versions of Windows allows you to use your voice to issue commands to your computer, such as to launch programs, switch to a different open program, close a window, and so forth. You can also use it in application programs—such as your e-mail program or Microsoft Word—to dictate text to the computer, as well as to edit and format already typed text.

To use Windows Speech Recognition, you need to have a microphone connected to your computer and then run through the setup process to test your microphone, adjust the volume, and so forth (choose *Ease of Access and then Speech Recognition Options* to start the setup process). Once Speech Recognition is set up and enabled, you will see the *Speech Recognition microphone bar* on your screen (see the accompanying

illustration). When the system is "sleeping," you need to say "Start Listening" to wake it up. After that point, until you say "Stop Listening," the system will respond to your voice commands. For instance, speaking text that is not an official command will cause that text to be typed in the program in the active window. Speaking a command (such as "Undo" to undo the last change, "Select *word*" to select that word in your document, or "Correct *word*" to correct the spelling of a particular word) will carry out that command. To see a list of possible commands, say "What can I say?" and the system will display a *Speech Reference Card* on your screen.

If there are multiple possibilities for a command or correction that you issue (refer again to the accompanying illustration), the system displays a numbered list of possibilities and waits for your selection. If the system doesn't understand a command, it will display a "What was that?" message.

While there are numerous speech recognition software programs on the market, for basic dictation and voice commands Windows Speech Recognition does the trick.

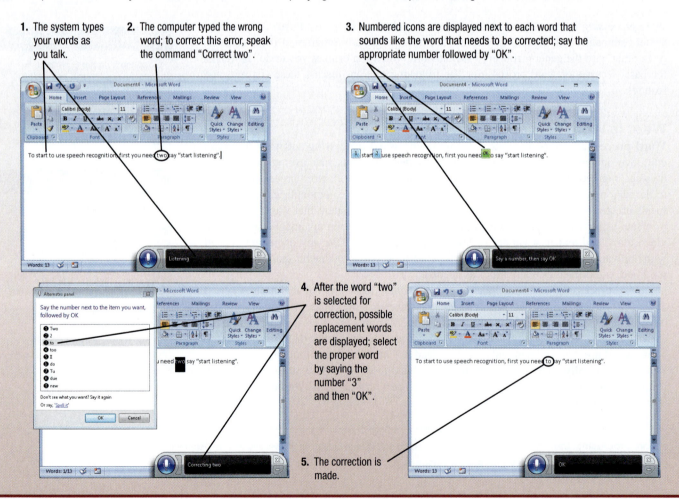

1. The system types your words as you talk.

2. The computer typed the wrong word; to correct this error, speak the command "Correct two".

3. Numbered icons are displayed next to each word that sounds like the word that needs to be corrected; say the appropriate number followed by "OK".

4. After the word "two" is selected for correction, possible replacement words are displayed; select the proper word by saying the number "3" and then "OK".

5. The correction is made.

Virtually all formal writing today is performed using a word processing program. Among today's most frequently used word processing programs are *Microsoft Word*, *Corel WordPerfect*, and *Apple Pages*—all part of the software suites mentioned earlier in this chapter. Most word processing programs offer hundreds of features, but virtually all support a core group of features used to create, edit, and format documents. Some of these basic features are described in the next few sections, using Microsoft Word 2007 as the example. Recent versions of Word save documents using the *.docx* extension by default, although other file formats (including the original *.doc* Word 97–2003 format for files that need to be opened in older versions of Word, the more universal *Rich Text Format* (*.rtf*), and several Web page formats) can be used instead when needed.

Creating a Word Processing Document

Every word processing program contains an assortment of operations for creating and editing documents, including commands to insert text, graphics, and other items, and then move, copy, delete, or otherwise edit the content, as needed. Some features in a typical word processing program are shown in Figure 6-12.

When entering text in a word processing document, it is important to know when to press the Enter key. Word processing programs use a feature called **word wrap**, which means the insertion point automatically moves to the beginning of the next line when the

FIGURE 6-12

Some features in a typical word processing program.

SW

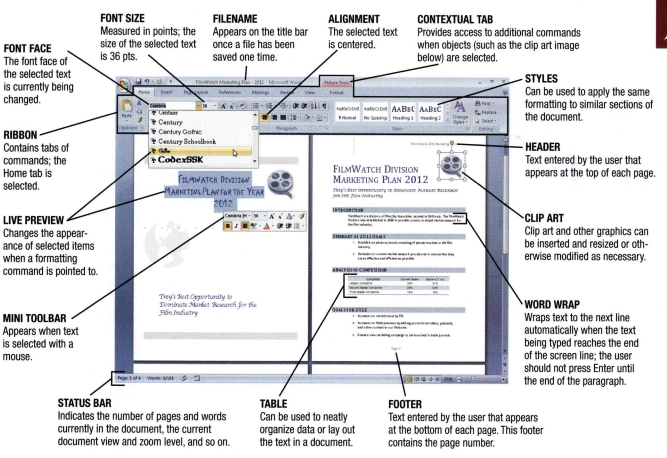

FONT FACE
The font face of the selected text is currently being changed.

RIBBON
Contains tabs of commands; the Home tab is selected.

LIVE PREVIEW
Changes the appearance of selected items when a formatting command is pointed to.

MINI TOOLBAR
Appears when text is selected with a mouse.

FONT SIZE
Measured in points; the size of the selected text is 36 pts.

FILENAME
Appears on the title bar once a file has been saved one time.

ALIGNMENT
The selected text is centered.

CONTEXTUAL TAB
Provides access to additional commands when objects (such as the clip art image below) are selected.

STYLES
Can be used to apply the same formatting to similar sections of the document.

HEADER
Text entered by the user that appears at the top of each page.

CLIP ART
Clip art and other graphics can be inserted and resized or otherwise modified as necessary.

WORD WRAP
Wraps text to the next line automatically when the text being typed reaches the end of the screen line; the user should not press Enter until the end of the paragraph.

STATUS BAR
Indicates the number of pages and words currently in the document, the current document view and zoom level, and so on.

TABLE
Can be used to neatly organize data or lay out the text in a document.

FOOTER
Text entered by the user that appears at the bottom of each page. This footer contains the page number.

> **Word wrap.** The feature in a word processing program that automatically returns the insertion point to the next line when the end of the screen line is reached.

TIP

When typing text in a word processing program, you should only press Enter after a short line (like a title), at the end of a paragraph, and to leave a blank line between paragraphs.

TIP

To save paper, always preview your documents before printing and use Word's *Shrink One Page* option if the document has a mostly blank last page.

end of the screen line is reached. Consequently, the Enter key should not be pressed until it is time to begin a new paragraph or leave a blank line. With word wrap, when changes are made to the document—such as adding, modifying, or deleting text or changing the text size or page margins—the program will automatically adjust the amount of text on each screen line, as long as the Enter key was not pressed at the end of each line.

In most word processing programs, formatting can be applied at the character, paragraph, and document levels. *Character formatting* changes the appearance of individual characters, such as to change the font face, size, style, or color. To format characters, you usually select them with the mouse, and then apply the appropriate format. In recent versions of Word, for instance, you can use the command buttons on the Ribbon's Home tab or the *Mini toolbar* (which appears when text is selected and is designed to allow easy text formatting), or you can click the *Font Dialog Box Launcher* (a small arrow at the bottom right corner of the *Font group* of the Home tab) to open the *Font dialog box*. As shown in Figure 6-12, Word includes a *Live Preview* feature, which allows the user to see the results of many formatting commands before they are applied, such as watching selected text change as the user scrolls through a list of font faces or sizes.

Paragraph formatting changes an entire paragraph at one time, such as specifying the *line spacing* for a particular paragraph. To format paragraphs, you usually select the paragraph with the mouse, and then apply the appropriate format. In Word, for instance, you can use the command buttons in the *Paragraph group* on the Ribbon's Home tab or you can click the *Paragraph Dialog Box Launcher* to open the *Paragraph dialog box*. The most common types of paragraph formatting include *line spacing*, *indentation*, and *alignment*. Line spacing is the amount of blank space between lines of text—usually set to 1 for single spacing or 2 for double spacing. Indentation is the distance between the paragraph and the left or right margin. Alignment indicates how the paragraph is aligned in relation to the left and right margins of the document, such as *left*, *center*, *right*, or *justify* (flush with both the left and right edges of the document as in this textbook). *Tabs* are set locations to which the insertion point is moved when the Tab key on the keyboard is pressed. Usually the tab settings are preset to every one-half inch, but the tab settings can be changed by the user. *Styles*—named format specifications—can also be applied on a paragraph-by-paragraph basis. Styles are used to keep a uniform appearance for related parts of a document. Once a paragraph has been assigned a style (such as one of Word's predefined styles, like Heading 1, or a new style defined by the user), all other paragraphs formatted with that style will appear the same and any formatting changes made to the style will be applied to all paragraphs using that style.

Most word processing programs also have a variety of *page formatting* options, such as changing the *margins*, the *paper size* being used, and whether you want the page to use the traditional *portrait orientation* (8.5 inches wide by 11 inches tall on standard paper) or the wider *landscape orientation* (11 inches wide by 8.5 inches tall on standard paper). In recent versions of Word, most page formatting options are found on the *Page Layout tab* on the Ribbon. You can also use the *Insert tab* on the Ribbon to add page numbers at the top or bottom of the page, or to specify a *header* or *footer*. As shown in Figure 6-12, a header or a footer is specified text or images that print automatically on every page; a header appears at the top of every page and a footer appears at the bottom of every page. Many of these options can be applied to an individual page as page formatting or to the entire document (called *document formatting*). Other types of document formatting include generating *footnotes* and *end notes*, a *table of contents*, or an *index*, as well as applying a *background* or a *theme* to the entire document.

CAUTION CAUTION CAUTION CAUTION CAUTION CAUTION CAUT

To avoid the embarrassment of distributing a document with hidden text, internal comments, and other data you may not wish to pass onto others, click the Office button, then *Prepare*, and then *Inspect Document* to check for and remove this data before distribution.

INSERT TAB
Used to insert a table, picture, shape, or other object into the document.

TABLE TOOLS CONTEXTUAL TABS
Used to change the design or layout of a table; available only when a table is selected.

PICTURE TOOLS CONTEXTUAL TAB
Used to format a picture object, such as to crop it or change its size, color, or border; available only when an image is selected.

Tables, Graphics, and Templates

Most word processing programs today have advanced features to help users create documents or add special features to documents. For instance, a *table* feature allows content to be organized in a table consisting of *rows* and *columns*. Tables can be used as basic data tables, such as the one shown in Figure 6-12; they can also be used to lay out documents, such as when creating a newsletter, résumé, or Web page. Once a table has been created, shading, borders, and other formatting can be applied to the table and/or its contents, and rows and columns can be inserted or deleted, as needed. There are a number of Ribbon tabs that can be used in Word to help users insert and modify tables. For instance, the Insert tab (shown in Figure 6-13) is used to insert tables (as well as pictures, shapes, charts, text boxes, and other objects). Once a table is created and selected, the *Table Tools* contextual tabs (*Design* and *Layout*—Layout is the active tab in Figure 6-13) appear on the Ribbon and contain commands that can be used to modify the table.

Graphics or *drawing* features are also commonly found in word processing programs. Virtually all word processing programs allow images (such as a photograph, a drawing from another program, a geometric shape, or a *clip art image* like the one in Figure 6-12) to be inserted into a document. Once an image is inserted into a document, it can be modified (such as changing the brightness or contrast of a digital photo, cropping an image, converting a color image to grayscale, compressing an image to reduce the file size of the document, or adding borders). The *Picture Tools* contextual tab, which is used in Word for these purposes and is displayed on the Ribbon whenever an image is selected, is shown in Figure 6-13. Once images are inserted into a document, they can be copied, moved, deleted, or otherwise modified, just like any other object in the document.

To help users create new documents quickly, many word processing programs have a variety of *templates* available. A template is a document that is already created and formatted to fit a particular purpose, such as a fax cover sheet, résumé, memo, business card, calendar, business plan, newsletter, or Web page. Usually placeholder text is included for text that can be customized so that all the user needs to do is to replace the placeholder text with the appropriate content.

Word Processing and the Web

Most word processing programs today include Web-related features, such as the ability to send a document as an e-mail message via the word processing program, the inclusion of Web page hyperlinks in documents, and the ability to create or modify Web pages or blogs. The latest versions of Office also include the ability to collaborate with others online.

FIGURE 6-13
Ribbon tabs used to insert and modify tables and images.

SW

TIP
When using a table for layout purposes, change the table borders to *None* after the document is finished to make the table outline invisible.

TIP
Additional templates are often available free of charge through software manufacturer Web sites, such as Microsoft's *Office Online* Web site.

TIP
To open the Web page associated with a hyperlink included in a document (assuming you have an active Internet connection), hold down the Control key and then click the hyperlink.

SPREADSHEET CONCEPTS

Another widely used application program is *spreadsheet software*. Spreadsheet software is commonly used by a variety of businesses and employees, including CEOs, managers, assistants, analysts, and sales representatives. Basic spreadsheet concepts and features are described next.

What Is a Spreadsheet?

A **spreadsheet** is a group of values and other data organized into rows and columns, similar to the ruled paper worksheets traditionally used by bookkeepers and accountants. **Spreadsheet software** is the type of application software used to create computerized spreadsheets, which typically contain a great deal of numbers and mathematical calculations. Most spreadsheets include *formulas* that are used to compute calculations based on data entered into the spreadsheet. All formula results are updated automatically whenever any changes are made to the data. Consequently, no manual computations are required, which increases accuracy. In addition, the automatic recalculation of formulas allows individuals to modify spreadsheet data as often as necessary either to create new spreadsheets or to experiment with various possible scenarios (called *what-if analysis*, as discussed shortly) to help make business decisions. Spreadsheet software typically includes a variety of data analysis tools, as well as the ability to generate charts.

The most widely used spreadsheet programs today are *Microsoft Excel*, *Corel Quattro Pro*, and *Apple Numbers*—again, all are part of their respective software suites mentioned near the beginning of this chapter. Some of the basic features supported by all spreadsheet programs are described in the next few sections, using Microsoft Excel 2007 as the example. Recent versions of Excel save spreadsheet files with the *.xlsx* extension by default.

Creating a Spreadsheet

A single spreadsheet document is often called a **worksheet**. Most spreadsheet programs allow multiple worksheets to be saved together in a single spreadsheet file, called a **workbook**. Worksheets are divided into **rows** and **columns**. The intersection of a row and a column is called a **cell**. Each cell is identified by its *cell address*, which consists of the column letter followed by the row number, such as B4 or E22. The *cell pointer* is used to select a cell; the selected cell is called the *active cell* or *current cell* and has a border around it so it is easy to identify. You can enter content into the active cell, as well as apply formatting to content already in the active cell. The cell pointer can be used to select more than one cell; if so, the selected cells are called a *range* or *block*. Ranges are always rectangular and are identified by specifying two opposite corners of the range, such as D8 through E9 for the four cells in the range shown in Figure 6-14 (and usually typed as *D8:E9* or *D8..E9*, depending on the spreadsheet program being used). As with Word, the Excel interface uses the Ribbon, contextual tabs, the Mini toolbar, and Live Preview for editing and formatting.

Entering Data into a Spreadsheet Cell

Data is entered directly into worksheet cells by clicking a cell to make it the active cell and then typing the data to be contained in that cell. The contents of the active cell can be erased by pressing the Delete key or by typing new content, which replaces the old contents of that cell. The data entered into a cell is usually a *label*, a *constant value*, a *formula*,

>**Spreadsheet.** A document containing a group of values and other data organized into rows and columns; also called a worksheet in a spreadsheet program. >**Spreadsheet software.** Application software used to create spreadsheets, which typically contain a great deal of numbers and mathematical computations organized into rows and columns. >**Worksheet.** A single spreadsheet document in a spreadsheet program. >**Workbook.** A collection of worksheets saved in a single spreadsheet file. >**Row.** In a spreadsheet program, a horizontal group of cells on a worksheet. >**Column.** In a spreadsheet program, a vertical group of cells on a worksheet. >**Cell.** The location at the intersection of a row and column on a worksheet into which data can be typed.

NAME BOX
Identifies the active cell, which is the location of the cell pointer.

COLUMNS
Run vertically and are identified by letters.

FORMULA BAR
Lists the contents of the active cell, in this case the formula entered into cell E8.

RIBBON
Contains tabs of commands grouped by function; the Home tab is selected.

CELL HEIGHT AND WIDTH
Can be changed to a specific value or to automatically fit the content.

NUMBER FORMATS
Used to specify the appearance of the numbers on a worksheet.

ACTIVE CELL/RANGE
Identifies the active cell or range; in this case the active cell is E8, and the range D8:E9 is selected.

ROWS
Run horizontally and are identified by numbers.

WORKSHEET AREA
Contains the worksheet itself.

GRAPHS
Are typically based on worksheet data and can be inserted into the worksheet area.

WORKSHEET TABS
Identify the different worksheets saved in a single spreadsheet (workbook) file.

CELL FORMATTING
Can be applied to cells (this cell is shaded blue with a double bottom border) and to cell content (such as currency with two decimal places).

or a *function*. **Labels** are words, column headings, and other nonmathematical data, such as *Profit Statement* and *January* in Figure 6-14. **Constant values** are numbers (such as *105* or *12740.25*) and are entered into a cell without any additional characters (such as a dollar sign or comma). A **formula** performs mathematical operations using the content of other cells (such as adding or multiplying the values in the specified cells) and displays the result in the cell containing the formula. A **function** is a named, preprogrammed formula, such as to compute the average of a group of cells or to calculate a mortgage payment amount. There are literally hundreds of functions that can be used in spreadsheets for statistical, date and time, engineering, math, logical, and text-based computations. The standard mathematical operators used in formulas and functions are shown in Figure 6-15; some examples of commonly used spreadsheet functions are listed in Figure 6-16.

When entering a formula or function into a cell, most spreadsheet programs require that you begin with some type of mathematical symbol—usually the equal sign (=). You can then enter the cell addresses and mathematical operators to create the formula, or you can type the appropriate function name and *arguments* (such as a cell or range address). When creating formulas and functions, it is important to always use the cell addresses of the numbers you want to include in the calculation (such as =B8+C8+D8 for the formula used to calculate the value displayed in cell E8 in Figure 6-14), rather than the numbers themselves (such as =4700+4950+5220). If the actual numbers are used in the formula instead of the cell addresses, the result of that formula (such as the total in cell E8) will not be correctly updated if one of the numbers (such as January payroll expenses in cell B8) is changed. When a

FIGURE 6-14
Some features in a typical spreadsheet program.

FIGURE 6-15
Universal mathematical operators.

SYMBOL	OPERATION
+	Addition
−	Subtraction
*	Multiplication
/	Division
^	Exponentiation

> **Label.** A text-based entry in a worksheet cell that identifies data on the worksheet. > **Constant value.** A numerical entry in a worksheet cell.
> **Formula.** An entry in a worksheet cell that performs computations on worksheet data and displays the results. > **Function.** A named formula that can be entered into a worksheet cell to perform some type of calculation or to extract information from other cells in the worksheet.

EXAMPLES OF FUNCTIONS

= SUM (range)	Calculates the sum of all values in a range.
= MAX (range)	Finds the highest value in a range.
= MIN (range)	Finds the lowest value in a range.
= AVERAGE (range)	Calculates the average of values in a range.
= FV (rate, number of payments, payment amount)	Calculates the future value of an annuity at a specified interest rate.
= PMT (rate, number of payments, loan amount)	Calculates the periodic payment for a loan.
= IF (conditional expression, value if true, value if false)	Supplies the values to be displayed if the conditional expression is true or if it is false.
= NOW ( )	Inserts the current date and time.

FIGURE 6-16
Common spreadsheet functions.

FIGURE 6-17
Relative vs. absolute cell referencing.

proper formula (using the cell references instead of the actual numbers) is used, the formula will be recomputed automatically every time any data in any of the cells used in that formula is changed. The appearance of numeric content (such as constant values or the result of a formula or numeric function) in a cell is determined by the *number format* applied to a cell (such as *Currency*, *Comma*, or *Percent*).

Absolute vs. Relative Cell Referencing

The Copy command can be used to copy content from one cell to another, in order to create a spreadsheet more quickly. This is especially true for cells containing formulas because the cells in a column or row often contain similar formulas (such as to add the values in the cells in the three columns to the left of the Total cells in column E in the spreadsheet shown in Figure 6-14) and typing formulas can be time-consuming. Labels and constant values are always copied exactly to the new location; what happens to formulas when they are copied depends on whether they use *relative cell referencing* or *absolute cell referencing*.

Relative cell references are used in most spreadsheet programs by default. When a formula containing relative cell references is copied, the cell addresses in the copied formula are adjusted to reflect their new location, so the formula performs the same operation (such as adding the two cells to the left of the cell containing the formula) but in the new location. In other words, the formula in the new location does the same *relative* operation as it did in the original location. For example, in the left screen in Figure 6-17, the formula in cell D2 (which uses relative cell references to add the two cells to the left of the cell containing the formula) is copied to cells D3 and D4. Because the cell references are all relative, when the formula is copied to the new cells, the cell references are adjusted to continue to add the two cells to

---

COPYING WITH RELATIVE CELL REFERENCES
In most formulas, cell addresses are relative and will be adjusted as the formula is copied.

Formula in cell D2 =B2+C2

	A	B	C	D
1		Cones	Sundaes	Total
2	April	600	200	800
3	May	800	500	1300
4	June	1500	600	2100
5	Total			
6				

Formula in cell D4 is =B4+C4.

Results when the formula in cell D2 is copied to cells D3 and D4.

COPYING WITH ABSOLUTE CELL REFERENCES
A dollar sign ($) marks a cell reference as absolute; it will be copied exactly as it appears in the source cell.

Formula in cell D2 =$B$2+$C$2

	A	B	C	D
1		Cones	Sundaes	Total
2	April	600	200	800
3	May	800	500	800
4	June	1500	600	800
5	Total			
6				

Results when the formula in cell D2 is copied to cells D3 and D4.

Formula in cell D4 is =$B$2+$C$2.

IMPROPER USE

Formula in cell E2 =D2/$D$5

	A	B	C	D	E
1		Cones	Sundaes	Total	Percent
2	April	600	200	800	19.05%
3	May	800	500	1300	30.95%
4	June	1500	600	2100	50.00%
5	Total			4200	100.00%
6					

Results when the formula in cell E2 is copied to cells E3 and E4.

PROPER USE

Formula in cell E4 is =D4/$D$5.

the left of the formula cell. For instance, the formula in cell D3 is updated automatically to =B3+C3 and the formula in cell D4 is updated automatically to =B4+C4. Relative cell references are also adjusted automatically when a row or column is inserted or deleted.

In contrast, when *absolute cell references* are used, formulas are copied exactly as they are written (see the rightmost screens in Figure 6-17). It is appropriate to use an absolute cell reference when you want to use a specific cell address in all copies of the formula—such as always multiplying by a constant value (perhaps a sales tax rate or overtime rate located in a particular cell on the worksheet) or always dividing by a total in order to compute a percentage. In other words, whenever you do not want a cell address to be adjusted when the formula is copied, you must use an absolute cell reference in the formula. To make a cell reference in a formula absolute, a special symbol—usually a dollar sign ($)—is placed before each column letter and row number that should not change. For example, both of the cell references in the formula in cell D2 in the top right screen in Figure 6-17 are absolute, resulting in the formula =$B$2+$C$2 being placed in both cells (D3 and D4) when the formula is copied. Obviously, this is not the correct formula for these cells—the formulas in these cells need to use relative cell references in order to display the proper totals. In cells E2 through E4 in the bottom right screen, however, an absolute cell reference is correctly used for cell D5 (and written as $D$5) in order to divide the total sales for each month (located in cells D2, D3, and D4, respectively) by the total sales for all three months (located in cell D5) to compute the percent of total sales. An absolute reference for cell D5 is necessary if the formula in cell E2 is to be copied to cells E3 and E4, since the denominator in all three cells should be D5.

Charts and What-If Analysis

Most spreadsheet programs include some type of *charting* or *graphing* capability. Because the data to be included in many business charts is often already located on a spreadsheet, using that program's charting feature eliminates reentering that data into another program. Instead, the cells containing the data to be charted are selected, and then the type of chart—as well as titles and other customizations—can be specified. Charts are inserted into an Excel spreadsheet using the commands in the *Charts group* on the Insert tab on the Ribbon. Finished charts can be moved like other graphical objects to the desired located on the worksheet (refer again to Figure 6-14). Selecting an existing chart displays three *Chart Tools* contextual tabs on the Ribbon. These three tabs can be used to change the design, layout, or format of the chart.

Because spreadsheet programs automatically recalculate all formulas on a worksheet every time the content of a cell on the worksheet is edited, spreadsheet programs are particularly useful for *what-if analysis* (also called *sensitivity analysis*)—a tool frequently used to help make business decisions. For example, suppose you want to know *what* profit would have resulted for January in Figure 6-14 *if* sales had been $15,000 instead of $10,570. You can simply enter the new value (15000) into cell B5, and the spreadsheet program automatically recalculates all formulas, allowing you to determine (from looking at the new value in cell B13) that the profit would have been $5,739.63. This ability to enter new numbers and immediately see the result allows businesspeople to run through many more possibilities in a shorter period of time before making decisions than in the past when all such calculations had to be performed by hand. Another type of sensitivity analysis (called *goal seeking* in Microsoft Excel) involves having the spreadsheet compute the amount a constant value would need to be in order for the result of a particular formula to become a specified amount (such as the total sales required to obtain a January profit of $5,000 if all of the expenses stayed the same).

Spreadsheets and the Web

As with word processors, most spreadsheet programs have built-in Web capabilities. Although they are used less commonly to create Web pages, many spreadsheet programs include the option to save the current worksheet as a Web page, and hyperlinks can be inserted into worksheet cells. Microsoft Word includes the ability to send a document as an e-mail message and to collaborate online; ranges of cells can also be copied to a Web publishing or word processing program to insert spreadsheet data into a document as a table.

DATABASE CONCEPTS

People often need to retrieve specific data rapidly while on the job. For example, a customer service representative may need to locate a customer's order status quickly while the customer is on the telephone. The registrar at a university may have to look up a student's grade point average or rapidly determine if the student has any outstanding fees before processing his or her class registration. A clerk in a video store may need to determine if a particular DVD is available for rental and, if not, when it is scheduled to be returned. The type of software used for such tasks is a *database management system*. Computer-based database management systems are rapidly replacing the paper-based filing systems that people used in the past to find information. The most common type of database used with personal computers today is a *relational database*. The basic features and concepts of this type of database software are discussed next. Other types of database programs are discussed in Chapter 14.

What Is a Database?

A **database** is a collection of related data that is stored on a computer and organized in a manner that enables information to be retrieved as needed. A *database management system (DBMS)*—also called **database software**—is the type of program used to create, maintain, and organize data in a database, as well as to retrieve information from it. Typically data in a database is organized into *fields*, *records*, and *files*. A **field** (today more commonly called a **column**) is a single type of data, such as last name or telephone number, to be stored in a database. A **record** (today more commonly called a **row**) is a collection of related fields—for example, the ID number, name, address, and major of Phyllis Hoffman (see Figure 6-18).

FIGURE 6-18

Paper-based vs. computerized databases. Data is organized into fields (columns), records (rows), and tables.

One student's record stored in the Addresses file.

Data is organized into fields.

16231

ID: 16231
Name: Hoffman, Phyllis
Street: 706 Elm Street
City: New Milford
State: NJ
Major: Business

PAPER-BASED DATABASE

Student database

Addresses file

Grades file

Schedules file

ADDRESSES

GRADES

SCHEDULES

COMPUTERIZED DATABASE

Fields (columns)   Table

Record (row)

Schedules
Grades
Addresses

ID	Name	Street	City	State	Major
15265	Michaels, Jane	111 First Avenue	Boston	MA	Math
16231	Hoffman, Phyllis	706 Elm Street	New Milford	NJ	Business
48595	Adams, Jose	45 Center Street	New York	NY	Business
49658	Gomez, Maria	3699 Lincoln	Boston	MA	Nursing
78982	Rivera, Cynthia	122 Morton	Martinez	CA	Chemistry
79856	Jenkins, Paul	789 White Avenue	Hamilton	NJ	Pre-Med

Record: 2 of 919   No Filter   Search

> **Database.** A collection of related data that is stored in a manner enabling information to be retrieved as needed; in a relational database, a collection of related tables. > **Database software.** Application software that allows the creation and manipulation of an electronic database. > **Field.** A single category of data to be stored in a database, such as a person's last name or telephone number. Also called a column. > **Column.** In a database, a field. > **Record.** A collection of related fields in a database. Also called a row. > **Row.** In a database program, a record.

A **table** is a collection of related rows (such as all student address data, all student grade data, or all student schedule data). One or more related tables can be stored in a database file.

The most commonly used *relational database management systems* (*RDBMSs*) include *Microsoft Access* (part of the Microsoft Office software suite), as well as *Oracle Database* and IBM's *DB2*. Some of the basic features of relational database programs in general are described in the next few sections, using Microsoft Access 2007 as the example. Recent versions of Access save database files with the *.accdb* extension by default.

Creating a Database

An Access database can contain a variety of *objects*. *Tables* are the objects that contain the database data. Other types of objects (such as *forms*, *queries*, and *reports*, discussed shortly) can be created and used in conjunction with tables when needed. As shown in Figure 6-19, a list of the various objects stored in a database file is displayed when the file is opened. However, you do not see the content of a database object until you open that object.

To create a database, you create the database file first, and then you create the database objects you want the database to contain. Each time Access is launched, you have the option of creating a new blank database file, creating a database file from a template, or opening an existing database file. If you choose to create a new blank database file, a new blank table opens in *Datasheet view* (which displays the table in rows and columns similar to a spreadsheet—see the top screen in Figure 6-20).

DATABASE FILE
Contains the Inventory database objects.

RIBBON
Contains tabs of commands grouped by function; the Create tab, which is used to create new database objects, is selected.

DATABASE OBJECTS
Include Tables (for storing data), Forms (for viewing and editing table data), and Queries and Reports (for retrieving information from tables).

FIGURE 6-19
Typical database objects. Common database objects include tables, forms, queries, and reports. The first object to be created is the table.

FIGURE 6-20
Creating a database table.

DATASHEET VIEW

As data is entered into a new table using Datasheet view, the structure of the table is created.

The table has been saved as "Product" and is in Design view.

This field was renamed "Product Name" and is a Text field.

Click to select Design View.

Properties of the Product Name field.

DESIGN VIEW

>**Table.** In a relational database, a collection of related records or rows.

As data is entered into a new table using Datasheet view, the *structure* of the table (the fields and their properties) is created. Each column becomes a new field and is given a temporary *field name* (an identifying name unique within the table, such as *Field1*) and is assigned an appropriate *data type* (which identifies the type of data to be contained in the field; for example, text, a number, or a date) based on the data initially entered into that field. These properties can be changed by selecting the field and using the commands on the *Datasheet tab* of the Ribbon (such as selecting the *Rename* option to rename the field or selecting a different data type in the *Data Type* box). Each field should be given a descriptive field name and the data type should be changed if the data type set by default is not correct. A field can also be declared a *required* field if the field should not be left blank. *Design view* (shown in the bottom screen in Figure 6-20) can be used to change other field properties, such as the *field size* (which is the maximum number of characters allowed for the content of that field), the *default value* (which is the initial content of that field that remains until it is changed), the field *description*, and the *format* (which describes how the field content should be displayed, such as including commas or dollar signs with numeric data). When the table is saved, it is given a name by the user and both the table data and table structure are saved in that table object.

To add new data to an existing table, to edit data, or to delete data, either a *form* or Datasheet view can be used. As shown in Figure 6-21, a form (which is created by the user for a particular table) typically displays one record at a time, while Datasheet view displays several records at one time. However, either Datasheet view or a form can be used to change the data in the table. Data can be edited by clicking inside the appropriate field and then making the necessary edits. A record can be deleted by clicking to the left of the first field in the appropriate Datasheet row or on the left edge of a form to select that record, and then pressing the Delete key. A field can be deleted in Datasheet view by selecting the appropriate field (column), and then pressing the Delete key. The *Record buttons* at the bottom of the form or Datasheet view window can be used to move through the records as needed.

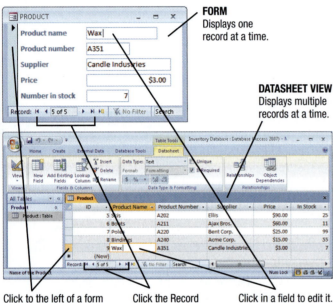

FORM
Displays one record at a time.

DATASHEET VIEW
Displays multiple records at a time.

Click to the left of a form or table record to select that record.

Click the Record buttons to display other records.

Click in a field to edit it.

FIGURE 6-21
Table data can be modified using a form or the Datasheet view.

Queries and Reports

To retrieve information from a database, *queries* and *reports* are used. A *query* is a question, or, in database terms, a request for specific information from the database. Like other database objects, each query object is created and then saved using an appropriate name as a part of the database file. A query object is associated with a particular table and contains *criteria*—specific conditions that must be met in order for a record (row) to be included in the query results—as well as instructions regarding which fields (columns) should appear in the query results. For instance, the query shown in Figure 6-22 is designed to retrieve information from the Product table shown in Figure 6-21. The query retrieves all products in that table that have prices less than $25, and the query results display only the Product Name, Product Number, and Price fields. Whenever the query is opened, only the records meeting the specified criteria at the time the query is opened are displayed, and only the specified fields for those records are listed. For instance, the query results shown in Figure 6-22 contain only two records from the Product table in Figure 6-21 because only two records in that table contain products with prices less than $25. If a new product priced less than $25 is added to the database, three records will be displayed the next time the query is opened.

When a more formal output is required, *reports* are used. Reports can contain page and column headings, as well as a company logo or other graphics, and can be formatted and customized as desired. Reports are associated with a database table or query and can be easily created using the *Report button* or *Report Wizard button* on the *Create tab* on the Ribbon. Existing reports can be modified using the *Report Design button*. Whenever a report object is opened, the corresponding data is displayed in the specified location in the report. Consequently, just as with queries, reports always display the data contained in a table at the time the report is generated. Queries and reports are discussed in more detail in Chapter 14.

Databases and the Web

Databases are often used on the Web. Many Web sites use one or more databases to keep track of inventory; to allow searching for people, documents, or other information; to place real-time orders; and so forth. For instance, any time you type keywords in a search box on a search site or hunt for a product on a retail store's Web site using its search feature, you are using a Web database. Web databases are explained in more detail in Chapter 14.

QUERY DESIGN SCREEN
This query will display only the records that meet the specified criteria each time the query is retrieved.

Only these three fields will be displayed in the query results.

Only the records in which the price is less than $25 will be displayed in the query results.

QUERY RESULTS
The two records meeting the specified criteria are displayed.

FIGURE 6-22
Creating and using a database query.

FIGURE 6-23
Examples of presentation graphics.

PRESENTATION GRAPHICS CONCEPTS

If you try to explain to others what you look like, it may take several minutes. Show them a color photograph, on the other hand, and you can convey the same information within seconds. The saying "a picture is worth a thousand words" is the cornerstone of *presentation graphics*. The basic concepts and features of presentation graphics are discussed in the next few sections.

What Is a Presentation Graphic?

A **presentation graphic** (see Figure 6-23) is an image designed to enhance a presentation (such as an *electronic slide show* or a printed report) visually, typically to convey information more easily to people. A variety of software (including spreadsheet programs, *image editing programs*, and *presentation graphics software*) can be used to create presentation graphics. Presentation graphics often take the form of electronic **slides** containing images,

COLUMN CHART

PIE CHART

ORGANIZATIONAL CHART

DRAWN OBJECTS

> **Presentation graphic.** An image, such as a graph or text chart, designed to visually enhance a presentation. > **Slide.** A one-page presentation graphic that can be displayed in a group with others to form an electronic slide show.

text, video, and more that are displayed one after the other in an **electronic slide show**. Electronic slide shows are created with **presentation graphics software** and can be run on individual computers or presented to a large group using a computer projector; for instance, they are frequently used for business and educational presentations. Some of today's most common presentation graphics programs are *Microsoft PowerPoint*, *Corel Presentations*, and *Apple Keynote*—again, all part of their respective software suites. The next few sections discuss creating an electronic slide show, using Microsoft PowerPoint 2007 as the example. Recent versions of PowerPoint save files with the *.pptx* extension by default.

Creating a Presentation

A presentation graphics program, such as the one shown in Figure 6-24, contains an assortment of tools and operations for creating and editing slides. For instance, new slides can be added to a new or existing presentation (preformatted *slide layouts* containing placeholders for text and charts and other elements in a slide can be used, if desired). Text, photographs, tables, shapes, charts, and more can then be added to slides using the Insert tab and formatted as needed using the *Format tab*. To create more exciting and dynamic presentations, multimedia objects and animation effects can be used. For instance, video and audio clips

FIGURE 6-24

Some features in a typical presentation graphics program.

NEW SLIDES
Use the Home tab to add a new slide.

SLIDES TAB
Click to see thumbnails of the slides in the presentation.

OUTLINE TAB
Click to see the titles and main text contained on the slides.

TEXT
Can be formatted using commands on the Ribbon or the Mini toolbar, like in other Office programs.

RIBBON
Contains tabs of commands grouped by function; the Insert tab is selected.

CLIP ART AND OTHER GRAPHICS
Can be inserted and resized or otherwise modified.

SLIDES
Can contain elements such as text, clip art, photographs, bulleted lists, charts, and video clips. Often a theme, color scheme, or design layout is used to apply a universal appearance to all slides.

DRAWN OBJECTS
Can be added, formatted, and resized; include lines, shapes, and more.

VIDEO CLIPS
Can be inserted into slides and set up to play automatically when the slide is loaded or when the video placeholder is clicked.

STATUS BAR
Includes information such as the current slide number and the total number of slides.

SOUND CLIPS
Can be inserted into slides and set up to play automatically when the slide is loaded or when the sound placeholder is clicked.

NOTES
Can be added so they can be seen by the presenter during the slide show or included on printouts.

SLIDE SHOW BUTTON
Click to run the slide show beginning with the current slide.

> **Electronic slide show.** A group of electronic slides that are displayed one after the other on a computer monitor or other display device.
> **Presentation graphics software.** Application software used to create presentation graphics and electronic slide shows.

can be inserted into a slide and set up to play automatically each time the slide containing those elements is displayed, or, alternatively, to play when certain objects on the slide are clicked. Text or other objects can be *animated* so that a special effect (such as *flying* the text in from the edge of the screen or *dissolving* the text in or out on a slide) is used to display that text or object each time the slide is viewed. *Animation settings* can be specified to indicate the sequence in which objects are displayed (such as to build a bulleted list one item at a time), whether or not a video loops continuously, and more.

Once the basic slides in a presentation have been created, the overall appearance of the entire slide show can be changed by applying a *theme* (a combination of colors, fonts, and effects that can be applied to an entire slide show at one time) to the presentation using the *Design tab*. In addition, *transitions*—special effects used between slides—can be applied to specific slides, or random transitions can be selected for the entire slide show. In PowerPoint, animations and transitions are both specified using the *Animations tab*.

Finishing a Presentation

Once all of the slides in a slide show have been created and the desired animation and transition effects have been applied, the slide show is ready to be finalized. To preview the slides and rearrange them if needed, presentation graphics programs typically have a special view, such as PowerPoint's *slide sorter view*, that shows thumbnails of all the slides in a presentation. Using this view, slides can easily be rearranged by dragging them with the mouse to their new location in the presentation. When the slide show is run, the slides are displayed in the designated order. The slides advance either automatically or manually, depending on how the presentation is set up. For an *automatic slide show*, the amount of time each slide should be displayed is specified using the *Slide Show tab* on the Ribbon before the presentation is saved. For a *manual slide show*, the speaker (or person viewing the slide show, for a stand-alone presentation) moves to the next slide by pressing the spacebar or by clicking anywhere on the screen using the mouse. If desired, PowerPoint allows narration to be recorded and played back when the slide show is run, and *speaker notes* can be added to the slides, as needed.

PowerPoint, like many other presentation software programs, also has a variety of *speaker tools*. For instance, the speaker can choose a ballpoint pen, felt tip pen, or highlighter tool and "write" on the slides while the slide show is running, perhaps to circle a particular sentence for emphasis or to draw an arrow pointing to one part of the slide. Recent versions of PowerPoint also include a *Presenter View* (see Figure 6-25) that can be used when two display devices are available (such as when a data projector is connected to the notebook computer being used to run the presentation). The regular slide show is projected in full screen for the audience on one display device (such as projected onto a large screen via the data projector), while a special Presenter View version of the slide show (containing a smaller version of the current slide along with speaker notes, thumbnails of surrounding slides, a timer, and so forth) is displayed for the presenter on the second display device (such as the notebook computer's display screen). Most presentation software programs can also print the speaker notes, as well as the slides (either full-sized or miniature versions printed several to a page) to create overhead transparencies or audience handouts.

FIGURE 6-25
Running an electronic slide show.

SLIDE SHOW VIEW
Displays the slide show for the audience in full screen with the software interface hidden. Slides can be advanced at predetermined intervals or by clicking the mouse or pressing the spacebar.

PRESENTER VIEW
Seen only by the presenter on a different display device; includes thumbnails, a timer, speaker notes, annotation tools, and so forth.

Presentation Graphics and the Web

As with the other application programs discussed so far, presentation graphics programs can be used to generate Web pages or Web page content, and slides can include hyperlinks. When a slide show is saved as a series of Web pages and displayed using a Web browser, generally forward and backward navigational buttons are displayed on the slides to allow the user to control the presentation.

GRAPHICS AND MULTIMEDIA CONCEPTS

Graphics are graphical images, such as digital photographs, clip art, scanned drawings, and original images created using a software program. *Multimedia* technically refers to any application that contains more than one type of media (as discussed in Chapter 10), but is often used to refer to audio and video content. There are a variety of software programs designed to help individuals create or modify graphics, edit digital audio or video files, play media files, burn CDs and DVDs, and so forth, as discussed next. Some programs focus on just one task; others are designed to perform multiple tasks, such as to import and edit images, audio, and video, and then create a finished DVD.

Graphics Software

Graphics software—also called *digital imaging software*—is used to create or modify images. Graphics software programs are commonly distinguished by whether they are primarily oriented toward painting, drawing, or image editing, although these are general categories, not strict classifications.

  Painting programs traditionally create *bitmap images*, which are created by coloring the individual pixels in an image. One of the most common painting programs is *Microsoft Paint* (shown in Figure 6-26). Painting programs are often used to create and modify simple

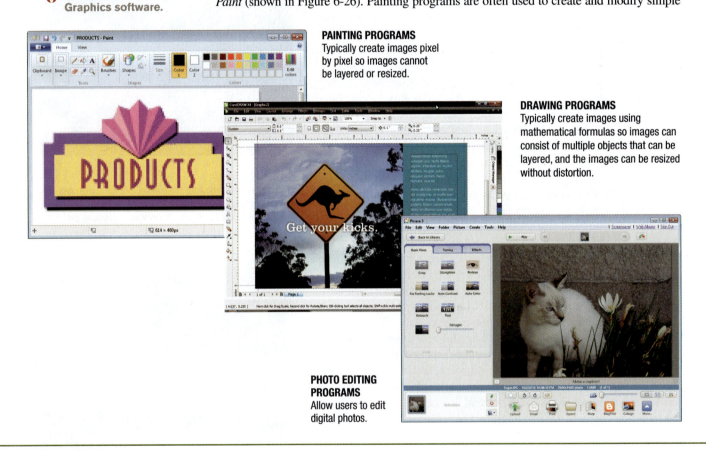

FIGURE 6-26
Graphics software.

PAINTING PROGRAMS
Typically create images pixel by pixel so images cannot be layered or resized.

DRAWING PROGRAMS
Typically create images using mathematical formulas so images can consist of multiple objects that can be layered, and the images can be resized without distortion.

PHOTO EDITING PROGRAMS
Allow users to edit digital photos.

>**Graphics software.** Application software used to create or modify images.

images, but, unless the painting program supports *layers* and other tools discussed shortly, use for these programs is relatively limited. This is because when something is drawn or placed on top of a bitmap image, the pixels in the image are recolored to reflect the new content so whatever was beneath the new content is lost. In addition, bitmapped images cannot be enlarged and still maintain their quality, since the pixels in the images just get larger, which makes the edges of the images look jagged. Some painting programs today (such as *Corel Painter*) do support layers and so are more versatile. Painting tools are also increasingly included in other types of software, such as in office suites and the drawing programs discussed next.

Drawing programs (also referred to as *illustration programs*) typically create *vector graphics*, which use mathematical formulas to represent image content instead of pixels. Unlike bitmap images, vector images can be resized and otherwise manipulated without loss of quality. Objects in drawing programs can also typically be *layered* so, if you place one object on top of another, you can later separate the two images if desired. Drawing programs are often used by individuals and small business owners to create original art, logos, business cards, and more; they are also used by professionals to create corporate images, Web site graphics, and so forth. Popular drawing programs include *Adobe Illustrator* and *CorelDRAW* (shown in Figure 6-26).

Image editing or *photo editing programs* are drawing or painting programs that are specifically designed for touching up or modifying images, such as original digital images and digital photos. Editing options include correcting brightness or contrast, eliminating red eye, cropping, resizing, and applying filters or other special effects. Most programs also include options for *optimizing* images to reduce the file size. Optimization techniques include reducing the number of colors used in the image and converting the image to another file format. Some of the most widely used consumer image editing and photo editing programs are *Adobe Photoshop Elements*, *Ulead Photo Express*, *Apple iPhoto*, *Corel Paint Shop Pro Photo X2*, *Microsoft Office Picture Manager*, and the free *Picasa 3* program (shown in Figure 6-26). For professional image editing, *Adobe Photoshop* is the leading program.

Audio Capture and Editing Software

For creating and editing audio files, *audio capture* and *audio editing* software is used. To capture sound from a microphone, *sound recorder* software is used; to capture sound from a CD, *ripping software* is used. In either case, once the audio is captured, it can then be modified, as needed. For instance, background noise or pauses can be removed, portions of the selection can be edited out, multiple segments can be spliced together, and special effects such as fade-ins and fade-outs can be applied. There are also specialized audio capture and editing programs designed for specific applications, such as creating podcasts or musical compositions. Professional audio capture and editing software (such as *Sony Creative Software Sound Forge 9* and *Adobe Audition 3*) is used to create professional audio for end products, Web pages, commercial podcasts, presentations, and so forth. Common consumer audio capture and editing programs include *Windows Sound Recorder*, *Apple GarageBand*, and *Sony Creative Software Sound Forge Audio Studio* software (see Figure 6-27).

Video Editing and DVD Authoring Software

It is common today for individuals to want to create finished videos, such as to create a video to upload to YouTube or to edit home videos and transfer them to a DVD. Businesses also often find the need for *video editing*, such as to prepare video clips for presentations and Web sites. Most video capture today is in digital form; if so, the video can be imported directly into a video editing program by connecting the camera to the computer or by inserting the storage media containing the video (such as a DVD) into the computer. Once the video has been imported, video editing (such as deleting or rearranging scenes, adding voice-overs, and adding other special effects) can be performed (see Figure 6-28). Some video editing software today can edit video in high definition format.

DVD authoring refers to organizing content to be transferred to DVD, such as importing video clips and then creating the desired menu structure for the DVD to control the playback of those videos. *DVD burning* refers to recording data (such as a collection of songs or a finished video) on a recordable or rewritable DVD. DVD authoring and burning capabilities

◬ FIGURE 6-27
Audio editing software.

◭ FIGURE 6-28
Video creation software. Often includes both video editing and DVD authoring capabilities.

VIDEO EDITING
Allows users to import and edit video; the finished video can be stored in a file or included in a DVD presentation.

Click to burn the finished presentation to a DVD.

The DVD includes the video clips and uses the titles and appearance designated by the user.

Video clips can be edited as needed; the timeline is used to crop out sections of the current video clip.

DVD AUTHORING
Allows users to import and organize photos, video, and music into a finished DVD presentation.

are commonly included with video editing capabilities in *video creation software*; there are also stand-alone *DVD authoring programs*, and DVD burning capabilities are preinstalled on computers containing a recordable or rewritable optical drive. Many file management programs (such as Windows Explorer) include CD and DVD burning capabilities, as well.

Consumer video creation software includes *Serif MoviePlus X3* (shown in Figure 6-28), *Roxio Creator 2009*, *Roxio MyDVD 10*, *Apple iMovie* and *iDVD*, *Windows Movie Maker*, *Ulead VideoStudio X2*, *Ulead DVD MovieFactory 6 Plus*, and *Sony Creative Software Vegas Movie Studio 9*. Professional products include *Adobe Premiere Pro*, *Sony Creative Software Vegas Pro*, and *Sonic CineVision*.

Media Players

Media players are programs designed to play audio and video files. They are used to play media available via your computer—such as music CDs, downloaded music, or video streamed from the Internet. Many media players are available for free, such as *RealPlayer* (see Figure 6-29), *Windows Media Player*, and *QuickTime Player*. Media players typically allow you to arrange your stored music and videos into *playlists*, and then transfer them to CDs or portable digital music players. Some also include the ability to download video from the Web and/or purchase and download music via an associated *music store*.

My Library is selected; use the other options to listen to radio, purchase music, and so on.

Use these options to view the media files stored on your computer.

Click to play a disc in your computer's CD or DVD drive.

Use these options to burn a CD or DVD.

This video file is currently playing.

FIGURE 6-29
A typical media player program.

It is important when using digital music to adhere to copyright laws, such as only transferring music from CDs that you have purchased and only downloading digital music files from sites that compensate the artists and record labels. While most music download sites today are legal and charge around $1 per title, illegal *peer-to-peer* (*P2P*) MP3 file exchanges do exist. Copyrights and P2P networks are discussed in more detail in later chapters.

Graphics, Multimedia, and the Web

Graphics and multimedia software are often used by individuals and businesses alike to create Web sites or content to be shared or distributed via the Web. In addition, games, tutorials, videos, demonstrations, and other multimedia content available on the Web are often created with multimedia software. Multimedia elements and creating multimedia Web sites are the focus of Chapter 10.

OTHER TYPES OF APPLICATION SOFTWARE

There are many other types of application software available today. Some are geared for business or personal productivity; others are designed for entertainment or educational purposes. Still others are intended to help users with a particular specialized application, such as preparing financial reports, issuing prescriptions electronically, designing buildings, controlling machinery, and so forth. A few of the most common types of application software not previously covered are discussed next.

Desktop and Personal Publishing Software

Desktop publishing refers to using a personal computer to combine and manipulate text and images to create attractive documents that look as if they were created by a

FIGURE 6-30

Desktop publishing software. Allows users to create publication-quality documents.

professional printer (see Figure 6-30). Although many desktop publishing effects can be produced using a word processing program, users who frequently create publication-style documents usually find a desktop publishing program a more efficient means of creating those types of documents. Some popular desktop publishing programs are *Adobe InDesign*, *Microsoft Publisher*, and *Serif PagePlus X3*. *Personal publishing* refers to creating desktop-publishing-type documents—such as greeting cards, invitations, flyers, calendars, certificates, and so forth—for personal use. There are also specialized personal publishing programs for particular purposes, such as to create scrapbook pages, cross stitch patterns, CD and DVD labels, and so forth.

Educational, Entertainment, and Reference Software

A wide variety of educational and entertainment application programs are available. *Educational software* is designed to teach one or more skills, such as reading, math, spelling, a foreign language, and world geography, or to help prepare for standardized tests. *Entertainment software* includes games, simulations, and other programs that provide amusement. A hybrid of these two categories is called *edutainment*—educational software that also entertains. *Reference software* includes encyclopedias, dictionaries, atlases, mapping/travel programs, cookbook programs, and other software designed to provide valuable information. Although still available as stand-alone software packages, reference information today is also obtained frequently via the Internet.

FIGURE 6-31

Note taking software. Allows individuals to record and organize important data.

Note Taking Software and Web Notebooks

Note taking software is used by both students and businesspeople to take notes during class lectures, meetings, and similar settings. It is used most often with tablet computers and other devices designed to accept pen input. Typically, note taking software (such as Microsoft *OneNote*, Agilix Labs *GoBinder*, or Circus Ponies *Notebook 3.0* program shown in Figure 6-31) supports both typed and handwritten input; handwritten input can usually be saved in its handwritten form as an image or converted to typed text. Note taking software contains features designed specifically to make note taking—and, particularly, retrieving information from the notes—easier. Like a paper notebook, tabbed sections can be created (such as one tab per course) and files, notes, Web links, and any other data are stored under the appropriate tabs. The built-in search tools allow you to find the information that you need quickly and easily. Online versions of these programs (such as *Google Notebook* and *Zoho Notebook*) are referred to as *Web notebooks* and are designed to help organize your online research, including text, images, Web links, search results, and other content located on Web pages.

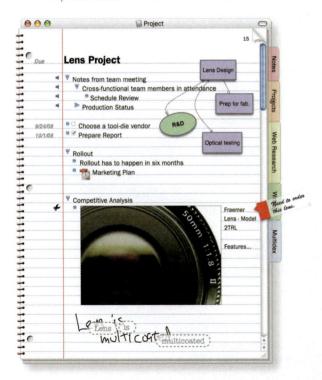

CAD and Other Types of Design Software

As discussed in more detail in Chapter 12, *computer-aided design (CAD) software* enables designers to design objects on the computer. For example, engineers or architects can create designs of buildings or other objects and modify the designs as often as needed. Increasingly, CAD programs are including capabilities to analyze designs in terms of how well they meet a number of design criteria, such as testing how a building design will hold up during an earthquake or how a car will perform under certain conditions. Besides playing an important role in the design of finished products, CAD is useful in fields such as art, advertising, law, architecture, and movie production. In addition to the powerful CAD programs used in business, there are also design programs designed for home and small business use, such as for designing new homes, and for making remodeling plans, interior designs, and landscape designs.

Accounting and Personal Finance Software

Accounting software is used to automate some of the accounting activities that need to be performed on a regular basis. Common tasks include recording purchases and payments, managing inventory, creating payroll documents and checks, preparing financial statements, and keeping track of business expenses (see Figure 6-32). *Personal finance software* is commonly used at home by individuals to write checks and balance checking accounts, track personal expenses, manage stock portfolios, and prepare income taxes. Increasingly, personal finance activities are becoming Web-based, such as the *online banking* and *online portfolio management* services available through many banks and brokerage firms and discussed in more detail in Chapter 8.

FIGURE 6-32
Accounting software. This iPhone application helps individuals keep track of business expenses.

Project Management, Collaboration, and Remote Access Software

Project management software is used to plan, schedule, track, and analyze the tasks involved in a project, such as the construction of a building or the schedule for preparing a large advertising campaign for a client. Project management capabilities are often included in *collaboration software*—software that enables a group of individuals to work together on a project—and are increasingly available as Web-based software programs.

Remote access software enables individuals to access content on another computer they are authorized to access, via the Internet. Some programs allow you to control the remote computer directly; others allow you to access your media files (such as recorded TV shows or music) from any Web-enabled device while you are away from home. For instance, the *Slingbox* product gives you access to and control over your cable box and DVR via the Internet (as discussed in Chapter 7), and *Orb* software allows you to access the files on your computer (documents, as well as recorded TV shows and music) from any Web-enabled device while you are away from home. Other remote access software automatically backs up all data files on your main computer to a secure Web server so they can be accessed from any Web-enabled device (such as a portable computer or mobile phone, in some cases), as well as shared with others for collaboration purposes. To make it easier to share single large files with others, you can use Web-based *file sending applications* (such as *YouSendIt* shown in Figure 6-33).

FIGURE 6-33
File sending applications. This Web-based application allows you to easily send large files to others via the Internet.

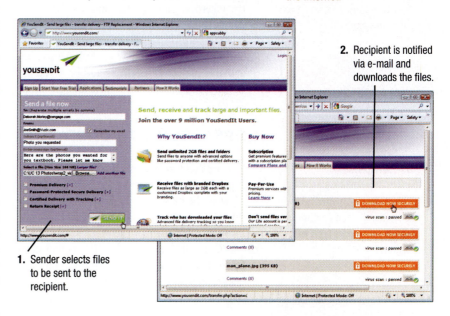

2. Recipient is notified via e-mail and downloads the files.

1. Sender selects files to be sent to the recipient.

SUMMARY

THE BASICS OF APPLICATION SOFTWARE

Chapter Objective 1:
Describe what application software is, the different types of ownership rights, and the difference between installed and Web-based software.

Application software is software designed to carry out a specific task. Common types of application software include games, Web browsers, word processing programs, multimedia software, and more. Many application software programs today are **commercial software** programs that are developed and sold for a profit. When a software program is purchased, individual users receive a **software license** authorizing them to use the software. Some commercial software is available in a *demo* or *trial version*. Other software is available as **shareware**, **freeware**, or **public domain software**. **Open source software** is the term for programs whose source code is available to the general public. Software is designed as either *desktop software* or *mobile software*. **Installed software** is installed on a local computer or network server; **Web-based software**, which is also called **Software as a Service (SaaS)** and **cloudware**, is run from the Internet instead. Organizations that provide Web-based software are referred to as *application service providers* (*ASPs*).

Many office-oriented programs are sold bundled together as a **software suite**. One of the most widely used software suites is **Microsoft Office**. Although they are used for different purposes, most application software programs share some of the same concepts and functions, such as similar document-handling operations and help features. For instance, documents are commonly *opened*, *saved*, *printed*, *edited,* and *formatted* in a similar manner. **Editing** a document changes its content; **formatting** a document changes its appearance (such as by changing the *font face*, *font size*, or *font style* of text, or by changing the *line spacing* or *margins*. Commands can be issued via a variety of methods, such as by using *menus*, *toolbars*, **keyboard shortcuts,** or the Microsoft Office **Ribbon**—the **insertion point** typically looks like a blinking vertical line and identifies the current position in a document. Online help is available in many programs.

WORD PROCESSING CONCEPTS

Chapter Objective 3:
Discuss word processing and explain what kinds of documents are created using this type of program.

Word processing refers to using a computer and **word processing software** to create, manipulate, and print written documents, such as letters, contracts, and so forth. When creating or editing a word processing document, the **word wrap** feature automatically moves the insertion point to the next line when the end of the screen line is reached. Formatting can be applied at the character, paragraph, or document level. Other enhancements found in most word processing programs include the ability to include graphical images and *tables*, and to use *styles*, *templates*, or *wizards* for more efficient document creation. Documents can also include hyperlinks and be saved as Web pages in many programs. Most word processors also include a spelling and grammar check feature and other useful tools.

SPREADSHEET CONCEPTS

Chapter Objective 4:
Explain the purpose of spreadsheet software and the kinds of documents created using this type of program.

Spreadsheet software is used to create documents (**spreadsheets** or **worksheets**) that typically include a great deal of numbers and mathematical computations; a collection of worksheets stored in the same spreadsheet file is called a **workbook**. A worksheet is divided into **rows** and **columns** that intersect to form **cells**, each of which can be accessed through a *cell address*, such as B3. A rectangular group of cells is referred to as a *range*.

Content is entered into individual cells and may consist of **labels**, **constant values**, **formulas**, or **functions**. Formulas can be typed using *relative cell* or *absolute cell references*, depending on the type of computation required. Once created, the content of individual cells may be edited and formatted. *Numeric formats* are used to change the appearance

Chapter Objective 2:
Detail some concepts and commands that many software programs have in common.

of numbers, such as adding a dollar sign or displaying a specific number of decimal places. Spreadsheet programs commonly include a *charting* or *graphing* feature and the ability to perform *what-if analysis*. Some spreadsheet programs allow worksheets to be saved in the form of a Web page and the inclusion of hyperlinks in cells.

DATABASE CONCEPTS

A *database management system* (*DBMS*) or **database software** program enables the creation of a **database**—a collection of related data stored in a manner so that information can be retrieved as needed. In a relational DBMS (the most common type found on personal computers), a **field** or **column** is a collection of characters that make up a single piece of data, such as a name or phone number; a **record** or **row** is a collection of related fields; and a **table** is a collection of related records. One or more tables can be stored in a database file.

A relational database typically contains a variety of *objects*, such as tables, *forms* to input or view data, *queries* to retrieve specific information, and *reports* to print a formal listing of the data stored in a table or the results of a query. When a table is created, the table fields are specified along with their characteristics, such as *field name*, *field size*, and *data type*. This structure, as well as the data, are saved in the table and can be modified when needed. Databases are commonly integrated into the Web, such as to keep track of inventory and to facilitate online ordering.

Chapter Objective 5:
Identify some of the vocabulary used with database software and discuss the benefits of using this type of program.

PRESENTATION GRAPHICS CONCEPTS

Presentation graphics are images used to visually enhance the impact of information communicated to other people. **Presentation graphics software** can be used to create presentation graphics and **electronic slide shows** consisting of electronic **slides**. The individual slides in the slide show are created, and then they can be edited and formatted, as can the overall appearance of the presentation. Multimedia elements, such as images and video clips, can also be included. After all slides have been created for a presentation, the order of the slides can be rearranged and *transitions* between the slides can be specified. It is becoming increasingly common to find slide-based presentations available through the Web. Web-based slide shows can include multimedia elements, as well as hyperlinks and other navigational buttons.

Chapter Objective 6:
Describe what presentation graphics and electronic slide shows are and when they might be used.

GRAPHICS AND MULTIMEDIA CONCEPTS

Graphics are graphical images, such as digital photographs, clip art, and original art. *Multimedia* refers to applications that include more than one type of media, but often refers to audio and video content. To create graphics, **graphics software**—such as a *painting*, a *drawing*, or an *image editing program*—can be used. *Audio editing*, *video editing*, and *DVD authoring software* are common types of multimedia programs, as are the *media player* programs used to play audio and video files. *CD* and *DVD burning software* can be used to burn songs or other data on a CD or DVD disc.

Chapter Objective 7:
List some types of graphics and multimedia software that consumers use frequently.

OTHER TYPES OF APPLICATION SOFTWARE

Other types of application software include *desktop publishing* and *personal publishing* programs, *computer-aided design* (*CAD*) and other types of *design software*, *accounting software*, *personal finance software*, and *project management software*. The use of *collaboration*, *remote access*, and *note taking software* is growing. *Educational*, *entertainment*, and *reference software* are very popular with home users.

Chapter Objective 8:
Name several other types of application software programs and discuss what functions they perform.

SW

REVIEW ACTIVITIES

KEY TERM MATCHING

a. cell

b. database

c. field

d. formula

e. label

f. public domain software

g. record

h. shareware

i. software license

j. workbook

Instructions: Match each key term on the left with the definition on the right that best describes it.

1. _____ A collection of related data that is stored in a manner enabling information to be retrieved as needed.

2. _____ A collection of related fields in a database. Also called a row.

3. _____ A collection of worksheets saved in a single spreadsheet file.

4. _____ An agreement, either included in a software package or displayed on the screen during installation, that specifies the conditions under which a buyer of the program can use it.

5. _____ An entry in a worksheet cell that performs computations on worksheet data and displays the results.

6. _____ A single category of data to be stored in a database, such as a person's name or telephone number. Also called a column.

7. _____ A text-based entry in a worksheet cell that identifies data on the worksheet.

8. _____ Copyrighted software that is distributed on the honor system; consumers should either pay for it or uninstall it after the trial period.

9. _____ Software that is not copyrighted and may be used without restriction.

10. _____ The location at the intersection of a row and column on a worksheet into which data can be typed.

SELF-QUIZ

Instructions: Circle **T** if the statement is true, **F** if the statement is false, or write the best answer in the space provided. **Answers for the self-quiz are located in the References and Resources Guide at the end of the book.**

1. **T F** Microsoft Office is one example of a software suite.

2. **T F** Changing the font size in a document is an example of a formatting operation.

3. **T F** In a word processing document, the Enter key is always pressed at the end of each screen line to move down to the next line.

4. **T F** The formula =A2+B2 located in cell C2 would multiply the two cells to the left of cell C2.

5. **T F** Software can be installed on both personal computers and servers.

6. With a(n) _____ program, the source code for the program is made available to the public and so can be modified by others.

7. The blinking vertical line displayed on the screen that indicates the current location in a document, such as where the next change will be made to the document in a word processing program, is called the _____.

8. A named formula (such as @SUM) in a spreadsheet program is called a(n) _____.

9. In a relational database, the database object that contains the actual data is the _____.

10. Match each application with its type of application program, and write the corresponding number in the blank to the left of each application.

a. _____ Listening to a music CD.

b. _____ Creating a child's birthday invitation.

c. _____ Creating a home movie DVD.

1. DVD authoring software

2. Media player

3. Personal publishing software

EXERCISES

1. List the programs included in the Microsoft Office software suite that fit in the following categories.

a. Spreadsheet software _____

b. Presentation graphics software _____

c. Word processing software _____

d. Database software _____

2. Match each spreadsheet element with its term and write the corresponding number in the blank to the left of each term.

a. _____ An absolute cell address

b. _____ A relative cell address

c. _____ A function

1. =SUM(A1:A2)

2. $D$4

3. B6

3. For a customer database containing 50 customers and recording data about the customer's number, last name, street, city, state, ZIP code, and current balance, answer the following questions.

a. How many records are in the database? _____

b. How many fields are in the database? _____

c. To display a list of all customers who live in Texas and have a current balance of less than $10, what database tool should be used? _____

4. Write the number of the presentation graphic that best matches each of the following possible uses in the blank to the left of each use.

a. _____ Adding an arrow to highlight a point located on a slide.

b. _____ Illustrating the percent of sales coming from each sales territory.

c. _____ Conveying the key points in an educational lecture.

1. Pie chart
2. Slide
3. Drawn object

5. Would rearranging the paragraphs in a document using a word processing program be an editing operation or a formatting operation? Explain your answer.

DISCUSSION QUESTIONS

1. There are an increasing number of Web-based applications available and the new version of Office will be available in both installed and Web versions. What are the advantages and disadvantages of Web-based software? Which do you prefer to use for school-related documents? Why? If you prefer installed software, what would have to change about Web-based software in the future to change your opinion?

2. Open source software is usually reviewed and improved at no cost. Proponents of open source software believe that if programmers who are not concerned with financial gain work on an open source program, they will produce a more useful and error-free product much faster than the traditional commercial software development process. As open source use continues to grow, will it force existing commercial software companies to cut costs to better compete with open source products? Or will they strive to produce products that are better and more reliable than open source competitors? Or will commercial software companies simply go out of business? Will commercial software manufacturers be justified in raising their prices to make up for revenue lost to open source competitors? Do you think open source software will have an overall positive or negative impact on the quality of software?

PROJECTS

HOT TOPICS

1. Natural Input As pen and voice input technologies continue to improve, these types of more natural input methods are increasingly being supported by software programs.

For this project, research either pen input or voice input and its use in conjunction with application software. How frequently is it used today with desktop and portable computers? Select one office application (such as a word processor or spreadsheet program) and determine what hardware or software is needed to use your selected method of input. What are the advantages of your input method? The disadvantages? Would you prefer to use a keyboard and mouse or your selected method of input with this program? Explain. At the conclusion of your research, prepare a one- to two-page summary of your findings and opinions and submit it to your instructor.

SHORT ANSWER/ RESEARCH

2. Software Search Just as with toys, movies, and music, the price of a software program can vary tremendously, based on where you buy it, sales, rebates, and more. Although most packages claim a manufacturer's suggested retail price, it is almost always possible to beat that price—sometimes by a huge amount—with careful shopping.

For this project, select one software program that you might be interested in buying and research it. By reading the program specifications either in a retail store or on a Web page, determine the program's minimum hardware and software requirements. By checking in person, over the phone, or via the Internet, locate three price quotes for the program, including any sales tax and shipping, and check availability and estimated delivery time. Do any of the vendors have the option to download the software? If so, do you have to register the program online or enter a code to activate the product after it is downloaded? At the conclusion of this task, prepare a one-page summary of your research and submit it to your instructor. Be sure to include a recommendation of where you think it would be best to buy your chosen product and why.

HANDS ON

3. Online Tours There are many online tours and tutorials for application programs. Some are available through the software company's Web site; others are located on third-party Web sites.

For this project, select one common software program (such as Word, Excel, PowerPoint, Chrome, Google Docs, or Paint). Locate a free online tour or tutorial for the program you selected (go to the Further Exploration links at the Chapter 6 page at **www.cengage.com/ computerconcepts/np/uc13** for some suggestions) and work your way through one tour or tutorial. How useful is it? Is it easy to use and understand? Did you encounter any errors or other problems? Are there multiple versions for varying levels of difficulty? Would you recommend this tour or tutorial to others? At the conclusion of this task, prepare a one-page summary of your efforts and submit it to your instructor.

4. **Emotion Recognition Software** An emerging application is *emotion recognition software*, which uses camera input to try to read a person's current emotion. The first expected application of such a system is for ATM machines, since they already have cameras installed. Possibilities include changing the advertising display based on the customer's emotional response to displayed advertising, and enlarging the screen text if the customer appears to be squinting. Is it ethical for businesses using emotion recognition software to read the emotions of citizens without their consent? Proponents of the technology argue that it is no different than when human tellers or store clerks interpret customers' emotions and modify their treatment of the customer accordingly. Do you agree? Why or why not? Is this a worthy new technology or just a potential invasion of privacy? Would you object to using an ATM machine with emotion-recognition capabilities? Why or why not?

   For this project, form an opinion about the ethical ramifications of emotion recognition systems and be prepared to discuss your position (in class, via an online class discussion group, in a class chat room, or via a class blog, depending on your instructor's directions). You may also be asked to write a short paper expressing your opinion.

ETHICS IN ACTION

5. **Compatibility** Files created by an application program are often upward-compatible, but not always downward-compatible. For example, a *.docx* file created in Microsoft Word 2007 cannot be opened in Word 2003, but a Word 2003 *.doc* file can be opened in Word 2007. Most application programs feature a "Save As" option that can be used to save a file in one of several formats.

   For this project, select one widely used software program and determine in which file formats the program can save documents and which file formats the program can open. If there are older versions of the program, are documents upward-compatible? Downward compatible? Research *plain text* (*.txt*) and the *Rich Text Format* (*.rtf*) and determine their purposes, the programs in which documents saved in each of these formats can be opened, and any disadvantages for using these formats. Have you ever experienced a compatibility problem with a document? If so, how was the problem resolved? Share your findings with the class in the form of a short presentation. The presentation should not exceed 10 minutes and should make use of one or more presentation aids, such as the chalkboard, handouts, overhead transparencies, or a computer-based slide presentation (your instructor may provide additional requirements). You may also be asked to submit a summary of the presentation to your instructor.

PRESENTATION/ DEMONSTRATION

Instructions: Go to the Chapter 6 page at **www.cengage.com/computerconcepts/np/uc13** to work the following Web Activities.

6. **Interactive Activities** Work the interactive **Crossword Puzzle**, watch the **Video Podcasts** and **Online Videos,** and explore the **Further Exploration** links associated with this chapter.

   If you have a SAM user profile, you may have access to hands-on instruction, practice, and assessment of the skills covered in this chapter. Check with your instructor for instructions and the correct URL/Web site to access those assignments.

7. **Student Edition Labs** Work the following interactive **Student Edition Labs**.

   ➤ **Word Processing**   ➤ **Spreadsheets**
   ➤ **Databases**   ➤ **Presentation Software**

8. **Test Yourself** Review the **Online Study Guide** for this chapter, then test your knowledge of the terms and concepts covered in this chapter by completing the **Key Term Matching** exercise, the **Self-Quiz,** the **Exercises,** and the **Practice Test**.

WEB ACTIVITIES

Student Edition Labs

Microsoft®

Graham Watson is a Senior Community Lead in the Technical Audience Group Marketing Team at Microsoft. He has worked for Microsoft for 16 years, initially as an enterprise infrastructure consultant. In all, he has over 30 years of experience working in the computer industry, beginning as a computer operator and then as a support engineer. Graham has a Bachelor of Arts degree in Computer Studies and runs a blog at blogs.technet.com/ grahamtwatson.

A conversation with GRAHAM WATSON
Senior Community Lead, Technical Audience Global Marketing, Microsoft

"*. . . as computers become smaller, more powerful, and more connected, additional opportunities open up.*"

My Background . . .

I actually got started with computers at school when I discovered I could either take a lesson where I played with a computer terminal or one involving cross-country running in winter! I quickly worked out that the computer was more fun! I'm now part of the Technical Audience Global Marketing Group at Microsoft. My specific responsibilities include making sure that the IT Professional and Developer User Groups around the world—representing over four million people—have the connection they need with Microsoft.

It's Important to Know . . .

About computer systems. No matter how directly you will be involved with computer systems in your career, everyone will need to know enough about systems to be able to make appropriate decisions as to how to use technology to help them in their work and daily lives in general. For example, everyone needs to know how to at least send an e-mail and create, edit, and print a document. Think about the business tasks you need to complete each day, and make sure you can efficiently use the right tools on your computer to help you work more effectively.

The impact of Windows 7. One of the biggest impacts on society that Windows 7 will have is enhanced security for users. One problem with the connectivity that computers provide is that it can also provide thieves and other miscreants with access to you. Each version of Windows improves on previous versions and, although Windows Vista was the most secure mass-marketed operating system when it was launched, Windows 7 continues this evolution and its use will further improve resilience against most forms of attack.

How IT affects your chosen career. It is important to understand the business impact and future trends within the IT space and how it can affect your chosen career. For example, think about the way the retail sales industry has changed over the past ten years. Depending on your chosen career, computer power, graphics, communications capabilities, or mobility may be particularly important to you. You will also need to keep abreast of the latest trends and understand the benefits, costs, risks, and details of how to implement solutions to business problems successfully, taking into account the needs of the customer and the user.

How I Use this Technology . . .

There are two main areas where computers affect me personally. The first one is the most obvious—it provides me with highly enjoyable employment! It's interesting, though, how my current role is more related to computers as a social tool, given my responsibilities toward technical communities. The second one is the same as for many people—my family and friends are all connected, and I often communicate with my wife and children via e-mail or IM. I also do most of my shopping via the Internet—I think I got most of my Christmas shopping done last year without leaving my desk. It's hard to imagine how I would live my life without Windows!

What the Future Holds...

Connectivity is probably the biggest thing—not just between people, but also between parts of computer applications. Web services will continue to grow in importance, and Windows 7, together with .NET 3.0 and Microsoft "Azure," will further enable the ability to develop applications quickly by "stitching together" services obtained from a variety of companies and building on them to fulfill specific needs. Mobility is another interesting area—as computers become smaller, more powerful, and more connected, additional opportunities open up. On one hand, we are finding some devices becoming more general purpose (for example, your cell phone may also take pictures and play music), but at the same time there is an opposite movement toward more dedicated devices which work better. Some people just want a simple-to-use cell phone.

I expect that the software we know today will continue to evolve and get more sophisticated but be simpler to use—for example, Microsoft Office continues to improve on its ability to create professional documents very easily. There will probably be at least one "left field" innovation—something that will be obvious once it's taken off, but almost unnoticed until that time. Examples of this from the last few years include digital video recorders (such as TiVo or Windows Media Center Edition), Voice over IP, and social media tools (such as Twitter). One possibility for the future is intelligent search–something that Microsoft is making significant progress on with *Bing* (imagine being able to ask your computer almost any question in the same way you would ask a friend, and get a single, correct answer). Another possibility we'll likely see in the near future is improved connectivity between computers and devices (imagine phoning friends and arranging to meet them, and then automatically getting directions given to you by your car, meetings set up and moved, flights booked, etc.).

> *"Use technology to become a better informed and connected person and use the information and connections gained to move forward in your chosen career."*

My Advice to Students...

Use technology to become a better informed and connected person and use the information and connections gained to move forward in your chosen career. Technology should be used as an enabler to achieve your goals, improve your life, and improve the lives of others.

Discussion Question

Graham Watson believes that every employee needs to know at least how to send an e-mail and how to create, edit, and print a document. Think about the jobs available today. Are there any that may not require computer skills? If so, would computer skills give that employee an advantage, even if it's not required? Should companies be required to teach any necessary computer skills or is it reasonable to require basic computer skills for any job today? Be prepared to discuss your position (in class, via an online class discussion group, in a class chat room, or via a class blog, depending on your instructor's directions). You may also be asked to write a short paper expressing your opinion.

>**For more information on Microsoft, visit www.microsoft.com. For interesting IT-related information, visit technet.microsoft.com and msdn.microsoft.com. To check if your PC is Windows 7 ready, go to www.microsoft.com/windows/windows-7/get/upgrade-advisor.aspx.**

Networks and the Internet

From telephone calls, to home and business networks, to Web surfing and online shopping, networking and the Internet are deeply embedded in our society today. Because of this, it is important for individuals to be familiar with basic networking concepts and terminology, as well as with the variety of activities that take place today via networks—including the Internet, the world's largest network. It is also important for all individuals to be aware of the potential problems and risks associated with networks and our networked society.

The purpose of Chapter 7 is to introduce basic networking principles, including what a computer network is, how it works, and what it can be used for. The Internet and World Wide Web are the topics of Chapter 8. Although they were introduced in Chapter 1, Chapter 8 explains in more detail how the Internet and World Wide Web originated, and looks more closely at common Internet activities, including how to search the Web effectively for information. This chapter also discusses the various options for connecting to the Internet, as well as how to select an Internet service provider (ISP). Chapter 9 takes a look at some of the risks related to network and Internet use, and explains measures computer users can take to lessen these risks.

in this module

". . . the more and more "connected" data and applications become, the more important it becomes to secure them."

For more comments from Guest Expert **Collin Davis** of Symantec Corporation, see the **Expert Insight on . . . Networks and the Internet** feature at the end of the module.

chapter 7

Computer Networks

After completing this chapter, you will be able to do the following:

1. Define a network and its purpose.

2. Describe several uses for networks.

3. Understand the various characteristics of a network, such as topology, architecture, and size.

4. Understand characteristics about data and how it travels over a network.

5. Name specific types of wired and wireless networking media and explain how they transmit data.

6. Identify the most common communications protocols and networking standards used with networks today.

7. List several types of networking hardware and explain the purpose of each.

OVERVIEW

The term *communications*, when used in a computer context, refers to *telecommunications*; that is, data sent from one device to another using communications media, such as telephone lines, privately owned cables, and the airwaves. Communication usually takes place over a private (such as a home or business) network, the Internet, or a telephone network and it is an integral part of our personal and professional lives today.

The purpose of Chapter 7 is to introduce you to the concepts and terminology associated with computer networks. First, a computer network is defined, followed by a look at some common networking applications. Next, a number of technical issues related to networks are discussed, including general characteristics of data and data transmission, and the types of transmission media in use today. We then proceed to an explanation of the various communications protocols and networking standards, which help explain the ways networked devices communicate with one another. The chapter closes with a look at the various types of hardware used with a computer network. ■

NET

WHAT IS A NETWORK?

A *network*, in general, is a connected system of objects or people. As discussed in Chapter 1, a **computer network** is a collection of computers and other hardware devices connected together so that network users can share hardware, software, and data, as well as communicate with each other electronically. Today, computer networks are converging with *telephone networks* and other *communications networks*, with both data and voice being sent over these networks. Computer networks range from small private networks to the Internet and are widely used by individuals and businesses today (see Figure 7-1).

In most businesses, computer networks are essential. They enable employees to share expensive resources, access the Internet, and communicate with each other, as well as with business partners and customers. They facilitate the exchange and collaboration of documents and they are often a key component of the ordering, inventory, and fulfillment systems used to process customer orders. In homes, computer networks enable individuals to share resources, access the Internet, and communicate with others. In addition, they allow individuals to access a wide variety of information, services, and entertainment, as well as share data (such as digital photos, downloaded movies, and music) among the networked

FIGURE 7-1
**Common uses for
computer networks.**

USES FOR COMPUTER NETWORKS

Sharing an Internet connection among several users.

Sharing application software, printers, and other resources.

Facilitating Voice over IP (VoIP), e-mail, video-conferencing, IM, and other communications applications.

Working collaboratively, such as sharing a company database or using collaboration tools to create or review documents.

Exchanging files among network users and over the Internet.

Connecting the computers and the entertainment devices (such as TVs, gaming consoles, and stereo systems) located within a home.

>**Computer network.** A collection of computers and other hardware devices that are connected together to share hardware, software, and data, as well as to communicate electronically with one another.

INSIDE THE INDUSTRY

Wireless Power

Imagine recharging your notebook computer or mobile phone automatically, without plugging it into an electrical outlet. That scenario may soon be possible with *wireless power*. Researchers have been working on the concept of wireless power transmission for decades, but recent developments indicate that the concept may be feasible in the relatively near future. For instance, researchers recently demonstrated making a 60-watt light bulb glow with 75% efficiency from an energy source 3 feet away—an important development because one of the biggest challenges in transmitting power wirelessly is preventing too much power from escaping during transit. Other challenges are ensuring that wireless power is safe for humans and other living things in the areas where power will be broadcast, as well as creating a standard for wireless power so that multiple devices from different manufacturers can be charged at the same time using the same technology.

One company working toward this standard is Fulton Innovation. This company, along with other members of the *Wireless Power Consortium* (such as Olympus, Philips, and Texas Instruments), supports wireless power technology that uses *magnetic induction* to transfer power wirelessly from a charging power supply device to a target device containing the appropriate receiving technology. Ideally, wireless power systems will power devices without any direct physical contact, will automatically adjust the power transmitted to each device being charged to meet the needs of that device, and will deactivate the charging process when the device is fully charged.

Initial consumer applications for wireless power will likely be wireless charging bases that recharge devices (such as mobile phones, digital media players, remote controls, notebook computers, and small kitchen appliances) located on or near them—called *near-field wireless power transfer*. These charging bases could be stand-alone devices or they could be built into car consoles (see the accompanying illustration), desks, kitchen countertops, and other objects. As the technology matures and if the safety issues can be resolved, future wireless power applications could even include charging transmitters built into walls and furniture to power all of the devices located in the home on a continual basis.

ONLINE VIDEO

Go to the Chapter 7 page at
www.cengage.com/ computerconcepts/np/uc13
to watch the "Wireless Power: eCoupled Overview" video clip.

devices in a home. On the go, networks enable individuals to work from remote locations, locate information whenever and wherever it is needed, and stay in touch with others.

NETWORKING APPLICATIONS

Today, there are a wide variety of important networking applications used by businesses and individuals for communications, information retrieval, and other applications. Some of the most common networking applications are described next. For a look at an emerging networking application—*wireless power*—see the Inside the Industry box.

The Internet

As previously discussed, the Internet is the largest computer network in the world. Many networking applications today (such as information retrieval, shopping, entertainment, and e-mail) take place via the Internet. Accessing Web pages and exchanging e-mail were discussed in Chapter 1; additional Internet-based activities are covered in Chapter 8.

Telephone Service

The original telephone network, sometimes called the *plain old telephone service* (*POTS*), was one of the first communications networks. This network is still used today to provide telephone service to conventional and cordless *landline phones*, and is used for some types of Internet connections.

Mobile phones (also called *wireless phones*) are phones that use a wireless network for communications instead of the regular telephone network. Billions of mobile phones are in use worldwide and approxi-

CELLULAR PHONES
Can be used wherever cellular phone coverage is available.

DUAL-MODE PHONES
Can be used with both cellular and Wi-Fi networks.

SATELLITE PHONES
Can be used virtually anywhere.

FIGURE 7-2
Types of mobile phones.

NET

mately 75% of Americans and close to half of the world's population use mobile phones. In fact, there are over twice as many mobile phones in use worldwide than landline phones, according to one estimate, and mobile phones may be the only telephone alternative in developing countries and other locations with a poor landline telephone infrastructure. Even in developed countries, however, many individuals—nearly 20% of all Americans, according to a recent Nielsen Mobile report—are dropping their conventional landline telephone service in favor of using their mobile phones as their primary telephones.

In addition to making telephone calls, most mobile phones today can be used for a wide variety of other purposes, such as exchanging e-mail and text messages, viewing Web information, taking digital photos, and watching TV shows. Some mobile phones can also be used to pay for goods or services and to unlock doors. These types of applications are more prominent in countries like Asia and Europe that have a longer history of mobile phone use than the United States, but they are beginning to become available in the U.S. as well.

The most common type of mobile phone is the **cellular (cell) phone** (see Figure 7-2), which communicates via *cellular technology*. Cell phone service is available in most populated areas of the U.S., but coverage varies depending on location because cell phones need to be within range of a *cell tower* to function, as described later in this chapter. Some cell phones today are **dual-mode phones**—phones that allows users to make telephone calls using more than one communications network, such as via both a *cellular* and a *Wi-Fi network*. This allows users to carry a single device (such as the one shown in Figure 7-2) and, at any given time, use the network that is available, least expensive, or has the needed capabilities. For example, as an individual using a *cellular/Wi-Fi dual-mode phone* moves in and out of range of a Wi-Fi network, the phone is able to switch seamlessly between the Wi-Fi network and a cellular network, such as using a home or office Wi-Fi network (and that network's

---

> **Mobile phone.** A phone, such as a cellular or satellite phone, that uses a wireless network. > **Cellular phone.** A mobile phone that communicates via a cellular network; also called a **cell phone**. > **Dual-mode phone.** A mobile phone that can be used with more than one communications network, such as with both a cellular and Wi-Fi network.

Internet connection) when the caller is indoors and then switching to a cellular network when the individual leaves the building. Cellular/Wi-Fi dual-mode phones are expected to experience rapid growth in the near future. In fact, Juniper Research predicts that cellular/Wi-Fi dual-mode phones will eventually dominate the mobile phone market worldwide.

Another, but less common, type of mobile phone is the **satellite phone** (refer again to Figure 7-2), which communicates via *satellite technology*, also described in detail later in this chapter. Although more expensive than cellular service, satellite phone coverage is typically much broader, often on a country-by-country basis, and some satellite phone services cover the entire earth. Consequently, satellite phones are most often used by individuals—such as soldiers, journalists, wilderness guides, and researchers—traveling in remote areas where continuous cellular service might not be available. They are also useful during times when cellular service might be interrupted, such as during a hurricane or other emergency. An emerging option is the *cellular/satellite dual-mode phone* that can be used with cellular service when it is available and then switches to satellite service when cellular service is not available.

Television and Radio Broadcasting

Two other original communications networks are *broadcast television networks* and *radio networks*. These networks are still used to deliver TV and radio content to the public, though some of this content is also available via the Internet today. Other networks involved with television content delivery are *cable TV networks*, *satellite TV networks*, and the private *closed-circuit television* (*CCTV*) systems used by businesses for surveillance and security purposes. Cable and satellite TV networks are also used today to provide access to the Internet.

Global Positioning System (GPS) Applications

The **global positioning system** (**GPS**) network consists of 24 Department of Defense *GPS satellites* (in orbit approximately 12,000 miles above the earth) that are used for location and navigation purposes. A *GPS receiver* measures the distance between the receiver and four GPS satellites simultaneously to determine the receiver's exact geographic location; these receivers are accurate to within 3 meters (less than 10 feet).

GPS receivers (see some examples in Figure 7-3) are commonly used by individuals to determine their geographic location while hiking and to obtain driving directions while traveling. GPS receivers are also commonly used on the job, such as by surveyors, farmers, and fishermen. In addition to just relaying location information, GPS can be used to guide vehicles and equipment (for example, to locate and dispatch ambulances, police cars, and other emergency vehicles, or to guide bulldozers and other construction equipment automatically according to a project's preprogrammed instructions) and GPS is used by the military to guide munitions. GPS capabilities are also built into consumer devices that are designed for specific purposes, such as fitness devices that use GPS technology to record workout data for runners or bicyclists. In addition to their practical uses, GPS receivers can also be used for entertainment. For example, *geocaching*, in which individuals use GPS receivers to locate secret caches hidden by others, is growing in popularity, particularly among families. To find the secret caches, participants follow the coordinates posted on a geocaching Web site.

>**Satellite phone.** A mobile phone that communicates via satellite technology. >**Global positioning system (GPS).** A system that uses satellites and a receiver to determine the exact geographic location of the receiver.

HANDHELD GPS RECEIVERS

CAR-MOUNTED GPS RECEIVERS

GPS RECEIVERS INTEGRATED INTO MOBILE PHONES

One recent concern regarding GPS technology is the possibility that the aging GPS satellites might fail (and, consequently, interrupt GPS services) before new replacement satellites can be launched. A recent General Accountability Office (GAO) report concluded that there is an 80% chance that full GPS service will be operational until 2014. Currently, there are 30 GPS satellites in orbit—six more than the 24 GPS satellites needed to ensure continuous coverage of the entire earth.

FIGURE 7-3

GPS receivers. Allow people to determine their exact geographical location, usually for safety or navigational purposes.

Monitoring Systems

Monitoring systems use networking technology to determine the current location or status of an object. Some monitoring systems in use today use the RFID tags and RFID readers discussed in Chapter 4 to monitor the status of the objects (such as shipping boxes, livestock, or expensive equipment) to which the RFID tags are attached. Other monitoring systems use GPS technology. For instance, the *OnStar* system built into many GM cars uses GPS to locate vehicles when the occupant activates the service or when sensors indicate that the car was involved in an accident. There are also *vehicle monitoring systems* that are installed in cars by parents and employers to monitor the use of the vehicles (by children or employees, respectively) using networking technology. These monitoring systems typically record factors such as where the vehicle was driven and how fast it was driven; some also allow the location of a vehicle to be tracked in real time via a Web site (see Figure 7-4). Some vehicle monitoring systems can even be used to set up a "virtual fence" for the car or a maximum allowable speed; the parent or employer is notified (usually via a text message) anytime the vehicle leaves the prescribed geographical area or exceeds the maximum designated speed. Monitoring systems are also available for GPS-enabled mobile phones to allow parents to track their child's location or be notified if their child's mobile phone leaves a designated area.

FIGURE 7-4

GPS-based vehicle monitoring systems. Allow parents or employers to track a vehicle in real time.

1. A GPS monitor like this is installed inside the car.

2. The location and speed of the car is available online.

NET

⚠ **FIGURE 7-5**

Home medical monitoring systems.

Go **FURTHER EXPLORATION**

Go to the Chapter 7 page at **www.cengage.com/ computerconcepts/np/uc13** for links to information about GPS, RFID, and monitoring systems.

▼ **FIGURE 7-6**

Placeshifting.

Products like the Slingbox are used to placeshift multimedia content to the user's current location.

Another area in which monitoring systems are frequently used is home healthcare. With the U.S. population aging, a variety of home medical monitoring systems are available to monitor elderly or infirm individuals and notify someone if a possible problem is detected. For instance, *electronic medical monitors* (see Figure 7-5) take the vital signs of an individual (such as weight, blood-sugar readings, or blood pressure) or prompt an individual to answer questions (such as if he or she ate yet that day, took prescribed medication, or feels well). These monitors then transfer readings or the individual's responses to a healthcare provider via the Internet or a telephone network for evaluation and feedback and to detect potential problems as early as possible.

Other monitoring systems use *sensors*—devices that respond to a stimulus (such as heat, light, or pressure) and generate an electrical signal that can be measured or interpreted. The sensors (sometimes called *motes*) are usually small and lightweight; contain the necessary hardware and software to sense and record the appropriate data, as well as transmit the data to a central computer and/or the other motes in the network; and include a power source (typically a battery). Sensors can be included in a network anytime there is a situation with measurable criteria that needs precise, automatic, and continual monitoring. For example, *sensor networks* can be used during transport to monitor the temperature inside cargo containers to ensure that products stay within the allowable temperature range, in pharmaceutical plants to monitor temperature and relative humidity in the drug development process, and in homes to manage and control smart devices such as smart appliances and home automation systems.

Multimedia Networking

A growing use of home networks is to deliver digital multimedia content (such as digital photos, digital music, home movies, downloaded movies, and recorded TV shows) to devices (such as computers, televisions, and home entertainment systems) on that network. A number of *multimedia networking* devices (such as *digital media receivers*) can be used to share and deliver digital content throughout the home via a multimedia network. Some are also able to connect to the Internet to deliver Internet content via the network. Two alternatives to a digital media receiver are *Windows Media Center Extenders*, which allow Windows Media Center computer users to access content from their computers and display it on their TVs via their home network, and *Apple TVs*, which stream content from the iTunes libraries of up to five computers to one TV set.

Other multimedia networking devices (such as the *Slingbox* shown in Figure 7-6) are designed to *placeshift* multimedia content—that is, to allow individuals to view their multimedia content at a more convenient location. For instance, an individual with a Slingbox installed at home can use a portable computer or mobile phone (along with software and his or her Slingbox ID code) to remotely control his or her cable box, satellite receiver, or digital video recorder (DVR) and transfer that content to his or her current location via the Internet. For instance, he or she can watch local news while out of town, watch a recorded TV show while at the beach, or start recording a TV show from the office.

1. Slingbox device is connected to the user's home TV system.

2. SlingPlayer Mobile software allows the user to watch and control his or her home TV and DVR.

Videoconferencing, Collaborative Computing, and Telecommuting

Videoconferencing is the use of networking technology to conduct real-time, face-to-face meetings between individuals physically located in different places. While videoconferencing can take place via a personal computer and the Internet (sometimes called *online conferencing* and discussed in more detail in Chapter 8), it can also take place via a dedicated videoconferencing setup, such as the one in Figure 7-7. As shown in this figure, videoconferencing technology is continuing to improve to more closely mimic a real-time meeting environment—a trend referred to as *telepresence videoconferencing*. Although telepresence videoconferencing setups are expensive, with travel becoming increasingly more expensive and time-consuming, many businesses view videoconferencing as a viable replacement for face-to-face meetings involving individuals in different locations. Videoconferencing is also used in educational settings and to provide language translation services (particularly for nonverbal languages such as American Sign Language that cannot be translated via a telephone) in locations such as airports and hospitals.

Life-size video images of remote participants appear on the display screen.

FIGURE 7-7
Telepresence videoconferencing.

Networking technology is also widely used today with collaborative software tools to enable individuals to work together on documents and other project components. This trend toward online collaboration is usually called *workgroup computing* or *collaborative computing*. For many industries, collaboration is a very important business tool. For example, engineers and architects commonly collaborate on designs; advertising firms and other businesses often route proposals and other important documents to several individuals for comments before preparing the final version of a client presentation; and newspaper, magazine, and book editors must read and edit drafts of articles and books before they are published. Instead of these types of collaborations taking place on paper, as in the not-too-distant past, collaboration tools (such as the Microsoft Office *markup tools* and specialized *collaboration software*) are used in conjunction with networking technology (typically a company network or the Internet) to allow multiple individuals to edit and make comments in a document without destroying the original content. Once a document has been reviewed by all individuals and is returned to the original author, he or she can

ASK THE EXPERT

Google **Rajen Sheth,** Senior Product Manager, Google Enterprise

How will Web 2.0 impact the daily life of the average individual?

Web 2.0 means that users can create and share content easily using blogs, social networks, and collaborative tools online. Compare that with the Web a decade ago: at that time, it was difficult to publish information; you needed to know HTML just to push things onto the Web. Now we're starting to see user-driven content and collaboration taking off across multiple communities, starting with consumers, but also extending into work environments.

Technologies driving this trend include (1) user tools such as blogs, wikis, and social networking sites and (2) Web technology itself, including AJAX and JavaScript.

It used to be that the interface of Web applications was inferior to the interface of desktop client applications. Now it's arguably superior on the Web in terms of how rich and dynamic the functionality is.

NET

>**Videoconferencing.** The use of computers, video cameras, microphones, and networking technologies to conduct face-to-face meetings over a network.

read the comments and accept or reject changes that others have made. Some collaboration software incorporates shared calendars, project scheduling, and videoconferencing tools in addition to document sharing.

The increased availability of videoconferencing, collaborative computing, and other tools (such as the Internet, e-mail, and mobile phones) has made **telecommuting** a viable option for many individuals. With telecommuting, individuals work from a remote location (typically their homes) and communicate with their places of business and clients via networking technologies. Telecommuting allows the employee to be flexible, such as working nontraditional hours or remaining with the company after a relocation. It also enables a company to save on office and parking space, as well as office-related expenses such as utilities. As an environmental plus, telecommuting helps cut down on the traffic and pollution caused by traditional work commuting. In addition, it gives a business the possibility to continue operations during situations that may affect an employee's ability to get to the office, such as during hurricanes, during a bridge or highway closure, or during a flu outbreak. As a result, many experts suggest businesses include telecommuting procedures in their *business continuity plans*, even if they don't intend to use telecommuting on a regular basis. Business continuity plans and disaster recovery are discussed in detail in Chapter 15.

▼ **FIGURE 7-8**
Examples of telemedicine applications.

REMOTE CONSULTATIONS
Using remote-controlled teleconferencing robots, physicians can "virtually" consult with patients or other physicians in a different physical location (left); the robot transmits video images and audio to and from the doctor (via his or her computer) in real time (right).

REMOTE DIAGNOSIS
At remote locations, such as the New York childcare center shown here, trained employees provide physicians with the real-time data (sent via the Internet) they need to make a diagnosis.

TELESURGERY
Using voice or computer commands, surgeons can now perform operations via the Internet; a robotic system uses the surgeon's commands to operate on the patient.

Telemedicine

Telemedicine is the use of networking technology to provide medical information and services and is most often used to provide care to individuals who may not otherwise have access to that care, such as allowing individuals living in remote areas to consult with a specialist. For instance, physicians can use videoconferencing to communicate remotely with other physicians or with hospitalized patients (see Figure 7-8). Physicians can also use telemedicine to perform remote diagnosis of patients (for example, healthcare workers at rural locations, childcare facilities, and other locations can use video cameras, electronic stethoscopes, and other devices to send images and vital statistics of a patient to a physician located at a medical facility).

Another example of telemedicine is **telesurgery**—a form of *robot-assisted surgery* (where a robot controlled by a physician operates on the patient) in which at least one of the surgeons performs the

---

operation by controlling the robot remotely over the Internet or another network (refer again to Figure 7-8). Robot-assisted surgery systems typically use cameras to give the human surgeon an extremely close view of the surgical area. As a result, robot-assisted surgery is typically more precise and results in smaller incisions than those made by a human surgeon, allowing for less invasive surgery (for example, not having to crack through the rib cage to access the heart) and resulting in less pain for the patient, a faster recovery time, and fewer potential complications.

Telemedicine has enormous potential for providing quality medical care to individuals who live in rural or underdeveloped areas and who do not have access to sufficient medical care. Telemedicine will also be necessary for future long-term space explorations—such as a trip to Mars and back that may take three years or more—since astronauts will undoubtedly need medical care while on the journey. In fact, NASA astronauts and physicians recently performed telesurgery experiments in the Aquarius Undersea Laboratory 50 feet below the ocean surface to help in the development of a robotic unit that will eventually allow physicians to perform surgery remotely on patients who are in outer space. Some individuals envision the eventual use of portable robot-assisted telesurgery units in space, war zones, and other environments where access to surgeons is extremely limited.

NETWORK CHARACTERISTICS

Networks can be identified by a variety of characteristics, including whether they are designed for wired or wireless access, their *topology*, their *architecture*, and their *size* or *coverage area*. These topics are described in the next few sections.

Wired vs. Wireless Networks

Networks can be designed for access via *wired* and/or *wireless* connections. With a **wired network** connection, the computers and other devices on the network are physically connected (via cabling) to the network. With a **wireless network** connection, wireless (usually radio) signals are used to send data through the air between devices, instead of using physical cables. Wired networks include the conventional telephone network, cable TV networks, and the wired networks commonly found in schools, businesses, and government facilities. Wireless networks include conventional television and radio networks, cellular telephone networks, satellite TV networks, and the wireless networks commonly found in homes, schools, and businesses. Wireless networks are also found in many public locations (such as coffeehouses, businesses, airports, hotels, and libraries) to provide Internet access to users while they are on the go via public *wireless hotspots*. For a look at how to connect a Windows computer to a public *Wi-Fi hotspot*, see the How It Works box.

Many networks today are accessible via both wired and wireless connections. For instance, a business may have a wired main company network to which the computers in employee offices are always connected, as well as provide wireless access to the network for visitors and employees to use while in waiting rooms, conference rooms, and other locations. A home network may have a wired connection between one computer and the devices needed to connect that computer to the Internet (such as a *router*), plus wireless access for other devices (such as computers, printers, and portable gaming devices) that may need to access the home network wirelessly.

Wired networks tend to be faster and more secure than wireless networks, but wireless networks have the advantage of allowing easy connections in locations where physical wiring is impractical or inconvenient (such as inside an existing home or outdoors), as well

ONLINE VIDEO

Go to the Chapter 7 page at **www.cengage.com/ computerconcepts/np/uc13** to watch the "Telemedicine in Action" video clip.

NET

>**Wired network.** A network in which computers and other devices are connected to the network via physical cables. >**Wireless network.** A network in which computers and other devices are connected to the network without physical cables; data is typically sent via radio waves.

HOW IT WORKS

Connecting to a Wi-Fi Hotspot

To connect to a Wi-Fi hotspot, all you need is a device (such as a mobile phone or a notebook computer) with a Wi-Fi adapter installed and enabled. (Note: Some notebook computers have a switch located on the case to turn off wireless networking and some power settings disable it—check these things if you can't connect using the following steps.) On a Windows computer that has a Wi-Fi adapter installed, there should be an icon in the system tray representing your wireless network connection. When you are within range of a Wi-Fi hotspot, click this icon and choose "View Available Wireless Networks" or "Connect to a Network" (depending on which version of Windows you are using) to see all of the Wi-Fi access points in the area (see the accompanying illustration). If there is more than one hotspot listed, select the appropriate one and then click the Connect button. For free hotspots that are in range, you should be connected shortly and can then open your browser and perform Internet activities. For secured networks, you will be asked to supply the appropriate passphrase before you can connect to the Internet via that hotspot, as discussed in more detail in Chapter 9. For most fee-based hotspots (and some free ones, as well, such as networks at a hotel or conference center designed for registered guests only), you will see a logon screen and will need to obtain an appropriate username and password from a hotspot representative and enter that information via the logon screen before being connected. Security issues related to public hotspot use are discussed in more detail in Chapter 9.

2. Select the desired network and click Connect.

3. When selecting an unsecured network, you may see a warning notice.

1. Click the wireless network icon and select the Connect option to view the available wireless networks in range.

4. The connection is established.

as giving users much more freedom regarding where they can use their computers. With wireless networking, for example, you can surf the Web on your notebook computer from anywhere in your house, access the Internet with your portable computer or mobile phone while you are on the go, and create a home network without having to run wires among the rooms in your house.

Network Topologies

The physical *topology* of a computer network indicates how the devices in the network are arranged. Three of the most common physical topologies are *star*, *bus*, and *mesh* (see Figure 7-9).

> ➤ **Star network**—used in traditional mainframe environments, as well as in small office, home, and wireless networks. All the networked devices connect to a central device (such as a server or a *switch*, discussed later in this chapter) through which all network transmissions are sent. If the central device fails, then the network cannot function.

>**Star network.** A network that uses a host device connected directly to several other devices.

> **Bus network**—uses a central cable to which all network devices connect. All data is transmitted down the bus line from one device to another so, if the bus line fails, then the network cannot function.

> **Mesh network**—uses a number of different connections between network devices so that data can take any of several possible paths from source to destination. With a *full mesh topology* (such as the one shown in Figure 7-9), each device on the network is connected to every other device on the network. With a *partial mesh topology*, some devices are connected to all other devices, but some are connected only to those devices with which they exchange the most data. Consequently, if one device on a mesh network fails, the network can still function, assuming there is an alternate path available. Mesh networks are used most often with wireless networks.

Many networks, however, don't conform to a standard topology. Some networks combine topologies and connect multiple smaller networks, in effect turning several smaller networks into one larger one. For example, two star networks may be joined together using a bus line.

Network Architectures

Networks also vary by their *architecture*; that is, the way they are designed to communicate. The two most common network architectures are *client-server* and *peer-to-peer* (*P2P*).

Client-Server Networks

Client-server networks include both *clients* (computers and other devices on the network that request and utilize network resources) and *servers* (computers that are dedicated to processing client requests). Network servers are typically powerful computers with lots of memory and a very large hard drive. They provide access to software, files, and other resources that are being shared via the network. Servers typically perform a variety of tasks. For example, a single server can act as a *network server* to manage network traffic, a *file server* to manage shared files, a *print server* to handle printing-related activities, and/or a *mail server* or *Web server* to manage e-mail and Web page requests, respectively. For instance, there is only one server in the network illustrated in Figure 7-10, and it is capable of performing all server tasks for that network. When a client retrieves files from a server, it is called *downloading*; transferring data from a client to a server is called *uploading*.

Peer-to-Peer (P2P) Networks

With a *peer-to-peer* (*P2P*) *network*, a central server is not used (see Figure 7-11). Instead, all the computers on the network work at the same functional level, and users have direct access to the computers and other devices attached to the network. For instance, users can access files stored on a peer computer's hard drive and print using a peer computer's printer, provided those devices have been designated as *shared devices*. Peer-to-peer networks are less expensive and less complicated to implement than client-server networks because there are no dedicated servers, but they may not have the same performance as client-server

STAR NETWORKS
Use a central device to connect each device directly to the network.

BUS NETWORKS
Use a single central cable to connect each device in a linear fashion.

MESH NETWORKS
Each computer or device is connected to multiple (sometimes all of the other) devices on the network.

FIGURE 7-9
Basic network topologies.

>**Bus network.** A network consisting of a central cable to which all network devices are attached. >**Mesh network.** A network in which there are multiple connections between the devices on the network so that messages can take any of several possible paths.

CLIENT — CLIENT — THE INTERNET

NETWORK SERVER
(provides client devices
with network services,
such as file, print, e-mail,
and Internet access)

SHARED NETWORK
PRINTER

CLIENT

FIGURE 7-10

Client-server networks.
With this type of network,
client computers
communicate through one
or more servers.

FIGURE 7-11

Peer-to-peer networks.
With this type of network,
computers communicate
directly with one another.

P2P HOME NETWORKS
Devices connect and communicate via the home
network.

INTERNET P2P NETWORKS
Devices connect and communicate
via the Internet.

networks under heavy use. Peer-to-peer capabilities are built into many personal operating systems and are often used in conjunction with small office or home networks.

Another type of peer-to-peer networking—sometimes called *Internet peer-to-peer* (*Internet P2P*) *computing*—is performed via the Internet. Instead of placing content on a Web server for others to view via the Internet, content is exchanged over the Internet directly between individual users via a peer-to-peer network. For instance, one user can copy a file from another user's hard drive to his or her own computer via the Internet. Internet P2P networking is commonly used for exchanging music and video files with others over the Internet—an illegal act if the content is copyright-protected and the exchange is unauthorized, although legal Internet P2P networks exist. Copyright law, ethics, and other topics related to peer-to-peer file exchanges are covered in Chapter 16.

> **CAUTION CAUTION CAUTION CAUTION CAUTION CAUTION CAUT**
>
> Do not enable sharing for folders that you do not want others on your network to see. And, if you choose to use a P2P network, be sure to designate the files in your shared folder as *read-only* to prevent your original files from being overwritten by another P2P user.

Network Size and Coverage Area

One additional way networks are classified is by the size of their coverage area. This also impacts the types of users the network is designed to service. The most common categories of networks are discussed next; these networks can use both wired and wireless connections.

Personal Area Networks (PANs)

A **personal area network (PAN)** is a network of personal devices for one individual (such as his or her portable computer,

> **Personal area network (PAN).** A network that connects an individual's personal devices that are located close together.

mobile phone, headset, digital camera, portable digital media player, and printer) that is designed to enable those devices to communicate and share data. PANs can be set up to work together automatically as soon as the devices get within a certain physical distance of each other. For instance, a PAN can be used to synchronize portable devices automatically with a desktop computer as soon as the individual returns home or to the office. The range of a PAN is very limited, so devices in a PAN must be physically located close together. Wireless PANs (see Figure 7-12), sometimes called *wireless personal area networks* (*WPANs*), are more common today than wired PANs.

Local Area Networks (LANs)

A **local area network** (**LAN**) is a network that covers a relatively small geographical area, such as a home, office building, or school. LANs allow users on the network to exchange files and e-mail, share printers and other hardware, and access the Internet. The client-server network shown in Figure 7-10 is an example of a LAN.

FIGURE 7-12
WPANs. Wireless PANs connect and synchronize an individual's devices wirelessly.

Metropolitan Area Networks (MANs)

A **metropolitan area network** (**MAN**) is a network designed to service a metropolitan area, typically a city or county. Most MANs are owned and operated by a city or by a network provider in order to provide individuals in that location access to the MAN. Some wireless MANs (often referred to as *municipal Wi-Fi* projects—see Figure 7-13) are created by cities or large organizations (including Microsoft and Google) to provide free or low-cost Internet access to area residents; these projects are typically supported by local taxes. In addition, some Internet service providers (such as Comcast) are experimenting with setting up free wireless MANs in select metropolitan areas for their subscribers to use when they are on the go.

NET

Wide Area Networks (WANs)

A **wide area network** (**WAN**) is a network that covers a large geographical area. Typically, a WAN consists of two or more LANs that are connected together using communications technology. The Internet, by this definition, is the world's largest WAN. WANs may be publicly accessible, like the Internet, or they may be privately owned and operated. For instance, a company may have a private WAN to transfer data from one location to another, such as from each retail store to the corporate headquarters. Large WANs, like the Internet, typically use a mesh topology.

FIGURE 7-13
Municipal Wi-Fi. This MAN covers downtown Riverside, California.

Intranets and Extranets

An **intranet** is a private network (such as a company LAN) that is designed to be used by an organization's employees and is set up like the Internet (with data posted on Web pages that are accessed with a Web browser). Consequently, little or no employee training is required to use an intranet, and intranet content can be accessed using a variety of devices. Intranets today are used for many purposes, such as coordinating internal e-mail and communications, making company publications (such as contact information, manuals, forms,

---

>**Local area network (LAN).** A network that connects devices located in a small geographical area, such as within a building. >**Metropolitan area network (MAN).** A network designed to service a metropolitan area. >**Wide area network (WAN).** A network that connects devices located in a large geographical area. >**Intranet.** A private network that is set up similar to the Internet and is accessed via a Web browser.

ASK THE EXPERT

Marian Merritt, Internet Safety Advocate, Symantec Corporation

How can an individual surf safely at a public Wi-Fi hotspot?

First, install Internet security software that includes antivirus, local firewall, and intrusion protection. Next, know the name of your Wi-Fi provider, create a unique username for that connection, and use a complex password comprised of random letters and numbers. When connecting through a logon page, view the site's certificate presented by the browser to verify that the site is operated by the expected organization.

In addition, turn off file and printer sharing to make it harder for a stranger to check your wireless activities, and avoid sending any confidential information (Social Security numbers, bank account passwords, and so on) over a Wi-Fi connection. If you can delay doing your online shopping or banking until you are back at home or the office, then do so! Unless you are connected to the Internet over an encrypted connection, assume that someone could potentially gain access to your personal information. Lastly, when possible, use a Virtual Private Network (VPN), which provides stronger protection against a variety of risks.

job announcements, and so forth) available to employees, facilitating collaborative computing, and providing access to shared calendars and schedules.

A company network that is accessible to authorized outsiders is called an **extranet**. Extranets are usually accessed via the Internet, and they can be used to provide customers and business partners with access to the data they need. Access to intranets and extranets is typically restricted to employees and other authorized users, similar to other company networks.

Virtual Private Networks (VPNs)

A **virtual private network (VPN)** is a private, secure path across a public network (usually the Internet) that is set up to allow authorized users private, secure access to the company network. For instance, a VPN can allow a traveling employee, business partner, or employee located at a satellite office or public wireless hotspot to connect securely to the company network via the Internet. A process called *tunneling* is typically used to carry the data over the Internet; special *encryption* technology is used to protect the data so it cannot be understood if it is intercepted during transit (encryption is explained in Chapter 9). Essentially, VPNs allow an organization to provide secure, remote access to the company network without the cost of physically extending the private network.

DATA TRANSMISSION CHARACTERISTICS

Data transmitted over a network has specific characteristics, and it can travel over a network in various ways. These and some other characteristics related to data transmission are discussed next.

Bandwidth

As discussed in Chapter 2, the term *bandwidth* (also called *throughput*) refers to the amount of data that can be transferred (such as over a certain type of networking medium) in a given time period. Text data requires the least amount of bandwidth; video data requires the most. Just as a wide fire hose allows more water to pass through it per unit of time than a narrow garden hose allows, a networking medium with a high bandwidth allows more data to pass through it per unit of time than a networking medium with a low bandwidth. Bandwidth is usually measured in the number of *bits per second* (*bps*), *Kbps* (thousands of bits per second), *Mbps* (millions of bits per second), or *Gbps* (billions of bits per second).

> **Extranet.** An intranet that is at least partially accessible to authorized outsiders. > **Virtual private network (VPN).** A private, secure path over the Internet that provides authorized users a secure means of accessing a private network via the Internet.

Analog vs. Digital Signals

Data can be represented as either *analog* or *digital* signals. Voice and music data in its natural form, for instance, is analog, and data stored on a computer is digital. Most networking media send data using **digital signals**, in which data is represented by only two *discrete states*: 0s and 1s (see Figure 7-14). **Analog signals**, such as those used by the conventional telephone system, represent data with *continuous waves*. The data to be transmitted over a networking medium must match the type of signal (analog or digital) that the medium supports; if it doesn't originally, then it must be converted before the data is transmitted. For instance, analog data that is to be sent using digital signals (such as analog music broadcast by a digital radio station) must first be converted into digital form, and digital data to be sent using analog signals (such as computer data sent over a conventional analog telephone network) must be converted into analog form before it can be transmitted. The conversion of data between analog and digital form is performed by networking hardware.

Transmission Type and Timing

Networking media can also use either *serial transmission* or *parallel transmission*. With **serial transmission**, data is sent one bit at a time, one after the other along a single path (see Figure 7-15). When **parallel transmission** is used, the message is sent at least one byte at a time, with each bit in the byte taking a separate path (refer again to Figure 7-15). While parallel transmission is frequently used within computer components (such as for buses) and is used for some wireless networking applications, networking media typically use serial transmission.

When data is sent using serial transmission, a technique must be used to organize the bits being transferred so the data can be reconstructed after it is received. Three ways of timing serial transmissions are by using *synchronous*, *asynchronous*, and *isochronous* connections (see Figure 7-16). Although all three of these methods send data one bit at a time, the methods vary with respect to how the bits are organized for transfer.

> *Synchronous transmission*—data is organized into groups or blocks of data, which are transferred at regular, specified intervals. Since the transmissions are synchronized, both devices know when data can be sent and when it should arrive. Most data transmissions within a computer and over a network are synchronous transmissions.

> *Asynchronous transmission*—data is sent when it is ready to be sent, without being synchronized. To identify the bits that belong in each byte, a *start bit* and *stop bit* are used at the beginning and end of the byte, respectively. This overhead makes asynchronous transmission less efficient than synchronous transmission and so it is not as widely used as synchronous transmission.

> *Isochronous transmission*—data is sent at the same time as other related data to support certain types of real-time applications that require the different types of data to be delivered at the proper speed for that application. For example, when transmitting a video file, the audio data must be received at the proper time in order for it to be played with its corresponding video data. To accomplish this with isochronous transmission, the sending and receiving devices first communicate to determine the bandwidth and other factors needed for the transmission, and then the necessary bandwidth is reserved just for that transmission.

ANALOG SIGNALS

DIGITAL SIGNALS

FIGURE 7-14
Analog vs. digital signals.

FIGURE 7-15
Serial vs. parallel transmissions.

01000001

SERIAL TRANSMISSIONS
All the bits in one byte follow one another over a single path.

PARALLEL TRANSMISSIONS
The eight bits in each byte are transmitted over separate paths at the same time.

NET

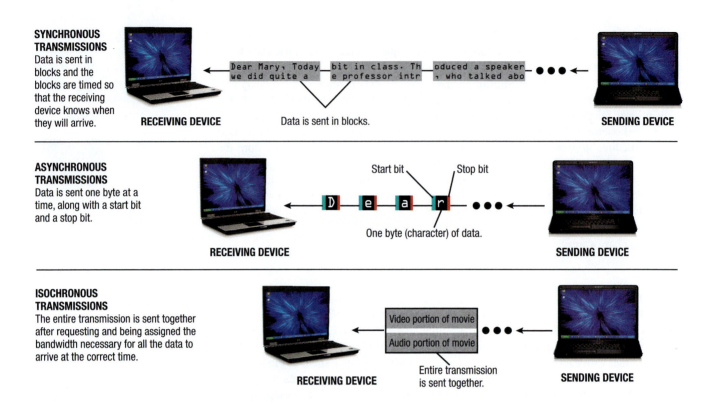

SYNCHRONOUS TRANSMISSIONS
Data is sent in blocks and the blocks are timed so that the receiving device knows when they will arrive.

RECEIVING DEVICE

Dear Mary, Today we did quite a | bit in class. The professor intr | oduced a speaker, who talked abo

Data is sent in blocks.

SENDING DEVICE

ASYNCHRONOUS TRANSMISSIONS
Data is sent one byte at a time, along with a start bit and a stop bit.

RECEIVING DEVICE

Start bit   Stop bit

D e a r

One byte (character) of data.

SENDING DEVICE

ISOCHRONOUS TRANSMISSIONS
The entire transmission is sent together after requesting and being assigned the bandwidth necessary for all the data to arrive at the correct time.

RECEIVING DEVICE

Video portion of movie
Audio portion of movie

Entire transmission is sent together.

SENDING DEVICE

FIGURE 7-16

Transmission timing. Most network transmissions use synchronous transmission.

Another distinction between types of transmissions is the direction in which transmitted data can move.

> *Simplex transmission*—data travels in a single direction only (like a doorbell). Simplex transmission is relatively uncommon in data transmissions since most devices that are mainly one-directional, such as a printer, can still transmit error messages and other data back to the computer.

> *Half-duplex transmission*—data can travel in either direction, but only in one direction at a time (like a walkie-talkie where only one person can talk at a time). Some network transmissions are half-duplex.

> *Full-duplex transmission*—data can move in both directions at the same time (like a telephone). Many network and most Internet connections are full-duplex; sometimes two connections between the sending device and receiving device are needed to support full-duplex transmissions.

Delivery Method

When data needs to travel across a large network (such as a WAN), typically one of three methods is used (see Figure 7-17). With *circuit switching*, a dedicated path over a network is established between the sender and receiver and all data follows that path from the sender to the receiver. Once the connection is established, the physical path or circuit is dedicated to that connection and cannot be used by any other device until the transmission is finished. The most common example of a circuit-switched network is the conventional telephone system.

The technique used for data sent over the Internet is *packet switching*. With packet switching, messages are separated into small units called *packets*. Packets contain information about the sender and the receiver, the actual data being sent, and information about how to reassemble the packets to reconstruct the original message. Packets travel along the network separately, based on their final destination, network traffic, and other network conditions. When the packets reach their destination, they are reassembled in the proper order (refer again to Figure 7-17). Another alternative is *broadcasting*, in which data is sent out (typically in packets) to all nodes on a network and is retrieved only by the intended recipient. Broadcasting is used primarily with LANs.

◀ **FIGURE 7-17**

Circuit-switched, packet-switched, and broadcast networks.

CIRCUIT-SWITCHED NETWORKS
Data uses a dedicated path from the sender to the recipient.

PACKET-SWITCHED NETWORKS
Data is sent as individual packets, which are assembled at the recipient's destination.

BROADCAST NETWORKS
Data is broadcast to all nodes within range; the designated recipient retrieves the data.

NETWORKING MEDIA

To connect the devices in a network, either *wired media* (physical cables) or *wireless media* (typically radio signals) can be used. The most common wired and wireless networking media are discussed next.

Wired Networking Media

The most common types of wired networking media are *twisted-pair*, *coaxial*, and *fiber-optic cable*.

Twisted-Pair Cable

A **twisted-pair cable** is made up of pairs of thin strands of insulated wire twisted together (see Figure 7-18). Twisted-pair is the least expensive type of networking cable and has been in use the longest. In fact, it is the same type of cabling used inside most homes for telephone communications. Twisted-pair cabling can be used with both analog and digital data transmission and is commonly used for LANs. Twisted-pair cable is rated by *category*, which indicates the type of data, speed, distance, and other factors that the cable supports. *Category 3* (*Cat 3*) twisted-pair cabling is regular telephone cable; higher speed and quality cabling—such as *Category 5* (*Cat 5*), *Category 6* (*Cat 6*), and *Category 7* (*Cat 7*)—is frequently used for home or business networks. The pairs of wires in twisted-pair wire are twisted together to reduce interference and improve performance. To further improve performance it can be *shielded* with a metal lining. Twisted-pair cables used for networks have different connectors than those used for telephones. Networking connectors are typically *RJ-45* connectors, which look similar to but are larger than telephone *RJ-11* connectors.

Coaxial Cable

Coaxial cable (also known as *coax*) was originally developed to carry a large number of high-speed video transmissions at one time, such as to deliver cable TV service. A coaxial cable (see Figure 7-18) consists of a relatively thick center wire surrounded by insulation and then covered with a shield of braided wire to block electromagnetic signals from entering the cable. Coaxial cable is commonly used today in computer networks, for short-run

---

The entire cable is covered by a plastic covering.

Pairs of copper wires are insulated with a plastic coating and twisted together; most cables contain at least two pairs.

TWISTED-PAIR CABLES

The entire cable is covered by a plastic covering.

Outer conductor is made out of woven or braided metal.

White insulating material surrounds the copper wire.

The innermost part of the cable is a single copper wire.

COAXIAL CABLES

The entire cable is surrounded by strengthening material and covered by a plastic covering.

The core of each fiber is a single glass or plastic tube, which is surrounded by a reflective cladding.

A protective plastic coating protects each fiber; a cable contains multiple fibers.

FIBER-OPTIC CABLES

FIGURE 7-18
Wired network transmission media.

telephone transmissions outside of the home, and for cable television delivery. Although more expensive than twisted-pair cabling, it is much less susceptible to interference and can carry more data more quickly. While not used extensively for networking home computers at the moment, that may change with the relatively new option of networking via the existing coax in a home. Coax is also growing in popularity for home multimedia networks. The most common types of connectors used with coaxial cable are the slotted *BNC connectors* that are turned once to lock or unlock them into place (and are on the cable shown in Figure 7-18) and the threaded *F connectors* frequently used with cable TV and antenna applications.

Fiber-Optic Cable

Fiber-optic cable is the newest and fastest of these three types of wired transmission media. It contains multiple (sometime several hundred) clear glass or plastic fiber strands, each about the thickness of a human hair (refer again to Figure 7-18). Fiber-optic cable transfers data represented by light pulses at speeds of billions of bits per second. Each strand has the capacity to carry data for several television stations or thousands of voice conversations, but each strand can only send data in one direction so two strands are needed for full-duplex data transmissions.

Fiber-optic cable is commonly used for the high-speed backbone lines of a network, such as to connect networks housed in separate buildings or for the Internet infrastructure. It is also used for telephone backbone lines and, increasingly, is being installed by telephone companies all the way to the home or business to provide super-fast connections directly to

> **Fiber-optic cable.** A networking cable that utilizes hundreds of thin transparent fibers over which lasers transmit data as light.

the end user. The biggest advantage of fiber-optic cabling is speed; the main disadvantage of fiber-optic cabling is the initial expense of both the cable and the installation. Fiber-optic connectors are less standardized than connectors for other types of wired media, so it is important to use cables with the connectors that match the hardware with which the cable will be used. Common connectors include the push-pull *SC connector* (shown in Figure 7-18) and the slotted *ST connector* that works similarly to a BNC connector.

Wireless Networking Media

Wireless networks usually use *radio signals* to send data through the airwaves. Depending on the networking application, radio signals can be short range (such as to connect a wireless keyboard or mouse to a computer), medium range (such as to connect a computer to a wireless LAN or public hotspot), or long range (such as to provide Internet access or cell phone coverage to a relatively large geographic area or to broadcast TV or radio shows). The radio signals used in wireless networks and the types of technologies used to transmit them are discussed next.

The Electromagnetic and Wireless Spectrums

All wireless applications in the United States—such as wireless networks, mobile phones, radio and TV broadcasts, sonar and radar applications, and GPS systems—use specific *frequencies* as assigned by the Federal Communications Commission (FCC). Frequencies are measured in *hertz* (*Hz*) and the frequencies that comprise the *electromagnetic spectrum*—the range of common *electromagnetic radiation* (energy)—are shown in Figure 7-19. Different parts of the spectrum have different properties (such as the distance a signal can travel, the amount of data a signal can transmit in a given period of time, and the types of objects a signal can pass through), which make certain frequencies more appropriate for certain applications. As illustrated in this figure, most wireless networking applications use frequencies located in the *radio frequency* (*RF*) band at the low end (up to 300 GHz) of the electromagnetic spectrum—this range is sometimes referred to as the *wireless spectrum*.

The frequencies assigned to an application, such as FM radio or cell phone service, typically consist of a range of frequencies to be used as needed for that application. For instance, FM radio stations broadcast on frequencies from 88 MHz to 108 MHz and each radio station in a particular geographic area is assigned its own frequency. Most radio frequencies in the U.S. are licensed by the FCC and can only be used for that specific application by the licensed individuals in their specified geographic areas. However, the 900 MHz, 2.4 GHz, 5 GHz, and 5.8 GHz frequencies used by many cordless landline phones, garage door openers, and other consumer devices—as well as for *Wi-Fi*, *WiMAX*, and *Bluetooth* wireless networking—fall within an unlicensed part of the spectrum and, therefore, can be used by any product or individual. A frequency range can be further broken down into multiple *channels*, each of which can be used simultaneously by different users. There are also ways to combine multiple signals to send them over a transmission medium at one time to allow more users than would otherwise be possible.

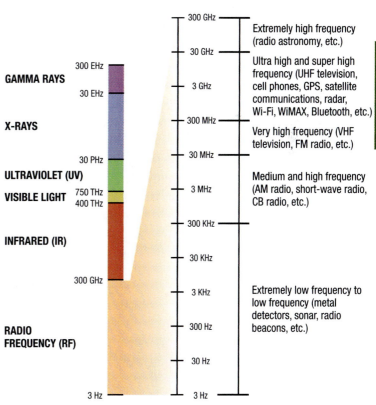

NET

FIGURE 7-19
The electromagnetic spectrum. Each type of communication is assigned specific frequencies within which to operate.

Because the number of wireless applications is growing all the time and there is a limited amount of the parts of the spectrum appropriate for today's wireless networking applications, the wireless spectrum is relatively crowded and frequencies are in high demand. One benefit of the 2009 switch from analog to digital television broadcasts is that it freed up some of the VHF and UHF frequencies for other applications. While some of these frequencies were allocated to public safety communications applications, a large portion were auctioned off in 2008 and are expected to be used for new wireless networks and applications—particularly for mobile users.

Cellular Radio Transmissions

Cellular radio transmissions are used with cell phones and are sent and received via *cellular (cell) towers*—tall metal poles with antennas on top. Cellular service areas are divided into honeycomb-shaped zones called *cells*; each cell contains one cell tower (see Figure 7-20). When a cell phone user begins to make a call, it is picked up by the appropriate cell tower (the one that is located in the cell in which the cell phone is located and that belongs to the user's mobile phone provider). That cell tower then forwards the call to the mobile phone company's *Mobile Telephone Switching Office* (*MTSO*), which routes the call to the recipient's telephone via his or her mobile or conventional telephone service provider (depending on the type of phone being used by the recipient). When a cell phone

FIGURE 7-20

How cellular phones work.

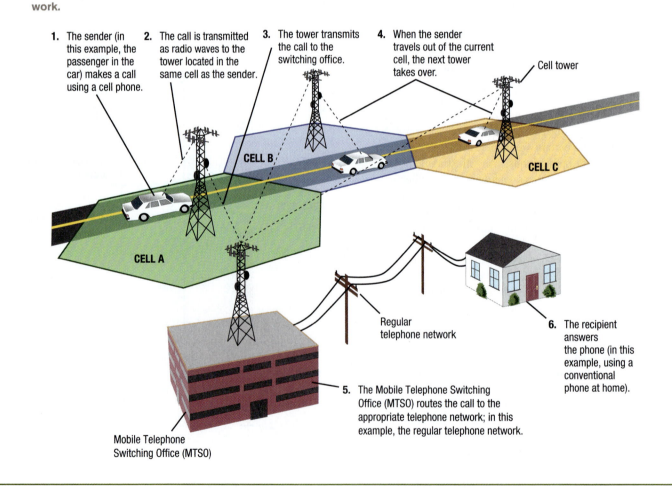

1. The sender (in this example, the passenger in the car) makes a call using a cell phone.

2. The call is transmitted as radio waves to the tower located in the same cell as the sender.

3. The tower transmits the call to the switching office.

4. When the sender travels out of the current cell, the next tower takes over.

Cell tower

CELL B

CELL C

CELL A

Regular telephone network

6. The recipient answers the phone (in this example, using a conventional phone at home).

5. The Mobile Telephone Switching Office (MTSO) routes the call to the appropriate telephone network; in this example, the regular telephone network.

Mobile Telephone Switching Office (MTSO)

>**Cellular radio.** A form of broadcast radio designed for use with cellular telephones that broadcasts using antennas located inside honeycomb-shaped cells.

user moves out of the current cell into a new cell, the call is passed automatically to the appropriate cell tower in the cell that the user is entering. Data (such as e-mail and Web page requests) sent via cell phones works in a similar manner. The speed of cellular radio transmissions depends on the type of *cellular standard* being used, as discussed later in this chapter.

Microwave and Satellite Transmissions

Microwaves are high-frequency radio signals that can send large quantities of data at high speeds over long distances. Microwave signals can be sent or received using *microwave stations* or *communications satellites*, but must travel in a straight line from one station or satellite to another without encountering any obstacles, since microwave signals are *line of sight*. **Microwave stations** are earth-based stations that can transmit microwave signals directly to each other over distances of up to about 30 miles. To avoid buildings, mountains, and the curvature of the earth obstructing the signal, microwave stations are usually placed on tall buildings, towers, and mountaintops. Microwave stations typically contain both a dish-shaped *microwave antenna* and a transceiver. When one station receives a transmission from another, it amplifies it and passes it on to the next station. Microwave stations can exchange data transmissions with *communications satellites*, discussed next, as well as with other microwave stations. Microwave stations designed specifically to communicate with satellites (such as for satellite TV and satellite Internet services) are typically called *satellite dishes*. Satellite dishes are usually installed permanently where they are needed, but they can also be mounted on trucks, boats, RVs, and other types of transportation devices when portable transmission capabilities are necessary or desirable, such as for military or recreational applications.

Communications satellites are space-based devices launched into orbit around the earth to receive and transmit microwave signals to and from earth (see the satellite Internet example in Figure 7-21). Communications satellites were originally used to facilitate microwave transmission when microwave stations were not economically viable (such as over large, sparsely populated areas) or were physically impractical (such as over large bodies of water). Today, communications satellites are used to send and receive transmissions to and from a variety of other devices, such as personal satellite dishes used for satellite television and Internet service, GPS receivers, satellite radio receivers, and satellite phones.

FIGURE 7-21
How satellite Internet works.

3. An orbiting satellite receives the request and beams it down to the satellite dish at the ISP's operations center.

2. The request is sent up to a satellite from the individual's satellite dish.

1. Data, such as a Web page request, is sent from the individual's computer to the satellite dish via a satellite modem.

4. The ISP's operations center receives the request (via its satellite dish) and transfers it to the Internet.

THE INTERNET

5. The request travels over the Internet as usual. The requested information takes a reverse route back to the individual.

> **Microwave station.** An earth-based device that sends and receives high-frequency, high-speed radio signals. > **Communications satellite.** An earth-orbiting device that relays communications signals over long distances.

Traditional communications satellites maintain a *geosynchronous* orbit 22,300 miles above the earth; since they travel at a speed and direction that keeps pace with the earth's rotation, they appear (from earth) to remain stationary over any given spot. Because these satellites are so far above the surface of the earth, there is a slight delay while the signals travel from earth, to the satellite, and back to earth again. This delay—less than one half-second—is not normally noticed by most users (such as individuals who receive Internet or TV service via satellite), but it does make geosynchronous satellite transmissions less practical for voice, gaming, and other real-time communications. Because of this delay factor, *low earth orbit* (*LEO*) satellite systems were developed for use with satellite telephone systems. LEO satellites typically are located anywhere from 100 to 1,000 miles above the earth and, consequently, provide faster transmission than traditional satellites. *Medium earth orbit* (*MEO*) systems typically use satellites located about 1,000 to 12,000 miles above the earth and are used most often for GPS.

Infrared (IR) Transmissions

One type of wireless networking that does not use signals in the RF band of the electromagnetic spectrum is **infrared (IR) transmission**, which sends data as infrared light rays over relatively short distances. Like an infrared television remote control, infrared technology requires line-of-sight transmission. Because of this limitation, many formerly infrared devices (such as wireless mice and keyboards) now use RF radio signals instead. Infrared transmissions are still used with remote controls (such as for computers that contain TV tuners). They are also used to beam data between some mobile devices, as well as between some game consoles, handheld gaming devices, and other home entertainment devices.

COMMUNICATIONS PROTOCOLS AND NETWORKING STANDARDS

A *protocol* is a set of rules to be followed in a specific situation; in networking, for instance, there are *communications protocols* that determine how devices on a network communicate. The term *standard* refers to a set of criteria or requirements that has been approved by a recognized standards organization (such as the *American National Standards Institute* (*ANSI*), which helps to develop standards used in business and industry, or *IEEE*, which develops networking standards) or is accepted as a de facto standard by the industry. Standards are extremely important in the computer industry because they help hardware and software manufacturers ensure that the products they develop can work with other computing products. *Networking standards* typically address both how the devices in a network physically connect (such as the types of cabling that can be used) and how the devices communicate (such as the communications protocols that can be used). Communications protocols and the most common wired and wireless networking standards are discussed in the next several sections.

TCP/IP and Other Communications Protocols

The most widely used communications protocol today is **TCP/IP**. TCP/IP is the protocol used for transferring data over the Internet and actually consists of two protocols: *Transmission Control Protocol* (*TCP*), which is responsible for the delivery of data, and *Internet Protocol* (*IP*), which provides addresses and routing information. TCP/IP uses packet switching to transmit data over the Internet; when the packets reach their destination, they are reassembled

---

>**Infrared (IR) transmissions.** A wireless networking medium that sends data as infrared light rays. >**TCP/IP.** A networking protocol that uses packet switching to facilitate the transmission of messages; the protocol used with the Internet.

in the proper order (see Figure 7-22). Support for TCP/IP is built into virtually all operating systems, and IP addresses are commonly used to identify the various computers and devices on networks such as LANs.

The first widely used version of IP—*Internet Protocol Version 4 (IPv4)*—was standardized in the early 1980s. IPv4 uses 32-bit addresses and so allows for 2^{32} possible unique addresses. While still widely used today, IPv4 was never designed to be used with the billions of devices that access the Internet today and, consequently, a newer version of IP (*IPv6*) was developed. IPv6 uses 128-bit addresses (and so allows for 2^{128} possible unique addresses) and adds many improvements to IPv4 in areas such as routing, data security, and network autoconfiguration. While IPv4 and IPv6 are expected to coexist for several years until IPv6 eventually replaces IPv4, the U.S. government has mandated that all federal agencies be capable of switching to IPv6. Experts suggest that businesses perform a network audit to determine what hardware and software changes will be needed to switch to IPv6 so that the business is prepared when the change is deemed necessary.

While TCP/IP is used to connect to and communicate with the Internet, other protocols are used for specific Internet applications. For instance, as discussed in Chapter 1, *HTTP (Hypertext Transfer Protocol)* and *HTTPS (Secure Hypertext Transfer Protocol)* are protocols used to display Web pages, and *FTP (File Transfer Protocol)* is a protocol used to transfer files over the Internet. Protocols used to deliver e-mail over the Internet include *SMTP (Simple Mail Transfer Protocol)* and *POP3 (Post Office Protocol)*.

1. Each message is split into packets.

SUE'S PC

2. The packets are addressed to the same destination.

From: SueG@usc.edu
0¢
To: JimS@cu.edu

From: SueG@usc.edu
0¢
To: JimS@cu.edu

From: SueG@usc.edu
0¢
To: JimS@cu.edu

4. The packets are reassembled into the message at the destination.

JIM'S PC

3. The packets may travel the same or different routes to the destination.

University of Colorado (CU)

University of Southern California (USC)

FIGURE 7-22
How TCP/IP works.
TCP/IP networks (like the Internet) use packet switching.

Ethernet (802.3)

Ethernet (802.3) is the most widely used standard for wired networks. It is typically used with LANs that have a star topology (though it can also be used with WANs and MANs) and can be used in conjunction with twisted-pair, coaxial, or fiber-optic cabling. Ethernet

>**Ethernet (802.3).** A widely used wired LAN networking standard.

STANDARD	MAXIMUM SPEED
10BASE-T	10 Mbps
Fast Ethernet (100BASE-T or 100BASE-TX)	100 Mbps
Gigabit Ethernet (1000BASE-T)	1,000 Mbps (1 Gbps)
10 Gigabit Ethernet (10GBASE-T)	10 Gbps
40 Gigabit Ethernet*	40 Gbps
100 Gigabit Ethernet*	100 Gbps
Terabit Ethernet**	1,000 Gbps (1 Tbps)

* Expected by 2010
** Expected by 2015

FIGURE 7-23
Ethernet standards.

PoE SWITCH

PoE CAMERA

PoE ADAPTER

NON-PoE OUTDOOR WIRELESS ACCESS POINT

POWER CABLE
ETHERNET CABLE

FIGURE 7-24

With Power over Ethernet (PoE), devices are powered through the Ethernet connection.

was invented in the mid-1970s and has continued to evolve over the years; about every three years the new approved amendments are incorporated into the existing IEEE 802.3 Ethernet standard to keep it up to date. Figure 7-23 summarizes the various Ethernet standards; of these, the most common today are *Fast Ethernet*, *Gigabit Ethernet*, and *10 Gigabit Ethernet*. The even faster standards shown in Figure 7-23 are currently under development and are expected to be used for connections between servers, as well as for delivering video, digital X-rays and other digital medical images, and other high-speed, bandwidth-intensive networking applications.

Early Ethernet networks were half-duplex and used a set of procedures collectively called *CSMA/ CD* (*Carrier Sense Multiple Access/Collision Detection*) to avoid multiple messages from being sent at one time and to detect any collisions of messages as they occur. Beginning in 1997, Ethernet became full-duplex and so collisions no longer occur.

A recent Ethernet development is *Power over Ethernet* (*PoE*), which allows electrical power to be sent along the cables in an Ethernet network (often referred to as *Ethernet cables*) along with data (see Figure 7-24). Consequently, in addition to sending data, the Ethernet cable can be used to supply power to the devices on the network. PoE is most often used in business networks with remote wired devices (such as outdoor net-working hardware, security cameras, and other devices) that are not located near a power outlet. It can also be used to place networked devices near ceilings or other locations where a nearby power outlet may not be available. Using PoE requires special hardware and devices designed for PoE but it eliminates the need for access to power outlets for that portion of the network. Regular Ethernet-enabled devices can be powered via PoE if a special *PoE adapter*, such as the one shown in Figure 7-24, is used.

Phoneline, Powerline, G.hn, and Broadband over Powerline (BPL)

Two alternatives to the Ethernet standard for wired home networks are the *Phoneline* and *Powerline standards*. Phoneline (also called the *Home Phoneline Networking Association* or *HomePNA standard*) allows computers to be networked through ordinary telephone wiring and telephone jacks (without interfering with voice telephone calls), as well as over existing home coaxial cable wiring. The newest version of this standard—*HomePNA 3.0*—supports speeds up to 320 Mbps and is designed to network both the computers and the home entertainment devices within a home. The Powerline (also called *HomePlug*) standard allows computers to be networked over existing power lines using conventional electrical outlets. Similar to Phoneline networks, Powerline networks are quick and easy to set up and are relatively fast (up to 200 Mbps). In addition, they have the advantage that houses usually have many more power outlets than phone outlets. Similar to the newest Phoneline standard, the newest Powerline standard—named *HomePlug AV*—can be used to network home entertainment devices in addition to computers.

The *G.hn* standard is an emerging standard designed as a unified worldwide standard for creating home networks over phone lines, power lines, and coaxial cable. It is being promoted by the HomeGrid Forum and is supported by the Home Phoneline Networking Association. Once the standard is finalized (expected by 2010), products that support all three types of home networking connections discussed in this section (via phone lines, power lines, and coaxial cable) can be developed.

An emerging technology based on the Powerline standard that is under development and that is designed to deliver broadband Internet to homes via the existing outdoor power lines (with the addition of some new hardware at the power poles) is *broadband over powerline* (*BPL*). BPL service is only available in limited areas at the moment (available through the area's power company), but BPL has great potential for delivering broadband Internet access to virtually any home or business that has access to electricity.

Wi-Fi (802.11)

One of the most common networking standards used with wireless LANs is **Wi-Fi (802.11)**—a family of wireless networking standards that use the IEEE 802.11 standard. Wi-Fi (sometimes called *wireless Ethernet* because it is designed to easily connect to a wired Ethernet network) is the current standard for wireless networks in the home or office, as well as for public Wi-Fi hotspots. Wi-Fi hardware is built into virtually all portable computers sold today; it is also built into many mobile phones to allow faster Web browsing via Wi-Fi when the user is within range of a Wi-Fi network. In addition to portable computers and mobile phones, Wi-Fi capabilities are becoming increasingly integrated into everyday products, such as printers, digital cameras, portable digital media players, handheld gaming devices, and gaming consoles (see Figure 7-25), to allow those devices to wirelessly network with other devices or to access the Internet. For a look at a new Wi-Fi-enabled consumer product you can use to automatically upload digital photos to your favorite photo-sharing sites—Wi-Fi flash memory cards—see the Technology and You box.

The speed of a Wi-Fi network and the area it can cover depend on a variety of factors, including the *Wi-Fi standard* and hardware being used, the number of solid objects (such as walls, trees, or buildings) between the access point and the computer or other device being used, and the amount of interference from cordless phones, baby monitors, microwave ovens, and other devices that also operate on the same radio frequency as Wi-Fi (usually 2.4 GHz). In general, Wi-Fi is designed for medium-range data transfers—typically between 100 and 300 feet indoors and 300 to 900 feet outdoors. Usually both speed and distance degrade with interference. The distance of a Wi-Fi network can be extended using additional *antennas* and other hardware designed for that purpose.

ONLINE VIDEO

Go to the Chapter 7 page at
**www.cengage.com/
computerconcepts/np/uc13**
to watch the "How to Create a
Powerline Network" video clip.

FIGURE 7-25
Wi-Fi enabled products. Many consumer products today contain built-in Wi-Fi connectivity.

PORTABLE COMPUTERS

MOBILE PHONES

DIGITAL CAMERAS

PORTABLE DIGITAL MEDIA PLAYERS

GAMING CONSOLES

NET

> **Wi-Fi (802.11).** A widely used networking standard for medium-range wireless networks.

TECHNOLOGY AND YOU

Wi-Fi SD Cards

One interesting new Wi-Fi product that became available recently is the *Wi-Fi SD card*. These cards (such as the *Eye-Fi cards* shown in the accompanying illustration) are designed to upload photos wirelessly and automatically from your camera to your computer via a Wi-Fi network. Some cards can also *geotag* your photos with location information (based on geographic coordinates) as you take them to show where the photos were taken; others can automatically upload your photos to photo sharing Web sites like Flickr, Facebook, or Picasa.

For instance, all three Eye-Fi cards in the accompanying photo wirelessly transfer your photos from your digital camera to your home computer as soon as the camera is within range of your home Wi-Fi network. The *Eye-Fi Share* and the *Eye-Fi Pro* cards can also wirelessly upload photos to your favorite photo sharing Web site, and the Eye-Fi Pro card automatically geotags your photos. In addition, the Eye-Fi Pro card can upload videos and uncompressed *RAW* files in addition to photos, send images to photo sharing Web sites and your home computer via a wireless hotspot when you are away from home, and upload photos directly to your computer while on the go (without a wireless router via a peer-to-peer connection) whenever the camera is in range of your computer.

In addition to allowing you to share your photos immediately with others (such as while on a vacation or at a special event), using a Wi-Fi SD card for your digital photos can also give you the peace of mind that your photos are backed up on your home computer and/or online. This is especially beneficial if your camera is stolen or the card becomes damaged. In fact, using an Eye-Fi card enabled one woman to catch the individual who stole her camera gear while she was on vacation—her photos, along with images of the thief with the camera gear, were uploaded to her home computer and the police were able to apprehend the thief and recover the stolen gear.

FIGURE 7-26
Wi-Fi standards.

WI-FI STANDARD	DESCRIPTION
802.11b	An early Wi-Fi standard; supports data transfer rates of 11 Mbps.
802.11a	Supports data transfer rates of 54 Mbps, but uses a different radio frequency (5 GHz) than 802.11g/b (2.4 GHz), making the standards incompatible.
802.11g	A current Wi-Fi standard; supports data transfer rates of 54 Mbps and uses the same 2.4 GHz frequency as 802.11b, so their products are compatible.
802.11n	The newest Wi-Fi standard; supports speeds up to about 300 Mbps and has twice the range of 802.11g. It can use either the 2.4 GHz or 5 GHz frequency.
802.11s*	Designed for Wi-Fi mesh networks.
802.11u*	Includes additional security features.
802.11z*	Designed for direct (ad hoc) networking between advices.
802.11ac and 802.11ad**	Designed to increase throughput.

* Expected by 2010
** Expected no earlier than 2012

A summary of the different Wi-Fi standards in use and under development is shown in Figure 7-26; of these, the most widely used today are *802.11g* and *802.11n*. The 802.11n standard is currently the fastest Wi-Fi standard today. Its use of *MIMO* (*multiple in, multiple out*) *antennas* to transfer multiple streams of data at one time, in addition to other improvements, allows for data transmissions typically about five times as fast as 802.11g and about twice the range.

Typically, 802.11g and 802.11n products can be used on the same network and the products are backward-compatible (so computers using older 802.11g hardware can connect to 802.11n networks, for instance, though they will only connect at 802.11g speeds). To ensure that hardware from various vendors will work together, consumers can look for products that are certified by the *Wi-Fi Alliance* (see Figure 7-27).

While Wi-Fi is very widely used today, it does have some limitations—particularly its relatively limited range. For instance, an individual using a Wi-Fi hotspot inside a Starbucks coffeehouse will lose that Internet connection when he or she moves out of range of that network and will need to locate another hotspot at his or her next location. In addition, many businesses may be physically too large for a Wi-Fi network to span the entire organization. While hardware can be used to extend a Wi-Fi network, an emerging possibility for creating larger wireless networks is *WiMAX*, discussed next.

FIGURE 7-27
Wi-Fi CERTIFIED logo.

WiMAX and Mobile WiMAX

WiMAX (*Worldwide Interoperability for Microwave Access*) is a series of standards designed for longer range wireless networking connections. Similar to Wi-Fi, WiMAX (also known as *802.16a*) is designed to provide Internet access to fixed locations (sometimes called *hotzones*), but the coverage is significantly larger (a typical hotzone radius is close to 2 miles, though WiMAX can transmit data as far as 6 miles or so without line of sight). With WiMAX, it is feasible to provide coverage to an entire city or other geographical area by using multiple WiMAX towers (see Figure 7-28), similar to the way cell phone cells overlap to provide continuous cell phone service. WiMAX can use licensed radio frequencies, in addition to unlicensed frequencies like Wi-Fi, to avoid interference issues.

Mobile WiMAX (*802.16e*) is the mobile version of the WiMAX wireless networking standard. It is designed to deliver broadband wireless networking to mobile users via a mobile phone, portable computer, or other WiMAX-enabled device. WiMAX capabilities are beginning to be built into portable computers and other devices, and WiMAX is currently being used to provide Internet access to selected geographical areas by a number of companies in over 135 countries. In the U.S., for instance, Sprint Nextel's WiMAX division and WiMAX leader Clearwire have merged and are in the process of building a new WiMAX-based nationwide high-speed network designed to deliver both fixed and mobile WiMAX-based Internet service to businesses and individuals. This new network is expected to be able to provide service to at least 140 million users by 2010.

- ● WiMAX hotzone
- ● Wi-Fi hotspot

FIGURE 7-28
WiMAX vs. Wi-Fi. WiMAX hotzones can provide service to anyone in the hotzone, including mobile users, while the range of Wi-Fi hotspots is fairly limited.

NET

Cellular Standards

Cellular standards have evolved over the years to better fulfill the demand for mobile Internet, mobile multimedia delivery, and other relatively recent mobile trends. The original *first-generation phones* were analog and designed for voice data only. Newer cell phones, starting with *second-generation (2G) phones*, are digital, support both data and voice, and are faster. Common *2G wireless standards* include *GSM (Global System for Mobile*

ONLINE VIDEO
Go to the Chapter 7 page at **www.cengage.com/computerconcepts/np/uc13** to watch the "WiMAX vs. Wi-Fi" video clip.

>**WiMAX.** An emerging wireless networking standard that is faster and has a greater range than Wi-Fi. >**Mobile WiMAX.** A version of WiMAX designed to be used with mobile phones.

ASK THE EXPERT

Dave Weick, Senior Vice President, Chief Information Officer, McDonald's Corporation

i'm lovin' it

How has the emergence of Wi-Fi affected companies such as McDonalds?

The emergence of Wi-Fi has fueled our customers' expectations of having immediate access to information. Our customers and employees love the convenience and relevance of McDonald's "hotspots." Through wireless connectivity, Wi-Fi is creating a more modern and relevant experience for our customers. The ability to conveniently check e-mail or download music or games can be a deciding factor in choosing a place to eat—a trend we don't see ending anytime soon.

FIGURE 7-29

Mobile broadband.
3G networks provide mobile phone users with broadband access to multimedia content.

> **✓ TIP**
>
> While many mobile phones are locked to a particular cellular provider, buying an *unlocked mobile phone* allows you to switch providers and keep your same phone, as well as carry your contacts and other data with you to a new unlocked phone just by moving the *SIM card* containing that data to the new phone.

communications) and *CDMA* (*Code Division Multiple Access*). Both of these standards are designed for voice traffic and both support speeds up to 14.4 Kbps, though some wireless providers have developed technologies such as *EDGE* (*Enhanced Data Rates for GSM Evolution*) that can be used with 2G networks to provide faster service (for instance, EDGE supports speeds up to 135 Kbps). These interim developments are sometimes referred to as *2.5G cellular standards*. Both GSM and CDMA are used in the United States (but are not compatible with each other, although some phones are available that can be used with both standards). GSM is also widely used overseas, though with different frequencies so international travelers will need to ensure their 2G phone supports the frequencies used in their destination location—some 2G phones support multiple frequencies to permit international roaming.

The current standard for cellular networks today in the U.S. and many other countries is *3G* (*third generation*). *3G cellular standards* use packet-switching (like TCP/IP) instead of circuit-switching (like conventional telephones and earlier mobile phones) and are designed to support both data and voice. Users of 3G mobile phones and other 3G mobile devices can access broadband Internet content (such as online maps, music, games, TV, videos and more—see Figure 7-29) at relatively fast speeds—up to about 1.7 Mbps at the present time, with speeds expected to reach 3 Mbps in the near future. These speeds are equivalent to the speeds many home broadband Internet users experience; consequently, Internet access via a 3G network is often referred to as *mobile broadband*. In addition to mobile phones, computers can access the Internet via a 3G network with appropriate hardware.

Virtually all mobile phone providers today have, or are in the process of building, a 3G network. The 3G standard used with a network depends on the type of cellular network. For instance, GSM mobile networks (like AT&T Wireless and T-Mobile) typically use the *HSDPA* (*High Speed Downlink Packet Access*)/*UMTS* (*Universal Mobile Telecommunications System*) 3G standards for their 3G networks; CDMA networks (like *Verizon Wireless* and *Cricket Wireless*) typically use the *EV-DO* (*Evolution Data Optimized*) 3G standard instead. To get 3G speeds, mobile users need to be in range of their providers' 3G network; typically, users outside the coverage area can still get service, but only at 2G speeds.

The next generation for mobile networks—*4G* (*fourth generation*)—is under development and two standards have emerged at the present time: the mobile WiMAX standard already discussed and *Long Term Evolution* (*LTE*). LTE (supported by AT&T Wireless, Verizon Wireless, and T-Mobile) is a cellular standard and is based on UMTS. LTE networks are expected to arrive in the U.S. by 2011. While mobile WiMAX is not a cellular standard, the new national WiMAX network being built in the U.S. by Sprint Nextel and Clearwire will be used to provide 4G mobile phone service to subscribers, in addition to Internet service.

Bluetooth, Ultra Wideband (UWB), and Other Short-Range Wireless Standards

There are several wireless networking standards in existence or being developed that are designed for short-range wireless networking connections. Most of these are used to facilitate PANs or very small, special-purpose home networks, such as connecting home entertainment devices or appliances within a home. The most common of these standards are discussed next.

Bluetooth and Wireless USB

Bluetooth is a wireless standard that is designed for very short-range (10 meters, approximately 33 feet, or less) connections. It is designed to replace cables between devices, such as to connect a wireless keyboard or mouse to a desktop computer, to send print jobs wirelessly from a portable computer to a printer, or to connect a mobile phone to a wireless headset (see Figure 7-30). Bluetooth devices automatically recognize and network with each other when they get within transmission range. For instance, Bluetooth enables a portable computer or mobile phone to be synchronized with a desktop computer automatically on entering the home or office, or a wireless keyboard to be connected to a computer automatically as soon as the computer is powered up. Bluetooth signals can transmit through clothing and other nonmetallic objects, so a mobile phone or other device in a pocket or briefcase can connect with Bluetooth hardware (such as a headset) without having to be removed from the pocket or briefcase. In addition, some industry experts predict that major household appliances will be Bluetooth-enabled in the future, resulting in an automatic, always connected, smart home.

Bluetooth works using radio signals in the frequency band of 2.4 GHz, the same as Wi-Fi, and traditionally supports data transfer rates up to 3 Mbps, though the newest *Bluetooth 3.0* standard incorporates 802.11 technology to support transfers up to 24 Mbps. Once two Bluetooth-enabled devices come within range of each other, their software identifies each other (using their unique identification numbers) and establishes a link. Because there may be many Bluetooth devices within range, up to 10 individual Bluetooth networks (called *piconets*) can be in place within the same physical area at one time. Each piconet can connect up to eight devices, for a maximum of 80 devices within any 10-meter radius. To facilitate this, Bluetooth divides its allocated radio spectrum into multiple channels of 1 MHz each. Each Bluetooth device can use the entire range of frequencies, jumping randomly (in unison with the other devices in that piconet) on a regular basis to minimize interference between piconets, as well as from other devices (such as garage-door openers, Wi-Fi networks, and some cordless phones and baby monitors) that use the same frequencies. Since Bluetooth transmitters change frequencies 1,600 times every second automatically, it is unlikely that any two transmitting devices will be on the same frequency at the same time.

As the use of Bluetooth grows, the standard is evolving to meet new needs. For instance, *Bluetooth 2.1* includes support for *Near Field Communications* (*NFC*), a standard for making payments via mobile phone, as discussed in more detail in Chapter 11, and the newest Bluetooth 3.0 standard is fast enough to support multimedia applications, such as transferring music, photos, and videos between computers, mobile phones, and other devices. One interesting emerging Bluetooth application is intended to protect teenagers from texting or talking on their mobile phones while driving—a special Bluetooth-enabled car key prevents the driver's mobile phone from being used while the car is on.

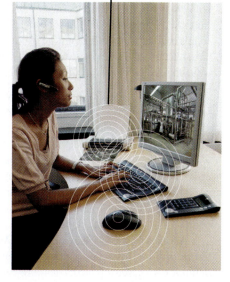

The desktop computer, keyboard, printer, and mouse form a piconet to communicate with each other. The headset and cell phone (not shown in this photo) belong to another piconet.

The headset and cell phone form a piconet when they are within range to communicate with each other.

FIGURE 7-30

Bluetooth. Bluetooth is designed for short-range wireless communications between computers or mobile devices and other hardware.

NET

ONLINE VIDEO

Go to the Chapter 7 page at **www.cengage.com/ computerconcepts/np/uc13** to watch the "What Is Bluetooth?" video clip.

>**Bluetooth.** A networking standard for very short-range wireless connections; the devices are automatically connected once they get within the allowable range.

A new standard that is designed to connect peripheral devices, similar to Bluetooth, but that transfers data more quickly is **wireless USB**. The speed of wireless USB depends on the distance between the devices being used, but is approximately 100 Mbps at 10 meters (about 33 feet) or 480 Mbps at 2 meters (about 6.5 feet). While Bluetooth and wireless USB can be used for similar applications, it is possible they might coexist. For example, wireless USB might be used to connect computer hardware in more permanent setups, while Bluetooth might be used in short-range mobile situations with portable computers and mobile devices. One of the first wireless USB devices to come on the market was the wireless USB hub, shown in Figure 2-17 in Chapter 2.

Ultra Wideband (UWB), WirelessHD (WiHD), and TransferJet

There are several wireless technologies being developed to transfer multimedia content quickly between nearby devices. One example is **Ultra Wideband (UWB)**. Similar to wireless USB (since wireless USB is based on UWB), UWB speeds vary from 100 Mbps at 10 meters (about 33 feet) to 480 Mbps at 2 meters (about 6.5 feet). UWB is especially appropriate for applications that require high-speed transfers over short distances, such as wirelessly delivering multimedia content—such as video, music, and photos—between computers, TVs, digital cameras, DVD players, and more.

Another possibility is **wirelessHD (WiHD)**. Similar to UWB, WiHD is designed for fast transfers of high-definition video between home consumer electronic devices (such as high-definition TVs, set-top boxes, gaming consoles, and DVD players) but it is faster. Backed by seven major electronics companies, WiHD is designed to transfer full-quality uncompressed high-definition audio, video, and data within a single room at speeds up to 25 Gbps, though those speeds have not been obtained yet. WiHD operates at 60 GHz and incorporates a smart antenna system that allows the system to steer the transmission, allowing for non-line-of-sight communications. WiHD aims to help users create an easy to manage wireless video network. Devices that include WiHD capabilities began to become available in 2009.

A new wireless standard designed for very fast transfers between devices that are extremely close together (essentially touching each other) is **TransferJet**. Developed by Sony, TransferJet is designed to quickly transfer large files (such as digital photos, music, and video) between devices as soon as they come in contact with each other, such as to transfer data between mobile phones or between digital cameras, to download music or video from a consumer kiosk or digital signage system to a mobile phone or other mobile device, or to transfer images or video from a digital camera to a TV set or printer. At a maximum speed of 560 Mbps, TransferJet is fast enough to support the transfer of video files. TransferJet-compatible devices are expected to be available by 2010.

ZigBee

An emerging networking standard designed for inexpensive and simple short-range networking (particular sensor networks) is *ZigBee (802.15)*. ZigBee is intended for applications that require low data transfer rates and several years of battery life. For instance, ZigBee can be used for home and commercial automation systems to connect a wide variety of devices (such as appliances and lighting, heating, cooling, water, filtration, and security systems), and allows for their control from anywhere in the world. ZigBee is also used in industrial plant manufacturing, personal home healthcare, device tracking, telecommunications, and wireless sensor networks.

ZigBee is designed to accommodate more than 65,000 devices on a single network and supports speeds from 20 Kbps to 250 Kbps, depending on the frequency being used

FURTHER EXPLORATION

Go to the Chapter 7 page at **www.cengage.com/ computerconcepts/np/uc13** for links to information about wireless networking standards.

>**Wireless USB.** A wireless version of USB designed to connect peripheral devices. >**Ultra Wideband (UWB).** A networking standard for very short-range wireless connections among multimedia devices. >**WirelessHD (WiHD).** An emerging wireless networking specification designed for connecting home consumer devices. >**TransferJet.** A networking standard for very short-range wireless connections between devices; devices need to touch in order to communicate.

CATEGORY	EXAMPLES	INTENDED PURPOSE	APPROXIMATE RANGE
Short range	Bluetooth Wireless USB	To connect peripheral devices to a mobile phone or computer.	33 feet
	Ultra Wideband (UWB) WirelessHD (WiHD) TransferJet	To connect and transfer multimedia content between home consumer electronic devices (computers, TVs, DVD players, etc.).	1 inch–33 feet
	ZigBee	To connect a variety of home, personal, and commercial automation devices.	33 feet–328 feet
Medium range	Wi-Fi (802.11)	To connect computers and other devices to a local area network.	100–300 feet indoors; 300–900 feet outdoors
Long range	WiMAX Mobile WiMAX	To provide Internet access to a large geographic area for fixed and/or mobile users.	6 miles non-line of sight; 30 miles line of sight
	Cellular standards (2G and 3G)	To connect mobile phones and mobile devices to a cellular network for telephone and Internet service.	10 miles

(several different frequencies are available for ZigBee networks). ZigBee has a range of 10 to 100 meters (about 33 to 328 feet) between devices, depending on power output and environmental characteristics; a wireless mesh configuration can be used to greatly extend the range of the network.

For a summary of the wireless networking standards just discussed, see Figure 7-31.

FIGURE 7-31
Summary of common wireless networking standards.

NETWORKING HARDWARE

Various types of hardware are necessary to create a computer network, to connect multiple networks together, or to connect a computer or network to the Internet. The most common types of networking hardware used in home and small office networks are discussed next.

Network Adapters and Modems

A **network adapter**, also called a **network interface card** (**NIC**) when it is in the form of an expansion card, is used to connect a computer to a network (such as a home or business network). A **modem** (derived from the terms *modulate* and *demodulate*) is used to connect a computer to a network over telephone lines. Technically, to be called a *modem*, a device must convert digital signals (such as those used by a computer) to modulated analog signals (such as those used by conventional telephone lines) and vice versa. However, in everyday use, the term *modem* is also used to refer to any device that connects a computer to a broadband Internet connection, such as a *cable modem* used for cable Internet service. In addition, the term *modem* is often used interchangeably with *network adapter* when describing devices used to obtain Internet access via certain networks, such as cellular or WiMAX networks.

Most computers and mobile devices today come with a network adapter and/or modem built in; the type of network adapter and modem used depends on the type of network (such as Ethernet, Wi-Fi, or 3G) and Internet access being used. For instance, to connect a computer to an Ethernet network, an Ethernet network adapter is used. To connect a

TIP

If your Internet connection slows down, try *power cycling* your modem and router: Unplug the modem and router for 30 seconds, then plug in the modem and wait for 30 seconds, then plug in the router.

> **Network adapter.** A network interface, such as an expansion card or external network adapter. > **Network interface card (NIC).** An expansion card through which a computer can connect to a network. > **Modem.** A device that enables a computer to communicate over analog networking media, such as connecting to the Internet via telephone lines.

Port for twisted-pair Ethernet cable

PCI EXPRESS GIGABIT ETHERNET ADAPTERS FOR DESKTOP COMPUTERS

Connects to USB port

USB WI-FI ADAPTERS FOR DESKTOP OR NOTEBOOK COMPUTERS

Connects via a cable to USB port

Connects to a power outlet

USB POWERLINE ADAPTERS FOR DESKTOP OR NOTEBOOK COMPUTERS

Slides into ExpressCard slot

EXPRESSCARD WI-FI ADAPTERS FOR NOTEBOOK COMPUTERS

Connects to USB port

USB 3G EV-DO MODEMS FOR DESKTOP OR NOTEBOOK COMPUTERS

Incoming coaxial cable from cable provider and either a USB or Ethernet cable coming from the computer or router connect to the back of the modem.

USB/ETHERNET CABLE MODEMS

FIGURE 7-32
Network adapters and modems.

computer to a cable Internet connection, typically both a cable modem and an Ethernet network adapter are used. To connect a computer to a Wi-Fi or WiMAX network or public hotspot, a Wi-Fi or WiMAX network adapter, respectively, is used.

When selecting a network adapter or modem, the type of device being used and the expansion slots and ports available on that device need to be considered as well. For example, network adapters and modems for desktop computers typically come in PCI, PCI Express (PCIe), or USB format, and network adapters and modems for portable computers usually connect via USB or an ExpressCard slot. In addition, the network adapter or modem needs to support the type of networking media (such as twisted-pair cabling, coaxial cabling, or wireless signal) being used. Some examples of network adapters and modems are shown in Figure 7-32.

Switches, Routers, and Other Hardware for Connecting Devices and Networks

A variety of networking hardware is used to connect the devices on a network, as well as to connect multiple networks together. For instance, as mentioned earlier in this chapter, networks using the star topology need a central device to connect all of the devices on the network. In a wired network, this device was originally a *hub*. A hub transmits all data received to all network devices connected to the hub, regardless of which device the data is being sent to, so the bandwidth of the network is shared and the network is not extremely efficient. Today, the central device in a wired network is usually a **switch**. A switch contains ports to which the devices on the network connect (typically via networking cables) and facilitates communications between the devices, similar to a hub. But, unlike hubs, switches identify which device connected to the switch is the one the data is intended

> **Switch.** A device used to connect multiple devices on a single (typically wired) network; forwards packets to only the intended recipient.

for and send the data only to that device, rather than sending data out to all connected devices. Consequently, switches are more efficient than hubs.

To connect multiple networks (such as two LANs, two WANs, or a LAN and the Internet), a **router** is used. Routers pass data on to the intended recipient only and can plan a path through the network to ensure the data reaches its destination in the most efficient manner possible, and are used to route traffic over the Internet.

A **wireless access point** is a device used to grant network access to wireless client devices. In home and small business networks, typically the capabilities of a switch, router, and wireless access point are integrated into a single **wireless router** device. A wireless router (such as the one shown in Figure 7-33) is commonly used to connect both wireless (via Wi-Fi) and wired (via Ethernet cables) devices to a network and to connect that network to an Internet connection. Some broadband modems today include wireless router capabilities to create a wireless network and to provide Internet access using a single piece of hardware. To connect just two LANs together, a **bridge** can be used. The most common use for a bridge in a home network is to wirelessly connect a wired device (such as a home audio/video system, DVR, or gaming console) to a home network via a wireless connection.

There are also routers and other devices used to connect multiple devices to a cellular network. For instance, *3G mobile broadband routers* are used to share a 3G mobile wireless Internet connection with multiple devices (such as your cell phone, personal computer, and handheld gaming device)—essentially creating a Wi-Fi hotpot that connects to your 3G Internet connection. For a closer look at one possibility for wirelessly creating a personal mobile hotspot wherever you are—see the Trend box. Other devices (sometimes called *femtocells*) can be used to route cell phone calls over a broadband network in order to provide better cellular coverage while indoors.

An example of how the devices discussed in this section, as well as the other networking hardware discussed in the next section, might be used in a network is shown in Figure 7-34.

Other Networking Hardware

Additional networking hardware is often needed to extend the range of a network and to share networking media, as discussed next.

Repeaters, Range Extenders, and Antennas

Repeaters are devices that amplify signals along a network. They are necessary whenever signals have to travel farther than would be otherwise possible over the networking medium being used. Repeaters are available for both wired and wireless networks; repeaters for a wireless network are often called **range extenders**. Range extenders usually connect wirelessly to the network and repeat the wireless signal to extend coverage of that network outside or to an additional floor of a building, or to eliminate *dead spots*—areas within the

Wireless devices connect wirelessly

A shared USB printer or external hard drive can connect here

Wired devices connect here

Modem connects here

FIGURE 7-33
Wireless routers.
Typically allow both wired and wireless users access to each other and an Internet connection.

> **Router.** A device that connects multiple networks together; routes packets to their next location in order to efficiently reach their destination.
> **Wireless access point.** A device on a wireless network that connects wireless devices to that network. > **Wireless router.** A router with a built-in wireless access point; most often used to connect wireless devices to a network and an Internet connection and often contains a built-in switch. > **Bridge.** A device used to bridge or connect two LANs; most often used to connect wired devices wirelessly to a network. > **Repeater.** A device on a network that amplifies signals. > **Range extender.** A repeater for a wireless network.

DIAL-UP CUSTOMER

DIAL-UP CUSTOMER

DIAL-UP CUSTOMER

GAMING DEVICES

COMPUTER

COMPUTER

COMPUTER

WIRELESS ROUTER
(with built-in 4-port switch)

CABLE MODEM

COMPUTER

HOME NETWORKS
(containing both wired and wireless devices)

ISP'S CONCENTRATOR

ISP

ROUTER

ROUTER

THE INTERNET

ROUTER

ISP

OUTDOOR WIRELESS ACCESS POINT

SWITCH

WIRELESS BRIDGE

SWITCH

MODEM

WIRELESS ROUTER

WIRELESS BRIDGE

SCHOOLS OR BUSINESSES WITH MULTIPLE LANS

FIGURE 7-34

Networking hardware.
As shown in this example, many different types of hardware are used to connect networking devices.

normal network range that don't have coverage. Some *WDS* (*Wireless Distribution System*) wireless access points can be used as range extenders by extending the network coverage from one access point to another.

Another alternative for increasing the range of a Wi-Fi network is using a *higher-gain* (stronger) **antenna**. The MIMO antennas used by many 802.11n routers allow for faster connections and a greater range than typically experienced by 802.11g wireless networks, but sometimes this still isn't enough. Using a network adapter designed for the router being used typically helps the network range to some extent; so does replacing the antenna on the router with a higher-gain antenna or adding an *external antenna* to a networking adapter, if the adapter contains an antenna connector.

> **Antenna.** A device used for receiving or sending radio signals; often used to increase the range of a network.

TREND

Personal Mobile Hotspots

You know you can access Wi-Fi hotspots in many locations, but how about creating your own hotspot whenever you need it? That's now possible with several emerging products designed to create personal mobile hotspots that can be used with any Wi-Fi device, such as notebook computers, mobile phones, and portable gaming devices.

One such product is Verizon Wireless's *MiFi Intelligent Mobile Hotspot*, shown in the accompanying illustration. After its initial setup, this product (about the size of several stacked credit cards) creates a mobile hotspot by just powering up the device. The MiFi device connects to Verizon Wireless's 3G mobile network and provides access to that network for up to five Wi-Fi devices. To those devices, the MiFi hotspot appears as any other Wi-Fi hotspot, so users connect as they normally would. While the cost per MB is relatively expensive and there is currently no unlimited data plan, this device is useful for many situations—such as iPhone users who need to quickly download files larger than the limit allowed via a cellular connection

and so need to use a Wi-Fi connection instead, and families who want to all access the Internet while traveling in a car. With a recent poll indicating that 90% of consumers surveyed prefer Internet access to DVD video players in their cars, it appears that mobile personal hotspots are hot.

Antennas come in a variety of formats and are classified as either *directional antennas* (antennas that concentrate the signal in a particular area) or *omnidirectional antennas* (antennas that are equally effective in all directions). Directional antennas have a farther range than omnidirectional antennas, but have a more limited delivery area. The strength of an antenna is measured in *decibels* (*dB*). For applications where a large Wi-Fi coverage area is needed (such as in a large business or a hotel), high-gain outdoor antennas can be used (in conjunction with outdoor range extenders and access points, if needed) to enable the network to span a larger area than the hardware would normally allow.

> **TIP**
>
> When buying an external antenna for a device, be sure they are compatible. For instance, 802.11n MIMO routers with three antennas cannot use a single antenna designed for 802.11g devices.

Multiplexers and Concentrators

High-speed communications lines are expensive and almost always have far greater capacity than a single device can use. Because of this, signals from multiple devices are often combined and sent together to share a single communications medium. A *multiplexer* combines the transmissions from several different devices and sends them as one message. For instance, multiple analog signals can be sent at one time by using multiple frequencies, and multiple optical signals can be sent at one time by using multiple wavelengths. Regardless of how the signals are sent, when the combined signal reaches its destination, the individual messages are separated from one another. Multiplexing is frequently used with fiber-optic cables and other high-capacity media to increase data throughput. For instance, if eight signals are multiplexed and sent together over each fiber in one fiber-optic cable, then the throughput of that cable is increased by a factor of eight.

A *concentrator* is a type of multiplexer that combines multiple messages and sends them via a single transmission medium in such a way that all the individual messages are simultaneously active, instead of being sent as a single combined message. For example, ISPs often use concentrators to combine the signals from their conventional dial-up modem customers to be sent over faster communications connections to their Internet destinations.

> **TIP**
>
> There are also range extenders and antennas designed to extend the range of a cellular network, such as to boost reception inside a home in order to use a cell phone as a primary home telephone.

SUMMARY

WHAT IS A NETWORK?

Communications refers to data being sent from one device to another over a distance—such as over long-distance phone lines, via privately owned cables, or by satellite. A **computer network** is a collection of computers and other hardware devices that are connected together to share hardware, software, and data, as well as to facilitate electronic communications. Computer networks include home networks, business networks, and the Internet.

NETWORKING APPLICATIONS

Some of the oldest networking applications are conventional telephone service and television and radio broadcasting. Many of today's networking applications take place via the Internet. There are, however, a variety of other important business and personal applications that utilize networks. For making phone calls while on the go, **mobile phones**—namely, **cellular (cell)** and **satellite phones**—are used; **dual-mode phones** can utilize more than one network, such as placing calls via both a cellular and Wi-Fi network. There are a variety of **global positioning system (GPS)** and monitoring system applications used by individuals and businesses; many homes today also have a *multimedia network*. To communicate and work with others remotely, **videoconferencing**, *collaborative computing*, and **telecommuting** applications are used; **telesurgery** and other **telemedicine** applications can be used to provide remote medical care.

NETWORK CHARACTERISTICS

Networks can be either **wired networks** (where devices are physically connected) or **wireless networks** (where devices are connected with wireless signals). Wired networks are found in businesses and some homes; wireless networks are becoming very common in both businesses and homes, and are frequently found in public locations to provide a wireless connection to the Internet. Networks can be classified in terms of their *topology* or physical arrangement (such as a **star network**, **bus network**, or **mesh network**). They can also be classified according to their *architecture* (such as *client-server* networks, which consist of *server* devices that provide network services to *client* computers, or *peer-to-peer* (*P2P*) networks, in which the users' computers and the shared peripherals in the network communicate directly with one another instead of through a server). With *Internet peer-to-peer* (*P2P*) *computing*, files are exchanged directly with other peers via the Internet.

Networks can also be classified by size. **Personal area networks** (**PANs**) connect the devices immediately around an individual; **local area networks** (**LANs**) connect geographically close devices, such as within a single building; **metropolitan area networks** (**MANs**) provide Internet access to cities; and **wide area networks** (**WANs**) span relatively wide geographical areas. Networks classified as **intranets** are private networks that implement the infrastructure and standards of the Internet and the World Wide Web, **extranets** are private networks accessible to authorized outsiders, and **virtual private networks** (**VPNs**) are used to transfer private information over a public communications system.

DATA TRANSMISSION CHARACTERISTICS

Data that travels over a network can use **analog signals** (where data is sent as continuous waves) or **digital signals** (where data is coded as 0s and 1s). Data transmissions can also be characterized by their *bandwidth* (the amount of data that can be transferred at one time), whether it uses **serial transmission** or **parallel transmission**, how serial transmissions are timed (namely, *synchronous*, *asynchronous*, or *isochronous transmission*), and whether it transmits in *simplex*, *half-duplex*, or *full-duplex* directions. Data can also be transferred using *circuit switching*, *packet switching*, or *broadcasting*.

NETWORKING MEDIA

Networking media used with wired networks include **twisted-pair**, **coaxial**, and **fiber-optic cable**. Wireless networks typically send messages through the air in the form of *radio signals* and typically use the frequencies in the *radio frequency* (*RF*) band of the *electromagnetic spectrum*. Wireless signals can be sent using **cellular radio** transmissions (which send and receive data via *cell towers* located within designated areas or *cells*), using **microwave stations** and/or **communications satellites** (which send and receive data to and from microwave stations and satellites), or using **infrared** (**IR**) **transmissions** (which send data over short distances as infrared light rays).

Chapter Objective 5:
Name specific types of wired and wireless networking media and explain how they transmit data.

COMMUNICATIONS PROTOCOLS AND NETWORKING STANDARDS

A *communications protocol* determines how the devices on a network communicate; a networking standard typically addresses both how the devices connect and the communications protocols used. The most common communications protocol is **TCP/IP**—the protocol used with the Internet. The most common networking standard for wired networks is **Ethernet (802.3)**, which is available in a variety of speeds, as well as the *Power over Ethernet* (*PoE*) standard, which allows both power and data to be transferred via an Ethernet network. Alternatives for wired networks increasingly being used within the home include the *Phoneline* and *Powerline* standards and the emerging universal *G.hn* standard. *Broadband over powerline* (*BPL*) can be used to deliver Internet via the existing power pole infrastructure.

The most common networking standard for home and business wireless LANs is **Wi-Fi** (**802.11**). Wi-Fi is designed for medium-range wireless transmissions, and there are various versions of the standard that support different speeds and distances. When a network with a greater range is needed, **WiMAX** and **mobile WiMAX** can be used. There are a variety of *cellular standards* used with mobile phones; the newest and fastest are *3G* and *4G standards*. For very short-range applications (such as wirelessly connecting a keyboard to a computer), **Bluetooth** can be used. Other standards used to connect devices wirelessly include **Ultra Wideband** (**UWB**) and **WirelessHD** (**WiHD**), which are most often used to connect home electronic devices; **wireless USB**, which is a wireless version of USB used to connect peripheral devices to a computer; and **TransferJet**, which is used to transfer data between devices as they are touched together.

Chapter Objective 6:
Identify the most common communications protocols and networking standards used with networks today.

NETWORKING HARDWARE

Computer networks require a variety of hardware. Computers usually connect to a network through either a **network adapter** (called a **network interface card** (**NIC**) when it is in the form of an expansion card); a **modem** is used to connect to a network via telephone lines, though many devices that connect a computer to the Internet today are commonly referred to as *modems*. The type of network adapter or modem used depends on the type of computer, connection, and networking media being used.

A **switch** is used to connect multiple (typically wired) devices to a network. **Routers** connect multiple devices together; **wireless routers** typically include a router, switch, and **wireless access point** to connect both wireless and wired devices to a network and the Internet. A **bridge** can be used to connect two LANs or a wired device to a wireless network. **Repeaters**, **range extenders**, and **antennas** can be used to extend the range of a network; *multiplexers* and *concentrators* are most commonly used with larger networks.

Chapter Objective 7:
List several types of networking hardware and explain the purpose of each.

REVIEW ACTIVITIES

KEY TERM MATCHING

a. antenna

b. Bluetooth

c. computer network

d. digital transmission

e. Ethernet

f. global positioning system (GPS)

g. mesh network

h. switch

i. TCP/IP

j. WiMAX

Instructions: Match each key term on the left with the definition on the right that best describes it.

1. _____ A collection of computers and other hardware devices that are connected together to share hardware, software, and data, as well as to communicate electronically with one another.

2. _____ A device used for receiving or sending radio signals; often used to increase the range of a network.

3. _____ A device used to connect multiple devices on a single (typically wired) network; forwards packets to only the intended recipient.

4. _____ A networking standard for very short-range wireless connections; the devices are automatically connected once they get within the allowable range.

5. _____ A network in which there are multiple connections between the devices on the network so that messages can take any of several possible paths.

6. _____ An emerging wireless networking standard that is faster and has a greater range than Wi-Fi.

7. _____ A networking protocol that uses packet switching to facilitate the transmission of messages; the protocol used with the Internet.

8. _____ A system that uses satellites and a receiver to determine the exact geographic location of the receiver.

9. _____ A type of data transmission where the data is represented by 0s and 1s.

10. _____ A widely used wired LAN networking standard.

SELF-QUIZ

Instructions: Circle **T** if the statement is true, **F** if the statement is false, or write the best answer in the space provided. **Answers for the self-quiz are located in the References and Resources Guide at the end of the book.**

1. **T   F**   GPS systems are used only by the government.

2. **T   F**   With serial transmissions, each bit of data is sent individually.

3. **T   F**   The Internet is an example of a LAN.

4. **T   F**   The type of cable used inside most homes for telephone service is twisted-pair wire.

5. **T   F**   A router is a type of modem.

6. With a(n) _____ network topology, all devices are connected in a line to a central cable.

7. A(n) _____ phone can be used with more than one communications network, such as with both a cellular and Wi-Fi network.

8. A small network designed to connect the personal devices for an individual (such as via Bluetooth) is called a(n) _____.

9. A(n) _____ is a network that transfers private information securely over the Internet or other public network.

10. Match each description to its networking application, and write the corresponding number in the blank to the left of the description.

a. _____ To diagnose a patient from a distance.

b. _____ To work for a company in New York when you live in California.

c. _____ To watch a TV show in the living room that is recorded on your computer.

d. _____ To receive telephone calls while you are out shopping.

e. _____ To determine your physical location while hiking in the mountains.

1. Multimedia networking
2. GPS
3. Telemedicine
4. Telecommuting
5. Cellular phone

EXERCISES

1. Match each description to its networking hardware, and write the corresponding number in the blank to the left of each description.

a. _____ A device used to connect network devices via cabling.

b. _____ A device that enables a computer to communicate over telephone lines.

c. _____ A device used to connect wireless devices to a wired network.

d. _____ A device used to amplify signals on a network.

1. Repeater
2. Modem
3. Switch
4. Wireless access point

2. Match each description to the networking standard most suited for this purpose, and write the corresponding number in the blank to the left of each description.

a. _____ To connect a portable computer to a wireless hotspot.

b. _____ To connect a wireless keyboard to a computer.

c. _____ To create a wired home or business network.

d. _____ To wirelessly connect home entertainment devices.

1. Bluetooth
2. Wi-Fi
3. Ultra Wideband (UWB)
4. Ethernet

3. If you need to transfer a 35 MB file from one computer to another over a Fast Ethernet network that supports data transfer rates of 100 Mbps, how long should it take to download the file? What real-world conditions might affect this download time?

4. What is the most common use of the TCP/IP networking standard?

5. Explain the difference between Wi-Fi and Bluetooth, including speed, range, and the purpose of each networking standard.

DISCUSSION QUESTIONS

1. As discussed in the chapter, Internet peer-to-peer (P2P) networking involves sharing files and other resources directly with other computers via the Internet. While some content is legally exchanged via an Internet P2P network, some content (such as movies and music) is exchanged illegally. Should Internet P2P networks be regulated to ensure they are used for only legal activities? Why or why not? If a P2P network set up for legitimate use is used for illegal purposes, should the organization or person who set up the P2P network be responsible? Would you want to use an Internet P2P network?

2. Interference with wireless devices is happening much more often than in the past. For instance, unlicensed walkie-talkies used on TV sets have interfered with police radios, and British air traffic control transmissions have been interrupted by transmissions from nearby baby monitors. If devices that use unlicensed radio frequencies interfere with each other, whose fault is it? The individual for buying multiple products that use the same radio frequency? The manufacturers for not ensuring their products can switch channels as needed to use a free channel? The government for allowing unregulated airwaves? Is there a solution to this problem? Who, if anyone, should be responsible for fixing this problem?

NET

PROJECTS

HOT TOPICS

1. **WiMAX vs. Wi-Fi** As discussed in the chapter, WiMAX and Wi-Fi are both wireless networking standards.

   For this project, research WiMAX and Wi-Fi to determine their current status and the differences between the two standards. Are they designed for the same or different purposes? Explain. How are they being used today? Do you think the standards will coexist in the future, or will one eventually replace the other? At the conclusion of your research, prepare a one-page summary of your findings and opinions and submit it to your instructor.

SHORT ANSWER/ RESEARCH

2. **Unwired** As discussed in the chapter, home networks—particularly wireless home networks— are becoming very common today.

   For this project, suppose that you have a home desktop computer and you are planning to buy a notebook computer to use at home, as well as on the go. You would like to network the two computers wirelessly. Determine the hardware you will need to accomplish this. Create a labeled sketch of the network and a list of the hardware you would need to acquire. Next, research the approximate cost of the hardware to determine the overall cost of the network. Does the cost seem reasonable for the benefits? Would you want to network your home computers in this manner? If you also wanted to use a printer with both computers, would you need any additional hardware? Why or why not? At the conclusion of your research, prepare a one-page summary of your findings and submit it to your instructor, along with your sketch and list of hardware.

HANDS ON

3. **Geocaching** Geocaching is a GPS application that is essentially a form of high-tech hide and seek—someone hides a water-tight container filled with a "treasure" (usually toys or cheap collectors' goodies) and posts the location of the cache (in GPS coordinates) on a geocaching Web site. Other individuals use their GPS equipment to find the cache and then sign a log (if one is included in the cache), take an item from the cache, and put another object into the cache as a replacement.

   For this project, find out how to geocache, including the required equipment and any "rules" or courtesies common among geocachers regarding listing or finding a cache, by searching online or visiting a geocaching Web site (such as **www.geocaching.com**). Next, use a geocaching site to find information about a cache currently hidden close to your city and determine what you would need to do in order to find it. At the conclusion of your research, prepare a one-page summary of your findings and submit it to your instructor.

4. **Net Neutrality and Your ISP** The term *net neutrality* refers to the equality of data as it is transferred over the Internet. For instance, the data from an individual and the data from Microsoft are treated the same. A recent controversy surrounding the cable giant Comcast brought up the possibility of ISPs interfering with the delivery of Internet data. According to complaints by customers, Comcast has been blocking the use of P2P sites like BitTorrent to download movies, music, and other large files. Comcast, like most ISPs, includes a statement in its terms of service that allows it to use tools to "efficiently manage its networks", in order to prevent those customers using a higher than normal level of bandwidth from interfering with the access of other customers. However, the Comcast issue was considered by many to be a blatant net neutrality issue—blocking access to multimedia from sources other than its own cable sources. Do you think the actions taken by Comcast were ethical? Does an ISP have a right to block selected Internet traffic? Why or why not? Was there a more ethical way Comcast could have handled the problem of some users consuming a higher than normal level of bandwidth?

For this project, form an opinion about the ethical ramifications of ISPs blocking selected Internet traffic and be prepared to discuss your position (in class, via an online class discussion group, in a class chat room, or via a class blog, depending on your instructor's directions). You may also be asked to write a short paper expressing your opinion.

ETHICS IN ACTION

5. **Wired Home Network** If you have two or more computers at home and want to share files, an Internet connection, or a printer, you will need to set up a home network. Although a wireless network is an option, wired networks still exist and new options for wired networks are emerging.

For this project, suppose that you want to set up a wired home network. Create a scenario (real or fictitious) that describes the number of computers and other devices involved, where each item is located, and the tasks for which the network will be used. Select a wired networking option (such as Ethernet, Powerline, or Phoneline) and determine the steps and equipment necessary to implement that network for your scenario. Be sure to include the cost of the necessary hardware and how the network would be physically installed. Share your findings (including a diagram of your proposed network) with your class in the form of a presentation. The presentation should not exceed 10 minutes and should make use of one or more presentation aids, such as the chalkboard, handouts, overhead transparencies, or a computer-based slide presentation (your instructor may provide additional requirements). You may also be asked to submit a summary of the presentation to your instructor.

PRESENTATION/ DEMONSTRATION

Instructions: Go to the Chapter 7 page at **www.cengage.com/computerconcepts/np/uc13** to work the following Web Activities.

6. **Interactive Activities** Work the interactive **Crossword Puzzle**, watch the **Video Podcasts** and **Online Videos**, and explore the **Further Exploration** links associated with this chapter.

If you have a SAM user profile, you may have access to hands-on instruction, practice, and assessment of the skills covered in this chapter. Check with your instructor for instructions and the correct URL/Web site to access those assignments.

7. **Student Edition Labs** Work the following interactive **Student Edition Labs.**
   - ➤ **Networking Basics** ➤ **Wireless Networking**

8. **Test Yourself** Review the **Online Study Guide** for this chapter, then test your knowledge of the terms and concepts covered in this chapter by completing the **Key Term Matching** exercise, the **Self-Quiz**, the **Exercises**, and the **Practice Test.**

WEB ACTIVITIES

SAM

Student Edition Labs

chapter 8

The Internet and the World Wide Web

After completing this chapter, you will be able to do the following:

1. Discuss how the Internet evolved and what it is like today.

2. Identify the various types of individuals, companies, and organizations involved in the Internet community and explain their purposes.

3. Describe device and connection options for connecting to the Internet, as well as some considerations to keep in mind when selecting an ISP.

4. Understand how to search effectively for information on the Internet and how to cite Internet resources properly.

5. List several ways to communicate over the Internet, in addition to e-mail.

6. List several useful activities that can be performed via the Web.

7. Discuss censorship and privacy, and how they are related to Internet use.

outline

OVERVIEW

With the prominence of the Internet in our personal and professional lives today, it is hard to believe that there was a time not too long ago that few people had even heard of the Internet, let alone used it. But technology is continually evolving and, in fact, it is only relatively recently that it has evolved enough to allow the use of multimedia applications—such as downloading music and movies, watching TV and videos, and playing multimedia interactive games—over the Internet to become everyday activities. Today, the Internet and the World Wide Web are household words, and, in many ways, they have redefined how people think about computers, communications, and the availability of news and information.

Despite the popularity of the Internet, however, many users cannot answer some important basic questions about it. What makes up the Internet? Is it the same thing as the World Wide Web? How did the Internet begin, and where is it heading? How can the Internet be used to find specific information? This chapter addresses these types of questions and more.

Chapter 8 begins with a discussion of the evolution of the Internet, followed by a look at the many individuals, companies, and organizations that make up the Internet community. Next, the chapter covers different options for connecting to the Internet, including the types of devices, Internet connections, and ISPs that are available today. Then, one of the most important Internet skills you should acquire—efficient Internet searching—is discussed. To help you appreciate the wide spectrum of resources and activities available over the Internet, we also take a brief look at some of the most common applications available via the Internet. The chapter closes with a discussion of a few of the important societal issues that apply to Internet use. ■

EVOLUTION OF THE INTERNET

The **Internet** is a worldwide collection of separate, but interconnected, networks accessed daily by millions of people using a variety of devices to obtain information, disseminate information, access entertainment, or communicate with others. While *Internet* has become a household word only during the past two decades or so, it has actually operated in one form or another for much longer than that.

From ARPANET to Internet2

The roots of the Internet began with an experimental project called *ARPANET*. The Internet we know today is the result of the evolution of ARPANET and the creation of the *World Wide Web* (WWW).

> **Internet.** The largest and most well-known computer network, linking millions of computers all over the world.

ARPANET

The U.S. Department of Defense *Advanced Research Projects Agency* (*ARPA*) created **ARPANET** in 1969. One objective of the ARPANET project was to create a computer network that would allow researchers located in different places to communicate with each other. Another objective was to build a computer network capable of sending or receiving data over a variety of paths to ensure that network communications could continue even if part of the network was destroyed, such as in a nuclear attack or by a natural disaster.

Initially, ARPANET connected four supercomputers and enabled researchers at a few dozen academic institutions to communicate with each other and with government agencies. As the project grew during the next decade, students were granted access to ARPANET as hundreds of college and university networks were connected to it. These networks consisted of a mixture of different computers so, over the years, protocols were developed for tying this mix of computers and networks together, for transferring data over the network, and for ensuring that data was transferred intact. Additional networks soon connected to ARPANET, and this *internet*—or network of networks—eventually evolved into the present day Internet.

The Internet infrastructure today can be used for a variety of purposes, such as researching topics of interest; exchanging e-mail and instant messages; participating in videoconferences and making telephone calls; downloading software, music, and movies; purchasing goods and services; watching TV and video online; accessing computers remotely; and sharing files with others. Most of these activities are available through the primary Internet resource—the *World Wide Web* (*WWW*).

The World Wide Web

In its early years, the Internet was used primarily by the government, scientists, and educational institutions. Despite its popularity in academia and with government researchers, the Internet went virtually unnoticed by the public and the business community for over two decades because 1) it required a computer and 2) it was hard to use (see the left image in Figure 8-1). As always, however, computer and networking technology improved and new applications quickly followed. Then, in 1989, a researcher named *Tim Berners-Lee* proposed the idea of the **World Wide Web** (**WWW**). He envisioned the World Wide Web as a way to organize information in the form of pages linked together through selectable text or images (today's hyperlinks) on the screen. Although the introduction of Web pages did not replace all other Internet resources (such as e-mail and collections of downloadable files), it became a popular way for researchers to provide written information to others.

In 1993, a group of professors and students at the University of Illinois *National Center for Supercomputing Applications* (*NCSA*) released the *Mosaic* Web browser. Soon after, use

FIGURE 8-1

Using the Internet: Back in the "old days" versus now.

EARLY 1990s
Even at the beginning of the 1990s, using the Internet for most people meant learning how to work with a cryptic sequence of commands. Virtually all information was text-based.

TODAY
Today's Web organizes much of the Internet's content into easy-to-read pages that can contain text, graphics, animation, video, and interactive content that users access via hyperlinks.

> **ARPANET.** The predecessor of the Internet, named after the Advanced Research Projects Agency (ARPA), which sponsored its development.
> **World Wide Web (WWW).** The collection of Web pages available through the Internet.

of the World Wide Web began to increase dramatically because Mosaic's graphical user interface (GUI) and its ability to display images on Web pages made using the World Wide Web both easier and more fun than in the past. Today's Web pages are a true multimedia, interactive, experience (see the right image in Figure 8-1). They can contain text, graphics, animation, sound, video, and three-dimensional virtual reality objects.

A growing number of today's Web-based applications and services are referred to as *Web 2.0* applications. Although there is no precise definition, Web 2.0 generally refers to applications and services that use the Web as a platform to deliver rich applications that enable people to collaborate, socialize, and share information online. Some Web 2.0 applications (such as cloud computing) have been discussed in previous chapters; others (such as *social networking sites, RSS feeds, podcasts, blogs*, and *wikis*) are covered later in this chapter.

Although the Web is only part of the Internet, it is by far the most widely used part. Today, most companies regard their use of the Internet and their World Wide Web presence as indispensable competitive business tools, and many individuals view the Internet—and especially the Web—as a vital research, communications, and entertainment medium.

One remarkable characteristic of both the Internet and World Wide Web is that they are not owned by any person or business, and no single person, business, or organization is in charge. Web pages are developed by individuals and organizations, and are hosted on Web servers owned by individuals, schools, businesses, or other entities. Each network connected to the Internet is privately owned and managed individually by that network's administrator, and the primary infrastructure that makes up the *Internet backbone* is typically owned by communications companies, such as telephone and cable companies. In addition, the computers and other devices used to access the Internet belong to individuals or organizations. So, while individual components of the Internet are owned by individuals and organizations, the Internet as a whole has no owner or network administrator. The closest the Internet comes to having a governing body is a group of organizations that are involved with issues such as establishing the protocols used on the Internet, making recommendations for changes, and encouraging cooperation between and coordinating communications among the networks connected to the Internet.

ASK THE EXPERT

Dave Weick, Senior Vice President, Chief Information Officer, McDonald's Corporation

How important is it for a business to have a Web site today if it doesn't sell products and services online?

For McDonald's, our online presence is about extending the McDonald's experience to our customers. Mcdonalds.com allows our customers another channel to engage with our brand without ever entering a restaurant. Through our Web site, customers can find promotions and nutritional information on all of our products. On the Open for Discussion blog, customers are talking about McDonald's corporate sustainability efforts. Happymeal.com is connecting kids across the globe in fun, interactive, and uniquely McDonald's ways. Finally, customers can download podcasts about food safety.

For McDonald's, our Web site allows us the opportunity to connect with our customers on topics that are important to them and in the way that they want to connect. In addition, in some parts of the world you can order off the menu located on our Web site and have it delivered to your door. As our customers demand even more convenience and control over the "ordering process," this may become even more prevalent in the future.

Internet2

Internet2 is a consortium of researchers, educators, and technology leaders from industry, government, and the international community that is dedicated to the development of revolutionary Internet technologies. Internet2 uses high-performance networks linking over 200 member institutions to deploy and test new network applications and capabilities. It is important to realize, however, that the Internet2 network is not a new network designed to eventually replace the Internet—it is simply a research and development tool to help develop technologies that ensure the Internet in the future can handle tomorrow's applications. Much of Internet2 research is focused on speed. For instance, the *Internet2 Land Speed Record* is an ongoing contest for the highest-bandwidth end-to-end network. The current record is an average speed of 9.08 Gbps while transferring 20.42 TB of data across about 30,000 miles of network.

The Internet Community Today

The Internet community today consists of individuals, businesses, and a variety of organizations located throughout the world. Virtually anyone with a computer or other Web-enabled device can be part of the Internet, either as a user or as a supplier of information or services. Most members of the Internet community fall into one or more of the following groups.

Users

Users are people who use the Internet to retrieve content or perform online activities, such as to look up a telephone number, read the day's news headlines or top stories, browse through an online catalog, make an online purchase, download a music file, watch an online video, make a phone call, or send an e-mail message. According to the Pew Internet & American Life Project, approximately 75% of the United States population are Internet users, using the Internet at work, home, school, or another location. The availability of low-cost computers, low-cost or free Internet access (such as at libraries, school, and other public locations), and bundled pricing for obtaining Internet service in conjunction with telephone and/or television service has helped Internet use begin to approach the popularity and widespread use of telephones and TVs.

Internet Service Providers (ISPs)

Internet service providers (**ISPs**) are businesses or other organizations (see some examples in Figure 8-2) that provide Internet access to others, typically for a fee. ISPs (sometimes called *wireless ISPs* or *WISPs* when referring to ISPs that offer service via a wireless network) include most communications and media companies, such as conventional and mobile phone companies, cable providers, and satellite providers. Some ISPs (such as cable and cellular phone companies) offer Internet service over their private networks; other ISPs provide Internet service over the regular telephone lines or the airwaves. While many ISPs (such as Road Runner and EarthLink) provide service nationwide, others provide service to a more limited geographical area. Regardless of their delivery method and geographical coverage, ISPs are the onramp to the Internet, providing their subscribers with access to the World Wide Web, e-mail, and other Internet resources. In addition to Internet access, some ISPs provide proprietary online services available only to their subscribers. A later section of this chapter covers ISPs in more detail, including factors to consider when selecting an ISP.

ⓥ FIGURE 8-2

Companies that provide Internet access today include telephone, cable, and satellite companies.

Internet Content Providers

Internet content providers supply the information that is available through the Internet. Internet content providers can be commercial businesses, nonprofit organizations, educational institutions, individuals, and more. Some examples of Internet content providers are listed next.

> ➤ A photographer who posts samples of her best work on a Web page.

> ➤ An individual who publishes his opinion on various subjects to an online journal or *blog*.

> **Internet service provider (ISP).** A business or other organization that provides Internet access to others, typically for a fee. > **Internet content provider.** A person or an organization that provides Internet content.

> ➤ A software company that creates a Web site to provide product information and software downloads.

> ➤ A national news organization that maintains an online site to provide up-to-the-minute news, feature stories, and video clips.

> ➤ A television network that develops a site for its TV shows, including episode summaries, cast information, and links to watch past episodes online.

Application Service Providers (ASPs) and Web Services

Application service providers (**ASPs**) are companies that manage and distribute Web-based software services to customers over the Internet. Instead of providing access to the Internet like ISPs do, ASPs provide access to software applications via the Internet. In essence, ASPs rent access to software programs to companies or individuals—typically, customers pay a monthly or yearly fee to use each application. As discussed in Chapter 6, this software can be called *Web-based software, Software as a Service* (*SaaS*), and *cloudware*. Common ASP applications for businesses include office suites, collaboration and communications software, accounting programs, and e-commerce software.

One type of self-contained business application designed to work over the Internet or a company network is a **Web service**. A Web service can be added to Web pages to provide a service that would otherwise not be feasible (such as the inclusion of mapping information on a Web site or in a Web application using Microsoft's *MapPoint .NET Web service*). A Web service can also be used to provide a service via a user's computer and the Internet. For instance, the *FedEx QuickShip Web service* allows users to create a shipment to any Microsoft Outlook contact from within Microsoft Outlook (by right-clicking the contact's name, as shown in Figure 8-3, or using the FedEx QuickShip toolbar displayed in Microsoft Outlook); the toolbar can also be used to track packages, order pickups, check rates, and more. It is important to realize that Web services are not stand-alone applications and, therefore, do not have a user interface—they are simply a standardized way of allowing different applications and computers to share data and processes via a network so they can work together with other Web services and be used with many different computer systems. A company that provides Web services is sometimes referred to as a *Web services provider*.

FIGURE 8-3

Web services. Once downloaded and installed, this Web service allows users to create and manage FedEx shipments from within Microsoft Outlook.

The QuickShip toolbar can be used for a variety of shipping tasks.

Right-click a contact to create a shipment to that individual.

Infrastructure Companies

Infrastructure companies are the enterprises that own or operate the paths or "roadways" along which Internet data travels, such as the Internet backbone and the communications networks connected to it. Examples of infrastructure companies include conventional and mobile phone companies, cable companies, and satellite Internet providers.

Hardware and Software Companies

A wide variety of hardware and software companies make and distribute the products used with the Internet and Internet activities. For example, companies that create or sell the software used in conjunction with the Internet (such as Web browsers, e-mail programs, e-commerce

---

> **Application service provider (ASP).** A company that manages and distributes software-based services over the Internet. > **Web service.** A self-contained business application that operates over the Internet.

and multimedia software, and Web development tools) fall into this category. So, too, do the companies that make the hardware (network adapters, modems, cables, routers, servers, computers, and mobile phones, for instance) that is used with the Internet.

The Government and Other Organizations

Many organizations influence the Internet and its uses. Governments have the most visible impact; their laws can limit both the information made available via Web servers located in a particular country and the access individuals residing in that country have to the Internet. For example, in France, it is illegal to sell items or post online content related to racist groups or activities; in China there are tight controls imposed on what information is published on Web servers located in China, as well as on the information available to its citizens. And in the United States, anything illegal offline (illegal drugs, child pornography, and so forth) is illegal online.

Legal rulings also can have a large impact on the communications industry in general. For example, the 1968 *Carterfone Decision* allowed companies other than AT&T to utilize the AT&T infrastructure and the 1996 *Telecommunications Act* deregulated the entire communications industry so that telephone companies, cable TV and satellite operators, and firms in other segments of the industry were free to enter each other's markets. A petition to apply the Carterfone Decision to wireless networks in order to allow open access to wireless networks so that any phone can be used with any network is under consideration now by the Federal Communications Commission (FCC). In addition to making these types of decisions, the FCC also greatly influences the communications industry through its ability to allocate radio frequencies (as discussed in Chapter 7) and to implement policies and regulations related to interstate and international communications via radio, television, wire, satellite, and cable. The ability of the government to approve or block potential mergers between communications companies and to break apart companies based on antitrust law to prevent new monopolies also impacts the Internet and communications industry.

Key Internet organizations are responsible for many aspects of the Internet. For example, the *Internet Society* (*ISOC*) provides leadership in addressing issues that may impact the future of the Internet. It also oversees the groups responsible for Internet infrastructure standards, such as determining the protocols that can be used and how Internet addresses are constructed. *ICANN* (*Internet Corporation for Assigned Names and Numbers*) coordinates activities related to the Internet's naming system, such as IP address allocation and domain name management. The *World Wide Web Consortium* (*W3C*) is a group of over 450 organizations dedicated to developing new protocols and specifications to promote the evolution of the Web and to ensure its interoperability. In addition, many colleges and universities support Internet research and manage blocks of the Internet's resources.

Myths About the Internet

Because the Internet is so unique in the history of the world—and its content and applications keep evolving—several widespread myths about it have surfaced.

Myth 1: The Internet Is Free

This myth stems from the fact that there has traditionally been no cost associated with accessing online content—such as news and product information—or with e-mail exchange, other than what the Internet users pay their ISPs for Internet access. And many people—such as students, employees, and consumers who opt for free Internet service or use free access available at public libraries or other public locations—pay nothing for Internet access. Yet it should also be obvious that someone, somewhere, has to pay to keep the Internet up and running.

Businesses, schools, public libraries, and most home users pay Internet service providers flat monthly fees to connect to the Internet. In addition, businesses, schools, libraries, and other large organizations might have to lease high-capacity communications lines (such as from a telephone company) to support their high level of Internet traffic.

Mobile users that want Internet access while on the go typically pay hotspot providers or mobile phone providers for this access. ISPs, phone companies, cable companies, and other organizations that own part of the Internet infrastructure pay to keep their parts of the Internet running smoothly. ISPs also pay software and hardware companies for the resources they need to support their subscribers. Eventually, most of these costs are passed along to end users through ISP fees. ISPs that offer free Internet access typically obtain revenue by selling on-screen ads that display on the screen when the service is being used.

Another reason that the idea the Internet is free is a myth is the growing trend of subscription or per-use fees to access Web-based resources. For instance, downloadable music and movies are very common today (see Figure 8-4) and some journal or newspaper articles require a fee to view them online. In fact, some newspapers and magazines have moved entirely online and most charge a subscription fee to view the level of content that was previously published in a print version. In lieu of a mandatory fee, some Web sites request a donation for use of the site. Many experts expect the use of fee-based Internet content to continue to grow at a rapid pace.

FIGURE 8-4
Fee-based Web content. The use of fee-based Web content, such as downloadable movies and music, is growing.

Myth 2: Someone Controls the Internet

As already discussed, no single group or organization controls the Internet. Governments in each country have the power to regulate the content and use of the Internet within their borders, as allowed by their laws. However, legislators often face serious obstacles getting legislation passed into law—let alone getting it enforced. Making governmental control even harder is the "bombproof" design of the Internet itself. If a government tries to block access to or from a specific country or Web site, for example, users can use a third party (such as an individual located in another country or a different Web site) to circumvent the block. This occurred recently in Iran when the Iranian government blocked access to social networking sites after the 2009 elections—some Iranian citizens were able to send and read Twitter updates via third-party sites.

Myth 3: The Internet and the World Wide Web Are Identical

Since you can now use a Web browser to access most of the Internet's resources, many people think the Internet and the Web are the same thing. Even though in everyday use many people use the terms *Internet* and *Web* interchangeably, they are not the same thing. Technically, the Internet is the physical network, and the Web is the collection of Web pages accessible over the Internet. A majority of Internet activities today take place via Web pages, but there are Internet resources other than the Web that are not accessed via a Web browser. For instance, files can be uploaded and downloaded using an *FTP* (*File Transfer Protocol*) *program* and conventional e-mail can be accessed using an e-mail program.

GETTING SET UP TO USE THE INTERNET

Getting set up to use the Internet typically involves three decisions—determining the type of device you will use to access the Internet, deciding which type of connection is desired, and selecting the Internet service provider to be used. Once these determinations have been made, your computer can be set up to access the Internet.

Type of Device

The Internet today can be accessed using a variety of devices. The type of device used depends on a combination of factors, such as the devices available to you, if you need

NET

INSIDE THE INDUSTRY

ISP Bandwidth Limits

Internet traffic has increased tremendously recently as individuals are watching TV and videos online, downloading music and movies, playing online multiplayer gaming, using online backup services, and otherwise performing high-bandwidth activities (see the accompanying illustration). This has created the issue of ISPs potentially running out of bandwidth available for customers, resulting in outages or delays. In response, some ISPs have, at times, blocked selected traffic to and from their customers, such as cable giant Comcast blocking the use of P2P sites like BitTorrent that is often used to download movies, music, and other large files. Other ISPs are slowing down traffic to and from heavy users during peak Internet usage periods or experimenting with *bandwidth caps* as Internet usage management tools. For instance, Comcast is currently testing slowing down traffic to and from heavy users during peak periods, Time Warner Cable is testing tiered pricing based on usage in certain areas, and AT&T is testing bandwidth caps for new customers in certain areas. With a bandwidth cap, customers either temporarily lose Internet access or are charged an additional fee if they exceed their download limit (often 5 GB to 150 GB per month).

Comcast, like most ISPs, includes a statement in its terms of service agreement that allows it to use tools to "efficiently manage its networks" in order to prevent customers from using a higher than normal level of bandwidth. However, many considered Comcast's blocking of P2P content to be a blatant *net neutrality* issue since Comcast was blocking access to multimedia from a source other than its own cable source and the Internet is designed for all content to be treated equally. There are also concerns about bandwidth caps and that overcharges will grow to an unreasonable level—particularly by cable companies and other providers who may want to stifle Internet multimedia to protect their TV advertising revenues. To protect against this, the *Broadband Internet Fairness Act* has been introduced in the U.S. to require broadband providers to submit tiered pricing plans to the FTC to ensure they are not unreasonable or discriminatory. While it is unclear at this time as to the outcome of this bill, as well as whether or not bandwidth caps will be part of the future of home Internet service, it is clear that, as Internet usage by the average consumer continues to grow, the issue of a finite amount of Internet bandwidth versus an increasing demand for online multimedia content will remain.

Online TV, videos, and other multimedia content require a great deal of bandwidth.

access just at home or while on the go, and what types of Internet content you want to access. Some possible devices are shown in Figure 8-5 and discussed next.

Personal Computers

Most users who have access to a personal computer (such as a desktop or notebook computer) at home, work, or school will use it to access the Internet. One advantage of using personal computers for Internet access is that they have relatively large screens for viewing Internet content, and they typically have a full keyboard for easier data entry. They can also be used to view or otherwise access virtually any Web page content, such as graphics, animation, music files, games, and video clips. In addition, they typically have a large hard drive and are connected to a printer so Web pages, e-mail messages, and downloaded files can be saved and/or printed easily.

Mobile Phones

Mobile phones are increasingly being used to view Web page content, exchange e-mail and instant messages, and download music and other online content. In fact, mobile Web

PERSONAL COMPUTERS   **MOBILE PHONES**   **TELEVISIONS**

use—or *wireless Web*, as it is sometimes called—is one of the fastest growing uses of the Internet today. While mobile phones are convenient to use on the go, they typically have a relatively small display screen. Some devices include a built-in or sliding keyboard for easier data entry; others utilize pen or touch input instead.

FIGURE 8-5
A variety of devices can be used to access the Internet.

Gaming Devices and Televisions

Another option is using a gaming device (such as a gaming console or handheld gaming device) to access Web content, in addition to using that device to play games. For instance, the Sony PlayStation 3, Sony PSP, Nintendo Wii, and Nintendo DSi all have Web browsers that can be used to access Web content. In addition to gaming consoles that can connect to television sets to display Internet content, an emerging option is *broadband-enabled TVs* that have Internet capabilities built-in in order to display Web pages and other Web content (such as the weather, stock quote, and other information displayed at the bottom of the TV screen shown in Figure 8-5) without any additional hardware.

Type of Connection and Internet Access

In order to use the Internet, your computer needs to be connected to it. Typically, this occurs by connecting the computer or other device you are using to a computer or a network (usually belonging to your ISP, school, or employer) that is connected continually to the Internet.

As discussed in Chapter 7, there are a variety of wired and wireless ways to connect to another device. Most types of connections today are *broadband* or high-speed connections. In fact, more than 60% of all home Internet connections in the U.S. are broadband connections, and that percentage is expected to climb to 77% by 2012, according to a recent Gartner study. As applications requiring high-speed connections continue to grow in popularity, access to broadband Internet speeds are needed in order to take full advantage of these applications. For instance, high-definition television, video-on-demand (VOD), and other multimedia applications all benefit from fast broadband connections (see Figure 8-6). For a look at a topic related to the increased use of multimedia Internet content—*ISP bandwidth limits*—see the Inside the Industry box.

The difference between *dial-up* and *direct* Internet connections are discussed next, followed by an overview of the most common types of Internet connections used for personal use today; these types of Internet connections are also summarized in Figure 8-7. Many providers today offer bundles (such as cable TV, telephone, and Internet service) to lower an individual's overall total cost for the services. Additional home Internet alternatives—such

FIGURE 8-6
Length of time to download a 1.5 GB movie using different home Internet options.

NET

TYPE OF INTERNET CONNECTION	AVAILABILITY	APPROXIMATE MAXIMUM SPEED*	APPROXIMATE MONTHLY PRICE
Conventional dial-up	Anywhere there is telephone service	56 Kbps	Free–$20
Cable	Virtually anywhere cable TV service is available	5–20 Mbps	$40–60
DSL	Within 3 miles of a switching station that supports DSL	1–7 Mbps	$20–40
Satellite	Anywhere there is a clear view to the southern sky and where a satellite dish can be mounted and receive a signal	1–1.5 Mbps	$60–80
Fixed wireless	Selected areas where service is available	1–2 Mbps	$40–60
Broadband over fiber (BoF)	Anywhere fiber has been installed to the building	10–50 Mbps	$50–145
Mobile wireless (3G)	Virtually anywhere cellular phone service is available	700 Kbps–1.7 Mbps	Varies greatly; often bundled with mobile phone service

* Download speed; most connections have slower upload speeds.

FIGURE 8-7

Typical home Internet connection options.

TIP

Sign up for and set up your computer to use a free dial-up Internet account (such as from NetZero) to have a backup Internet service if your regular Internet service ever goes down.

as the emerging *broadband over power lines* (*BPL*) standard discussed in Chapter 7, which allows people to connect to the Internet through their power outlets—will likely be available in the future.

Dial-Up vs. Direct Connections

While some Internet connections are *dial-up connections* (in which your computer dials up and connects to your ISP's computer only when needed), most are *direct* (or *always-on*) *connections* (in which you have a continuous connection to your ISP).

Dial-up connections usually work over standard telephone lines. To connect to the Internet, your computer dials its modem and then connects to a modem attached to a computer belonging to your ISP via the telephone lines. While you are connected to your ISP, your computer can access Internet resources. To end your Internet session, you disconnect from your ISP. One advantage of a dial-up connection is security. Since you are not continually connected to the Internet, it is much less likely that anyone (such as a *hacker*, as discussed in Chapter 9) will gain access to your computer via the Internet, either to access the data located on your computer or, more commonly, to use your computer in some type of illegal or unethical manner. However, dial-up connections are much slower than other types of connections; they are also inconvenient, since you have to instruct your computer to dial up your ISP every time you want to connect to the Internet. Also, your telephone line will be tied up while you are accessing the Internet, unless you have a second phone line. The most common type of dial-up Internet service is *conventional dial-up*.

Direct connections keep you continually connected to your provider and, therefore, continually connected to the Internet. With a direct connection (such as *cable*, *DSL*, *satellite*, or *fixed wireless*), you access the Internet simply by opening a Web browser, such as Internet Explorer, Chrome, or Firefox. Direct Internet connections are typically broadband connections, are commonly used in homes and businesses, and are often connected to a LAN to share the Internet connection with multiple devices within the home or business. Because direct connections keep your computer connected to the Internet at all times (as long as your computer is powered up), it is important to protect your computer from unauthorized access or hackers. Consequently, all computers with a direct Internet connection should use a *firewall* program. Firewall programs block access to a computer from outside computers and enable each user to specify which programs on his or her computer are allowed to have access to the Internet. Firewalls, as well as other network and Internet security precautions, are discussed in more detail in Chapter 9.

>**Dial-up connection.** A type of Internet connection in which the computer or other device must dial up and connect to a service provider's computer via telephone lines before being connected to the Internet. >**Direct connection.** A type of Internet connection in which the computer or other device is connected to the Internet continually.

Conventional Dial-Up

Conventional dial-up Internet access uses a conventional dial-up modem connected to a standard telephone jack with regular twisted-pair telephone cabling. Conventional dial-up Internet service is most often used with home computers for users who don't need, or do not want to pay for, broadband Internet service. Advantages include inexpensive hardware, ease of setup and use, and widespread availability. The primary disadvantage is slow connection speed, since conventional dial-up modems connect to the Internet at a maximum of 56 Kbps.

Cable

Cable Internet access uses a direct connection and is the most widely used type of home broadband connection, with over half of the home broadband market. Cable connections are very fast (typically between 5 and 20 Mbps, though some faster services are available for a premium fee) and are available wherever cable TV access is available, provided the local cable provider supports Internet access. Consequently, cable Internet is not widely available in rural areas. Cable Internet service requires a cable modem.

DSL

DSL (Digital Subscriber Line) Internet access is a type of direct connection that transmits via standard telephone lines, but it does not tie up your telephone line. DSL requires a DSL modem and is available only to users who are relatively close (within three miles) to a telephone switching station and who have telephone lines capable of handling DSL. DSL speeds are about one-half of cable speeds and the speed of the connection degrades as the distance between the modem and the switching station gets closer and closer to the three-mile limit. Consequently, DSL is usually only available in urban areas. Download speeds are typically between 1 and 7 Mbps.

Satellite

Satellite Internet access uses a direct connection, but is slower and more expensive than cable or DSL access (typically up to around 1.5 Mbps). However, it is often the only broadband option for rural areas. In addition to a satellite modem, it requires a *transceiver* satellite dish mounted outside the home or building to receive and transmit data to and from the satellites being used. Installation requires an unobstructed view of the southern sky (to have a clear line of sight between the transceiver and appropriate satellite), and performance might degrade or stop altogether during very heavy rain or snowstorms.

FIGURE 8-8
WiMAX towers. This tower is installed at the peak of Whistler Mountain in British Columbia.

Fixed Wireless

Fixed wireless Internet access uses a direct connection and is similar to satellite Internet in that it uses wireless signals, but it uses radio transmission towers (either stand-alone towers like the one shown in Figure 8-8 or transmitters placed on existing cell phone towers) instead of satellites. Fixed wireless Internet access requires a modem and, sometimes, an outside-mounted transceiver. Fixed wireless companies typically use Wi-Fi and/or WiMAX technology to broadcast the wireless signals to customers. Speeds are typically up to about 2 Mbps, though the speed depends somewhat on the distance between the tower and the customer, the types and number of obstacles in the path, and the type and speed of the connection between the wireless transmitter and the Internet.

Broadband over Fiber (BoF)

A new type of direct connection available to homes and businesses in areas where there is fiber-optic cabling available all the way to the building is generically called **broadband over fiber (BoF)** or **fiber-to-the-premises (FTTP) Internet access**, with other names being used by individual providers, such as Verizon's *fiber-optic service* (*FiOS*). These fiber-optic networks are most often installed by telephone companies in order to upgrade their overall infrastructures and, where installed, are used to deliver telephone and TV service, in addition to Internet service. However, some cities are creating fiber-optic MANs that include connections to businesses and homes to provide very fast broadband Internet services. Where available, download speeds for BoF service typically range between 10 Mbps and 50 Mbps and the cost varies accordingly. BoF requires a special networking terminal installed at the building to convert the optical signals into electrical signals that can be sent to a computer or over a LAN.

Mobile Wireless

Mobile wireless Internet access is the type of direct connection most commonly used with mobile phones and other mobile devices to keep them connected to the Internet via a mobile phone network, even as they are carried from place to place. Some mobile wireless services can be used with notebook computers and other computers as well. For instance, AT&T's DataConnect service allows you to access the Internet on your notebook or netbook computer via the AT&T wireless network, and some mobile phones can be connected to a notebook computer to act as a modem to connect that computer to the mobile phone's wireless network. As discussed in Chapter 7, the speed of mobile wireless depends on the cellular standard being used—3G networks typically have speeds between 1 and 1.7 Mbps. Costs for mobile wireless Internet access vary widely, with some packages including unlimited Internet, some charging by the number of minutes of Internet use, and some charging by the amount of data transferred.

Wi-Fi Hotspots

While not typically used for primary Internet access, another option for Internet access is a **Wi-Fi hotspot**—a location with a direct Internet connection and a wireless access point that allows users to connect wirelessly (via Wi-Fi) to the hotspot to use its Internet connection (see Figure 8-9). Public Wi-Fi hotpots are widely available

V FIGURE 8-9

Wi-Fi hotspots.
Hotspots are used to wirelessly connect to the Internet via the Internet connection belonging to a business, city, school, or other organization.

COFFEEHOUSES AND OTHER PUBLIC LOCATIONS
Often fee-based, though some are available for free.

HOSPITALS, BUSINESSES, AND OTHER ORGANIZATIONS
Usually designed for employees but are sometimes also available free to visitors.

COLLEGE CAMPUSES
Usually designed for students and faculty; sometimes used directly in class for student assignments, as shown here.

> **Broadband over fiber (BoF) Internet access.** Very fast, direct Internet access via fiber-optic networks; also referred to as **fiber-to-the-premises (FTTP) Internet access.** >**Mobile wireless Internet access.** Internet access via a mobile phone network. >**Wi-Fi hotspot.** A location that provides wireless Internet access to the public.

today, such as at many coffeehouses and restaurants; at hotels, airports, and other locations frequented by business travelers; and in or nearby public areas such as libraries, subway stations, and parks. Some public Wi-Fi hotspots are free; others charge per hour, per day, or on a subscription basis. College campuses also typically have Wi-Fi hotspots to provide Internet access to students; many businesses and other organizations have Wi-Fi hotspots for use by employees in their offices, as well as by employees and guests in conference rooms, waiting rooms, lunchrooms, and other onsite locations.

FURTHER EXPLORATION   Go

Go to the Chapter 8 page at **www.cengage.com/ computerconcepts/np/uc13** for links to information about types of Internet access and ISPs.

Selecting an ISP and Setting Up Your Computer

Once the type of Internet access to be used is determined, the final steps to getting connected to the Internet are selecting an ISP and setting up your system. While this discussion is geared primarily toward a home Internet connection used with a personal computer, some of the concepts apply to business or mobile users as well.

Selecting an ISP

The type of device used (such as a personal computer or mobile phone), the type of Internet connection and service desired (such as cable Internet or mobile wireless), and your geographical location (such as metropolitan or rural) will likely determine your ISP options. The pricing and services available through any two ISPs will probably differ somewhat, based on the speed of the service, as well as other services available. The questions listed in Figure 8-10 can help you narrow your ISP choices and determine the questions you want answered before you decide on an ISP. A growing trend is for ISPs to offer a number of *tiers*; that is, different levels (speeds) of service for different prices so users requiring faster service can get it, but at a higher price.

FIGURE 8-10
Choosing an ISP.
Some questions to ask before making your final selection.

Setting Up Your Computer

The specific steps for setting up your computer to use your selected type of Internet connection depend on the type of device, the type of connection, and the ISP you have chosen to use. Some types of Internet connections, such as satellite and broadband over fiber, require professional installation, after which you will be online; with other types, you can install the necessary hardware (typically a modem that connects to your computer or wireless router via an Ethernet cable) yourself. You will usually need to select a username and your desired payment method at some point during the ordering or setup process. This username is needed to log on to some types of Internet connections; it is also used in your e-mail address that will be associated with that Internet service.

After one computer is successfully connected to the Internet, you may need to add additional hardware to connect other computers and devices that you want to be able to access the Internet. For instance, to

AREA	QUESTIONS TO ASK
Services	Is the service compatible with my device?
	Is there a monthly bandwidth limit?
	How many e-mail addresses can I have?
	What is the size limit on incoming and outgoing e-mail messages and attachments?
	Do I have a choice between conventional and Web-based e-mail?
	Is there dial-up service that I can use when I'm away from home?
	Are there any special member features or benefits?
	Does the service include Web site hosting?
Speed	How fast are the maximum and usual downstream (ISP to my PC) speeds?
	How fast are the maximum and usual upstream (my PC to ISP) speeds?
	How much does the service slow down under adverse conditions, such as high traffic or poor weather?
Support	Is 24/7 telephone technical support available?
	Is Web-based technical support (such as via e-mail) available?
	Is there ever a charge for technical support?
Cost	What is the monthly cost for the service? Is it lower if I prepay a few months in advance? Are different tiers available?
	Is there a set-up fee? If so, can it be waived with a 6-month or 12-month agreement?
	What is the cost of any additional hardware needed, such as modem or transceiver? Can the fee be waived with a long-term service agreement?
	Are there any other services (telephone service, or cable or satellite TV, for instance) available from this provider that I have or want and that can be combined with Internet access for a lower total cost?

NET

share a broadband connection, you can connect other computers directly to the modem (via an Ethernet cable or Wi-Fi connection) if the modem contains a built-in switch or wireless router. If the modem does not include switching or wireless routing capabilities, you will need to connect a switch or wireless router to the modem (typically via an Ethernet cable), and then connect your devices to the switch or router, in order to share the Internet connection with those devices.

SEARCHING THE INTERNET

Most people who use the Internet turn to it to find specific information. For instance, you might want to find out the lowest price of the latest *Pirates of the Caribbean* DVD, the flights available from Los Angeles to New York on a particular day, a recipe for clam chowder, the weather forecast for the upcoming weekend, a video of President Obama's inaugural address, or a map of hiking trails in the Grand Tetons. The Internet provides access to a vast array of interesting and useful information, but that information is useless if you cannot find it when you need it. Consequently, one of the most important skills an Internet user can acquire today is how to search for and locate information on the Internet successfully. Basic Internet searching was introduced in Chapter 1, but understanding the various types of search sites available and how they work, as well as some key searching strategies, can help you perform more successful and efficient Internet searches. These topics are discussed next.

Search Sites

Search sites (such as *Google, Bing, Yahoo! Search, Microsoft Live Search, Ask.com, Cuil*, and so forth) are Web sites designed specifically to help you find information on the Web. Most search sites use a **search engine**—a software program—in conjunction with a huge database of information about Web pages to help visitors find Web pages that contain the information they are seeking. Search site databases are updated on a regular basis; for example, Google estimates that its entire index is updated about once per month. Typically, this occurs using small, automated programs (often called *spiders* or *webcrawlers*) that use the hyperlinks located on Web pages to jump continually from page to page. At each Web page, the spider program records important data about the page into the search site's database, such as the page's URL, its title, the keywords that appear frequently on the page, and the keywords and descriptive information added to the page's code by the Web page author when the page was created. Spider programs can be tremendously fast, visiting millions of pages per day. In addition to spider programs, search site databases also obtain information from Web page authors who submit Web page URLs and keywords associated with their Web sites to the search site, as discussed more in Chapter 11. The size of the database used varies with each particular search site, but typically includes information collected from several billion Web pages; at the time of this writing, for instance, the spider used with the Cuil search site had crawled a total of 186 billion Web pages.

To begin a search using a search site, type the URL for the desired search site in the Address bar of your browser. Most search sites today are designed for *keyword searches*; some sites allow *directory searches* as well. These two types of searches are discussed next. In addition, as the ability to search becomes more and more important, new types of searching are being developed. One emerging possibility is *real-time search engines* that search the Web

> **Search site.** A Web site designed to help users search for Web pages that match specified keywords or selected categories. > **Search engine.** A software program used by a search site to retrieve matching Web pages from a search database.

live, instead of relying on a search site database (one such service—called *MyLiveSearch*—was in development at the time of this writing). Another emerging search site—*ChaCha Search*—uses human guides that you can chat with via the ChaCha Search page if you can't find the information you are looking for. Searching by mobile phone is another growing area, including *mobile voice search*, which is discussed in the Chapter 6 Technology and You box.

Keyword Search

The most common type of Internet search is the **keyword search**—that is, when you type appropriate **keywords** (one or more key terms) describing what you are looking for into a search box. The site's search engine then uses those keywords to return a list of Web pages (called *hits*) that match your search criteria; you can view any one of these Web pages by clicking its corresponding hyperlink (see Figure 8-11). Search sites differ in determining how close a match must be between the specified search criteria and a Web page before a link to that page is displayed, so the number of hits from one search site to another may vary. To reduce the number of hits displayed, good search strategies (discussed shortly) can be used. Search sites also differ with respect to the order in which the hits are displayed. Some sites list the most popular sites (usually judged by the number of Web pages that link to it) first; others list Web pages belonging to organizations that pay a fee to receive a higher rank (typically called *sponsored links*) first.

The keyword search is the most commonly used search type. It is used not only on conventional search sites like the Google search site shown in Figure 8-11, but also on many other Web sites. For instance, Web pages like the one shown in Figure 8-12 often include a keyword search box so visitors can search that Web site to find information (such as items for sale via the site or specific documents or Web pages located on that site). Many of these Web site searches are powered by search engine technology, such as by *Google Site Search*.

Directory Search

An alternate type of Internet search available on some search sites is the **directory search**, which uses lists of categories instead of a search box. To perform a directory search, click the category that best matches what you are looking for in order to display a list of more specific subcategories within the main category. You can then click specific subcategories to drill down to more specific topics until you see hyperlinks to Web pages matching the information you are looking for.

1. Type appropriate keywords in the search box to display the search results.

2. Click the hyperlink for a Web page in the search results to display that page.

⚠ FIGURE 8-11
Using a search site.

▽ FIGURE 8-12
Web page keyword searches. Allow users to search the Web site for the desired content.

Search box

NET

FUNCTION	EXPLANATION
Calculator	Enter a mathematical expression or a conversion to see the result.
Currency converter	Enter an amount and currency type to see the corresponding value.
Dictionary	Enter the term *define* followed by a term to view definitions for that term from online sources.
Flight information	Enter an airline and a flight number to see status information.
Movie showtimes	Enter the term *movie* followed by a ZIP code to view movies showing in that area.
Number search	Enter a UPS, FedEx, or USPS tracking number; an area code; or a UPC code to view the associated information.
Phonebook	Enter a name followed by a city and a state, a ZIP code, or an area code to look up that person's address and phone number.
Reverse phonebook	Enter a telephone number to look up the person or business associated with that number.
Stock quotes	Enter one or more stock ticker symbols to retrieve stock quotes.
Street maps	Enter an address to find a map to that location.
Time	Enter the term *time* followed by a city name to see the current time in that city.
Travel conditions	Enter an airport code followed by the term *airport* to view current conditions at that airport.
Weather	Enter the term *weather* followed by a city name or ZIP code to view the weather for that location.
Yellow pages	Enter a type of business and city name or ZIP code to view businesses in that local area.

EXAMPLES:

10 miles in feet — Search

10 miles = 52 800 feet

time paris — Search

10:10pm Wednesday (CEST)
Time in **Paris**, France

weather san francisco — Search

Weather for **San Francisco, CA**
68°F
Mostly Cloudy
Wind: NW at 1 mph
Humidity: 76%

Wed	Thu	Fri
65°F | 50°F	68°F | 52°F	70°F | 52°F

FIGURE 8-13
Google search tools.

Search Site Tools

Many search sites contain a variety of tools that can be used to find specific types of information. For instance, many search sites include links next to the search box that allow you to search for items other than Web pages, such as music files, videos, images, maps, news articles, products for sale—even files on your computer. Google is one of the most versatile search sites at the present time and is continually adding new search options. In addition to the options just listed, Google allows a variety of special searches to be conducted by typing specific search criteria in its search box to find other useful information, such as to quickly track a shipped package, look up a telephone number, check on the status of an airline flight, or make a calculation or conversion. Some examples of search tools that can be performed using the Google search box are listed in Figure 8-13.

Search Strategies

There are a variety of strategies that can be used to help whittle down a list of hits to a more manageable number (some searches can return billions of Web pages). Some search strategies can be employed regardless of the search site being used; others are available only on certain sites. Some of the most useful search strategies are discussed next.

Using Phrases

One of the most straightforward ways to improve the quality of the hits returned is to use *phrase searching*—essentially typing more than one keyword in a keyword search. Most search engines automatically list the hits that include all the keywords first, followed by hits matching most of the keywords, continuing down to hits that fit only one of the keywords. To force this type of sorting, virtually all search engines allow you to use some type of character—often quotation marks—to indicate that you want to search for the entire phrase together. Because search options vary from site to site, it is best to look for a search tips link on the search site you are using; the search tips should explain all of the search options available for that site. Examples of the results based on different search phrases to find Web pages about hand signals used with dogs and conducted at two search sites are listed in Figure 8-14. Notice that while the last two search phrases shown in Figure 8-14

SEARCH PHRASE USED	SEARCH SITE	NUMBER OF PAGES FOUND	TITLE OF FIRST TWO NONSPONSORED PAGES FOUND*
dogs	Google	48,600,000	Dogs & Puppies – Next Day Pets Dogs – Dog Information, Pictures and Reviews for over 350 Dogs
	Yahoo!	633,000,000	American Kennel Club (AKC) Animal Planet's Dog Guide
hand signals	Google	58,600,000	Hand Signals Bicycle Safety – Hand Signals
	Yahoo!	45,100,000	Hand Signals – Wikipedia, the free encyclopedia Bicycle Safety – Hand Signals
dog hand signals	Google	1,010,000	DDEAF Training Hand Signals How to Teach a Dog Hand Signals | eHow.com
	Yahoo!	7,660,000	How to Train a Dog Using Hand Signals | eHow.com Dog Training – Hand Signals – Amazingdogtrainingman.com
"dog hand signals"	Google	713	How to Teach a Dog Hand Signals | eHow.com D for Dog – Deaf dog hand signals sign language
	Yahoo!	213	How to Train a Dog Using Hand Signals | eHow.com Dog Training – Hand Signals – Amazingdogtrainingman.com

* Highlighted entries indicate Web pages about dog hand signals.

both returned relevant (and similar) Web pages, the number of Web pages found varied dramatically (hundreds of pages versus millions).

FIGURE 8-14

Examples of phrase searching. Using different search phrases and different search sites can dramatically change the search results.

Using Boolean Operators

To further specify exactly what you want a search engine to find, *Boolean operators*—most commonly AND, OR, and NOT—can often be used in keyword searches. For example, if you want a search engine to find all documents that cover *both* the Intel and AMD microprocessor manufacturers, you can use the search phrase *Intel AND AMD* if the search engine supports Boolean operators. If, instead, you want documents that discuss *either* of these companies, the search phrase *Intel OR AMD* can be used. On the other hand, if you want documents about microprocessors that are cataloged with no mention of Intel, *microprocessors NOT Intel* can be used. Just as with other operators, the rules for using Boolean operators might vary from search site to search site (for instance, Google automatically assumes the AND operator as the default operator any time more than one search term is listed and uses a minus sign (–) instead of the word *NOT*). Be sure to check the search tips for the search site that you are using to see what operators can be used on that site. Some search sites also include an *Advanced Search* option that helps you specify Boolean conditions and other advanced search techniques using a fill-in-the-blank form.

Using Multiple Search Sites

Most users have a favorite search site that they are most comfortable using. However, as illustrated in Figure 8-14, different search sites can return different results. It is important to realize that sometimes a different search site might perform better than the one you use regularly. If you are searching for something and are not making any progress with one search site, then try another search site.

Using Appropriate Keywords, Synonyms, Variant Word Forms, and Wildcards

When choosing the keywords to be used with a search site, it is important to select words that represent the key concept you are searching for. For example, if you want to find out about bed and breakfasts located in the town of Leavenworth, Washington, a keyword

NET

TIP

When searching, be efficient—if an appropriate Web page is not included among the first page or two of hits, redo the search using more specific criteria or a different search strategy.

FIELD TYPE	EXAMPLE	EXPLANATION
Title	title:"tax tips"	Searches for Web pages containing the words "tax tips" in the page title.
URL	url:taxtips	Searches for Web pages containing "taxtips" in the page URL.
Text	text:"tax tips"	Searches for Web pages containing "tax tips" in the text of the page.
Site	forms site:irs.gov	Searches for Web pages associated with the keyword "forms" that are located only on the irs.gov Web site.
Domain	tax tips site:*.gov	Searches for Web pages associated with the keywords "tax tips" that are located on government Web sites (they can have anything for the first part of the domain name, but must have a .gov TLD).

FIGURE 8-15

Field searching.

Field searches limit search results to just those pages that match specific field criteria, in addition to any specified search criteria.

phrase (such as *Leavenworth Washington bed and breakfast*) should return appropriate results. If your initial search does not produce the results you are hoping for, you can try *synonyms*—words that have meanings similar to other words. For example, you could replace *bed and breakfast* with *hotel* or *lodging*. To use synonyms in addition to the original keywords, Boolean operators can be used, such as the search phrase *"bed and breakfast" OR hotel OR lodging AND Leavenworth AND Washington*.

Variant—or alternate—word forms are another possibility. Try to think of a different spelling or form of your keywords, if your search still does not work as desired. For example, *bed and breakfast* could be replaced or supplemented with the variants *bed & breakfast* and *B&B*, and the *hand signals* keywords used in Figure 8-14 could be replaced with the variants *hand signal* and *hand signaling*. Using alternative spellings is a form of this strategy, as well. Another strategy that is sometimes used with keywords is the *wildcard* approach. A wildcard is a special symbol that is used in conjunction with a part of a word to specify the pattern of the terms you want to search for. For instance, the asterisk wildcard (*) is used to represent one or more letters at the asterisk location, so on many sites searching for *hand sign** would search for *hand sign, hand signal, hand signals, hand signaling*, and any other keywords that fit this specific pattern.

Using Field Searches

Another strategy that can be used when basic searching is not producing the desired results is *field searching*. A field search limits the search to a particular search characteristic (or *field*), such as the page title, URL, page text, top-level domain, or Web site (see Figure 8-15). When a field search is performed, only the hits associated with the Web pages that match the specified criteria in the specified field are displayed. You can also use field searching in conjunction with regular search terms, such as to search for a particular keyword on just Web sites that use a specific domain. Many, but not all, search engines support some type of field searching. Check the search tips for the particular search site you are using to see if it has that option.

Evaluating Search Results

Once a list of Web sites is returned as the result of a search, it is time to evaluate the sites to determine their quality and potential for meeting your needs. Two questions to ask yourself before clicking a link in the search results are as follows:

➤ Does the title and listed description sound appropriate for the information you are seeking?

➤ Is the URL from an appropriate company or organization? For example, if you want technical specifications about a particular product, you might want to start with information on the manufacturer's Web site. If you are looking for government publications, stick with government Web sites.

After an appropriate Web page is found, the evaluation process is still not complete. To determine if the information can be trusted, you should evaluate both the author and the

FURTHER EXPLORATION

Go

Go to the Chapter 8 page at **www.cengage.com/ computerconcepts/np/uc13** for links to information about citing online references.

TYPE OF RESOURCE	CITATION EXAMPLE
Web page article (magazine)	Dvorak, John (2009, May 5). Data Mining and the Death of Privacy. *PC Magazine*. Retrieved February 14, 2010, from http://www.pcmag.com/article2/0,1895,2346287,00.asp
Web page article (journal)	Sensmeier, Joyce (2009, March). Advancing the EHR (Electronic Health Record): Are We There Yet? *Nursing Management*, 40 no. 3. Retrieved June 21, 2010, from http://www.nursingcenter.com/library/JournalArticle.asp?Article_ID=850211
Web page article (not appearing in a periodical)	Baldor, Lolita (2009, May 6). Air Traffic Systems Vulnerable to Cyber Attack. MSNBC. Retrieved March15, 2010, from http://www.msnbc.msn.com/id/30602242
Web page content (not an article)	*Browse the Web Safely*. (n.d.) Retrieved April 11, 2010 from http://www.symantec.com/norton/security_response/browsewebsafely.jsp
E-mail (cited in text, not reference list)	Maria Rodriquez (personal communication, March 28, 2010).

source to decide if the information can be considered reliable and whether or not it is biased. Be sure to also check for a date to see how up-to-date the information is—many online articles are years old. If you will be using the information in a report, paper, or other document in which accuracy is important, try to verify the information with a second source.

Citing Internet Resources

According to the online version of the Merriam-Webster Dictionary, the term *plagiarize* means "to steal and pass off the ideas or words of another as one's own" or to "use another's production without crediting the source." To avoid plagiarizing Web page content, you need to credit Web page sources—as well as any other Internet resources—when you use them in papers, on Web pages, or in other documents.

The guidelines for citing Web page content are similar to those for written sources. In general, the author, date of publication, and article or Web page title are listed along with a "Retrieved" statement listing the date the article was retrieved from the Internet and the URL of the Web page used to retrieve the article. Some citation examples based on the guidelines obtained from the *American Psychological Association (APA)* Web site are shown in Figure 8-16. If in doubt when preparing a research paper, check with your instructor as to the style manual (such as APA, *Modern Language Association (MLA)*, or *Chicago Manual of Style*) he or she prefers you to follow and refer to that guide for direction.

FIGURE 8-16

Citing Web sources.
It is important to properly credit your Web sources. These examples follow the American Psychological Association (APA) citation guidelines.

FIGURE 8-17

Online messaging programs can often be used to perform a variety of communications tasks.

1. After signing in to your messaging program, select a contact in order to start an IM or initiate a voice call, video call, game, or other activity with that individual.

BEYOND BROWSING AND E-MAIL

In addition to basic browsing and e-mail (discussed in Chapter 1), there are a host of other activities that can take place via the Internet. Some of the most common of these Web-based applications are discussed next.

Other Types of Online Communications

Many types of online communications methods exist. E-mail, discussed in Chapter 1, is one of the most common; other types of online communications are discussed in the next few sections. While originally the programs that supported the various types of online communications discussed next were dedicated to a single task, today's programs often can be used for a variety of types of online communications. For instance, many *instant messaging (IM) programs* today (such as the one shown in Figure 8-17) can also be used to exchange *text messages*,

2. IMs show up on both the sender's and the recipient's computers.

NET

make voice calls via *Voice over Internet Protocol* (*VoIP*), and make *video phone calls*, and many *VoIP programs* today can be used to exchange instant messages and text messages, in addition to making voice phone calls. This online communications convergence trend is found in both personal and business applications; in business, it is referred to as *unified communications* (*UC*). With UC, the various channels of business communications (such as e-mail, instant messaging, and telephone calls) are tied together and work with a single unified mailbox and interface. For instance, UC enables you to receive voice mail messages and faxes in your e-mail Inbox, listen to e-mail messages and calendar items over the phone, call a contact by clicking that person's name in your online contact list, view the availability status of co-workers before initiating a phone call, and so forth. UC is expected to be nearly a $50 billion business by 2012, according to Wainhouse Research.

Instant Messaging (IM) and Text Messaging

Instant messaging (**IM**) allows you to exchange real-time typed messages with people on your *buddy list*—a list of individuals (such as family, friends, and business associates) that you specify. *Instant messages* (*IMs*) can be sent via computers and mobile phones using installed *messaging programs* (such as *AIM, Windows Live Messenger, Yahoo! Messenger*, or *Google Talk*), Web-based messaging services (such as *Meebo.com* or Web versions of AIM, Yahoo! Messenger, or Google Talk), or other online communications programs that support instant messaging. Originally a popular communications method among friends, IM has also become a valuable business tool.

In order to send an IM, you must be signed in to your IM service. You can then select an online buddy and send an IM, which then appears immediately on your buddy's computer (refer again to Figure 8-17). You can also typically engage in other types of activities with an online buddy via the IM program, such as sending a photo or file, starting a voice or video conversation, or playing an online game. Instant messaging capabilities are also sometimes integrated into Web pages, such as to ask questions of a customer service representative or to start a conversation with one of your friends via a social networking site; this type of messaging is sometimes referred to as *chat*.

Because IM applications display the status of your buddies (such as if they are online, or if they have set their status to "Busy" or "In a meeting"), IM is an example of an application that uses *presence technology*—technology that enables one computing device to identify the current status of another device. Presence technology is increasingly being integrated into devices and applications and is discussed in more detail in Chapter 15. For a look at a growing presence application—*geobrowsing*—that you may use to keep track of your friends and family while they are on the go, see the Trend box.

Text messaging is a form of messaging frequently used by mobile phone users. Also called *Short Message Service* or *SMS*, text messaging is used to send short (less than 160 character) text-based messages via a cellular network. The messages are typically sent to the recipient via his or her mobile phone number (though some mobile phones can receive text messages sent via an e-mail address). Individuals may incur a fee for exchanging IMs and text messages, if these services are not included in their mobile phone plan.

Twittering and Other Types of Status Updates

Twittering is a relatively new way of staying in touch and connected with your friends' current activities. Sometimes referred to as *microblogging*, this free service allows

---

> **Instant messaging (IM).** A way of exchanging real-time typed messages with other individuals. > **Text messaging.** A way of exchanging real-time typed messages with other individuals via a cellular network and, typically, cell phones. > **Twittering.** Sending short status updates about your current activities via the Twitter service.

TREND

Geobrowsing

One of the biggest trends in mobile Web services today is geobrowsing—that is, information that is displayed based on the physical location of your phone (typically determined by the phone's GPS coordinates). Because most mobile phones today can be tied to location information and because most individuals carry a mobile phone with them at all times, geo-browsing services are becoming available at a record pace. Some geobrowsing applications and services (such as *GyPSii and Buddy Beacon*—see the accompanying illustration) allow you to broadcast your current location to friends and view the names and mapped locations of your friends that are near your current location. Others (such as *Eventful*) are designed to find businesses and events that are close to your current location.

Using the mobile phone to deliver location-based, real-time information seems like a natural evolution to many. And the trend shows no signs of slowing down. In fact, the Gartner Group predicts that location-based services will soon become mainstream and the market will grow to 300 million users worldwide (and more than $8 billion annually) by 2011.

members (both individuals and businesses) to post short (up to 140 character) updates (called *tweets*) about what they are doing at any moment (see Figure 8-18). The updates can be sent via text message, IM, or e-mail and are posted to the member's Twitter.com page. Tweet updates can also be sent to your friends' mobile phones if they have set up their accounts to follow you via text updates (standard text messaging rates apply when a mobile phone is used to send or receive tweets). Members can also search the Twitter Web site to find tweets of interest.

Features similar to Twitter tweets (generally referred to as *status updates*) are available on some social networking sites to keep your friends up to date on your current activi-
ties, as discussed shortly. The use of status updates is growing—a recent report by the Pew Internet & American Life Project found that 11% of online adults use Twitter or another online service to post status updates—and it is changing the way some people communicate online. Twitter is used today to get updates on the weather, to ask for assistance with problems or to conduct information searches—even for personal safety purposes. For instance, the U.S. State Department recently began using Twitter to issue traveling advisories and one Berkeley graduate student used Twitter to send the tweet "Arrested" as he was being arrested in Egypt for photographing an antigovernment protest. After being notified by the student's Twitter friends, the U.S. embassy was able to secure his release.

▽ **FIGURE 8-18**

Twitter. Allows individuals to post tweets via computer, mobile phone, or Xbox (as shown here).

Message Boards

For asking questions of, making comments to, or initiating discussions with a large group of individuals, **message boards** (also called *discussion groups, newsgroups*, and *online forums*) can be used. Message boards are Web pages designed to facilitate written discussions between people on specific subjects, such as TV shows, computers, movies, investing, gardening, music, photography, or politics. When a participant posts a message, it is displayed for anyone accessing the message board to read and respond to. Messages are usually organized by topics (called *threads*); participants can post new messages in response to an existing message and stay within that thread, or they can post discussion group messages that start new threads. Participants in discussion groups do not have to be online at the same time because participants can post and respond to messages at their convenience.

Voice over Internet Protocol (VoIP)

Internet telephony is the original industry term for the process of placing telephone calls over the Internet. Today, the standard term for placing telephone calls over the Internet or any other type of data network is **Voice over Internet Protocol** (**VoIP**) and it can take many forms. At its simplest level, VoIP calls can take place from computer to computer, such as by starting a voice conversation with an online buddy using an IM program and a headset or microphone connected to the computer. Computer to computer calls (such as via the popular *Skype* service, as well as via messaging programs that support voice calls) are generally free. Often calls can be received from or made to conventional or mobile phones for a small fee, such as two cents per minute for domestic calls.

More permanent VoIP setups (sometimes referred to as *digital voice, broadband phone*, or *Internet phone service*) are designed to replace conventional landline phones in homes and businesses. VoIP is offered through some ISPs, such as cable, telephone, and mobile phone companies; it is also offered through dedicated VoIP providers, such as *Vonage*. Permanent VoIP setups require a broadband Internet connection and a *VoIP phone adapter* (also called an *Internet phone adapter*) that goes between a conventional phone and a broadband router, as shown in Figure 8-19. Once your phone calls are routed through your phone adapter and router to the Internet, they travel to the recipient's phone, which can be another VoIP phone, a mobile phone, or a landline phone. VoIP phone adapters are typically designed for a specific VoIP provider. With these more permanent VoIP setups, most users switching from landline phone service can keep their existing telephone number.

The biggest advantage of VoIP is cost savings, such as unlimited local and long-distance calls for as little as $25 per month, or cable and VoIP services bundled together for about $50 per month. One of the biggest disadvantages of VoIP at the present time is that it does not function during a power outage or if your Internet connection (such as your cable connection for cable Internet users) goes down.

Web Conferences and Webinars

As discussed in Chapter 7, the term *videoconferencing* refers to the use of computers, video cameras, microphones, and other communications technologies to

Ⓥ FIGURE 8-19

Voice over IP (VoIP). Permanent VoIP setups allow telephone calls to be placed via a broadband Internet connection using a conventional telephone.

THE INTERNET

1. A conventional phone is plugged into a VoIP adapter, which is connected to a broadband modem.

2. Calls coming from the VoIP phone travel over the Internet to the recipient's phone.

>**Message board.** A Web page that enables individuals to post messages on a particular topic for others to read and respond to; also called a discussion group or online forum. >**Voice over Internet Protocol (VoIP).** The process of placing telephone calls via the Internet.

conduct face-to-face interactive meetings between people in different locations. Videoconferencing that takes place via the Internet is often called *Web conferencing* or *online conferencing*. **Web conferences** typically take place via a personal computer or mobile phone and are used by businesses and individuals. Basic Web conferences (such as a video call between individuals as in Figure 8-20) can be performed via any online communications program (such as an instant messaging program) that supports video phone calls. Business Web conferences that require multiple participants or other communication tools (such as a shared whiteboard or the ability for attendees to share the content on their computer screens) may need to use *Web conferencing software* or services instead. Business Web conferencing is often used for meetings between individuals located in different geographical locations, as well as for employee training, sales presentations, customer support, and other business applications.

Webinars (Web seminars) are similar to Web conferences, but typically have a designated presenter and an audience. Although interaction with the audience is usually included (such as question and answer sessions), a Webinar is typically more one-way communication than a Web conference.

FIGURE 8-20
Web conferencing. Allows individuals to talk with and see each other in real time, such as this student talking to her family from her dorm room.

Social Networking

A **social networking site** can be loosely defined as any site that creates a community of individuals who can communicate with and/or share information with one another. Some examples are *MySpace* and *Facebook* that allow users to post information about themselves for others to read, *Meetup.com* that connects people with common hobbies and interests, video sharing sites like *YouTube*, and photo sharing sites like *Flickr* and *Fotki*. Social networking can be performed via personal computers, though the use of *mobile social networking*—social networks accessed with a mobile phone or other mobile device—is growing rapidly. In fact, Jupiter Research predicts the number of active mobile social networking users will rise from 54 million today to 730 million in five years, and MySpace expects half of its traffic to come from mobile devices within a few years. Some reasons for this include that most individuals carry a mobile phone with them all the time, many individuals like to communicate with others via the Web while they are on the go, and the use of a mobile phones enables location applications to be integrated into the social networking experience.

Social networking sites are used most often to communicate with existing friends.

ASK THE EXPERT

THROW THE FIGHT

Ryan Baustert, Guitarist, Throw the Fight

What impact has the Internet and social networking sites had on your band's success?

The Internet has had a major impact on us. The best marketing is when the distance between artist and audience is short and direct. Due to sites like MySpace, Purevolume, and Facebook, we are able to stay better connected and interact with our fans on a more personal level. We can also gauge how our music is received by peoples' reactions and comments online.

It's much easier to promote shows, tours, and album releases, as well. More recently, with the explosion of Twitter, we can go one step further and give fans more insight into what is going on in our lives behind the scenes. This, in turn, helps us build brand loyalty.

> **Web conference.** A face-to-face meeting taking place via the Web; typically uses video cameras and microphones to enable participants to see and hear each other. > **Webinar.** A seminar presented via the Web. > **Social networking site.** A site that enables a community of individuals to communicate and share information.

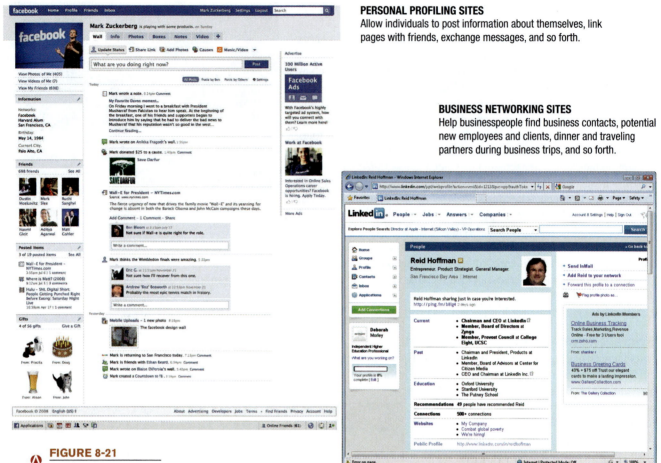

FIGURE 8-21
Social networking sites. A variety of social networking sites are available to meet different needs.

Facebook, for instance (shown in Figure 8-21), allows you to post photos, videos, music, and other content for your *Facebook friends* (individuals you have chosen to communicate with via Facebook) to view. You can also chat with your Facebook friends who are currently online, and publish notes and status updates (similar to Twitter tweets) on your *Facebook wall*, as well as the walls of your friends' Facebook pages. For privacy purposes, you can limit access to your Facebook page to the individuals you identify (such as just to your Facebook friends). To help keep track of all your friends' social networking activities, *social networking management services* can help, as discussed in the Technology and You box.

In addition to being used to communicate with existing friends, social networking sites are also used to learn about individuals you currently don't know. For instance, one new application for social networks like Facebook is their use by college-bound students to meet other incoming freshmen before the school year starts. Class pages for many colleges in the United States emerge prior to the fall semester so that incoming freshmen can "facestalk" (view the profiles of) other students in their graduating class, look up the profiles of their dorm roommates, find fellow students with common interests, and more—all before actually setting foot on campus.

In addition to being used for personal use, social networking sites today are also viewed as a business marketing tool. For instance, MySpace, Facebook, and YouTube are often used by businesses, political candidates, emerging musicians, and other professionals or professional organizations to increase their online presence. There are also business social networking sites designed for business networking. These sites (such as LinkedIn shown in Figure 8-21) are used for recruiting new employees, finding new jobs, building professional contacts, and other business activities. Other specialized social networking sites include sites designed for children (these usually work in a manner similar to

TECHNOLOGY AND YOU

Social Networking Management Services

With the popularity of social networking sites comes the problem of trying to keep up with the seemingly end-less stream of input (such as Flickr photos, Twitter tweets, MySpace messages, Facebook posts, and so forth) gener-ated by friends and contacts. There are a number of differ-ent *social networking management tools* available now that can help. These tools typically display new content from your friends and contacts (such as from your Facebook friends and/or people in your IM or e-mail contact list) in a central location to make it easier to follow all of your friends' activi-ties at one time.

Some social networking management capabilities are built into portal pages and IM programs. For instance, the *What's New* area at the bottom of the *Windows Live Messenger* screens displays updates about activities the people you have specified as being in your Live network have performed recently, such as new blog posts or new uploaded photos. Other ser-vices are more universal, such as the *Yoono* browser plug-in that contains various widgets located on the left side of your browser to conveniently display different types of information aggregated from the Web. The *Friends Widget* (shown in the accompanying illustration) displays your friend's social network-ing activities continuously, and the updates can be displayed in chronological order, by social network, or by friend. The Friends Widget also provides one-click access to e-mail and IM, and allows you to upload media to your favorite social networks.

With the popularity and use of social networks still growing at an astounding rate, expect to see many more types of social management services in the future.

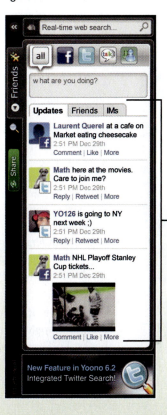

Most recent activity (Facebook posts and Twitter tweets in this example) by friends.

MySpace, but they have safeguards in place to prevent personal information from being posted, to monitor language, and so forth) and families (such as to exchange messages, view online tasks lists, and access a shared family calendar).

When using a social networking site, adults and children should be cautious about revealing too much personal information via these sites, both for personal safety reasons and to prevent the information from being used in personalized, targeted *spear phishing* attacks, discussed in Chapter 9. In addition, social networking content is increasingly being monitored by colleges (to find inappropriate behavior by students and to research college applicants) and employers (to find unprofessional behavior by current employees and to research potential job candidates). Because of this, all individuals should be careful about the types of photos and other content they post online. There have been numerous cases over the past few years of students being disciplined or not admitted to a college, and individuals being fired or not hired, due to content posted to a social networking site. Consequently, it is a good idea for individuals to take a close look at their online posts and photos and remove anything that might be potentially embarrassing if viewed by current or future employers, a future partner, or other people important to them now or in the future.

Another emerging issue is what happens to social networking content when some-one dies unexpectedly, since family members and heirs cannot access the sites without logon information or access to the deceased's e-mail for password recovery purposes. In response, some special services have emerged to help individuals store information about their online assets and to designate a beneficiary—the person designated to receive that information upon the individual's death. These services can be used to store logon information for Web sites and e-mail accounts and to leave e-mail messages to be distributed to designated individuals when the individual dies, such as to loved ones, online and offline friends, online gaming companions, and other individuals. An alternative is for individuals to leave the necessary online contact and access information, as well as instructions regarding how to notify online friends and sites, with a trusted friend or relative who is instructed to use the information only in the event of the individual's death.

TIP

The data on online auction pages is typically not updated automatically once it is displayed on your screen. To get updated information—such as the current bid for an auction and auction time remaining—use your browser's Refresh or Reload button to redisplay the page.

Online Shopping and Investing

Online shopping and *online investing* are examples of *e-commerce*—online financial transactions. It is very common today to order products, buy and sell stock, pay bills, and manage financial accounts online. However, since *online fraud, credit card fraud*, and *identity theft* (a situation in which someone gains enough personal information to pose as another person) are continuing to grow at a rapid pace, it is important to be cautious when participating in online financial activities. To protect yourself, use a credit card or *online payment service* such as *PayPal* (discussed in Chapter 11) whenever possible when purchasing goods or services online so that any fraudulent activities can be disputed. Also, be sure to enter your payment information only on a *secure Web page* (look for a URL that begins with *https* instead of *http*). Online financial accounts should also be protected with *strong user passwords* that are changed frequently. Internet security and strong passwords are discussed in detail in Chapter 9, and e-commerce is the topic of Chapter 11.

Online Shopping and Online Auctions

Online shopping is commonly used to purchase both physical products (such as clothing, books, DVDs, shoes, furniture, and more) and downloadable products (such as software, movies, music, and e-books) via Web pages. Typically, shoppers locate the items they would like to purchase using an online shopping site (one example is shown in Figure 8-22),

FIGURE 8-22

Online shopping. Allows you to purchase goods and services online.

and then they add those items to their online *shopping carts* or *shopping bags*. The site's *checkout* process—including supplying the necessary billing and shipping information—is then used to complete the sale. After the payment is processed, the item is either shipped to the customer (if it is a physical product), or the customer is given instructions on how to download it (if it is a downloadable product). Forrester Research predicts that U.S. online sales will reach approximately $335 billion by 2012.

Online auctions are the most common way to purchase items online from other individuals. Sellers list items for sale on an auction site (such as *eBay* or *Yahoo! Auctions*) and pay a small listing fee (and a commission to the auction site if the item is sold). Individuals can visit the auction site and enter bids on auction items until the end of the auction. At that time, the person with the highest bid is declared the successful bidder (provided the minimum selling price, if one was established, was met) and arranges payment for and delivery of the item directly with the seller. Online auctions are described in more detail in Chapter 11. Another common way to purchase items from other individuals is via online classified ads, such as those posted on the popular *Craigslist* site.

Online Banking and Online Investing

Many banks today offer **online banking** as a free service to their customers to enable customers to check balances on all their accounts (such as checking, credit cards, mortgage, and investment accounts), view cashed checks and other transactions, transfer funds between accounts, pay bills electronically, and perform other activities related to their bank accounts. Online banking is continually growing—according to the Pew Internet & American Life Project, close to one-half of all U.S. adults now bank online.

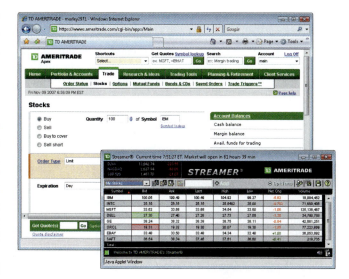

Buying and selling of stocks, bonds, mutual funds, and other types of securities is referred to as **online investing**. Although it is common to see stock quote capabilities on many search and news sites, trading stocks and other securities requires an *online broker*. The biggest advantages of online investing include lower transaction fees and the ability to quickly buy or sell stock when desired—a convenience for those investors who do a lot of trading. Common online investing services include the ability to order sales and purchases; access performance histories, corporate news, and other useful investment information; and set up an *online portfolio* that displays the status of the stocks you specify. On some Web sites, stock price data is delayed 20 minutes; on other sites, real-time quotes are available. Like other Web page data, most stock price data is current at the time it is retrieved via a Web page, but it will not be updated (and you will not see current quotes, for instance) until you reload the Web page using your browser's Refresh or Reload toolbar button. An exception to this rule is if the Web page is designed to refresh the content automatically on a regular basis. For example, the portfolio shown in Figure 8-23 uses a *Java applet*—a small program built into a Web page—to redisplay updated data continuously.

FIGURE 8-23

Online investing.

Allows you to buy and sell stock, view your portfolio, get real-time quotes, and more.

NET

Online Entertainment

There are an ever-growing number of ways to use the Web for entertainment purposes, such as listening to music, watching TV and videos, and playing online games. Some applications can be accessed with virtually any type of Internet connection; others are only practical with a broadband connection. Many online entertainment applications require the use of a *media player program* or *plug-in* (such as *QuickTime Player* or *Silverlight*) to deliver multimedia content.

Online Music

There are a number of options available today for **online music**, such as listening to live radio broadcasts via an *online radio station*, watching music videos on *MTV.com* or *Yahoo! Music*, or downloading music from *online music stores*, such as the *iTunes Music Store, Rhapsody MP3 Store*, or *Wal-Mart MP3 Music Downloads*. Online radio

---

> **Online banking.** Performing banking activities via the Web. > **Online investing.** Buying and selling stocks or other types of investments via the Web. > **Online music.** Music played or obtained via the Web.

stations typically allow you to listen to music free of charge on your computer; online music stores allow you to purchase and then download music singles and albums to your computer, mobile phone, or portable digital media player. Music files downloaded to your computer can be played from your computer's hard drive; they can also be copied to a CD to create a custom music CD or transferred to a portable digital media player or mobile phone provided the download agreement does not preclude it. *Mobile music downloads* is a rapidly growing market, and Juniper Research predicts it will exceed $17.5 billion business by 2012.

Online TV, Videos, and Movies

Watching TV shows, videos, and movies online is another very popular type of online entertainment. **Online videos** (such as news videos and movie trailers, videos posted to Web sites belonging to businesses and other organizations, personal videos posted to blogs and social networking pages, and videos shared via YouTube and Google Video) have been available to watch online for a number of years. Today, however, you also have the option of **online TV** and **online movies**. The availability of live online TV has been fairly limited in the past, but is growing. Some Web sites (such as *CNN.com Live*) offer live news coverage, and some TV shows and sporting events can be delivered in real time to mobile phones (referred to as *mobile TV* and shown in Figure 8-24). As demand for live TV keeps rising (for instance, it is estimated that more than 70 million people watched the 2009 Presidential Inauguration live coverage online), its availability is expected to grow.

There is also a wide variety of recorded TV content (such as episodes of current TV shows after they have been aired) available through the respective television network Web sites for viewing online. There are also a number of Web sites, such as *Hulu, TV.com, Fancast,* and *CastTV* (see Figure 8-24), that provide free access to many prime time TV

FIGURE 8-24

Online TV and movies.

MOBILE TV
Both live and recorded TV shows can be delivered directly to a mobile phone.

ONLINE TV AND MOVIES
TV shows and movies can be watched online for free via a variety of Web sites.

VIDEO-ON-DEMAND (VOD)
Fee-based feature films and other content can be delivered to a computer or TV.

>**Online video.** Video watched or downloaded via the Web. >**Online TV.** Live or recorded TV shows available via the Web. >**Online movies.** Feature films available via the Web.

shows, a wide variety of older TV shows, and many full-length feature films. In addition, YouTube and the *Internet Movie Database* (*IMDb*) recently added full-length TV shows and movies that visitors can watch for free, and Comcast is currently testing a new *On Demand Online* service designed to provide TV subscribers with free online TV content. A new trend is the development of original TV series, sometimes referred to as *telewebs*, that are only available online. Typically, online TV and online movies are streaming media, in which the video plays from the server when it is requested. Consequently, you need an Internet connection in order to view the video.

Another entertainment option is renting video via the Internet—typically referred to as **video-on-demand** (**VOD**). With VOD, individuals order movies and television shows via a VOD provider (such as the individuals' cable company or a Web site such as *CinemaNow, iTunes, BLOCKBUSTER OnDemand, Netflixs,* or *Amazon Video On Demand*). Rentals typically cost $3.99 or less; purchasing a movie costs around $15. In either case, the movies are downloaded to a computer, to a DVR or other device (such as the *Roku* digital media player shown in Figure 8-24) that is connected to your TV, or to a mobile phone or mobile device to be watched while on the go. Rented movies can usually be viewed only for a limited time; some services allow movies downloaded to a computer to be transferred to a portable digital media player or other mobile device during the allowable viewable period.

Many believe the future of delivering TV content over the Internet (sometimes referred to as *Internet Protocol Television* or *IPTV*) will be the delivery of content via the Internet directly to your television. Digital media players that can download VOD movies, gaming consoles that can be used to access Internet content, and multimedia networks that allow Internet content to be streamed from your computer to your TV are a step in that direction. A new option just becoming available—*broadband-enabled TVs* that connect to your Internet connection without any additional hardware—go one step farther. These TVs can be used to view Web pages, watch online TV and videos, and display *widgets* or *gadgets*—small pieces of current information such as sport scores, news headlines, or product information (as shown in Figure 8-5 earlier in this chapter). The demand for Web-to-TV content is expected to grow at an astounding pace with 24 million U.S. households expected to be viewing Internet content on their TVs by 2013, according to a report by In-Stat.

Online Gaming

Online gaming refers to games played over the Internet. Many sites—especially children's Web sites—include games for visitors to play. There are also sites whose sole purpose is hosting games that can be played online. Some of the games are designed to be played alone or with just one other person. Others, called *online multiplayer games*, are designed to be played online against many other online gamers. Online multiplayer games (such as *Doom, EverQuest, Final Fantasy*, and *City of Heroes*) are especially popular in countries, such as South Korea, that have readily available high-speed Internet connections and high levels of Internet use in general. Internet-enabled gaming consoles (such as the PlayStation 3, Xbox 360, and Wii) and portable gaming devices (such as the Sony PSP and Nintendo DSi) that have built-in Internet connectivity can also be used for multiplayer online gaming. Online gaming is also associated quite often with *Internet addiction*— the inability to stop using the Internet or to prevent extensive use of the Internet from interfering with other aspects of one's life. Internet addiction is a growing concern and is discussed in more detail in Chapter 16.

NET

>**Video-on-demand (VOD).** The process of downloading movies and television shows, on demand, via the Web. >**Online gaming.** Playing games via the Web.

Online News, Reference, and Information

There is an abundance of news and other important information available through the Internet. The following sections discuss some of the most widely used news, reference, and information resources.

News and Reference Sites

News organizations, such as television networks, newspapers, and magazines, nearly always have Web sites that are updated on a continual basis to provide access to current local and world news, as well as sports, entertainment, health, travel, politics, weather, and other news topics (see Figure 8-25). Many news sites also have searchable archives to look for past articles, although some require a fee to view back articles. Once articles are displayed, they can typically be saved, printed, or sent to other individuals via e-mail. A growing trend is for newspapers and magazines to abandon print subscriptions and to provide Web-only service—primarily for cost reasons. Although some subscribers miss the print versions, there are some advantages to digital versions, such as the ability to easily search through content in some digital publications. Other online news resources include news radio programs that are broadcast over the Internet, as well as the wide variety of news video clips available through many Web sites.

News can also be delivered via gadgets displayed on computer desktops, TVs, dashboards, and other objects. News gadgets typically display headlines, and clicking a headline displays that news story. Recent versions of Windows include a number of gadgets that can be added to the Windows desktop, as discussed in Chapter 5.

Reference sites are designed to provide users access to specific types of useful information. For example, reference sites can be used to generate maps (see Figure 8-25), check the weather forecast, look up the value of a home, or provide access to encyclopedias, dictionaries, ZIP code directories, and telephone directories. One potential downside to the increased availability of online reference sites is use by criminals. For instance, one California lawmaker has introduced a bill requiring mapping sites to blur out details of schools, churches, and government buildings after being informed that some terrorists have used these maps to plan bombings and other attacks.

FIGURE 8-25

Online news and reference.

NEWS SITES
News organizations typically update their sites several times per day to provide access to the most current news and information.

REFERENCE SITES
Reference Web sites provide access to specific types of useful information, such as the maps and driving directions available via this Web site.

Portal Pages, RSS Feeds, and Podcasts

Portal Web pages are Web pages designed to be selected as a browser's home page and visited on a regular basis. Portal pages typically include search capabilities, news headlines, weather, and other useful content, and can usually be customized by users to display their requested content (see Figure 8-26). Once the portal page is customized, each time the user visits the portal page, the specified information is displayed. Popular portals include *My Yahoo!*, *iGoogle*, *My MSN*, and *AOL.com*.

RSS (**Really Simple Syndication**) is an online news tool designed for facilitating the delivery of news articles and other content regularly published to a Web site. Provided the content has an associated *RSS feed*, individuals can *subscribe* (usually for free) to that feed. You typically subscribe to an RSS feed by clicking a *subscribe* link on the associated Web page to add the feed content to your browser feed list or by copying the URL for the RSS feed to your portal page. To view the feed content, you can select that feed from your browser's feed list (such as the *Favorites Feeds* list in Internet Explorer) or you can click the appropriate link on your portal page, such as the links shown on the portal page in Figure 8-26. In either case, as new content for the subscribed feed becomes available, it will be accessible via the feed links. In addition to computers, RSS feeds today can also be delivered to mobile phones and other mobile devices. In the future, we will likely see RSS feeds delivered directly to televisions—and perhaps even to watches, refrigerators, and other consumer devices that have a display screen.

Another Web resource that can provide you with useful information is a **podcast**—a recorded audio or video file that can be downloaded via the Internet, such as the audio and video podcasts available for download via the Web site that accompanies this text. The term *podcast* is derived from the iPod portable digital media player (the first widely used device for playing digital audio files), although podcasts today can also be listened to using a computer or mobile phone.

Podcasting (creating a podcast) enables individuals to create self-published, inexpensive Internet radio broadcasts, such as to share their knowledge, express their opinions on particular subjects, or share original poems, songs, or short stories with interested individuals. Originally created and distributed by individuals, podcasts are now also being created and distributed by businesses. Some commercial radio stations are making portions of their broadcasts available via podcasts, and a growing number of news sites and corporate sites now have regular podcasts available. In fact, some view podcasts as the new and improved radio since it is an easy way to listen to your favorite radio broadcasts on your own schedule. Podcasts are typically uploaded to the Web on a regular basis, and RSS feeds can be used to notify subscribers when a new podcast is available. For a look at how to create an audio podcast, see the How It Works box.

Content is customized for each user

Search capabilities

Access to Web mail

RSS feed subscriptions

Social networking updates

Selected news headlines

Selected weather

Other gadgets

FIGURE 8-26
Portal pages. Portal pages can contain a wide variety of customized news and information.

VIDEO PODCAST

Go to the Chapter 8 page at **www.cengage.com/ computerconcepts/np/uc13** to download or listen to the "How To: Create an RSS Feed" video podcast.

VIDEO PODCAST

Go to the Chapter 8 page at **www.cengage.com/ computerconcepts/np/uc13** to download or listen to the "How To: Create a Podcast" video podcast.

>**Portal Web page.** A Web page designed to be designated as a browser home page; typically can be customized to display personalized content.
>**RSS (Really Simple Syndication).** A tool used to deliver selected Web content to subscribers as the content is published to a Web site.
>**Podcast.** A recorded audio or video file that can be played or downloaded via the Web.

HOW IT WORKS

Podcasting

To create an audio podcast, you need a microphone or headset connected to your computer and audio capture software, such as the free *Audacity* program shown in the accompanying illustration. You can then record your podcast content and save it. You can also import additional audio files to mix in with your recorded content and otherwise edit the podcast as needed, such as arranging the order of the tracks, transition opening or closing segments by fading in or out, editing out sneezes or long stretches of silence, adding sound effects, and so forth.

Once the podcast is finished, it is typically saved in the MP3 format (the Audacity program requires you to download the free *LAME* MP3 encoder in order to save files in the MP3 format). During the save process, you should add *ID3 tags*, which include important details about your show, such as the title of the show, your name, your URL, a copyright notice, and other relevant information. The ID3 information is displayed when the podcast is played; it is also used to help your podcast be located easily by podcasting search sites and directories.

Finished podcasts can be uploaded to a podcast hosting site or your own Web site. If you use a podcast hosting site (such as the free hosting site shown in the accompanying illustration), you typically just upload the file and the site creates the download link for you automatically. If you are hosting the podcast on your own site, you will need to upload the file to your site and create the download link on the appropriate Web page yourself. If you would like individuals to be able to subscribe to your podcast via an RSS feed, you also need to create a *podcast feed*—an RSS file that contains the information needed for users to subscribe to your podcast. RSS files can be created in a text editing program like Windows Notepad and saved with an *.rss* file extension. There are also Web sites that can generate a podcast feed for you, and some podcast editing programs include the ability to create a podcast feed. To be safe, you should test your download link and/or podcast feed to make sure they work properly. Once your podcast is ready to go, you can submit it to podcast directories, such as Podcast Alley, so people can find and download it.

1. Record the podcast, then import additional audio tracks and edit as needed.

The introductory segment plays first and then fades out.

The podcast track was moved to start when the opening segment is fading out.

ID3 tags are added during the save process.

2. Save the podcast file as an MP3 file.

3. Upload the files to the appropriate Web site, such as the free podcasting hosting site shown here.

4. The podcast is available for download

Product, Corporate, Government, and Other Information

The Web is a very useful tool for locating product and corporate information. Manufacturer and retailer Web sites often include product specifications, instruction manuals, and other information that is useful to consumers before or after they purchase a product. There are also numerous consumer review sites (such as *Epinions.com*) to help purchasers evaluate their options before buying a product online or in a physical store. For investors and consumers, a variety of corporate information is available online, from both company Web sites and sites (such as *Hoovers.com*) that offer free or fee-based corporate information.

Government information is also widely available on the Internet. Most state and federal agencies have Web sites to provide information to citizens, such as government publications, archived documents, forms, and legislative bills. You can also perform a variety of tasks, such as downloading tax forms and filing your tax returns online. In addition, many cities, counties, and states allow you to pay your car registration fees, register to vote, view property tax information, or update your driver's license online.

There is also a wide variety of information available from various organizations, such as non-profit organizations, conservation groups, political parties, and more. For instance, many sites dedicated to energy conservation and saving the environment have emerged over the past few years to bring awareness to this issue, and the 2008 presidential race brought numerous online resources for learning the positions of political candidates and other information important to voters. For example, the nonpartisan *FactCheck.org* Web site shown in Figure 8-27 is dedicated to monitoring the factual accuracy of what is being said by major U.S. political candidates and elected officials and reporting it, in an attempt to reduce the level of deception and confusion in U.S. politics. According to a study by the Pew Internet & American Life Project, more than one-half of U.S. adults used the Internet in conjunction with the 2008 Election, such as to share political content with others, research issues, or watch political videos.

Online Education and Writing

Online education—using the Internet to facilitate learning—is a rapidly growing Internet application. The Internet can be used to deliver part or all of any educational class or program; it can also be used to supplement or support traditional education. In addition, many high school and college courses use Web content—such as online syllabi, schedules, discussion boards, podcasts, and tutorials—as required or suggested supplements. For example, the Web site that supplements this book contains an online study guide, online quizzes, online hands-on labs,

FIGURE 8-27

FactCheck.org. This Web site can be used to check the accuracy of political statements.

NET

ASK THE EXPERT

INSTITUTE FOR POLITICS DEMOCRACY & THE INTERNET www.ipdi.org

Julie Barko Germany, Director, Institute for Politics, Democracy, & the Internet

What is the most significant way that the Internet affects politics today?

The Internet and its applications—from Twitter to social networking sites to blogs to videos—have a significant impact on the invisible primary in American politics, as well on the elections. Today, technologically-savvy candidates and politicians use the Internet to push information out to voters, to fundraise, to solicit opinions from constituents, and to gain media coverage. One of the most valuable ways that politicians can use the Internet today, but that I believe is underutilized, is to listen to voters and each other. Really listening to the issues and concerns important to their constituents helps elected officials create better public policy and gain trust. When our leaders don't listen, we can then use the Internet (from blogs to Twitter to video to email) to get their attention—and to mobilize to vote them out of office, if necessary.

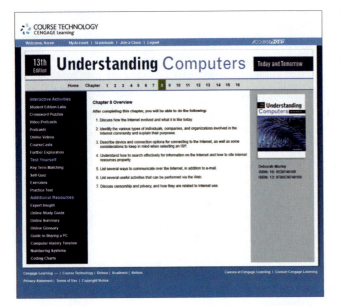

FIGURE 8-28

Web-based learning.

The Understanding
Computers Web site
provides a variety of
Web-based learning
opportunities for
readers of this textbook.

Web links, downloadable audio and video podcasts, streaming videos, and other online resources for students taking a course that uses this textbook (see Figure 8-28). There are also Web-based *learning management systems* (such as *Blackboard*) that can be used to deliver course content, manage assignments and grades, and more; and the use of *student response systems*— where students use a special device or their mobile phone to respond to surveys or review questions during in-class lectures is growing. The next few sections take a look at some of the most widely used online education applications.

Web-Based Training and Distance Learning

The term **Web-based training** (**WBT**) refers to any instruction delivered via the Web. It is commonly used for employee training, as well as for delivering instruction in an educational setting. **Distance learning** occurs whenever students take classes from a location—often home or work—which is different from the one where the delivery of instruction takes place. Distance learning today typically includes Web-based training or other online learning tools (and so is also called *online learning* and *e-learning*) and is available through many high schools, colleges, and universities, as well as organizations that provide professional certifications. Distance learning can be used to learn just one task or new skill; it can also be used to complete a college course or an entire degree program. Typically the majority of distance learning coursework is completed over the Internet via class Web pages, YouTube videos, Webinars, podcasts, discussion groups, and e-mail, although schools might require some in-person contact, such as sessions for orientation and testing.

The biggest advantage of Web-based training and distance learning is that they are typically experienced individually and at the user's own pace. Online content for Web-based training components is frequently customized to match the pace of each individual user and can be completed at the user's convenience. Web-based content can be updated as needed and online content and activities (such as exercises, exams, and animations) typically provide immediate feedback to the student. One disadvantage is the possibility of technological problems—since students need a working computer and Internet connection to access the material, they cannot participate if they have no access to a computer or if their computer, their Internet connection, or the Web server hosting the material goes down. Another concern among educators is the lack of face-to-face contact, and security issues—such as the difficulty in ensuring that the appropriate student is completing assignments or taking exams. Some possible solutions for this later concern are discussed in the next section.

Online Testing

In both distance learning and traditional classes, *online testing*—which allows students to take tests via the Internet—is a growing trend. Both objective tests (such as those containing multiple choice or true/false questions) and performance-based exams (such as those given in computer classes to test student mastery of software applications) can be administered and taken online. For instance, there are *SAM* (*Skills Assessment Manager*)

>**Web-based training (WBT).** Instruction delivered on an individual basis via the Web. >**Distance learning.** A learning environment in which the student is physically located away from the instructor and other students; commonly, instruction and communications take place via the Web.

tests available for use in conjunction with this textbook to test both Microsoft Office software skills and computer concepts. Typically online tests are graded automatically, freeing up the instructor's time for other activities, as well as providing fast feedback to the students.

One challenge for online testing is ensuring that an online test is taken by the appropriate individual and in an authorized manner, in order to avoid cheating. Some distance learning programs require students to go physically to a testing center to take the test or to find an acceptable test proctor (such as an educator at a nearby school or a commanding officer for military personnel). Other options are using smart cards, fingerprint scans, and other means to authenticate students taking an online exam from a remote location. For instance, one secure testing solution being used at a number of schools nationwide to enable students to take online tests from their remote locations while still ensuring the integrity of the exams is the *Securexam Remote Proctor* system shown in Figure 8-29. This system uses a device that first authenticates the individual taking the test via a fingerprint scan, and then captures real-time audio and video during the exam. The device's camera points to a reflective ball, which allows it to capture a full 360-degree image of the room, and the recording is uploaded to a server so it can be viewed by the instructor from his or her location. The Securexam software locks down the computer so that it cannot be used for any purpose not allowed during the test (such as performing an Internet search). It also flags suspicious behavior (such as significant noises or movements) in the recording so that the instructor can review those portions of the recording to see if any unauthorized behavior (such as leaving the room or making a telephone call) occurred during the testing period.

1. The device authenticates the individual via a fingerprint scan before the exam can begin.

2. The device captures real-time audio and video during the exam.

3. The computer is locked down during the exam so it can only be used for authorized activities.

FIGURE 8-29
Secure online testing.

FIGURE 8-30
Blogs. Allow individuals to post entries to an online personal journal.

Blogs, Wikis, and Other Types of Online Writing

A **blog**—also called a *Web log*—is a Web page that contains short, frequently updated entries in chronological order, typically as a means of expression or communication (see Figure 8-30). In essence, a blog is an online personal journal accessible to the public that is usually created and updated by one individual. Blogs are written by a wide variety of individuals—including ordinary people, as well as celebrities, writers, students, and experts on particular subjects—and can be used to post personal commentary, research updates, comments on current events, political opinions, celebrity gossip, travel diaries, television show recaps, and more.

Blogging software, which is available via blogging sites such as Blogger.com, is usually used to easily create and publish blogs and blog updates to the Web. Blogs are also frequently published on school, business, and personal Web sites. Blogs

---

> **Blog.** A Web page that contains short, frequently updated entries in chronological order, typically by just one individual.

TIP

There are numerous online blog search engines and directories— such as Technorati.com—to help you find blogs that meet your interests.

are usually updated frequently, and entries can be posted via computers, e-mail, and mobile phones. Blogs often contain text, photos, and video clips. With their increased use and audiences, bloggers and the *blogosphere* (the complete collection of blogs on the Internet) are beginning to have increasing influence on businesses, politicians, and individuals today. One new ethical issue surrounding blogging relates to bloggers who are paid to blog about certain products. Although some Web sites that match up bloggers with advertisers require that the blogger reveal that he or she receives payment for "sponsored" posts, some believe that commercializing blogging will corrupt the blogosphere. Others, however, view it as a natural evolution of word-of-mouth advertising.

Another form of online writing sometimes used for educational purposes is the **wiki**. Wikis, named for the Hawaiian phrase *wiki wiki* meaning *quick*, are a way of creating and editing collaborative Web pages quickly and easily. Similar to a blog, the content on a wiki page can be edited and republished to the Web just by pressing a Save or Submit button. However, wikis are intended to be modified by others and so are especially appropriate for collaboration, such as for class Web pages or group projects. To protect the content of a wiki from sabotage, the entire wiki or editing privileges for a wiki can be password protected.

One of the largest wikis is *Wikipedia* (shown in Figure 8-31), a free online encyclopedia that contains over eight million articles written in 250 languages, is updated by more than 75,000 active contributors, and is visited by hundreds of thousands of individuals each day. While most Wikipedia contributors edit articles in a responsible manner, there are instances of erroneous information being added to Wikipedia pages intentionally. As with any resource, visitors should carefully evaluate the content of a Wikipedia article before referencing it in a report, Web page, or other document, as discussed earlier in this chapter.

FIGURE 8-31

Wikis. Wikis, such as the Wikipedia collaborative online encyclopedia shown here, can be edited by any authorized individual.

An **e-portfolio**, also called an *electronic portfolio* or *digital portfolio*, is a collection of an individual's work accessible through a Web site. Today's e-portfolios are typically linked to a collection of student-related information, such as résumés, papers, projects, and other original works. Some e-portfolios are used for a single course; others are designed to be used and updated throughout a student's educational career, culminating in a comprehensive collection of information that can be used as a job-hunting tool.

CENSORSHIP AND PRIVACY ISSUES

There are many important societal issues related to the Internet. One important issue— network and Internet security—is covered in Chapter 9. Two other important issues— *censorship* and *privacy*—are discussed next, in the context of Internet use. Other societal issues—including computer security, ethics, health, and the environment—related to computer use are discussed in further detail in Chapters 15 and 16.

>**Wiki.** A collaborative Web page that is designed to be edited and republished by a variety of individuals. >**E-portfolio.** A collection of an individual's work accessible via the Web.

Censorship

The issue of Internet censorship affects all countries that have Internet access. In some countries, Internet content is filtered by the government, typically to hinder the spread of information from political opposition groups, to filter out subjects deemed offensive, or to block information from sites that could endanger national security. Increasingly, some countries are also blocking information (such as blogs and personal Web pages) from leaving the country, and have occasionally completely shut down Internet access to and from the country during political protests to stop the flow of information in and out of that country.

In the United States, the First Amendment to the U.S. Constitution guarantees a citizen's right to free speech. This protection allows people to say things to others without fear of arrest. But how does the right to free speech relate to potentially offensive or indecent materials available over the Internet where they might be observed by children or by people who do not wish to see them? There have been some attempts in the United States and other countries to regulate Internet content—what some would view as *censorship*—in recent years, but the courts have had difficulty defining what is "patently offensive" and "indecent" as well as finding a fair balance between protection and censorship. For example, the *Communications Decency Act* was signed into law in 1996 and made it a criminal offense to distribute patently indecent or offensive material online in order to protect children from being exposed to inappropriate Web content. In 1997, however, the Supreme Court overturned the portion of this law pertaining to indecent material on the basis of free speech, making this content legal to distribute via the Internet and protecting Web sites that host third-party content from being liable for that content.

Another example of legislation designed to protect children from inappropriate Web content is the *Children's Internet Protection Act* (*CIPA*). CIPA requires public libraries and schools to implement Internet safety policies and technologies to block children's access to inappropriate Web content in order to receive certain public funds. While this law was intended to protect children, it was fought strenuously by free speech advocacy groups and some library associations on the basis that limiting access to some Internet content violates an individual's First Amendment rights to free speech. While CIPA was ruled unconstitutional by a federal court in 2002, the Supreme Court reversed the lower court decision in 2003 and ruled that the law is constitutional because the need for libraries to prevent minors from accessing obscene materials outweighs the free speech rights of library patrons and Web site publishers. However, the Court also modified the law to require the library to remove the technologies for an adult library patron at the patron's request.

One technology commonly used to conform to CIPA regulations, as well as by parents and employees, is **Internet filtering**—the act of blocking access to particular Web pages or types of Web pages. It can be used on home computers (for instance, by individuals to protect themselves from material they would view as offensive or by parents to protect their children from material they feel is inappropriate). It is also commonly used by employers to keep employees from accessing non-work-related sites, by some ISPs and search sites to block access to potentially objectionable materials, and by many schools and libraries to control the Web content that children are able to view. Internet filtering typically restricts access to Web pages that contain offensive language, sex/pornography, racism, drugs, or violence (based on either the keywords contained

> **Internet filtering.** Using a software program or browser option to block access to particular Web pages or types of Web pages.

PARENTAL CONTROLS
Affect a particular user account, such as "Kids" in this example.

CONTENT ADVISOR
Affects all users on this computer.

FIGURE 8-32

Internet filtering.

Browser settings can be changed to deny access to Web pages with objectionable content.

on each site or a database of URLs containing restricted content). It can also be used to block access to specific sites (such as social networking sites, YouTube, or eBay), as well as to restrict the total number of hours or the time of day that the Internet can be used.

Most browsers include some Internet filtering options. For instance, Internet Explorer's *Content Advisor* (see Figure 8-32) can be used to filter the Web sites displayed for all users of a particular computer (although blocked Web sites can be viewed if the user knows the appropriate password); and *Parental Controls* can be used to set restrictions for individual users, such as the Web sites that can be viewed, whether or not the user can download files, and so forth. More comprehensive Internet filtering can be obtained with stand-alone filtering programs, such as *NetNanny* or *Safe Eyes*.

Web Browsing Privacy

Privacy, as it relates to the Internet, encompasses what information about individuals is available, how it is used, and by whom. As more and more transactions and daily activities are being performed online, there is the potential for vast amounts of private information to be collected and distributed without the individual's knowledge or permission. Therefore, it is understandable that public concern regarding privacy and the Internet is on the rise. Although personal privacy will be discussed in more detail in Chapter 15, a few issues that are of special concern to Internet users regarding Web browsing privacy and e-mail privacy are discussed in the next few sections.

Cookies

Many Web pages today use **cookies**—small text files that are stored on your hard drive by a Web server—to identify return visitors and their preferences. While some individuals view all cookies as a potential invasion of privacy, Web sites can read only their own cookie files and the use of cookies can provide some benefits to consumers. For example, cookies can enable a Web site to remember preferences for customized Web site content (for instance, displaying customized content on a portal page, such as the one shown in Figure 8-26), as well as to retrieve a shopping cart containing items selected during a previous session. Some Web sites also use cookies to keep track of which pages on their Web sites each person has visited, in order to recommend products on return visits that match that person's interests. A use of cookies that is more objectionable to some is the use of *third-party cookies* (cookies placed on your hard drive by a company other than the one associated with the Web page that you are viewing—typically a Web advertising company). Third-party cookies target advertisements to Web site visitors based on their activities on the site (such as products viewed or advertisements clicked).

The information stored in a cookie file typically includes the name of the cookie, its expiration date, and the domain that the cookie belongs to. In addition, a cookie contains either personal information that you have entered while visiting the Web site or an ID number assigned by the Web site that allows the Web site's server to retrieve your personal information from its database. Such a database can contain two types of information: *personally identifiable information* (*PII*) and *non-personally identifiable information* (*Non-PII*). Personally identifiable information is connected with a specific user's identity—such as his or her name and address—and is typically given during the process of ordering goods or services. Non-personally identifiable information is anonymous data—such as which product pages were viewed or which advertisements located on the site were clicked—that is not directly associated with the visitor's name or another personally identifiable characteristic.

Cookies stored on your computer's hard drive can be looked at, if desired, although sometimes deciphering the information contained in a cookie file is difficult. Internet Explorer users can view and/or delete cookies and other temporary files by using Internet Explorer's Tools menu to open the Internet Options dialog box and selecting the appropriate options in the *Browsing history* section on the General tab. The Privacy tab in this dialog box (shown in Figure 8-33) can be

FIGURE 8-33

Browser cookie management. The desired cookies settings can be specified in the browser settings.

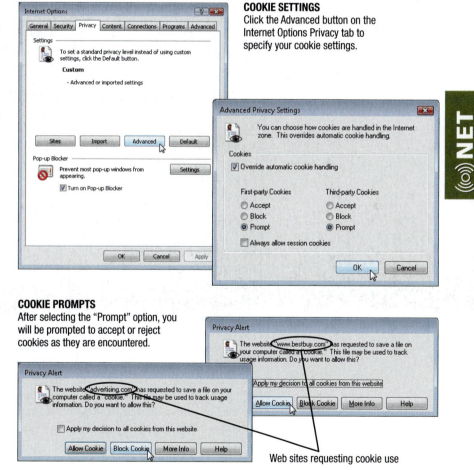

COOKIE SETTINGS
Click the Advanced button on the Internet Options Privacy tab to specify your cookie settings.

COOKIE PROMPTS
After selecting the "Prompt" option, you will be prompted to accept or reject cookies as they are encountered.

Web sites requesting cookie use

NET

> **Cookie.** A small file stored on a user's hard drive by a Web server; commonly used to identify personal preferences and settings for that user.

used to specify which type of cookies (if any) are allowed to be used, such as permitting the use of regular cookies, but not third-party cookies or cookies using personally identifiable information.

Turning off cookies entirely might make some features—such as a shopping cart—on some Web sites inoperable. The *Medium High* privacy option in Internet Explorer is a widely used setting since it allows the use of regular cookies but blocks third-party cookies that use personally identifiable information without explicit permission. Users who want more control over their cookies can choose to accept or decline cookies as they are encountered in most browsers. Although this option interrupts your Web surfing frequently, it is interesting to see the cookies generated from each individual Web site. For example, the two cookie prompts shown in the bottom of Figure 8-33 were generated while visiting the BestBuy.com Web site. Although one cookie request is from the BestBuy.com Web site directly, the other is a third-party cookie from an online marketing company.

Another alternative is the *private browsing* option available with many Web browsers, including Internet Explorer, Chrome, and Safari. As discussed more in Chapter 15, this option allows you to browse the Web without leaving any history (including browsing history, form data, cookies, usernames, and passwords) on the computer you are using. Private browsing is useful for individuals using school, library, or other public computers to visit password-protected sites, research medical information, or perform other tasks that the user may prefer to keep private. Individuals using a computer to shop for presents or other surprises for family members who share the same computer may find the feature useful, as well.

CAUTION CAUTION CAUTION CAUTION CAUTION CAUTION CAUT

Cookies (typically placed by advertising companies) that attempt to track your activities across a Web site or the Web sites belonging to an advertising network are referred to as *tracking cookies*. If your security software includes tracking cookie protection, be sure it is enabled to avoid these cookies from being stored on your computer. Setting your browser's privacy settings to block third-party cookies can offer you some additional protection against tracking cookies.

Spyware and Adware

Spyware is the term used for any software program that is installed without the user's knowledge and that secretly gathers information about the user and transmits it through his or her Internet connection. Spyware is sometimes used to provide advertisers with information used for marketing purposes, such as to help select advertisements to display on each person's computer. The information gathered by the spyware software is usually not associated with a person's identity. But spyware is a concern for privacy advocates because it is typically installed without a user's direct knowledge (such as at the same time another program is installed, often when a program is downloaded from a Web site or a P2P service) and conveys information about a user's Internet activities. Spyware can also be used by criminals to retrieve personal data stored on your computer for use in criminal activities, as discussed in more detail in Chapter 9.

>**Spyware.** A software program that is installed without the user's permission and that secretly gathers information to be sent to others.

Unfortunately, spyware use is on the rise and can affect the performance of a computer (such as slowing it down or causing it to work improperly), in addition to its potential security risks. And the problem will likely become worse before it gets any better. Some spyware programs—sometimes referred to as *stealthware*—are getting more aggressive, such as delivering ads regardless of the activity you are doing on your computer, changing your browser home page or otherwise altering your browser settings (referred to as *browser hijacking*), and performing other annoying actions. The worst spyware programs rewrite your computer's main instructions—such as the Windows registry—to change your browser settings back to the hijacked settings each time you reboot your computer, undoing any changes you may have made to your browser settings.

A related type of software is *adware*, which is free or low-cost software that is supported by on-screen advertising. Many free programs that can be downloaded from the Internet, such as the free version of the *NetZero* e-mail program, include some type of adware, which results in on-screen advertising. The difference between spyware and adware is that adware typically does not gather information and relay it to others via the Internet (although it can), and it is not installed without the user's consent. Adware might, however, be installed without the user's direct knowledge, since many users do not read licensing agreements before clicking OK to install a new program. When this occurs with a program that contains adware, the adware components are installed without the user's direct knowledge.

Both spyware and adware can be annoying and use up valuable system resources, in addition to revealing data about individuals. As discussed in detail in Chapter 9, *firewalls* and *antispyware programs* can be used to protect against spyware.

E-Mail Privacy

Many people mistakenly believe that the e-mail they send and receive is private and will never be read by anyone other than the intended recipient. Since it is transmitted over public media, however, only *encrypted* (electronically scrambled) e-mail can be transmitted safely, as discussed in Chapter 9. Although unlikely to happen to your personal e-mail, *nonencrypted* e-mail can be intercepted and read by someone else. Consequently, from a privacy standpoint, a nonencrypted e-mail message should be viewed more like a postcard than a letter (see Figure 8-34).

It is also important to realize that your employer and your ISP have access to the e-mail you send through those organizations. Businesses and ISPs typically archive (keep copies of) e-mail messages that travel through their servers and are required to comply with subpoenas from law enforcement agencies for archived e-mail messages.

FIGURE 8-34

You cannot assume e-mail messages are private, unless they are encrypted.

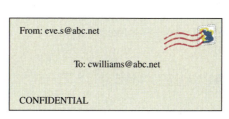

Chris,

The meeting is Monday at 2 pm. Please bring all related personnel files detailing the anticipated firing of Joe D.

Eve

To: cwilliams@abc.net
From: eve.s@abc.net

From: eve.s@abc.net

To: cwilliams@abc.net

CONFIDENTIAL

REGULAR (NONENCRYPTED E-MAIL) = POSTCARD   **ENCRYPTED E-MAIL = SEALED LETTER**

SUMMARY

EVOLUTION OF THE INTERNET

The origin of the **Internet**—a worldwide collection of interconnected networks that is accessed by millions of people daily—dates back to the late 1960s. At its start and throughout its early years, the Internet was called **ARPANET**. It was not until the development of the **World Wide Web** (**WWW**) that public interest in the Internet began to soar. Most companies have Web sites today and consider the Web to be an indispensable business tool. While the Web is a very important and widely used Internet resource, it is not the only one. Over the years, *protocols* have been developed to download files, send e-mail messages, and perform other tasks, in addition to using Web pages. Today, the term *Internet* has become a household word and, in many ways, has redefined how people think about computers and communications. The next significant improvement to the Internet infrastructure may be the result of projects such as *Internet2*.

The Internet community is made up of individual *users*; companies, such as **Internet service providers** (**ISPs**), **Internet content providers**, **application service providers** (**ASPs**), *infrastructure companies*, and a variety of software and hardware companies; the government; and other organizations. Virtually anyone with a computer with communications capability can be part of the Internet, either as a user or supplier of information or services. **Web services** are self-contained business functions that operate over the Internet.

Because the Internet is so unique in the history of the world—and it remains a relatively new and ever-changing phenomenon—several widespread myths about it have surfaced. Three such myths are that the Internet is free, that it is controlled by some central body, and that it is synonymous with the World Wide Web.

GETTING SET UP TO USE THE INTERNET

Most Internet connections today are **direct connections** (always connected to the Internet), though some are **dial-up connections** (which need to dial up and connect to the Internet to provide access). Dial-up connections are typically **conventional dial-up Internet access**; common types of direct Internet connections include **cable**, **DSL** (**Digital Subscriber Line**), **satellite**, **fixed wireless**, **mobile wireless**, and **broadband over fiber** (**BoF**)—also called **fiber-to-the-premises** (**FTTP**)—**Internet access**. Individuals can also connect to the Internet via a **Wi-Fi hotspot**. When preparing to become connected to the Internet, you need to decide which type of device (personal computer or mobile phone, for instance), which type of Internet connection, and which specific Internet service provider to use. Once all these decisions are made, you can acquire the proper hardware and software and set up your system for Internet access.

SEARCHING THE INTERNET

Search sites are Web sites that enable users to search for and find information on the Internet. They typically locate pages using a **keyword search** (in which the user specifies **keywords** for the desired information)—a **search engine** retrieves the list of matching Web pages from a database. A **directory search** (in which the user selects categories corresponding to the desired information) is another possibility. Search site databases are generally maintained by automated *spider* programs.

There are a variety of search strategies that can be used, including typing phrases instead of single keywords; using *Boolean operators*; trying the search at multiple search sites; and using *synonyms, variant word forms, wildcards*, and *field searches*. Once a list of links to Web pages matching the search criteria is displayed, the hits need to be evaluated for their relevancy. If the information found on a Web page is used in a paper, report, or other original document, the source should be credited appropriately.

BEYOND BROWSING AND E-MAIL

The Internet can be used for many different types of activities in addition to basic Web browsing and e-mail exchange. Common types of online communications include **instant messaging** (**IM**) and **text messaging** (sending real-time typed messages via a computer or mobile phone, respectively), **Twittering** (sending short status updates via Twitter), **message boards** (online locations where people post messages on a particular topic for others to read and respond to), **Web conferencing** (real-time meetings taking place via the Web that typically use video cameras and microphones to enable participants to see and hear each other), and **Webinars** (seminars presented over the Web). **Social networking sites** also allow the members of an online community to communicate and exchange information. **Voice over Internet Protocol** (**VoIP**) refers to making voice telephone calls over the Internet.

Common Web activities for individuals include a variety of consumer *e-commerce* activities, such as **online shopping**, **online auctions**, **online banking**, and **online investing**. When performing any type of financial transaction over the Internet, it is very important to use only *secure* Web pages.

Online entertainment applications include **online gaming**, downloading music files and other types of **online music**, and **online TV**, **online movies**, and other types of **online video**. Selecting and receiving TV shows and movies via the Web is called **video-on-demand** (**VOD**). A wide variety of news, reference, government, product, and corporate information is available via the Web as well. News, reference, and search tools are commonly found on **portal Web pages**; RSS (**Really Simple Syndication**) feeds can be used to deliver current news, **podcasts**, and other Web content to individuals as it becomes available.

Online education options include **Web-based training** (**WBT**) and **distance learning**. *Online testing* can be used for both objective and performance-based exams and can be secured by a variety of means. Online writing includes **blogs** (Web pages that contain frequently updated entries by individuals), **wikis** (Web pages designed to be created and edited by multiple individuals), and **e-portfolios** (collections of an individual's work).

CENSORSHIP AND PRIVACY ISSUES

Among the most important societal issues relating to the Internet are *censorship* and *privacy*. Web content is not censored as a whole, but **Internet filtering** can be used by parents, employers, educators, and anyone wishing to prevent access to sites they deem objectionable on computers for which they have control. *Privacy* is a big concern for individuals, particularly as it relates to their Web activity. **Cookies** are typically used by Web sites to save customized settings for that site and can also be used for advertising purposes. Another item of possible concern is **spyware** (software installed without the user's permission that sends information to others). Unless an e-mail message is *encrypted*, it should not be assumed to be completely private.

Chapter Objective 5:
List several ways to communicate over the Internet, in addition to e-mail.

Chapter Objective 6:
List several useful activities that can be performed via the Web.

Chapter Objective 7:
Discuss censorship and privacy, and how they are related to Internet use.

NET

REVIEW ACTIVITIES

KEY TERM MATCHING

a. cookie

b. dial-up connection

c. direct connection

d. distance learning

e. Internet

f. keyword

g. podcast

h. search engine

i. video-on-demand (VOD)

j. World Wide Web (WWW)

Instructions: Match each key term on the left with the definition on the right that best describes it.

1. _____ A learning environment in which the student is physically located away from the instructor and other students; commonly, instruction and communications take place via the Web.

2. _____ A type of Internet connection in which the computer or other device is connected to the Internet continually.

3. _____ A small file stored on a user's hard drive by a Web server; commonly used to identify personal preferences and settings for that user.

4. _____ A software program used by a search site to retrieve matching Web pages from a search database.

5. _____ A type of Internet connection in which the computer or other device must dial up and connect to a service provider's computer via telephone lines before being connected to the Internet.

6. _____ A recorded audio or video file that can be played or downloaded via the Web.

7. _____ A word typed in a search box on a search site to locate information on the Internet.

8. _____ The collection of Web pages available through the Internet.

9. _____ The largest and most well-known computer network, linking millions of computers all over the world.

10. _____ The process of downloading movies and television shows, on demand, via the Web.

SELF-QUIZ

Instructions: Circle **T** if the statement is true, **F** if the statement is false, or write the best answer in the space provided. **Answers for the self-quiz are located in the References and Resources Guide at the end of the book**.

1. **T F** When the Internet was first developed, it was called Mosaic.

2. **T F** On the Internet, an *access provider* and a *content provider* are essentially the same thing.

3. **T F** With a direct connection, you need only open your browser to start your Internet session.

4. **T F** A Wi-Fi hotspot is used to provide Internet access to individuals via a wireless connection.

5. **T F** A Webinar is a Web site designed to allow individuals to easily create and publish blogs.

6. _____ is a type of always-on broadband Internet service that transmits data over standard telephone lines but does not tie up your phone line.

7. With a(n) _____ search, keywords are typed into the search box; with a(n) _____ search, users select categories to find matching Web pages.

8. A(n) _____ is a Web site (such as Facebook) designed to enable a community of individuals to communicate and exchange information.

9. With a(n) _____ , people bid on products over the Internet, and the highest bidder purchases the item.

10. Match each Internet application to its possible situation, and write the corresponding number in the blank to the left of each situation.

a. _____ To communicate with a friend in a different state.

b. _____ To pay only as much as you specify for an item purchased through the Internet.

c. _____ To pay a bill without writing a check.

d. _____ To find Web pages containing information about growing your own Bonsai trees.

1. Online banking
2. E-mail
3. Internet searching
4. Online auction

EXERCISES

1. Match each type of Internet access to its description, and write the corresponding number in the blank to the left of each description.

a. _____ A common type of home broadband connection; does not use standard phone lines.

b. _____ Provides access to the Internet via a very fast fiber-optic network.

c. _____ Accesses the Internet via standard phone lines and ties up your phone; the maximum speed is 56 Kbps.

1. Conventional dial-up
2. BoF
3. Cable

2. What would each of the following searches look for?

a. hot AND dogs _____

b. snorkel* _____

c. text:"Internet privacy" domain:*.gov _____

3. List three different sets of keywords that could be used to search for information on how to maintain a trumpet.

4. Explain the difference between a blog, a wiki, and a podcast.

5. List one advantage and one disadvantage of the use of Web site cookies.

DISCUSSION QUESTIONS

1. Twittering became virtually an overnight sensation, but some question its usefulness. Do you want to know the routine activities your friends (or other individuals you choose to follow) are doing during the day? Is it useful information to tweet that you are stuck in traffic or having a bad day? Do you follow anyone on Twitter or tweet regularly? Why or why not? Since Twitter updates have to be very short, some may think that twittering on the job does not take up enough time to be a concern, but what about the distraction factor? Should employers allow employees to use Twitter, Facebook, and other popular online activities during work hours? Why or why not?

2. Some courtrooms today are becoming high-tech, such as using videoconferencing systems to allow defendants and witnesses to participate in proceedings from remote locations. Allowing defendants to participate remotely from the jail facility saves travel time and expense, as well as eliminates any risk of flight. Remote testimony from witnesses can save both time and money. But, could having defendants and witnesses participate remotely affect the jury's perspective? If the videoconference takes place via the Internet, can it be assured that proceedings are confidential? Do you think the benefits of these systems outweigh any potential disadvantages?

PROJECTS

HOT TOPICS

1. **Social Network Addiction** As discussed in the chapter, social networks (such as Facebook and MySpace) are very popular with individuals. However, it has become apparent recently that some individuals are moving from casual social networking use to compulsive or addictive behavior.

   For this project, investigate either Facebook addiction or Internet addiction. How common is it? What are some of the warning signs? Is there an actual medical disorder associated with it? If so, what is it and how is it treated? Find one example in a news or journal article of a person who was "addicted" to using a social networking site or other online activity—why was their behavior considered addictive? Were they able to modify their behavior? Have you ever been concerned about becoming addicted to any Internet activities? At the conclusion of your research, prepare a one-page summary of your findings and opinions and submit it to your instructor.

**SHORT ANSWER/
RESEARCH**

2. **Online Travel Planning** Planning and booking travel arrangements online is a very popular Internet activity today and there are a number of sites that can be used.

   For this project, review two popular travel sites, such as Expedia.com and Travelocity.com, to see what services they offer and how easy it is to locate the information needed to plan and book a flight via those sites. Select a destination and use one of the sites to obtain a quote for a particular flight on a particular day. Next, go to the Web site for the airline of the flight and use the site to obtain a quote for the same flight. Is there a difference in price or flight availability? Could you make a reservation online through both sites? Would you feel comfortable booking an entire vacation yourself online, or are there services that a travel agent could provide that you feel would be beneficial? Do you think these sites are most appropriate for making business travel plans or vacation plans, or are they suited to both? At the conclusion of your research, prepare a one-page summary of your findings and submit it to your instructor.

HANDS ON

3. **Web Searching** Search sites can be used to find Web pages containing specific information, and there are strategies that can be used to make Web searching an efficient and useful experience.

   For this project, go to the Google search site and perform the following searches, then submit your results and printouts to your instructor. (Note: Some of the answers will vary from student to student.)

   a. Search for *rules*. How many pages were found? What is the name of the first page in the list of hits? Next, search for *backgammon rules*. How many pages were found? Use the hits to find a picture of how a backgammon board is initially set up, then, print that page.

   b. Search to find a recipe for Buffalo Chicken Wings; a map of where your house, apartment, or dorm is located; and the ZIP code for 200 N. Elm Street, Hinsdale, IL and print the pages containing this information.

   c. Go to the Advanced Search option. Use the form fields to perform a search for Web pages that contain all of the words *hiking trails Sierras*, do not contain the word *horse*, and have the domain *.gov*. After the hits are displayed, record the actual search phrase that is listed in the search box along with the name and URL of the first page displayed in the list of hits.

4. **Paid Bloggers** Blogs are traditionally online personal journals where the blogger expresses his or her opinion on desired topics. Unlike professional journalists, bloggers typically post because they want to, not because they have been hired to do so. However, as discussed in the chapter, bloggers are increasingly being paid or "sponsored" to blog. Is this ethical? If a blogger is paid to post his or her honest opinion about a product or service, does that lessen the credibility of that post? Does it change your opinion if the blogger reveals that it is a sponsored blog? If you based a purchase on a review posted in a blog that you later found out was sponsored, would you feel misled? How, if at all, do sponsored posts affect the blogosphere as a whole?

For this project, form an opinion about the ethical ramifications of paid blogging and be prepared to discuss your position (in class, via an online class discussion group, in a class chat room, or via a class blog, depending on your instructor's directions). You may also be asked to write a short paper expressing your opinion.

ETHICS IN ACTION

5. **Wi-Fi Hotspots** There are an increasing number of public locations offering Wi-Fi hotspots available for public use.

For this project, find one location in your local area that offers public Wi-Fi access and either visit the location or call the provider on the phone to find out the how the hotspot works, in terms of fees and access. Is there a fee to use the hotspot? If so, do you have to subscribe on a regular basis, or can you pay only when you want to use the hotspot? Where and how is payment made? Do you need any special software to access the hotspot? Do you need to be assigned a username or key (such as a *WEP*, *WPA*, or *WPA 2* key) before you can use the service? Share your findings and opinions with the class in the form of a short presentation. The presentation should not exceed 10 minutes and should make use of one or more presentation aids, such as the chalkboard, handouts, overhead transparencies, or a computer-based slide presentation (your instructor may provide additional requirements). You may also be asked to submit a summary of the presentation to your instructor.

PRESENTATION/ DEMONSTRATION

Instructions: Go to the Chapter 8 page at **www.cengage.com/computerconcepts/np/uc13** to work the following Web Activities.

6. **Interactive Activities** Work the interactive **Crossword Puzzle**, watch the **Video Podcasts** and **Online Videos**, and explore the **Further Exploration** links associated with this chapter.

If you have a SAM user profile, you may have access to hands-on instruction, practice, and assessment of the skills covered in this chapter. Check with your instructor for instructions and the correct URL/Web site to access those assignments.

7. **Student Edition Labs** Work the following interactive **Student Edition Labs**.
   ➤ **Connecting to the Internet**   ➤ **Getting the Most Out of the Internet**

8. **Test Yourself** Review the **Online Study Guide** for this chapter, then test your knowledge of the terms and concepts covered in this chapter by completing the **Key Term Matching** exercise, the **Self-Quiz**, the **Exercises**, and the **Practice Test**.

WEB ACTIVITIES

NET

chapter 9

Network and Internet Security

After completing this chapter, you will be able to do the following:

1. Explain why computer users should be concerned about network and Internet security.

2. List several examples of unauthorized access and unauthorized use.

3. Explain several ways to protect against unauthorized access and unauthorized use, including access control systems, firewalls, and encryption.

4. Provide several examples of computer sabotage.

5. List how individuals and businesses can protect against computer sabotage.

6. Discuss online theft, identity theft, spoofing, phishing, and other types of dot cons.

7. Detail steps an individual can take to protect against online theft, identity theft, spoofing, phishing, and other types of dot cons.

8. Identify personal safety risks associated with Internet use.

9. List steps individuals can take to safeguard their personal safety when using the Internet.

10. Discuss the current state of network and Internet security legislation.

OVERVIEW

As discussed in the last few chapters, networks and the Internet help many of us be more efficient and effective workers, as well as add convenience and enjoyment to our personal lives. However, there is a downside, as well. The widespread use of home and business networks and the Internet increases the risk of unauthorized computer access, theft, fraud, and other types of computer crime. In addition, the vast amount of business and personal data stored on computers accessible via company networks and the Internet increases the chances of data loss due to crime or employee errors. Some online activities can even put your personal safety at risk, if you are not careful.

This chapter looks at a variety of security concerns stemming from the use of computer networks and the Internet in our society, including unauthorized access and use, computer viruses and other types of sabotage, and online theft and fraud. Safeguards for each of these concerns are also covered, with an explanation of precautions that can be taken to reduce the chance that these security problems will happen to you. Personal safety issues related to the Internet are also discussed, and the chapter closes with a look at legislation related to network and Internet security. ■

NET

WHY BE CONCERNED ABOUT NETWORK AND INTERNET SECURITY?

From a *computer virus* making your computer function abnormally, to a *hacker* using your personal information to make fraudulent purchases, to someone harassing you online in a discussion group, a variety of security concerns related to computer networks and the Internet exist. Many Internet security concerns today can be categorized as **computer crimes**. Computer crime—sometimes referred to as *cybercrime*—includes any illegal act involving a computer. Many computer crimes today are committed using the Internet or another computer network and include theft of financial assets or information, manipulating data (such as grades or account information), and acts of sabotage (such as releasing a computer virus or shutting down a Web server). Cybercrime is an important security concern today. It is a multibillion-dollar business that is often performed by seasoned criminals. In fact, according to the FBI, organized crime organizations in many countries are increasingly turning to computer crime to target millions of potential victims easily, and *phishing attacks* and other *Internet scams* (discussed shortly) are expected to increase in reaction to the recent troubled economy. These and other computer crimes that are carried out via the Internet or another computer network are discussed in this chapter. Other types of computer crime (such as using a computer to create counterfeit currency or make illegal copies of a DVD) are covered in Chapter 15.

>**Computer crime.** Any illegal act involving a computer.

With some security concerns, such as when a spyware program changes your browser's home page, the consequence may be just an annoyance. In other cases, such as when someone steals your identity and purchases items using your name and credit card number, the consequences are much more serious. And, with the growing use of wireless networks, Web 2.0 applications (such as social networking sites), and individuals accessing company networks remotely, paired with an increasing number of security and privacy regulations that businesses need to comply with, network and Internet security has never been more important. Consequently, all computer users should be aware of the security concerns surrounding computer network and Internet use, and they should take appropriate precautions. The most common types of security risks related to network and Internet use, along with some corresponding precautions, are discussed throughout this chapter.

UNAUTHORIZED ACCESS AND UNAUTHORIZED USE

Unauthorized access occurs whenever an individual gains access to a computer, network, file, or other resource without permission—typically by *hacking* into the resource. **Unauthorized use** involves using a computer resource for unauthorized activities. Often, they happen at the same time, but unauthorized use can occur when a user is authorized to access a particular computer or network but is not authorized for the particular activity the user performs. For instance, while a student may be authorized to access the Internet via a campus computer lab, some use—such as viewing pornography—would likely be deemed off-limits. If so, viewing that content from a school computer would be considered unauthorized use. For employees of some companies, checking personal e-mail or visiting personal Facebook pages at work might be classified as unauthorized use.

Unauthorized access and many types of unauthorized use are criminal offenses in the United States and many other countries. They can be committed by both *insiders* (people who work for the company whose computers are being accessed) and *outsiders* (people who do not work for that company). Whether or not a specific act constitutes unauthorized use or is illegal depends on the circumstances, as well as the specific company or institution involved. To explain acceptable computer use to their employees, students, or other users, many organizations and educational institutions publish guidelines for behavior, often called *codes of conduct* (see Figure 9-1). Codes of conduct typically address prohibited activities, such as playing games, installing personal software, violating copyright laws, causing harm to computers or the network, and snooping in other people's files.

▼ FIGURE 9-1

A sample code of conduct.

Hacking

Hacking refers to the act of breaking into a computer or network. It can be performed in person by hacking into a computer the *hacker* has physical access to, but it is more often performed via the Internet or another network. Unless authorized (such as when a company

---

hires a *professional hacker* to test the security of its system), hacking in the United States and many other countries is a crime.

Typically, the motivation for hacking is to steal data, sabotage a computer system, or perform some other type of illegal act. In particular, the theft of consumer data (such as credit card numbers and cardholder information) has increased dramatically over the past several years—one breach, discovered in 2009, compromised the data of millions of debit and credit cards. Another growing trend is to hack into a computer and "hijack" it for use in an illegal or unethical act, such as generating spam or hosting pornographic Web sites. Hackers are also increasingly aiming attacks at very specific individuals, such as product designers and other individuals who have access to valuable corporate data.

In addition to being a threat to individuals and businesses, hacking is also considered a very serious threat to national security in the United States. The increased number of systems that are controlled by computers and are connected to the Internet, along with the continually improving abilities of hackers and the increasing availability of sets of tools (sometimes called *rootkits*) that allow hackers to access a system, has led to an increased risk of *cyberterrorism*—where terrorists launch attacks via the Internet. Current concerns include attacks against the computers controlling vital systems (such as the nation's power grids, banks, and water filtration facilities), as well as computers related to national defense, the airlines, and the stock market. In fact, outsiders attempt to access U.S. Pentagon computers millions of times each day, and military leaders are concerned about the potential of cybersecurity threats from other countries. As a result, President Obama has made cybersecurity a priority, including setting up a cybersecurity task force and czar, and stating, "It's now clear this cyber threat is one of the most serious economic and national security challenges we face as a nation."

Today, hackers often gain access via a wireless network. This is because wireless networks are becoming increasingly common and it is easier to hack into a wireless network than a wired network. In fact, as discussed in Chapter 7, it is possible to gain access to a wireless network just by being within range (about 100 to 300 feet, depending on the Wi-Fi standard being used) of a wireless access point, unless the access point is sufficiently protected. Although security features are built into wireless routers and other networking hardware, they are typically not enabled by default. As a result, many wireless networks belonging to businesses and individuals—some estimates put the number as high as 70% of all Wi-Fi networks—are left unsecured. Securing a Wi-Fi network is discussed shortly.

ASK THE EXPERT

Moshe Vardi, Rice University, Co-Chair of the ACM Globalization and Offshoring of Software Taskforce

Is there a national security risk to outsourcing/offshoring software development?

Offshoring magnifies existing risks and creates new and often poorly understood threats. When businesses offshore work, they increase not only their own business-related risks (e.g., intellectual property theft) but also risks to national security and to individuals' privacy. While it is unlikely these risks will deter the growth of offshoring, businesses and nations should employ strategies to mitigate the risks. Businesses have a clear incentive to manage these new risks to suit their own interests, but nations and individuals often have little awareness of the exposures created. For example, many commercial off-the-shelf (COTS) systems are developed offshore, making it extremely difficult for buyers to understand all of the source and application code in the systems. This creates the possibility that a hostile nation or nongovernmental hostile agent (such as a terrorist or criminal) could compromise these systems. Individuals are also often exposed to loss of privacy or identity theft due to the number of business processes being offshored today and managed under laws that are much less restrictive than in most developed countries.

War Driving and Wi-Fi Piggybacking

Unauthorized use of a Wi-Fi network is called **war driving** or **Wi-Fi piggybacking**, depending on the location of the hacker at the time. War driving typically involves driving in a car with a portable computer looking for unsecured Wi-Fi networks to connect to. Wi-Fi piggybacking refers to accessing someone else's unsecured Wi-Fi network from the hacker's current location (such as inside his or her home, outside a Wi-Fi hotspot location, or near a local business). Both war driving and Wi-Fi piggybacking are ethically—if not legally—questionable acts. They can also lead to illegal behavior, such as individuals deciding to use data (credit card numbers, for instance) they run across while war driving for fraudulent purposes, as was the case with two men who illegally accessed a Lowe's wireless network during a war drive and later decided to steal credit card numbers via that network. War driving and Wi-Fi piggybacking can also have security risks, both for the hacker and the owner of the Wi-Fi network that is being used. For instance, they both risk the introduction of computer viruses (either intentionally or unintentionally) and unauthorized access of the data located on their computers. In addition, the owner may experience reduced performance or even the cancellation of his or her Internet service if the ISP limits bandwidth or the number of computers allowed to use a single Internet connection.

While there are products and services available to help mobile users locate legitimate public Wi-Fi hotspots (see Figure 9-2), laws in some countries, such as the U.K., are clear that unauthorized access of a Wi-Fi connection is illegal. In the United States, federal law is not as clear, although some states (such as Michigan) have made using a Wi-Fi connection without permission illegal. In fact, a Michigan man was found guilty, fined, and sentenced to community service in 2007 for using the free Wi-Fi service offered to customers at a local café because he was using the service from his parked car located on the street outside the café to check his e-mail on a regular basis.

Advocates of war driving and Wi-Fi piggybacking state that, unless individuals or businesses protect their access points, they are welcoming others to use them. Critics compare that logic to that of an unlocked front door—you cannot legally enter a home just because the front door is unlocked. Some wireless network owners do leave their access points unsecured on purpose and some communities are creating a collection of wireless access points to provide wireless Internet access to everyone in that community. However, it is difficult—if not impossible—to tell if an unsecured network is that way intentionally, unless connecting to the wireless network displays a welcome screen stating that it is a free public Wi-Fi hotspot.

Some feel the ethical distinction of using an unsecured wireless network is determined by the amount of use, believing that it is acceptable to borrow someone's Internet connection to do a quick e-mail check or Google search, but that continually using a neighbor's Internet connection to avoid paying for your own is crossing over the line. Others feel that allowing outsiders to share an Internet connection is acceptable use, as long as the subscriber does not charge the outsider for that access. Still others believe that an Internet connection is intended for use only by the subscriber and that sharing it with others is unfair to the subscriber's ISP. This issue is beginning to be addressed by the courts and

FIGURE 9-2

Wi-Fi finders. Some online mapping services list the Wi-Fi hotspots for a particular geographic area.

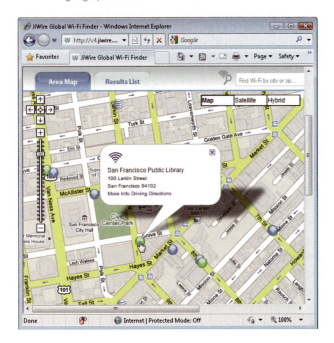

>**War driving.** Driving around an area with a Wi-Fi-enabled computer or mobile device to find a Wi-Fi network to access and use without authorization. >**Wi-Fi piggybacking.** Accessing an unsecured Wi-Fi network from your current location without authorization.

ISPs, and some answers regarding the legality of "Wi-Fi borrowing" and Internet connection sharing will likely be forthcoming in the near future. However, the ethical questions surrounding this issue may take longer to resolve.

Interception of Communications

Instead of accessing data stored on a computer via hacking, some criminals gain unauthorized access to data, files, e-mail messages, VoIP calls, and other content as it is being sent over the Internet. For instance, *unencrypted* (unsecured) messages, files, logon information, and more sent over a wireless network (such as while using a public Wi-Fi hotspot or over an unsecured home or business Wi-Fi network) can be captured and read by anyone within range using software designed for that purpose. Once intercepted, the data can be used for unintended or fraudulent purposes.

Although it is unlikely that anyone would be interested in intercepting personal e-mail sent to friends and relatives, proprietary corporate information and sensitive personal information (such as credit card numbers and Web site logon information) is at risk if it is sent unsecured over the Internet or over a wireless home or corporate network. The widespread use of wireless networks, as well as the increased use of wireless connections to transmit data via mobile phones and other portable devices, has opened up new opportunities for data interception. For instance, the data on mobile devices with Bluetooth capabilities enabled can be accessed by other Bluetooth devices that are within range.

A new trend is criminals intercepting credit and debit card information during the card verification process; that is, intercepting the data from a card in real time as a purchase is being authorized. In several recent cases, this occurred via *packetsniffing* software installed at payment terminals (such as restaurant cash registers or gas station credit/debit card readers) by hackers—the packetsniffing software gathered the data during transactions and then sent it to the hackers. The increased occurrence of real-time attacks may be partly because of the new *Payment Card Industry Data Security Standard* (*PCI DSS*) rules that require companies to limit the credit card data stored on company servers and to *encrypt* the data that is allowed to be stored. Consequently, hackers may be moving away from targeting data stored on company servers and focusing on stealing data in real time during credit card and debit card transactions.

PROTECTING AGAINST UNAUTHORIZED ACCESS AND UNAUTHORIZED USE

The first step in protecting against unauthorized access and unauthorized use is controlling access to an organization's facilities and computer networks to ensure that only authorized individuals are granted access. In addition, steps need to be taken to ensure that authorized individuals access only the resources that they are supposed to access.

Access Control Systems

Access control systems are used to control access to facilities, computer networks, company databases, individual Web site accounts, and other assets. They can be *identification systems*, which verify that the person trying to access the facility or system is listed as an authorized user, and/or *authentication systems*, which determine whether or not the person attempting access is actually who he or she claims to be. In businesses, access control systems are often integrated into a comprehensive *identity management (IDM) system* designed to manage users' access to enterprise systems, such as to grant them secure and appropriate access to the systems they are allowed to access in as convenient a manner as possible to the end user. The three most common types of access control systems are discussed next, followed by a discussion of additional considerations for controlling access to wireless networks.

FIGURE 9-3

Passwords.

Passwords are used to log on to computers, networks, Web sites, and other computing resources.

FIGURE 9-4

Strategies for creating good passwords.

PASSWORD STRATEGIES

Make the password at least eight characters, if possible. A five-character password can be cracked by a computer program in less than one minute. A ten-character password, in contrast, has about 3,700 trillion possible character permutations and is considerably safer.

Choose passwords that are not in a dictionary—for instance, mix numbers and special characters with abbreviations or unusual words you will remember, but that do not conform to a pattern a computer can readily figure out.

Do not use your name, your kids' or pets' names, your address, your birthdate, or any other public information as your password.

Determine a *passphrase* that you can remember and use corresponding letters and symbols (such as the first letter of each word) for your password. For instance, the passphrase "My son John is five years older than my daughter Abby" could be used to remember the corresponding strong password "Msji5yotMd@".

Do not keep a written copy of the password in your desk or taped to your monitor. If you need to write down your password, create a password-protected file on your computer that contains all your passwords so you can look them up as needed.

Use a different password for your highly sensitive activities (such as online banking or stock trading) than for Web sites that remember your settings or profile (such as online news, auction, shopping, or bookstore sites). If a hacker determines your password on a low-security site (which is easier to break into than a site located on a secure Web server), he or she can use it on an account containing sensitive data if you use the same password on both accounts.

Change your passwords frequently.

Possessed Knowledge Access Systems

A **possessed knowledge access system** is an identification system that requires the individual requesting access to provide information that only the authorized user is supposed to know. *Passwords* and *cognitive authentication systems* fall into this category.

Passwords, the most common type of possessed knowledge, are secret words or character combinations associated with an individual. They are typically used in conjunction with a *username* (often a variation of the person's first and/or last names or the individual's e-mail address). Username/password combinations are often used to restrict access to networks, computers, Web sites, routers, and other computing resources—the user is granted access to the requested resource only after supplying the correct information. While usernames and e-mail addresses are not secret, passwords are and, for security purposes, typically appear as asterisks or dots as they are being entered so they cannot be viewed (see Figure 9-3). For some applications (such as ATM machines), a *PIN* or *personal identification number*—a secret combination of numeric digits selected by the user—is used instead of a password. Numeric passwords are also referred to as *passcodes*.

One of the biggest disadvantages of password-based systems is that passwords can be forgotten. Another disadvantage is that any individual possessing the proper password will be granted access to the system because the system recognizes the password, regardless of whether or not the person using the password is the authorized user, and passwords can be guessed or deciphered by a hacker or a hacker's computer easily if secure password selection strategies are not applied. For example, many hackers are able to access networking hardware and databases because the system administrator passwords for those resources are still the default passwords (the ones assigned during manufacturing) and so are commonly known; some insiders gain unauthorized access to systems using passwords written down on sticky notes attached to a user's monitor. Consequently, it is important to select passwords that are *strong passwords* but are also easy to remember without writing them down. Strong passwords are passwords that are at least eight characters long; use a combination of letters, numbers, and symbols; and do not form words found in the dictionary or that match the username that the password is associated with. Some strategies for selecting good passwords are listed in Figure 9-4.

A growing trend in possessed knowledge access systems is the use of *cognitive authentication systems* instead of, or in conjunction with, usernames and passwords. Cognitive authentication systems use information that an individual should know or can remember easily.

> **Possessed knowledge access system.** An access control system that uses information only the individual should know to identify that individual.
> **Password.** A secret combination of characters used to gain access to a computer, computer network, or other resource.

Some systems use personal information about the individual (such as his or her city of birth, first elementary school attended, or amount of home mortgage) that was pulled from public databases or the company database and the individual must supply the correct answer in order to be granted access. Other systems (such as the password recovery systems used by many secure Web sites to verify individuals when they forget their password) allow the individual to supply answers to questions when the account is created and then the individual can supply those answers again for authentication purposes when needed.

Possessed knowledge systems are often used in conjunction with the *possessed object access systems* and *biometric access systems* that are discussed next. Using two different methods to authenticate a user is called **two-factor authentication**. Typically, the methods used are some type of possessed knowledge (something you know) along with either a *possessed object* (something you have) or a *biometric feature* (something you are). Two-factor authentication adds an additional level of security to an access control system, since hackers are much less likely to be able to gain access to two different required factors. One emerging type of two-factor authentication used to protect access to sensitive online accounts (such as online banking accounts) uses a conventional username/password combination in conjunction with an access card (such as the one shown in Figure 9-5) that displays a *one-time password (OTP)* when the button on the card is pressed. The OTP changes each time the button is pressed and the current OTP must be entered on the logon screen along with the username/password in order to log on to the account. Two-factor authentication systems are common in many countries and use is growing in the United States. In fact, a federal guideline that went into effect in 2007 instructs banks, credit unions, and other financial institutions to replace single-factor authentication systems (typically username/password systems) with systems using two-factor authentication, and some banks (such as Bank of America) offer two-factor authentication protection via an OTP access card or an OTP sent on demand to your mobile phone. Many other countries are considering or implementing similar guidelines or mandates.

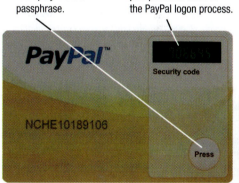

FIGURE 9-5

Two-factor authentication. With this system, the user must have both the access card (to obtain the OTP) and his or her conventional username/password combination, in order to log on to his or her online account.

1. Press the button to display the OTP passphrase.

2. The displayed OTP passphrase is used in the PayPal logon process.

> **⚠ CAUTION**
>
> Don't supply answers to the cognitive authentication questions (like your high school or your pet's name) used in the password recovery process of many Web sites that a hacker may be able to guess based on information found on your Facebook page, an online database, or another online source. Instead, supply answers that you can remember but that also follow secure password rules. For instance, if your dog's name is Spot, you could enter *MDN1s$pOT* as the answer to a question about your pet's name and remember it as "My dog's name is Spot."

Possessed Object Access Systems

Possessed object access systems use physical objects for identification purposes and they are frequently used to control access to facilities and computer systems. Common types of possessed objects are smart cards, RFID-encoded badges, and magnetic cards that are swiped through or placed close to a reader to be read (see Figure 9-6). Increasingly, *USB security keys* (also called *USB security tokens*)—USB flash drives that are inserted into a computer to grant access to a network, to supply Web site usernames and passwords, or

---

> **Two-factor authentication.** Using two different methods to authenticate a user. > **Possessed object access system.** An access control system that uses a physical object an individual has in his or her possession to identify that individual.

SMART CARDS
Are read by a smart card reader to provide access to a facility or computer system.

USB SECURITY TOKENS
Are inserted into one of the computer's USB ports to provide access to that computer system.

FIGURE 9-6

Possessed objects. Help protect against unauthorized access; some can also store additional security credentials.

to provide other security features—are also being used. Access cards (like the one shown in Figure 9-5) and other devices used to supply the OTPs used to log on to Web sites and other resources are another type of *security token* possessed object.

One disadvantage of using possessed objects is that the object can be lost or, like passwords, can be used by an unauthorized individual if that individual has possession of the object. This latter disadvantage can be overcome by using a second factor, such as requiring the user to supply a username/password combination or be authenticated by a fingerprint or other type of *biometric* data in order to use the possessed object.

Biometric Access Systems

Biometrics is the study of identifying individuals using measurable, unique physiological or behavioral characteristics. **Biometric access systems** typically identify users by a particular unique biological characteristic (such as a fingerprint, a hand, a face, or an iris), although personal traits are used in some systems. For instance, some systems today use *keystroke dynamics* to recognize an individual's unique typing pattern to authenticate the user as he or she types in his or her username and password; other systems identify an individual via his or her voice, signature, or gait. Because the means of access (usually a part of the body) cannot typically be used by anyone other than the authorized individual, biometric access systems can perform both identification and authentication.

To identify and authenticate an individual, biometric access systems typically use a biometric reader (such as a *fingerprint reader* or *hand geometry reader* to identify an individual based on his or her fingerprint or hand image) or a digital camera (to identify an individual based on his or her face or iris), in conjunction with software and a database. The system matches the supplied biometric data with the biometric data that was stored in the database when the individual was enrolled in the system and authenticates the individual if the data matches. To speed up the process, many biometric access systems require users to identify themselves first (such as by entering a username or swiping a smart card), and then the system uses that identifying information to verify that the supplied biometric data matches the identified person.

Biometric access systems are used to control access to secure facilities (such as corporate headquarters and prisons); to log users on to computers, networks, and secure Web sites (by using an external reader or one built into the computer); to punch employees in and out of work; and to confirm consumers' identities at ATM machines and check-cashing services. Biometric readers are also increasingly being built into notebook computers, external hard drives (like the one shown in Figure 4-20 in Chapter 4), USB flash drives, and other hardware to prevent unauthorized use of those devices.

>Biometric access system. An access control system that uses one unique physical characteristic of an individual (such as a fingerprint, face, or voice) to authenticate that individual.

In addition to being used to control access to computers, networks, and other resources, biometrics are an important part of the systems used by law enforcement agencies and the military to identify individuals. For instance, the border control systems in many countries use biometrics to identify citizens, travelers, criminal suspects, and potential terrorists, and biometric identification systems are used extensively by law enforcement agencies and the military in areas of conflict. For example, biometric identification systems are being used in Iraq to identify members of the Iraqi police and military, prisoners, prison guards, authorized gun owners, citizens, contract employees, known criminals, and criminal suspects. In addition, *face recognition systems* (biometric systems that use cameras and a database of photos to attempt to identify individuals as they walk by the cameras) are used in many airports and other public locations to help identify known terrorists and criminal suspects.

Biometric access systems are very accurate. In fact, the odds of two different individuals having identical irises is 1 in 10^{78} and the statistical probability of two different irises being declared a match are 1 in 1.2 million—even identical twins (who have the same DNA structure) have different fingerprints and irises. Systems based on biological characteristics (such as a person's iris, hand geometry, face, or

FINGERPRINT RECOGNITION SYSTEMS
Typically used to protect access to office computers, to automatically supply Web site passwords on home computers, and to pay for products or services.

HAND GEOMETRY SYSTEMS
Typically used to control access to facilities (such as government offices, prisons, and military facilities) and to punch in and out of work.

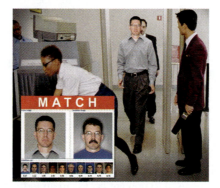

FACE RECOGNITION SYSTEMS
Typically used to control access to highly secure areas, as well as to identify individuals for law enforcement purposes.

IRIS RECOGNITION SYSTEMS
Typically used to control access to highly secure areas and by the military; also beginning to be used to authenticate ATM users and other consumers.

fingerprint) tend to be more accurate than those based on a personal trait (such as a person's voice or written signature) because biological traits do not change, but physical traits might change (such as an individual's voice, which might be affected by a cold, or a written signature, which might be affected by a broken wrist). In addition, biometric characteristics cannot be lost (like an access card), cannot be forgotten (like a password), and do not have to be pulled out of a briefcase or pocket (like an access card or other type of possessed object).

The primary disadvantages of biometric access systems are that much of the necessary hardware and software is expensive, and the data used for authentication (such as a fingerprint or an iris image) cannot be reset if it is compromised. In addition, fingerprint and hand geometry systems typically require contact with the reader device, though some systems under development (such as one that identifies individuals based on the veins in their hands) are contactless systems.

Some examples of the most commonly used types of biometric access and identification systems are shown in Figure 9-7.

FIGURE 9-7
Types of biometric access and identification systems.

VIDEO PODCAST

Go to the Chapter 9 page at **www.cengage.com/computerconcepts/np/uc13** to download or listen to the "How To: Use Face Recognition with Your Computer" video podcast.

NET

Controlling Access to Wireless Networks

As already discussed, wireless networks—such as Wi-Fi networks—are less secure, in general, than wired networks. There are Wi-Fi security procedures, however, that can be used to protect against unauthorized use of a wireless network and to *encrypt* data sent over the network so that it is unreadable if it is intercepted. The original Wi-Fi security standard was

Because the SSID is being broadcast, the user can select the network from the list.

The user must supply the appropriate network key or passphrase in order to connect to the network.

If the SSID isn't broadcast, the user must add the network manually, using its SSID, in order to log on.

▲ **FIGURE 9-8**
Accessing a Wi-Fi network. To access a secure network, the appropriate passphrase must be supplied.

WEP (*Wired Equivalent Privacy*). WEP is now considered insecure and has been replaced with the more secure *WPA* (*Wi-Fi Protected Access*) and the even more secure *WPA2* standards. However, Wi-Fi security features only work if they are enabled. Most Wi-Fi hardware today is shipped with the security features switched off, and many network owners never enable them, leaving those networks unsecured.

To protect against unauthorized access, Wi-Fi network owners should secure their networks by changing the router or access point settings to enable one of the encryption standards and to assign a *network key* or *passphrase* (essentially a password) that must be supplied in order to access the secured network. In addition, the name of the network (called the *SSID*) can be hidden from view by switching off the SSID broadcast feature. While hiding the network name will not deter serious hackers, it may reduce the number of casual war drivers or neighbors accessing the network. Once a network is secured, users who want to connect to that network need to either select or supply the network SSID name (depending on whether or not the SSID is being broadcast) and then enter the network key assigned to that network (see Figure 9-8). For an overview of how you can secure your wireless home router, see the How It Works box.

Firewalls, Encryption, and Virtual Private Networks (VPNs)

In addition to the access control systems just discussed, there are a number of other tools that can be used to prevent access to an individual computer or to prevent data from being intercepted in an understandable form during transit. These tools are discussed next.

Firewalls

A **firewall** is a security system that essentially creates a barrier between a computer or network and the Internet in order to protect against unauthorized access. Firewalls are typically two-way, so they check all incoming (from the Internet to the computer or the network) and outgoing (from the computer or the network to the Internet) traffic and allow only authorized traffic to pass through the firewall. *Personal firewalls* are typically software-based systems that are geared toward protecting home computers from hackers attempting to access those computers through their Internet connections. All computers with direct Internet connections (such as DSL, cable, satellite, or fixed wireless Internet access) should use a firewall (computers using dial-up Internet access only are relatively safe from hackers). Personal firewalls can be stand-alone programs (such as the free *ZoneAlarm* program); they are also built into many operating systems (such as the *Windows Firewall* program shown in Figure 9-9). Many routers, modems, and other pieces of networking hardware also include built-in firewall capabilities to help secure the networks these devices are used with. Firewalls designed to protect business networks may be software-based, hardware-based, or a combination of the two. They can typically be used both to prevent network access by hackers and other outsiders, as well as to control employee Internet access.

✓ **TIP**

If a legitimate application installed on your computer needs to access the Internet but cannot, check your firewall settings—you may need to unblock that program.

>**Firewall.** A collection of hardware and/or software intended to protect a computer or computer network from unauthorized access.

HOW IT WORKS

Securing a Wireless Home Router

If you have a home wireless network, it is important to secure it properly so it cannot be used by unauthorized individuals. Security settings are specified in the router's configuration screen, such as the one shown in the accompanying illustration. To open your router's configuration screen to check or modify the settings, type the IP address assigned to that device (such as 192.168.0.1— check for a sticker on the bottom of your router or your router's documentation for its default IP address and username) in your browser's Address bar. Use the default password listed in your router documentation to log on the first time, and then change the password using the configuration screen to prevent unauthorized individuals from changing your router settings. To secure the router, enter the network name (SSID) you want to have associated with the router, select the appropriate security mode (such as WEP, WPA, or WPA2) to be used, and then type a secure passphrase to be used in order to log on to the network.

For additional security, *MAC (Media Access Control) address filtering* can be used to allow only the devices whose network adapter MAC addresses you enter into your router's settings access to the network. Because hackers can "spoof" MAC addresses by changing the MAC addresses of their devices to match an authorized MAC address (once the hacker determines those addresses), MAC address filtering should not be considered an alternative to using WPA or WPA2 encryption. However, it does add another layer of protection. Other precautions include designating specific times (such as when you are away from home) that the router will deny access to any device, and reducing the strength of the wireless signal if its current strength reaches farther than you need.

Use the router's IP address to display the router's configuration screen.

Use this tab to enable MAC address filtering.

Use this tab to change the administrator password used to access this configuration screen.

Type your desired SSID here.

Enable SSID broadcast here.

Select the desired security mode here.

Type your desired network key here.

Firewalls work by closing down all external *communications port addresses* (the electronic connections that allow a computer to communicate with other computers) to unauthorized computers and programs. While business firewalls are set up by the network administrator and those settings typically cannot be changed by end users, individuals may choose to change the settings for their personal firewall. For example, the user can choose to be notified when any application program on the computer is trying to access the Internet, to specify the programs that are allowed to access the Internet, or to block all incoming connections temporarily. In addition to protecting your computer from outside access, firewall programs also protect against

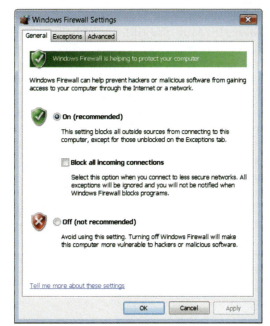

ONLINE VIDEO

Go to the Chapter 9 page at **www.cengage.com/computerconcepts/np/uc13** to watch the "Securing Your Wireless Router" video clip.

FIGURE 9-9

A personal firewall program. The firewall is on, so only authorized traffic can access the computer.

1. Click to run the security scan.

2. No threats were found.

FIGURE 9-10
Online security scans can check your system for vulnerabilities.

any spyware, computer viruses, or other malicious programs located on your computer that are designed to send data from your computer (such as credit card numbers, Web site passwords, and other sensitive data stored on your hard drive) to a hacker at the hacker's request.

A related type of security system increasingly being used by businesses today is an *intrusion prevention system (IPS)*. Whereas a firewall tries to block unauthorized traffic, an IPS continuously monitors and analyzes the traffic allowed by the firewall to try to detect possible attacks as they are occurring. If an attack is in progress, IPS software can immediately block it.

After installing and setting up a firewall (and an IPS if needed), individuals and businesses should test their systems to determine if vulnerabilities still exist. Individuals can use online security tests—such as the *Symantec Security Check* shown in Figure 9-10 or the tests at Gibson Research's *Shields Up* site—to check their computers; businesses may wish to hire an outside consultant to perform a comprehensive security assessment.

Encryption

Encryption is a way of temporarily converting data into a form, known as a *cipher*, which is unreadable until it is *decrypted* (unscrambled) in order to protect that data from being viewed by unauthorized individuals. As previously discussed, secure Wi-Fi networks use encryption to secure data that is transferred over the network. **Secure Web pages** use encryption so that sensitive data (such as credit card numbers) sent via the Web page is protected as it travels over the Internet. The most common security protocols used with secure Web pages are *Secure Sockets Layer (SSL)* and *Extended Validation Secure Sockets Layer (EV SSL)*. The URL for Web pages using either form of SSL begins with *https:* instead of *http:*.

Some Internet services (such as *Skype VoIP* calls and *HushMail* Web-based e-mails) use built-in encryption. Encryption can also be added manually to a file or an e-mail message before it is sent over the Internet to ensure that the content is unreadable if the file or message is intercepted during transit. In addition to securing files during transit, encryption can be used to protect the files stored on a hard drive so they will be unreadable if opened by an unauthorized person (such as if a hacker accesses a file containing sensitive data or if a computer containing sensitive files is lost or stolen). Increasingly, computers and hard drives (particularly those used with portable computers) are *self-encrypting*; that is, encrypting all data automatically and invisibly to the user. Windows, Mac OS, and other current operating systems support encryption and businesses are increasingly turning to encryption to prevent data loss, if a data breach should occur.

✓ **TIP**

Sensitive information (such as credit card numbers, account numbers, and Web site passwords) should only be entered on secure Web pages to prevent that data from being intercepted by a criminal.

✓ **TIP**

An emerging encryption standard thay may eventually replace SSL is *Transport Layer Security* (*TLS*).

> **Encryption.** A method of scrambling the contents of an e-mail message or a file to make it unreadable if an unauthorized user intercepts it.
> **Secure Web page.** A Web page that uses encryption to protect information transmitted via that Web page.

The two most common types of encryption in use today are *public key encryption* (often used with content being transmitted over the Internet, such as secure Web pages and encrypted e-mail) and *private key encryption* (most often used to encrypt files or the content of a hard drive or other device). **Private key encryption**, also called *symmetric key encryption*, uses a single secret *private key* (essentially a password) to both encrypt and decrypt the file or message. It is often used to encrypt files stored on an individual's computer, since the individual who selects the private key is likely the only one who will need to access those files. Private key encryption can also be used to send files securely to others, provided both the sender and recipient agree on the private key that will be used to access the file. Private key encryption capabilities are incorporated into a variety of programs today, including Microsoft Office, the WinZip file compression program, and Adobe Acrobat (the program used to create PDF files). To encrypt a document in Microsoft Word, for instance, you use the *Prepare* option on the Office menu, choose *Encrypt Document*, type the desired password (private key), and then save the file. To open that document again (or any copies of the file, such as those sent via e-mail), the password assigned to that file must be entered correctly.

Public key encryption, also called *asymmetric key encryption*, utilizes two encryption keys to encrypt and decrypt documents. Specifically, public key encryption uses a pair of keys (a private key and a *public key*) that are related mathematically to each other and have been assigned to a particular individual. An individual's public key is not secret and is available for anyone to use, but the corresponding private key is used only by the individual to whom it was assigned. Documents or messages encrypted with a public key can only be decrypted with the matching private key.

Public/private key pairs are generated by the program being used to perform the encryption or they are obtained via the Internet through a *Certificate Authority*, such as VeriSign or Thawte. Once obtained, encryption keys are stored in your browser, e-mail program, and any other program with which they will be used—this is typically done automatically for you when you obtain your key pairs. Obtaining a business public/private key pair usually requires a fee, but free key pairs for personal use are available through some Certificate Authorities. If a third-party encryption program is used (such as *Pretty Good Privacy* or *PGP*), the program typically takes care of obtaining and managing your keys for you.

To send someone an encrypted e-mail message or file using public key encryption, you need his or her public key. If that person has previously sent you his or her public key (such as via an e-mail message), it was likely stored by your e-mail program in your address book or contacts list, or by your encryption program in a central key directory used by that program. In either case, that public key is available whenever you want to send that person an encrypted document. If you do not already have the public key belonging to the individual to whom you wish to send an encrypted e-mail or file, you will need to request it from that individual. Once the recipient's public key has been used to encrypt the file or e-mail message and that document is received, the recipient uses his or her private key to decrypt the encrypted contents (see Figure 9-11).

To avoid the need to obtain the recipient's public key before sending that person an encrypted e-mail, *Web-based encrypted e-mail* can be used. Web-based encrypted e-mail works similarly to regular Web-based e-mail (in which e-mail is composed and viewed on a Web page belonging to a Web-based e-mail provider), but Web-based encrypted e-mail systems use secure Web servers to host the Web pages that are used to compose and read e-mail messages. Some Web-based encrypted e-mail systems—such as the popular free *HushMail* service that automatically encrypts all e-mail sent through the

VIDEO PODCAST

Go to the Chapter 9 page at **www.cengage.com/ computerconcepts/np/uc13** to download or listen to the "How To: Create an Encrypted Partition On Your Hard Drive" video podcast.

NET

FURTHER EXPLORATION Go

Go to the Chapter 9 page at **www.cengage.com/ computerconcepts/np/uc13** for links to information about encryption.

> **Public key encryption.** A type of encryption that uses key pairs to encrypt and decrypt the file or message. > **Private key encryption.** A type of encryption that uses a single key to encrypt and decrypt the file or message.

1. The e-mail message (including any attached files) is created by the sender, who then uses the recipient's public key to encrypt the e-mail (including any attached files) using the Message Options dialog box.

2. The e-mail (including any attached files) is transmitted over the Internet in its encrypted form.

```
!!START
GjTw4rbwFGeyqiLR77MBiBapKS0Ka0:3ss5CyASSEzw3lXj8V
khzIAFfLylqyiuwo:uZKx4ECQNq5kLnQ;lwa81bhckhXNgHAj
YUPO;6TTJozHMvYU7rEBlXfZcU7GoIYXDd7h8XjERAmP9r
yi:th30MeZt7QdcVwXfdAo7Ey3eUEX19nmxjTul;qqxwGows9
OwWZcJ0Y:euiQEDbgVGdWTjSan3UjpVCyXcXEODNhnNP
wYCdjMeG1dFOrsuFc4CUniQ1UVR0ML51N2LJ8uXsYwsrzP
psn3f2zJCCEiGun59VEc4dUBMF1he1UFC7IE0RkSZ22gAAQ
UEsgWB5pWYUsuWLc1kmQ:AHzejiWRRLDkG3LwqB6qaQJ
AGmu2Pap8uW8PgQ0J74G5BNEjgy0O3wceuYeApaNE
END!!
```

3. The recipient receives the encrypted message and opens it using an e-mail program. When prompted by the program, the recipient enters his or her private key to decrypt the e-mail (including any attached files) so it becomes readable again.

Joe's public key

Joe's private key

FIGURE 9-11
Using public key encryption to secure an e-mail message.

service—require both the sender and recipient to have accounts. Others require only the sender to have an account and the recipient is sent an e-mail containing instructions regarding how to view the message on a secure Web page.

There are various strengths of encryption available; the stronger the encryption, the more difficult it is to crack. Older 40-bit encryption (which can only use keys that are 40 bits or 5 characters long) is considered *weak encryption.* Stronger encryption is available today, such as *strong 128-bit encryption* (which uses 16-character keys) and *military-strength 2,048-bit encryption* (which uses 256-character keys), although not without some objections from law enforcement agencies and the government because they state that terrorists routinely use encryption methods to communicate.

Virtual Private Networks (VPNs)

While e-mail and file encryption can be used to transfer individual messages and files securely over the Internet, a **virtual private network (VPN)** is designed to be used when a continuous secure channel over the Internet is needed. A VPN provides a secure private tunnel from the user's computer through the Internet to another destination and is most often used to provide remote employees with secure access to a company network. VPNs use encryption and other security mechanisms to ensure that only authorized users can access the remote network and that the data cannot be intercepted during transit. Since it uses the Internet instead of an expensive private physical network, a VPN can provide a secure environment over a large geographical area at a manageable cost. Once a VPN is set up, the user just needs to log on (such as with a username/password combination or a security token) in order to use the VPN.

VPNs are often used by both businesses and individuals at public Wi-Fi hotspots to prevent data interception when connecting to the Internet via the hotspot. While businesspeople will typically use a VPN set up by their companies, individuals can create *personal VPNs* using software designed for that purpose. This software automatically encrypts all inbound and outbound Internet traffic, including Web pages, e-mail messages, IMs, VoIP calls, and

✓ **TIP**

Unless it is absolutely necessary and you are using a VPN, do not perform sensitive transactions (such as shopping or banking) at a public hotspot.

> **Virtual private network (VPN).** A private, secure path over the Internet that provides authorized users a secure means of accessing a private network via the Internet.

so forth, and also acts as a personal firewall. Using a personal VPN at a public hotspot can help individuals from becoming the victim of a growing trend—*evil twin* Wi-Fi access points, discussed in the Trend box.

Additional Public Hotspot Precautions

The precautions already discussed (such as using firewall software, secure Web pages, VPNs, and encryption) are a good start for protecting against unauthorized access and unauthorized use at a public Wi-Fi hotspot. However, there are additional precautions individuals can use to avoid data (both that which is on their computers and that which is being sent over the Internet) from being compromised. These precautions are listed in Figure 9-12.

Sensible Employee Precautions

A significant number of business security breaches—over 60%, according to a recent University of Washington study—are the responsibility of insiders. Sometimes the employee deliberately performs the act; other times the employee makes a mistake, such as losing a portable computer or removable storage medium, or inadvertently providing access to sensitive data. Consequently, it pays for employers to be cautious with their employees. Some suggestions to avoid security breaches by employees are listed next.

PUBLIC HOTSPOT PRECAUTIONS

Turn off automatic connections and pay attention to the list of available hotspots to try to make sure you connect to a legitimate access point (not an evil twin).

Use a personal firewall to control the traffic going to and from your computer and temporarily use it to block all incoming connections.

Use a virtual private network (VPN) to secure all activity between your computer and the Internet.

Only enter passwords, credit card numbers, and other data on secure Web pages using a VPN.

If you're not using a VPN, encrypt all sensitive files before transferring or e-mailing them.

If you're not using a VPN, avoid online shopping, banking, and other sensitive transactions.

Turn off file sharing so others can't access the files on your hard drive.

Turn off Bluetooth and Wi-Fi when you are not using them.

Disable *ad hoc* capabilities to prevent another computer from connecting to your computer directly without using an access point.

Use antivirus software and make sure your operating system is up to date.

FIGURE 9-12
Sensible precautions for public Wi-Fi hotspot users.

Screen Potential New Hires Carefully

Employers should carefully investigate the background of all potential employees. Some people falsify résumés to get jobs. Others may have criminal records or currently be charged with a crime. One embarrassing mistake made by Rutgers University was to hire David Smith, the author of the *Melissa* computer virus, as a computer technician when he was out on bail following the arrest for that crime.

Watch for Disgruntled Employees and Ex-Employees

The type of employee who is most likely to commit a computer crime is one who has recently been terminated or passed over for a promotion, or one who has some reason to want to "get even" with the organization. Limiting access for each employee to only the resources needed for his or her job (referred to as the *Principle of Least Privilege*) and monitoring any attempts to access off-limit resources can help prevent some types of problems, such as unauthorized access of sensitive files, unintentional damage like deleting or changing files inadvertently, or sabotage like deleting or changing company files intentionally. In addition, it is vital that whenever an employee leaves the company for any reason, all access to the system for that individual (username, password, e-mail address, and so forth) should be removed immediately. For employees with high levels of system access, simultaneously removing access while the termination is taking place is even better. Waiting even a few minutes can be too late, since just-fired employees have been known to barricade themselves in their office immediately after being terminated in order to change passwords, sabotage records, and perform other malicious acts. Some wait slightly longer, such as one computer administrator at a Houston organ and tissue donation center who recently pled guilty to accessing the company computer system the evening of and day after being fired and intentionally deleting numerous software applications and important files, such as organ donation records, accounting files, and backup files. She was charged with one

NET

TREND

Evil Twins

An *evil twin* is a fake Wi-Fi hotspot set up by a thief to masquerade as a legitimate Wi-Fi hotspot in order to gather personal or corporate information from individuals who connect to that hotspot thinking it is the legitimate one. Typically, the thief selects a legitimate hotspot and moves within range of that hotspot, uses software to discover the network name (SSID) and radio frequency being used by the legitimate hotspot, and then broadcasts his or her hotspot using the same SSID as the legitimate one. To the end user, the evil twin looks like the legitimate hotspot because it uses the same SSID and settings as the "good twin" it is impersonating. If an end user connects to the evil twin to access the Internet, the thief can intercept sensitive data sent to the Internet, such as passwords or credit card information. That information can then be used for *identity theft* and other fraudulent activities.

Because of the increased use of Wi-Fi hotspots and the availability of software enabling a would-be thief to set up an evil twin hotspot, evil twins are an increasing threat. To make matters worse, some evil twins are able to disconnect users from the legitimate hotspot in hopes the users will be reconnected automatically to the evil twin instead of the legitimate hotspot. To protect yourself, set up your portable computer to only connect manually to hotspots so you cannot be connected to an evil twin hotspot inadvertently. In addition, refrain from performing sensitive transactions (such as shopping and banking) at public hotspots. Businesspeople should use a VPN when connecting to the company server via a Wi-Fi hotspot; individuals needing to perform sensitive transactions should use a personal VPN, such as the one shown in the accompanying figure.

count of unauthorized computer access, sentenced to two years in prison, and ordered to pay more than $94,000 in restitution.

Develop Policies and Controls

All companies should develop policies and controls regarding security matters. As already mentioned, employees should be granted the least amount of access to the company network that they need to perform their job. Employees should be educated about the seriousness and consequences of hacking, data theft, and other computer crimes, and they should be taught what to do when they suspect a computer crime has been committed. Employees should also be instructed about proper computer and e-mail usage policies—such as whether or not downloading and installing software on company computers is allowed, whether or not employees are responsible for updating their computers, and the types of removable storage mediums (such as USB flash drives or portable digital media players) that may be used with company computers—in order to avoid inadvertently creating a security problem. Policies for removing computers and storage media containing sensitive data from the premises should also be implemented and enforced, and sensitive documents should be shredded when they are no longer needed. In addition, policies should be updated as needed to respond to new types of threats. For instance, the Pentagon banned USB flash drives in late 2008 due to a computer virus threat; it is unknown at this time when or if their use will be allowed again.

Employees who work from home or otherwise access the company network via the Internet also need to be educated about security policies for remote access and the proper precautions that need to be taken. These precautions include keeping their operating system and security software up to date, and using only encrypted storage devices (such as self-encrypting USB flash drives) when transporting documents between work and home. In addition, telecommuting workers and outside contractors should not be allowed to have peer-to-peer (P2P) software on computers containing company documents, since data is increasingly being exposed through the use of P2P networks. For instance, classified data about the U.S. presidential helicopter was discovered recently on a computer in Iran and traced back to a P2P network and the computer of a military contractor in Maryland, and the Social Security numbers and other personal data belonging to about 17,000 current and former Pfizer workers were leaked onto a P2P network in 2007 after an employee installed unauthorized P2P software on a company notebook computer provided for use at her home.

Use Data-Leakage Prevention and Enterprise Rights-Management Software

As employees are increasingly bringing portable devices (such as mobile phones, portable digital media players, and USB flash drives) that can interact with business networks to the office, the challenge of securing these devices (and the company network against these devices) has grown. Some companies now prohibit all portable devices; others allow only company-issued devices so they can ensure appropriate security measures, such as encryption, password protection, and the ability to wipe the device clean remotely if it is lost or stolen, are implemented.

To protect against employees copying or sending confidential data to others either intentionally or accidentally, *data-leakage prevention systems* can be used. Data-leakage prevention systems are available as software and/or hardware systems, and have a range of capabilities, but the overall goal is to prevent sensitive data from exposure. For instance, some systems control which devices (such as USB flash drives and portable digital media players) can be connected to an employee's computer (see Figure 9-13) in order to prevent sensitive data from being taken home inadvertently or intentionally. Other data-leakage prevention systems—sometimes also called *outbound-content monitoring systems*—scan all outgoing communications (e-mail, transferred files, instant messages, and so forth) for documents containing Social Security numbers, intellectual property, and other confidential information. Some can also continually scan network devices to locate sensitive data in documents stored on computers to ensure that sensitive files are not on the computer of an employee who should not have access to them. For even stronger protection of confidential company documents, *enterprise rights-management software*, which encrypts confidential documents and limits functions such as printing, editing, and copying the data to only authorized users with the appropriate password, can be used.

FIGURE 9-13
Data-leakage prevention software can control which devices can be connected to an employee's computer.

Ask Business Partners to Review their Security

In this networked economy, many organizations provide some access to internal resources for business partners. If those external companies are lax with their security measures, however, attacks through the business partners' computers (such as via an employee or hacker) are possible. Consequently, businesses should make sure that their business partners maintain adequate security policies and controls. Regulations—such as the *Sarbanes-Oxley Act of 2002*—increasingly require businesses to ensure that adequate controls are in place to preserve the integrity of financial reports. This includes outside companies—such as business partners and *outsourcing companies* (outside vendors for specific business tasks, as discussed in Chapter 12)—if they have access to sensitive corporate data. Companies that utilize cloud computing also need to ensure that the cloud vendor's policies (such as for protecting access to stored data, using adequate encryption techniques and backup procedures, submitting to necessary audits, and storing data in locations with the desired security and privacy laws) match the company's requirements.

COMPUTER SABOTAGE

Computer sabotage—acts of malicious destruction to a computer or computer resource—is another common type of computer crime today. Computer sabotage can take several forms, including launching a *computer virus* or a *denial of service (DoS) attack*, altering the content of a Web site, or changing data or programs located on a computer. A common tool used to perform computer sabotage is a *botnet*, discussed next. Computer sabotage is illegal in the United States, and acts of sabotage are estimated to cost individuals and organizations billions of dollars per year, primarily for labor costs related to correcting the problems caused by the sabotage, lost productivity, and lost sales.

Botnets

A computer that is controlled by a hacker or other computer criminal is referred to as a **bot** or *zombie computer*; a group of bots that are controlled by one individual and can work together in a coordinated fashion is called a **botnet**. According to the FBI, an estimated one million U.S. computers are currently part of a botnet; consequently, botnets are a major security threat. Criminals (called *botherders*) are increasingly creating botnets to use for computer sabotage, such as to spread *malware* and to launch *denial of service (DoS) attacks*, discussed shortly. Botherders also often sell their botnet services to send spam and launch Internet attacks on their clients' behalf, as well as use them to steal identity information, credit card numbers, passwords, corporate secrets, and other sensitive data, which are then sold to other criminals or otherwise used in an illegal manner.

Computer Viruses and Other Types of Malware

Malware is a generic term that refers to any type of malicious software. Malware programs are intentionally written to perform destructive acts, such as damaging programs, deleting files, erasing an entire hard drive, or slowing down the performance of a computer. This damage can take place immediately after a computer is *infected* (that is, the malware software is installed) or it can begin when a particular condition is met. A malware program that activates when it detects a certain condition, such as when a particular keystroke is pressed or an employee's name is deleted from an employee file, is called a *logic bomb*. A logic bomb that is triggered by a particular date or time is called a *time bomb*.

Writing a computer virus or other type of malware or even posting the malware code on the Internet is not illegal, but it is considered highly unethical and irresponsible behavior. Distributing malware, on the other hand, is illegal, and virus writers who release their malware are being vigorously prosecuted. Malware can be very costly in terms of the labor costs associated with removing the viruses and correcting any resulting damage, as well as the cost of lost productivity of employees. One type of malware often used by computer criminals to send sensitive data secretly from

---

ASK THE EXPERT

symantec. **Marian Merritt,** Internet Safety Advocate, Symantec Corporation

How can individuals tell if their computers are part of a botnet?

Bots were created to steal your personal information or take control of your computer without you knowing. Because of that, they are silent in nature. The only way computer users can tell their computers are infected by a bot is by using a security solution with bot detection capabilities.

>**Computer sabotage.** An act of malicious destruction to a computer or computer resource. >**Bot.** A computer that is controlled by a hacker or other computer criminal. >**Botnet.** A group of bots that are controlled by one individual. >**Malware.** Any type of malicious software.

infected computers to the criminal—spyware—was discussed in Chapter 8. The most common other types of malware are discussed next.

Computer Viruses

One type of malware is the **computer virus**—a software program that is installed without the permission or knowledge of the computer user, that is designed to alter the way a computer operates, and that can replicate itself to infect any new media it has access to. Computer viruses are often embedded into program or data files (often games, videos, and music files downloaded from Web pages or shared via a P2P service). They are spread whenever the infected file is downloaded, is transferred to a new computer via an infected removable storage medium, or is e-mailed to another computer (see Figure 9-14). Viruses can also be installed when a recipient clicks a link in an e-mail message (often in an unsolicited e-mail message that resembles a legitimate e-mail message that normally contains a link, such as an electronic greeting card e-mail that contains a link to view the card), as well as through links in instant messages. Regardless of how it is obtained, once a copy of the infected file reaches a new computer it typically embeds itself into program, data, or system files on the new computer and remains there, affecting that computer according to its programmed instructions, until it is discovered and removed.

FIGURE 9-14
How a computer virus or other type of malicious software might spread.

1. A computer virus originates when an unscrupulous programmer intentionally creates it and embeds it in a file. The infected file is then posted to a Web page where it will be downloaded via the Internet or is sent as an e-mail attachment to a large group of people.

THE INTERNET

COMPANY NETWORK

NET

3. A virus can spread very quickly because every computer that comes in contact with the virus—whether through an infected removable storage medium, infected downloaded file, or infected e-mail attachment—becomes infected, unless virus-protection software is used to prevent it.

2. When the infected file is opened on a computer, the virus copies itself to that computer's hard drive and the computer becomes infected. The virus may then e-mail itself to people in the newly infected computer's e-mail address book or copy itself to any removable storage medium inserted into the that computer.

>**Computer virus.** A software program installed without the user's knowledge and designed to alter the way a computer operates or to cause harm to the computer system.

ONLINE VIDEO

Go to the Chapter 9 page at **www.cengage.com/computerconcepts/np/uc13** to watch the "How Worms Spread Using AutoPlay" video clip.

Computer Worms

Another common form of malware is the **computer worm**. Like a computer virus, a computer worm is a malicious program that is typically designed to cause damage. Unlike a computer virus, however, a computer worm does not infect other computer files on the infected computer in order to replicate itself; instead, it spreads by creating copies of its code and sending those copies to other computers via a network. Often, the worm is sent to other computers as an e-mail attachment. Usually after the infected e-mail attachment is opened by an individual, the worm inflicts its damage and then automatically sends copies of itself to other computers via the Internet or a private network, typically using addresses in the e-mail address book located on the newly infected computer. When those e-mail messages and their attachments are opened, the new computers become infected and the cycle continues. Because of its distribution method, a worm can spread very rapidly. For instance, the *Mydoom* worm (which was released in 2004 and is considered one of the fastest spreading worms ever) spread so rapidly that, at one point, one out of every 10 e-mails contained the worm.

Some newer worms do not require any action by the users (such as opening an e-mail attachment) to infect their computers. Instead, the worm scans the Internet looking for computers that are vulnerable to that particular worm and sends a copy of itself to those computers to infect them. Other worms just require the user to view an infected e-mail message or insert an infected removable storage medium (such as a USB flash drive) into the computer, in order to infect the computer. Still other worms are specifically written to take advantage of newly discovered *security holes* (vulnerabilities) in operating systems and e-mail programs. Worms and other types of malware that are designed to take advantage of a security hole and are released at a time when no security patch to correct the problem is available are referred to as *zero-day attacks*. Unfortunately, as malware writing tools become more sophisticated, zero-day attacks are becoming more common.

Trojan Horses

A **Trojan horse** is a type of malware that masquerades as something else—usually an application program (such as what appears to be a game or utility program). When the seemingly legitimate program is downloaded or installed, the malware part of the Trojan horse infects the computer. Many recent Trojan horses masquerade as normal ongoing activities (such as the Windows Update service or an *antivirus* or *antispyware program* telling you to download a file containing program updates) when they are installed to try to trick unsuspecting users into downloading another malware program or buying a useless program. For instance, after a *rogue antivirus program* like the one shown in Figure 9-15 is installed (usually without the user's direct knowledge or permission), the malware takes over the computer displaying warning messages or scan results (see Figure 9-15) indicating the computer is infected with malware. In addition, the rogue antivirus program typically prevents access to any Web sites other than its own and prompts the user to buy a fake antimalware program to get rid of the "malware." Usually the only malware on the computer is the rogue program,

FIGURE 9-15

Rogue antivirus programs. These programs try to trick victims into purchasing subscriptions to remove nonexistent malware supposedly installed on their computers.

> **Computer worm.** A malicious program designed to spread rapidly to a large number of computers by sending copies of itself to other computers.
> **Trojan horse.** A malicious program that masquerades as something else.

but it is often very intrusive (such as displaying constant messages on the desktop and in pop-up windows and hiding the options needed to change the hijacked settings back to normal), and it is extremely hard to remove.

Unlike viruses and worms, Trojan horses cannot replicate themselves. Trojan horses are usually spread by being downloaded from the Internet, though they may also be sent as an e-mail attachment, either from the Trojan horse author or from individuals who forward it, not realizing the program is a Trojan horse. Some Trojan horses today act as spyware and are designed to find sensitive information about an individual (such as a Social Security number or a bank account number) or about a company (such as corporate intellectual property like mechanical designs, electronic schematics, and other valuable proprietary information) located on infected computers and then send that information to the malware creator to be used in illegal activities. One emerging type of Trojan horse is called a *RAT* (*Remote-Access Trojan*). RATs are typically installed via small files obtained from an Internet download, such as free software, games, or electronic greeting cards. Once installed, RATs are designed to record every keystroke made on the infected computer and then send the sensitive information they recorded (such as account numbers and passwords) to criminals.

Mobile Malware

In addition to computers, malware also can infect mobile phones, portable digital media players, printers, and other devices that contain computing hardware and software. In fact, some GPS devices and portable digital media players (including some video iPods) shipped recently had malware already installed on them. Mobile phones with Bluetooth capabilities in particular are vulnerable since they can be infected via a Bluetooth connection just by being within range (about 30 feet) of a carrier. Some *mobile malware* is designed to crash the phone's operating system; others are designed to be a nuisance by changing icons or otherwise making the device more difficult to use. Still others are money-oriented, such as malware designed to steal credit card data located on the mobile phone. According to IBM, more malware directed to mobile phones and other devices—such as cars—that contain embedded computers is expected in the near future as those devices continue to incorporate more software components and, consequently, become more vulnerable to malware. However, the lack of a universal operating system for mobile devices (compared with the relatively few operating systems used with personal computers) at the present time limits the amount of mobile malware currently in circulation.

Denial of Service (DoS) Attacks

A **denial of service (DoS) attack** is an act of sabotage that attempts to flood a network server or Web server with so many requests for action that it shuts down or simply cannot handle legitimate requests any longer, causing legitimate users to be denied service. For example, a hacker might set up one or more computers to *ping* (contact) a server continually with a request to send a responding ping back to a false return address, or to request nonexistent information continually. If enough useless traffic is generated, the server has no resources left to deal with legitimate requests (see Figure 9-16). An emerging trend is DoS attacks aimed at mobile wireless networks. These attacks typically involve repeatedly establishing and releasing connections with the goal of overloading the network to disrupt service.

ONLINE VIDEO

Go to the Chapter 9 page at **www.cengage.com/ computerconcepts/np/uc13** to watch the "Demonstration of a Rogue Antivirus Program Spread via Skype" video clip.

FURTHER EXPLORATION Go

Go to the Chapter 9 page at **www.cengage.com/ computerconcepts/np/uc13** for links to information about malware and malware detection.

NET

>**Denial of service (DoS) attack.** An act of sabotage that attempts to flood a network server or a Web server with so much activity that it is unable to function.

1. Hacker's computer sends several simultaneous requests; each request asks to establish a connection to the server but supplies false return information. In a distributed DoS attack, multiple computers send multiple requests at one time.

Hello? I'd like some info...

Hello? I'd like some info...

2. The server tries to respond to each request but can't locate the computer because false return information was provided. The server waits for a short period of time before closing the connection, which ties up the server and keeps others from connecting.

I'm busy, I can't help you right now.

I can't find you, I'll wait and try again...

LEGITIMATE COMPUTER

HACKER'S COMPUTER

3. The hacker's computer continues to send new requests, so as a connection is closed by the server, a new request is waiting. This cycle continues, which ties up the server indefinitely.

Hello? I'd like some info...

4. The server becomes so overwhelmed that legitimate requests cannot get through and, eventually, the server usually crashes.

WEB SERVER

FIGURE 9-16
How a denial of service (DoS) attack might work.

DoS attacks today are often directed toward popular sites (for example, Twitter was recently shut down for two hours due to a DoS attack) and typically are carried out via multiple computers (referred to as a *distributed denial of service attack* or *DDoS attack*). DDoS attacks are typically performed by botnets created by hackers; the computers in the botnet participate in the attacks without the owners' knowledge. Because home computers are increasingly using direct Internet connections but tend to be less protected than school and business computers, hackers are increasingly targeting home computers for botnets used in DDoS attacks and other forms of computer sabotage.

Denial of service attacks can be very costly in terms of business lost (such as when an e-commerce site is shut down), as well as the time and expense required to bring the site back online. Networks that use VoIP are particularly vulnerable to DoS attacks since the real-time nature of VoIP calls means their quality is immediately affected when a DoS attack slows down the network.

Data, Program, or Web Site Alteration

Another type of computer sabotage occurs when a hacker breaches a computer system in order to delete data, change data, modify programs, or otherwise alter the data and programs located there. For example, a student might try to hack into the school database to change his or her grade; a hacker might change a program located on a company server in order to steal money or information; or a disgruntled or former employee might perform a vengeful act, such as altering programs so they work incorrectly, deleting customer records or other critical data, or randomly changing data in a company's database. Like other forms of computer sabotage, data and program alteration is illegal.

Data on Web sites can also be altered by hackers. For instance, individuals sometimes hack into and alter other people's social networking accounts. In early 2009, for instance, the Twitter accounts of over 30 high-profile individuals (including then President-elect Obama) were accessed by an unauthorized individual who sent out fake (and sometimes embarrassing) tweets posing as those individuals. It is also becoming more common for hackers to compromise legitimate Web sites and then use those sites to perform malware attacks. Typically, a hacker alters a legitimate site to display an official-looking message that informs the user that a particular software program must be downloaded, or the hacker posts a rogue banner ad on a legitimate site that redirects the user to a malware site instead of the site for the product featured in the banner ad. According to a report released this year by security company Websense, more than half of the Web sites classified as malicious are actually legitimate Web sites that have been compromised.

PROTECTING AGAINST COMPUTER SABOTAGE

One of the most important protections against computer sabotage is using *security software*, and ensuring that it is kept current.

Security Software

To protect against becoming infected with a computer virus or other type of malware, all computers and other devices used to access the Internet or a company network in both homes and offices should have **security software** installed. Security software typically includes a variety of security features, including a firewall, protection against spyware and bots, and protection against some types of *online fraud*, discussed shortly. One of the most important components is **antivirus software**, which protects against computer viruses and other types of malware.

Antivirus software typically runs continuously whenever the computer is on to perform real-time monitoring of the computer and incoming e-mail messages, instant messages, Web page content, and downloaded files, in order to prevent malicious software from executing. Many antivirus programs also automatically scan any devices as soon as they are connected to a USB port in order to guard against infections from a USB flash drive, a portable digital media player, or other USB device. Antivirus software helps prevent malware from being installed on your computer since it deletes or *quarantines* (safely isolates) any suspicious content (such as e-mail attachments or downloaded files) as they arrive; regular full system scans can detect and remove any viruses or worms that find their way onto your computer (see Figure 9-17).

According to McAfee Security, a manufacturer of antivirus and security software, there are millions of threats in existence today, and research firm IDC estimates that 450 new viruses and other types of malware are released each day. Consequently, it is vital to keep your antivirus program up to date. Antivirus software is usually set up to download new *virus definitions* automatically from its associated Web site on a regular basis, as often as several times per day—a very important precaution. Most fee-based antivirus programs come with a year of access to free updates; users should purchase additional years after that to continue to be protected or they should switch to a free antivirus program, such as *AVG Free*, that can be updated regularly at no cost. Schools and businesses should also ensure

FIGURE 9-17
Security software.
Most security software is set up to monitor your system on a continual basis, removing threats as they are discovered.

NET

ANTIVIRUS SOFTWARE

Both programs typically monitor your system on a continual basis, as well as periodically scanning your entire computer.

If malware is found during a scan or as you use your computer, the software removes it.

If spyware is found, the software recommends quarantining or removing it.

ANTISPYWARE SOFTWARE

>**Security software.** Software, typically a suite of programs, used to protect your computer against a variety of threats. >**Antivirus software.** Software used to detect and eliminate computer viruses and other types of malware.

VIRUS PREVENTION STRATEGIES

Use antivirus software to check incoming e-mail messages and files, and download updated virus definitions on a regular basis.

Limit the sharing of flash memory cards, USB flash drives, and other removable storage media with others.

Only download files from reputable sites.

Only open e-mail attachments that come from people you know and that do not have an executable file extension (such as .exe, .com, .bat, or .vbs); double-check with the sender before opening an unexpected, but seemingly legitimate, attachment.

For any downloaded file you are unsure of, upload it to a Web site (such as VirusTotal.com) that tests files for viruses before you open them.

Keep the preview window of your e-mail program closed so you will not view messages until you determine that they are safe to view.

Regularly download and install the latest security patches available for your operating system, browser, and e-mail programs.

Avoid downloading files from P2P sites.

FIGURE 9-18
Sensible precautions can help protect against computer virus infections.

TIP

If you suspect you are infected with a malware program that your antivirus software cannot detect or remove, try a software program that specializes in removing hard-to-remove malware, such as the free *MalwareBytes Anti-Malware* program.

that students and employees connecting to the campus or company network with personal computers are using up-to-date antivirus software so they will not infect the network with malware inadvertently. Some colleges now require new students to go through a *quarantine process*, in which students are not granted access to the college network until they complete a security process that checks their computers for security threats, updates their operating systems, and installs antivirus software. Some additional virus-prevention strategies are listed in Figure 9-18.

Many ISPs today also offer some malware protection to their subscribers. Typically, ISP antivirus software scans all incoming e-mail messages at the mail server level to filter out messages containing a virus. If a message containing a virus is detected, it is usually deleted and the recipient is notified that the message contained a virus and was deleted. Another type of program, which is currently in development and which is designed to protect against viruses sent via e-mail, is an *e-mail authentication system*. E-mail authentication systems are designed to tell recipients exactly where e-mail messages come from to help them determine which messages are safe to open and which might contain malware. For a look at an emerging tool in the fight against malware—*people-driven security* and *whitelisting*—see the Inside the Industry box.

Other Security Precautions

Individuals and businesses can protect against some types of computer sabotage (such as program, data, or Web site alteration) by controlling access to their computers and networks, as discussed earlier in this chapter. Intrusion protection systems can help businesses detect and protect against denial of service (DoS) attacks. For extra protection against spyware, rogue antivirus programs, and other specialized malware, specialized security programs (such as the antispyware program shown in Figure 9-17 for detecting and removing spyware) can be used. In addition, most Web browsers have security settings that can be used to help prevent programs from being installed on a computer without the user's permission, such as prompting the user for permission whenever a download is initiated. Enabling these security settings is a wise additional precaution.

ONLINE THEFT, ONLINE FRAUD, AND OTHER DOT CONS

A booming area of computer crime involves online fraud, theft, scams, and related activities designed to steal money or other resources from individuals or businesses—these are collectively referred to as **dot cons**. According to a report by the *Internet Crime Complaint Center (IC3)*, a joint venture of the FBI and the National White Collar Crime Center that receives cybercrime complaints from consumers and reports them to the appropriate law enforcement agency, online crime hit a record high in 2008. In all, more than

> **Dot con.** A fraud or scam carried out through the Internet.

INSIDE THE INDUSTRY

New Tools to Fight Malware

People-driven security refers to using the judgments of individuals to identify new threats. For instance, Google has a page where users can submit URLs of Web sites they believe are malicious (see the accompanying illustration), and antivirus companies like Symantec and McAfee rely on malware samples that they receive from users to help keep their virus lists and programs current. Many security experts believe that user involvement is crucial today in the fight against malware and phishing. People-driven security is also being used today to identify spammers.

The idea behind *whitelisting* is the opposite of blocking potentially dangerous applications from running on your computer; with whitelisting, only known good programs are allowed to run. While some users believe that whitelisting is annoying (because trying to run a program not on the whitelist requires responding to a pop-up alert message), many security companies believe that keeping track of known good software might be easier than trying to keep track of all the malware in existence today. Both Symantec and Kaspersky Lab are advocates of whitelisting and Kaspersky recently integrated the database

of Bit9, a company that maintains a list of over six billion known good applications, into its antivirus programs. While antivirus companies are currently working on maintaining their own whitelists to use in conjunction with their products, some view a central whitelist maintained by a neutral group and available to everyone as the most efficient solution for consumers.

275,000 reports were received with an average individual loss of $931. Some of the most common types of dot cons are discussed next.

Theft of Data, Information, and Other Resources

Data theft or *information theft* is the theft of data or information located on or being sent from a computer. It can be committed by stealing an actual computer (as discussed in more detail in Chapter 15); it can also take place over the Internet or a network by an individual gaining unauthorized access to that data by hacking into the computer or by intercepting the data in transit. Common types of data and information stolen via the Internet or another network include customer data (such as Web site passwords or credit card information) and proprietary corporate information. Over the past years, there have been numerous examples of hackers stealing information from company databases. For instance, one hacker obtained the contact information of more than 1.6 million users of the Monster.com online job search service; another breached the systems of the Heartland credit and debit card processor and several retail stores, stealing more than 130 million credit and debit card numbers, according to the charges filed against the hacker. Stolen consumer data is often used in fraudulent activities, such as *identity theft*, as discussed shortly.

Money is another resource that can be stolen via a computer. Company insiders sometimes steal money by altering company programs to transfer small amounts of money—for example, a few cents' worth of bank account interest—from a very large number of transactions to an account controlled by the thieves. This type of crime is sometimes called *salami shaving*. Victims of salami-shaving schemes generally are unaware that their funds have been accessed because the amount taken from each individual is very small. However, added together, the amounts can be substantial. Another example of monetary theft performed via computers involves hackers electronically transferring money illegally from online bank accounts, traditional bank accounts, credit card accounts, or accounts at online payment services (such as *PayPal*, which is discussed more in Chapter 11).

Identity Theft, Phishing, and Pharming

A growing dot con trend is obtaining enough information about an individual to perform fraudulent financial transactions. Often, this is carried out in conjunction with *identity theft*; techniques frequently used to obtain the necessary personal information to commit identity theft are *phishing*, *spear phishing*, and *pharming*. These topics are discussed next.

Identity Theft

Identity theft occurs when someone obtains enough information about a person to be able to masquerade as that person—usually to buy products or services in that person's name (see Figure 9-19). Typically, identity theft begins with obtaining a person's name, address, and Social Security number, often from a discarded or stolen document (such as a preapproved credit card application that was sent in the mail), from information obtained via the Internet (such as from a résumé posted online), or from information located on a computer (such as on a stolen computer or hacked server, or information sent from a computer via a computer virus or spyware program installed on that computer). The thief may then order a copy of the individual's birth certificate, obtain a "replacement" driver's license, make purchases and charge them to the victim, and/or open credit or bank accounts in the victim's name. Identity theft is illegal and, in 1998, the federal government passed the *Identity Theft and Assumption Deterrence Act*, which made identity theft a federal crime.

Assuming the thief requests a change of address for these new accounts after they are opened, it may take quite some time—often until a company or collections agency contacts the victim about overdue bills—for the victim to become aware that his or her identity has been stolen. Although identity theft often takes place via a computer today, information used in identity theft can also be gathered from trash dumpsters, mailboxes, and other locations. Other commonly used techniques are *skimming* and *social engineering*. Skimming involves stealing credit card or debit card numbers by using an illegal device attached to an ATM machine or credit card reader that reads and stores the card numbers to be retrieved by the thief

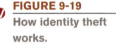

TIP

To help prevent identity theft, do not include your Social Security number on your résumé or any other document posted online.

FIGURE 9-19
How identity theft works.

1. The thief obtains information about an individual from discarded mail, employee records, credit card transactions, Web server files, or some other method.

2. The thief uses the information to make purchases, open new credit card accounts, and more in the victim's name. Often, the thief changes the address on the account to delay the victim's discovery of the theft.

3. The victim usually finds out by being denied credit or by being contacted about overdue bills generated by the thief. Clearing one's name after identity theft is time-consuming and can be very difficult and frustrating for the victim.

>**Identity theft.** Using someone else's identity to purchase goods or services, obtain new credit cards or bank loans, or otherwise illegally masquerade as that individual.

at a later time. Social engineering involves pretending—typically via phone or e-mail—to be a bank officer, potential employer, or other trusted individual in order to get the potential victim to supply personal information. One recent social engineering scheme placed phony parking tickets on cars instructing the owners to go to a particular Web site; going to that site installed software on the users' computers to capture their keystrokes.

Unfortunately, identity theft is a very real danger to individuals today. According to the Federal Trade Commission (FTC), millions of Americans have their identity stolen each year. Identity theft can be extremely distressing for victims, can take years to straighten out, and can be very expensive. Some identity theft victims, such as Michelle Brown, believe that they will always be dealing with their "alter reality" to some extent. For a year and a half, an identity thief used Brown's identity to obtain over $50,000 in goods and services, to rent properties—even to engage in drug trafficking. Although the culprit was eventually arrested and convicted for other criminal acts, she continued to use Brown's identity and was even booked into jail using Brown's stolen identity. As a final insult after the culprit was in prison, U.S. customs agents detained the real Michelle Brown when she was returning from a trip to Mexico because of the criminal record of the identity thief. Brown states that she has not traveled out of the country since, fearing an

ASK THE EXPERT

symantec. **Marian Merritt**, Internet Safety Advocate, Symantec Corporation

What is the single most important thing computer users should do to protect themselves from online threats?

The single most important step to protect computer users from online threats is to make sure their Internet security solution is current and up to date. There are several all-in-one security solutions available, such as Symantec's Norton 360, which combine PC security, antiphishing capabilities, backup, and tuneup technologies.

It's also pivotal to maintain a healthy wariness when receiving online communications. Do not click on links in suspicious e-mails or instant messages (IMs). These links will often direct you to sites that will ask you to reveal passwords, PINs, or other confidential data. Genuine organizations or institutions do not send such e-mails, nor do they ask for confidential data (like your Social Security number) for ordinary business transactions. If you're unsure whether or not an e-mail is legitimate, type the URL directly in your browser or call the institution to confirm they sent you that e-mail. Finally, do not open attachments in e-mails of questionable origin, since they may contain viruses.

arrest or some other serious problem resulting from the theft of her identity, and estimates she has spent over 500 hours trying to correct all the problems related to the identity theft.

Phishing and Spear Phishing

Phishing (pronounced "fishing") is the use of a *spoofed* e-mail message (an e-mail appearing to come from eBay, PayPal, Bank of America, or another well-known legitimate organization, but is actually sent from a phisher) to trick the recipient into revealing sensitive personal information (such as Web site logon information or credit card numbers). Once obtained, this information is used in identity theft and other fraudulent activities. A phishing e-mail typically looks legitimate and it contains links in the e-mail that appear to go to the Web site of the legitimate business, but these links go to the phisher's Web site that is set up to look like the legitimate site instead—an act called *Web site spoofing*. Phishing e-mails are typically sent to a wide group of individuals and usually include an urgent message stating that the individual's credit card or account information needs to be updated and instructing the recipient of the e-mail to click the link provided in the e-mail in order

> **Phishing.** The use of spoofed e-mail messages to gain credit card numbers and other personal data to be used for fraudulent purposes.

The link is for an insecure Web page and does not use the bofa.com domain.

This e-mail looks legitimate, but the link goes to a spoofed Web page.

⚠ **FIGURE 9-20**

Phishing. Phishing schemes use legitimate-looking e-mails to trick users into providing private information.

to keep the account active (see Figure 9-20). If the victim clicks the link and supplies the requested information via the spoofed site, the criminal gains access to all information provided by the victim, such as account numbers, credit card numbers, and Web site passwords. Phishing attempts can occur today via IM, text messages (called *smishing*), fake messages sent via eBay or MySpace, Twitter tweets, and pop-up security alert windows, in addition to via e-mail. Phishers also frequently utilize spyware; typically, clicking the link in the phishing e-mail installs the spyware on the victim's computer, and it will remain there (transmitting passwords and other sensitive data to a phisher) until it is detected and removed.

To fool victims into using the spoofed Web site, phishing e-mails and the spoofed Web sites often look legitimate. To accomplish this, phishers typically use copies of the spoofed organization's logo and other Web site content from the legitimate Web site. For spoofed banking Web pages and other pages where the victim would expect to see a secure Web page, some criminals use a secure connection between the victim and the criminal's server so the Web page looks secure with an *https:* in the Address bar. The domain name of the legitimate company (such as *ebay* for an eBay phishing page) is also often used as part of the URL of the phishing link (such as a URL starting with the text *ebay* even though the URL's domain is not ebay.com) to make it appear more legitimate. Other phishing schemes use a technique called *typosquatting*, which is setting up spoofed Web sites with addresses slightly different from legitimate sites. For example, a spoofed Web site using the URL www.amazom.com might be used to catch shoppers intending to reach the Amazon.com Web site located at www.amazon.com in hopes that customers making this error when typing the URL will not notice it and will supply logon information via the spoofed site when they arrive at it.

Another recent trend is the use of more targeted, personalized phishing schemes, known as **spear phishing**. Spear phishing e-mails are directly targeted to a specific individual and typically appear to come from an organization or person that the targeted individual has an association with. They also often include personalized information (such as the potential victim's name) to make the spear phishing e-mails seem even more legitimate. Several recent spear phishing attacks were targeted at users of social networking sites like MySpace since the personal information (name, age, hobbies, friends list, favorite music, and so forth) typically included on these sites makes them a good resource for spear phishers. Some of these attacks used spoofed logon pages for the social networking sites to obtain an individual's logon information and password. Since many individuals use the same logon information for a variety of sites, once a scammer has a valid username/password combination, he or she can try it on a variety of common e-commerce sites, such as shopping sites, online banking sites, and online payment services like PayPal. If the scammer is able to log on successfully to one of these sites, he or she can buy products, transfer money, and perform other types of financial transactions posing as the victim. Another recent tactic is to use the victim's social networking site logon information to log on to the victim's account and then post comments or send messages containing phishing links (posing as the victim) to the victim's friends, who are much more likely to click on the links because they appear to come from a friend.

> **Spear phishing.** A personalized phishing scheme targeted at an individual.

Spear phishers also target employees of selected organizations by posing as someone within the company, such as a human resources or technical support employee. These spear phishing e-mails often request confidential information (such as logon IDs and passwords) or direct the employee to click a link to supposedly reset his or her password. The goal for corporate spear phishing attacks is usually to steal intellectual property, such as software source code, design documents, or schematics. It can also be used to steal money. For instance, in one recent case, a grocery store received fraudulent e-mails that appeared to come from two approved suppliers. The e-mails instructed the grocery store chain to send future payments to new bank accounts listed in the e-mail—the grocery store chain deposited more than $10 million into two fraudulent bank accounts before the scam was discovered.

Pharming and Drive-By Pharming

Pharming is another type of scam that uses spoofing—specifically spoofed domain names used to obtain personal information for use in fraudulent activities. With pharming, the criminal reroutes traffic intended for a commonly used Web site to a spoofed Web site set up by the pharmer. Sometimes pharming takes place via malicious code sent to a computer via an e-mail message or other distribution method. More often however, it takes place via changes made to a *DNS server*—a computer that translates URLs into the appropriate IP addresses needed to display the Web page corresponding to a URL. This type of pharming can take place at one of the 13 *root DNS servers* (the DNS servers used in conjunction with the Internet), but it more often takes place at a *company DNS server* (the DNS server for that company used to route Web page requests received via company Web site URLs to the appropriate company server). After hacking into a company DNS server (typically for a company with a commonly used Web site), the pharmer changes the IP addresses used in conjunction with a particular company URL (called *DNS poisoning*) so any Web page requests made via the legitimate company URL is routed (via the company's poisoned DNS server) to a phony spoofed Web page located on the pharmer's Web server. So, even though a user types the proper URL to display the legitimate company Web page in his or her browser, the spoofed page is displayed instead.

Since spoofed sites are set up to look like the legitimate sites, the user typically does not notice any difference, and any information sent via that site is captured by the pharmer. To avoid suspicion, some pharming schemes capture the user's account name and password as it is entered the first time on the spoofed site, and then display a password error message. The spoofed site then redirects the user back to the legitimate site where he or she is able to log on to the legitimate site, leaving the user to think that he or she must have just mistyped the password the first time. But, by then, the pharmer has already captured the victim's username and password and can use that information to gain access to the victim's account.

A recent variation of pharming is *drive-by pharming*. The goal is still to redirect victims to spoofed sites; however, the pharmer accomplishes this by changing the victim's designated DNS server (which is specified in the victim's router settings) to the pharmer's DNS server in order to direct the victim to spoofed versions of legitimate Web sites when the victim enters the URLs for those sites. Typically, the pharmer uses malicious JavaScript code placed on a Web page to changes the victim's DNS settings to use the pharmer's DNS server; this change can only occur on a router in which the default administrator password was not changed.

Online Auction Fraud

Online auction fraud (sometimes called *Internet auction fraud*) occurs when an online auction buyer pays for merchandise that is never delivered, or that is delivered but it is

---

not as represented. Online auction fraud is an increasing risk for online auction bidders. According to the Internet Crime Complaint Center (IC3), online auction fraud accounted for about 25% of all reported online fraud cases in 2008 for an average loss of around $600. Like other types of fraud, online auction fraud is illegal, but similar to many types of Internet cons, prosecution is difficult for online auction fraud because multiple jurisdictions are usually involved. Although most online auction sites have policies that suspend sellers with a certain number of complaints lodged against them, it is very easy for those sellers to come back using a new e-mail address and identity.

Other Internet Scams

There is a wide range of other scams that can occur via Web sites or unsolicited e-mails. The anonymity of the Internet makes it very easy for con artists to appear to be almost anyone they want to be, including a charitable organization or a reputable-looking business. Common types of scams include loan scams, work-at-home cons, pyramid schemes, bogus credit card offers and prize promotions, and fraudulent business opportunities and franchises. These offers typically try to sell potential victims nonexistent services or worthless information, or they try to convince potential victims to voluntarily supply their credit card details and other personal information, which are then used for fraudulent purposes. Some scammers use hacking as a means of obtaining a list of e-mail addresses for potential targets for a scam (such as stealing contact information from sites related to investing for a stock market scam) to increase the odds of a potential victim falling for the scam. A recent trend involves scammers who hack into Web mail and social networking accounts and send messages (posing as the victim) to the victim's entire contact list requesting money or urging recipients to buy specific products.

One ongoing Internet scam is the *Nigerian letter fraud* scheme. This scheme involves an e-mail message that appears to come from the Nigerian government and that promises the potential victim a share of a substantial amount of money in exchange for the use of the victim's bank account. Supposedly the victim's bank account information is needed to facilitate a wire transfer (but the victim's account is emptied instead) and/or up-front cash is needed to pay for nonexistent fees (that is kept by the con artist with nothing given in return). The theme of these scams often changes to fit current events, such as the war in Iraq or the Katrina hurricane. However, the scams always involve a so-called fortune that is inaccessible to the con artist without the potential victims' help (see Figure 9-21) and the victims always lose money when they pay fees or provide bank account information in the hope of sharing in the wealth. Despite the fact that this con is well known, people are still falling for it and with heavy losses—at $1,650, the Nigerian letter fraud scam had the third highest average dollar loss per individual for 2008 complaints, according to a report issued by the Internet Crime Complaint Center (IC3).

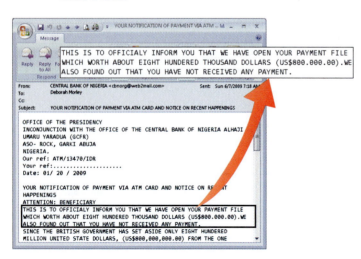

FIGURE 9-21
A Nigerian letter fraud e-mail.

Other schemes involve con artists who solicit donations after disasters and other tragic events, but who keep the donations instead of giving them to any charitable organization. Another common scam involves setting up a pornographic site that requires a valid credit card, supposedly to prove that the visitor is of the required age (such as over 18), but which is then used for credit card fraud. A relatively new type of scam involves posting fake job listings on job search sites to elicit personal information (such as Social Security numbers) from job seekers. An even more recent twist is to hire individuals through online job sites for seemingly legitimate positions involving money handling (such as bookkeeping or accounting positions), but then use those individuals—often without their knowledge—as illegitimate go-betweens to facilitate Internet auction scams and other monetary scams.

PROTECTING AGAINST ONLINE THEFT, ONLINE FRAUD, AND OTHER DOT CONS

In a nutshell, the best protection against many dot cons is protecting your identity; that is, protecting any identifying information about you that could be used in fraudulent activities. There are also specific precautions that can help protect against online theft, identity theft, online auction fraud, and other types of dot cons, as discussed next. With any dot con, it is important to act quickly if you think you have been a victim. For instance, you should work with your local law enforcement agency, credit card companies, and the three major consumer credit bureaus (*Equifax*, *Experian*, and *TransUnion*) to close any accessed or fraudulent accounts, place fraud alerts on your credit report, and take other actions to prevent additional fraudulent activity while the fraud is being investigated.

Arrests and prosecutions by law enforcement agencies may also help cut down on cybercrimes. Prosecution of online scammers has been increasing and sentences are not light. For instance, one man—the first person convicted by a jury under the *CAN-SPAM Act of 2003* for operating a phishing scheme—was sentenced in mid-2007 to 70 months in federal prison and ordered to pay over one million dollars to his victims.

Protecting Against Data and Information Theft

Businesses and individuals can both help to prevent some types of data and information theft. For instance, businesses should use good security measures to protect the data stored on their computers. Individuals should be vigilant about protecting their private information by sending sensitive information via secure Web servers only and not disclosing personal information—especially a Social Security number or a mother's maiden name—unless it is absolutely necessary and they know how the information will be used and that it will not be shared with others. In addition, individuals should never give out sensitive personal information to anyone who requests it over the phone or by e-mail—businesses that legitimately need bank account information, passwords, or credit card numbers will not request that information via phone or e-mail. Encrypting computers and other hardware containing sensitive information, so it will not be readable if the hardware is lost or stolen, is another important precaution.

Protecting Against Identity Theft, Phishing, and Pharming

Some of the precautions used for other types of online theft (such as being careful to disclose your personal information only when it is necessary and only via secure Web pages) can help reduce the chance that identity theft will happen to you. So can using security software (and keeping it up to date) to guard against computer viruses, spyware, and other malware that can be used to send information from your computer or about your activities (the Web site passwords that you type, for example) to a criminal. In addition, to prevent someone from using the preapproved credit card offers and other documents containing personal information that frequently arrive in the mail, shred them before throwing them in the trash. To prevent the theft of outgoing mail containing sensitive information, don't place it in your mailbox—mail it at the post office or in a USPS drop box.

To avoid phishing schemes, never click a link in an e-mail message to go to a secure Web site—always type the URL for that site in your browser (not necessarily the URL shown in the e-mail message) instead. Phishing e-mails typically sound urgent and often contain spelling and grammatical errors—see Figure 9-22 for some tips to help you recognize phishing e-mails. Remember that

FIGURE 9-22
Tips for identifying phishing e-mail messages.

A PHISHING E-MAIL OFTEN . . .

Tries to scare you into responding by sounding urgent, including a warning that your account will be cancelled if you do not respond, or telling you that you have been a victim of fraud.

Asks you to provide personal information, such as your bank account number, an account password, credit card number, PIN number, mother's maiden name, or Social Security number.

Contains links that do not go where the link text says it will go (point to a hyperlink in the e-mail message to view the URL for that link).

Uses legitimate logos from the company the phisher is posing as.

Appears to come from a known organization, but one you may not have an association with.

Appears to be text or text and images but is actually a single image; it has been created that way to avoid being caught in a spam filter (a program that sorts e-mail based on legitimate e-mail and suspected spam) since spam filters cannot read text that is part of an image in an e-mail message.

Contains spelling or grammatical errors.

NET

TIPS FOR AVOIDING IDENTITY THEFT

Protect your Social Security number—give it out only when necessary.

Be careful with your physical mail and trash—shred all documents containing sensitive data.

Secure your computer—update your operating system and use up-to-date security (antivirus, antispyware, firewall, etc.) software.

Be cautious—never click on a link in an e-mail message or respond to a too-good-to-be-true offer.

Use strong passwords for your computer and online accounts.

Verify sources before sharing sensitive information—never respond to e-mail or phone requests for sensitive information.

Be vigilant while on the go—safeguard your wallet, mobile phone, and portable computer.

Watch your bills and monitor your credit reports—react immediately if you suspect fraudulent activity.

Use security software or browser features that warn you if you try to view a known phishing site.

FIGURE 9-23

Tips to reduce your risk of identity theft.

TIP

You can order your free credit reports online quickly and easily via Web sites like *AnnualCreditReport.com*.

FIGURE 9-24

Unsafe Web site alerts.

spear phishing schemes may include personalized information (such as your name)—do not let that fool you into thinking the phishing e-mail is legitimate. If you think an unsolicited e-mail message requesting information from you may be legitimate (for instance, if the credit card you use to make an automatic payment for an ongoing service is about to expire and you receive an e-mail message asking you to update your credit card information), type the URL for that site in your browser to load the legitimate site and then update your account information. To prevent a drive-by pharming attack, all businesses and individuals should change the administrator password for routers, access points, and other networking hardware from the default password to a strong password.

Keeping a close eye on your credit card bills and credit history is also important to make sure you catch any fraudulent charges or accounts opened by an identity thief as soon as possible. Make sure your bills come in every month (some thieves will change your mailing address to delay detection), and read credit card statements carefully to look for unauthorized charges. Be sure to follow up on any calls you get from creditors, instead of assuming it is just a mistake. Most security experts also recommend ordering a full credit history on yourself a few times a year to check for accounts listed in your name that you did not open and any other problems. The *Fair and Accurate Credit Transactions Act (FACTA)* enables all Americans to get a free copy of their credit report, upon request, each year from the three major consumer credit bureaus. Ideally, you should request a report from one of these bureaus every four months to monitor your credit on a regular basis. These reports contain information about inquiries related to new accounts requested in your name, as well as any delinquent balances or other negative reports. For another tool that you can use to help detect identity theft—*online financial alerts*—see the Technology and You box. You can also use browser-based *antiphishing* tools and *digital certificates* to help guard against identity theft and the phishing and pharming schemes used in conjunction with identity theft, as discussed next. Some additional tips for minimizing your risk of identity theft are listed in Figure 9-23.

Antiphishing Tools

Antiphishing tools are built into many e-mail programs and Web browsers to help notify users of possible phishing Web sites. For instance, some e-mail programs will disable links in e-mail messages identified as questionable, unless the user overrides it; many recent browsers warn users when a Web page associated with a possible phishing URL is requested (see Figure 9-24); and antiphishing capabilities are included in many recent security suites.

In addition, some secure Web sites are adding additional layers in security to protect against identity thieves. For example, some online banking sites analyze users' habits to look for patterns that vary from the norm, such as accessing accounts online at an hour unusual for that individual or a higher than normal level of online purchases. If a bank suspects the account may be compromised, it contacts the owner for verification. Bank of America and some other financial institutions have also added an additional step in their logon process—displaying an image or word preselected by the user and stored on the bank's server—to prove to the user that the site being viewed is the legitimate (not a phishing) site. In addition, if the system does not recognize the

TECHNOLOGY AND YOU

Online Financial Alerts

Want to know as soon as possible when a transaction that might be fraudulent is charged to your credit card? Well, *online financial alerts* might be the answer.

Many online banking services today allow users to set up e-mail alerts for credit card activity over a certain amount, low balances, and so forth. For individuals wishing to monitor multiple accounts, however, online money management aggregator services (such as *Mint.com*) make it easier. Once you have set up a free Mint.com account with your financial accounts (including credit cards and checking, savings, and PayPal accounts) and their respective passwords, you can see the status of all your accounts through the Mint.com interface. You can also set up alerts for any of the accounts based on your desired criteria, such as any transaction over a specified amount (see the accompanying illustration). The alerts are sent to you via e-mail or text message, depending on your preference, to help notify you as soon as possible if a suspicious activity occurs. And timeliness is of the essence, because the sooner identity theft is discovered, the less time the thief has to make additional fraudulent transactions. For security purposes, Mint. com doesn't store online banking usernames and passwords; instead, a secure online financial services provider is used to connect Mint.com to the appropriate financial institutions as needed to update your activity. In addition, the Mint.com Web site cannot be used to move money out of or between financial accounts—it can be used only to view information.

Unusual Spending and Large Purchases alerts can help you detect fraudulent charges to your financial accounts.

computer that the user is using to log on to the system, the user is required to go through an authentication process (typically by correctly answering cognitive authentication questions) before being allowed to access the system via that computer. The questions used are specifically designed to be "out of wallet" questions—easy for the individual to answer but difficult for hackers to guess the correct answer or find in a stolen wallet. Bank of America is also one bank offering customers the option of adding the use of one-time passwords (autogenerated by a security token like the one shown in Figure 9-5 or sent via text message to the individual's mobile phone) to their online banking logon procedure.

Digital Certificates and Digital Signatures

The purpose of a **digital certificate** is to authenticate the identity of an individual or organization. Digital certificates are granted by Certificate Authorities and typically contain the name of the person, organization, or Web site being certified along with a certificate serial number and an expiration date. Digital certificates also include a public/private key pair. In addition to being used by the certificate holder to encrypt files and e-mail messages (as discussed earlier in this chapter), these keys and the digital certificate are used with secure Web pages to guarantee the Web pages are secure and actually belong to the stated organization (so users can know for sure who their credit card number or other sensitive data is really being sent to, in order to protect against some online scams).

> **Digital certificate.** A group of electronic data that can be used to verify the identity of a person or organization; includes a key pair that can be used for encryption and digital signatures.

Red indicates a problem with the site's digital certificate.

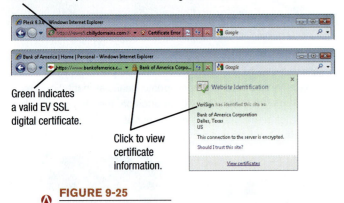

Green indicates
a valid EV SSL
digital certificate.

Click to view
certificate
information.

FIGURE 9-25
EV SSL certificates.
The browser's Address
bar reflects information
about the digital
certificate being used.

Secure Web sites can obtain either a normal *SSL digital certificate* or a newer *Extended Validation (EV) SSL digital certificate* that was developed to provide consumers with a higher level of trust while online. While both digital certificates require an application process, the verification process to obtain an EV SSL digital certificate is more thorough, requiring the use of reputable third-party sources to verify that the company has the right to use the Web site domain name in question and that the business requesting the certificate is authorized to do so. With both types of certificates, individuals can click the secure Web page icon in their browser window to view that site's digital certificate in order to ensure that the certificate is valid and issued to the company associated with the Web site being viewed. If an EV SSL certificate is used, however, additional information is displayed when the Web site is viewed in an EV-compliant browser, such as recoloring the Address bar green to indicate a site using a valid EV SSL certificate and displaying certificate information in the *Security Status bar* to the right of the Address bar, as shown in Figure 9-25.

The keys included in a digital certificate can also be used to authenticate the identity of a person sending an e-mail message or other document via a **digital signature**. To digitally sign an e-mail message or other document, the sender's private key is used and that key, along with the contents of the document, generates a unique digital signature; consequently, a digital signature is different with each signed document. When a digitally signed document is received, the recipient's computer uses the sender's public key to verify the digital signature. Since the document is signed with the sender's private key (that only the sender should know) and the digital signature will be deemed invalid if even one character of the document is changed after it is signed, digital signatures guarantee that the document was sent by a specific individual and that it was not tampered with after it was signed.

Digital signatures are an important component of the emerging *e-mail authentication systems* (such as the *DomainKeys* system used by Yahoo!, eBay, Google, PayPal, and other companies) that may help prevent some types of online fraud in the future as these systems become more widely used. These systems are designed to authenticate e-mail messages via digital signatures and so can help ISPs block phishing e-mails because messages coming from a participating company must be digitally signed by that company in order to be deemed authentic.

Protecting Against Online Auction Fraud and Other Internet Scams

The best protection against many dot cons is common sense. Be extremely cautious of any unsolicited e-mail messages you receive and realize that if an offer sounds too good to be true, it probably is. You should also be cautious when dealing with individuals online through auctions and other person-to-person activities. Before bidding on an auction item, check out the feedback rating of the seller to see comments written by other auction sellers and buyers. Always pay for auctions and other online purchases using a credit card or an online payment service (such as PayPal) that accepts credit card payments so you can dispute the transaction through your credit card company, if needed. Using an online payment service that bills the charge to your credit card, instead of allowing the seller to charge your credit card, has the extra advantage of keeping your credit card information private.

> **Digital signature.** A unique digital code that can be attached to a file or an e-mail message to verify the identity of the sender and guarantee the file or message has not been changed since it was signed.

In addition, some auction sites and online payment services offer free buyer protection against undelivered items or auction items that are significantly different from the description provided in the auction information. For instance, most eBay purchases paid for via PayPal have at least $200 of buyer protection coverage at no additional cost. For expensive items, consider using an *escrow service*, which allows you to ensure that the merchandise is as specified before your payment is released to the seller.

PERSONAL SAFETY ISSUES

In addition to being expensive and inconvenient, cybercrime can also be physically dangerous. Although most of us may not ordinarily view using the Internet as a potentially dangerous activity, cases of physical harm due to Internet activity do happen. For example, children and teenagers have become the victims of pedophiles who arranged face-to-face meetings by using information gathered via e-mail, message boards, social networking sites, or other online sources. There are also a growing number of incidents in which children are threatened by classmates via e-mail, Web site posts, or text messages. Adults may fall victim to unscrupulous or dangerous individuals who misrepresent themselves online, and the availability of personal information online has made it more difficult for individuals to hide from people who may want to do them harm, such as abused women trying to hide from their abusive husbands. Two of the most common ways individuals are harassed online—*cyberbullying* and *cyberstalking*—are discussed next.

Cyberbullying and Cyberstalking

Children and teenagers bullying other children or teenagers via the Internet—such as through e-mail, a text message, a social networking site, a blog, or other online communications method—is referred to as **cyberbullying**. Unfortunately, cyberbullying is common today—by some estimates, it affects as many as one-half of all U.S. teenagers. Cyberbullying can take place via direct online communication (such as with an e-mail or instant message), as well as via more subtle means. For instance, there have been cases of students posting videos on YouTube of other students being bullied and cases of individuals hacking into a student's MySpace or Facebook account and changing the content on the student's pages to harass that student. In one tragic instance, a 13-year-old girl hanged herself after the mother of one of the girl's classmates arranged to have a MySpace profile created for a nonexistent teenage boy in order to determine what the victim was saying about her daughter, and then cruelly ended the friendship. While the mother was convicted of three misdemeanor charges of unauthorized access to computers in conjunction with the case, her conviction was dismissed in 2009. However, the case prompted many states and schools to look at harassment statutes and bullying policies and resulted in several states implementing new laws or amending existing harassment laws to address cyberbullying.

Repeated threats or other harassment carried out online between adults is referred to as **cyberstalking**. Cyberstalkers sometimes find their victims online; for instance, someone in a discussion group who makes a comment or has a screen name that the cyberstalker does not like, or bloggers who are harassed and threatened with violence or murder because of their blogging activities. Other times, the attack is more personal, such as employers who are stalked online by ex-employees who were fired or otherwise left their position under adverse conditions, and celebrities who are stalked online by fans.

Cyberstalking typically begins with online harassment—such as sending harassing or threatening e-mail messages or unwanted files to the victim, posing as the victim in order to

FURTHER EXPLORATION   Go

Go to the Chapter 9 page at **www.cengage.com/ computerconcepts/np/uc13** for links to information about how to prevent and deal with identity theft and online auction fraud.

NET

>**Cyberbullying.** Children or teenagers bullying other children or teenagers via the Internet. >**Cyberstalking.** Repeated threats or harassing behavior between adults carried out via e-mail or another Internet communications method.

sign the victim up for pornographic or otherwise offensive e-mail newsletters, publicizing the victim's home address and telephone number, or hacking into the victim's social networking pages to alter the content. Cyberstalking can also lead to offline stalking and possibly physical harm—in at least one case, it led to the death of the victim. While there are as yet no specific federal laws against cyberstalking, all states have made it illegal (and it is being increasingly prosecuted), and some federal laws do apply if the online actions include computer fraud or another type of computer crime, suggest a threat of personal injury, or involve sending obscene e-mail messages. Many cyberstalkers are not caught, however, due in part to the anonymity of the Internet, which assists cyberstalkers in concealing their true identities.

Online Pornography

A variety of controversial and potentially objectionable material is available on the Internet. Although there have been attempts to ban this type of material from the Internet, they have not been successful. For example, the *Communications Decency Act*, signed into law in 1996—which made it a criminal offense to distribute patently indecent or offensive material online—was ruled unconstitutional in 1997 by the U.S. Supreme Court. However, like its printed counterpart, online pornography involving minors is illegal. Because of the strong link they believe exists between child pornography and child molestation, many experts are very concerned about the amount of child pornography that can be found and distributed via the Internet. They also believe that the Internet makes it easier for sexual predators to act out, such as by striking up "friendships" with children online and convincing these children to meet them in real life. And this can have devastating consequences, as it did for a 13-year-old girl from Connecticut who was strangled to death in 2002 by a 25-year-old man she met originally online and eventually in person. Although the man confessed, he maintains that the strangling was accidental. The man was sentenced in late 2003 to a total of 40 years in prison for state and federal charges relating to the crime.

PROTECTING AGAINST CYBERBULLYING, CYBERSTALKING, AND OTHER PERSONAL SAFETY CONCERNS

The growing increase in attention to cyberbullying and cyberstalking is leading to more efforts to improve safeguards for children. For instance, social networking sites have privacy features that can be used to protect the private information of their members. In addition, numerous states in the U.S. have implemented cyberbullying and cyberstalking laws. While there is no surefire way to protect against cyberbullying, cyberstalking, and other online dangers completely, some common-sense precautions can reduce the chance of a serious personal safety problem occurring due to online activities.

Safety Tips for Adults

It is wise to be cautious and discreet online—especially in online profiles, message boards, and other online locations where individuals communicate with strangers. To protect yourself against cyberstalking and other types of online harassment, use gender-neutral, nonprovocative identifying names, such as *jsmith*, instead of *janesmith* or *iamcute*. Be careful about the types of photos you post of yourself online and do not reveal personal information—such as your real name, address, or telephone number—to people you meet online. In addition, do not respond to any insults or other harassing comments you may receive online. You may also wish to request that your personal information be removed from online directories—especially those associated with your e-mail address or other online identifiers.

Safety Tips for Children and Teens

Most experts agree that the best way to protect children from online dangers is to stay in close touch with them as they explore the Internet. In order for parents to be able to monitor

TIP

Search for yourself using search sites and online telephone books to see what personal information is available about you on the Internet.

TIP

Both adults and children should avoid including personal information on social networking sites that could be used by an online stalker.

their children's online activities, children and teenagers should use a computer in a family room or other public location, instead of their bedroom, and they should be told which activities are allowed, which types of Web sites are off-limits, and why. In addition, it should be made clear that they are never to reveal personal information about themselves online without a parent's permission. They should also be instructed to tell a parent (or teacher if at school) if an individual ever requests personal information or a personal meeting, or threatens or otherwise harasses the child, via any type of online communications medium. Older children should also be cautioned about sending compromising photos of themselves to others. This practice—referred to as *sexting*—is a growing problem. In one recent study, for instance, more than 20% of teens reported sending nude or seminude photos of them-

▼ **FIGURE 9-26**

Computer network and Internet security legislation.

selves to others. Part of the problem is that many young people don't realize they lose control of photos and other compromising content once that information has been sent to others and, in one case, a teenage girl committed suicide after the nude photos she had sent her boyfriend were sent to other students once the couple broke up. Sexting has also resulted in child pornography charges being filed against teens for sending their own photos to others or having compromising photos of other children on their mobile phones.

NETWORK AND INTERNET SECURITY LEGISLATION

Although new legislation is passed periodically to address new types of computer crimes, it is difficult for the legal system to keep pace with the rate at which technology changes. In addition, there are both domestic and international jurisdictional issues because many computer crimes affect businesses and individuals located in geographic areas other than the one in which the computer criminal is located, and hackers can make it appear that activity is coming from a different location than it really is. Nevertheless, computer crime legislation continues to be proposed and computer crimes are being prosecuted. A list of selected federal laws concerning network and Internet security is shown in Figure 9-26.

DATE	LAW AND DESCRIPTION
2004	**Identity Theft Penalty Enhancement Act** Adds extra years to prison sentences for criminals who use identity theft (including the use of stolen credit card numbers) to commit other crimes, including credit card fraud and terrorism.
2003	**CAN-SPAM Act** Implements regulations for unsolicited e-mail messages.
2003	**Fair and Accurate Credit Transactions Act (FACTA)** Amends the Fair Credit Reporting Act (FCRA) to require, among other things, that the three nationwide consumer reporting agencies (Equifax, Experian, and TransUnion) provide to consumers, upon request, a free copy of their credit report once every 12 months.
2003	**PROTECT Act** Includes provisions to prohibit virtual child pornography.
2003	**Health Insurance Portability and Accountability Act (HIPAA)** Includes a Security Rule that sets minimum security standards to protect health information stored electronically.
2002	**Homeland Security Act** Includes provisions to combat cyberterrorism, including protecting ISPs against lawsuits from customers for revealing private information to law enforcement agencies.
2002	**Sarbanes-Oxley Act** Requires archiving a variety of electronic records and protecting the integrity of corporate financial data.
2001	**USA PATRIOT Act** Grants federal authorities expanded surveillance and intelligence-gathering powers, such as broadening the ability of federal agents to obtain the real identity of Internet users, intercept e-mail and other types of Internet communications, follow online activity of suspects, expand their wiretapping authority, and more.
1998	**Identity Theft and Assumption Deterrence Act of 1998** Makes it a federal crime to knowingly use someone else's means of identification, such as name, Social Security number, or credit card, to commit any unlawful activity.
1997	**No Electronic Theft (NET) Act** Expands computer piracy laws to include distribution of copyrighted materials over the Internet.
1996	**National Information Infrastructure Protection Act** Amends the Computer Fraud and Abuse Act of 1984 to punish information theft crossing state lines and to crack down on network trespassing.
1994	**Computer Abuse Amendments Act** Amends the Computer Fraud and Abuse Act of 1984 to include computer viruses and other harmful code.
1986	**Computer Fraud and Abuse Act of 1986** Amends the 1984 law to include federally regulated financial institutions.
1984	**Computer Fraud and Abuse Act of 1984** Makes it a crime to break into computers owned by the federal government. This act has been regularly amended over the years as technology has changed.

NET

SUMMARY

WHY BE CONCERNED ABOUT NETWORK AND INTERNET SECURITY?

Chapter Objective 1:
Explain why computer users should be concerned about network and Internet security.

There are a number of important security concerns related to computers and the Internet. Many of these are **computer crimes**. Because computers and networks are so widespread and many opportunities for criminals exist, all computer users should be aware of the risks of using networks and the Internet so they can take appropriate precautions.

UNAUTHORIZED ACCESS AND UNAUTHORIZED USE

Chapter Objective 2:
List several examples of unauthorized access and unauthorized use.

Two risks related to networks and the Internet are **unauthorized access** and **unauthorized use**. **Hacking** is using a computer to break into a computer. **War driving** and **Wi-Fi piggybacking** refer to the unauthorized use of unsecured Wi-Fi network. Data can be intercepted as it is transmitted over the Internet or a wireless network.

PROTECTING AGAINST UNAUTHORIZED ACCESS AND UNAUTHORIZED USE

Chapter Objective 3:
Explain several ways to protect against unauthorized access and unauthorized use, including access control systems, firewalls, and encryption.

Access control systems are used to control access to a computer, network, or other resource. These include **possessed knowledge access systems** that use **passwords** or other types of possessed knowledge; **possessed object access systems** that use physical objects; and **biometric access systems** that identify users by a particular unique biological characteristic, such as a fingerprint. Passwords should be *strong passwords*; **two-factor authentication systems** that use multiple factors are more effective than single-factor systems.

To protect wireless networks, they should be secured; **firewalls** protect against unauthorized access. Sensitive transactions should be performed only on **secure Web pages**; sensitive files and e-mails should be secured with **encryption**. **Public key encryption** uses a private key and matching public key; **private key encryption** uses only a private key. A **virtual private network (VPN)** can be used to provide a secure remote connection to a company network, as well as to protect individuals at public Wi-Fi hotspots. Employers should take appropriate precautions with current and former employees to limit the risk of unauthorized access and use, as well as accidental exposure of sensitive information.

COMPUTER SABOTAGE

Chapter Objective 4:
Provide several examples of computer sabotage.

Computer sabotage includes **malware** (**computer viruses**, **computer worms**, and **Trojan horses** designed to cause harm to computer systems), **denial of service (DoS) attacks** (designed to shut down a Web server), and data and program alteration. Computer sabotage is often performed via the Internet, increasingly by the **bots** in a **botnet**.

PROTECTING AGAINST COMPUTER SABOTAGE

Chapter Objective 5:
List how individuals and businesses can protect against computer sabotage.

Protection against computer sabotage includes using appropriate access control systems to keep unauthorized individuals from accessing computers and networks, as well as using **security software**. In particular, **antivirus software** protects against computer viruses and other types of malware. It is important to keep your security software up to date.

ONLINE THEFT, ONLINE FRAUD, AND OTHER DOT CONS

There are a variety of types of theft, fraud, and scams related to the Internet—collectively referred to as **dot cons**—that all Internet users should be aware of. Data, information, or money can be stolen from individuals and businesses. A common crime today is **identity theft**, in which an individual poses as another individual—typically to steal money or make purchases posing as the victim. The information used in identity theft is often gathered via **phishing**, **spear phishing**, and **pharming**. **Online auction fraud** is another common dot con.

Chapter Objective 6:
Discuss online theft, identity theft, spoofing, phishing, and other types of dot cons.

PROTECTING AGAINST ONLINE THEFT, ONLINE FRAUD, AND OTHER DOT CONS

To protect against identity theft, individuals should guard their personal information carefully. To check for identity theft, watch your bills and credit history. When interacting with other individuals online or buying from an online auction, it is wise to be conservative and use a credit card whenever possible. To avoid other types of dot cons, be very wary of responding to unsolicited offers and e-mails, and steer clear of offers that seem too good to be true. Never click a link in an e-mail message to update your personal information. To verify a Web site, a **digital certificate** can be used. To verity the sender of a document, a **digital signature** can be used. Digital certificates include key pairs that can be used to both digitally sign documents and to encrypt files.

Chapter Objective 7:
Detail steps an individual can take to protect against online theft, identity theft, spoofing, phishing, and other types of dot cons.

PERSONAL SAFETY ISSUES

There are also personal safety risks for both adults and children stemming from Internet use. **Cyberbullying** and **cyberstalking**—online harassment that frightens or threatens the victim—is more common in recent years, even though most states have passed laws against it. Cyberbully is a growing risk for children, as is the potential exposure to online pornography and other materials inappropriate for children, and the growing *sexting* trend.

Chapter Objective 8:
Identify personal safety risks associated with Internet use.

PROTECTING AGAINST CYBERBULLING, CYBERSTALKING, AND OTHER PERSONAL SAFETY CONCERNS

To protect their personal safety, adults and children should be cautious in online communications. They should be wary of revealing any personal information or meeting online acquaintances in person. To protect children, parents should keep a close watch on their children's online activities, and children should be taught never to reveal personal information to others online without a parent's consent.

Chapter Objective 9:
List steps individuals can take to safeguard their personal safety when using the Internet.

NETWORK AND INTERNET SECURITY LEGISLATION

The rapid growth of the Internet and jurisdictional issues have contributed to the lack of network and Internet security legislation. However, computer crime legislation continues to be proposed and computer crimes are actively prosecuted.

Chapter Objective 10:
Discuss the current state of network and Internet security legislation.

NET

REVIEW ACTIVITIES

KEY TERM MATCHING

a. computer virus

b. denial of service (DoS) attack

c. dot con

d. encryption

e. firewall

f. hacking

g. identity theft

h. password

i. phishing

j. Trojan horse

Instructions: Match each key term on the left with the definition on the right that best describes it.

1. _____ A collection of hardware and/or software intended to protect a computer or computer network from unauthorized access.

2. _____ A fraud or scam carried out through the Internet.

3. _____ A malicious program that masquerades as something else.

4. _____ A method of scrambling the contents of an e-mail message or a file to make it unreadable if it is intercepted by an unauthorized user.

5. _____ A secret combination of characters used to gain access to a computer, computer network, or other resource.

6. _____ A software program installed without the user's knowledge and designed to alter the way a computer operates or to cause harm to the computer system.

7. _____ An act of sabotage that attempts to flood a network server or a Web server with so much activity that it is unable to function.

8. _____ The use of spoofed e-mail messages to gain credit card numbers and other personal data to be used for fraudulent purposes.

9. _____ Using a computer to break into another computer system.

10. _____ Using someone else's identity to purchase goods or services, obtain new credit cards or bank loans, or otherwise illegally masquerade as that individual.

SELF-QUIZ

Instructions: Circle **T** if the statement is true, **F** if the statement is false, or write the best answer in the space provided. **Answers for the self-quiz are located in the References and Resources Guide at the end of the book.**

1. **T F** A computer virus can only be transferred to another computer via a storage medium.

2. **T F** An access control system that uses passwords is a possessed knowledge access system.

3. **T F** Using a password that is two characters long is an example of two-factor authentication.

4. **T F** Secure Web pages use encryption to securely transfer data sent via those pages.

5. **T F** Cyberstalking is the use of spoofed e-mail messages to gain credit card numbers and other personal data to be used for fraudulent purposes.

6. Driving around looking for a Wi-Fi network to access is referred to as _____.

7. _____ access control systems use some type of unique physical characteristic of a person to authenticate that individual.

8. A(n) _____ can be used at a Wi-Fi hotspot to create a secure path over the Internet.

9. A(n) _____ can be added to a file or an e-mail message to verify the identity of the sender and guarantee the file or message has not been changed.

10. Match each computer crime to its description, and write the corresponding number in the blank to the left of the description.

a. _____ A person working for the Motor Vehicle Division deletes a friend's speeding ticket from a database.

b. _____ An individual does not like someone's comment on a message board and begins to send that individual harassing e-mail messages.

c. _____ An individual sells the same item to 10 individuals via an online auction site.

d. _____ A person accesses a computer belonging to the IRS without authorization.

1. Online auction fraud

2. Hacking

3. Data or program alteration

4. Cyberstalking

1. Write the appropriate letter in the blank to the left of each term to indicate whether it is related to unauthorized access (U) or computer sabotage (C).

a. _____ Time bomb   **c.** _____ Malware   **e.** _____ War driving

b. _____ DoS attack   **d.** _____ Wi-Fi piggybacking

2. Is the password *john1* a good password? Why or why not? If not, suggest a better password.

3. Supply the missing words to complete the following statements regarding public/private key pairs.

a. With an encrypted e-mail message, the recipient's _____ key is used to encrypt the message, and the recipient's _____ key is used to decrypt the message.

b. With a digital signature, the sender's _____ key is used to sign the document, and the sender's _____ key is used to validate the signature.

4. To secure files on your computer so they are unreadable to a hacker who might gain access to your computer, what type of encryption (public key or private key) would be the most appropriate? Explain.

5. List two precautions that individuals can take to secure a wireless router against unauthorized access.

1. The term *hacktivism* is sometimes used to refer to the act of hacking into a computer system for a politically or socially motivated purpose. While some view hacktivists no differently than they view other hackers, hacktivists contend that they break into systems in order to bring attention to political or social causes. Is hacktivism a valid method of bringing attention to specific causes? Why or why not? Should hacktivists be treated differently than other types of hackers when caught?

2. According to security experts, several worms released in past years contain more than just the virus code—they contain code to remove competing malware from the computers they infect and messages taunting other virus writers. The goal seems to be not only to gain control of an increasing number of infected machines—a type of "bot war" to build the biggest botnet—but also to one-up rivals. If this trend continues, do you think it will affect how hackers and other computer criminals will be viewed? Will they become cult heroes or be viewed as dangerous criminals? Will continuing to increase prosecution of these individuals help or hurt the situation?

PROJECTS

HOT TOPICS

1. **Wi-Fi Hotspot Safety** As discussed in the chapter, it is possible to inadvertently connect to an evil twin instead of the legitimate Wi-Fi hotspot you intended to connect to and, even if you are connected to a legitimate hotspot, any data you send unsecured via the hotspot can be intercepted by a criminal. In either case, if the thief intercepts your credit card number, Web site passwords, or other sensitive data, it can be used for identity theft and other criminal activities.

   For this project, research these and any other possible risks you can think of related to using a Wi-Fi hotspot. For each risk, identify a possible precaution that can be taken to guard against that risk. If you have ever used a Wi-Fi hotspot, were you at risk? Knowing what you do now, would you take any new precautions the next time you use one? Is it possible to surf safely using a Wi-Fi hotspot? At the conclusion of your research, prepare a one-page summary of your findings and opinions and submit it to your instructor.

SHORT ANSWER/ RESEARCH

2. **New Viruses** Unfortunately, new computer viruses and other types of malware are released all the time.

   For this project, identify a current virus or worm (most security companies, such as Symantec and McAfee, list the most recent security threats on their Web sites) and answer the following questions: When was it introduced? What does it do? How is it spread? How many computers have been affected so far? Is there an estimated cost associated with it? Is it still in existence? At the conclusion of your research, prepare a one-page summary of your findings and submit it to your instructor.

HANDS ON

3. **Virus Check** There are several Web sites that include a free virus check, as well as other types of diagnostic software.

   For this project, find a free virus check available on the Web site of a company that makes antivirus software (such as the Symantec Security Scan at **security.symantec.com**) and run the free virus check. NOTE: The programs may require temporarily downloading a small program or an ActiveX component. If you are unable to perform this task on a school computer, ask your instructor for alternate instructions. If the check takes more than 10 minutes and there is an option to limit the check to a particular drive and folder, redo the check but scan only part of the hard drive (such as the Documents folder) to save time. After the virus scan is completed, print the page displaying the result. Did the program find any viruses or other security threats? At the conclusion of this task, submit your printout with any additional comments about your experience to your instructor.

4. **Teaching Computer Viruses** Some college computer classes include instruction on writing computer viruses. At one university, precautions for containing code created during this course include only allowing fourth year students to take the course, not having a network connection in the classroom, and prohibiting the removal of storage media from the classroom. Do you think these precautions are sufficient? Should writing virus code be allowed as part of a computer degree curriculum? Some believe that students need to know how viruses work in order to be able to develop antivirus software; however, the antivirus industry disagrees, and most antivirus professionals were never virus writers. Is it ethical for colleges to teach computer virus writing? Is it ethical for students to take such a course? Will teaching illegal and unethical acts (such as writing virus code) in college classes help to legitimize the behavior in society? Would you feel comfortable taking such a course? Why or why not?

   For this project, form an opinion about the ethical implications of including the instruction of writing virus code in college classes and be prepared to discuss your position (in class, via an online class discussion group, in a class chat room, or via a class blog, depending on your instructor's directions). You may also be asked to write a short paper expressing your opinion.

5. **Virus Hoaxes** In addition to the valid reports about new viruses found in the news and on antivirus software Web sites, reports of viruses that turn out to be hoaxes abound on the Internet. In addition to being an annoyance, virus hoaxes waste time and computing resources. In addition, they may eventually lead some users to routinely ignore all virus warning messages, leaving them vulnerable to a genuine, destructive virus.

   For this project, visit at least two Web sites that identify virus hoaxes, such as the Symantec or McAfee Web sites and Snopes.com. Explore the sites to find information about recent virus hoaxes, as well as general guidelines for identifying virus hoaxes and other types of online hoaxes. Share your findings with the class in the form of a short presentation. The presentation should not exceed 10 minutes and should make use of one or more presentation aids, such as the chalkboard, handouts, overhead transparencies, or a computer-based slide presentation (your instructor may provide additional requirements). You may also be asked to submit a summary of the presentation to your instructor.

Instructions: Go to the Chapter 9 page at **www.cengage.com/computerconcepts/np/uc13** to work the following Web Activities.

6. **Interactive Activities** Work the interactive **Crossword Puzzle**, watch the **Video Podcasts** and **Online Videos**, and explore the **Further Exploration** links associated with this chapter.

   If you have a SAM user profile, you may have access to hands-on instruction, practice, and assessment of the skills covered in this chapter. Check with your instructor for instructions and the correct URL/Web site to access those assignments.

7. **Student Edition Labs** Work the following interactive **Student Edition Lab**.

   ➤ **Keeping Your Computer Virus Free**

8. **Test Yourself** Review the **Online Study Guide** for this chapter, then test your knowledge of the terms and concepts covered in this chapter by completing the **Key Term Matching** exercise, the **Self-Quiz**, the **Exercises**, and the **Practice Test**.

SAM

Student Edition Labs

expert insight on . . .
Networks and the Internet

A conversation with COLLIN DAVIS
Senior Development Manager, Consumer Product Solutions, Symantec Corporation

" Cyber criminals aren't in it for just notoriety anymore; they want your money—or worse, your identity. "

symantec.

Collin Davis is a Senior Development Manager in the Consumer Product Solutions Group at Symantec Corporation. He has worked for Symantec for nine years, initially as a Software Development Intern while in college. He has over 12 years of experience working with computer systems, networks, and other computer-related areas. Collin has a Bachelor of Science degree in Computer Science from the UCLA Henry Samueli School of Engineering.

My Background . . .

I have been working in the computer security industry for nine years. I started in 2001 as a Software Development Intern while studying at UCLA. After earning my Bachelor's degree in computer science from the University of California, Los Angeles, Henry Samueli School of Engineering, I joined Symantec as an engineer on the Norton AntiVirus product team and helped develop and ship six iterations of that product. I then joined the team responsible for the creation of Symantec's all-in-one security solution, Norton 360. Most recently, I lead the development of OnlineFamily. Norton, a new, unique family safety solution that helps parents protect their kids online and fosters communication about their online activities.

It's Important to Know . . .

To use a layered security system. A layered security system consists of multiple layers of protection to guard against intrusions and other threats. You should use a secure wireless router and advanced firewall and antivirus technologies. You should also ensure that all your passwords are secure and change them often.

That you need to stay up to date. The threat landscape is constantly changing. There are actually more "bad" files today than "good" ones. This has led some security software makers to rely less on signature-based detection. Instead, they use a combination of whitelisting and advanced reputation engines to trust only the good files and block everything else. Use software with this type of technology if possible. Regardless, it is critical that you keep your security products up to date to stay protected from the latest threats. It's fairly easy for computer users to do this since most products download updates automatically or notify you when you need to download a new version. Don't ignore these notifications.

To think before you act. The online world is no different from the real one. If a link seems suspicious, proceed with caution before clicking it or seek information and services elsewhere.

How I Use this Technology . . .

I use this technology every day in my personal life. I also realize that the more and more "connected" data and applications become, the more important it becomes to secure them. Every time I connect to the Internet to send an e-mail, bank online, or view family photos, I am using the networking and Internet technologies discussed in this module to make the connection, and I am using the security technologies listed in this module to ensure my private data is protected. I don't always see these technologies as they do their job (this is a good thing!), but the fact that they are there gives me the confidence to take advantage of all the other great technologies being offered today.

What the Future Holds . . .

Our lives are becoming increasingly more and more dependent on technology. We store our documents and photos online. We work online and even date and form social networks online. All of this introduces increased privacy and security concerns that we must be aware of. It's important to be aware of what data is stored online and to use appropriate protection measures to secure it.

One of the biggest Internet-related risks today is that threats have evolved to exploit people for financial gain. Cyber criminals aren't in it for just notoriety anymore; they want your money—or worse, your identity. People need to be particularly cautious about whom they give their personal information (like credit card and Social Security numbers) to online. Everyone should check their bank and credit card statements often to monitor for fraudulent charges and change their passwords frequently.

In the future, we can expect to see businesses moving toward delivering an even more connected online experience. Personal computers are moving back toward their past role as simple "terminals" that provide a connection to the Internet where a wide array of data and applications are hosted. The line between what is stored and run from your local computer and what is "online" is being blurred. One impact of our online and local content becoming more interconnected is that we will be able to access our own personalized application experience from anywhere in the world, with many different types of devices. Wherever we are, our experience will remain consistent, according to our preferences and our content. However, security will remain essential. If people cannot trust that their information is secure and protected, they will be unable to take advantage of all the exciting services and benefits being offered today.

> *"The online world is no different from the real one. If a link seems suspicious, proceed with caution before clicking it or seek information and services elsewhere."*

My Advice to Students . . .

Be curious—explore every facet of a technology that interests you. Try to learn everything about its inner workings but don't lose sight of the big picture. If you're interested in a career in a particular field, get an internship. There is no better way to learn something than to do it.

Discussion Question

Collin Davis stresses the importance of people trusting that their information is secure and protected. Think about the systems that contain personal data about you. How would you feel if those systems were breached and your information was stolen? Does your viewpoint change if the information was monetary (such as credit card information) versus private information (such as grades or health information)? What security precautions, if any, do you think should be imposed by laws? Are organizations that hold your personal data morally responsible for going beyond the minimum requirements? What types of security measures would you implement to protect these systems? Be prepared to discuss your position (in class, via an online class discussion group, in a class chat room, or via a class blog, depending on your instructor's directions). You may also be asked to write a short paper expressing your opinion.

>**For more information on Symantec, visit www.symantec.com. To view the latest Symantec Internet Security Threat Report results, go to www.symantec.com/business/ theme.jsp?themeid=threatreport.**

REFERENCES AND RESOURCES
GUIDE

INTRODUCTION

When working on a computer or taking a computer course, you often need to look up information related to computers. For instance, you may need to find out when the IBM PC was first invented, you may want tips about what to consider when buying a computer, or you may want to find out more about how numbering systems work. To help you with the tasks just mentioned and more, this References and Resources Guide brings together in one convenient location a collection of computer-related references and resources. These resources plus additional resources (such as a variety of interactive activities and study tools) are located on this textbook's Web site, at www.cengage.com/computerconcepts/np/uc13.

OUTLINE

The earliest recorded calculating device, the abacus, is believed to have been invented by the Babylonians sometime between 500 B.C. and 100 B.C. It and similar types of counting boards were used solely for counting.

Blaise Pascal invented the first mechanical calculator, called the Pascaline Arithmetic Machine. It had the capacity for eight digits and could add and subtract.

Dr. John V. Atanasoff and Clifford Berry designed and built ABC (for Atanasoff-Berry Computer), the world's first electronic computer.

500 B.C.   1642   1937

Precomputers and Early Computers

1621   1804   1944

French silk weaver Joseph-Marie Jacquard built a loom that read holes punched on a series of small sheets of hardwood to control the weave of the pattern. This automated machine introduced the use of punch cards and showed that they could be used to convey a series of instructions.

The Mark I, considered to be the first digital computer, was introduced by IBM. It was developed in cooperation with Harvard University, was more than 50 feet long, weighed almost five tons, and used electromechanical relays to solve addition problems in less than a second; multiplication and division took about 6 and 12 seconds, respectively.

The slide rule, a precursor to the electronic calculator, was invented. Used primarily to perform multiplication, division, square roots, and the calculation of logarithms, its wide-spread use continued until the 1970s.

Precomputers and Early Computers (before approximately 1945)

Most precomputers and early computers were mechanical machines that worked with gears and levers. Electromechanical devices (using both electricity and gears and levers) were developed toward the end of this era.

First Generation (approximately 1946–1957)

Powered by vacuum tubes, these computers were faster than electromechanical machines, but they were large and bulky, generated excessive heat, and had to be physically wired and reset to run programs. Input was primarily on punch cards; output was on punch cards or paper. Machine and assembly languages were used to program these computers.

The UNIVAC 1, the first computer to be mass produced for general use, was introduced by Remington Rand. In 1952, it was used to analyze votes in the U.S. presidential election and correctly predicted that Dwight D. Eisenhower would be the victor only 45 minutes after the polls closed, though the results were not aired immediately because they weren't trusted.

The COBOL programming language was developed by a committee headed by Dr. Grace Hopper.

The first floppy disk (8 inches in diameter) was introduced.

IBM unbundled some of its hardware and software and began selling them separately, allowing other software companies to emerge.

UNIX was developed at AT&T's Bell Laboratories; Advanced Micro Devices (AMD) was formed; and ARPANET (the predecessor of today's Internet) was established.

1951   1960   1967   1969

First Generation	Second Generation	Third Generation

1947   1957   1964   1968

The FORTRAN programming language was introduced.

Robert Noyce and Gordon Moore founded the Intel Corporation.

John Bardeen, Walter Brattain, and William Shockley invented the transistor, which had the same capabilities as a vacuum tube but was faster, broke less often, used less power, and created less heat. They won a Nobel Prize for their invention in 1956 and computers began to be built with transistors shortly afterwards.

The first mouse was invented by Doug Engelbart.

The IBM System/360 computer was introduced. Unlike previous computers, System/360 contained a full line of compatible computers, making upgrading easier.

Second Generation (approximately 1958–1963)

Second-generation computers used transistors instead of vacuum tubes. They allowed the computer to be physically smaller, more powerful, more reliable, and faster than before. Input was primarily on punch cards and magnetic tape; output was on punch cards and paper; and magnetic tape and disks were used for storage. High-level programming languages were used with these computers.

Third Generation (approximately 1964–1970)

The third generation of computers evolved when integrated circuits (IC)—computer chips—began being used instead of conventional transistors. Computers became even smaller and more reliable. Keyboards and monitors were introduced for input and output; magnetic disks were used for storage. The emergence of the operating system meant that operators no longer had to manually reset relays and wiring.

The first microprocessor, the Intel 4004, was designed by Ted Hoff. The single processor contained 2,250 transistors and could execute 60,000 operations per second.

Bill Gates and Paul Allen wrote a version of BASIC for the Altair, the first computer programming language designed for a personal computer. Bill Gates dropped out of Harvard to form Microsoft with Paul Allen.

Software Arts Inc's Visi-Calc, the first electronic spreadsheet and business program for personal computers, was released. This program is seen as one of the reasons personal computers first became widely accepted in the business world.

IBM introduced the IBM PC. This DOS-based PC used a 4.77 MHz 8088 CPU with 64 KB of RAM and quickly became the standard for business personal computers.

1971

1975

1979

1981

Fourth Generation

1972

1976

1980

The C programming language was developed by Dennis Ritchie at Bell Labs.

Seymour Cray, called the "father of supercomputing," founded Cray Research, which would go on to build some of the fastest computers in the world.

Steve Wozniak and Steve Jobs' founded Apple computer and released the Apple I (a single-board computer), followed by the Apple II (a complete personal computer that became an instant success in 1977). They originally ran the company out of Jobs' garage.

Sony Electronics introduced the 3.5-inch floppy disk and drive.

Seagate Technology announced the first Winchester 5.25-inch hard disk drive, revolutionizing computer storage.

IBM chose Microsoft to develop the operating system for its upcoming personal computer. That operating system was PC-DOS.

Fourth Generation (approximately 1971–present)

The fourth generation of computers began with large-scale integration (LSI), which resulted in chips that could contain thousands of transistors. Very large-scale integration (VLSI) resulted in the microprocessor and the resulting microcomputers. The keyboard and mouse are predominant input devices, though many other types of input devices are now available; monitors and printers provide output; storage is obtained with magnetic disks, optical discs, and memory chips.

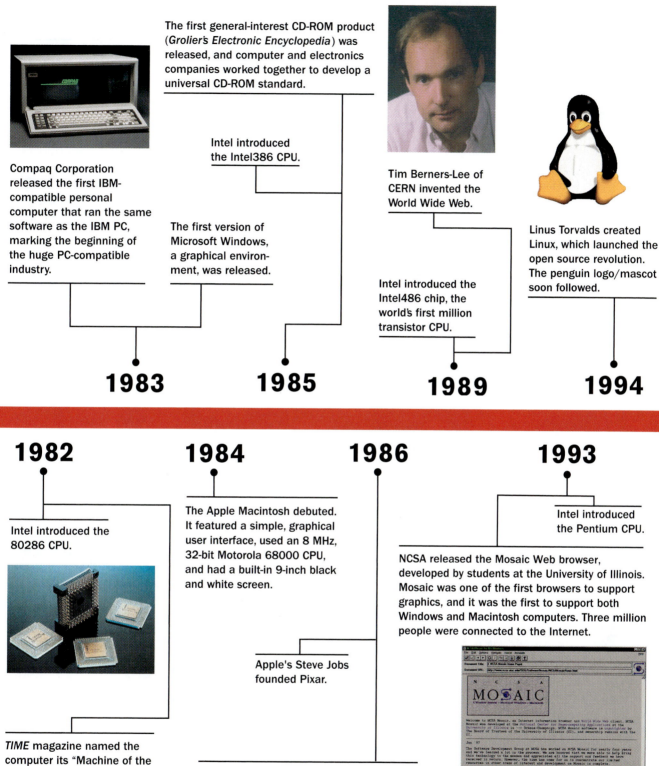

The first general-interest CD-ROM product (*Grolier's Electronic Encyclopedia*) was released, and computer and electronics companies worked together to develop a universal CD-ROM standard.

Intel introduced the Intel386 CPU.

Compaq Corporation released the first IBM-compatible personal computer that ran the same software as the IBM PC, marking the beginning of the huge PC-compatible industry.

The first version of Microsoft Windows, a graphical environment, was released.

Tim Berners-Lee of CERN invented the World Wide Web.

Intel introduced the Intel486 chip, the world's first million transistor CPU.

Linus Torvalds created Linux, which launched the open source revolution. The penguin logo/mascot soon followed.

1983　1985　1989　1994

1982　1984　1986　1993

Intel introduced the 80286 CPU.

The Apple Macintosh debuted. It featured a simple, graphical user interface, used an 8 MHz, 32-bit Motorola 68000 CPU, and had a built-in 9-inch black and white screen.

Intel introduced the Pentium CPU.

NCSA released the Mosaic Web browser, developed by students at the University of Illinois. Mosaic was one of the first browsers to support graphics, and it was the first to support both Windows and Macintosh computers. Three million people were connected to the Internet.

Apple's Steve Jobs founded Pixar.

TIME magazine named the computer its "Machine of the Year" for 1982, emphasizing the importance the computer had already reached in our society at that time.

Microsoft was listed on the New York Stock Exchange and began to sell shares to the public; Bill Gates became one of the world's youngest billionaires.

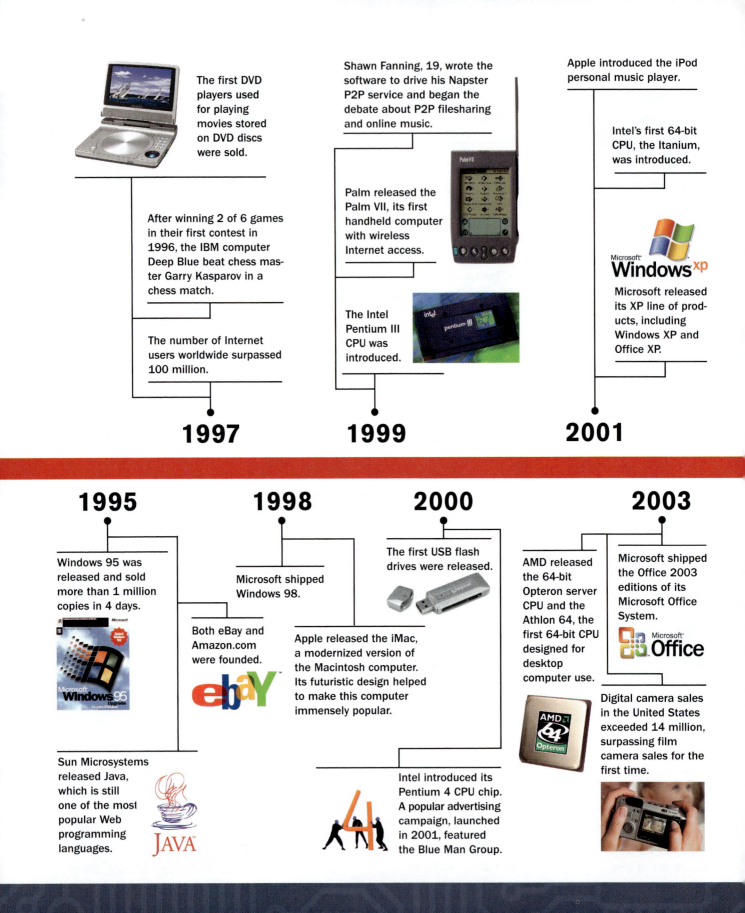

The first DVD players used for playing movies stored on DVD discs were sold.

After winning 2 of 6 games in their first contest in 1996, the IBM computer Deep Blue beat chess master Garry Kasparov in a chess match.

The number of Internet users worldwide surpassed 100 million.

Shawn Fanning, 19, wrote the software to drive his Napster P2P service and began the debate about P2P filesharing and online music.

Palm released the Palm VII, its first handheld computer with wireless Internet access.

The Intel Pentium III CPU was introduced.

Apple introduced the iPod personal music player.

Intel's first 64-bit CPU, the Itanium, was introduced.

Microsoft released its XP line of products, including Windows XP and Office XP.

1997

1999

2001

1995

1998

2000

2003

Windows 95 was released and sold more than 1 million copies in 4 days.

Both eBay and Amazon.com were founded.

Microsoft shipped Windows 98.

The first USB flash drives were released.

Apple released the iMac, a modernized version of the Macintosh computer. Its futuristic design helped to make this computer immensely popular.

AMD released the 64-bit Opteron server CPU and the Athlon 64, the first 64-bit CPU designed for desktop computer use.

Microsoft shipped the Office 2003 editions of its Microsoft Office System.

Sun Microsystems released Java, which is still one of the most popular Web programming languages.

Intel introduced its Pentium 4 CPU chip. A popular advertising campaign, launched in 2001, featured the Blue Man Group.

Digital camera sales in the United States exceeded 14 million, surpassing film camera sales for the first time.

Delivery of TV shows and other media to mobile phones became more common.

Netbooks were introduced.

New Internet-enabled gaming consoles, like the Wii shown here, were released.

Blu-ray Disc and HD-DVD movies, discs, and players became available in the U.S.

facebook

The Internet and wireless networks enabled people to work and communicate with others while on the go.

Use of the Internet for online shopping, as well as downloads of music, movies, games, and television shows, continued to grow.

Google introduced the Chrome operating system.

Use of social networking sites exploded; Facebook announced it had more than 100 million users.

Spyware became a major problem; some studies indicated that over 80% of computers had spyware installed.

Broadband Internet access approached the norm and improvements to wireless networking (such as WiMAX) continued to be developed.

The HD-DVD format was discontinued, leaving Blu-ray Disc the HD format winner.

2004

2006

2008

2005

2007

2009

Phishing and identity theft became household words as an increasing number of individuals fell victim to these Internet scams.

Portable media players, such as the iPod, were common; digital music capabilities were built into a growing number of objects and devices.

The Twitter microblogging service was launched.

Apple released the revolutionary iPhone.

Microsoft released Windows Vista and Office 2007.

Geobrowsing applications became more prominent; 4G phones became available.

Cloud computing entered the mainstream for both individuals and businesses.

The capabilities of mobile devices continued to grow; Palm's LifeDrive came with a 4 GB hard drive and built-in Wi-Fi and Bluetooth support.

Windows Vista

Intel and AMD their first dual-core CPUs both released

Quad-core CPUs were released by both Intel and AMD.

Microsoft released Windows 7.

Windows 7

R-7

Before buying a new computer, it is important to give some thought to what your needs are, including what software programs you wish to run, any other computers with which you need to be compatible, how you might want to connect to the Internet, and how much portability is needed. This section of the References and Resources Guide explores topics related to buying a new personal computer. ■

Analyzing Needs

When referring to a computer system, a need refers to a functional requirement that the computer system must be able to meet. For example, at a video rental store, a computer system must be able to enter barcodes automatically from videos or DVDs being checked in and out, identify customers with overdue movies, manage movie inventories, and do routine accounting operations. Portability is another example of a possible need. For example, if you need to take your computer with you as you travel or work out of the office, you will need a portable computer instead of a desktop computer.

Selecting a computer for home or business use must begin with the all-important question "What do I want the system to do?" Once you have determined what tasks the system will be used for and the amount of portability that is needed, you can choose among the software and hardware alternatives available. Making a list of your needs in the areas discussed in the next few sections can help you get a picture of what type of system you are shopping for. If you are not really sure what you want a system to do, you should think twice about buying one yet—you can easily make expensive mistakes if you are uncertain about what you want a system to do. Some common decision categories are discussed next; Figure R-1 provides a list of questions that can help you define the type of computer that will meet your needs.

FIGURE R-1

Questions to consider when getting ready to buy a personal computer.

POSSIBLE QUESTIONS

What tasks will I be using the computer for (writing papers, accessing the Internet, watching TV, making telephone calls, composing music, playing games, etc.)?

Do I prefer a Mac or a PC-compatible? Are there any other computers I need my documents and storage media to be compatible with?

How fast do I need the system to be?

Do I need portability? If so, do I need a powerful desktop replacement or will a netbook or UMPC suffice?

What size screen do I need? Do I need two monitors?

What removable storage media will I need to use (such as DVDs, flash memory cards, or USB flash drives)?

What types of Internet access will I be using (such as conventional dial-up, DSL, cable, satellite, or mobile wireless)?

Do I need to be able to connect the computer to a network? If so, is it a wired or wireless network and what type of network adapter is needed to connect to that network?

What additional hardware do I need (scanner, printer, TV tuner/antenna, wireless router, or digital camera, for example)?

What brand(s) do I prefer? When do I need the computer?

Do I want to pay extra for a better warranty (such as a longer time period, more comprehensive coverage, or on-site service)?

Application Software Decisions

Determining what functions you want the system to perform will also help you decide which application software is needed. Most users start with an application suite containing a word processor, spreadsheet, and other programs. In addition, specialty programs, such as tax preparation, drawing, home publishing, reference software, games, and more, may be needed or desired.

Not all software is available for all operating systems. Consequently, if a specific piece of software is needed, that choice may determine which operating system you need to use. In addition, your operating system and application software decisions may already be made for you if your documents need to be compatible with those of another computer (such as other office computers or between a home and an office computer).

Platforms and Configuration Options

If your operating system has already been determined, that is a good start in deciding the overall platform you will be looking for—most users will choose between the PC-compatible and Apple Macintosh platform. PC-compatible computers usually run either Windows or Linux; Apple computers almost always use Mac OS.

Configuration decisions initially involve determining the size of the machine desired (see Figure R-2). For nonportable systems, you have the choice between tower, desktop, or all-in-one configurations; in addition, the monitor size needs to be determined. Fully functioning personal computers can be notebook or tablet computers. For tablet computers, you need to decide if you will require keyboard use on a regular basis; if so, a convertible tablet computer would be the best choice. If a powerful fully functioning computer is not required, you may decide to go with a more portable option, such as a netbook or UMPC.

You should also consider any other specifications that are important to you, such as the size of the hard drive, types of other storage devices needed, amount of memory required, and so forth. As discussed in the next section, these decisions often require reconciling the features you want with the amount of money you are willing to spend.

Power vs. Budget Requirements

As part of the needs analysis, you should look closely at your need for a powerful system versus your budgetary constraints. Most users do not need a state-of-the-art system. Those who do should expect to pay more than the average user. A computer that was top of the line six months or a year ago is usually reasonably priced and more than adequate for most users' needs. Individuals who want a computer only for basic tasks, such as using the Internet and word processing, can likely get by with an inexpensive computer designed for home use.

When determining your requirements, be sure to identify the features and functions that are absolutely essential for your primary computing tasks (such as a large hard drive and lots of memory for multimedia applications, a fast video card for gaming, a fast Internet connection, a TV tuner card for individuals who wish to use the computer as a TV set, and so forth). After you have the minimum configuration determined, you can add optional or desirable components, as your budget allows.

Listing Alternatives

After you consider your needs and the questions mentioned in Figure R-1, you should have a pretty good idea of the hardware and software you will need. You will also know what purchasing options are available to you, depending on your time frame (while some retail stores have systems that can be purchased and brought home the same day, special orders or some systems purchased online will take longer). The next step is to get enough information from possible vendors to compare and contrast a few alternative systems that satisfy your stated needs. Most often, these vendors are local stores (such as computer stores, warehouse clubs, and electronic stores) and/or online stores (such as manufacturer Web sites and e-tailers). To compare prices and specifications for possible computer systems, find at least three systems that meet or exceed your needs by looking through newspaper advertisements, configuring systems online via manufacturer and e-tailer Web sites, or calling or visiting local stores. A comparison sheet listing your criteria and the systems you are considering, such as the one in Figure R-3, can help you summarize your options. Although it is sometimes very difficult to compare the prices of systems since they typically have somewhat different configurations and some components (such as CPUs) are difficult to compare, you can assign an approximate dollar value to each extra feature a system has (such as $50 for an included printer or a larger hard drive). Be sure to also include any sales tax and shipping charges when you compare the prices of each total system.

If your budget is limited, you will have to balance the system you need with extra features you may want. But do not skimp on memory or hard drive space because sufficient memory can help your programs to run faster and with fewer problems and hard

DESKTOPS

NOTEBOOKS

NETBOOKS

ULTRA-MOBILE PCS (UMPCs)

FIGURE R-2
Types of personal computers.

COMPONENT	EXAMPLE OF DESIRED SPECIFICATIONS	SYSTEM #1 VENDOR:	SYSTEM #2 VENDOR:	SYSTEM #3 VENDOR:
Operating system	Windows 7 Home Premium			
Manufacturer	HP or Dell			
Style	Notebook			
CPU	Intel dual core			
RAM	2 GB or higher			
Hard drive	500 GB or higher			
Removable storage	8-in-1 and flash memory card reader			
Optical drive	DVD-RW			
Monitor	Widescreen 15.4" minimum			
Video card and video RAM	Prefer dedicated video RAM			
Keyboard/mouse	Portable USB mouse with scroll wheel			
Sound card/speakers	No preference			
Modem	None			
Network card	Wi-Fi (802.11n)			
Printer	Ink-jet if get deal on price with complete system			
Included software	Microsoft Office			
Warranty	3 years min. (1 year onsite if not a local store)			
Other features	3 USB ports minimum, TV tuner, ExpressCard module			
Price				
Tax				
Shipping				
TOTAL COST				

FIGURE R-3

Comparing computer alternatives. A checklist such as this one can help to organize your desired criteria and evaluate possible systems.

drive space is consumed quickly. Often for just a few extra dollars, you can get additional memory, a faster CPU, or a larger hard drive—significantly cheaper than trying to upgrade any of those features later. A good rule of thumb is to try to buy a little more computer than you think you need. On the other hand, do not buy a top-of-the-line system unless you fall into the power user category and really need it. Generally, the second or third system down from the top of the line is a very good system for a much more reasonable price. Some guidelines for minimum requirements for most home users are as follows:

> ➤ A relatively fast multi-core CPU (generally, any multi-core CPU currently being sold today is fast enough for most users).

> ➤ 3 GB of RAM for desktop and notebook users.

> ➤ 320 GB or more hard drive space.

> ➤ Recordable or rewritable DVD drive.

> ➤ Network adapter or modem for the desired type(s) of Internet access.

> ➤ Sound card and speakers.

> ➤ At least 3 USB ports.

> ➤ A built-in flash memory media reader.

A LOOK AT NUMBERING SYSTEMS

As discussed in Chapter 2 of this text, a numbering system is a way of representing numbers. People generally use the *decimal numbering system* explained in Chapter 2 and reviewed next; computers process data using the *binary numbering system*. Another numbering system related to computer use is the *hexadecimal numbering system*, which can be used to represent long strings of binary numbers in a manner more understandable to people than the binary numbering system. Following a discussion of these three numbering systems, we take a look at conversions between numbering systems and principles of computer arithmetic, and then close with a look at how to perform conversions using a scientific calculator. ■

The Decimal and Binary Numbering System

The *decimal (base 10)* numbering system uses 10 symbols—the digits 0, 1, 2, 3, 4, 5, 6, 7, 8, and 9—to represent all possible numbers and is the numbering system people use most often. The *binary (base 2)* numbering system is used extensively by computers to represent numbers and other characters. This system uses only two digits—0 and 1. As illustrated in Figure 2-3 in Chapter 2, the place values (columns) in the binary numbering system are different from those used in the decimal system.

▼ FIGURE R-4
Hexadecimal characters and their decimal and binary equivalents.

The Hexadecimal Numbering System

Computers often output diagnostic and memory-management messages and identify network adapters and other hardware in *hexadecimal (hex)* notation. Hexadecimal notation is a shorthand method for representing the binary digits stored in a computer. Because large binary numbers—for example, 11010100010011101—can easily be misread by people, hexadecimal notation groups binary digits into units of four, which, in turn, are represented by other symbols.

The hexadecimal numbering system is also called the *base 16 numbering system* because it uses 16 different symbols. Since there are only 10 possible numeric digits, hexadecimal uses letters instead of numbers for the additional 6 symbols. The 16 hexadecimal symbols and their decimal and binary counterparts are shown in Figure R-4.

The hexadecimal numbering system has a special relationship to the 8-bit bytes of ASCII and EBCDIC that makes it ideal for displaying addresses and other data quickly. As you can see in Figure R-4, each hex character has a 4-bit binary counterpart, so any combination of 8 bits can be represented by exactly two hexadecimal characters. For example, the letter N (represented in ASCII by 01001110) has a hex representation of *4E* (see the Binary Equivalent columns for the hexadecimal characters *4* and *E* in Figure R-4).

HEXADECIMAL CHARACTER	DECIMAL EQUIVALENT	BINARY EQUIVALENT
0	0	0000
1	1	0001
2	2	0010
3	3	0011
4	4	0100
5	5	0101
6	6	0110
7	7	0111
8	8	1000
9	9	1001
A	10	1010
B	11	1011
C	12	1100
D	13	1101
E	14	1110
F	15	1111

Converting Between Numbering Systems

In Figure 2-3 in Chapter 2, we illustrated how to convert from binary to decimal. Three other types of conversions are discussed next.

Hexadecimal to Decimal

As shown in Figure R-5, the process for converting a hexadecimal number to its decimal equivalent is similar to converting a binary number to its decimal equivalent, except the base number is 16 instead of 2. To determine the decimal equivalent of a hexadecimal number (such as 4F6A, as shown in Figure R-5), multiply the decimal equivalent of each individual hex character (determined by using the table in Figure R-4) by the appropriate power of 16 and then add the results to obtain the decimal equivalent of that hex number.

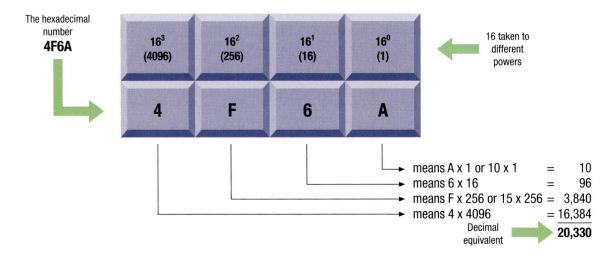

FIGURE R-5

The hexadecimal (base 16) numbering system. Each digit in a hexadecimal number represents 16 taken to a different power.

Hexadecimal to Binary and Binary to Hexadecimal

To convert from hexadecimal to binary, we convert each hexadecimal digit separately to 4 binary digits (using the table in Figure R-4). For example, to convert F6A9 to binary, we get

F	6	A	9
1111	0110	1010	1001

or 1111011010101001 in binary representation. To convert from binary to hexadecimal, we go through the reverse process. If the number of digits in the binary number is not divisible by 4, we add leading zeros to the binary number to force an even division. For example, to convert the binary number 1101101010011 to hexadecimal, we get

0001	1011	0101	0011
1	B	5	3

or 1B53 in hexadecimal representation. Note that three leading zeros were added to change the initial 1 to 0001 before making the conversion.

Decimal to Binary and Decimal to Hexadecimal

To convert from decimal to either binary or hexadecimal, we can use the *remainder method*. To use the remainder method, the decimal number is divided by 2 (to convert to a binary number) or 16 (to convert to a hexadecimal number). The *remainder* of the division operation is recorded and the division process is repeated using the *quotient* as the next dividend, until the quotient becomes 0. At that point, the collective remainders (written backwards) represent the equivalent binary or hexadecimal number (see Figure R-6).

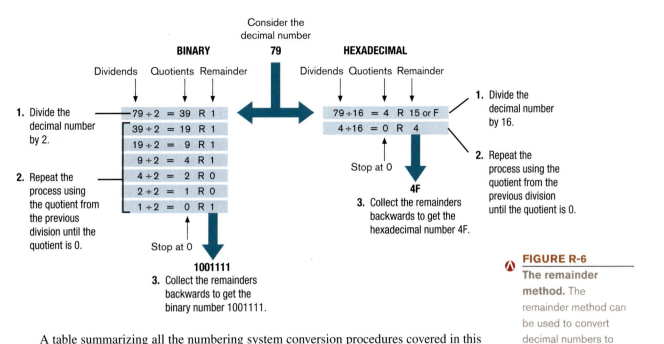

1. Divide the decimal number by 2.

2. Repeat the process using the quotient from the previous division until the quotient is 0.

Consider the decimal number
79

BINARY

Dividends   Quotients   Remainder

79 ÷ 2 = 39 R 1
39 ÷ 2 = 19 R 1
19 ÷ 2 =   9 R 1
 9 ÷ 2 =   4 R 1
 4 ÷ 2 =   2 R 0
 2 ÷ 2 =   1 R 0
 1 ÷ 2 =   0 R 1

Stop at 0

1001111

3. Collect the remainders backwards to get the binary number 1001111.

HEXADECIMAL

Dividends   Quotients   Remainder

79 ÷ 16 = 4 R 15 or F
 4 ÷ 16 = 0 R 4

Stop at 0

4F

3. Collect the remainders backwards to get the hexadecimal number 4F.

1. Divide the decimal number by 16.

2. Repeat the process using the quotient from the previous division until the quotient is 0.

FIGURE R-6

The remainder method. The remainder method can be used to convert decimal numbers to binary or hex format.

A table summarizing all the numbering system conversion procedures covered in this text is provided in Figure R-7.

FIGURE R-7
Summary of conversions.

FROM BASE	TO BASE		
	2	**10**	**16**
2		Starting at the right-most digit, multiply binary digits by 2^0, 2^1, 2^2, etc., respectively, and then add products.	Starting at the right-most digit, convert each group of four binary digits to a hex digit.
10	Divide repeatedly by 2 using each quotient as the next dividend until the quotient becomes 0, and then collect the remainders in reverse order.		Divide repeatedly by 16 using each quotient as the next dividend until the quotient becomes 0, and then collect the remainders in reverse order.
16	Convert each hex digit to four binary digits.	Starting at the right-most digit, multiply hex digits by 16^0, 16^1, 16^2, etc., respectively, and then add products.	

Computer Arithmetic

To most people, decimal arithmetic is second nature. Addition and subtraction of binary and hexadecimal numbers is not much different than the process used with decimal numbers—just the number of symbols used in each system varies. For instance, the digits in each column are added or subtracted and you carry to and borrow from the column to the left as needed as you move from right to left. Instead of carrying or borrowing 10, however—as you would in the decimal system—you carry or borrow 2 (binary) or 16 (hexadecimal).

Figure R-8 provides an example of addition and subtraction with decimal, binary, and hexadecimal numbers.

FIGURE R-8
Adding and subtracting with the decimal, binary, and hexadecimal numbering systems.

	DECIMAL	BINARY	HEXADECIMAL
	1	1 1 1	1
	144	100101	8E
	+ 27	+ 10011	+ 2F
Addition	171	111000	BD
	3	0 0	7
	1 4̶ 4	1̶ 0 0 1̶ 0 1	8̶ E
	− 27	− 10011	− 2F
Subtraction	117	10010	5F

Using a Scientific Calculator

A scientific calculator can be used to convert numbers between numbering systems, or to check conversions performed by hand. Many conventional calculators have different numbering system options; scientific calculator programs can be used for this purpose, as well. For example, Figure R-9 shows how to use the Windows Calculator program to double-check the hand calculations performed in Figure R-6 (the Scientific option must be selected using the View menu to display the options shown in the figure). Arithmetic can also be performed in any numbering system on a calculator, once that numbering system is selected on the calculator. Notice that, depending on which numbering system is currently selected, not all numbers on the calculator are available—only the possible numbers are displayed, such as only 0 and 1 when the binary numbering system is selected, as in the bottom screen in the figure.

> **FIGURE R-9**
>
> **Using a scientific calculator.** A physical calculator or calculator program can be used to convert between numbering systems, as well as to perform arithmetic in different numbering systems.

WINDOWS CALCULATOR
The Calculator program is typically located under Accessories on the Windows Start menu; select the *Scientific* option using the Calculator's View menu.

1. After entering a number (such as the decimal number 79 with the decimal numbering system selected shown here), select the numbering system to which the number should be converted (hex in this example).

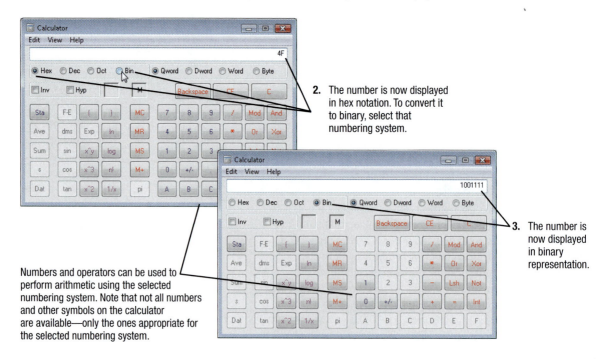

2. The number is now displayed in hex notation. To convert it to binary, select that numbering system.

3. The number is now displayed in binary representation.

Numbers and operators can be used to perform arithmetic using the selected numbering system. Note that not all numbers and other symbols on the calculator are available—only the ones appropriate for the selected numbering system.

CODING CHARTS

As discussed in Chapter 2 of this text, coding systems for text-based data include ASCII, EBCDIC, and Unicode. ■

ASCII and EBCDIC

Figure R-10 provides a chart listing the 8-digit ASCII and EBCDIC representations (in binary) for most of the symbols found on a typical keyboard.

FIGURE R-10
ASCII and EBCDIC binary codes for typical keyboard symbols.

SYMBOL	ASCII	EBCDIC	SYMBOL	ASCII	EBCDIC	SYMBOL	ASCII	EBCDIC
A	0100 0001	1100 0001	e	0110 0101	1000 0101	8	0011 1000	1111 1000
B	0100 0010	1100 0010	f	0110 0110	1000 0110	9	0011 1001	1111 1001
C	0100 0011	1100 0011	g	0110 0111	1000 0111	(	0010 1000	0100 1101
D	0100 0100	1100 0100	h	0110 1000	1000 1000	)	0010 1001	0101 1101
E	0100 0101	1100 0101	i	0110 1001	1000 1001	/	0010 1111	0110 0001
F	0100 0110	1100 0110	j	0110 1010	1001 0001	-	0010 1101	0110 0000
G	0100 0111	1100 0111	k	0110 1011	1001 0010	*	0010 1010	0101 1100
H	0100 1000	1100 1000	l	0110 1100	1001 0011	+	0010 1011	0100 1110
I	0100 1001	1100 1001	m	0110 1101	1001 0100	,	0010 1100	0110 1011
J	0100 1010	1101 0001	n	0110 1110	1001 0101	.	0010 1110	0100 1011
K	0100 1011	1101 0010	o	0110 1111	1001 0110	:	0011 1010	0111 1010
L	0100 1100	1101 0011	p	0111 0000	1001 0111	;	0011 1011	0101 1110
M	0100 1101	1101 0100	q	0111 0001	1001 1000	&	0010 0110	0101 0000
N	0100 1110	1101 0101	r	0111 0010	1001 1001	\	0101 1100	1110 0000
O	0100 1111	1101 0110	s	0111 0011	1010 0010	$	0010 0100	0101 1011
P	0101 0000	1101 0111	t	0111 0100	1010 0011	%	0010 0101	0110 1100
Q	0101 0001	1101 1000	u	0111 0101	1010 0100	=	0011 1101	0111 1110
R	0101 0010	1101 1001	v	0111 0110	1010 0101	>	0011 1110	0110 1110
S	0101 0011	1110 0010	w	0111 0111	1010 0110	<	0011 1100	0100 1100
T	0101 0100	1110 0011	x	0111 1000	1010 0111	!	0010 0001	0101 1010
U	0101 0101	1110 0100	y	0111 1001	1010 1000			0111 1100	0110 1010
V	0101 0110	1110 0101	z	0111 1010	1010 1001	?	0011 1111	0110 1111
W	0101 0111	1110 0110	0	0011 0000	1111 0000	@	0100 0000	0111 1100
X	0101 1000	1110 0111	1	0011 0001	1111 0001	_	0101 1111	0110 1101
Y	0101 1001	1110 1000	2	0011 0010	1111 0010	'	0110 0000	1011 1001
Z	0101 1010	1110 1001	3	0011 0011	1111 0011	{	0111 1011	1100 0000
a	0110 0001	1000 0001	4	0011 0100	1111 0100	}	0111 1101	1101 0000
b	0110 0010	1000 0010	5	0011 0101	1111 0101	~	0111 1110	1010 0001
c	0110 0011	1000 0011	6	0011 0110	1111 0110	[	0101 1011	0100 1010
d	0110 0100	1000 0100	7	0011 0111	1111 0111	]	0101 1101	0101 1010

A 0041	N 004E	a 0061	n 006E	o 0030	(007B	* 002A	■ 25A0	অ 0985
B 0042	O 004F	b 0062	o 006F	1 0031	| 007C	+ 002B	□ 25A1	প 0997
C 0043	P 0050	c 0063	p 0070	2 0032	} 007D	, 002C	▲ 25B2	ে 09C7
D 0044	Q 0051	d 0064	q 0071	3 0033	~ 007E	- 002D	% 2105	৶ 09F6
E 0045	R 0052	e 0065	r 0072	4 0034	! 0021	. 002E	℞ 211E	چ 0685
F 0046	S 0053	f 0066	s 0073	5 0035	" 0022	/ 002F	⅓ 2153	ڴ 06B4
G 0047	T 0054	g 0067	t 0074	6 0036	# 0023	£ 20A4	⅔ 2154	ڪ 06AA
H 0048	U 0055	h 0068	u 0075	7 0037	$ 0024	Σ 2211	♛ 2655	α 03B1
I 0049	V 0056	i 0069	v 0076	8 0038	% 0025	Ø 2205	☂ 2602	β 03B2
J 004A	W 0057	j 006A	w 0077	9 0039	& 0026	√ 221A	❑ 2750	Δ 0394
K 004B	X 0058	k 006B	x 0078	[005B	' 0027	∞ 221E	☀ 2742	φ 03A6
L 004C	Y 0059	l 006C	y 0079	\ 005C	(0028	≤ 2264	➲ 27B2	Ω 03A9
M 004D	Z 005A	m 006D	z 007A	] 005D	) 0029	≥ 2265	♥ 2665	Ÿ 03AB

FIGURE R-11

Selected Unicode codes.

FIGURE R-12

Using Unicode.

Unicode

Since consistent worldwide representation of symbols is increasingly needed today, use of Unicode is growing rapidly. Unicode can be used to represent every written language, as well as a variety of other symbols. Unicode codes are typically listed in hexadecimal notation—a sampling of Unicode is shown in Figure R-11.

The capability to display characters and other symbols using Unicode coding is incorporated into many programs. For instance, when the Symbol dialog box is opened using the Insert menu in Microsoft Office Word, the Unicode representation (as well as the corresponding ASCII code in either decimal or hexadecimal representation) can be viewed (see Figure R-12). Some programs allow you to enter a Unicode symbol using its Unicode hexadecimal value. For instance, in Microsoft Office programs you can use the Alt+X command when the insertion point is just to the right of a Unicode hex value to convert that hex value into the corresponding symbol. For example, the keystrokes

2264Alt+X

result in the symbol corresponding to the Unicode code 2264 (the less than or equal sign ≤) being inserted into the document; entering 03A3 and then pressing Alt+X inserts the symbol shown in the Word screen in Figure R-12.

Unicode representation for Greek capital letter sigma Σ symbol.

UNICODE REPRESENTATION

The Symbol dialog box shown here lists the Unicode representation of each symbol as it is selected. If preferred, the ASCII representation can be displayed.

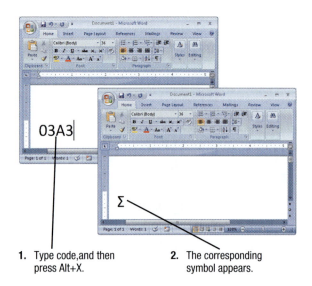

1. Type code, and then press Alt+X.

2. The corresponding symbol appears.

INSERTING SYMBOLS USING UNICODE

In Microsoft Office programs, typing the hexadecimal Unicode code for a symbol and then pressing Alt+X displays the corresponding symbol.

ANSWERS TO SELF-QUIZ

Chapter 1
 1. T 2. F 3. F 4. F 5. T 6. Input 7. tablet 8. Virtualization 9. electronic mail or e-mail 10. a. 4 b. 2 c. 1 d. 3

Chapter 2
 1. T 2. F 3. T 4. T 5. F 6. 13 7. quad-core 8. port 9. multiprocessing 10. a. 6 b. 2 c. 4 d. 9 e. 7 f. 1 g. 8 h. 5 i. 3

Chapter 3
 1. F 2. T 3. F 4. T 5. F 6. C 7. volatile 8. 650 MB 9. smart card 10. flash memory

Chapter 4
 1. F 2. T 3. T 4. T 5. F 6. handwriting recognition 7. scanner, optical scanner, flatbed scanner, or portable scanner 8. pixel 9. flat-panel or LCD; cathode-ray tube or CRT 10. a. 2 b. 5 c. 1 d. 4 e. 3

Chapter 5
 1. T 2. F 3. T 4. F 5. F 6. Multitasking 7. Linux 8. file compression 9. back up 10. a. 3 b. 4 c. 2 d. 1

Chapter 6
 1. T 2. T 3. F 4. F 5. T 6. open source 7. insertion point or cursor 8. function 9. table 10. a. 2 b. 3 c. 1

Chapter 7
 1. F 2. T 3. F 4. T 5. F 6. bus 7. dual-mode 8. personal area network or PAN 9. virtual private network or VPN 10. a. 3 b. 4 c. 1 d. 5 e. 2

Chapter 8
 1. F 2. F 3. T 4. T 5. F 6. Digital Subscriber Line or DSL 7. keyword; directory 8. social networking site 9. online auction 10. a. 2 b. 4 c. 1 d. 3

Chapter 9
 1. F 2. T 3. F 4. T 5. F 6. war driving 7. Biometric 8. virtual private network or VPN 9. digital signature 10. a. 3 b. 4 c. 1 d. 2

CREDITS

Throughout the modules: Screen shots of Microsoft Access®, Excel®, Paint®, PowerPoint®, Visual Basic®, Word®, and Windows® reprinted with permission from Microsoft Corporation. Copyright © Microsoft Explorer® reprinted with permission from Microsoft Corporation.

Chapter 1

Figure 1-1a, Photo courtesy of Nokia; Figure 1-1b, Courtesy Microsoft Corporation; Figure 1-2a, Courtesy Dell Inc.; Figure 1-2b, Courtesy Epson America; Figure 1-2c, Courtesy of Nintendo; Figure 1-3a, Courtesy Intel Corporation; Figure 1-3b, Courtesy General Dynamics Itronix; Figure 1-3c, Courtesy U.S. Army; Figure 1-4a, Courtesy of iStockphoto © Steve Cole; Figure 1-4b, Courtesy General Dynamics Itronix; Figure 1-4c, BlackBerry®, RIM®, Research In Motion®, SureType®, SurePress™ and related trademarks, names and logos are the property of Research In Motion Limited and are registered and/or used in the U.S. and countries around the world.; Figure 1-4d, Courtesy Ingersoll Rand Security Technologies; You box, Courtesy Abilene Christian University; Figure 1-5a, Courtesy Bluetooth SIG; Figure 1-5b, Courtesy 3M Touch Systems; Figure 1-5c, Courtesy MasterCard Worldwide; Figure 1-5d, Courtesy Ingersoll Rand Security Technologies; Figure 1-7acde, Courtesy IBM Corporate Archives; Figure 1-7b, Courtesy U.S. Army; Figure 1-9a, Courtesy of Gateway, Inc.; Figure 1-9b, Courtesy, Hewlett-Packard Company; Figure 1-9c, ©2009 Logitech. All rights reserved. Images/materials on page 15 used with permission from Logitech.; Figure 1-9d, Courtesy D-Link Systems, Inc.; Figure 1-9e, Courtesy Kingston Technology Company, Inc.; Figure 1-11c, Courtesy RedLobster.com; Trend box a, Courtesy of HTC; Trend box b, Courtesy Acer America Corporation; Trend box c, Courtesy Microsoft Corporation; Trend box d, Courtesy Dell Inc.; Figure 1-12, Courtesy Volvo Cars of North America; Figure 1-13, Courtesy of HTC; Figure 1-14a, Courtesy, Hewlett-Packard Company; Figure 1-14b, Courtesy Dell Inc.; Inside box, Courtesy of iStockphoto © Carsten Madsen; Figure 1-15a, Courtesy Belkin International, Inc.; Figure 1-15b, Courtesy Fujitsu America; Figure 1-15c, Courtesy MSI Computer Corporation; Figure 1-15d, Courtesy General Dynamics Itronix; Figure 1-16a, Photo by Dom Miguel Photography for Seaport; Figure 1-16b, Courtesy Chumby Industries. Chumby and the Chumby Logo are the registered trademarks of Chumby Industries, Inc.; Figure 1-16c, Courtesy of Nintendo; Figure 1-17a, Courtesy Ergotron Inc.; Figure 1-17b, Courtesy Dell Inc.; Figure 1-18, Courtesy of IBM; Figure 1-19, Courtesy of IBM; Figure 1-20acd, Courtesy of Gateway, Inc.; Figure 1-20b, Courtesy Dell Inc.; Figure 1-20e, Courtesy, Hewlett-Packard Company; Figure 1-21a, Image ©2009 by Kelty; Figure 1-21b, Google screenshot © Google Inc. and used with permission.; Figure 1-21c, Used by Permission of Clear Channel Radio.; Figure 1-21e, Courtesy Classmates.com; Figure 1-21f, Courtesy CastTV; Figure 1-23a, Courtesy of Gateway, Inc.; How box, Courtesy e2Campus by Omnilert, LLC; Figure 1-25, Courtesy of Stanford University; Figure 1-26, Google Chrome screenshot © Google Inc. and used with permission.; Figure 1-27ac, Courtesy of Gateway, Inc.; Figure 1-27b, Courtesy Dell Inc.; Figure 1-28, The Survivor: Tocantins Logo is a registered trademark of Survivor Productions, LLC. CSB.com website contents © CBS Broadcasting Inc. Used by permission. CBS and the CBS Eye are registered trademarks of CBS Broadcasting Inc.; Figure 1-29, Courtesy of Symantec Corp; Figure 1-31, Courtesy www.snopes.com; Ask the Expert 2, Courtesy Jack in the Box Inc.; Ask the Expert 3, Courtesy TabletKiosk; Expert Insight, Courtesy D-Link Systems, Inc.

Chapter 2

Figure 2-8ad, Courtesy of Intel Corporation; Figure 2-8bc, (C) 2003, 2005, 2006 2007 Advanced Micro Devices, Inc., Reprinted with permission. AMD, the AMD Arrow logo, AMD Opteron, AMD Turion and combinations thereof as well as certain other marks listed at http://www.amd.com/legal/trademarks.html are trademarks of Advanced Micro Devices, Inc.; How box, Courtesy of IBM; Figure 2-11, Courtesy Kingston Technology Company, Inc.; Figure 2-13a, Courtesy of ABS Computer Technologies Inc. All rights reserved.; Figure 2-13b, Courtesy Belkin International, Inc.; Figure 2-14a, Courtesy D-Link Systems, Inc.; Figure 2-16a, Courtesy Dell Inc.; Figure 2-16b-f, Courtesy of Belkin International, Inc.; Figure 2-16g, Courtesy Cables To Go; Figure 2-17, Courtesy D-Link Systems, Inc.; Figure 2-18a, Courtesy Fujitsu America; Figure 2-18b, Courtesy Socket Mobile, Inc.; Figure 2-18c, Courtesy Kingston Technology Company, Inc.; Inside box, Courtesy Intel Corporation; Trend box, Courtesy TAEUS International Corporation; Figure 2-21, © 2009 Micron Technology, Inc. All Rights Reserved. Used with permission.; Figure 2-23, Copyright IMEC; You box, Photo courtesy of Nokia; Figure 2-25, Courtesy BMC Cycling; Figure 2-26, Image reproduced by permission of IBM Research, Almaden Research Center. Unauthorized use not permitted.; Figure 2-27, Courtesy Intel Corporation; Figure 2-28, Courtesy of IBM; Ask the Expert 1, Courtesy Unicode Inc.; Ask the Expert 2, Courtesy Tom's Hardware; Ask the Expert 3, Courtesy Kingston Technology Company, Inc.

Chapter 3

Figure 3-1, Courtesy of Gateway, Inc.; Figure 3-4a, Courtesy of Hitachi Global Storage Technologies; Figure 3-4b, Courtesy Western Digital; Inside box, Courtesy of DriveSavers, Inc. www.drivesavers.com; Figure 3-6, SanDisk is a trademark of SanDisk Corporation, registered in the United States and other countries. Other brand names mentioned herein are for identification purposes only and may be the trademarks of their respective holder(s).; Figure 3-7ab, Copyright © Iomega Corporation. All Rights Reserved. Iomega, the stylized "i" logo and all product images are property

of Iomega Corporation in the United States and/or other countries.; Figure 3-7cd, Courtesy Transcend Information USA; Figure 3-8, Courtesy of Seagate Technology LLC; Figure 3-11, Copyright © Iomega Corporation. All Rights Reserved. Iomega, the stylized "i" logo and all product images are property of Iomega Corporation in the United States and/or other countries.; Figure 3-12ab, Courtesy Verbatim America LLC; Figure 3-12c, Courtesy CD Digital Card www.cddigitalcard.com; Figure 3-13, © 2006 Danjaq, LLC, United Artists Corporation and Columbia Pictures Industries, Inc. All Rights Reserved.; Figure 3-14a, Courtesy Verbatim America LLC; Figure 3-14b, Courtesy Memorex Products, Inc.; Figure 3-14c, Courtesy of Sony Electronics Inc.; Trend box, Courtesy IronKey; Figure 3-15a, Courtesy of Sony Electronics Inc.; Figure 3-15c, © 2009 Micron Technology, Inc. All Rights Reserved. Used with permission.; Figure 3-16adfg, SanDisk, the SanDisk logo, SanDisk Extreme and ImageMate are trademarks of SanDisk Corporation, registered in the United States and other countries. SD and SDHC are trademarks. SanDisk is an authorized licensee of the xD trademark. Other brand names mentioned herein are for identification purposes only and may be the trademarks of their respective holder(s).; Figure 3-16b, Courtesy Kingston Technology Company, Inc.; Figure 3-16c, Courtesy of Sony Electronics Inc.; Figure 3-16e, © 2009 Micron Technology, Inc. All Rights Reserved. Used with permission.; Figure 3-17a, Courtesy Kingston Technology Company, Inc.; Figure 3-17bc, Courtesy CustomUSB.com; You box a, Courtesy Kingston Technology Company, Inc.; You box b, Courtesy PortableApps.com; Figure 3-18b, Copyright © Iomega Corporation. All Rights Reserved. Iomega, the stylized "i" logo and all product images are property of Iomega Corporation in the United States and/or other countries.; Figure 3-20, Photo by HID Global Corporation; Figure 3-21, Courtesy InPhase Technologies; Figure 3-22, Courtesy 3PARdata, Inc.; Figure 3-24, Courtesy Data Robotics; Figure 3-25, Courtesy Imation; Ask the Expert 1, Courtesy of Seagate Technology LLC; Ask the Expert 2, Courtesy Kingston Technology Company, Inc.; Ask the Expert 3, Copyright © Iomega Corporation. All Rights Reserved. Iomega, the stylized "i" logo and all product images are property of Iomega Corporation in the United States and/or other countries.

Chapter 4

Figure 4-1, ©2009 Logitech. All rights reserved. Images/materials on page 130 used with permission from Logitech.; Figure 4-2a, Photo courtesy of Nokia; Figure 4-2b, Courtesy of HTC; Figure 4-2c, Courtesy Verizon Wireless; Figure 4-3a, ©2009 Logitech. All rights reserved. Images/materials on page 131 used with permission from Logitech.; Figure 4-3b, Courtesy 3Dconnexion; Figure 4-4b, Courtesy Kensington; Trend box, Courtesy GestureTek; Figure 4-5a, Courtesy Intermec Technologies; Figure 4-5b, Courtesy Motion Computing; Figure 4-5c, Courtesy Wacom Technology Corp.; Figure 4-6, Courtesy of Mi-Co; Figure 4-7a, Courtesy Livescribe; Figure 4-7b, Courtesy Wacom Technology Corp.; Figure 4-7c, Courtesy of NCR Corporation; Figure 4-8a, Courtesy Dell Inc.; Figure 4-8b, Courtesy of Sony Electronics Inc.; Figure 4-8c, Courtesy Microsoft Corporation; Figure 4-8d, Courtesy of NCR Corporation; Figure 4-9a, ©2009 Logitech. All rights reserved. Images/materials on page 137 used with permission from Logitech.; Figure 4-9b, SanDisk is a trademark of SanDisk Corporation, registered in the United States and other countries. Other brand names mentioned herein are for identification purposes only and may be the trademarks of their respective holder(s).; Figure 4-9c, © Fujitsu Siemens Computers; How box, Courtesy 3M Touch Systems; Figure 4-10a, Courtesy General Dynamics Itronix; Figure 4-10b, Courtesy of Motorola; Figure 4-11a, Courtesy, Hewlett-Packard Company; Figure 4-11b, Courtesy WizCom Technologies; Figure 4-11c, Courtesy of NCR Corporation; Figure 4-13abe, Courtesy of Motorola; Figure 4-14a, Courtesy of NCR Corporation; Figure 4-14b, Courtesy of Motorola; Figure 4-14c, Photo courtesy of Nokia; Figure 4-15, Courtesy Intermec Technologies; Figure 4-16a, Courtesy Intermec Technologies; Figure 4-16b, Courtesy of teamaxess.com; Figure 4-16c, Courtesy MasterCard Worldwide; Figure 4-16d, © AP Images/Denis Poroy; Figure 4-17, Courtesy Scantron Corporation®; Figure 4-18, Courtesy of NV Energy; You box, Courtesy of Mitek Systems; Figure 4-19, Courtesy of NCR Corporation; Figure 4-20a, Courtesy of UPEK, Inc.; Figure 4-20b, Courtesy LaCie Ltd.; Figure 4-21a, Courtesy Canon USA; Figure 4-21b, Courtesy Kingston Technology Company, Inc.; Figure 4-21c, Courtesy of Sony Electronics Inc.; Figure 4-21d, BlackBerry®, RIM®, Research In Motion®, SureType®, SurePress™ and related trademarks, names and logos are the property of Research In Motion Limited and are registered and/or used in the U.S. and countries around the world.; Figure 4-22a, Courtesy of Sony Electronics Inc.; Figure 4-22b, Courtesy of iStockphoto; Figure 4-23a, Courtesy David Shopper and Nuance Communications, Inc.; Figure 4-23b, Courtesy Dell Inc.; Figure 4-24, Courtesy Ergotron Inc.; Figure 4-25a, Courtesy of Gateway, Inc.; Figure 4-25b, Courtesy Bluetooth SIG; Figure 4-25ce, Courtesy of Sony Electronics Inc.; Figure 4-25d, Courtesy of HTC; Figure 4-25f, Courtesy of Clear Channel Spectacolor; Figure 4-26, Courtesy CineMassive Displays; Figure 4-27a, Courtesy Acer America Corporation; Figure 4-28, Courtesy ZOTAC; Figure 4-29, Courtesy Kensington; Figure 4-30, Courtesy Lumus Ltd.; Inside box a, Courtesy of Sony Electronics Inc.; Inside box b, Courtesy E Ink Corporation; Figure 4-31a, Courtesy of Sony Electronics Inc.; Figure 4-32, Courtesy of Universal Display Corporation; Figure 4-33, Courtesy of QUALCOMM MEMS Technologies, Inc.; Figure 4-34a, Courtesy of ViewSonic Corporation; Figure 4-34b, Courtesy Microvision, Inc.; Figure 4-34c, Courtesy Laser Magic Productions, Inc.; Figure 4-35, Courtesy InfoPrint Solutions Company; Figure 4-36, Courtesy, Hewlett-Packard Company; Figure 4-37, Courtesy Epson America; Figure 4-39b, Courtesy, Hewlett-Packard Company; Figure 4-40a, Courtesy, Hewlett-Packard Company; Figure 4-40b, Courtesy of Intermec Technologies; Figure 4-40c, Courtesy ZINK Imaging; Figure 4-40d, Courtesy Canon USA; Figure 4-40e, Courtesy Stratasys Inc.; Figure 4-41a, Courtesy of Altec Lansing; Figure 4-41b, Courtesy NordicTrack; Figure 4-41c, Courtesy Plantronics; Ask the Expert 1, Courtesy TabletKiosk; Ask the Expert 2, Courtesy GestureTek; Ask the

Expert 3, SanDisk is a trademark of SanDisk Corporation, registered in the United States and other countries. Other brand names mentioned herein are for identification purposes only and may be the trademarks of their respective holder(s).; **Expert Insight,** Courtesy Acer America Corporation.

Chapter 5
Figure 5-1a, Courtesy Bluetooth SIG; **Figure 5-8a,** Courtesy Kingston Technology Company, Inc.; **Figure 5-8b,** Courtesy Western Digital; **Figure 5-11a,** Courtesy Dell Inc.; **Figure 5-11b,** Courtesy of Gateway, Inc.; **Figure 5-11c,** Courtesy InfoPrint Solutions Company; **Trend box a,** Courtesy ASUS Computer International (ACI); **Trend box b,** Courtesy Mini-Box.com; **Figure 5-16,** Courtesy Novell, Inc.; **Inside box,** Courtesy, Volvo Cars of North America, LLC; **Figure 5-17a,** Courtesy of HTC; **Figure 5-17b,** Courtesy T-Mobile USA; **Figure 5-17c,** Courtesy Belkin International, Inc.; **Figure 5-17d,** BlackBerry®, RIM®, Research In Motion®, SureType®, SurePress™ and related trademarks, names and logos are the property of Research In Motion Limited and are registered and/or used in the U.S. and countries around the world.; **Figure 5-18,** Courtesy of Symantec; **How box,** WinZip is a registered trademark of WinZip International LLC. All rights reserved.; **Figure 5-21,** WinZip is a registered trademark of WinZip International LLC. All rights reserved.; **Figure 5-22b,** Courtesy of Mozy; **You box,** Google Docs screenshot (c) Google Inc. and used with permission.; **Ask the Expert 1,** Courtesy Strike Fighter Weapons School Pacific, NAS Lemoore; **Ask the Expert 2,** Courtesy The Linux Foundation; **Ask the Expert 3,** Courtesy of DriveSavers, Inc. www.drivesavers.com.

Chapter 6
Figure 6-1a, Courtesy of Symantec Corp; **Figure 6-1b,** Courtesy Holersoft; **Inside box,** Courtesy OpenOffice.org; **Figure 6-3,** Courtesy of Tucows; **Figure 6-4a,** Courtesy DataViz, Inc.; **Figure 6-4b,** Courtesy Microsoft Corporation; **Figure 6-4cd,** Courtesy Ilium Software; **Figure 6-4e,** Courtesy T-Mobile USA; **Figure 6-5,** Courtesy of Symantec Corp.; **Figure 6-6a,** Courtesy Zoho; **Figure 6-6b,** Courtesy Zillow; **Figure 6-6c,** Courtesy Soonr; **You box,** Courtesy Yahoo! Inc.; **Figure 6-7a,** Courtesy Microsoft Corporation; **Figure 6-7b,** Box shot reprinted with permission of Corel Corporation; **6-7c,** Courtesy of Apple Inc.; **Trend box,** Courtesy Microsoft Corporation; **Figure 6-26b,** Courtesy Corel Corporation; **Figure 6-26c,** Google Picassa screenshot (c) Google Inc. and used with permission. Courtesy Nick Morley; **Figure 6-27,** Courtesy of Sony Creative Software Inc. Sony Sound Forge Audio Studio 9.0 is a trademark/registered trademark of Madison Media Software, Inc. All rights reserved.; **Figure 6-28,** © Serif (Europe) Limited 2009 - www.serif.com; **Figure 6-29,** © 1995-2009 RealNetworks, Inc. All rights reserved. RealNetworks, Real.com, RealAudio, RealVideo, RealSystem, RealPlayer, RealJukebox and RealMedia are trademarks or registered trademarks of RealNetworks, Inc.; **Figure 6-30,** © Serif (Europe) Limited 2009 - www.serif.com; **Figure 6-31,** Courtesy Circus Ponies Software, Inc. All Rights Reserved.; **Figure 6-32,** Courtesy The Application Cubby LLC and Courtesy Belkin International; **Figure 6-33,** Courtesy YouSendIt; **Ask the Expert 1,** Courtesy of Tucows; **Ask the Expert 2,** Courtesy OpenOffice.org; **Ask the Expert 3,** Courtesy Bark Animation Co.; **Expert Insight,** Courtesy Microsoft, Inc.

Chapter 7
Inside box, © 2009 Fulton Innovation LLC. All Rights Reserved. Used with Permission.; **Figure 7-2a,** Courtesy of Motorola; **Figure 7-2b,** T-Mobile USA; **Figure 7-2c,** Courtesy Iridium; **Figure 7-3a,** Courtesy Magellan; **Figure 7-3b,** Courtesy Volvo Cars of North America; **Figure 7-3c,** Courtesy Garmin International; **Figure 7-4,** Courtesy LiveViewGPS Inc. www.liveviewgps.com; **Figure 7-5,** Courtesy Intel Corporation; **Figure 7-6,** Courtesy Sling Media; **Figure 7-7,** Courtesy Cisco Systems, Inc.; **Figure 7-8a,** Courtesy InTouch Health, Inc.; **Figure 7-8b,** Courtesy, University of Rochester; **Figure 7-8c,** Photo made available by St. Joseph's Healthcare Hamilton; **Figure 7-9a,** Courtesy, Hewlett-Packard Company; **Figure 7-9b,** Courtesy of Cisco Systems Inc.; **Figure 7-9c,** Courtesy InfoPrint Solutions Company; **Figure 7-10a,** Courtesy, Hewlett-Packard Company; **Figure 7-10b,** Courtesy of Linksys; **Figure 7-10c,** Courtesy InfoPrint Solutions Company; **Figure 7-11a,** Courtesy, Hewlett-Packard Company; **Figure 7-11b,** Courtesy of Cisco Systems Inc.; **Figure 7-11c,** Courtesy InfoPrint Solutions Company; **Figure 7-12,** Courtesy Intel Corporation; **Figure 7-13,** Courtesy City of Riverside; **Figure 7-16a,** Courtesy, Hewlett-Packard Company; **Figure 7-18abcf,** Courtesy of Black Box Corporation; **Figure 7-18de,** Courtesy Belkin International, Inc.; **Figure 7-21abde,** Photo(s) courtesy of Hughes Network Systems, LLC.; **Figure 7-21c,** Courtesy, Hewlett-Packard Company; **Figure 7-22a,** Courtesy of Gateway, Inc.; **Figure 7-22c,** Courtesy Acer America; **Figure 7-24,** Courtesy D-Link Systems, Inc.; **Figure 7-25a,** Courtesy Dell Inc.; **Figure 7-25b,** Courtesy Verizon Wireless; **Figure 7-25c,** Courtesy of Sony Electronics Inc.; **Figure 7-25d,** Courtesy ARCHOS; **Figure 7-25e,** Courtesy of Nintendo; **You box,** Courtesy Eye-Fi; **Figure 7-27,** Courtesy Wi-Fi Alliance. The Wi-Fi CERTIFIED logo is a registered trademark of the Wi-Fi Alliance; **Figure 7-29,** Courtesy Sprint Nextel; **Figure 7-30,** Courtesy Bluetooth SIG; **Figure 7-32af,** Courtesy D-Link Systems, Inc.; **Figure 7-32bcd,** Courtesy Belkin International, Inc.; **Figure 7-32e,** Courtesy Cricket Wireless; **Figure 7-33,** Courtesy D-Link Systems, Inc.; **Figure 7-34a,** Courtesy, Hewlett-Packard Company; **Figure 7-34b,** Courtesy D-Link Systems, Inc.; **Figure 7-34c,** Courtesy of Cisco Systems Inc.; **Figure 7-34d,** Courtesy of Nintendo; **Figure 7-34e,** Courtesy of Gateway, Inc.; **Figure 7-34f,** Courtesy Data Comm for Business Inc.; **Figure 7-34g,** Courtesy Dell Inc.; **Figure 7-34h,** Photo courtesy of Nokia; **Figure 7-34i,** Courtesy of Apple Inc.; **Trend box,** Courtesy Verizon Wireless; **Ask the Expert 1,** Courtesy of Google Inc.; **Ask the Expert 2,** Courtesy of Symantec; **Ask the Expert 3,** Courtesy McDonald's Corporation.

Chapter 8
Figure 8-1a, Courtesy of Gateway, Inc.; **Figure 8-1b,** The Survivor: Tocantins Logo is a registered trademark of Survivor Productions, LLC. CSB.com website contents © CBS Broadcasting Inc. Used by permission. CBS and the CBS Eye are registered trademarks of CBS Broadcasting Inc.; **Figure 8-2a,** Use of the AT&T logo is granted under permission by AT&T Intellectual Property.; **Figure 8-2b,** Courtesy of Verizon Communications; **Figure 8-2c,** Courtesy Comcast; **Figure 8-2d,** Photo(s) courtesy of Hughes Network Systems, LLC; **Figure 8-2e,** Courtesy EarthLink, Inc.; **Figure 8-2f,** Courtesy Clearwire; **Figure 8-4,** Courtesy CinemaNow; **Inside box,** Courtesy U.S. Air Force; **Figure 8-5a,** Courtesy of Gateway, Inc.; **Figure 8-5b,** Courtesy of HTC; **Figure 8-5c,** Courtesy of Yahoo!; **Figure 8-8,** Courtesy Tranzeo Wireless USA; **Figure 8-9a,** Courtesy of iStockphoto © Sean Locke; **Figure 8-9b,** Courtesy Fujitsu America; **Figure 8-9c,** Courtesy Abilene Christian University; **Figure 8-11ab,** Google screenshot (c) Google Inc. and used with permission.; **Figure 8-13b,** Google screenshot (c) Google Inc. and used with permission.; **Figure 8-17,** Courtesy Microsoft Corporation; **Trend box,** Courtesy of Helio By Virgin Mobile USA; **Figure 8-18a,** Courtesy of Yahoo!; **Figure 8-18b,** Courtesy Microsoft Corporation; **Figure 8-19b,** Courtesy Vonage; **Figure 8-19c,** Courtesy D-Link Systems, Inc.; **Figure 8-20,** Courtesy of Intel Corporation; **Figure 8-21a,** Courtesy Facebook, Inc.; **Figure 8-21b,** Courtesy LinkedIn; **You box,** Courtesy Yoono; **Figure 8-24a,** Courtesy MobiTV; **Figure 8-24b,** Courtesy CastTV; **Figure 8-24c,** Courtesy Roku, Inc.; **Figure 8-25b,** MapQuest and the MapQuest logo are registered trademarks of MapQuest, Inc. Map content (c) 2009 by MapQuest, Inc. and its respective copyright holders. Used with permission.; **Figure 8-26,** iGoogle screenshot (c) Google Inc. and used with permission.; **How box a,** "Audacity" is a trademark of Dominic Mazzoni; **Figure 8-27,** Courtesy FactCheck.org; **Figure 8-29,** Courtesy Software Secure, Inc.; **Figure 8-30,** Courtesy of Zach Sunderland www.zacsunderland.com; **Ask the Expert 1,** Courtesy McDonald's Corporation; **Ask the Expert 2,** Courtesy Throw the Fight www.myspace.com/throwthefight, www.throwthefight.com.; **Ask the Expert 3,** Courtesy of IDPI.

Chapter 9
Figure 9-2, Courtesy JiWire, Inc.; **Figure 9-6a,** Courtesy ActivIdentity; **Figure 9-6b,** Joseph Mehling, Dartmouth College; **Figure 9-7a,** Courtesy Fujitsu America; **Figure 9-7b,** Courtesy Ingersoll Rand Security Technologies; **Figure 9-7c,** Courtesy L-1 Identity Solutions; **Figure 9-7d,** DoD photo by Staff Sgt. Jonathan C. Knauth, U.S. Marine Corps.; **How box,** Courtesy D-Link Systems, Inc.; **Figure 9-10,** Courtesy of Symantec; **Trend box,** Courtesy WiTopia and Viscosity; **Figure 9-13,** Courtesy Centennial Software Limited; **Figure 9-14ad,** Courtesy of Gateway, Inc.; **Figure 9-14bcf,** Courtesy Acer America Corporation; **Figure 9-14e,** Courtesy Kingston Technology Company, Inc.; **Figure 9-15,** Courtesy BleepingComputer.com; **Figure 9-16ac,** Courtesy, Hewlett-Packard Company; **Figure 9-16b,** Courtesy Dell Inc.; **Figure 9-17a,** Courtesy of Symantec; **Figure 9-17b,** Courtesy Lavasoft AB; **Inside box,** Google screenshot (c) Google Inc. and used with permission.; **You box,** Courtesy Mint.com; **Ask the Expert 1,** Courtesy ACM; **Ask the Expert 2,** Courtesy of Symantec; **Ask the Expert 3,** Courtesy of Symantec; **Expert Insight,** Courtesy of Symantec.

References and Resources Guide
Computer History Timeline: 1, 2, 5, 6, 9, 11, 15, Courtesy of IBM Archives; **3,** Courtesy Iowa State University; **4,** Courtesy Jim Bready; **7,** Courtesy Unisys Corporation; **8,** Courtesy U.S. Navy; **10,** Courtesy of Bootstrap Institute/Alliance; **12, 21, 25, 31,** Courtesy of Intel Corporation; **13, 35,** Courtesy Microsoft Corporation; **14,** Courtesy of Dan Bricklin. (c) www.jimraycroft.com **16,** Courtesy Cray Inc.; **18, 34,** Courtesy, Hewlett-Packard Company; **19,** Fabian Bachrach, courtesy W3C; **20,** Courtesy Larry Ewing lewing@isc.tamu.edu and The GIMP; **22,** Courtesy NCSA/University of Illinois; **23,** Courtesy of Panasonic; **24,** Image courtesy of Palm, Inc. Palm, Treo, Zire, Tungsten, logos, stylizations, and design marks associated with all the preceding, and trade dress associated with Palm, Inc.'s products, are among the trademarks or registered trademarks owned by or licensed to Palm. Inc.; **26, 32, 42, 45,** Microsoft, Windows and the Windows logo are either registered trademarks or trademarks of Microsoft Corporation in the United States and/or other countries.; **27,** Courtesy Microsoft Museum; **28,** The eBay logo is a trademark of eBay Inc.; **29,** Java and the Java Coffee Cup logo are trademarks or registered trademarks of Sun Microsystems, Inc.; **30,** Courtesy Kingston Technology Company Inc.; **33,** (C) 2003, 2005, 2006 2007 Advanced Micro Devices, Inc., Reprinted with permission. AMD, the AMD Arrow logo, AMD Opteron, AMD Turion and combinations thereof as well as certain other marks listed at http://www.amd.com/legal/trademarks.html are trademarks of Advanced Micro Devices, Inc.; **36,** Photo courtesy of Nokia. Copyright © 2007 Nokia. All rights reserved. Nokia and Nokia Connecting People are registered trademarks of Nokia Corporation; **37,** Courtesy Nintendo; **38,** Courtesy Dell Inc.; **39,** Courtesy Facebook, Inc.; **40, 43.** Google image (c) Google Inc. and used with permission.; **41,** Courtesy Belkin International, Inc.; **44,** Courtesy T-Mobile USA; **R-1a,** Courtesy Dell Inc.; **R-1b,** Courtesy Belkin International, Inc.; **R-1c,** Courtesy MSI Computer Corporation; **R-1d,** Courtesy General Dynamics Itronix.

GLOSSARY/INDEX